The

Proof Texts of the Catechism

with a

Practical Commentary

By

LOUIS WESSEL, D. D.

Professor at Concordia Theological Seminary
Springfield, Ill.

St. Louis, Mo.
CONCORDIA PUBLISHING HOUSE
1927

PUBLISHERS' PREFACE

Prof. Augustus L. Graebner, D. D., originated this book by the serial publication of its first six chapters in the *Theological Quarterly* (now the *Theological Monthly*) in 1898. Subsequently Prof. W. H. T. Dau, D. D., his successor as editor, continued the instalments, embracing chapter seven, thereafter passing on the task to Professor Louis Wessel, D. D. When the publication of these contributions to the *Theological Quarterly* was discontinued, Doctor Wessel carried the work to its conclusion, and in 1920 the Concordia Supply Company of the Springfield Concordia Seminary published a complete edition in two volumes.

This edition is now exhausted, and the present publishers have acquired all publication rights of this valuable text- and reference book. This edition is a zinco-photographic reproduction, a process that does not permit of any changes or improvements in the typography, but makes it possible for the publishers to offer the book at a price much more reasonable than would have been possible if it had been reset.

FOREWORD

"The Proof Texts of the Catechism with a Practical Commentary" is the caption of a series of articles now running in the "Theological Quarterly" for well-nigh twenty-two years. The commentary was begun by Dr. A. Graebner of our St. Louis theological seminary in 1898. Advocating a thorough exegetical study of the texts as essential to thorough *preparation* for the work in the class room, and desiring "to be of some assistance toward such preparatory work in the minister's study," he "offered a series of specimens, according to which others might continue the work and prepare for themselves an exegetical commentary of all the proof texts of the catechism." Since they were to be specimens only, the articles were discontinued. What happened? Dr. Graebner says: "From the time we discontinued our articles to the present day so many requests for a resumption of our humble efforts came to us from individual brethren and entire conferences that we are inclined to take up the series where we left it in 1899 and continue these commentaries for the benefit of such as may have use for them in the service of the Master." (Theol. Quart., Vol. V., p. 91.)

Upon the death of this brilliant scholar in December 1904, Prof. W H. T. Dau, the successor of Dr. Graebner in the editorial chair of the Theological Quarterly, continued the commentary during the year 1906. His many duties becoming too onerous, he prevailed upon Prof. Louis Wessel, of our Springfield theological seminary, to carry on the work. Prof. Wessel began his labors in 1907 and still continues the good work to this day.

When the commentary on the proof passages of the Third Article was nearing completion, requests from ministers, teachers, and students became more and more insistent to publish the commentary in book form.

Complying with this demand, we diffidently undertook the task. In the present volume all the passages in our Synodical Catechism (Dr. Schwan's) have been covered from *The Introduction* down to the close of the *Third Article*.

From the many encouraging letters we have received, hailing our enterprise with joy, we infer that our fond hope of rendering a distinct service to the brethren in the ministry and to the teachers in our church schools by the publication of the Proof Texts has been realized. May God's blessing accompany the study of this book.

EDWARD A. WESTCOTT, '20.

PAUL HILGENDORF, '20.

Concordia Theological Seminary, Springfield, Ill.
March 24, 1920.

GENERAL REMARKS

Proof texts, in a Catechism, serve a twofold purpose. In the first place, they are adduced as *sources* from which the various points of doctrine exhibited in the questions and answers of the catechism are drawn. Then, again, inasmuch as catechisms present these doctrines in terms chosen and arranged by the authors of such catechisms, the texts are added with a view of showing that these statements of doctrine are in full agreement with the *norm* of Christian doctrine, the holy Scriptures. As these texts, or many of them, are to be memorized by the catechumens, they should not be longer than is necessary for a complete statement of the point or points they are to substantiate. But their brevity does not render them unavailable for their purpose in the catechism; for every plain statement of Scripture is "Scripture" that "cannot be broken" (John 10, 35), and "profitable for doctrine" (2 Tim. 3, 16). Besides, the catechetical instructor is not, in his exposition of the texts, enjoined from entering upon the context and turning its light upon the words adduced in the book; on the contrary, remembering that the exposition and application of the proof texts is the more important part of his work, he will feel thoroughly prepared for his lesson only after careful exegetical preparation for this part of his task. It may be needless to say that we do not think of recommending or inculcating a learned grammatico-historical and theological exegesis before a class of catechumens. But we do recommend a thorough exegetical study of the texts as essential to thorough *preparation* for the work in the class room, and the desire to be of some assistance toward such preparatory work in the minister's study prompts us to offer the following specimens.

INTRODUCTION

1 Pet. 2, 2: *As newborn babes, desire the sincere milk of the word, that ye may grow thereby.*

These words are addressed to Christians (1 Pet. 1, 1.2), who were born again by the word of God (1 Pet. 1, 23), which by the gospel is preached to them (1 Pet. 1, 25). In view of this new birth, they are called *newborn babes*, who have recently entered into spiritual life, not, however, that they should remain babes, but that they should grow. The proper nourishment of a babe, without which it will not grow, but pine away and perish, is milk, and young babes crave that nourishment and eagerly accept the offered breast. And the proper food whereby the spiritual children of God may be nourished and strengthened and preserved and increased is, of course, *spiritual*. Thus Luther correctly understands the Greek *logikon*, when, in his commentary published in 1539, he says: "These are, again, figurative words; for he does not speak of material milk, but of another kind of milk, which is logical, that is, 'spiritual, which is taken with the soul and sucked with the heart." The English Bible, rendering *logikon* "of the word," while it fails in the interpretation of the adjective, gives a correct comment, stating properly what the figurative term, *logikon gala, spiritual* milk, implies; for this food of the children of the Spirit is indeed the word of God (1 Cor. 3, 1.2).

But the apostle adds another adjective, *adolon, sincere, unadulterated.* Thus St. Paul warns the Christians against those who *corrupt the word of God* (2 Cor. 2, 17). False doctrine does not come alone, but as an adulteration of sound doctrine, and is all the more dangerous as it comes with the appearance of milk, the proper spiritual food of God's children.

The pure, sincere milk of divine truth is what St. Peter would have us *desire*, as a sucking child eagerly craves its mother's breast, and drinks until its hunger is appeased, and craves again after a few short hours. So we, likewise, should seek with eagerness the spiritual milk of the word, largely and frequently partaking thereof.

And this do, says the apostle, *that ye may grow thereby.* By *hina* he indicates that our spiritual growth should be not only a consequence, but an end and purpose of our craving for and partaking of the spiritual food prepared for us in the word. And when he says *en auto*, he says more forcibly than he would by *di autou*, that the word is not only the means whereby, but the power *wherein* we should grow into spiritual maturity.

This text, then, should be made to furnish, at the very outset of this course of instruction, an exhortation and admonition to the catechumens that they would earnestly and assiduously and with the proper end and aim apply themselves to the study of this compend of Christian doctrine, the Catechism.

2 Pet. 1, 21: *Holy men of God spake as they were moved by the Holy Ghost.*

This text is a part of the dictum classicum beginning with v. 19 and asserting the firmness or reliability of the divine word of Scripture by emphasizing the fact that it is the word not of man, but of God. The English Bible fails to indicate the emphasis which, in the original, lies on the words *hupo pneumatos hagiou, by the Holy Ghost.* These words, which, in the translation, occupy the last place, the place they would also occupy in Greek if they were not emphasized, are placed first in the original, even before the verb, *feromenoi, moved, driven.* What the apostle would inculcate is that the word of Scripture is not human but divine, the word of GOD. The *holy men of God,* holy and men of God as they were, were not the authors of this word of prophecy. They wrote not under the promptings of their holiness or godliness; they were *driven* to write what they wrote, as ships are driven by the wind that swells their sails; and he who drove, impelled them, was God, the Holy Ghost. And when the apostle says *elalesan,* he thereby refers not to the thoughts only to which they gave utterance, which he might have done by *elegon,* but to the *words* they pronounced and the sounds of which those words consist, or the characters representing those sounds. They are called *holy* men of *God,* because they were the instruments of God, and the emphasized words indicate that it was the Holy Ghost who used them as His instruments, as by and through them He gave utterance to the words of prophecy, which were not their own but His own.

2 Tim. 3, 15-17: *And that from a child thou hast known the holy scriptures, which are able to make thee wise unto salvation through faith which is in Christ Jesus. All scripture is given by inspiration of God, and is profitable for doctrine, for reproof, for correction, for instruction in righteousness; that the man of God may be perfect, thoroughly furnished unto all good works.*

This text is not quoted here for the purpose of inculcating the early training of children in the nurture and admonition of the Lord, though that may be incidentally pointed out as implied in the opening words of v. 15. What the words here quoted should teach is the nature and use of the holy Scriptures. The term *ta hiera grammata, the holy writings,* is used only here to denote the Old Testament Scriptures, the more common terms being *he grafe, hai grafai,* or *hai grafai hagiai.* The form *ta hiera grammata* is more expressive of the nature of the holy books as a revelation of God laid down in *written characters, grammata,* as distinguished from spoken words, and by the article, *ta,* these writings are presented as a fixed quantity, the books which were known and acknowledged as *the holy writings.* The adjective, *hiera,* denotes a relation to God, and distinguishes these writings from secular literature. But while these books may be termed *holy* in various respects, as to their contents and purposes, they are related to God in a peculiar way indicated by another adjective, *theopneustos,* v. 16.

The English Bible correctly renders *theopneustos given by inspiration of God,* Luther, *von Gott eingegeben.* The two versions disagree as to the syntactical relation of the adjective, the English Bible taking it as the predicate of the subject, *pasa grafe,* and supplying the copula accordingly: *All Scripture IS given by inspiration of God;* while Luther takes *theopneustos* as the attribute of *pasa grafe* and, making *pasa grafe theopneustos* the subject, and *ofelimos,* etc., the predicate, supplies the copula after *theopneustos* and translates: *Alle Schrift von Gott eingegeben IST nuetze, etc.* Either construction is grammatically admissible. But as the divine inspiration of the Scriptures was not at issue, and the apostle evidently means to state more explicitly than in the previous verse the *use* of the holy Scriptures, Luther's construction would seem to deserve the preference. The *kai* before *ofelimos,* which neither version has noticed, must then be given by *also,* and we would translate, *All Scripture, given by inspiration of God, is also profitable, etc.* Since, however, what is an attribute of a thing can also be predicated of that thing, the text teaches the divine inspiration of all Scripture, whether *theopneustos* be attributively or predicatively construed, just as holiness is ascribed to the church, whether we say, *the church is holy,* or, *the holy church.*

The words *pasa grafe* are in both translations correctly rendered, *all Scripture, alle Schrift; for the entire Scripture, die ganze Schrift,* would be *pasa he grafe.* But if whatever is holy Scripture is given by inspiration of God, then the entire Scripture is thus given. There is, however, a significance in *pasa grafe* which would not be found in *pasa he grafe.* The latter form, *the whole Scripture,* would be understood to refer to the body of the Old Testament Scriptures as it was then in the hands of the Jews and had been known to Timotheus from his youth as *he grafe.* All Scripture, *pasa grafe,* says more; it includes not only the Scriptures that had been handed down, Moses and the Prophets, but also the Scriptures that were then being given by inspiration of God through the Apostles and Evangelists. Scripture (Old and New), *whatever is Scripture given by inspiration of God, is also profitable, etc.:* this is what the apostle here says.

Of the *purposes* of Scripture, the apostle here teaches that it is profitable, 1. *for doctrine,* i. e., to teach, to communicate truth to such as would or should learn and know the truth, to give knowledge of those things which are therein set forth (Rom. 15, 4); 2. *for reproof,* i. e., to convict sinners of their sinfulness and the erring and gainsaying of their error (Titus 1, 9.13. I Tim. 5, 20. Titus 2, 15; 3. *for correction, for our admonition,* 1 Cor. 10, 11, that we may amend our evil ways in accordance with the divine norm of right and truth; 4. *for instruc-*

tion in righteousness, our spiritual *education* toward that ripeness of spiritual manhood which should be the aim of every child of God. Of the ulterior purpose of the written word the apostle has said before, v. 15: it is *man's salvation* through faith which is in Christ Jesus.

The *perspicuity* of the Bible is asserted when the apostle says that Scripture is profitable for doctrine, and that not only to readers of ripe understanding and profound learning, but even to a child, v. 15.16.

The *efficacy* and *sufficiency* of Scripture is also apparent, when it is said to be able to make *wise unto salvation,* and to make the man of God *perfect, thoroughly furnished unto all good works.* The *man of God* is every man who is of the household of God, either in the ministry or otherwise. Whatever duties may be encumbent upon a Christian, he may be fitted for their performance by the word of Scripture, and by the same means he may obtain his soul's salvation. Such is the efficacy and sufficiency of the Book of books.

Thus, then, we have in this text a compend of Bibliology and an earnest admonition to use the Scriptures with all diligence and unceasingly all the days of our lives.

1 Cor. 2, 13: *Which things also we speak, not in the words which man's wisdom teacheth, but which the Holy Ghost teacheth, comparing spiritual things with spiritual.*

The apostle, having in the preceding context declared that he and his fellow apostles were by the Spirit of God imbued with a *knowledge* of spiritual things, now proceeds to state that the utterance of these things was not in words of human wisdom, but that the same Spirit who taught them to know whereof they spoke, also taught them to speak of what they knew, so that when they spoke they uttered the thoughts of the Holy Ghost in the words of the Holy Ghost. The progress from *eidomen* to *laloumen* is marked by *kai, also,* and *laloumen* more expressly than *legomen* denotes the utterance in words, *logois.* The verb *sugkrinein,* which the English Bible renders *compare,* and Luther, *richten,* means to *match together.* Uttering the *things* of the Holy Spirit in *words* of the Holy Spirit, the apostles match or join together spiritual things with spiritual, both the things and the words being of the Spirit of God.

John 5, 39: *Search the Scriptures; for in them ye think ye have eternal life: and they are they which testify of me.*

This in an endorsement of the entire Old Testament as a revelation of God to teach the way of salvation and to testify of Christ, the Savior. The plural, *tas grafas,* refers to the various books of Scripture, *the Scriptures,* the writings of Moses and the Prophets, and Christ approves them all without exception or restriction. The verb, *ereunate,* is of peculiar force, denoting a thorough search as distinguished from a superficial view or hasty persual. *Ereunate* may be either indicative or imperative. If the latter, it is an injunction, if the former, an approval, of the study of the written Word, not for the purpose of Higher Criticism, for which this text leaves no room, but that the reader may be made wise unto salvation through faith which is in Christ Jesus.

Luke 11, 28: *Blessed are they that hear the word of God, and keep it.*

A voice out of the multitude had pronounced the mother of Jesus blessed because of her motherhood. The Lord accepts the macarism, but gives a different reason. Mary was indeed blessed, but not because she had been made the mother of Jesus. Elizabeth, filled with the Holy Ghost, had given the proper reason, saying, *Blessed is she that BE-LIEVED* (Luke 1, 45). Mary had believed the word that came to her by the angel in the annunciation (Luke 1,38), the words that the shepherds reported in the night of the nativity (Luke 2, 19), the words of the boy Jesus spoken in the temple (Luke 2, 51), the words spoken to the fathers of old (Luke 5, 54.55), and we are repeatedly told that she *kept* these sayings and things and *pondered* them in her heart (Luke 2, 19.51). Such was the manner of Mary's blessedness. Not by immaculate conception, not because of her virgin motherhood, but by the word of divine grace which she had heard and kept, was she blessed. And this blessedness was not open to her alone, but to all who would likewise hear and accept and keep the word of God in which we have eternal life.

THE TEN COMMANDMENTS

Micah 6, 8: *He hath showed thee, O man, what is good; and what doth the Lord require of thee, but to do justly, and to love mercy, and to walk humbly with thy God?*

This text closes the first act of *the Lord's controversy* with His people (Micah 6, 2ff). The Lord has challenged the ungrateful people to state what grievance they may have against Him who has done them no evil and only good (Micah 6, 3-5). Thereupon Israel, knowing and acknowledging that the people cannot lay charges against the Lord, but that, on the contrary, the Lord has just claims to make against His people, answered the question, "What have I done to thee?" with the counter question, "What are we to do to the Lord? What does He demand of us? Would He have sacrifices of calves, of thousands of rams, of ten thousand rivers of oil, of our first born?" (Micah 6, 6.7). The climax is very emphatically expressive of the people's readiness to balance their account with God, to be even with Him at any cost. To humble the pride and arrogance hidden in this offer of the conscience-stricken people, the prophet steps in with the words of our text. He accosts the speaker, *O man, adam,* as if to say, "What manner of language is this? Hast thou forgotten what thou art, *man,* taken from the dust of the earth, flesh born of the flesh? Wouldst thou place thyself on a level with the Lord, thy Maker, and barter with Him? What wouldst .thou give Him that is not already His own? It is *thyself* thou owest Him, thy body and soul, and in order that thou shouldst serve Him in righteousness, He hath shown thee what is good, and requires of thee to live according to His commandments, not in arrogant self-righteousness, but loving mercy and walking humbly with thy God." *With thy God* is not the same as *before* thy God, but indicates that our ways should be the ways of God, He being ever with us and we with Him, *walking*, that is, moving forward step by step, as He directs us and leads us by His commandments. And this conformity with the commandments of God should not be of outward works only, but also of heart and soul, a heart that *loves mercy*, and a soul that is *humble* and trusts in God, *its* God. This is more than all whole burnt offerings and sacrifices (Mark 12, 23).

Deut. 6, 6.7: *And these words, which I command thee this day, shall be in thine heart: and thou shalt teach them diligently unto thy children.*

The words referred to are the words of the *Law*, and the present admonition is addressed to Israel, the people of God (Deut. 6, 4.5). The speaker is Moses, by whom God promulgated His Law in Israel, and what he here says is itself an injunction to all those to whom he was, under God, the lawgiver of the people. It is a maxim of human law that the first demand the law makes is that it should be known. And here the duty to know the law and to bear it in mind is imposed upon all whom the law concerns. Ignorance of the law is no excuse, but is itself a violation of the law. And inasmuch as a father is responsible for his children and bound to see to their welfare, it is also his duty to teach the law to his children, and to do this with all diligence, lest his children, being ignorant of the law, in and by such ignorance offend against the law. Again, the children also are not excused by ignorance of the law, and if it is the parent's duty to teach them the law, it is their duty with all diligence to learn the law and to keep it in mind at all times and everywhere. See continuation, Deut. 6, 7-9.

Rom. 2, 14.15: *For when the Gentiles, which have not the law, do by nature the things contained in the law, these, having not the law, are a law unto themselves: which show the work of the law written in their hearts, their conscience also bearing witness, and their thoughts the mean while accusing or else excusing one another.*

The text is here quoted to substantiate the statement that God, in the creation of man, wrote the law in man's heart. St. Paul speaks of the Gentiles and describes them as *having not the law*. He thereby distinguishes them from the Jews, who had the law, that is, the written law as it was codified and promulgated through Moses, the lawgiver of Israel. And yet the Gentiles are not without the law. While they have not the law written in the book of the law, they *are a law unto themselves*, a norm of right and wrong which is really and truly *law*, *nomos*, the published will of the lawgiver, of equal stringency with the law of Sinai, but differing in form and in the mode of publication. Through Moses the law was published as a code of statutes written in the book of law, or as words or commandments graven in tablets of stone. The Gentiles, too, had the moral law, but differently published, *written in their hearts*, and in a different form, *showing the* WORKS *of the law*, indicating in every instance of internal or external human action what was in accordance with the will of God, so that, whatever any man would do or forbear, commit or omit, he might, by consulting the moral norm inscribed in his heart, know whether such act or work was good or evil, in conformity or at variance with the divine will. Thus the Gentiles, when they obeyed their superiors and maintained conjugal fidelity, or when they abstained from murder and theft and fornication, *did the things contained in the law*. And doing these things *by nature*, they showed the works of the law written in their hearts, a natural law handed down from generation to generation, not by traditional statutes, but by natural propagation, inheriting with their nature the natural law. And as at no time a new race of men had been created from which the Gentiles had taken their origin, but as *from one blood all nations of men* have come (Acts 17,26), the natural law must have come down to the later generations of men from the same source from which their common nature was descended, from Adam and Eve, our common ancestors, in whose hearts as in those of their natural descendants the natural law must have been written by the Creator's hand.

That this natural law is really *law*, a stringent and authoritative norm of right, is evinced by man's *conscience*, which *bears witness* to the law and testifies to every man that he is subject to that law and responsible to him who has given it and, as a jealous God, watches over and vindicates its dignity. As a law, it is not an aesthetical, but an ethical norm, not a rule determining what is pleasing and beautiful or the contrary, but what is right and wrong, and, therefore, the thoughts that are set astir by the voice of this law and the testimony of man's conscience are not of aesthetical, but of ethical concern, *accusing or else excusing one another.*

1 Tim. 1, 5: *Now the end of the commandment is charity out of a pure heart.*

The *commandment*, *parangelia*, here spoken of is the doctrine which Christian ministers are charged to preach concerning those things which the Christians should observe in holiness of life. The *end*, *telos*, that to which it should tend or lead, is said to be *charity, agape, love, out of a pure heart*. Sin, the transgression of the law, proceeds out of the heart, the impure, evil heart (Matt. 15, 19). Thus, also, the fulfillment of the law should proceed from the heart, a pure heart sanctified by the Spirit of God. While, according to this text, compliance with the law may seem a very simple and easy thing, only love and nothing more, the text teaches that the fulfilling of the law is not only difficult, but impossible, to the natural man, who lacks precisely that from which the fulfilling of the law must spring, *a pure heart.*

Rom. 13, 10: *Therefore love is the fulfilling of the law.*

In the 8th verse of the chapter St. Paul has said, *He that loveth another hath fulfilled the law.* This he has proved in the 9th verse by showing that all the special commandments of the law are summed up, *anakefalaioutai,* are briefly recapitulated, in the word, *Thou shalt Love thy neighbor as thyself.* For this he gives a reason when he says, v. 10, *Love worketh no ill to his neighbor.* To work ill to his neighbor is the manner of an enemy, who hates his neighbor, while love is kind, *chrestenetai,* (1 Cor. 13, 4), a disposition to do good, to benefit others. Now, every commandment of the law which regulates our relations to our neighbor serves as a safeguard and protection to the neighbor's interests, his dignity, life, spouse, property, and honor, his welfare in general. *Hence,* the apostle concludes in our text, *love is the fulfillment of the law,* as already stated in the words above, *He that loveth another hath fulfilled the law,* and not only the commandments of the second, but also those of the first table, since only *he who loveth God loveth his brother also* (1 John 4, 21).

THE FIRST COMMANDMENT.

Is. 42, 8: *I am the Lord: that is my name: and my glory will I not give to another, neither my praise to graven images.*

The text condemns idolatry of every kind, gross and fine. To give to any person or thing besides God the honor and praise we owe to God, is idolatry. This is a sin for which there is no excuse. God has revealed Himself to man as *the one personal (Ani, I,) Supreme Being;* this is His *name,* whereby we should *know Him* as what He is and would be *to us, and* whereby He would be called by us, *Thou, the Lord, my God.* Instead of this, the idolater turns around and says *to the fine gold, Thou art my confidence (Job 31, 24),* or *cries out, saying, Great is Diana of the Ephesians (Acts 19, 28),* giving honor and praise to a graven image. Such is idolatry.

Matt. 4, 10: *Thou shalt worship the Lord thy God, and Him only shalt thou serve.*

This text pertains to the words of Answer 15: *actually to adore a creature as God.*

Satan had tempted Jesus in the desert to commit idolatry by worshiping him, and this is a part of Christ's reply to the tempter.

Being Himself God, He might have said: "Get thee down before Me, Satan, and worship Me." But being man, *made of a woman and made under the Law* (Gal. 4, 4), in His state of humiliation, He gave as the reason for His refusal to comply with the devil's demand a commandment of God saying, *It is written, Thou shalt, etc.* He refers to such passages as Deut. 6, 13 and 10,20; and thus His refusal to worship Satan is stamped as an act of obedience to the Law of God. But if this Law, though it does not mention Satan, prohibits the worship of Satan, it also prohibits the *worship* of all other creatures, all manner of idolatry.

Ps. 115, 3.4: *But our God is in the heavens; He hath done whatsoever he hath pleased. Their idols are silver and gold, the work of men's hands.*

This text sets forth the blasphemous perverseness and foolishness of idolaters, who, instead of trusting in God, the almighty Maker of heaven and earth, who from His celestial throne governs the universe, repose their trust and confidence in what is so far beneath themselves as they are beneath God, idols of silver and gold, the work of their own or other men's hands. This ungodly foolishness is more at length described and derided in the verses following our text, as also in Is. 44, 9-19 and Jer. 10, 3-9. Such foolishness is also practised by those who seek help and succor before the statues or pictures of saints, etc.

Matt. 10, 28: *Fear not them which kill the body, but are not able to kill the soul: but rather fear Him which is able to destroy both soul and body in hell.*

The context shows that these words are specially directed to those who are threatened or afflicted with persecution because of their confession of the Christian faith (Matt. 10, 16-39). God is almighty and omniscient; He has numbered the very hair of our heads and promised us His protection (Matt. 10,30.31), while, on the other hand, Christ will deny those who deny Him, and he that finds his life by denying Him shall lose it (Matt. 10, 31.39) under the just judgment of Him who *is able to destroy both soul and body in hell.* On the other hand, our enemies and persecutors are creatures who may, at their utmost, kill the body, and that only with the permission of Him without whom no sparrow falls to the ground (Matt. 10, 29.30). In view of all this it is evident idolatry to fear the creature instead of fearing the Creator, the Father Almighty, and putting our trust in Him.

Matt. 10, 37: *He that loveth father or mother more than me is not worthy of me: and he that loveth son or daughter more than me is not worthy of me.*

That children should love their parents, and that parents should love their children, is proper according to the will and commandment of God. But filial and parental love is perverted into a sin when it infringes upon the love we owe our Savior and our God. He is Supreme, over all, God blessed forever (Rom. 9, 5); and hence, to love any inferior being more than God is clearly idolatrous, placing that creature not only beside but even above God. The judgment which Christ pronounces upon such idolaters is, They are *not worthy of Me.* The meaning of these words appears from the parallel text, Luke 14, 26: If any man come to Me, and hate not his father and mother......, *he cannot be My disciple.* Christ loved the Father above all things, also above His mother according to the flesh (Luke 2, 48.49), even above His own life (John 14, 31), and His disciples must do likewise. Hence an idolater cannot be a disciple of Christ; and he who is not with Christ, is against Him, an enemy of Christ under the wrath of God.

Prov. 3, 5: *Trust in the Lord with all thine heart; and lean not unto thine own understanding.*

God is the supreme Intelligence. *The Lord by wisdom hath founded the earth; by understanding hath He established the heavens* (Prov. 3, 19). Hence, to lean to our own inferior understanding instead of trusting in the Lord with all our heart is idolatry. As in the previous text God does not prohibit filial and parental love, but its perversion into idolatry, so also here God does not forbid the ordinate *use* of our understanding, but its idolatrous *abuse.*

Jer. 17, 5: *Cursed be the man that trusteth in man, and maketh flesh his arm, and whose heart departeth from the Lord.*

The continuation of this text is, *For he shall be like the heath in the desert, and shall not see when good cometh; but shall inhabit the parched places in the wilderness, in a salt land and not inhabited.*

Blessed is the man that trusteth in the Lord, and whose hope the Lord is. For he shall be as a tree planted by the waters, and that spreadeth out her roots by the river, and shall not see when heat cometh, but her leaf shall be green; and shall not be careful in the year of drought, neither shall cease from yielding fruit. (Jer. 17, 6-8).

Here, then, we have two parallel statements, the one beginning with, *Cursed be the man,* and the other with, *Blessed is the man.* The blessing is pronounced on *the man that trusteth in the Lord,* and his blessed state is then described as a state of prosperity such as God only, the Almighty, can give. The curse is, correspondingly, pronounced on him who in his heart *departeth from the Lord* and places his trust in man and his reliance on flesh, making that *his arm,* i. e., his strength (Cf. Ps. 84, 5), and when God in His wrath leaves these idolaters to their gods, their lot is as the prophet describes it, *like the heath in the desert,* etc.

Eph. 5, 5: *For this ye know, that no whoremonger, or unclean person, nor covetous man, who is an idolater, hath any inheritance in the kingdom of Christ and of God.*

The statement in point is that the covetous man is an idolater and cannot inherit the kingdom of God. The covetous man, *pleonektes*, is he who craves for MORE *possession (pleou echein)*. The German *habsuechtig* or *habgierig* comes near the Greek word, but does not quite cover it. But why is covetousness, *pleonexia*, a species of idolatry? Because the insatiable love which the covetous man bears toward created things is greater love than that which man may bear toward God. For the love of God satisfies the soul, so that having Him the heart will want no more. But the covetous man is never satisfied, but, having much, wants more, and still more, and infinitely more. Thus covetousness, *pleonexia*, is in its very nature idolatry, placing silver and gold not only beside, but above God, and justly excludes the covetous from that inheritance of which the Psalmist says, *I shall be satisfied, when I awake, with thy likeness* (Ps. 17, 15).

Phil. 3, 19: *Whose God is their belly, and whose glory is in their shame, who mind earthly things.*

The form of idolatry here described is, like that of covetousness, largely prevalent in our day, as it was in the days of St. Paul. It is the sin of materialism, of those *who mind earthly things*, who are absorbed in the things of this world; whose maxim is, *Let us eat and drink, for tomorrow we die*, (1 Cor. 15, 32). Of such the apostle says they *serve not our Lord Jesus Christ, but their own belly* (Rom. 16,18), or, in our text, *whose God is their belly*. Man was made for God (1 Cor. 8, 6. *eis auton)*, and every man should say with St. Paul: *God, whose I am and whom I serve* (Acts 27, 23). Christ has died for all, *that they which live should not henceforth live unto themselves, but unto Him who died for them and rose again.* (2 Cor. 5, 15). To live for this world and to serve the belly instead of living unto Christ and God and serving Him is, therefore, manifest idolatry, and idolatry of a base kind, whereby the votaries of the belly seek their glory in what is their shame, disgracing themselves in dishonoring God.

Ps. 14, 1: *The fool hath said in his heart, There is no God. They are corrupt, they have done abominable works.*

The denial of God is also a violation of the first commandment, *Thou shalt have no other Gods before me;* for this implies that man should regard and adore as his God the one true God who places at the head of His commandments the statement, *I am the Lord thy God.* (Ex. 20, 2. Deut. 5, 6.) The text calls him who denies the existence of God a *fool*, whose sin is not only ungodly, but also unreasonable, being at variance with the joint testimony of all the creatures of the universe, the *fool* himself not excepted, whose very existence and nature would be impossible without a Maker of heaven and earth. But the text gives also the reason why such fools deny the existence of God: *They are corrupt; they have done abominable works.* Being wicked, they have an interest in denying the existence of a righteous, holy, and almighty God who will punish their *abominable works.* And this motive, their surpassing love of darkness which prompts them to hate the light again stamps them idolaters. (John 3, 19.20.)

John 5, 23: *That all men should honor the Son, even as they honor the Father. He that honoreth not the Son, honoreth not the Father which hath sent him.*

This text is directed against a species of idolatry also very prevalent in our day, especially in secret societies which perform religious rites and ceremonies, but exclude the worship of Jesus Christ, the Son of God and only Savior of mankind. It will not do to say, "We pray to the Father in the lodge and do not prevent others from praying to the Son without the lodge." *All men* should honor the Son *even as* they honor the Father, and he that does not honor the Son, not only withholds from the Son the honor which is His, but does not truly honor the Father whom he professes to worship. For *whosoever denieth the Son, the same hath not the Father.* (John 2, 23.) What has he then? An idol, the creature of his own imagination, a false, man-made God, no more the true God than any idol of wood or stone.

Gen. 17, 1: *I am the Almighty God; walk before Me and be thou perfect.*

This is a very remarkable text. Twenty-four years after God had led Abram from Haran to the land of Canaan and given him the promise that in him all the families of the earth should be blessed (Gen. 12, 1-3), these words were spoken. Abram was then a worshiper of the true God (Gen. 12, 7.8; 13, 4.18), who had declared Himself his shield and exceeding great reward. (Gen. 15, 1.) Abram then stood justified by faith. (Gen. 15, 6; Rom. 4, 3. Gal. 3, 6.) And this man it was to whom the words of our text were spoken. They consist of a statement and an injunction. The statement is, *I am the Almighty God.* The Hebrew El Shaddai designates God as the *Almighty Mighty One*, the *God of transcendent power.* The injunction is, *Walk before me, and be thou perfect.* What God demands of Abram is nothing less than perfect holiness; and to render such holiness, he is to walk before God, to take every step, perform every act, both external and internal, in thought, word, or deed, as before, under the very eyes of, God; and all that constantly remembering that He, under whose watchful eyes he walks, is the Almighty God, before whom even the holy man must stand in awe and with bated breath, under whose mighty scepter the righteous may abide in peace and perfect security, but who is to the unrighteous a consuming fire.

There is, perhaps, in all the Scriptures no other text which in words as brief as these inculcates the true fear of God as an incentive to true holiness of life in those who are the children of God by faith and in whom the renewal of the image of God is in progress.

Ps. 33, 8: *Let all the earth fear the Lord: let all the inhabitants of the world stand in awe of Him.*

This text, taken in conjunction with its context, has this in common with the preceding text that it points out the omnipotence and sovereign majesty of God with a view of inculcating due reverence and fear of God. In the previous context the psalmist speaks of the exhibition of divine power in the creation of the world and the government of the universe, as *By the word of the Lord the heavens were made, and all the host of them by the breath of his mouth. He gathereth the waters of the sea together as an heap; he layeth up the depth in storehouses.* And in the subsequent context he continues, FOR *He spake, and it was done; he commanded, and it stood fast. The Lord bringeth the counsel of the heathen to nought, he maketh the devices of the people of none effect.* And therefore, he says in our text, *let all the earth fear the Lord,* which, by a parallelism familiar in the psalms, he repeats, saying, *let all the inhabitants of the world stand in awe of Him,* the second member, as is frequently the case, dropping the figure of speech employed in the first member, substituting *the inhabitants of the world,* for *all the earth,* which stands for *the dwellers on the earth.*

But the argument of our text and context agrees with that of the text from Gen. 17 also in this that it makes the fear of God a mainspring of our obedience to the will of God as revealed in his commandments. Having called upon all men to fear God and stand in awe of Him, he continues, *For He* SPAKE, *and it was done; He* COMMANDED, *and it stood fast;* as if to say: Heaven and earth came into being in *obedience* to His *word* and in *compliance* with His *command,* as it was God, the Almighty One, who spoke and commanded. How much more should man, to whom God has revealed Hims.lf in many ways, be moved by the fear of God to obey Him and perform His holy will.

Gen. 39, 9: *How can I do this great wickedness, and sin against God?*

The sin which Joseph, then an inmate in the house of Potiphar, was here tempted to commit was the sin of adultery, by which Joseph would have violated the conjugal rights of his master and the trust which Potiphar had reposed in his Hebrew servant. This was in Joseph's mind when he said, *Behold, my master wotteth not what is with me in the house, and he hath committed all that he hath to my hand; there is none greater in this house than I; neither hath he kept back any thing from me but thee, because thou art his wife.* Yet Joseph does not continue in words as these: "How then should I commit this great sin against my master?" or, "What would Potiphar, my master and thy husband, say and do if I were to commit this grave offense against him?" Joseph knows that the eye of One who is greater than Potiphar is upon him, that by yielding to the temptation of this adulterous woman he would offend against the holy will of God, and it is the fear of God that prevails in him and puts into his mouth the words recorded in our text. Thus here, again, the fear of God is shown to be a cardinal virtue, a safeguard against all manner of sins, and a source of true holiness according to all the commandments of God.

Ps. 73, 25.26: *Whom have I in heaven but Thee? and there is none upon earth that I desire beside Thee. My flesh and my heart faileth: but God is the strength of my heart, and my portion forever.*

The love of God in a human heart is nowhere in the Scriptures uttered more forcibly than in this text. The love of God which is here described is so much a love of God above all things, that it is a love of God to the utter exclusion of all things. Aside of God heaven with all its host, its glory and bliss, is void and empty, and the earth with all its treasures and pleasures is vacant space to the psalmist, who in heaven and earth knows of but one object of his possession and desire, and that is God. Nor is this all. The psalmist loves God even with the exclusion of his own self. If his flesh and his heart, his body and soul, should fail him, that is, if he should be deprived of that wherein he exists, then he would still cling to God and live in spite of death and destruction, since God is his strength and his portion forever. This last sentiment is given by Paul Gerhardt in the words:

> Du sollst sein meines Herzens Licht,
> Und wann mein Herz in Stuecken bricht,
> Sollst du mein Herze bleiben,

And the whole text is exquisitely versified in the following words of Martin Schalling's hymn, *Herzliech lieb hab ich dich, o Herr:*

> I scorn the richest earthly lot,
> E'en heaven and earth attract me not,
> If only thou art near to me.
> Yea, though my heart be like to break,
> Thou shalt my trust that naught can shake,
> My portion and my comfort be.

Ps. 42, 11: *Why art thou cast down, O my soul? and why art thou disquieted within me? hope thou in God; for I shall yet praise Him, who is the health of my countenance, and my God.*

The psalm of which this text is the closing verse is a lamentation of an anguished soul, thirsting after God. The second section of the psalm begins with the words, *O my God, my soul is cast down within me: therefore will I remember thee,* v. 6. Finding no strength within himself and no help about himself, he lifts up his thoughts to God. And now he argues with his soul. He does not deny the power of his enemies nor his own weakness. Neither does he behold the helping hand of God already turning away the oppression of the enemy. And yet he reproaches his soul for being bowed down and moaning in trepidation and thus troubling him without cause. For is not God still *God,* a mighty helper above all his enemies? And so firm is his reliance on Him who is the health of his countenance, and his *God,* under whose protecting care no harm can befall him, that in the midst of his tribula-.

tions, and while he is yet exhorting his soul to wait for future help, he is, as it were, already tuning his harp to songs of praise and thanksgiving; for he *trusts in God.*

Ps. 118, 8: *It is better to trust in the Lord than to put confidence in man.*

Here, again, the power of the Lord is contrasted with the strength, or the weakness, of men. But the text is taken from a song of praise rising from the hearts and lips of those who have experienced the goodness and power of God. In v. 5, the psalmist points to a certain distress, from the midst of which, as in Ps. 42, the believer called upon the Lord; and the Lord answered him and helped him, so that from gladsome experience he could say, *The Lord is on my side; I will not fear: what can man do unto me? The Lord taketh my part with them that help me: therefore shall I see my desire upon them that hate me.* And now, as the psalmist contemplates the ways of men, who, when threatened or assailed by enemies, will look about for allies among men and the princes of men, he takes comfort in knowing that the Lord is on his side and takes his part as his ally against all his enemies. For while confidence reposed in men, even in princes, is often misplaced, and human aid is often by sad experience shown to be of no avail, his experience has taught him that *it is better to trust in the Lord than to put confidence in man; it is better to trust in the Lord than to put confidence in princes.*

But what is true as to men in general and princes in particular is also true as to physicians and their remedies, fathers and mothers, wealthy and influential friends and relatives, and whoever else may be looked upon as deserving of trust and confidence: it is better to trust in the Lord; and to confide in them instead of or above and before the Lord is idolatry.

THE SECOND COMMANDMENT.

Ps. 48, 10: *According to Thy name, O God, so is Thy praise unto the ends of the earth: Thy right hand is full of righteousness.*

The 48th psalm is a song of victory to celebrate a new manifestation of divine power and greatness in the protection of the city of God. *Great is the Lord, and greatly to be praised,* is the opening strain and the burden of the psalm. The name of God is that by which He is known, and we cannot know God unless He reveals or manifests Himself. Again, to praise God is to voice forth His name by extolling His deeds. The fame of God is, according to our text, in accordance with His name: that which may be said of Him is commensurate with what He has revealed of Himself. And His right hand is full of righteousness. Our right hand is our chief organ of action, the fighting hand in war and the working hand in peace. Thus the right hand of God again stands for His activity, whereby He manifests Himself as what He is, power, love, truth, or, what the text mentions, righteousness. And *righteousness* is a divine name; *this is His* NAME *whereby he* SHALL BE CALLED, *the Lord our righteousness.* (Jer. 23, 6; 33, 16.)

Lev. 24, 15.16: *Whosoever curseth his God, shall bear his sin. And he that blasphemeth the name of the Lord, he shall surely be put to death.*

The sin here proscribed is that of speaking evil against God and impugning His name. A son of an Israelitish woman and an Egyptian father, in a quarrel with a man of Israel in the camp, had committed this offense and was stoned pursuant to a special order of God, v. 10-14. Before this sentence was executed, v. 23, God caused the injunction set forth in our text to be published to all the children of Israel with the express statement that it should apply to the stranger as well as to him that was born in the land, v. 16.

Gal. 6, 7: *Be not deceived; God is not mocked.*

In the words preceding our text the apostle has enjoined upon the hearers of the word the duty of contributing from their temporal goods toward the support of their teachers. To render this command-ment all the more impressive, the apostle adds the solemn warning, *Be not deceived· God is not mocked,* or, in other words, God will not allow this commandment to be set aside with impunity. The verb *mukteridzein* signifies a contemptuous gesture, as an unruly inferior may turn up his nose and sneer at the command of a master whom he holds in contempt. Thus the apostle teaches that wilful disregard of the manifest will of God is also a manner of blasphemy which will not go unpunished, and that he who neglects or refuses to heed this will but deceive himself.

James 3, 9.10: *By the tongue bless we God, even the Father; and therewith curse we men, which are made after the similitude of God. Out of the same mouth proceed blessing and cursing. My brethren, these things ought not so to be.*

This text would, from two different points of view, teach all Christians to consider and comprehend the utter impropriety of cursing their fellow-men. In the first place, a Christian, whose duty and daily occupation is to bless God, would by cursing a fellow-man expose himself to such divine censure as this: "How canst thou, while praising Me, the Creator, at the same time curse my creature, made after My own similitude, in My own image? Gen. 1, 26.27. Is not this gross incon-sistency? Is not thy praise thereby turned into scoffing?" But cursing in a Christian is not only improper when the objects of his blessing and cursing are considered, but also, in the second place, in view of the sub-ject which performs these contrary and contradictory acts, and the nature of these acts themselves. God has given us our mouths as all other organs that we should use them in His service, in obedience to His commandments. But what consistency is there in blessing God in obedience to this Second Commandment, and abusing His name by cursing in open violation of this same commandment? Is it not mockery that these two acts, so incompatible with one another, should proceed from the same mouth, the mouth of a Christian? The same argument is continued in the subsequent context: *Doth a fountain send forth at the same place sweet water and bitter? Can the fig tree, my brethren, bear olive berries? either a vine, figs?* Thus, also, he would say, it is not in the proper nature of a Christian, not compatible with his fruit, that he should curse. And hence, these things ought, surely, not to be.

2 Cor. 1, 23: *Moreover, I call God for a record upon my soul.*

For *record* the Revised Version has substituted *witness*, the correct translation of the Greek *martura, Zeuge.* That whereto he calls upon God to testify is the truth of his assertion, *that to spare you I came not as yet unto Corinth.* The emphasis is on *feidomenos humon, to spare you,* which states the motive whereby the apostle was prompted to delay his return to Corinth. But a man's motives, which reside in his soul are known only to himself and God, and the apostle, as he is about to state his motive, calls upon God, who knows all things and is Himself the Truth, to be his witness and testify to the truth of his statement. This is the very essence of an oath sworn by God's name. And as it is an apostle of Christ who, under inspiration of the Holy Ghost, makes this solemn appeal, we may know that it is not under all circumstances wrong to "call upon God as the witness of truth or the avenger of falsehood."

Matt. 5, 33-37: *Again, ye have heard that it hath been said to them of old time, Thou shalt not forswear thyself, but shalt perform unto the Lord thine oaths; but I say unto you, Swear not at all; neither by heaven; for it is God's throne: nor by the earth; for it is his footstool: neither by Jerusalem; for it is the city of the great King. Neither shalt thou swear by thy head, because thou canst not make one hair white or black. But let your communication be, Yea, yea; Nay, nay: for whatsoever is more than these cometh of evil.*

To understand this text correctly, we must, in the first place, remember that it cannot be intended as an absolute prohibition of oaths, since lawful oaths are expressly sanctioned by divine commandment and example and by numerous appeals of the holy men of God, even under divine inspiration, to God as the witness and judge of the truth of their statements (Deut. 6, 13. Ex. 22, 11. Deut. 10,20. Is. 19, 18; 65, 16. Jer. 4, 2; 5, 7; 12, 16. Ps. 63, 11.—Gen. 22, 16. Hebr. 6, 13. 16. 17. Luke 1, 73. Matt. 26, 63.64.—Rom. 1, 9. Gal. 1, 20. Phil. 1, 8), and no interpretation of a text can be correct which conflicts with other clear texts of Scripture. In the second place we must consider the scope of this admonition. From the forms of oaths quoted by Christ, which were not judicial oaths, we see that the Lord here deals with the evil habit of irreverent swearing, of loading down commonplace conversations and assertions with all manner of oaths, a custom which to this day prevails among Jews and Mohammedans. In extenuation of this habit, the Jews distinguished between the solemn oaths by the holy name of God and such other oaths as, "By heaven," "By Jerusalem," "By my head," etc., and maintained that they kept within the law if they abstained from perjuring themselves by the Name expressly invoked. This attempted justification of an immoral practice is, together with the practice itself, discountenanced by the authentical Interpreter of the law, who in our text would lead the Jews to understand that their irreverent oaths were, in fact, no less abusive of the name of God than the forms which they avoided would have been under like circumstances, since those familiar oaths by heaven and earth and Jerusalem and their own heads were ultimately but so many invocations of Him who is the Ruler of the heavens, His throne, and of the earth, His footstool, and of Jerusalem, His own peculiar city, and holds dominion over every hair of our heads. Thus, then, the Pharisaical theory is shown to be utterly at variance with the law, which, while it does not prohibit, but enjoins, the proper use of the oath, condemns not only one form, but all forms of swearing besides and beyond that proper use, where *yea* should be simply *yea*, and *nay* should be simply *nay*, and what is more than these and partakes of the nature of an oath is a violation of the law and *cometh of evil*, just as killing in any form besides and beyond the proper use of the sword is murder, and carnal intercourse besides and beyond that which is proper in lawful marriage is lewdness, whether in the form of fornication, or of adultery, or of any other sin of uncleanness, though it be only that of looking at a woman to lust after her. (Matt. 5, 28.)

Deut. 6, 13: *Thou shalt fear the Lord thy God, and serve Him, and shalt swear by His name.*

This verse contains three injunctions, to fear God, to serve Him, and to swear by His name; and it is just as truly the will of God that we should swear by his name as it is that we should fear and serve Him. At the same time, the context shows that the oath is to be looked upon as an act of worship which must be performed to the true God only. For in the preceding verse we read, *Beware lest thou forget the Lord*, etc., and in the following verse, *Ye shall not go after other gods, of the gods of the people which are round about you.* Hence, in the light of our text, the oaths taken in societies which worship a man-made god instead of the Triune God are an idolatrous abomination as inconsistent with the Christian faith as an oath by or a prayer to the Mohammedan *Allah* or the heathen *Jupiter* would be in the mouth of a Christian.

Hebr. 6, 16: *For men verily swear by the greater: and an oath for confirmation is to them an end of all strife.*

These words are a part of an argument beginning in v. 13 and ending in v. 18. The argument is this: an oath is an appeal to the highest authority and is final in settling the point which it is to confirm. God, having no authority above Himself, swears by Himself. Men, being under God, swear by the greater, by God. In both cases the oath is conclusive, and if even among men a truth confirmed by an oath is considered beyond dispute, then, surely, when God has confirmed the immutability of his counsel by an oath, we have a strong consolation.— This argument incidentally sanctions the proper use of oaths for the settlement of disputes or litigations, or the confirmation of the truth where such confirmation is necessary for God's sake or for the benefit of others. It should be noted that the holy writer does not speak of past ages, but of the present time, the time of New Testament Christianity, which this epistle in other respects places into sharp contrast with the past dispensation of the Old Covenant. (Cf. chapters 8, 9, 10, 11.) And thus we learn that the commandment in Deut. 6, 13 is not revoked in the New Testament.

Deut. 18, 10-12: *There shall not be found among you any one that maketh his son or his daughter to pass through the fire, or that useth divination, or an observer of times, or an enchanter, or a witch, or a charmer, or a consulter with familiar spirits, or a wizard, or a necromancer. For all that do these things are an abomination unto the Lord: and because of these abominations the Lord thy God doth drive them out before thee.*

The law here enumerates the various forms of satanic art prevalent among the heathen nations. That the precise meaning of the various terms cannot now be ascertained is easily understood when we consider the occult character of these practices. Most of them seem to refer to the prediction of future events or the revelation of hidden things. But when at the head of the list we find those practices which were connected with the Canaanitic Moloch-worship, of which human sacrifices were a prominent feature (Lev. 18, 12. 2 Kings 16, 3; 17, 17; 21, 26; 23, 10. Jer. 7, 31; 32, 35. Ezek. 16, 20.21; 20,31), we are led to understand that all these arts and practices were and are satanic in their nature. For of those who practiced these abominations we read, *They were mingled among the heathen, and learned their works, and they served their idols, which were a snare unto them. Yea they sacrificed their sons and their daughters* UNTO DEVILS. (Ps. 106, 35-37. Cf.1 Cor. 10, 20. *These things which the Gentiles sacrifice, they sacrifice* TO DEVILS. Cf. Lev. 17, 7. Deut. 32, 17. Rev. 9, 20.) Yet these sins, as appears from texts quoted above, became a deep-rooted evil among the Israelites, who learned them from their heathen neighbors, very much as similar satanic arts have found their way from heathen ancestors and oriental nations into the Christian communities of the present day and largely baffle all efforts to eradicate them.

Jer. 23, 31: *Behold, I am against the prophets, saith the Lord, that use their tongues and say, He saith.*

These words of God spoken through the prophet are a proscription of all manner of false doctrine as an abuse of God's name. A prophet is a man by whom God would reveal Himself, His counsel and will, into whose mouth God gives *His* word, and whose tongue He makes *His* tongue. False prophets, however, *taking their own tongue*, and speaking their own words, *oracle forth oracles*, utter what they would have others receive and accept as the word of God. This is *"lying and deceiving by God's name."* And of such God says, *I am against them.* That there are conflicting doctrines in the world is not according to the will of God. He is the Truth and *shall destroy them that speak leasing.* (Ps. 5, 6.) He is against the false teachers and false doctrines at all times and everywhere; and this we should note and bear in mind. *Behold,* says our text; and the same word occurs twice more in the context, vv. 30-32, to make sure of attracting the reader's and hearers attention to these important words. And, furthermore, the Lord Himself gives us a commentary to our text in the subsequent verse: *Behold, I am against them that prophesy false dreams, saith the Lord, and to tell them, and cause my people to err by their lies, and by their lightness; yet I sent them not, nor commanded them: therefore they shall not profit this people at all, saith the Lord.*

Matt. 15, 8: *This people draweth nigh unto me with their mouth, and honoreth me with their lips; but their heart is far from me.*

These words are quoted from Is. 29, 13 and applied by Christ to the Jewish scribes and Pharisees who were, in doctrine and practice, religious hypocrites, substituting their traditions for the word of God and living ungodly lives under the pretense of surpassing sanctity. (Matt. 15, 1-6.) He who pretends to be what he is not, is a liar everywhere, and he who professes godliness with his mouth and is ungodly at heart lies and deceives by God's name. And how grave this offense against the holy name of God really is, and how fearful its consequences have been in God's dealing with religious hypocrites, appears from the context in Isaiah, where God says in the previous context, *The Lord hath poured out upon you the spirit of deep sleep, and hath closed your eyes: the prophets and your rulers, the seers hath he covered, and the vision of all is become as the words of a book that is sealed, etc.*, and, after the words quoted, he continues, *Therefore, behold, I will proceed to do a marvelous work among this people, even a marvelous work and a wonder: for the wisdom of their wise men shall perish, and the understanding of their prudent men shall be hid, etc.* Such is the consequence and punishment of religious hypocrisy, a heart which has become callous and benumbed, spiritual stupidity and blindness to an extraordinary degree.

Matt. 7, 21: *Not every one that saith unto me, Lord, Lord, shall enter into the kingdom of heaven; but he that doeth the will of my Father which is in heaven.*

The discourse from which these words are taken is the Sermon on the Mount, which is, in the main, an exposition of the Law; and the special subject dealt with in the section preceding our text pertains to the Second Commandment. Here, too, the Savior speaks of such as take the name of the Lord our God in vain. He warns His hearers to *beware of false prophets, which come to them in sheep's clothing, but inwardly are ravening wolves,* who professing to be prophets, messengers of God proclaiming His truth, teach error and falsehood, and thus "lie and deceive by God's name." Having closed this special warning with the repeated advice, *Wherefore by their fruits* ye shall know them, He now proceeds to take a more general view of the same sin, including the hearers as well as the teachers, and warning both not to take the name of the Lord in vain. TO SAY *Lord, Lord,* and at the same time to neglect or refuse to DO the will of the Father in heaven is a sin which excludes the sinners from the kingdom of heaven. This is more explicitly set forth in the subsequent context. That the text would not teach salvation by works is clear from the terms in opposition, which are not *faith* and *works,* but *saying* and *doing,. professing* to be servants of the Lord, and *being in fact* what saying *Lord, Lord,* should indicate, true servants of God, who do His will. That this is the import of the text, and that salvation by works is not thought of, appears from the subsequent context, which expressly rejects salvation by works, as it points out those who have performed external works, *wonderful works,* some of which they enumerate as having been done "in Christ's name." But these works prove of no avail to them, since their performance in Christ's name was again only taking the name of God in vain. These hypocrites had not in truth been what by their words and their deeds they had pretended to be, true servants of the Lord by faith in Christ, walking in righteousness and *true* holiness. (Eph. 4, 24.)

Ps. 50, 15: *Call upon me in the day of trouble: I will deliver thee, and thou shalt glorify me.*

The entire psalm from which these words are taken is a lesson on the worship and sacrifices acceptable to God. In the verses immediately preceding our text we read, *Will I eat the flesh of bulls, or drink the blood of goats? Offer unto God thanksgiving: and pay thy vows unto the most high: and,* continues the psalm, CALL UPON ME *in the day of trouble: I will deliver thee,* and THOU SHALT GLORIFY ME. Prayer and praise, then, are here pointed out as proper sacrifices to be offered up before God (Cf. v. 23:*Whoso* OFFERETH *praise glorifieth me*), as acts of worship acceptable in His sight. This being so, it is clear that communion of prayer is communion of worship and religion and is admissible only where all other exercises of religion and acts of worship might be performed in common. Communion of prayer with those who adhere to and profess false doctrine is taking away with one hand what is offered with the other, the hallowing of God's name. (This text occurs again in the exposition of the Lord's prayer, where it must be considered from a different point of view.)

Matt. 7, 7: *Ask, and it shall be given you; seek, and ye shall find; knock, and it shall be opened unto you.*

This text is also taken from the Sermon on the Mount, the Lawgiver's exposition of the Law. In the subsequent context the Father in heaven, to whom we should pray, is compared with human fathers with a view of showing that we should pray to God with all confidence, knowing that He is able and willing to hear our prayers and give us what we ask. Thus it appears to pray in the right spirit of filial confidence and veneration is to glorify the name of our *Father which is in heaven,* and thus to offer unto God an acceptable sacrifice and to worship Him as He alone deserves to be worshiped by His children. (The consideration of the climax in *ask, seek,* and *knock,* and of the promises embodied in the text, should also be reserved for the exposition of the Lord's prayer, where the text recurs.)

Ps. 103, 3: *Bless the Lord, O my soul: and all that is within me, bless his holy name.*

To bless, *barak,* as *eulogein,* when the object is God, is to *praise,* to acknowledge and extol the blessings which He has bestowed upon us. Thus, in the next verse, the psalmist says, *Bless the Lord, O my soul,* AND FORGET NOT ALL HIS BENEFITS, and in the subsequent verses he proceeds to enumerate a series of divine blessings which should induce his soul *to bless the Lord.* All these divine blessings are manifestations of the goodness and power and wisdom and truth of God, and to extol them is to magnify the *name* of God. It is of peculiar significance that the psalmist, a holy man of God, should exhort *his soul* to bless the Lord, and *all that is within him* to bless His holy name: for thus he sets an example to every Christian and, at the same time, leads us to understand that the best among us are far from perfection and have ample reason to let our first note of praise be, *Who forgiveth all thine iniquities.*

Ps. 118, 1: *O give thanks unto the Lord; for he is good; because his mercy endureth forever.*

Thanking differs from *praising* inasmuch as the latter refers more to the praiseworthy qualities of the object of praise, while *thanking* is rather an acknowledgment of the subject's indebtedness to the giver of that for which thanks are rendered. Thus we may *praise* God also for the blessings bestowed upon others, but we *thank* Him for blessings which in some way concern ourselves. But both terms have this in common, that they imply a recognition of something that is good and estimable in the object of praise and thanksgiving. Thus, in our text, the goodness of God and His everlasting grace are mentioned as the motives for giving thanks unto the Lord. The Hebrew *tob* also stands for what the Greek *chrestos, kind, guetig, freundlich,* express, goodness in manifestation, the disposition to do good to others, and *chesed, charis, grace, Gnade,* is the goodness that blesses of its own accord, freely gives what it gives, regardless of merits or demerits in those whom it blesses. Thus the goodness and grace of God, whereby God is an everlasting fountain of blessings freely given to sinful man, is most eminently a cause of thanks, unceasing thanks, the sacrifices of human hearts and lips; and offering thanks, especially for the goodness and grace of God, is most pertinently a work of the Second Commandment.

THE THIRD COMMANDMENT.

Matt. 12, 8: *The Son of man is Lord even of the sabbath day.*

The disciples of Christ, while passing through a cornfield with their Master on a sabbath day, and being hungry, had plucked ears of corn and eaten. For this the Pharisees had upraided Jesus and accused the disciples and Himself of an unlawful act. But Jesus justified His disciples and Himself and reproved the Pharisees for not knowing the letter or understanding the spirit of the law even as it was binding upon the Jews. Thus, the Mosaic laws prohibited all men but the priests to eat of the show bread in the temple; and yet King David and they who were with him had eaten of the show bread when they were hungry, and they committed no wrong. And, furthermore, he continues, does not the law itself, Lev. 24, 8. Num. 28, 9.10, permit to or even enjoin upon the priests the performance of certain duties in the temple on the sabbath day? Now, then, if the holiness of the temple permitted or even required such services in the face of the law, how can you reprimand My disciples for doing what they have done in My presence? "I say unto you that One greater than the temple is here," He in whom dwells the fullness of the Godhead bodily, Col. 2, 9.

Having thus shown them that they did not even properly know the letter of the Law, He proceeds to show them that they have even less knowledge of the spirit of the Law, according to which love, compassionate love, is the fulfillment of the Law. "For had ye known," says He, "what it means, I desire mercy and not sacrifice, ye would not have condemned the guiltless." And guiltless they certainly were; "for the Son of Man is Lord even of the sabbath day." This settles the whole question. He who understands the law of the sabbath as Christ understands it, and who observes it as Christ would have it observed, truly understands and observes it, no matter what the blind Pharisees and the like of them may say to the contrary. And when, finally, Christ sets aside or entirely abrogates the sabbath, it is set aside or abrogated by the Lord of the sabbath, and no authority in heaven or earth shall any longer make it binding on any man's conscience.

Col. 2, 16.17: *Let no man therefore judge you in meat, or in drink, or in respect of a holyday, or of the new moon, or of the sabbath days: which are the shadow of things to come; but the body is in Christ.*

The admonition of which this text is a part begins in v. 8 of the chapter, where the apostle says: "Beware lest any man spoil you through philosophy and vain deceit, after the tradition of men," etc. He then proceeds to show how Christ had done away with the rite of circumcision by substituting the spiritual "circumcision made without hands," especially in the sacrament of Baptism, vv. 11-13, how He abrogated the whole handwriting of ordinances, the Mosaic law, v. 14, and made us free from all manner of spiritual thraldom, v. 15. "*Therefore,*" oun, he continues, "since the law is taken from your necks and you are free children of God in and through Christ crucified, and complete in Him who is the Head of all principality and power, v. 10, let no man judge you in meat, or in drink, or in respect of a holyday, or of the new moon, or of the sabbath days, which are the shadow of things to come; but the body is in Christ." Judgment, he would say, is according to the law; where there is no law, there can be no judgment. Now the law of circumcision, of meat and drink, of holydays, new moons and the sabbath days, is cancelled and abrogated since Christ is come and the new dispensation, which was foreshadowed by the rites and sacraments of the old; and, therefore, the judaizing teachers, with their philosophy, v. 8, are entirely out of date and only endeavor to place a yoke on your necks which Christ would not have you bear, Acts 15, 10. Thus, then, the Augsburg Confession is in full accord with St. Paul when, having made reference to our text, it says in the 28th article: "Such is the observation of the Lord's day, of Easter, of Pentecost, and like holydays and rites. For they think that the observation of the Lord's day was appointed by the authority of the church, instead of the sabbath, as necessary, are greatly deceived. The Scripture, which teaches that all the Mosaic ceremonies can be omitted after the Gospel is revealed, has abrogated the sabbath."

Hebr. 10, 25: *Not forsaking the assembling of ourselves together, as the manner of some is.*

In the preceding verses the Christians are exhorted to draw near to God, or to offer divine worship, Hebr. 7, 25; 11, 6; 4, 16, in the house of God, the church of Christ, in which Christ is the great high priest, vv. 21 and 22. All the elements of Christian worship are implicitly or explicitly indicated in the words following. The full assurance of faith, the sanctifying of our bodies and souls, v. 22, must be wrought by the means of grace, the word and sacraments of the new covenant, prefigured by the ritual sprinkling and washing of the former dispensation. The profession of faith, the praise of God for all His bountiful goodness according to His promises, and works of brotherly love to which Christians provoke one another, are the acceptable sacrifices of

the children of God. And all this intercourse with God and with one
another we should exercise not only privately and individually, but *not
forsaking*, by non-attendance, *the assembling of ourselves together*.
Episunagoge cannot stand here for congregation, the local body of
Christian people, and *egkataleipein* cannot mean the separation from
such body by dissolution of church membership, since that could not be
described as *ethos*, a custom; but *episunagoge* is the assembling together in religious meetings for Christian worship, for common and
mutual edification and communication, from which even in those early
days some members of Christian congregations stood aloof. But it is
the will of God that Christians should thus assemble, though He has
not prescribed times and places when and where such meetings must
be held; and he who refuses to attend public worship when his brethren
the world over have appointed Sunday as the day of common edification
should know that he sins against the will of God, not because it is
Sunday, but because it is public worship, which he sets aside.

Acts 2, 42: *And they continued steadfastly in the apostles' doctrine and fellowship, and in breaking of bread, and in prayers.*

The second chapter of the Acts is a narrative of the origin of the
first Christian congregation at Jerusalem. To this whole congregation
the pronoun *they* in our text refers. In four things the members of
this church are said to have continued steadfastly. The first was the
apostles' doctrine, he didache ton apostolon. The apostles were the
teachers of the church, and all members of the congregation came to hear
them, and not only occasionally, but regularly and assiduously, paying
close attention to what they were permitted to hear: *esan proskart-
erountes*. To hear the doctrine of the apostles was from the beginning
of the church the chief element of public worship. The *communion,
koinonia*, mentioned next, is not the internal communion of Christians
inasmuch as they are united in Christ as members of His body by the
unity of faith, but, as the hearing of the word, the breaking of the
bread, and prayer, with which it is placed in line, a common occupation
of the members of the church, an outward manifestation of the internal
union and communion, existing also in the exercise of fraternal benevolence, which was from the beginning so prominent a feature in the religious life of the early church. Thus Rom. 15, 26. 2 Cor. 9, 13. Hebr.
13, 16 the contributions for the support of indigent brethren, as also of
the ministry, are especially called *koinonia*, in which sense also the verb
koinonein is used Rom. 12, 13. Gal. 6. 6; and 1 Cor. 16, 1.2 we learn that
these contributions were made on the common meeting day of the
Christians in apostolic times. Cf. Acts 4, 35.37; 5, 2. The *breaking of
the bread, klasis tou artou*, signifies the common meals and, in connection
therewith, the sacrament of the Lord's Supper, which constituted a part
of the regular public services in the early church; cf. v. 46. Acts 20, 7.
1 Cor. 10, 16; 11, 20-34. Of common *prayer* as an act of common worship we read Acts 4, 23.31; 6, 6; 13, 3. 1 Cor. 11, 4. 5; 14, 14ff. It is of

the meetings in which Christian congregations were occupied with these various religious exercises that the preceding text speaks, warning all Christians not to forsake the assembling of themselves together.

John 8, 47: *He that is of God heareth God's words: ye therefore hear them not, because ye are not of God.*

In the preceding verse Jesus had asked his enemies the question, "If I say the truth, why do ye not believe Me?" This was a question the Jews preferred not to answer, and Jesus answers it for them in our text. He had already told them that they are not of God, but of their father the devil, vv. 42 and 44, and now He argues along the same line. His first proposition is: *He that is of God heareth God's words.* Compared with v. 44, to be of God, *einai ek theou,* here means to be a child of God. To hear God's words does not mean merely to hear with the ears, but to hear and accept what God says; for the Jews were even then hearing Jesus, but not as God's word should be heard, since, when Jesus told them the truth, they did not believe Him, vv. 45 and 46. In a similar sense *to hear* is used Matt. 18, 15.17 and Luke 10, 16. What Jesus would say is, He that is a child of God hears, accepts, and believes the word of God. And now the question of v. 46 was easily answered. That the obstinate Jews were not of God had already been said and proven, vv. 42-44, and hence they were not the kind of men that hear the word of God as it should be heard. This is Christ's argument to the Jews. But Christ still speaks in His word, and His argument also applies to those who would be Christians, but do not hear and accept what God says in His word. They do not hear, because they are not of God. And, again, God speaks wherever His messengers and ministers preach His truth, and he who refuses to hear such preaching and yet considers himself a child of God, deceives himself.

Luke 10, 16: *He that heareth you heareth me; and he that despiseth you despiseth me; and he that despiseth me despiseth him that sent me.*

These words were spoken to the seventy disciples whom Christ had chosen to be preachers of the Gospel, and they are the closing words of His charge to them as His messengers. Thus also when He had commissioned His "twelve disciples" and was about to close. His charge to them, Matt. 10, 5-42, He said, "He that receiveth you receiveth me, and he that receiveth me, receiveth him that sent me," v. 40. God deals with man through human ministers, men with human frailties and shortcomings, when His word is preached. And knowing this we should not refuse but be ready and willing to hear them as we should gladly hear Christ in person and God Himself, and confidently trust in His word and willingly obey His commandments. For to despise the messengers of God is to despise God Himself whose message they carry. And especially when God has ordained that the Gospel should be preached by men who are called to the ministerial office, it is His holy will that men should not deem it sufficient to use the written word of God, but also hear the preaching of the word according to Christ's ordinance, knowing that a refusal to hear such preaching, however humble the messenger may be, is a disregard of Christ Himself.

Hos. 4, 6: *Because thou hast rejected knowledge, I will also reject thee.*

The entire verse of which this text is a part reads thus: "My people are destroyed for lack of knowledge: because thou hast rejected knowledge, I will also reject thee, that thou shalt be no priest to me: seeing thou hast forgotten the law of thy God, I will also forget thy children." From the opening words of the verse it appears that the censure here pronounced is not aimed at the ungodly world, but at the people of God, those among whom the Lord has established His worship and the preaching of His word, the people of whom St. Paul says Rom. 3, 2 that unto them were committed the oracles of God. But God has given His word that it should be known, and the knowledge here spoken of is not secular knowledge, but, as the parallelism of the verse shows, the knowledge of the revealed will of God, and God demands that those who would worship Him as His priestly people should know His will and keep it in remembrance. To hear and learn the word of God and to grow in spiritual wisdom and knowledge is the chief part of all true worship, and he who refuses to learn what God would teach him should know that his worship is an abomination in the sight of God, and that God will punish the contempt of His word by temporal and eternal penalties.

Is. 66, 2: *To this man will I look, even to him that is poor and of a contrite spirit, and trembleth at my word.*

In the preceding context God has spoken by the prophet of His supreme majesty, saying, "The heaven is my throne, and the earth is my footstool: where is the house that ye built unto me? and where is the place of my rest? For all those things hath mine hand made, and all those things have been, saith the Lord." In the subsequent context he speaks of those who bring sacrifices which are an abomination in the sight of God, but who, when God called, did not answer, and when He spoke, did not hear, vv. 1-4. But the true worshiper, upon whom God would look with divine pleasure, is described in our text as being poor and bowed down and of a contrite spirit and trembling at the word of God, the word of Him, whose throne is the heaven and whose footstool is the earth, the Maker and Preserver of all things, who would deal with us by His word, the word of the law, whereby He humbles the sinful heart, and of the Gospel, whereby He lifts with an everlasting grace those who have humbled themselves before Him. Blessed is he, who thus in the day of grace trembleth before the word of God; for he shall stand among the blessed of the Father rejoicing when others shall tremble at the word of the Lord when He shall fix His judgment throne in midheaven.

Eccl. 5, 1: *Keep thy foot when thou goest to the house of God, and be more ready to hear, than to give the sacrifice of fools: for they consider not that they do evil.*

This text also is a warning against the mere outward worship of those who go to the house of God, unmindful of the true purpose of public worship. Hence this admonition is also directed to the members of the visible church lest any deceive themselves. Not every outward worship is true worship. It may be the sacrifice of fools, who in their ignorance do evil where they and others imagine that they are doing what is good and acceptable before the Lord. *Keep thy foot,* says the Lord, that is, be not unmindful where thou goest when on the way to the house of God, knowing that it is the place where God would speak to thee to make thee wise unto salvation and thoroughly furnished unto all good works, and hence thy chief purpose in coming to the house of God should be to hear and to receive in a willing heart the word of God. To heed this admonition is the proper preparation for divine worship, and the neglect of such preparation is apt to deprive the worshiper of much or all the blessing which God has intended for him in the public administration of the means of grace.

Ps. 26, 6-8: *So will I compass thine altar, O Lord: that I may publish with the voice of thanksgiving, and tell of all thy wondrous works. Lord, I have loved the habitation of thy house, and the place where thine honor dwelleth.*

Here the psalmist utters his delight in public worship as an occupation of those who are priests of the Most High. It was the altar of the Lord about which the priests in the temple of Jehovah were occupied bringing sacrifice to the Lord and intonating the songs of praise and thanksgiving in which the congregation was to join, giving thanks and telling of the wondrous works of God. Thus in the worship of Israel God visited His people and graciously accepted the sacrifices of their hearts and lips and hands. And this was the beauty of the temple of the Lord, the habitation of His grace and the place where His honor dwelled. Such also is the public worship of Christian congregations today. There the peculiar people of God appear as a royal priesthood in the habitation of God's house, where He comes to them and dwells among them with His holy word, where those who speak tell of all His wondrous works and intonate the songs of praise and thanksgiving, spiritual sacrifices on the altar of the Lord. And hence we should also love this spiritual sanctuary of God and rejoice in the exercises for which Christians unite and hold joint communion with their God.

1 Thess. 2, 13: *When ye received the word of God which ye heard of us, ye received it not as the word of men, but, as it is in truth, the word of God.*

Where this text in the English Bible has the word *received*, the original Greek has two different words, *paralambanein* and *dechesthai*, and a more literal translation would be: "Receiving the word of preaching by us of God," or: "the word of God as it is preached by us, ye accepted it not as the word of men," etc. There are men who receive the word of God when and where it is preached, and this outward hearing, of which even the natural man is in a measure capable, is not superfluous; he who would not even outwardly hear the word, refuses to permit the blessings of divine grace to be brought even near his heart. And again, that which is outwardly received or heard, should be "the word of God" preached by the apostles or those who bring the doctrine of the apostles. False doctrine should not even be outwardly received, but avoided as endangering our salvation. But merely to hear the word is not sufficient, but hearing the word of God, *paralabontes*, we should also *dechesthai*, inwardly receive or accept it as the word of God, with due veneration, believing all its statements, relying on all its promises, and willingly obeying its demands. This, however, is not within the power of natural man, but a gift of God. This is indicated by the context, when the Apostle says: *"For this cause thank we God without ceasing,* because, when ye received the word of God," etc. And thus we also should thank God, when by His grace we have been led properly to receive and accept the word of God, which is able to save our souls, James 1, 21.

Col. 3, 16: *Let the word of Christ dwell in you richly in all wisdom; teaching and admonishing one another in psalms and hymns and spiritual songs, singing with grace in your hearts to the Lord.*

A Christian congregation is in this text likened to a house in which the word of Christ should find a habitation. The word of God should not only be an occasional guest, but should dwell continually, *enoikeito*, in the church, and not sparingly, but richly, *plousios*, abundantly, in excess of what is needful for the immediate wants of the children of the household for the mere sustenance of spiritual life. Christians should also grow according to the spirit, and should also yield forth to others what may quicken and nourish them unto salvation. In their endeavors to have the word of Christ richly among them, the Christians should seek various ways of voicing forth such word of God, and the Apostle comes to their aid by adding to his general admonition special advice. Not only by preaching the word, but by teaching and admonishing one another in psalms and hymns and spiritual songs the members of the church may yield forth spiritual blessing to each other. *Psalmoi* are religious songs in general, *humnoi*, songs of praise, *odai pneumatikai*, spiritual songs. Thus when, in our church, songs treating of the doctrines of the Christian religion, of God and His will and counsel, of Christ and His redemption, of the church and the means of grace, of faith and justification, of Christian life and hope, are sung by or to the congregation, such singing constitutes a most im-

pressive form of mutual instruction, admonition and edification, and
when and where the voice of spiritual song is lifted up it should find
its response within the hearts of those who sing and hear, and they
should "sing with their hearts to the Lord," as the Apostle here says.
But this again we cannot do of ourselves, but it must be done "with
grace" or "in the grace of God." *En te chariti* is in the English Bible
correctly construed with the following word *adontes*. They only who are
compassed about by the grace of God will sound the praises of that
grace within their hearts, being truly edified by the songs they hear
with their ears.

Luke 11, 28: *Blessed are they that hear the word of God, and
keep it.*

This text has already been considered in a different connection.
The words which should be particularly noted here are *hear* and *accept*,
akouontes kai fulassontes. We cannot keep the word of God without
hearing it, and hearing it ever anew. It is not sufficient to have
heard it in early youth, but it must be heard throughout our
lives, and that not only as a matter of form, but as a matter of necessity, without which we cannot spiritually prosper. Even Mary, the
mother of Christ, was no exception. But hearing alone will not suffice,
the word should also be kept or guarded. To guard a word is to pay
attention to what it means, demands, promises, gives, confers, and secures, and to lose no opportunity of gaining the full benefit which may
be derived therefrom. And only they who both hear and keep the
word of God are blessed here and hereafter.

Gal. 6, 6: *Let him that is taught in the word communicate unto
him that teacheth in all good things.*

This is one of a series of admonitions directed to a Christian congregation. The Apostle supposes that Christians are being instructed
in the word of God, not only by way of preparation, as of candidates
for Baptism or Confirmation, but also after they have become acknowledged members of the church, growing in grace by acquiring a more
extensive and intensive knowledge of divine truth as it is revealed in
Christ and His word. The utterance of this supposition is itself a word
of approval to those who are, and of reproof to those who are not, willing
learners of the word. This is the first admonition embodied in the
text. The second is, that those who are being instructed and thereby
receive spiritual blessings through the faithful labors of their teachers
should contribute of their temporal possessions to the support of those
who teach them and who, according to 1 Cor 9, 14, should live of the
Gospel while they preach the Gospel. The words *koinoneito en pasin
agathois* enjoin upon each member of the congregation the duty of
contributing according to his means toward the support of the ministry,
and the subsequent context shows that the Apostle is very earnest in
his admonition, adding a threat to those who will not, and a promise
to those who will, heed his words.

THE SECOND TABLE

Matt. 7, 12: *All things whatsoever ye would that men should do, to you, do ye even so to them: for this is the law and the prophets.*

The sermon on the mount, from which this text is taken, is an exposition of the law, not the exhibition or promulgation of a new law which should take the place of the law as it had been in force before the days of Christ, but the moral law of God, the manifestation of God's holy will to men. And of the law as far as it regulates our conduct toward our fellow-men Christ gives the sum and substance in this text. That the following words are a summary of the preceding discourse is indicated by *own*. That He would not here summarize a new law, but all the moral precepts for the conduct toward our neighbor laid down in the word of God, is expressly said in the words: *for this is the law and the prophets,* i. e., all the Scriptures inasmuch as they are law. The same summary had already been recorded Lev. 19, 18: *Thou shalt love thy neighbor as thyself;* cf. Matt. 22, 39. But the form here given by Christ is more explicit and practical, showing how we may apply the rule. The simple way of learning what in any given case we should do to our neighbor is, to enquire what we would that he or others should do to us if we were in his place. This is indeed a golden rule, easy of application, and unfailing if properly applied. But it is a gross abuse of this rule, to pervert this summary of the law into a summary of the Gospel by teaching that "to live up to the golden rule" is Christianity, the true religion. He who would be saved by living according to this rule will as surely be damned as a thief or murderer who refuses to believe in Christ Jesus. For if the law condemns all men, the summary of the law cannot save, but must certainly and summarily condemn.

Gal. 6, 10: *As we have therefore opportunity, let us do good unto all men, especially unto them who are of the household of faith.*

The word correctly rendered *opportunity, kairos,* is the present period of time with its peculiar circumstances, while *chronos* is time conceived as a line extending through a series of periods. The question, who is my neighbor? must be answered in consideration of times and circumstances, all men being our neighbors as we have opportunity to do them good. At the same time, however, the apostle points out a category of fellow-men in whose favor we should discriminate, when he says: *Especially unto them who are of the household of faith,* our brethren in Christ, the members of Christian congregations. In a similar way St. Paul points out such as should be provided for before others, when he says, 1 Tim. 5, 8: *But if any provide not for his own, and especially those of his own house, he hath denied the faith.* But while it is proper that we should exercise due discrimination in doing good, the text before us at the same time teaches that we should not restrict our benevolence to the members of our natural and spiritual household when we find opportunity to do good to others besides and beyond them.

Matt. 5, 44, 45: *Love your enemies, bless them that curse you, do good to them that hate you, and pray for them which despitefully use you, and persecute you; that ye may be the children of your Father which is in heaven: for he maketh his sun to rise on the evil and on the good, and sends rain on the just and on the unjust.*

The Jewish teachers had perverted the divine commandment, *Thou shalt love thy neighbor as thyself,* by drawing the false conclusion: If it is our neighbor we should love, we may, and even should, hate our enemy. This is what Christ has pointed out in the preceding context, v. 43, saying, *Ye have heard that it hath been said, Thou shalt love thy neighbor, and hate thine enemy;* and to refute this perversion of the law he continues, *But I say unto you, love your enemies, etc.* There is, however, need of inculcating this precept at all times, since the perverted nature not only of the Jews, but also of the Gentiles, prompted and prompts them to repay enmity with enmity. To love an enemy instead of hating him and being revenged or seeking revenge for injuries received was looked upon as a weakness unworthy of a man by the ancient Greeks and Romans, and is largely looked upon as cowardice and lack of selfrespect today. And thus today, to love our enemies and to bless those who curse us, to do good to them that hate us, and to pray for them that despitefully use us and persecute us, is not the conduct of natural man but of the children of God, who have from their Father in heaven received a mind which makes them akin to their Father, who also makes His sun to rise on the evil and on the good, and sends rain on the just and on the unjust. Yet even this is not a new law, but a restatement of and in full keeping with the spirit of the law which the Jews have perverted, and a summary of which we have seen in Matt. 7, 12; for no man desires that this enemy should retaliate evil for evil and inflict vengeance for every offense.

THE FOURTH COMMANDMENT

Prov. 30, 17: *The eye that mocketh at his father, and despiseth to obey his mother, the ravens of the valley shall pick it out, and the young eagles shall eat it.*

To mock a father and to refuse obedience to a mother is in this text forcibly pictured as a heinous sin, worthy not only of death, but of an ignominious death and the denial of decent burial. For to lie unburied, a prey to dogs and the fowl of the air, was, in Israel, and even among the Gentiles, looked upon as being under a curse, an object of divine wrath; I Kings 13, 22; 14, 11; 16, 4; Jer. 7, 33; 8, 2; 9, 22; 14, 16; 16, 4; 25, 33; Hezek. 29, 5. Ps. 79, 3ff. Even the dead bodies of executed criminals were to be taken down and buried before the night was over, Deut. 21, 22.23; and of the "cursed woman," Jezebel, it was recorded that nothing was left of her but a few bones when she was to be buried, 2 Kings 9, 35.

Rom. 13, 2: *Whosoever therefore resisteth the power, resisteth the ordinance of God: and they that resist shall receive to themselves damnation.*

In the previous context the apostle has inculcated obedience to the higher powers, especially to civil governments, for the reason that there is no power but of God and by divine ordinance. *Hence, hoste,* the apostle continues by way of argument, *ho antitassomenos te exousia,* who instead of *hupotassesthai,* of submitting himself or being subject to the powers, v. 1, sets himself against the government, resists not only the *anthropine ktisis,* 1 Pet. 2, 13, but *te tou theou diatage,* the divine ordinance, *tou theou* being emphasized by its position before *diatage.* And the *damnation, krisis, judgment,* which they shall receive, is not only the human penalty of rebellion or willful violation of the law, but divine judgment, imposed upon him who has rebelled against God by resisting those whom God has clothed with His own majesty. For this reason the apostle says, v. 5: "Ye must needs be subject also for conscience sake," that is, as those who deal with God in their conduct toward their civil superiors.

1 Pet. 2, 18: *Servants, be subject to your masters with all fear; not only to the good and gentle, but also to the froward.*

Servants, oiketai, is the milder term for *douloi,* slaves. They are here described as *hupotassomenoi,* subordinate. To supply *ete,* the imperative, *be,* of the English Bible, is an unnecessary and, therefore, undue liberty. The verb to which the participle is to be referred is either *timesate* or *timate,* v. 17, or *hupotagete,* v. 13, which opens this series of admonitions with a general injunction of submission to every *anthropine ktisis.* Servants should be subject to their masters *en panti fobo, in all fear.* *Fobos, fear,* is the consciousness of inferiority under a superior power or authority which it is dangerous to disregard. The reason why servants should submit themselves to their masters, not only to the good but also to the froward, *skolioi,* the *unfair* or *unjust,* the reverse of *dikaioi,* Prov. 28, 11, coll. Luke 3, 5, is stated in the subsequent context which says: "For this is thankworthy, if a man *for conscience toward God* endure grief." Servants should remember that by divine ordinance they are subject to their masters and should therefore submit themselves for conscience's sake, in the fear of God, who, no matter how their masters may be disposed toward them, has placed the superiors in authority.

Eph. 6, 2. 3: *Honor thy father and thy mother; which is the first commandment with promise; that it may be well with thee, and thou mayest live long on the earth.*

In the previous context, v. 1, the apostle enjoins upon all children obedience to their parents, because this is *dikaion, right,* according to the law of God, and, quoting this law of God in our text, he proceeds to describe the frame of mind whence such obedience should spring. Filial obedience should proceed from a heart which *honors* father and mother, holds them in high esteem.   And that such esteem is well founded, appears from the fact that God Himself has distinguished this commandment by making it *entole prote en epangelia, the first commandment in point of promise,* though not the first *en te taxei,* in order of arrangement, in which it is the fourth.   The promise in Ex. 26, 6. Deut. 5, 10, is not a promise attached to one special commandment, but pertains to the decalogue as a whole, wherefore Luther has correctly placed it at the end of the ten commandments.   The promise itself is given in v. 3, not in the Jewish form, Ex. 20, 12. Deut. 5, 16, where it is restricted to the land of Canaan for the children of Israel, but simply *epi tes ges,* on the earth, in this temporal life.   The promise here given has this in common with all temporal blessings, that it is under the wise providence of God, who adjusts the fulfillment of His promise to the higher interests of His children, and, being a temporal blessing, God often fulfills this promise also to such children as by unbelief forego His spiritual gifts, which are obtained only by faith in Christ.   But while God has reserved to Himself the mode and measure of temporal reward for filial veneration of father and mother, the distinction of the fourth commandment, as being the first in point of promise, remains undisputed as a special inducement to dutiful children to a more cheerful observance of this commandment.

Col. 3, 20: *Children, obey your parents in all things: for this is well pleasing unto the Lord.*

In vv. 18-25 of this chapter, and v. 1 of the next, the apostle inculcates the domestic virtues, the proper conduct of wives and husbands, children and parents, servants and masters.   In each case he addresses the inferiors, wives, children, servants, first and the superiors, husbands, fathers, masters, next.   In our text he speaks to the children, *ta tekna,* and the virtue he enjoins upon them is obedience, not to fathers only, but *tois goneusin,* to the parents.   This filial obedience is to be *kata panta,* concerning all things.   This is the rule.   It is not for children to choose whether they would obey or not, but in all things, great or small, they are not to consult their own inclinations but comply with a parent's will.   This is the nature of obedience, and in accordance with the rule.   The exceptions, according to Acts 5, 29, are understood.   To offer an inducement to cheerful obedience, especially where it may impose selfdenial, the apostle adds the words: *Touto gar euareston estin en kurio, for this is well pleasing in the Lord.*   The text does not say, TO *the Lord,* which would be *to kurio,* as the Elzevir text has by the way of uncritical emendation. Filial obedience is here described as an ornament fair and pleasing to behold among Christians, a beautiful token of true godliness. The same sentiment is more explicitly set forth Phil. 4, 8, where the apostle says: "Finally, brethren, whatsoever things are true, whatsoever things are honest, whatsoever things are just, whatsoever things are pure, whatsoever things are lovely, whatsoever things are of good report; if there be any virtue, and if there be any praise, think on these things."

Prov. 23, 22: *Hearken unto thy father that begat thee, and despise not thy mother when she is old.*

According to a well-known *parallelismus membrorum* the meaning of this text is: Hearken unto thy father and thy mother who have begotten thee, and do not despise them when they have grown old. The text combines the two injunctions, one of which is laid down in each of the two preceding texts, Eph. 6, 2, which would lead children to *honor*, and Col. 3, 20, which would induce them to *obey*, their parents; and as filial veneration is often neglected when parents have grown old and subject to the frailties of old age, a special admonition to the children of such parents was deemed needful by the Spirit of God for the sake of both parents and children.

1 Tim. 5, 4: *To requite their parents: for that is good and acceptable before God.*

The infinitive, *apodidonai*, is governed by *manthanetosan*, and the subject is *tekna kai ekgona, children and grandchildren*, who are here admonished to show piety *(eusebein)* toward their parents and grandparents who are of their household, and thus to requite their *progonoi*, to *repay* in a measure what parents and grandparents have done for them in former years. But this is a duty often neglected even among Christians, and Christian children in riper years must learn this lesson *(manthanetosan)*; and to incite us to heed his admonition the apostle adds: *for this is acceptable before God.* The words *kalon kai*, found in early editions, are spurious according to A, C, D, F, G, the testimony of ancient versions and fathers; they were carried over probably from 1 Tim. 2, 3. That the fulfillment of filial duties is acceptable before God should induce Christian children to do with all faithfulness what filial gratitude toward their greatest benefactors should suffice to prompt them to do.

Hebr. 13, 17· *Obey them that have the rule over you, and submit yourselves: for they watch for your souls, as they that must give account, that they may do it with joy, and not with grief for that is unprofitable for you.*

By *tois hegoumenois, which* the English Bible has rendered, *them that have the rule over you,* the pastors of congregations are designated as *leaders.* They march at the head of the congregations who are to follow their example, and especially their doctrine, whereby they lead or guide the flock of Christ in the ways of God. The obedience and submission of Christians toward their pastors should be commensurate with the leadership of their ministers, which is exercised by sound doctrine and good example, 2 Thess. 1, 8; 3, 14. Rom. 6, 17.—Phil. 3, 17. 2 Thess. 3, 9.—1 Pet. 5, 2. 3.—The reason *(gar)* why such obedience should be rendered, is given in the following words, *For they watch for your souls.* The souls of Christians are endangered by enemies, by ravenous wolves, and when faithful pastors perform the duties of their office, especially when they warn their flock against false doctrine, the wiles of Satan, and the allurements of the world, and their warning and admonitions are not heeded and obeyed, those who refuse to hear and heed them are in imminent peril of their souls. Or should pastors accomodate themselves to the obstinacy and waywardness of their people and decline to watch and warn while they know *they must give account?* Indeed, they might be tempted to neglect their duties when they see that their word is left unheeded or even resented by obstinate resistance. But if by painful experience, performing the works of their office with grief and not with joy, they should be discouraged from the faithful fulfillment of their pastoral duties, that would be unprofitable to the congregation and its members, and might result in the loss of their souls.

Rom. 13, 1: *Let every soul be subject unto the higher powers. For there is no power but of God: the powers that be are ordained of God.*

This text inculcates due submission to civil rulers and magistrates. They are here called *exousiai, powers;* for it is essential for a government to be a power, able to fulfill the fundamental purposes of civil governments, to afford protection to the members of the body politic. They are described as *exousiai huperechousai, superior powers, obrigkeitliche Maechte.* It is immaterial in what person or persons this superior power may be vested, whether in a monarch, or in a collegiate government, or in the people at large; wherever a sovereign government is established it is the duty of every soul subject to such superior power to acknowledge the superiority of those who are and rule in power. *For,* says the apostle, *there is no power but of God.* Governments, though established by men, represent a divine institution for the maintenance of order in human society. And thus, as St. Paul continues, *the powers that be are ordained of God,* they are God's ministers, Rom. 13, 6, and Christians are not exempt from civil duties, but are to render unto Caesar the things which are Caesar's, Matt. 22, 21; and while the ungodly submit to civil laws for selfish reasons, Christians will submit themselves to every ordinance of men for the Lord's sake, 1 Pet. 2, 13, knowing that by God kings reign and princes decree justice, Prov. 18, 15, and that it is He who removes kings and setteth up kings, Dan. 2, 21, even though such kings may be ungodly, as Nero was in the days of St. Paul. For even a corrupt government is better than no government at all, and an anarchist is not only an enemy of human society, but also a rebel against God.

Lev. 19, 32: *Thou shalt rise up before the hoary head and honor the face of the old man.*

This text is followed by the words, *And fear thy God: I am the Lord.* The admonition to venerate old age is not a rule of politeness and good manners only, but an utterance of the holy will of God, and, therefore, a commandment which is binding upon young people at all times, and which cannot be set aside without offending God. To rise up before the hoary head is but one of many ways in which the veneration we owe to the aged may be exercised in demeanor, words, and deeds; and such conduct is well pleasing in the sight of God.

Acts 5, 29: *We ought to obey God rather than men.*

This text is part of the answer given by Peter and the other apostles to the high priest and the captain of the temple and the chief priests at Jerusalem, men who administered not only the religious but also the municipal affairs of the city but who had forbidden the apostles to teach in the name of Jesus. Here, then, it was proper for the apostles to set aside the will and commandment of the civil rulers in order to obey the will and commandment of Him who is the King of kings and the Lord of lords. And thus all Christians should know that obedience to those who are in power under God must cease where such obedience would be or imply a transgression of a clear commandment of God, even when such refusal to obey human superiors would bring upon the inferiors temporal punishment, persecution, and even a violent death. It should be noted, however, that children and subjects are not emancipated from their filial and civil duties when parents or rulers in a given instance exceed their authority and demand what God has forbidden and forbid what God has enjoined. Though in such instance the inferior must disobey man in order to obey God, he still remains an inferior, bound to obey his parents and rulers in all things which they may rightfully demand.

THE FIFTH COMMANDMENT

Gen. 9, 6: *Whoso sheddeth man's blood, by man shall his blood be shed: for in the image of God made he man.*

The fifth commandment is a sacred enclosure drawn about human life for its protection and defense. In the words preceding our text God says, "Surely your blood of your lives will I require; at the hand of every beast will I require it, and at the hand of man; at the hand of every man's brother will I require the life of man." Here God threatens to visit His vindictive justice upon all who shall violate the sacredness of human life. In our text He makes provision for the execution of this threat by ordaining that the murderer's temporal punishment shall be a violent death inflicted by human hands. To impose capital punishment on the murderer is thus seen to be so far from being contrary to the will of God that it is rather expressly demanded by the positive law here enacted by the supreme Lawgiver and Judge Himself, and the refusal to mete out justice according to this ordinance is disobedience to the will of God. Even Cain's conscience told him that by slaying his brother he had forfeited his life, Gen. 4, 14, and it was by special provision of God and by a mark set on him that the first murderer's life was shielded from the avenging hand of man, Gen. 4, 15. By this special dispensation God, who is the lord of human life as of all other created things, would not, however, establish a rule for all times. The rule is established in our text, which states also a reason for this rule; *for in the image of God made he man.* Human life is not of the same kind with the life of brutes. Man does not differ from brutes as brutes differ from themselves, but is a being of a higher order, distinct from all brutes, the only visible creature originally made in the image of God. And while it is not contrary to the will of God that man should kill fowl, fishes, or beasts of the forest and domestic animals for food, Gen. 9, 2.3, the human life shall be held sacred, and the shedding of human blood shall be avenged by man. By whom among men, the subsequent texts will specify.

Matt. 26, 52: *All they that take the sword shall perish with the sword.*

Peter, the apostle of Christ, had drawn the sword in resentment of an act of violence committed against his Master. But Jesus, far from approving of Peter's intervention, has only words of rebuke for His disciple, not only because it was the will of God that Jesus should be led captive, to suffer and die,—and Peter's interference was, for this reason, out of time and place,—but because in using the sword Peter had arrogated to himself what was not his proper right and duty. Peter had *taken* the sword. It was not given him by authority. He was not a minister of God with power of the sword to execute wrath upon him that doeth evil, Rom. 13, 4, but a minister of the word with power to forgive and retain sins. Matt. 16, 19. And hence, instead of administering justice and punishing a crime, he was violating justice and committing a crime, exposing himself to punishment. Thus today, to avenge wrong without proper authority, as, to lynch a criminal, is *taking* the sword and deserving to perish with the sword, not only a crime against human law, but a sin against the divine commandment, *Thou shalt not kill.* On the other hand, this text also shows that it is not incumbent upon a Christian to deliver up for punishment a fellow Christian, who has, by offending the secular law, become liable to punishment, though it is a brother's duty to admonish the offending brother and lead him to repentance, as Christ admonished Peter but did not turn him over to the secular arm that he might perish with the sword. To punish crime is under God the province of civil government, as to remit or retain sins is under God a right and duty of the church.

Rom. 13, 4: *He beareth not the sword in vain: for he is the minister of God, a revenger to execute wrath upon him that doeth evil.*

The subject is *he exousia*, the civil power, of whom it is said *theou gar diakonos esti soi eis to agathon, he is the minister of God to thee for good.* The noun *theou* is here in emphasis, which is not reproduced in the English version. It is from *God*, not originally or primarily from the people, that civil governments derive their authority and power, and God has made them what they officially are. In such office the civil ruler is a minister of God, of whom the apostle here says *ou gar eike ten machairan forei, for not in vain doth he bear the sword. Gar* here refers to the preceding context: *But if thou do that which is evil, be afraid.* Fear, *fobos*, is the expectation of future or impending loss or pain. The right to inflict loss or pain, even the loss of life and the pain of death, upon the malefactor rests with the civil government, the minister of God. God alone primarily is the lord of life and death. But He has appointed His minister, the civil power, and has given him *ten machairan*, not simply *a* sword but *the* sword of His office. And this instrument of death the minister of God is not to take but to carry (*forein verbum est continuativum, ferein inceptivum*), and not *eike*, not *in vain*, but to use it for what it is made and given him. He is not to use it indiscriminately or arbitrarily, for private revenge or other unlawful purposes. He is not to put to the sword such as have not done evil to merit the sword. All this would not be use but abuse of the sword, and worse than carrying it in vain. But he is to use it as *a revenger to execute wrath upon him that doeth evil.* The punishment of crime is not a reformatory measure, but a vindication of the majesty of the law. Hence capital punishment is not incompatible with the true end and aim of punishment, but most appropriate where the severest penalty which can be inflicted by man is called for. Nor is it an unjust usurpation of divine authority, but the execution of justice under divine authority when inflicted on the criminal by civil government as the minister of God.

Rom. 12, 19: *Dearly beloved, avenge not yourselves, but rather give place unto wrath: for it is written, Vengeance is mine; I will repay, saith the Lord.*

Vengeance, retribution for evil, is properly an execution of divine justice: for it is written Deut. 32, 35 just as our text gives it, *emoi ekdikesis, ego antapodoso.* The pronouns *emoi* and *ego* are in emphasis, to indicate the more forcibly that he who takes vengeance in his own hand usurps that which is not his but God's. Hence we should, when we are offended or injured by our fellowmen, beware of avenging ourselves, but rather give place unto wrath. The Greek text has *te orge,*

THE. *wrath*. What wrath is meant appears from the subsequent context, the quotation from Deut. 32, which is annexed by *gar*. The wrath of God is the assertion and éxertion of His holiness in opposition to sin. To this we should *give place*, allow it to have its way in carrying out its designs. And the ways of God to work retribution are manifold, direct and indirect. He may punish through His minister, who carries the sword as a revenger to execute wrath, Rom. 13, 4. He may inflict punishment in a thousand other ways and *will repay* according as He will dispose. But He will also bring retribution on those who violate His majesty by avenging themselves, hurting or harming their neighbor for harm he may have inflicted upon them.

Matt. 5, 21.22: *Ye have heard that it was said by them of old time, Thou shalt not kill; and whosoever shall kill shall be in danger of the judgment: but I say unto you, That whosoever is angry with his brother without a cause shall be in danger of the judgment; and whosoever shall say to his brother, Raca, shall be in danger of the council; but whosoever shall say, Thou fool, shall be in danger of hellfire.*

This text, as the entire Sermon on the Mount, has often been grossly misconstrued, especially by such as would make a new lawgiver of Christ and find in this discourse a supplement to the law, and not what it truly is, an exposition and application of the law In the words, Ye have heard that it was said by, or better to, them of old time, he refers to the rèading and expounding of the Mosaic law in the synagogues, where the teachers of the people in those days were chiefly of the Pharisees. We know what the doctrine and life of the Pharisees was. Their righteousness was an outward observance of what they considered the precepts of the law; they considered only the gross violations of those precepts sinful in the meaning of the law and deserving of punishment. In this sense they would expound the old commandment, Thou ·shalt not kill, taking the word kill, to mean the violent destruction of human life, and declaring him, and. him only, who had committed such crime as liable to trial, sentènce, and punishment in the proper tribunals, the courts of the place, which according to Deut. 16, 18 were to "judge the people with just judgment." Such was the exposition of the fifth commandment as given by the Pharisees and heard in the synagogues. In opposition to this inadequate exhibition and inculcation of the law, and not as going beyónd the law itself, Christ says, *But I say unto you*, not what you hear from the Pharisees but what I am about to tell you is the true meaning of that old commandment, Thou shalt not kill. Sin is committed and judgment is merited and incurred not only by violently taking another's life, not only by the outward act, but even by the affections of the heart, anger rising within the soul against a brother. Such inward sin is as truly an offense against the commandment, Thou shalt not kill, as the outward act would be, and as truly deserving of punishment in the sight of God. Thus also bitter words employed against a brother, such as *raca, empty, vain*, and *fool,* are really and truly sins against that old commandment, bringing upon the offender the danger of council and of hellfire, which is, in fact, the punishment merited by all who transgress a law of God. The various efforts to establish a climax from "whosoever is angry" to "whosoever shall say, Thou fool," as from a lesser to a greater and still greater offense, are hardly to the point, since in that case bitterness and anger directed against a brother would appear to make the sinner liable to judgment in an inferior court, but not to hellfire, which it certainly does. What Christ would say is, that every evil thought or affection or word or deed consisting in, or flowing from, hatred against a fellow-man is really and truly sin, worthy of punishment, even to eternal damnation.

1 John 3, 15: *Whosoever hateth his brother is a murderer: and ye know that no murderer hath eternal life abiding in him.*

In the preceding context the apostle had referred to Cain, who slew his brother because his own works were evil and his brother's righteous, and to the world, which, being evil, hates the children of God, vv. 12 and 13. In the 14th verse he contrasts those who have passed from death into life, which appears from their love of the brethren, and him that abideth in death, since he loveth not his brother, and now he closes the argument, saying, Whosoever hateth his brother is a murderer. The word here employed is not *foneus*, murderer, but *anthropoktonos*, literally *manslayer*, the more graphic term of the two. Cain, who slew his brother, is evidently still in the apostle's mind, and what he would lead us to understand is that the commandment against which Cain sinned is not only transgressed by the actual violent destruction of human life, but also by hatred conceived or entertained in the heart. And hence as the murderer in deed has according to the law forfeited his own life, so the murderer in heart excludes himself from eternal life. And this is a truth which the apostle considers familiar to every Christian. Yet he does not deem it superfluous to remind them of what they already know. And thus today we are ever in need of being reminded of the true meaning of the law, also of the fifth commandment, lest, being unmindful of its import, we permit hatred and enmity to take root in our hearts and endanger the salvation of our souls, and in order that by the law properly understood there may be in us the knowledge of sin.

Matt. 15, 19: *Out of the heart proceed evil thoughts, murders, adulteries, fornications, thefts, false witness, blasphemies.*

The first man who was born on earth was a murderer, shedding his own brother's blood. Being the first murderer among men he was certainly not misled to the perpetration of his crime by evil example. Neither was he persuaded by any man's words, prompting him to slay his brother. How, then, came he to be a murderer? We have the answer in these words of Christ: *Out of the heart proceed evil thoughts,*

MURDERS, etc. Cain's heart was evil, his nature was wholly depraved, flesh born of the flesh. And from that evil heart proceeded evil thoughts, murderous thoughts, and finally atrocious murder itself. Thus there is a murderous root in every man's heart, which may at any time sprout forth, and when it bears its natural fruit that fruit is a murderous deed. In fact, every emotion of anger or hatred would naturally result in bloodshed, were it not held down by circumstances and conflicting interests under the providence of God. This is also indicated by the plural, *fonoi*, murders, employed in the text, which stands for various acts of the same kind as proceeding from one and the same heart. And though human justice may take cognizance only of the outward act, murder in the heart is just as truly sin before God; and the wages of sin is death.

Is. 58, 7: *Is it not to deal thy bread to the hungry, and that thou bring the poor that are cast out to thy house? when thou seest the naked, that thou cover him; and that thou hide not thyself from thine own flesh?*

This text is taken from a longer passage in which God censures His people for priding themselves on their righteousness in works of their own choice, while they had neglected to do works according to the will and commandment of God. Having especially repudiated their fasts and other measures of self-imposed penitence, the Lord continues, "Is not this the fast that I have chosen?" v. 6, and to the commendable works mentioned in the verse preceding our text He adds others, saying: "Is it not to deal thy bread to the hungry," etc. All these are works according to the fifth commandment, which enjoins upon us the duty of helping and befriending our neighbor in every bodily need. We should not look upon bread as being given us only to appease our own hunger, nor upon our house as only to shelter ourselves, nor upon the raiment we possess as intended to cover our own bodies only, but on the contrary, that others beside us are hungry, and that there are poor without shelter and without clothing, should be so many opportunities for us to do unto them as we would that others should do to us. It is worthy of note that the needy here recommended to our care are not described as the deserving poor or those who suffer innocently, but the motive given in our text for these works of charity is that the poor and needy are of our own flesh, human as we are. To point out the need of our fellowmen as being brought upon them by their own neglect and lack of foresight or economy is very often merely a pretext, behind which a heart void of mercy, and hands unwilling to part with what they hold, endeavor to hide themselves; thus, also, certain socalled benevolent societies, which are, in fact, based upon and determined by selfishness, are but hiding places and disguises for unwillingness to exercise true charity in works as those enjoined in this text.

Rom. 12, 20: *Therefore if thine enemy hunger, feed him; if he thirst, give him drink: for in so doing thou shalt heap coals of fire on his head.*

In the preceding verse the apostle has enjoined upon his readers to avenge not themselves, but rather to give place to the wrath of God who says, *Vengeance is mine, I will repay.* And now he continues: *Therefore*, since God has reserved wrath unto Himself, love only remains for us, love also toward the enemy, and hence, *if thine enemy hunger, feed him; if he thirst, give him drink.* Not to take but to preserve life, even the life of an enemy, behooves those who would live in obedience to the will of God. Hunger and thirst, as every other bodily need in a fellowman, should be an occasion for us to help and befriend him, not because we expect to be again befriended by him, or because we have experienced the same at his hands, but even though he be an enemy who has done us harm and may do us harm again. Yet, while punishment is not properly a reformatory measure, kindness bestowed upon an enemy may be, inasmuch as it may lead him more forcibly than revenge might have done to understand his wickedness and the wrong he has inflicted upon his benefactor. This conviction may be like coals of fire on his head, a painful consciousness of his evil deeds as they appear in sharp contrast with the acts of benevolence experienced at the hands of him whom he has wronged.

Matt. 5, 5.7.9: *Blessed are the meek: for they shall inherit the earth. Blessed are the merciful: for they shall obtain mercy. Blessed are the peacemakers: for they shall be called the children of God.*

The law, as has been shown, is transgressed not only by the outward act of shedding blood, but also by the sinful disposition of the heart, by unkind affections, anger and hatred, and by bitter words. Thus on the other hand conformity with the law may consist not only in the performance of outward acts of kindness, as feeding the hungry and clothing the naked, but also in a friendly disposition and kind affections, thoughts, and words, toward others. Three virtues pertaining to the fifth commandment are commended in these verses from the Sermon on the Mount. The first is meekness. *Praeis, the meek*, are those in whom cheerful kindness and mildness shuts out bitterness and selfish resentment. *Eleemones, the merciful*, are those who have compassion with another's misery. *Eirenopoioi, the peacemakers*, are those who, being opposed to sinful strife, not only as between themselves and others but also among their fellowmen, are bent upon establishing peace and good will wherever their influence goes. And as the penalty of sin is merited not only by the gross violation of the law but also by sins of the heart and in thoughts and words (see above, Matt. 5, 21.22. 1 John 3, 15), so the divine promises of grace and every blessing to all that keep His commandments apply not only to outward acts of obedience but also to conformity with the will of God in thoughts and words. Thus here blessings are pronounced over the meek, the merciful, and the peacemakers. But again it should be noted that while punishment is merited by the sinner and the *wages* of sin is death, the blessings bestowed upon them who keep the commandments are free gifts of divine goodness. This appears very clearly from the promises of this text. The meek shall *inherit* the earth, not obtain it as their merited remuneration. The time shall come when the meek shall hear the greeting, Come, ye blessed of my Father, inherit the kingdom prepared for you from the foundation of the world, Matt. 25, 34; according to the prophecy of Isaiah, They shall inherit the land forever, Is. 16, 21, when God shall create new heavens and a new earth, Is. 65, 17; 66, 22. 2 Pet. 3, 13. Rev. 21, 1. Again the merciful will obtain *mercy*, they shall experience the goodness of God in their own afflictions, temporal and spiritual. And the peacemakers shall be called the children of God. Things are known by their names and should be named what they are known to be. Thus the peacemakers by their endeavors to allay strife and establish peace shall appear and be known and acknowledged as children of God, bearing the likeness of their Father, who is the God of peace. And thus again this virtue is not here described as meritorious but as blessed by the goodness of God, whose children we are for Christ's sake, by faith.

Matt. 5, 25: *Agree with thine adversary quickly, whilst thou art in the way with him; lest at any time the adversary deliver thee to the judge, and the judge deliver thee to the officer, and thou be cast into prison.*

The imagery which underlies this text is taken from the relation of a debtor and his creditor, who in default of payment might take the debtor into court and have him sentenced and condemned to imprisonment for debt. This appears more clearly from the subsequent context, which speaks of payment to the uttermost farthing, v. 26. The adversary, then, with whom we should make haste to be reconciled, is not in this case, as some have assumed, one who has offended us—for that would make us the creditor—but one who has been offended by us and who therefore has an account against us which we are bound to satisfy. Thus the case is not the reverse of that described in v. 23, but the same, and the admonition is simply continued, inculcating the duty of being reconciled to those whom we have offended, to seek forgiveness of those whom we have wronged; and the special admonition here added is not to defer but to be prompt in our settlement with our adversary. For procrastination is also in such matters a very dangerous thing and may lodge him who refuses to be reconciled in the prison house of hell, where the last farthing shall never be paid. And here it should be noted that the sin against which this warning goes is not the original offense whereby the neighbor has been wronged, but the unwillingness to be reconciled, which is here pictured as a damnable sin.

THE SIXTH COMMANDMENT.

Eph. 5, 3.4: *But fornication, and all uncleanness, or covetousness, let it not be once named among you, as becomes saints; neither filthiness, nor foolish talking, nor jesting, which are not convenient: but rather giving of thanks.*

The conjunction *but* refers to the previous context, *Be ye therefore followers of God, as dear children; and walk in love, as Christ also hath loved us, and hath given himself for us an offering and a sacrifice to God for a sweetsmelling savor.* As altogether incompatible with the imitation of God and Christ in holy love the apostle mentions the things named or intimated in our text. *Porneia* is a gross form of what is named with the general term of *Pasa akatharsia.* All sin is uncleanness. Thus the psalmist prays, *Wash me thoroughly from mine iniquity and cleanse me from my sin* (Ps. 51, 2); and again, *Purge me with hyssop, and I shall be clean: wash me, and I shall be whiter than snow.* (Ps. 51, 7.) And Christ speaks of sin which dwells in and proceeds from the heart as that which defiles a man. (Matt. 15, 18-20.) But there is one class of sins which are of such a nature that, as the apostle indicates in our text, the mere naming of them is embarrassing to Christians; for we are *saints*, and holiness is purity, which would not even get near that which defiles. These sins are in a peculiar sense sins of uncleanness, the sins of unchastity, the sins forbidden in the sixth commandment. It is this class of sins which more than any other underlie the sense of shame, and the suggestion or consciousness of which drives or ought to drive the blush of shame to cheeks which, on the other hand, would be blanched by the pallor of fear caused by sins of a different type. Hence also the term of *aischrotes*, for which the English Bible has *filthiness*, but which is more exactly rendered by *shameful conduct*. It is this peculiar nature of these sins which causes them to be chiefly committed in secret. Where they are openly committed it is because the sense of shame, is in the individual or in a community, blunted in such a aegree as to react no longer as it should against these works of the flesh. Thus the modern theatre, the dance of today, many society games, are abominations to which no decent person should in any way become a party and which could not serve as amusements for decent people but for a prevailing obtuseness of the sense of shame. The terms *morologia* and *eutrapelia* are connected by *e, or,* which after the *kai* preceding both indicates that the two terms are descriptive of the same thing under different aspects. *Morologia* is foolish frivolity in words, *eutrapelia* is vain frivolity in demeanor, *leichtfertiges geschwaetz and Gebahren*, things which are *me anekonta, improper* for an earnest Christian, and of which one who would walk in Christ's footsteps should be ashamed. Of such improprieties a certain class of jokes and anecdotes and the immodest laughter they elicit, as well as certain immodesties in dress and deportment, may be especially mentioned. Such manner of merriment is unbecoming to a Christian, who should manifest the gladness of his heart in other ways, one which is named here by the apostle, the *giving of thanks*

Eph. 5, 12: *For it is a shame even to speak of those things which are done of them in secret.*

In the previous context we are admonished to *have no fellowship with the unfruitful works of darkness, but rather to reprove them.* The apostle has described the works of the heathen world of this day as works of darkness, thereby indicating that they are largely performed as secret sins, which even more than certain other sins shun the light of day and the eyes of witnesses not occupied with the same sins. Of this description are the sins of unchastity, and among them, again, certain sins of uncleanness before others. These secret sins were extensively practiced in the time of St. Paul and are widely practiced in our day, sins against nature so repulsive that the apostle only points toward them as from a distance and forbears to mention them more definitely, stating his reason in our text. He would not defile his mouth or the ears of his hearers by even speaking of them more particularly in an epistle intended for all classes of readers. This is a very emphatic way of impressing his readers with the shamefulness and repulsiveness of the sins here intimated, and with the abhorrence wherewith those should be viewed who not only speak of but practice such abominations.

Matt. 19, 6: *What therefore God hath joined together, let no man put asunder.*

The first married couple, Adam and Eve, were in a peculiar sense joined together in wedlock by God Himself, as we read in Gen. 2, 22. In a different sense, however, all those who entered into valid marriage have been joined together by God. For matrimony is of divine institution, and as such it is what God has made it, a union of a man and a woman for life. Thus married people are not bound together merely by a contract entered into by themselves as by their mutual consent, so that they might again by mutual consent revoke their agreement and dissolve their bond of marriage; but being united in a divine ordinance, the bond which unites them is of God's own making and must not be dissolved but by God alone or under the conditions determined by His will. This is true also where the state of marriage has been entered with some violation of the law of God in points not essential to valid marriage; for in such cases the sin or sins committed were not according to the will of God and least of all caused by God and should be duly repented of by those who sinned; but that the marriage bond thus assumed should be indissoluble is according to the will of God, and hence those whom God has joined together no man shall put asunder.

Matt. 19, 9: *Whosoever shall put away his wife, except it be for fornication, and shall marry another, committeth adultery.*

In these words Christ deals with those who, like the Pharisees of His day, looked upon marriage as being dissoluble by mutual consent or by the observation of a certain provision made by Moses for those who, in the hardness of their hearts, insisted upon severing before men the marriage bond by which they were bound before God. Such separations were looked upon as being legitimate dissolutions of marriage, whereby both parties were free to remarry with whom they might choose, provided that the proper form of divorcement had been observed, whatever the cause of such divorcement might have been, vv. 7-8. There is but one cause which justifies divorce before God, and that is fornication, whereby the innocent party is entitled to consider the bond of marriage dissolved, though he or she may also condone the offence and continue the union with the offending party. But for no other cause may a man put away his wife without offending against the word that what God has joined together no man should put asunder; and if, having put away his wife without sufficient cause, he should marry another, he would thereby commit adultery in becoming one flesh with a person not his wife.

2 Pet. 2, 14: *Having eyes full of adultery, and that cannot cease from sin.*

In the chapter from which this text is taken the apostle describes certain impious deceivers of the latter days, who by doctrine and practice mislead many into their evil ways. The apostle's prediction has been fulfilled in every point chiefly in popery and the various institutions peculiar to the synagogue of antichrist. One of the abominations which have rendered the Roman See and many other purported seats of exquisite holiness repulsive even in the eyes of Romanists themselves is that of all varieties of carnal licentiousness. Our text mentions one form of voluptuousness in describing those men as *having eyes full of adultery.* A more precise translation of the original would be *having eyes full of an adulteress,* that is, looking with intense pleasure upon an unchaste woman as a hungry man looks with gloating eyes upon an article of food, or as one who is parched with thirst looks at a cup of water as if he would drink it with his eyes. Thus unchastity has driven out modesty so that, instead of looking down abashed or turning away his eyes when immodest persons or things intrude themselves upon his gaze, a man will rather indulge in his evil lusts and derive pleasure from intently gazing upon what may inflame his licentious desires. This is the sin of those who seek and find enjoyment in witnessing unchaste performances on the theatrical stage, immodest paintings and statuary and other objects which must offend a modest eye and heart. Of course, if such abuse of the eyes is sinful it is no less sinful to provide for voluptuous eyes the objects whereon they would feast, to pander to licentiousness by immodest exposure, by the production or exhibition of immodest pictures or statues under the pretext or with the boast of dramatic or plastic or pictorial art.

Matt. 5, 27.28: *Ye have heard that it was said by them of old*

time, Thou shalt not commit adultery: but I say unto you, That who-
soever looketh upon a woman to lust after her hath already committed
adultery with her in his heart.

Here again Christ rebukes the conception and exposition of the
law as it was prevalent among the Pharisees of His day, who looked
upon the ommission of gross offences against the law or the performance
of outward works demanded by the law as adequate fulfillment of the
divine commandments. What He inculcates is that not only the consummation of the sin of adultery is a transgression of the sixth commandment, but that the unclean desire of the heart directed upon a
woman is before God adultery committed with that woman. Adultery,
as every other work of the flesh, originates in the heart, and every unclean desire would terminate in a gross work of the flesh if it were not
prevented by circumstances under the control of divine government.
Besides, God demands not only outward but also inward conformity
with His holy will, and as in His omniscience He sees the thoughts of
men and their desires and affections afar off, He is thereby offended just
as truly and consistently as by the outward acts which are performed
in the sight of men. This should be all the more assiduously inculcated
and remembered as concerning the sins of unchastity, since these sins
are more extensively practiced and indulged in by evil thoughts and
imaginations than many sins against other commandments of God.

Hebr. 13, 4: *Whoremongers and adulterers God will judge.*

All the words of this statement are in the original by their arrangement placed in emphasis: *Pornous de kai moichous krinei ho theos*,
while the regular order would be *ho theos krinei pornous kai moichous.*
The secular courts deal much more largely with open transgressors
of the laws against the security of person and property corresponding
to the fifth and seventh commandments, while fornication and adultery,
being naturally practiced in secret and under cover of darkness more
generally than other sins, are in comparison less frequently prosecuted
and punished by the secular arm. But be they ever so carefully guarded
and so secretly performed, these sins will not go unpunished. God
sees and records them all and will judge those against whom they
stand recorded in His book. And for still another reason God threatens
to punish these sins of unchastity. They are often made light of among
men. Profligate seducers and defilers of women, and women who by
voluptuous arts entice men from the path of virtue, even pride themselves with their so-called victories and conquests and are looked upon
by others as heroes and heroines in their way, by whose example others
are incited to like practices. But God puts a different estimate upon
these things. He will judge them not according to the perverse codes
of corrupt society, but according to the norm of His holy law. Hence
the emphasis on *krinei.* God will not condone and make light of sins
as these; much less will He justify and even extol them; but He will
judge them and bring condemnation upon those also who escape tem-

poral punishment.

Rom. 13, 13: *Let us walk honestly, as in the day; not in rioting and drunkenness, ont in chambering and wantonness, not in strife and envying.*

Komoi, which the English Bible renders *rioting,* is the word for *banquets,* which, among the heathen of those days, were generally occasions for immoderate eating, the guests being gorged with food and entertained with music, song, and dances. King Herod celebrated his birthday with a *komos,* Matt. 14, 6ff. On other occasions indulgence in excessive drinking, even to intoxication, was more prominent, and to this the apostle refers by *methai, drunken revelries.* These sins are in very extensive practice today in club houses and saloons, at weddings and anniversaries and other occasions, and are as little befitting a Christian today as they were in the apostle's day. They are in themselves gross works of the flesh and often lead to other works of the flesh. Of such, also, the apostle speaks as he continues, *me koitais kai aselgeiais, not in illicit carnal intercourse and lewd excesses.* These sins are often the outcome of those named before, and they, too, have their occasions and localities. Many a man and woman would not have fallen into these gross abominations if they had kept away from places and occasions where no Christian should be found. That even Christians are in danger of gross sins of unchastity appears from the divine admonition laid down in this text for Christians, who are here, on the other hand, called upon to walk *euschemonos, decently, as in the day.* Sins of uncleanness are preeminently works of darkness, shunning the light of day; but a Christian should so conduct himself in all things that he may have no cause of fleeing the light. A Christian should "lead a chaste and decent life in word and deed." This should be his *walk,* as with a steady step, moving forward in the way of the commandments of God, Ps. 119, 32, and with God's word as a lamp unto his feet, Ps. 119, 105, he walks through an evil world to his eternal home. Thus he will avoid the ways of sin.

Eph. 4, 29: *Let no corrupt communication proceed out of your mouth, but that which is good to the use of edifying, that it may minister grace unto the hearers.*

Pas logos sapros ek tou stomatos humon me ekporeuestho. Sapros, from the root *sap,* from which we have the words *sepo, to rot, or to make rotten, seps, rottenness,* means *rotten, foul, nasty.* Every child knows or feels what is meant by *nasty words.* These should not come out of a Christian's mouth, not any of them. How unbecoming to a Christian such words are is all the more clear from the contrast in which they stand to such words as befit the Christian. St. James shows how improper cursing is to a Christian by saying: *Out of the same mouth proceed blessing and cursing. My brethren, these things ought not so to be.* James 3, 10. Thus St. Paul here leads us to comprehend that indecent words are ill agreed with Christian decency in words. A Christian should speak that which is *agathon pros oikodomen tes chreias.* The genetive, *tes chreias,* is gen. relationis, and the whole phrase is, *That which is good, useful, for edification as the occasion may require, hina do charin tois akouousin, that he may render a welcome service to those who hear him.* All this is the very reverse of indecent words, which cannot edify but only demoralize. Hence, the more a Christian endeavors to make right use of his mouth according to the apostle's direction, the less will he be in danger of abusing and defiling it by unsavory speech, lewd songs, unclean anecdotes and puns, and the like. In the subsequent context the apostle gives two more reasons for abstaining from filthy words; they grieve the Holy Spirit and are altogether unworthy of the future state of glory and perfect holiness for which we are already sealed, v. 30.

1 Cor. 6, 19: *Know ye not that your body is the temple of the Holy Ghost which is in you, which ye have of God, and ye are not your own?*

In the previous context, v. 18, the apostle had said, *He that committeth fornication sinneth against his own body,* and had given this as a reason for his admonition, *Flee from fornication.* And to render the weight of this argument all the more clear to his readers, and especially to such as might not at once grasp the significance of the nature of these sins of unchastity, he proceeds to point out two reasons why a Christian should not defile his body. In the first place he reminds the Christian that his body is the temple of the Holy Spirit which is in him and which he has of God. To defile a temple was even among the heathen nations looked upon as a heinous sin, a sacrilegious crime, and that while the temples dedicated to the worship of pagan idols were the very reverse of dwellings of God, but, like the heathen sacrifices, devoted to devils, 1 Cor. 10, 20. But a Christian's body is truly a temple of God wherein the Holy Spirit dwells, sanctifying his abode by His divine presence. In view of this it must appear a most awful sacrilege to defile the body of a Christian man or woman, especially when that sin is committed by the Christian himself, who has within him the testimony of the Holy Spirit whereby He makes known His presence in various ways, as the Spirit of power, of hope, and of sanctification.— The second reason why a Christian should beware of polluting his body with the filth of carnal sin is stated in the words, *And ye are not your own,* which are further explained in the next verse, where the apostle continues, *For ye are bought with a price.* We have the same words again 1 Cor. 7, 23, and St. Peter is more explicit, saying, *Ye know that ye were not redeemed with corruptible things, as silver and gold, from your vain conversation received by tradition from your fathers; but with the precious blood of Christ, as of a lamb without blemish and without spot.* 1 Pet. 1, 18. 19. The same apostle also speaks of those who *deny the Lord who bought them.* 2 Pet. 2, 1. And in Rev. 5, 9 the saints say in the new song, *Thou wast slain, and hast redeemed us to God by thy blood.* Thus are we bought with a price, not only our souls but also our bodies. Thus are we not ours but Christ's, who has purchased us to Himself with His holy, precious blood and with His innocent suffering and death, that we should be His own, body and soul. And hence we should beware of defiling that body which is Christ's by rightful acquisition, and instead of polluting it we should rather *glorify God in our body and in our spirit, which are God's,* v. 20.

Ps. 51, 10: *Create in me a clean heart, o God; and renew a right spirit within me.*

That all manner of sin springs from man's evil heart has already appeared in the text quoted under the fifth commandment, Matt. 15, 19: *Out of the heart proceed evil thoughts, murders, adulteries, fornications, etc.* Hence a thorough reform whereby we may be cured from this leprosy also of unchastity must consist in a renewal of our hearts. But this is not within our power but a work of God. David had by sad experience learned that from his evil heart even the grossest sins, adultery and murder, might spring; and though he was truly penitent of what he had done, he knew that he was not secure from the recurrence of such atrocious sins while his heart was evil and unclean. Hence the psalmist's petition: *Create in me a clean heart, o God.*

Prov. 23, 31-33: *Look not thou upon the wine when it is red, when it giveth his color in the cup, when it moveth itself aright. At the last it biteth like a serpent and stingeth like an adder. Thine eyes shall behold strange women, and thine heart shall utter perverse things.*

This is a warning to those who are in danger of being enticed to excessive drink and its consequence. The *color of the wine* and its *sparkling and glittering in the cup* are apt to entice the man whose eyes are not guarded, and when the cup has gone to the lips the taste of the wine may add to the charm under which many have succumbed. The words, *When it moveth itself aright* is not rendered correctly in the English Bible. *When* has no equivalent in the text, and Luther's version, *Er gehet glatt ein,* is an exquisite idiomatic expression for the more literal: *He walks complacently on level ways.* The wine is here compared with a portly man who walks down the drinker's throat. But the wine, when taken in excess, will change its character and *bite like a serpent and sting like an adder.* What these words say in figurative speech, the following words state in proper terms: *Thine eyes shall behold strange women, and thine heart shall utter perverse things.* In the original the word *women* is not found, but has been supplied by many interpreters. But the sense certainly includes *strange women,* and the state of intoxication which is here described certainly does not exclude what the English words say, as voluptuousness is often kindled and fanned into flame by the influences of strong drink.

Prov. 1, 10: *My son, if sinners entice thee, consent thou not.*

The word here rendered *sinners* stands for those who have by continued practice become accustomed to, or adepts in, sin, in whom sin has grown into a vice, *Lasterknechte*, and the wise man warns his son not to have intercourse with such. This warning is all the more appropriate, as those who are given to any vice are generally very prone to enticing others to become their associates, and especially such as are yet uninitiated into the ways of sin with which their seducers are familiar. Very often those whom they have singled out for their victims are very little aware of the danger which threatens them; and this is vividly pictured in the form, *Consent not!* which, like the Latin *noli!* is in the manner of an outcry directed to one who stands on the verge of a precipice with but another step between him and a fearful descent into a yawning gulf. Thus should parents and others who may be aware of the dangers to which the young are exposed by intercourse with evil men and women raise their warning voices, and those who hear such warning should speedily heed it, lest they be precipitated into an abyss of sin and shame and even everlasting perdition.

THE SEVENTH COMMANDMENT.

Eph. 4, 28: *Let him that stole, steal no more: but rather let him labor, working with his hands the thing which is good, that he may have to give to him that needeth.*

The English form, *him that stole*, is not a precise rendering of the original, which is not *ho klepsas*, the aorist, but *ho klepton*, the present participle, which describes one who is in the habit of or practices stealing. The Apostle here evidently refers to such as were before their conversion given to theft, a sin very extensively practised in the days of Paul by people throughout all the strata of society, from the highest civil and military officers down to the slave and the beggar in the streets, while, on the other hand, honest toil was very generally looked upon as being unworthy of a free man. The Apostle, on the contrary, teaches his readers that one who has come from out of the ungodly world must abandon the occupation of a thief and earn an honest living by honest labor, as behooves a Christian. And this admonition is very pertinent in our day, when the acquisition of gain by a multitude of ways and means other than honest toil is again rampant in the world, while honest labor in the sweat of the brow is looked upon as an evil and a misfortune. It is this unwillingness to labor and to be content with honest earnings which also in our time makes thieves of many, men and women, young and old, thieves of many kinds, robbers and burglars, swindlers and gamblers, speculators and usurers, and those who live and fatten on the toil and sweat of others. Such disposition and the practises springing therefrom are unworthy of a Christian to-day as they were in the days of St. Paul.

But still another inducement to theft is indicated in our text; it is want and poverty, the lack of the necessaries of life. And a Christian should not only be himself honest, but also do what he can to keep his neighbor from dishonesty or from temptation thereto by *giving to him that needeth*. It should be noted, however, that what is given to the needy should also be honestly acquired. It will not do to steal from the rich in order to give to the poor, or to give alms from the profit made by any illicit trade. And no trade befits a Christian which is not *working the things which is good*, labor which redounds to the temporal and spiritual benefit of our neighbor and upon which a Christian may consistently ask God's blessing from on high.

Hab. 2, 6: *Woe unto him that increaseth that which is not his! How long? And to him that ladeth himself with thick clay.*

This is an imprecation upon all those who enrich themselves at the cost of others. The prophet would warn those who are apparently successful in accumulating wealth, while in fact their increase is not their own. Thus when the usurer exacts interest upon loans regardless of profit or loss accruing from the use of the loan, demanding and taking profit where no profit has been made or even where loss has been sustained by the debtor in the use of the loan, he takes that which is not rightfully his own, and though by usurious gain he may largely increase his wealth, the prophet cries out, *Woe unto him!* How long will he enjoy what he has thus acquired? Even though he remain in possession of his ill-gotten wealth, he has only burdened his soul with a heavy weight, as one who has laden himself with thick clay, and the time will come when he would fain be rid of his encumbrance.

1 Thess. 4, 6: *That no man go beyond and defraud his brother in any matter: because that the Lord is the avenger of all such.*

The infinitives, *huperbainein* and *pleonektein*, are syntactically connected with *touto gar estin thelema tou theou, for this is the will of God*, v. 3. In the preceding context the Apostle has inculcated the will of God that Christians should abstain from sins against the sixth commandment, vv. 3-5, and he now enjoins the seventh commandment as likewise the will of God. The verb *huperbainein, to go beyond, to exceed proper bounds*, is the general term, which is, then, specified by *kai pleonektein, to defraud, to enrich oneself at the cost of another*. The seventh commandment draws a sacred line about our neighbor's property, a line where honesty ceases and dishonesty begins. Beyond this line we must never go, neither by open theft nor by unfair dealings in business. That the brother, the fellow Christian, is here named does not imply license to practise dishonesty on such as are not brethren, but makes it a special point to warn against taking advantage of the fraternal trust and confidence with which a brother may and should deal with a brother in Christ. And though the unsuspecting brother may not be nor ever become aware of a fraud practised upon him by a brother, the day of reckoning will come; for *the Lord is the avenger of all such.* This warning should be most earnestly heeded among Christians. It is a disgrace to the name of Christ that Christians should by dishonest dealing of their brethren be induced to deal or trade with those who are without.

Lev. 19, 35. 36: *Ye shall do no unrighteousness in judgment, in .meteyard, in weight, or in measure. Just balances, just weights, a just ephah, and a just hin, shall ye have: I am the Lord your God.*

The previous text enjoins from all manner of dishonesty in matters of property and business. The present text deals more particularly with commercial transactions. Weights and measures are standards of quantity. *Ephah* was a dry measure of about 1 1-10 bushel; a *hin*, a liquid measure of about a gallon and a half. To change or manipulate weights or measures to the disadvantage of a customer is not smartness but *unrighteousness.* The same is true of all other commercial standards, such as coins, brands, grades, etc. Though these standards are fixed and maintained by the will of men, they must not be tampered with in violation of fairness and honesty. For when God, demanding just balances and weights, etc., adds the words, *I am the Lord your God,* He would thereby lead us to understand and remember that these human standards are under His divine surveillance, and that he will call to account those who abuse them for dishonest purposes.

Lev. 25, 36: *Take thou no usury of him, or increase; but fear thy God, that thy brother may live with thee.*

Usury is the exaction of interest on loans, generally on money, regardless of profit or loss accruing from the use of the loan. It is certainly fair that the owner should share the profit resulting from the use of his property; but it is just as certainly unfair that he should demand profit where no profit has been made and even where loss has been sustained by the debtor in the use of the loan. The creditor who demands and exacts interest where no increase has come to his money while in his creditor's hands, takes that which is not his, but his neighbor's. The plea that interest thus exacted was stipulated by contract only says that the contract itself was unfair and usurious. This form of illicit gain is not restricted to the loans of money. The text distinguishes between *usury,* where money is loaned, and *increase,* where provisions and other goods are to be returned in greater quantity. Even though such usurious transactions be sanctioned by human laws, as by a legal rate of interest, the usurer is not justified. *Fear thy God,* says the Lord in the text, and the day of reckoning will be a day of wrath also for usurers. Besides, usury is also in a temporal way a source of evil in human society, bringing poverty and woe upon the victims of usurers. This is indicated by the words, *That thy brother may live with thee.* The prohibition of usury in Israel was one of the provisions whereby the preservation of the people and the prosperity of the various families from generation to generation was to be secured and the enrichment of the few at the cost of the many prevented. In our day the troubles which confront us in commercial and industrial life are largely owing to the sin and evil of usury.

Jer. 22. 13: *Woe unto him that buildeth his house by unrighteousness, and his chambers by wrong; who uses his neighbor's services without wages, and giveth him not for his work.*

This text is very plain and very timely. The relation between an employer and an employee is a moral relation regulated by the will of God. The builder of a house may employ laborers to perform the work necessary for or incidental to the erection and furnishing of the edifice, and while others perform such work, he is properly the builder of the house. It is for *him that buildeth his house* to determine who shall perform the work according to the contract or contracts upon which he may agree by his free consent. The work performed by the employee is *service*, and he who serves must not presume to dictate and to enforce his will regardless of the rights of others and especially of the employer. And yet the employer, *he that buildeth his house,* is a responsible agent, responsible to God, and *when he uses his neighbor's service without wages, and giveth him not for his work, he buildeth his house by unrighteousness and his chambers by wrong.* Wages is the fair consideration or recompense for services rendered, and the full amount of such wages, when duly earned, belongs to the laborer, and to withhold his wages from the laborer is just as truly theft as to take his earnings out of his pocket after he has received them. Such unrighteousness and wrong is all the more damnable when the employer is rich. This is indicated by the subsequent context: "That saith, I will build me a wide house and large chambers, and cutteth him out windows; and it is ceiled with cedar, and painted with vermilion. Shalt thou reign, because thou closest thyself in cedar?" This is a portraiture of the overbearing rich man, who in his pride haughtily disregards the just claims of his laborer, a counterpart of many employers of our day, individuals and corporations, who crush and grind out the very life of the poor employees as if there were no God in heaven who cries out, *Woe unto him that buildeth his house by unrighteousness,* etc.

2 Thess. 3, 10: *If any would not work neither should he eat.*

This was a Jewish proverb based upon Gen. 3, 19, and adopted by St. Paul in his oral instruction and in his epistle as a true saying. It is God who gives us our daily bread; but He has so ordained that He would give us what we need as the proceeds of honest labor. Meanwhile God has not bound His hand by this ordinance any more than by any other. He gives food and raiment to many who are unable to work, as He feeds the sparrows and clothes the lilies. Hence the text does not say, *If any DO not work,* but, *If any WOULD not work, ei tis ou thelei ergadzesthai, neither should he eat.* The able-bodied man who is unwilling to work must not expect that God will feed him, while he who is unable to work need not fear that God will let him starve.

Ps. 37, 21: *The wicked borroweth and payeth not again.*

The Psalmist in the preceding and the subsequent context exhibits the difference between the godly and the wicked and shows that true happiness and prosperity is the lot of the former and not the latter. Thus, also, in the 21st verse he points out the difference between these two classes of men, saying, *The wicked borroweth and payeth not again, but the righteous showeth mercy and giveth.* There is no true prosperity with the ungodly. What they have is not sufficient to them; the property of others is in their hands and they frequently cannot do without it; and when they should repay what they have borrowed they are either unwilling or unable to refund what they owe. It is different with the godly and righteous. While they do not take and keep what rightfully belongs to others, they give from what is theirs, and are not thereby impoverished but are still in condition to show mercy. Thus do the wicked and the godly differ in the administration of this world's goods.

Prov. 29, 24: *Whoso is partner with a thief hateth his own soul.*

A Christian should not only shun the sin of theft in any form as a sin committed by himself, but should also beware of partaking in such sin when and where it is committed by others. Even the secular courts will hold the accomplice responsible with the principal perpetrator of an unlawful act, and the laws of those who are not able to kill the soul are not in this respect more stringent than the law of Him who is able to destroy both soul and body in hell. A Christian who becomes a partaker in transactions whereby his neighbor is deprived of his rightful property, though he be only a silent partner or a sharer in such illicit gain, risks the loss of his soul.

Matt. 5, 42: *Give to him that asketh thee, and from him that would borrow of thee turn not thou away.*

This text is taken from Christ's exposition of the law in the Sermon on the Mount. The connection in which the words stand with the previous context indicates that the Lord would here teach us to administer what is entrusted to us of this world's goods without selfishness. Man in his natural depravity is inclined to assert his right of possession regardless of the wants of others, and his natural selfishness is apt to be increased by every increase of wealth. Here, then, Christ teaches us that in our stewardship we should duly consider our neighbor's wants according as circumstances may permit or demand, giving where a gift, lending where a loan may be called for and proper.

Prov. 19, 17: *He that hath pity upon the poor lends to the Lord; and that which he hath given will He repay him again.*

This is an injunction and a promise combined. The injunction is that we should have pity upon the poor, not only by kind dealings and words, but also by giving to them according to our means and their need. This is indicated by the parallelism of the members of this text, according to which *having pity upon the poor* and *giving* belong together. The promise lies in the parallel statements, *Lends unto the Lord* and *He will repay him again.* This promise is not given in order that we should give to the poor merely to secure greater returns from the Lord, but to indicate how well pleasing our good stewardship in disposing of our temporal goods is in the sight of God, and to render us all the more cheerful in the exercise of benevolence as we remember whence all temporal blessings come.

Hebr. 13, 16: *But to do good, and to communicate, forget not: for with such sacrifices God is well pleased.*

This is a much needed admonition. Men, and also Christians, are not very apt to forget their opportunities for increasing their income and enjoying what they possess. But we are apt to be unmindful of the occasions and opportunities for Christian beneficence and even to take it with bad grace when others remind us of what we are pleased to forget. And hence this admonition is again coupled with a reference to the estimate which God places on our acts of benevolence. He looks upon them as sacrifices, that is, as offerings given, not to the poor and needy among our fellowmen or fellow-Christians, but to the Lord God Himself, who is well pleased with such sacrifices, and places them on our record for the day of reckoning, when He will before men and angels give us credit for every one of them, saying, "Inasmuch as ye have done it unto one of the least of these, my brethren, ye have done it unto me."

THE EIGHTH COMMANDMENT.

Zech. 8, 17: *Let none of you imagine evil in your hearts against his neighbor.*

In the previous context the Prophet enjoins works of righteousness according to the eighth commandment, v. 16, *These are the things that ye shall do; speak every man the truth to his neighbor; execute the judgment of truth and peace in your gates.* In the continuation of his admonition he speaks of things prohibited by the same commandment: *And let none of you imagine evil in your hearts against his neighbor; and love no false oath: for all these are things that I hate, saith the Lord.* The injunction in v. 16 implies that to speak the untruth and to execute deceitful judgment is sin. But according to our text God also hates transgressions of the eighth commandment committed in our hearts. To imagine evil against our neighbor is an absolute or relative violation of the truth, since what we do not *know,* but *imagine,* may be or is untrue, and he who loves his neighbor as himself will not hold him guilty of evil unless on full and sufficient proof. To assume or imagine to our neighbor's discredit what *may* be false implies a disregard of truth as well as the love we owe our neighbor, and is in the context placed on the same line with loving a false oath.

Eph. 4, 25: *Wherefore putting away lying, speak every man truth with his neighbor: for we are members one of another.*

The word *wherefore* refers to the previous context which is a general admonition to *put on the new man, which after God is created in righteousness and true holiness;* and our text is the first of a series of special exhortations under this head, and teaches us that lying is inconsistent with righteousness and true holiness and must therefore be put off as a work of the old man, and that one of the foremost endeavors of every one who would put on the new man must be to speak the truth with his neighbor. But while lying is thus seen to be wholly inconsistent with the new man within us, it is incompatible also with the relation we hold among each other as Christians; *for we are members one of another.* It is unnatural for the members of the body to deceive each other instead of doing by one another according to their true and actual wants, whatever these may be. Thus, also, it is unnatural for Christians to deceive each other, a denial of their relation with one another and with Christ, their common head. And note that the Apostle says, SPEAK *the truth.* To withhold the truth where it should be spoken is also a species of falsehood.

Prov. 19, 5: *A false witness shall not be unpunished, and he that speaketh lies shall not escape.*

It is of the very nature of a lie that it would go in the guise of truth and thus conceal its nature. A false witness, in order to be heard and believed, will naturally claim credit as a true witness, and a liar's first and fundamental endeavor is to deceive by his falsehood. But though man may be deceived and allow a false witness to go unpunished, God is not deceived and will visit also the liar's sin upon the sinner, and in God's judgment no false plea or testimony will avail; He will bring to light the hidden things of darkness. 1 Cor. 4, 5.

Prov. 11, 13: *A talebearer revealeth secrets: but he that is of a faithful spirit concealeth the matter.*

Those who reveal a neighbor's secret sins will often endeavor to justify themselves by the plea that what they have said is true. But this is no valid defense. To divulge a neighbor's hidden sin is not truthfulness, but the work of a *faithless heart;* for *he that is of a faithful spirit concealeth the matter,* that is, *keeps it secret.* Other people's secrets should not be looked upon as being at our free disposal, but as a sacred trust which should be conscientiously and faithfully guarded and kept as what it is, a trust not to be faithlessly betrayed.

James 4, 11: *Speak not evil one of another, brethren.*

The Apostle does not say, "Do not lie against one another, "but *me katalaleite allelon, do not speak against one another, to each other's damage.* Even the truth may be spoken in bad faith, and a statement concerning our neighbor, though true in substance, when made with evil intent, *kata,* is sinful, a sin which has blasted the good name of many a man and woman. Besides, experience teaches that those who speak evil of a brother are rarely very scrupulous in point of truthfulness. It is but natural that he who would damage his brother by evil reports should endeavor to give color to his statements even at the cost of truth in order to achieve his evil purpose.

Luke 6, 37: *Judge not, and ye shall not be judged: condemn not, and ye shall not be condemned.*

The key to this admonition is in the previous context, *Be ye therefore merciful, as your Father also is merciful,* v. 36. *Krinein, to judge,* is, here, *to sit in judgment,* while *katadikadzein, to condemn,* is *to pronounce guilty.* In both cases what is prohibited is a violation of the injunction: Be merciful. Our disposition should not be to mete out justice to the brother who has sinned, but to look upon him as one whose weakness appeals to our compassion and to whom we should stoop with an earnest desire to help him. This is God's disposition toward us, though He is the supreme judge and a consuming fire, who will in His time judge and condemn those who have unmercifully judged and condemned others. Besides, those who judge and condemn where they should show mercy will in most cases set aside both justice and mercy. As a rule the brother who has sinned is not even given a hearing by these self-constituted judges, but is judged and condemned without as much as semblance of a fair trial, and his good name may be damaged beyond repair before he even knows what is going on.

Matt. 18, 15: *If thy brother shall trespass against thee, go and tell him his fault between thee and him alone.*

Here our Lord shows us the proper way of exercising mercy on the brother who has sinned. To show mercy to the sinner is not to ignore his sin or to consider or call good that which is evil. The proper person, however, to speak to concerning a brother's sin is not his neighbor, nor his enemy, but *himself. Elenxon auton,* says Christ, lead him to know and acknowledge the sinfulness of what he has done. But do not publish his sin; tell him his fault *between thee and him alone.* If this rule were more carefully observed among us, there would be less backbiting and slander among Christians. And the fault lies not with the talebearer alone, but also with those who lend him their ear. When any one comes to us with an evil report concerning a brother, we should promptly refuse to hear him but *tell him his fault* and admonish him to do as Christ here directs us to do.

Ps. 50, 16, 19-22: *Unto the wicked God saith, Thou givest thy mouth to evil, and thy tongue frameth deceit. Thou sittest and speakest against thy brother; thou slanderest thine own mother's son. These things hast thou done, and I kept silence; thou thoughtest that I was altogether such an one as thyself: but I will reprove thee, and set them in order before thine eyes. Now consider this, ye that forget God, lest I tear you in pieces, and there be none to deliver.*

The *wicked* here is not one who has openly renounced religion and godliness, but one who is wicked at heart while he declares God's statutes and takes His covenant in his mouth, v. 16. Having charged him with sins against the seventh and the sixth commandments, God, with more words, reprimands him for his various offenses against the eighth commandment. The literal translation is *to let loose the mouth in evil*, as a reckless driver will let his horse rush along unchecked, when he should keep the reins in a firm and steady hand. Thus the tongue when it is not guarded and checked will rush headlong in evil ways. The imagery changes in the following words, *Thy tongue knitteth deceit.* This is the painstaking tongue, occupied in laying its threads with evil intent, as subtle slanderers are apt to do, choosing their words deliberately and often doing greater damage with what they intimate than by what they actually say. *Thou sittest......mother's son* is a portraiture of the talebearer who sits down and fills up the ears and hearts of his listeners with his slanderous gossip, sparing no one, not even his brother, though he be a brother by whole blood, having not only the same father, but also the same mother. The following verses describe God's attitude toward such sins. God is long suffering, and the slanderer may pursue his evil way for a long time, even to his hoary old age. But let him beware. The time will come when he will have to answer for what he may have long ago forgotten; for God keeps a record of every slanderous word, and the punishment of the evil tongue will be fearful; for the slanderer sins not only against his neighbor, but also against God, whose commandment he has set aside.

Prov. 31, 8, 9: *Open thy mouth for the dumb in the cause of all such as are appointed to destruction. Open thy mouth, judge righteously, and plead the cause of the poor and needy.*

The dumb in this text are not only those who are physically unable to speak, but all those who are not able to plead their own cause or make their own defense. The *children of perdition* are those who are in imminent danger of perishing. So then, when evil tongues assail the good name and fame of our neighbor, while he is, because of his absence or for some other reason, unable to defend himself, we should not listen in silence, but open our mouths and defend him as best we can. Again, while the wealthy generally find no difficulty in securing justice and more than justice and an advocate to plead their cause, the poor are often at a disadvantage in court and out of court. Hence we should deem it a special duty to *plead the cause of the poor and needy*, especially where they are in danger of being unjustly dealt with in court or out of court.

1 Pet. 4, 8: *Charity shall cover the multitude of sins.*

In Prov. 10, 12 we read, *Hatred stirreth up strife: but love covereth up all things,* and the verse from which our text is taken reads, *Above all things have fervent charity among yourselves: for,* etc. The parallelism between the two texts is evident. In both instances the neighbor is supposed to have offended, and not only once, but variously and repeatedly. In both instances the sins of the offender are looked upon as so many occasions, not for hatred which stirreth up strife, but for the exercise of love, fervent love. And this exercise of love should not consist in ignoring a brother's sin or making light of it. But knowing that our brother has sinned, we should not stir up strife on that account or bruit his sin abroad; for that would not be love but hatred toward him. On the contrary, true love will do what can be done toward keeping a brother's offenses from the knowledge of others who have no business to know of them. And this course should not only be pursued when a brother's sins are few, but all the more when they are manifold; for in such case he will be all the more in need of our protecting love. But to cover a *multitude* of sins requires *fervent charity.* The fulfillment of the eighth commandment is eminently a work of love according to the sum of the second table, "Thou shalt love thy neighbor as thyself."

1 Cor. 13, 7: *Charity believeth all things, hopeth all things, endureth all things.*

The Apostle would not say in these words that love is credulous and readily indulges in vain expectations and does not feel when it is ill-treated. But what he would say is that love is not suspicious but trusting and confiding and unwilling to injure a brother by assuming what is to his discredit. Love does not readily fear that a brother will do evil, but rather hopes that he will do what is proper while there is any foundation for such hope. And even where a brother has offended us, charity will not induce us to put the worst construction on what he has done and to fear that he will offend us still more grievously in the future, but readily believes what he or others may have to say in extenuation of his offense, and hopes that he will make good his promises of doing better in the future. On the contrary, suspicion and distrust concerning our neighbor's doings or intentions, and a lack of hopefulness for his reform, will chill and finally exterminate what little love we may have entertained towards him.

THE NINTH COMMANDMENT.

Is. 5, 8: *Woe unto them that join house to house, that lay field to field, till there be no place, that they may be placed alone in the midst of the earth.*

67

The ninth commandment, *Thou shalt not covet thy neighbor's house,* is a specification of the general precept, *Thou shalt not covet,* as we find it in Rom. 13, 9. It is in the nature of the perverted heart of fallen man to covet, and God would lead us to know that covetousness is sin in His sight. A Greek term for *covetousness, pleonexia,* (Luke 12, 15. Rom. 1, 29. Eph. 4, 19; 5, 3. Col. 3, 5), describes this sin as a craving for MORE possession, *pleon echein.* This is the nature of covetousness. The covetous man is never satisfied with what he has. When he has little he longs for more, and when he has more he craves for still more, and the more he has, the more he desires to have. This is most graphically pictured in our text. Here we have the owner of a house. But having succeeded in obtaining possession of one house, he is not satisfied; he longs for another house, and having acquired that, he longs for still another. Or he is possessed of a field, say eighty acres. But what are eighty acres? He must have 160; the adjoining farm must also be his own; and no sooner is the title to that good in his name, than he craves for still more if it seems at all within his reach. Thus he joins house to house, or lays field to field. How long? When will he be satisfied and cease to crave for more? Never, until there be *no place left,* and he *be placed alone in the midst of the earth.* Such is covetousness, an insatiable longing and craving for *more.* And this is sin, and God says, WOE *unto them* that are covetous, for this morbid appetite is itself an immoral perversion of the enjoyment of what God has given us into a greed for that which God has not given us but allotted to others. And this sinful lust and longing begets a multitude of other sins, as the following texts will show.

Matt. 23, 14: *Woe unto you, scribes and Pharisees, hypocrites! for ye devour widows' houses, and for a pretense make long prayer: therefore ye shall receive the greater damnation.*

This verse is not found in the best codices, nor in the ancient versions and the Fathers, and may have been taken over from Mark 12, 40, where it occurs in nearly the same words. It is, therefore, certainly a dictum of our Savior censuring the covetousness of the scribes and Pharisees. These men enriched themselves by gorging themselves with other people's property, taking what they could get by fair means or foul, not even stopping short at the possessions of widows. Under pretense of praying for them, they would take advantage of the credulity and devotion of women whom their husbands had left in possession of houses, but without a natural supporter and protector. But nothing is sacred to a covetous man. He craves and takes, no matter whence it may come, and is not satisfied until he has all that is to be had. This is indicated by *katesthiein, to eat UP (kataesthiein),* until nothing is left, like the greedy glutton, who, with an insatiable appetite, devours all he can to the very last morsel within his reach. And here, again, covetousness is marked as damnable sin which brings down upon the sinner the righteous wrath of God, not only upon the robber and murderer, but also upon the priest and the Levite, the man of prayer and outward godliness.

1 Tim. 6, 6-10: *But godliness with contentment is great gain. For we brought nothing into this world, and it is certain we can carry nothing out. And having food and raiment, let us be therewith content. But they that will be rich fall into temptations and a snare, and into many foolish and hurtful lusts, which drown men in destruction and perdition. For the love of money is the root of all evil: which while some coveted after, they have erred from the faith, and pierced themselves through with many sorrows.*

This is a remarkable text. In the verse preceding it, the Apostle has spoken of those who *suppose that gain is godliness*, or, more literally, that *godliness is a way of gain*, a *porismos*, *ein Gewerbe*, as Luther has it. He refers to those who put on the guise of godliness for filthy lucre's sake, as the scribes and Pharisees of the previous text and the mercenary ministers of whom Paul speaks in Tit. 1, 11. This is a form of covetousness of which the Apostle says, "From such withdraw thyself." And now he proceeds, *Estin de porismos megas he eusebeia meta autarkeias*, but indeed a great way of gain is godliness coupled with contentment. *Autarkeia, contentment*, is the very reverse of covetousness. He who is covetous never has enough, is never satisfied. He who is *autarkes*, Phil. 4, 11, always has enough, is always satisfied. And this is proper and reasonable. *For we brought nothing into this world, and it is certain we can carry nothing out.* Cf. Job 1, 21. Ps. 49, 17, 18. Eccles. 5, 14. Hence, whatever we have in this world is gain, is more than we brought when we came and more than we shall take with us when we go. Why, then, should we covet what we cannot claim as having brought it with us, nor have and hold to take it with us? *Having food and raiment, let us be therewith content.* It is really all we need, the means wherewith to sustain and to protect this body and life; and that God will give us this, we assume as a matter of course. If He, in His wisdom and goodness, will give us more, we thank Him; if He will give us this and nothing more, we likewise thank Him; and in either case we are gainers and rest content. This is the reverse of covetousness, and it is in every way far better to be godly with contentment than covetous. Why? *They that will be rich fall into temptation and a snare and into many foolish and hurtful lusts, which drown men in destruction and perdition.* The Apostle does not say, *They that ARE rich*, but *hoi boulomenoi ploutein, they that desire to be rich. Ploutos* is derived from the same root with *polu, much*, and *ploutein* is *to have much*, more than food and raiment, the necessities of our station in life. *Hoi boulomenoi ploutein* are simply the *covetous*, who *crave for more*. And this is an evil and, as all sin, leads to evil. This evil lust begets a progeny of other evil and *hurtful lusts*, and the end of this sin as of all other sins is *destruction and perdition*. The wages of sin is death. *Rhidza gar panton ton kakon estin he filarguria.* There is no article before *rhidza*. Paul would not here teach what is the root of all evil, but what follows from and grows out of *filarguria, the love of money,* and that is not good, but evil, and nothing but evil, as coming from an evil root, a sinful disposition and propensity, covetousness. And this evil root, this sinful propensity, is not only in the hearts of the ungodly, of unbelievers, but is found side by side with faith, the root of all that is good in us; and there, too, it is a dangerous thing, as sad experience has shown; for such coveting has caused some to err from the faith and to pierce themselves with many sorrows. Hence the warning following in v 11 is not superfluous even to such as Timothy, *Thou, O man of God, flee these things!* Beware of covetousness!

Phil. 2, 4: *Look not every man on his own things, but every man also on the things of others.*

Skopein, to look, is also used in the sense of *to pay attention to—, to care for—,* as 2 Cor. 4. 18, and secular authors, as Plato, Thucyd., Herod., use *skopein ta tinos* for *to see to the interest or advantage of—.* So here the Apostle exhorts the Philippians and all Christians to see not to their own interests but to those of others. The sum of all commandments, the fulfilling of the law, is love. Matt. 22, 39. Rom. 13, 10. 1 Tim. 1, 5. But *charity seeketh not her own.* 1 Cor. 13, 5. Thus coveting, which is the selfish care of one's own profit even to the loss of others, is seen to be the death of love and a root of all manner of violations of the law. To counterpoise this evil propensity, we should not only abstain from and put down our evil craving for advantages to ourselves even to the disadvantage of our neighbor, but also, *kai,* practice a continual care for the interests of our neighbor, even when in doing so we must deny ourselves. The fact, however, that this admonition, as that of the preceding text, is directed to Christians, clearly shows that we, too, are in need of such admonition. Why? Because our hearts, too, are not free from coveting.

Gal. 5, 13: *By love serve one another.*

Coveting tends to make all men and all things subservient to one's own interests regardless of the interests of others or the good will of God. Coveting will even lead to the perversion and abuse of the best and noblest gifts of God for the satisfaction of selfishness. Thus, Christians, as Paul says in the previous context, *have been called unto liberty, the liberty wherewith Christ hath made us free,* v. 1. But the flesh, *sarx,* our natural depravity, the residues of which are still within us, may abuse even this precious gift of God for taking advantage of our brethren by self-aggrandizement and other selfish ends, until those who are brethren and freedmen of Christ, even bite and devour one another, v. 15 Hence the warning, *Only use not liberty for an occasion to the flesh.* And now follows the admonition, *But by love serve one another.* The Greek word for *serve, douleuete,* connotes submission to another who holds the position of a master, *doulos,* from the root DA, *to give*, being an inferior who is not his own but belongs to a superior and is bound to serve his master's interests. And this submissive service shall be rendered *dia tes agapes, through the love* which Christians bear toward one another, and according to which they do not COVET, but rather deny themselves to serve the brethren.

Rom. 13, 9: *Thou shalt not covet.*

St. Paul quotes this commandment as the last in a series comprising four other commandments of the decalogue, given as the sixth, the fifth, the seventh, and the eighth, in our Catechism. The ninth and tenth commandments, both beginning with *Thou shalt not covet*, are in this selection of St. Paul, evidently quoted as one, *Ouk epithumeseis.* This verb, *epithumein*, the word used in the Septuagint, and the noun, *epithumia, desire*, do not always stand for *evil desire* or *lust*. Even our Savior says, *Epithumia epethumesa k. t. l. With desire I have desired to eat this passover with you*, Luke 22, 15. Hence, when God says, *Ouk epithumeseis, Thou shalt not desire, thou shalt not covet*, He clearly indicates that the human heart is depraved and its faculties are perverted. Man was created with a faculty of *epithumein*, of directing his affections upon, *epi*, objects which God had intended for his use, and all these ordinate desires were holy desires. But when Eve, under temptation, directed her desire upon the fruit of the forbidden tree, she sinned, and thenceforth her heart was depraved, the seat and source of evil desires, and her progeny inherited from her and her fallen husband a corrupt nature, a seat of impure, unholy desires. Man now covets his neighbor's wife, his man-servants and his maid-servants, his cattle, and all that is his neighbor's. And this depraved condition, and these corrupt desires, though the evil deeds of adultery and theft and other sins may not in every case ensue, are in themselves sinful; for God says, *Ouk epithumeseis, Thou shalt not covet.*

Rom. 7, 7: *I had not known lust, except the law had said, Thou shalt not covet.*

Here the question is answered, How do we know that *epithumia*, sinful desire, is *sin?* It is by the law. For the law is the moral norm, and sin is the transgression of the law. And now, the law, not only the Mosaic decalogue, but also the law written in the human heart, the natural law, says, *ouk epithumeseis.* Herodotus and Juvenal and other Gentiles knew that evil desire is itself damnable sin. When Jesus taught the Jews, in His Sermon on the Mount, Matt. 5, 21ff., that the evil desires of the heart are damnable before God, this was not extending the law to what it had not comprehended before, but a reassertion of the moral law which had been largely forgotten not only by the Gentiles, but also among the Jews under the influence of Pharisaic traditions and the doctrines of the lawyers. Thus Paul the Pharisee, too, had been in particular need of enlightenment on this subject, not by a new revelation, but by the law written in the Book of the Law and corroborated by the law as written in his heart, saying, *Thou shalt not çovet.* And hence, not only as regards this commandment, but because of our proneness to be forgetful or unmindful of all the commandments of God, we are in need of continually hearing and learning the law, by which is the *knowledge of sin,* Rom. 3, 20, not only of the sin of coveting, but of all sins, as Paul says in the context, Rom. 7, 7: *I had not known sin but by the law.*

James 1, 14, 15: *But every man is tempted, when he is drawn away of his own lust and enticed. Then, when lust hath conceived, it bringeth forth sin; and sin, when it is finished, bringeth forth death.*

The conjunction, *but,* points back to the previous context, which says that temptation to evil does not proceed from God. On the contrary, the source of evil is in man himself, who is tempted as by his own lust he is *exelkomenos kai deleadzomenos, drawn out and allured.* In these verbs man is pictured as a beast in its lair which is, by various means, induced to come forth and roused to action. Thus *deleadzein* is *to allure by a delear, a bait* attached to a hook or trap. Or both verbs may picture lust as a captivating woman who entices and allures men to have lewd intercourse with her. As a natural consequence of such intercourse, lust will conceive and bring forth a progeny of her own nature, sin, actual sins of various kinds; and sin, in its turn also fruitful, *apokuei,* brings forth that with which it was pregnant, death. And thus it appears that evil desire, which is in *every man's* heart, is not in itself a neutral thing, depending for its moral character or influence from without, but is, in its native state, sin, bringing forth a daughter of like nature, sin which again bears the fruit of sin, death. What St. James would here teach is not so much the genesis of sin and death, as rather the nature of lust, the enticing sinful mother of an evil progeny

Lev. 19, 2: *Ye shall be holy: for I the Lord your God am holy.*

These words were spoken to the people of Israel in connection with and at the head of a series of the statutes which God gave by Moses to His peculiar people. Most of these statutes refer to acts enjoined or prohibited, stating what the people of God should do or forbear. Here, however, the Lawgiver demands more; he utters His will not only as to what they should *do,* but as to how they should *be: Ye shall be holy.* Holiness is perfect purity from all ungodliness. And God Himself being holy, He cannot but demand holiness of those whose God He would be. It is against the will of God to have a heart defiled with evil propensities and evil desires, and such indwelling sinfulness as truly separates between unholy man and a holy God as any gross act committed in violation of any other commandment of God. For, *Ye shall be holy* is as truly and in the same sense a divine commandment as the commandment, *Thou shalt not kill,* or, *Thou shalt not steal.*

Matt. 5, 48: *Be ye therefore perfect, even as your Father which is in heaven is perfect.*

By *therefore, oun,* this text is marked as a conclusion drawn from the previous context, which enjoins love, true love, not toward our friends only, as the publicans may love, but also toward our enemies, doing good to them that hate us, even as our Father in heaven makes His sun to rise on the evil and on the good, and sends rain on the just and on the unjust. And we are our Father's children; therefore *we* should resemble, not the publicans, but our Father in heaven, who is perfect in His goodness, *teleios,* lacking nothing in quality or quantity. And this is not in our option. Christ is here preaching the law. Hence every imperfection in us is sin and damnable, though it be but a shortcoming in thought or desire.

Ps. 37, 4: *Delight thyself in the Lord; and He shall give thee the desires of thine heart.*

In the preceding verse the psalmist exhorts us to *trust in the Lord and* DO GOOD. All our works should be good, in conformity with the will of God expressed in His holy law. But not only our works should be holy; our desires and affections *also* should be godly, says the psalmist in our text. Our delight, too, should be in the Lord, and our heart's desires should be directed to those things only which God in His wisdom and goodness would give us. This is again but another form of the commandment, *Thou shalt not covet.* For he who covets does not delight himself in the Lord and is not content with what God gives him, but craves for that which God would not give him, and is displeased with the Lord when He withholds from him what his wicked, covetous heart desires.

THE CLOSE OF THE COMMANDMENTS.

James 4, 12: *There is one lawgiver, who is able to save and to destroy.*

The text followed by this translation is incomplete. The best manuscripts and most of the ancient versions add *kai krites, and judge,* after *ho nomothetes, the lawgiver.* What the Apostle says is this: *One* is the lawgiver and judge, and that is He who is able to save and to destroy, i. e., to execute His judgments according to the law. Human justice is imperfect. No human law is fully adequate to secure the ends of justice; for the lawgivers are human and their work can be no better than its makers. Again, the best of human laws may miscarry in the courts because the judges fail to apply the law to the nature and circumstances of the case. Or the ends of human justice may be frustrated at still a later stage; a righteous judgment may prove futile because the sentence cannot be executed. But divine justice is perfect as God Himself is perfect, a lawgiver of infinite wisdom and justice, whose laws are true utterances of His holy will, a judge who is never biased or deceived, whose judgments are true and in full conformity with the law, and an executor of unlimited knowledge and power, whose retribution is, in manner and measure, in full consistency with His judgments. Cf. Matt. 10, 28.

Deut. 27, 26: *Cursed be he that confirmeth not all the words of this law to do them: and all the people shall say, Amen.*

This is the last of a series of imprecations, eleven of which refer to particular sins, gross offenses against the first, fourth, fifth, sixth, seventh commandments of the decalogue. But this closing imprecation invokes a curse upon the transgressors of any commandment of God's holy law. The verb quoted here means *He will raise up, establish.* God has laid down the law in His commandments, and man is now called upon to set this law before his eyes as a rule of life, not a part of the law, but *all the words of the law,* not only to know them, but *to do them,* all of them. And such is the stringency of the law, of every word of the law, that the curse of God is here pronounced upon every one who comes short of compliance with this statute, and all the people shall acknowledge this and say *Amen.* Thus is the law the letter that killeth, the ministration of condemnation, 2 Cor. 3, 6. 9, that every mouth may be stopped, and all the world may become guilty before God. Rom. 3, 19.

Rom. 6, 23: *The wages of sin is death.*

Sin is here, as also in the previous context, pictured as a mistress or queen ruling over those who serve her; cf. vv. 12, 13, 14, 16, 17, 19, 20, 22; and in v. 13, where the members of the sinner are spoken of as *hopla adikias, weapons of unrighteousness,* the service of sin is pictured as military service. So here also. For *opsonia,* as the German *Sold,* denotes the pay of a soldier. The sinner, having undergone the hardships of a campaign with its marches and battles, at last, in consideration of his services, receives his well-earned wages, *death,* temporal and eternal death. Such is the service and recompense of Sin, the tyrant who rules over generations of slaves and wages war against God and His kingdom.

Ezek. 18, 20: *The soul that sinneth, it shall die. The son shall not bear the iniquity of the father, neither shall the father bear the iniquity of the son: the righteousness of the righteous shall be upon him, and the wickedness of the wicked shall be upon him.*

This text might seem to contradict the statement that "God is a jealous God, visiting the iniquity of the fathers upon the children unto the third and fourth generation." But both being words of God, there can be no real contradiction, and both must be true. The solution lies in the words, "of them that hate me." *There is no condemnation to them which are in Christ Jesus,* Rom. 8, 1, though their ancestors may have been steeped in iniquity. The godly son shall not bear the iniquity of an ungodly father any more than a godly father shall bear the iniquity of an ungodly son. But to the slave of sin, the wages of sin is death, because he rejects the gift of God, which is eternal life through Christ Jesus our Lord. Rom. 6, 23. Even the ungodly, who live and die in their sins, do not suffer death as a penalty of other men's sins, but *the soul that sinneth, it shall die: the wickedness of the wicked shall be upon him.* Yet God is not unjust, but a righteous judge, when, in meting out *temporal* punishment, as indicated by the words, "unto the third and fourth generation," He visits upon ungodly descendants His rightful wrath excited by the sins of ungodly ancestors, in whose footsteps He sees their children and children's children walk the same ways of iniquity, hating Him as their fathers hated Him. Thus were the wicked sons of wicked Canaan doomed to servitude, Gen. 9, 25; thus was the innocent blood of Jesus visited in wrath upon the wicked children of His murderers, because they refused to find grace and forgiveness in that blood which might have cleansed them too from *all* sin. Matt. 27, 25. 1 John 1, 7.

Luke 10, 28: *This do, and thou shalt live.*

These words were spoken to a lawyer who had tempted Jesus, saying, "Master, what shall I do to inherit eternal life?" The lawyer ought to have known better than to ask such a question; for inheritance does not come by works, but by virtue of the relation of parent and child or by the testator's will. Yet Jesus enters upon the lawyer's question, *What must I DO?* and points out to him a way which, being a way of works, would lead to eternal life those who performed such works. When the lawyer had correctly quoted the sum of the law, Jesus said to him, *Thou hast answered right; this DO, and thou shalt live.* God, in His goodness, has promised life to those who keep His commandments. Cf. Lev. 18, 5. Rom. 10, 5. Gal. 3, 12. And God would not fail to make His promise good, if any man rendered obedience, perfect obedience, to all commandments of His holy law. But Jesus was so far from teaching that any man may actually obtain eternal life by fulfilling the law, that by his answer He would rather lead the lawyer and others to understand that, being utterly unable to *do* all that the law demands, they cannot by their works obtain eternal life, but, being transgressors of the law, deserve eternal death, according to the word, *The soul that sinneth, it shall die.*

1 Tim. 4, 8: *Godliness is profitable unto all things, having promise of the life that now is, and of that which is to come.*

This is an exhortation to *godliness, eusebeia,* a life in the fear and love of God according to His holy will. In the preceding verse the Apostle has admonished Timothy, *Exercise thyself unto godliness.* With the notion of *gumnadzein,* to exercise, he associates in his mind the gymnastic exercises and training of the Greeks, of which we read in 1 Cor. 9, 24-27; and he continues in our verse: *For the bodily exercise profiteth little.* Even this bodily training he would not put down as altogether unprofitable; it may conduce to physical health and may secure a temporal, corruptible crown and transient glory. And in view of these things the aspirants endure hardships and privations and exert their utmost endeavors to win the prize, though it be of comparatively little value. *But,* he continues, *godliness is profitable unto all things.* "God promises grace and every blessing to all that keep His commandments." *Every* blessing. The promises of God hold out to us not only benefits pertaining to this temporal life, as in the promise attached to the fourth commandment, but also blessings of the life to come. Cf. Matt. 19, 20. To what purpose? "That we may love God and trust in Him and willingly do according to His commandments."

THE PURPOSES OF THE LAW.

Ps. 14, 3: *They are all gone aside, they are all together become filthy: there is none that doeth good, no, not one.*

These words comprise a threefold description of all men, not as they are or appear in the opinion or judgment of a human moralist or judge, but as they are and appear in the sight of God. For in the preceding verse the psalmist says, *The* LORD *looked down from heaven upon the children of men,* etc. And as God views the children of men, all of them, as He sees them from the throne of righteousness with the searching gaze of His omniscience, what does He find? The answer is given in three statements, the first of which is: *They are all gone aside,* that is, they have left the way of God's commandments. This is said of *all,* not of some men only, but of *all,* or, *the whole of them.* The next statement asserts the same truth in different and stronger terms: *They are all together become filthy.* The Hebrew word for *filthy* signifies a state of rottenness which renders things no longer available for their use. This state of thorough depravity is universal, predicated of all man should be just and righteous according to the law, doing good and of which is rotten to the core. This universality of human sinfulness is once more stated in the words, *There is none that doeth good, no, not one.* Lest any man should consider himself an exception, or though in the sight of men there might be a man of spotless rectitude, this text emphasizes that there is no exception, that all are sinners and none, no, not one, can in the sight of God appear righteous in himself. Thus St. Paul adduces this text in proof of what he has taught in Rom. 1 and 2, that we are all under sin, the Jews being no better than the Gentiles, Rom. 3, 9-12.

Eccl. 7, 20: *There is not a just man on earth, that doeth good and sinneth not.*

Righteousness, according to God's commandments, consists in doing

that which God has enjoined and avoiding that which God has forbidden. And as the law of God is intended for and binding upon all men, every men, the whole mass of them, like a whole barrel of apples every one sinning not. But such is the total and universal depravity of mankind, that the very reverse must be acknowledged. In all the world, on all the earth, among all nations, not only in the dens of vice, but also in temples and sanctuaries, there is not one just man, not one that doeth good, not one that sinneth not.

Is. 64, 6: *We are all as an unclean thing, and all our righteousnesses are as filthy rags.*

Here again the universality as well as the totality of human depravity is emphatically asserted. The prophet speaks of himself and his hearers or readers, *all* of them without exception, as being unclean before God, to whom he has in the preceding verse said, *Thou art wroth, for we have sinned.* This is universal depravity, including all men. And this depravity is total, every man, of himself, being wholly sinful even where he is rated after what is best in him. The prophet does not say, "Our sins are abominations," but, *Our righteousnesses,* and not only some, but *all* of them, *are as filthy rags.* What Jews and Gentiles would account as virtues are abominations before God, and even the good works of the regenerate are contaminated with sin, all of them, and would condemn us if we should be judged according to them at the tribunal of divine justice.

Job 14, 4: *Who can bring a clean thing out of an unclean? Not one.*

This text teaches that all men are sinful by nature, all, without a single exception. The chapter opens with the words, *Man that is born of woman is of few days and full of trouble;* and, having, in the third verse, plaintively referred to the fact that he, too, a woman's son, must face the judgment of God, Job confesses his innate sinfulness in the words of our text. He acknowledges that, even aside from anything he may have to answer for as committed or omitted by him in the course of his days, he must stand abashed before the righteous Judge, being unclean from his mother's womb. It is immaterial whether the form *Who can,* etc., be taken as a wish or as a rhetorical question; for the final *not one* either says that the wish can in no wise be fulfilled, or that the question must in all cases be denied.

Phil. 3, 12: *Not as though I had already attained, either were already perfect: but I follow after, if that I may apprehend that for which I am apprehended of Christ Jesus.*

The Apostle here, as appears more clearly in the subsequent context, especially v. 14, pictures himself as an athlete competing in the race for a prize, *brabeion,* which is in view but not yet within his grasp. The prize is the full and perfect conformity with Christ in the life to come. This he has not yet attained; he is not yet perfect, though he is already apprehended of Christ Jesus, a subject in Christ's kingdom, a living member of His spiritual body. Perfection, also in the regenerate, is not of this life, and even the great apostle and servant of Christ is no exception any more than was the servant of God speaking in the following text.

Ps. 143, 2: *Enter not into judgment with thy servant: for in thy sight shall no man living be justified.*

The psalmist is a servant of Jehovah. As a servant he has entered upon the performance of his Master's will according to His commandments. If this fulfillment of the will of God were perfect in all its parts, he might declare his readiness to render account to the Master and receive his reward. But the servant of the Lord knows that before Jehovah's awful throne he would be found wanting, and not he alone, but every other man living in this world and time. Hence his prayer and confession. He prays that the Lord would not enter into judgment with him, but deal with him in grace and mercy, vv. 8-12; for in the judgment of God, before whom no man living can be justified, he and all other men must surely be condemned, unless grace and mercy prevail.

James 2, 10: *Whosoever shall keep the whole law, and yet offend in one point, he is guilty of all.*

Law is the expressed will of the lawgiver. The divine law is the unalterable will of God. God is one, and His will is one, and to offend against any point of the divine law is to offend against the one God and His holy will. *For,* as the subsequent context says, *he that said, Do not commit adultery, said also, Do not kill.* Hence, one transgression of one commandment of God, even during a life of perfect righteousness in all other points, would constitute the transgressor a sinner and *enochos, guilty,* and damnable before God. A chain is broken, though but one link, and whatever link, have been broken; a garment is soiled, though one sleeve only may have been spattered with filth; and a body is wounded, perhaps to death, though one organ only may have been pierced. Even in a court of human justice a thief is not acquitted because he has not committed murder or arson. And one sin is sin and can never be anything but sin in time and eternity; and *the soul that sinneth, it shall die.* Ezek. 18, 4-20.

Rom. 3, 20: *By the law is the knowledge of sin.*

The law is here described as the means, *dia, by* or through which, a certain end is achieved, the knowledge of sin, *epignosis hamartias.* As sin is the transgression of the law, the law only can decide whether an act be sin or not. This is true everywhere. What is a crime in Missouri must be determined by the law, and by the law of Missouri, not by the law of China, which is not law in Missouri. And *where no law is, there is no transgression.* Rom. 4, 15. The divine law is law binding upon all men. It was published so that it can be known to all. The Lawgiver being one and unchangeable, there can be no conflict of laws in His statutes. Hence he who would obtain a knowledge of sin, and not a superficial, but a *thorough knowledge, epignosis,* of sin, must not apply traditions of men, man-made precepts or concessions, decisions or decrees of councils or courts, but the infallible law of God. Whatever is a transgression of this law is surely sin, though all the world should justify it. And whatever is not a transgression of this law is certainly not sin, though all the world should condemn it. Thus the law is as a good mirror which reflects the true image of the beholder, neither concealing nor adding blotch or blemish.

Rom. 7, 7: *I had not known sin, but by the law: for I had not known lust, except the law had said, Thou shalt not covet.*

This text contains a general and a particular statement. The general statement is, *I had not known sin, but by the law.* To know sin is to know that a certain act or state is at variance with the law of God. Though a man may be conscious of an act as such, he cannot, without the law, be cognizant of the sinfulness of the act, or of the sin committed in and by the act. Hence ignorance of the law, though it does not excuse the sinner, certainly excludes the knowledge of sin. Ignorance of the law is, therefore, since it does not excuse the sinner, a dangerous thing. On the other hand, the law, when known, not only reveals sin as sin, but also draws the sinner's attention to the sinful act and leads him to ponder its significance in the judgment of God. A thorough knowledge of the law is, therefore, a highly needful and commendable thing. All this is exemplified in the particular statement: *For I had not known lust, except the law had said, Thou shalt not covet.* Here the general truth before stated is applied to a particular commandment of the law. This commandment, though a precept of the moral law, was largely forgotten by Jews and Gentiles, and hence the evil desires of the heart were not known and regarded as evil lusts, as sinful before God and damnable. But here was the plain statute of the law, *Thou shalt not covet,* and the knowledge of this utterance of the holy will of God was to Paul and should be to others the way to the knowledge of evil lust in its damnable sinfulness, just as by the commandments, *Thou shalt not kill,* and *Thou shalt not steal,* they should know murder and theft as sins and damnable before God.

Ps. 119, 9: *Wherewith shall a young man cleanse his way? By taking heed thereto according to thy word.*

The text consists of a question and an answer. The psalmist asks, *Wherewith shall a young man cleanse his way?* Life is here pictured as a pilgrimage, and a young man's life is a period beset with peculiar dangers of moral defilement, temptations unknown to the child. Owing to his innate sinfulness, the young man will find his way a way of sin from day to day unless it be *cleansed,* that is, unless he sedulously shun and put off whatever *is corrupt according to the deceitful lusts,* Eph. 4, 22, and *cleanse himself from all filthiness of the flesh and spirit, perfecting holiness in the fear of God.* 2 Cor. 7, 1. How is he to do this? The psalmist's answer is, *By taking heed thereto according to thy word.* The word of God which he has in mind is the word of the law. This we learn from the subsequent context where, at the same time, he confesses his inability to accomplish this purity of life without assistance from the Lord, and prays for divine succor, saying, *With my whole heart have I sought Thee: O let me not wander from Thy commandments. Thy word have I hid in mine heart, that I might not sin against thee. Blessed art Thou, O Lord; teach me thy statutes.* Vv. 10-12. By continually and prayerfully growing in the knowledge of God's statutes and keeping them forever in his heart he secures to himself the rule of life according to which with the help of God he hopes and desires to cleanse his way.

OF SIN.

1 John 3, 4: *Whosoever committeth sin transgresseth also the law; for sin is the transgression of the law.*

The Apostle would in these words point out the nature of sin. The Greek text is, *Pas ho poion ten hamartian, kai ten anomian poiei, kai he hamartia estin he anomia.* In the first place, then, he says that every sinful act is also an unlawful act. The Greek *anomia,* like the English *lawlessness,* signifies not merely what is without the law, but what is in violation of the law. The law, *nomos,* is the expressed will of the lawgiver, and the Lawgiver of the moral law, the violation of which is sin, is God. What the Apostle would say is, therefore, that sin is in all cases—*pas ho poion ktl.*—a violation of the holy will of God as expressed in the law. And this cannot be otherwise; for *sin is the transgression of the law.* The two, *hamartia* and *anomia,* are simply convertible terms. Everything which is *hamartia* is also *anomia,* and everything which is *anomia* is also *hamartia,* and nothing is the one which is not the other. It is sacrilegious arrogance to stamp that sin which is not against the law of God, or to deny that to be sin which God has prohibited in His law. And as every sin is *anomia,* it is in itself damnable before God, no matter how insignificant it may be in the sight of men, or by whom it may have been committed, whether he be a saint or sot, a king or slave, a Peter or a Judas; for *whosoever committeth* sin, committeth *anomia,* a violation of the holy will of God.

1 John 3, 8: *He that committeth sin is of the devil; for the devil sinneth from the beginning.*

Whom the apostle would describe in the first part of this verse appears from the preceding verse, in which he says, *He that doeth righteousness is righteous, even as he is righteous.* The children of God, who walk after Christ in true righteousness, are the one class of men living in this world. In direct opposition to them there is another class, not *ho poion ten dikaiosunen,* but *ho poion ten hamartian, he that committeth sin.* Thus also in v. 10 he distinguishes between *tekna theou, children of God,* and *tekna tou diabolou, children of the devil.* Though not immediately begotten of the devil, yet the remote origin of that wherein and for which they live and which gives them their character, the very fountain-head of sin, lies even beyond the first natural ancestor of the human race. That they are evildoers they have, primarily and originally, *ek tou diabolou,* from the devil, *hoti ap' arches ho diabolos hamartanei, forasmuch as the devil sins from the beginning.* Man did not sin *ap' arches.* The beginning of sin was made before the fall of man, by the devil. He was the first origin and originator of sin. Though he too was made, as all the works of God, *very good,* Gen. 1, 31, he, in a manner which we cannot know or understand, set his will against the will of God and, sinning, made the beginning of sin. Then, seducing man to sin, he was also the first cause of the sin of humankind.

Rom. 5, 12: *By one man sin entered into the world, and death by sin.*

The apostle would not here point out the first origin or originator of sin, which was the devil, but the manner in which sin found its way into the world, the mass of sinful mankind. He does not say, *From one man, exhenos anthropou,* as he might have said *ek tou diabolou, from,* or *out of the devil,* but, *By,* or *through one man, di henos anthropou.* This one man was Adam, v. 14. For though Eve was first seduced and had sinned before Adam, yet Adam was the natural fountain-head of mankind, also of Eve, who was taken from him, and the progenitor of a sinful progeny bearing his likeness and image, Gen. 5, 3. Thus it was Adam's sin rather than Eve's which was propagated to the later generations of men, even as to him the commandment was given, *Thou shalt not eat of it,* and the threat, *For in the day that thou eatest thereof thou shalt surely die.* Gen. 2, 17. To this also the apostle refers in the words, *And death by sin,* death, the wages of sin, death which *reigned from Adam to Moses,* v. 14, and beyond Moses over all generations that have taken their origin from Adam, the sinful father of a sinful race.

Ps. 51, 5: *Behold, I was shapen in iniquity; and in sin did my mother conceive me.*

A grave and grievous sin committed by one of God's great saints and servants was the occasion for this psalm. But in his penitential prayer David not only confesses this sin and other actual sins; he acknowledges also the sinfulness of his nature from the first beginnings of his existence. What he says concerning his conception and birth does not refer to a sin similar to that which he himself had committed with Bathsheba; for he was conceived and born in lawful wedlock. Neither would he say that marriage and the begetting of children is in itself impure and sinful; for it is by the plan and ordinance of God that children are begotten and born in wedlock. What he clearly states, emphasizing the statement with *Behold*, is that he took his origin from a sinful source, that his very being is, from its beginning, contaminated and permeated with iniquity. And this he does not plead to exonerate himself or to extenuate his evil acts, but rather to add to his humiliation and the acknowledgment of his utter unworthiness, craving only that God in His grace and mercy would cleanse him. The corruption of his heart is also acknowledged in the petition, *Create in me a clean heart, O God,* v. 10. What he is by his first creation, flesh born of flesh, is thoroughly unclean to the very core, not only the members but the innermost heart.

John 3, 6: *That which is born of the flesh is flesh; and that which is born of the Spirit is spirit.*

Nicodemus was slow to comprehend how and why a man must be born again to see the kingdom of God, and Jesus endeavors to enlighten him. That which is requisite in order that a man should enter the kingdom of God is not in natural man. Even if he could and would *enter the second time into his mother's womb, and be born,* v. 4, such birth would avail him nothing. For it would be a birth like his first birth, flesh being born of the flesh, that is, corrupt human nature from a corrupt human nature, and, hence, unfit to enter the kingdom of God. Spirit, *the new man, which after God is created in righteousness and true holiness,* Eph. 4, 24, cannot come from the flesh, in which *dwelleth no good thing,* Rom. 7, 18, but must be born of the Spirit; and this is the new birth.

Gen. 8, 21: *The imagination of man's heart is evil from his youth.*

When God spoke these words He had before him the few righteous men and women who were saved from the water of the deluge. At the same time he looked forward to all the generations of men who were to live while the earth should endure. When He had seen the wickedness of man before the flood, and that *every imagination of the thoughts of his heart was only evil continually,* Gen. 6, 5, He had resolved to destroy man from the face of the earth. Now, after the flood, He saw that the progeny of the second ancestor of mankind to the end of time would again be corrupt by nature, that the hearts of all men would be from their youth fountains of evil from which evil would flow, and that He would find sufficient and abundant cause to destroy the second world as He did the first. Hence the special covenant, of which the bow in the cloud should be the token, that *the waters shall no more become a flood to destroy all flesh.* Gen. 8, 21ff.; 9, 14-16.

Rom 7, 18: *I know that in me (that is, in my flesh) dwelleth no good thing.*

These words were written by St Paul when he was no longer a

Pharisee and a persecutor of the church, but an apostle of Christ and *delighted in the law of God after the inward man*, v. 22. Still he complains of serving *with the flesh the law of sin*, v. 25, his flesh, the corrupt nature which he brought into the world, being evil throughout, so that no good thing dwelled therein. Thus we learn that the flesh of the regenerate is no better than that of the ungodly, and that, since flesh is what all men are by nature, and in the flesh of no man any good thing dwells, the natural depravity of man is both universal and total.

Eph. 2, 3: *And were by nature the children of wrath, even as others.*

This text teaches that the original sin, with which all men are by nature contaminated, is really and truly *sin*, whereby the wrath of God is kindled against us and we are liable to the penalty of sin, death, and damnation. The apostle describes himself and his readers and other men as being not only children of sin, but *children of wrath*, of God's holiness incensed over the sin that is within us. He does not here refer to the wrath of God aroused by the evil works we have done in our lives, but to the wrath to which we are subject as a child to an angry father from the very beginning of our existence, not by our works, but *by nature*. When he says, *tekna fusei orges*, the word *fusei* is in emphasis. He would emphatically state that when we were conceived and born in sin, we were, because of such hereditary and innate sin, already under the wrath of God, guilty and damnable in His sight, we and all other men, as many as are flesh born of the flesh.

Matt. 15, 19: *Out of the heart proceed evil thoughts, murders, adulteries, fornications, thefts, false witness, blasphemies.*

The corruption of man's heart is sin, *hamartia*. But man is a rational being endowed with a conscious will which prompts his acts, and these acts, being prompted by an evil heart inclined toward all that is evil, are sins, *hamartiai*. The plurals, *fonoi, moicheiai, porneiai, klopai, murders, adulteries, fornications, thefts*, are employed to indicate the various acts or cases of murder, theft, adultery, etc. The sinful acts here enumerated are of three kinds: 1. evil thoughts; 2. evil words, as false witness and blasphemies; and 3. evil deeds, as murders, thefts, etc. All these have their origin in the human heart, and every human heart is capable of bringing forth such fruits of the flesh.

James 4, 17: *Therefore to him that knoweth to do good, and doeth it not, to him it is sin.*

This verse states a general truth which St. James places at the close of a series of more particular admonitions. The meaning is not that sin were committed only by those who knew the law, while ignorance of what is good would excuse us from doing good. Ignorance of the law is nowhere an excuse for transgressing the law. What he would say is akin to his general admonition, *Be ye doers of the word, and not hearers only, deceiving your own selves*, ch. 1, 22. God would have us know his will, and not to know it is sin. But such knowledge alone will not avail; for to know to do good and not to do it is also sin and all the more damnable sin. It is our duty not only to avoid sins of commission, works prohibited by the law; but it is also our duty to beware of sins of omission committed by neglecting or refusing to do that which is good.

Rom. 10, 4: *Christ is the end of the law for righteousness to every one that believeth.*

The law says, *This do, and thou shalt live.* But since we are unable to do what the law demands, we cannot by the works of the law enter into life, and the curse of the law is upon us as long as we are under the law. The rule and dominion of the law signifies to every man transgression of the law, or sin, guilt, condemnation, wrath, death, eternal damnation. Christ says, "I have fulfilled the law; this believe, and thou shalt live." Christ signifies to every man who believes in Him a perfect vicarious fulfillment of the law; no sin, but righteousness; no guilt, but innocence; no condemnation, but justification; no wrath, but grace and mercy; no death, but life; no damnation, but everlasting blessedness. And thus is Christ, *in negotio salutis*, the end of the law.

THE CREED.

John 3, 16: *For God so loved the world, that he gave his only begotten Son, that whosoever believeth in him, should not perish, but have everlasting life.*

This text may be fitly called an epitome of all Scripture, both the law and the Gospel. It teaches that, left to itself, all the world must have perished, and no man could have obtained eternal life. For if salvation is by the love of God in Christ and through faith in Him, then by his own works man must be lost now and forever. But the text also teaches that God, the only true God, whose Son is the only begotten of the Father, the God whom no man can know but by revelation, is not only just but also merciful, that instead of condemning the world, as He might have done, He loved the world. That this is very remarkable is indicated by the emphasis which the original lays on the verb, *loved*, placing it before its subject, *houtos egapesen ho theos*. And this wonderful love of God is all the more wonderful, the more we consider and comprehend the state and condition of the objects of His love. The *world, kosmos*, the whole mass of fallen mankind, sinful, ungodly, rebellious in enmity against God, and damnable in His sight, was the object of His love. Love is the longing for union and communion with the object of such desire. The world was separated from God by sin (Is. 59, 2). But though man had turned his back upon God and neither could nor would return to Him, God longed to be reunited with the wayward race. In this God did not deny but reassert His holiness. He loved the world, not ignoring but taking away the sin which separated between Him and man, by laying that sin upon a substitute for man, a substitute whom He had Himself provided. He so longed to recover the fallen world into union with Himself, that He gave His only begotten Son, to be the Redeemer of the world, *that the world through Him might be saved* (John 3, 17), through *the Lamb of God which taketh away the sin of the world* (John 1, 29). And now, since God has provided a Savior for all the world, because He loved the world, it is His earnest will that by accepting this Savior and salvation in Him every sinner should have and enjoy the benefits of the redemption now and forever, that he should not suffer what by sin he has deserved, and which Christ has suffered in his stead, and that he should enjoy what he could not have procured for himself, but which Christ has secured for him by His vicarious obedience unto death, everlasting life. This is the sum and substance of the Gospel and of our Christian faith.

Rom. 1, 16: *I am not ashamed of the Gospel of Christ: for it is the power of God unto salvation to every one that believeth.*

The English word, gospel, is a literal translation of the Greek *euangelion,* good tidings, good spell, a gladsome story. It is the glad news the angel of the Lord brought to the shepherds, saying, *Fear not: for, behold, I bring you good tidings of great joy, which shall be to all people. For unto you is born this day in the city of David a Savior, which is Christ, the Lord.* Luke 2, 10f. But the Gospel is not a mere announcement of the goodness of God in Christ Jesus; it is also an exertion of the saving grace of God. The apostle describes it as being not only *dunamenon* or *dunaton*, mighty, powerful, but *dunamis*, a power, and not a human power, but a power of God, so that wherever it is preached and heard, God himself is active, working on and in the heart of the hearer. It is, furthermore, described as the power of God unto salvation. God is active with His power also in the physical world, as the almighty Preserver and Ruler of the universe. But whenever and wherever the Gospel is preached, God is active in the divine work of saving those who are lost. Salvation is the work of God performed by the Gospel. How? Not by teaching us what we must do to merit salvation, but by teaching us what God has done in Christ to procure our salvation, and by leading us to accept such salvation by faith. This is what the text says in describing the Gospel as the power of God unto salvation, not to every one that worketh, but to every one that believeth. Hence this Gospel of *Christ crucified is unto the Jews a stumblingblock, and unto the Greeks foolishness.* I Cor. 1, 23. For the self-righteous Jews and the self-wise Gentiles, the adherents of all false religions, teach salvation by works, by man's own endeavors, and despise and spurn a doctrine and way of salvation which gives all the glory to God and His saving grace in Christ. But with Paul and all true believers we are not ashamed of the Gospel of Christ, the power of God and the wisdom of God. 1 Cor. 1, 24.

THE FIRST ARTICLE.

John 4, 24: *God is a Spirit: and they that worship him must worship him in spirit and in truth.*

The Samaritan woman at Jacob's well was ignorant of the true God. She thought the difference between the Jews and the Samaritans consisted in their different places of worship. John 4, 20. But Jesus tells her, "Ye worship ye know not what." He then proceeds to teach her concerning the true God, and in doing this He speaks the words of our text. He says, *Pneuma ho theos,* God is spirit. The emphasis is on *pneuma,* Spirit. He would say, You are ignorant of the very nature of God. You suppose Him to be residing at a certain place like a corporeal being, and this false notion determines your notions of divine worship. But God is Spirit, a being without a body or the properties of material things. And it is needful for those who would worship God to know who and what God is. For God cannot be acceptably worshiped according to the false notions which men may entertain concerning Him, but must be worshiped in a manner corresponding with His nature, as He is, in spirit and truth. Thus our text refutes the error of all those who hold, as so many do in our day, that it were immaterial what notions a man had of God, if he only worshiped Him according to his views and convictions. Such worship is, in fact, idolatry and damnable before God.

Ps. 90, 1, 2: *Lord, thou hast been our dwelling place in all generations. Before the mountains were brought forth, or ever thou hadst formed the earth and the world, even from everlasting to everlasting, thou art God.*

The psalmist, Moses, here teaches that God is eternal. Men are born and die, generation following generation. But as parents, children, and grandchildren may successively dwell in the same mansion, so God has been the dwelling place where His children have found shelter from generation to generation. While they come and pass away one after another, He is and remains the same mighty fortress for all times. Nor is God of lasting existence only as compared with the fleeting generations of men. The massive mountains, too, have towered for ages above their changing surroundings, looking down in silent majesty upon the short-lived children of men. But God is of still longer duration.

The mountains, too, came into being and must pass away. But before the mountains were brought forth, before God had formed the earth and the whole world, the sun and moon and stars, which have been running their steady courses for ages, God is God. He was not only, but He is. In Him there is no past or future, but eternal to-day. And when the mountains and the earth and the universe shall pass away, God's existence will have no end. He, and He alone, is from everlasting to everlasting. He is eternal.

Ps. 102, 27: *Thou art the same.*

The Hebrew original is *thou art he.* The corresponding *I am he,* from the mouth of the Lord, occurs repeatedly in Isaiah, and in every instance it is an assertion of God's eternity and immutability. Thus when we read, *Who hath wrought and done it, calling the generations from beginning? I, the Lord, the first, and with the last, I am He.* Is. 41, 4. And again, *I am he: before me there was no God formed, neither shall there be after me.* Is 43, 10. And once more, *I am he, I am the first, I also am the last. Mine hand also hath laid the foundation of the earth.* Is. 48, 12.f. Our context is even more explicit. Here the psalmist says: *Thy years are throughout all generations. Of old hast thou laid the foundation of the earth: and the heavens are the work of thy hands. They shall perish, but thou shalt endure: yea, all of them shall wax old like a garment, as a vesture shalt thou change them, and they shall be changed: but thou art the same, and thy years shall have no end.* Thus the psalmist is his own best commentator.

Jer. 23, 23.24: *Am I a God at hand, saith the Lord, and not a God afar off? Can any hide himself in secret places that I shall not see him? saith the Lord. Do not I fill heaven and earth? saith the Lord.*

These words are taken from a longer passage in which the Lord rebukes the false prophets, who ran, though they had not been sent, and prophesied, though the Lord had not spoken to them. The audacity of these impostors was all the more astounding since their evil ways were known to God. *I have heard what the prophets said, that prophesy lies in my name,* says the Lord. For He is near and present everywhere, filling heaven and earth, so that there is no place so secret or remote as to serve as a hiding place from the presence of Him who is omnipresent, as our text says. This omnipresence of God is not expansion through space, as water fills a vessel. Where God is, He is whole and entire, not a part of Him in heaven and a part of Him in the earth. He fills the heavens, being everywhere in heaven, and He fills the earth, being everywhere on earth, and everywhere the Lord God, performing His divine works, whether amid the hosts of cherubim and seraphim, or in the heart of a little child. Hence, let false prophets and all workers of iniquity beware, and let all that seek His face take comfort.

Luke 1, 37: *With God nothing shall be impossible.*

These are words of Gabriel, the angel of the Lord who was sent to the virgin to announce to her that she was to be the mother of the Son of God. That the virgin's motherhood was not to come about in the course of nature, but by a special and particular act of divine power, was also made known to her, and as a token of the working of God's almighty power, her cousin Elisabeth was pointed out to her, by the angel. "For," continued Gabriel, "with God nothing shall be impossible." This is a general truth, by which the angel would corroborate his special announcements. The incarnation of the Son of God was one, but not the only, work of divine omnipotence. God's power has no limit. It is God Himself, and God is infinite. There is no contradiction between our text and such statements as, *It was impossible for God to lie.* For there never was nor could be such a thing as a lie in God. A lie in God is, in fact, no thing, nothing, and nothing is impossible with God. This is precisely what our text says in full agreement with the words from the Epistle to the Hebrews.

Ps. 139, 1-4: *Lord, thou hast searched me, and known me. Thou knowest my downsitting and mine uprising, thou understandeth my thought afar off. Thou compassest my path and my lying down, and art acquainted with all my words. For there is not a word in my tongue, but, lo, O Lord, thou knowest it altogether.*

The psalmist here teaches that God knows all things. He begins with an anthropopathism, in order to picture the thoroughness of God's knowledge. If a man would know a thing thoroughly, he must investigate or search it. Thus David here pictures God as having made a thorough investigation of him and thereby having learned to know all about him, all his present and future ways, and acts, and attitudes, and words, and thoughts, everything even beyond the psalmist's knowledge of himself. Remembering this we should walk in fear of God all the days of our lives, at the same time trusting that, knowing all our wants and weaknesses better than we can ever know them ourselves, He will provide for us as only an omniscient and omnipotent Father can provide for His children. Knowing all our ways and doings and words and thoughts, He also knows our prayers, even the desires of our hearts directed to Him, and He knows best how to adjust the fulfillment of our petitions to our temporal and eternal welfare.

Is. 6, 3: *Holy, holy, holy is the Lord of hosts: the whole earth is full of his glory.*

The holiness of God is His absolute purity, according to which all His affections, thoughts, will, and acts are in perfect consistency with His own nature, and in energetic opposition to everything that is not in conformity therewith. This is also the notion which Isaiah has of the holiness of God. For immediately after the description of the wonderful vision which embodied the great trishagion given in our text, the prophet continues: *Then said I, Woe is me! for I am undone; because I am a man of unclean lips, and I dwell in the midst of a people of unclean lips: for mine eyes have seen the King, the Lord of hosts.* God is holy, thrice holy, though not three holy ones, but one Holy One, in three persons, each of whom is what each of the others is, the Father the Holy One, the Son the Holy One, the Holy Ghost the Holy One, the Lord of hosts. He is the same everywhere: the whole earth is full of His, not *their*, but His, glory. Beside Him, the Holy One, in His divine purity and conformity with His divine nature, man, even though he be a prophet of the Lord, is of unclean lips, dwelling in the midst of people of unclean lips. And knowing that the Holy One is in energetic opposition to everything that is not of pure godliness like Himself, the prophet cries out, *Woe is me! for I am undone.* The wrath of God is the reaction of His holiness against all ungodliness.

Dan. 9, 7: *O Lord, righteousness belongeth unto thee, but unto us confusion of faces.*

These words are a part of the prophet's confession and penitential prayer beginning in the fourth verse of the chapter and continuing to the nineteenth verse. Throughout this prayer Daniel, confessing his sin and that of the people, also acknowledges that they have thereby incurred the righteous wrath of God, as when he says in v. 14. *Therefore hath the Lord watched upon the evil, and brought it upon us: for the Lord our God is righteous in all His works which He doeth: for we obeyed not His voice.* Thus standing with the blush of shame upon his downcast face before his God, the prophet by word and mien and attitude avows that in all the sin and guilt of men God has no share, but is and remains all righteousness, all His acts and judgments being in full accord with His holy will and the utterances thereof.

Ps. 33, 4: *The word of the Lord is right; and all his works are done in truth.*

God is truth inasmuch as He is as He manifests Himself in word and deed, and His works are in full agreement with His words. Men may deceive by word and deed, pretending to be what they are not, or saying what they do not mean or will not fulfill. But the word of God is a true manifestation of the mind of God, and His works bear out His words to the letter. He who trusts in what God has once spoken is never deceived. There is no crookedness in God or in His word. God is ever worthy of all confidence.

Ps. 145, 9: *The Lord is good to all: and His tender mercies are over all His works.*

The 145th psalm is a song of the royal psalmist to the King of kings, the Lord of unsearchable greatness and glorious majesty, mighty in terrible acts, vv. 1-6. But throughout the greater part of the psalm the theme is the goodness of the everlasting King toward His subjects, who are also His handiwork. Not only shall His saints bless

Him (v. 10) for His grace and mercy shown forth in spiritual blessings, but all His works have reason to praise Him as the Preserver of them all. The ancient church took the benediction over the noonday meal from this psalm: *The eyes of all wait upon thee*, etc., vv. 15.16. Thus the almighty Ruler of the universe, who will destroy all the wicked (v. 20), is the kind Provider of all blessings for every living thing, and our text sounds the keynote of the magnificent psalm.

Exod. 34, 6.7: *The Lord, the Lord God, merciful and gracious, long-suffering, and abundant in goodness and truth, keeping mercy for thousands, forgiving iniquity and transgression and sin.*

Moses had, in obedience to the word of God, prepared two stone tables like those he had broken, and taken them up on Mount Sinai. Then the Lord, the Son of God, stood with Moses and proclaimed the name of the Lord, as He was about to repeat the law of the tables. To proclaim the name of the Lord is to announce the will and counsel of God whereby He would be known by those to whom He manifests Himself. While dealing with Moses and the children of Israel as their Lawgiver, establishing with this people a covenant bound up with a stringent code of law, yet He would not be known even to this people in His legislative, judicial, and executive justice only, but also in His grace and mercy. God is merciful inasmuch as He has pity on the afflicted and bestows His benefits on the miserable. He is gracious as He confers His blessings regardless of the merits or demerits of those whom He would bless. He is long-suffering as He is not quickly provoked and has patience with those who offend Him. All these are so many aspects of the goodness of God, which, being God Himself, is infinite. Thus God is abundant in goodness, keeping mercy not for a few only, but for thousands, not punishing but forgiving offenses against His holy will, under whatever name they may come, iniquity, transgression, or sin.

1 John 4, 8: *God is love.*

These words occur twice in the same chapter, here and in the 16th verse, the Greek form being in both instances, *ho theos agape estin.* There are other texts in which we are told that God has loved us, loved the world (John 3, 16), loved the people (Deut. 33, 3), loved us with an everlasting love (Jer. 31, 3), with a love surpassing that of a mother toward her child (Is. 49, 15). But nowhere else in the Scriptures do we find this truth uttered with the terseness and force peculiar to this statement that *God is love.* The same can be said of no created being in heaven and in earth. If it could, it would still predicate but the finite love of such finite being. But to say that God is love is to say that this love is infinite as God Himself is infinite, a boundless, endless, illimitable ocean of incomprehensible love.

Rom. 1, 19.20: *Because that which may be known of God is mani-*

fest in them, for God hath showed it unto them, For the invisible things of him from the creation of the world are clearly seen, being understood by the things that are made, even his eternal power and Godhead, so that they are without excuse.

In the previous texts the nature and attributes of God are set forth as by divine revelation in the written word of God. But while certain things concerning God can be known only from the word of revelation, the existence and some of the attributes of God may, in a measure, be known and are thus *gnoston tou theou, what is knowable of God,* in the light of nature and human reason. God has, in a measure revealed Himself also to such as have no knowledge of the written word, who walk in the darkness of heathendom. For of such the apostle says that God has showed, *efanerosen, made manifest,* to them what is known to them concerning Him. God is a spirit, invisible to human eyes. But while the eyes of the body cannot see God, His divine nature and attributes, which are invisible, yet *nooumena kathoratai,* the eyes of the mind, human reason, can behold Him, His eternal power and Godhead, *theiotes,* as, from the works of creation, man, a rational being, may conclude that all the innumerable works that make up the universe must have an almighty maker, the Maker of heaven and earth. This revelation is as old as the world, *apo ktiseos kosmou,* since *the heavens declare the glory of God and the firmament showeth His handiwork* (Ps. 19, 1). A brute, which is without reason, can know nothing of God. But when man, a rational being, denies the existence of God and fails to search after a more extensive knowledge of Him, he is without excuse. Every page of the book of nature bears the stamp and imprint and teems with profound thoughts of its Author, though there be idiots and inebriates who cannot read.

(Prof. Dau's Articles Begin Here)

THE TRINITY.

Deut. 6, 4: *Hear, O Israel, the Lord our God is one Lord.*

Various renderings have been proposed for this passage, e. g.: "Jehovah is our God, Jehovah is one." Inasmuch as our Lord cites this passage Mark 12, 29 in exactly the same sense and construction as the Authorized Version has given to our text, it is futile to attempt a different rendering. This text declares the *unity of God.* God is *achad,* one, i. e., "beside me there is no God," Is. 44, 6; "there is none else," Is. 45, 5.6.14.18.22; "there is none like me," Is. 46, 9. Paganism acknowledges many gods; Israel's God is one Jehovah. And this very name He will not share with another, Is. 42, 8 ("that is my name"). God's name stands for the divine essence. God cannot be named by comparison with other similar beings. His name is as much His own exclusively as His attributes, properties, etc. God is one and Jehovah is His name, therefore, means: There is one eternal, one almighty, one omniscient, etc., Being or Essence. We cannot imagine two eternal, almighty, omnipresent Beings without imagining, at the same time, a constant conflict between the two. Or if they exist in harmony with one another, we imagine a power still higher than the two, which controls them, and thereby destroys their omnipotence.—A divine name, indeed, has been conferred on beings other than God. Moses is made *elohim*, a god, to his brother Aaron, Ex. 4, 16, to Pharaoh, Ex. 7, 1. The civil authorities, Ex. 12, 12; 22, 28; 23, 32; judges, Ex. 22, 8 (in Hebrew text v. 7: "the master of the house shall be brought unto elohim"); Ps. 82, 1.6; John 10, 34; people of influence, Ps. 89, 7, and the holy angels, Ps. 97, 7 (compare Hebr. 1, 6), are given the divine names *elohim* and *el.* Evidently this is done by a figure of speech. Scripture recognizes the fact that divine titles may be applied when the divine nature is wanting, Gal. 4, 8. Accordingly, when God claims the divine name for Himself alone, the term "name" is used as the exponent of the divine essence. He alone is all-wise, almighty, good, etc. Absolute goodness can be predicated of one Being only, that is God, Matt. 19,17; Mark 10, 18; Luke 18, 19. Luther's rendering in these three passages, "der einige Gott," is preferable to the literal rendering of the Authorized Version, because it expresses the mind of Christ more strikingly. Likewise in its religious relations mankind is restricted to one divine Being only; there is "one Lawgiver," James 4, 12; belief in the existence of one God is approved, James 2, 19. Christ mediated between mankind and one God, Gal. 3, 20. One God justifies Jew and Gentile, Rom. 3, 30. And so Paul teaches Christians: "There is none other God but one *(ei me eis).* For though there be that are called gods, whether in heaven or in earth (as there be gods many and lords many), but to us there is but one God" *(eis theos),* 1 Cor. 8, 4-6.

For his own sake, not for use in the class-room, the cathechist may note furthermore, that this text teaches also the *plurality of persons* in the One Godhead. "The Lord *Eloheinu* is one *Lord." Eloheinu* is the plural. In the same breath God declares Himself to be several and one.

"On this verse the Jews lay great stress; it is one of the four passages which they write on their phylacteries, and they write the last letter in the first and last words very large, for the purpose of exciting attention to the weighty truth it contains. It is perhaps in reference to this custom of the Jews that our blessed Lord alludes, Matt. 22, 38; Mark 12, 29.30, where He says, *This is the first and great commandment * * ** When this passage occurs in the Sabbath readings in the synagogues, the whole congregation repeat the last word *achad* (one) for several minutes together with the loudest vociferations: this, I suppose, they do to vent a little of their spleen against the Christians, for they suppose the latter hold three Gods, because of their doctrine of the Trinity * * * Were the Christians, when reading this verse, to vociferate *Eloheinu* for several minutes as the Jews do *achad*, it would apply more forcibly in the way of convic-tion to the Jews of the *plurality* of the persons in the Godhead, than the word *achad*, of *one*, against any pretended false tenet of Christianity, as every Christian receives the doctrine of the *unity* of God in the most conscientious manner." (Clarke, ibid.)

Matt. 28, 19: *Go ye therefore and teach all nations, baptizing them in the name of the Father, and of the Son, and of the Holy Ghost.*

Three appellatives are here introduced, but these three are *one* name *(eis to onoma, not to onomata)*. In a different view Father, Son, and Holy Ghost are three names. One person of the Godhead calls the other by the name here given, Ps. 2, 7; John 17, 1; Luke 23, 46; John 15, 26. But the three names here given are backed by one author-ity, one almighty power, one grace and love, all of which virtues are re-quired for the institution of a sacrament and its maintenance and abiding obligation upon men. (NB. This is not the place to show that *eis to onoma* means *into* the name; that is a matter that should be re-served when this text occurs again as the baptismal command; see Qu. 277.) This text, then, teaches that there are *three* persons in the God-head, not more nor less, and that these three share the name, dignity, power of God equally. Hence, there is a Trinity in Unity. God is three in one, triune.

"Baptism is not made in the name of a quality or attribute of the Divine nature. The orthodox, as they are termed, have generally considered this text as a decisive proof of the doctrine of the holy Trinity: and what else can they draw from it? Is it possible for words to convey a plainer sense than these do? And do they not direct every reader to consider the Father, the Son, and the Holy Spirit as three distinct persons? 'But this I can never believe.' I cannot help that— you shall not be persecuted by me for differing from my opinion. I cannot go over to *you;* I must abide by what I believe to be the mean-ing of the Scriptures." (Clarke ad loc.)

2 Cor. 13, 14: *The grace of the Lord Jesus Christ, and the love of God, and the communion of the Holy Ghost, be with you all.*

Numb. 6, 24-26: *The Lord bless thee, and keep thee: the Lord make His face to shine upon thee, and be gracious unto thee: the Lord lift up His countenance upon thee, and give thee peace.*

The preceding passage showed that there are in the Godhead three persons united in One Being. These two passages name and refer to the same persons, but show that they are distinct from each other. This was indicated also in the passage from Matthew by the definite article which is affixed to each person there named. The article ex-presses individuality, marks the person as distinct. But in these two passages the distinction is made · stronger, because each person is represented as holding to us a peculiar relation. We are taught to view God the Father as the One who loves us. He so loved us that He sent His Son to redeem us, John 3, 16. He blesses us and keeps us. We are taught to view Christ as the God who is gracious to sinners. In Him the grace of God which bringeth salvation hath appeared to all men, Tit. 2, 11. He makes His face shine upon us; He does not look at us with a sour, surly, wry face, but with a face beaming with tender affection, radiant with smiles, as a father looks upon his child. And we are taught to view the Holy Ghost as the God who brings us into communion with the Father and the Son by giving us peace with God. Thus these passages express to the mind what was exhibited to the senses at the Lord's baptism in Jordan, Matt. 3, 16.17.

The three persons of the Trinity are really persons, not attributes, energies, modes of manifestations, etc., of the One Supreme Being. Each person not only exists together with, but also distinct from, the other. The revelation which John witnessed at the baptism of Jesus "forcibly marks divine personality." (Clarke ad Matt, 3, 16.17.) As the Son was incarnate in Jesus of Nazareth, so the Spirit became visible also in a bodily shape, Luke 3, 22, like a dove, while the Father is distinct from both by the voice from heaven. Neither person in that moment was engaged in the same act as the other. Though by the unity of essence each cooperated, unseen by man's eyes, in the action of the other, yet each was engaged in a distinct act, as each also exhibited Himself in a different place from the other.

In conclusion, we note that the doctrine that there are three distinct Persons in one divine essence, is very old. We derive arguments for it from *both* Testaments. Adam, Moses, David, Isaiah, knew the true God to be triune, as well as did Peter, Paul, Luther, and any Christian child in our day. The Scriptures of the New Testament shed greater light on this truth, as they do on other truths, but the doctrine of the Trinity is recorded with sufficient distinctness on the very first page of the Bible. "God created," "the Spirit moved upon the face of the waters," "God said," (Gen. 1, 1-3), i. e., God spoke into being through His Word, who was with Him in the beginning and was God (John 1, 1-3)—thus God, from the beginning, has declared Himself to be One and Three. When Aaron and his successors were commanded to bless the children of Israel, a stated form for doing this was given them. Thrice they had to invoke the name of God in their blessing, and God Himself calls this act "putting His name upon the children of Israel," Numb. 6, 27. This act of blessing the people was considered an important priestly function as it is mentioned on a line with other functions, Lev. 9, 22; 1 Chron. 23, 13. Isaiah was made to hear the seraphims sing their "Thrice Holy." Thus God was at pains to have His people constantly put in mind that the God who is truly One is this God who is Three in One.

Ps. 2, 7: *Thou art my Son; this day have I begotten Thee.*

We had ascertained that the three persons of the Godhead are distinct each from the other. The distinctness of each is declared not only to us, but also within the circle of the Holy Trinity itself. It flows from certain acts which cause us to predicate something of one person that we cannot predicate of the other. Each person has a personal attribute which never passes over to either of the other persons, and thus fixes its distinctness forever. In Ps. 2, 7 we behold this difference in full operation as between the Father and the Son. The brief statement is in the form of an address: there is a party speaking and a party spoken to. I and Thou, my and Thee, as every child knows, refer to the first and second person. The relation of speaker and addressee is accidental. The speaker on one occasion may be the addressee on another. Thus we find the addressee in this text the speaker in John 17. However, the subject of the brief discourse between speaker and addressee in the text before us never changes hands, so to speak, between them. The speaker here states with regard to Himself: "I have begotten Thee," and with regard to the party spoken to: "Thou art my Son." He claims for Himself fatherhood, for the party spoken to sonship. This relation is never inverted between the first and second persons of the Godhead. True, Christ is also called Father, Is. 9, 6. A person may hold to one the relation of son, while to another he holds the relation of father. Christ is "the everlasting Father," or the eternity-Father, from whom eternity takes its origin (if we can speak of an origin of eternity!). He is the father of the raindrop, Job 38, 28, the "Father of lights, with whom is no variableness, neither shadow of turning," James 1, 17. He has created us and acts as a father to us. But He is not the father of the Father. This statement: "Today I have begotten Thee," cannot be made by any other than the first person of the Trinity. And this statement: "Thou art my Son," based on the ground here stated, cannot refer to any other than the second person of the Trinity. Angels are called "the sons of God," Job 1, 6; 2,1; 38, 7; also all men, Mal. 2, 10, especially those who walk in His ways, Gen. 6, 2.4. But Christ alone is the Son of God, because "He hath begotten Him"; He is "the only Begotten of the Father," John 1, 14.18; 3, 16.18; 1 John 4, 9. In an inscrutable and ineffable manner God has communicated His essence to His Son, who thus is "the brightness of His glory, and the express image of His person," Hebr. 1, 3. He is "the Firstbegotten," Hebr. 1, 6, "the image of the invisible God, the Firstborn of every creature," Col. 1,15. Luther rightly renders the genitive *pases ktiseos* by "vor" (*prae*, not *ante)* "allen Kreaturen." The Son's origin not only antecedes by the difference of eternity, but also excels by the difference of divine majesty that of every creature. He has taken His being directly from God and shares all God's attributes, being "one with the Father," John 10, 30. He addresses the first person of the Godhead as His Father, and the Father proclaims Him as His beloved Son. This relation constitutes the personal attribute of the Father and Son.

John 15, 26: *When the Comforter is come, whom I will send unto you from the Father, even the Spirit of truth, which proceedeth from the Father, He shall testify of me.*

Gal. 4, 6: *Because ye are sons, God hath sent forth the Spirit of His Son into your hearts, crying, Abba, Father.*

These passages state the personal attribute of the Holy Spirit. Christ speaks of Him as "another", John 14, 16, distinct from Himself and from the Father. He goes out from the Father *(ekporeuetai)*. Christ is also gone out from the Father *(exerchetai)*, John 8, 42; 16, 27ff; 17, 8. The choice of these two verbs, the former of which is always applied to the procession of the Spirit, while the latter is used to describe the advent of Christ into the world, shows that each is a different action. Virtually Christ, in John 15, 26, predicates of the Spirit both *exerchesthai* and *ekporeuesthai*, the former as an action to be expected by the disciples, the latter as an action which is already going on, the former as an official act of the Spirit, the latter as an action by which the Spirit is constituted in His essence and being. He is "the Spirit of God," *to pneuma tou theou* (1 Cor. 2, 11), i. e., as the next verse declares, "the Spirit which is of God," *to pneuma to ek tou theou.* The mode of this procession passes our comprehension. The allusion to breath issuing from the mouth (Ps. 33, 6; John 20,22), to the wind (John 3, 8), is helpful, but inadequate to express this act.

The procession is not from the Father alone, but also from the Son, but this latter fact is not as explicitly stated as the former. Still the genitive in Gal. 4, 6, whether it is understood as expressing ownership or origin, sufficiently indicates the procession also from the Son. Christ also speaks and acts in a manner indicating this procession, John 20, 22; 15, 26; 16, 7.

The reading of the Athanasian Creed, especially to applicants for confirmation, would serve the purpose of a resume or review of this doctrine.

FAITH

Each article of the Creed opens with the statement of an important fact: *I believe.* We use this expression every day and connect various meanings with it. According as we utter it with more or less emphasis and solemnity, according as the matters to which we apply the expression differ, and according as we are conscious of a greater or less authority for the statement, we can make the phrase *I believe* express, now a mere thought that flits through our mind, now a vague expectation, now a conjecture, now a personal judgment, now conviction, now reliance. What does this expression mean, what are its contents as used in the Three Articles?

Rom. 10, 14: *How shall they believe in Him of whom they have not heard?*

This question necessitates a negative answer: Believing without previous information is impossible. That which I believe must have been presented to me in such a manner that I was enabled to perceive its meaning and to understand its import. The Greek verb which denotes hearing in this place has the object in the genitive. Wilke says: "*akouein* cum genit. rei: vim et argumentum auditi percipere." ("To hear, when connected with an object denoting matter in the genitive, means to perceive the force and import of what one has heard.") To hear thus, means to note that something is actually so, that it has reality. When the high-priest at the trial of Jesus addressed his associates: "Ye have heard the blasphemy" (*tes Blasfemias*), Mark 14, 64, he meant to say: You are aware of the blasphemous nature of His remark; you have heard and you perceive what the words imply. When Paul from the temple-stairs at Jerusalem appealed to his countrymen: "Hear ye my defense" (*tes apologias*), Acts 22, 1, he asked permission to explain to them the situation in which he was placed, and to exhibit his innocence if they would only listen. The Lord describes the wise builder thus: "Whosoever cometh to me and heareth my saying (*ton logon*) and doeth them." If the hearing of the Lord's teaching induced in the hearers action suited to what they heard, the words must have carried a certain unmistakable meaning with them.

Faith, then, requires previous information and instruction by which *knowledge* of the subject-matter of faith is conveyed. The first impulse to believe comes to a person from without. Objects are presented to his perception, his attention is arrested, his intellect is set to work, and his judgment invited to pass on facts and truths communicated to him, and thus his mind and memory is stored with knowledge which he had not possessed previously. Hearing and believing are, therefore, Scripture correlatives: "Many of the Corinthians *hearing, believed*," Acts 18, 8. "God made choice among us" (i. e., the apostles; and He did so with this appointment) "that the Gentiles by my mouth should *hear* the Gospel and *believe*," Acts 15, 7. "Two disciples *heard* Him speak, and followed Jesus," John 1, 37. "Many more *believed because of* His own *word*, and said: Now we *believe*, not because of thy *saying* for we have *heard* Himself and *know* that this is indeed the Christ, the Savior of the world," John 4, 41f. This last passage, in particular, shows that knowing and believing are synonyms, and both result from hearing.

God has supplied the means whence faith derives its knowledge.

Rom. 10, 17: *So, then, faith cometh by hearing, and hearing by the Word of God.*

Luther's differs from this rendering: he substitutes for hearing *Predigt* and *Predigen*, just as in 1 Thess. 2, 13: *logon akoes tou theou*, "the Word of God *which ye heard of us*," "das Wort goettlicher *Predigt*," and in Gal. 3, 2: *ex akoes pisteos*, "by the *hearing* of faith," "durch die *Predigt* vom Glauben." In Hebr. 4, 2, both versions agree: *ho logos tes akoes,* "the word *preached,*" "das Wort der *Predigt.*" Wilke distinguishes between the first and second *akoe* in our text: the former he interprets "auditio cum fide conjuncta," hearing coupled with faith, and the latter, "quod auditur, vel auditum est," that which one hears, or has heard. Thus, *akoe,* in the first place, would have subjective force, *the act of hearing,* in the second, objective force, *the matter* heard. Now, the apostle in this connection cites Is. 53, 1: "Who hath believed our report?" (*akoe*), v. 16. The Septuagint renders the Hebrew term *angelia,* while the English version is "report" (in 1 Sam. 4, 19, "tidings"). This is decisive for establishing the meaning of *akoe* in the passage before us: it is objective, that which is proposed for hearing, the communication, the instruction, the sermon; Luther: *Predigt.* And there is no apparent reason why the meaning of the same word should be varied in the same verse. Faith cometh by that which is heard, i. e., by preaching, and that which is heard, preaching, cometh by the Word of God. God by His Word creates faith. "The Lord gave the Word: great was the company of them that published it," Ps. 68, 11. "How beautiful are the feet of them that preach the Gospel of peace, and bring glad tidings of good things!"—this very text is taken from the immediate context of our proof-passage. Faith, then, is from the Gospel,—this is what the passage substantiates. The Word of God, more particularly the Gospel, informs man of what God wants him to know for his salvation; it enables man to *know* the things that make for his peace, and it bestows that knowledge, enlightening man's understanding by its inherent power.

The knowledge of faith extends to all that God has had to communicate. John 17, 3 states the chief doctrines, that of the only true God, and that of the Savior and His work. But Rom. 10, 17 declares, by inference, that faith is from any word of God: for any word of God when preached can produce faith in the hearers. All communications of God to man are in the Holy Scriptures, the chief part of which is the Gospel of Jesus Christ: From this book faith obtains all its knowledge, and strives to know all that is in the Bible. Whatever is not Scripture cannot form the subject-matter of faith. We can believingly know only that which "cometh by the Word of God."

This knowledge is no small matter.

John 17, 3: *This is eternal life, that they might know Thee the only true God, and Jesus Christ whom Thou hast sent.*

Believing knowledge is the way of life, the true road to heaven. Knowledge is such an important characteristic of faith that faith is here called simply knowledge. Knowing of this kind and believing are equivalents. Hence, John declares: "These things have I written unto you that believe on the name of the Son of God; that ye may *know* that ye have eternal life, and that ye may *believe* in the name of the Son of God," 1 John 5, 13. And in John 2, 3 the statement: "We do know that we know Him" amounts to saying: We are aware that we believe in Him.

But faith is not knowledge only. It is not in the intellect alone; it is not of the head. Christ charges the Jews:

John 5, 46: *Had ye believed Moses, ye would have believed me: for he wrote of me.*

John 3, 36: *He that believeth not the Son shall not see life; but the wrath of God abideth on him.*

In both passages the Greek verbs for believe and not believe have the object in the dative, and that object is a person. There is an approach made from the believer to the person whom he believes: he recognizes the authority and benevolence of the person who speaks to him. Wilke (sub voce) interprets *pisteuein*, with the dative of a person thus: "alicui aliquid narranti, asseveranti, docenti fidem habere," to give credence to the narrative, claim, or teaching of some one; in a word, to believe a person's words. The believer coincides with the speaker, and declares his acquiescence in the speaker's statements. He is satisfied, not only that he has heard the truth, but that he likes the truth. He applauds it; he expresses, in some manner, his assent; he accepts what has been proposed to him. There is seen in such an act a more intimate and personal relation between the believer and the object of the believer's faith. The assenting believer not only perceives facts, but facts as they concern him, and perceives their relation to him with gladness. His heart is filled with joy and gratitude, while he declares: Yes, these things are so!

The assent of faith extends to all that Moses in the Old and Christ in the New Testament have published by God's direction. Moses (John 5, 46) and Christ (John 3, 36), by synecdoche, stand for the entire Scripture. The believer assents to just as much as he knows. He affixes his yea and amen to the whole Bible.

This assent is no small matter. This is shown by the two passages just quoted and by

James 2, 19: *Thou believest that there is one God; thou doest well: the devils also believe and tremble.*

The Jews did not lack knowledge of the contents of Moses' books. They read them every day and Sabbath day. They taught them to their children, wrote them on strips of paper, and tied them about their wrists and foreheads, carved them on the gables of their houses, and could recite entire sections from memory. Nor was there any doubt in their hearts that Moses was the author of these sayings, and that he had received them from God. But they did not accept the truth of these words, they perverted them by false interpretations, they denied their reference to Jesus of Galilee, they yielded no assent to what Moses had told them concerning the coming Messiah, who now rebukes them for their failure to give credence and a glad acceptance to the teachings of their ancient prophet. The consequence was: "The wrath of God abideth on them." It rests on the Jews to this day. Their case is similar to that of the devils, not one of whom is as great a fool as our modern atheists, who deny the existence of a personal God. The devils are fully convinced of the truth of the Scriptures, of the Christian religion, of the redeemership of Christ. But their heart is all the while opposed to the truths which they know to be truths. It is a fearful thing for them to be convinced of them; they tremble; they scorn, and yet dread God and His Christ. Failure to assent to the words which God and His Anointed have taught for the salvation of men, entails eternal damnation; approving of these words, assenting to them, and accepting what they state, brings eternal life.

But faith is still more than knowledge and assent.

Hebr. 11, 1: *Now faith is the substance of things hoped for, the evidence of things not seen.*

The objects of faith are removed from the believer's vision. They are immaterial. They cannot be verified by human sense and reason. And yet, they are not mere dreams and fancies, not castles in the air, not a beautiful mirage. They are very real, substantial, and evident to the believer. As to the force of *hupostasis*, the Septuagint renders Ps. 39, 8: "My hope is in Thee," *hupostasis mou para sou.* Geier: "David with these words replies to himself, having inwardly received from the Holy Ghost a certain new enlightenment and a confirmation of his future hope; as if to say: From Thee, O Lord, I promise myself all sufficiency, as well for this life as for that to come; in Thee I have all things. (See Ps. 37, 3; 73, 25.) However, the word hoped, expected, signifies an expectation, or hope, which one places in something, and it is found, besides in this place, five times in the Holy Scriptures: Prov. 10, 28: 'The hope of the righteous shall be gladness,' i. e., it shall be crowned at last with a glad outcome; ch. 11, 7: 'The expectation of a wicked man shall perish,' i. e., it shall be frustrated in its conclusion; ch. 13, 12: 'Hope deferred maketh the heart sick;' Job. 41, 1: 'The hope of him (who expects to capture leviathan) is in vain;' and finally, Lam. 3, 18: 'My hope and my strength is perished from the Lord.' Accordingly, also in the present place such a firm trust of the heart must be understood by which we rest immovably in God as in Him who only is good, true, almighty, the truth (or realization) of whose promises for the future we await unhesitatingly, and whose kind and fatherly affection we meanwhile embrace all the time with a filial mind. Hope and confidence are sometimes used interchangeably (*promiscue*) in the Holy Scriptures, says Flacius. Comp. Ps. 7, 1; 9, 10. And the Septuagint version, indeed, will shed not a little light on the passage Hebr. 11, 1, where faith is likewise called *hupostasis*, i. e., that which causes invisible matters to subsist as though they were present, etc. The Septuagint rendering, however, has been improperly reproduced by the Vulgate: 'Thou art my substance.'" As to the force of *elenchos*, the idea of cogent proof, reliability is contained in it. Matters of faith, the doctrines of Scripture, the promises of God are so perfectly sure to the believer, that he regards and speaks of them as quite evident, though he beholds not one of them with his natural eyes, nor grasps them with his natural reason.—This text, then, brings out the feature of confidence, trust, calm, firm, even proud repose, which fills the heart of the believer. All things with which his faith is occupied are quite plain and quite certain to him. He entertains no doubts either regarding affairs of the past that have been revealed, or affairs of the future which have been foretold. To his faith the world, its history, his own life present no problems.

This is illustrated by

2 Tim. 1, 12: *I know whom I have believed, and am persuaded that he is able to keep that which I have committed unto Him against that day.*

These words were spoken by the *suffering apostle*. He had been appointed a preacher and an apostle, and a teacher of the Gentiles in those things which were necessary for their faith. His vocation had brought him bonds and stripes, ignominy and persecution; he was in daily expectation of being put to death for having proclaimed the Gospel. Under these circumstances not only did the substance and evidence of his faith not appear, but, what was worse, the very opposite appeared to the eye of flesh. Nevertheless, the apostle's faith is undaunted: he declares, in these words, his complete faith; knowledge (*oida*), assent ("whom I have believed," *ho pepisteuka*), and confidence (*pepeismai*, i. e., I have been persuaded, I am assured).

The confidence of faith rests upon that evidence which the subject-matter of faith offers. This is the word and promise of God, who is able (*dunatos estin*) to make good every word He has spoken. Hence, faith relies upon Scripture, every part of it. Faith has sprung from God's Word, and ever returns to draw strength and support from that same Word. Faith is *from* the Word, and *in* the Word. The Bible is the mother which begets, the cradle which shelters, the home which nourishes, raises, supports, and protects faith. Upon any statement of Scripture the believer is willing to stake his life, the outward aspect of his earthly affairs to the contrary notwithstanding. See Rom. 8, 35—39.

It is plain that such confidence is no small matter. The apostle speaks in this passage of something "which he has committed unto Him who is able to keep it against that day." The English rendering at this place is very weak as compared to Luther's version: "Er kann mir meine Beilage bewahren." *Paratheke* is a deposit for safekeeping, a bailment. Of the five different sorts of bailment known to English law the one here intended comes nearest to the fourth kind, the *mandatum*, or *commission*, "the bailment of goods to another who undertakes gratuitously to do some act for the owner in regard to them." In this case the act is *fulaxai*, to stand guard over, "custodire ne quid auferatur, curare ne mihi eripiatur, seu tutum praestare," to guard something lest it be taken away, to exercise care lest it be snatched from me, or to render it safe. But what is *paratheke?* Wilke says: "Appellatur ita doctrina pura, Timotheo commissa," and he cites 2 Tim. 2, 2, to corroborate his view: "the things that thou hast heard of me among many witnesses, the same commit thou (*parathou*) to faithful men, who shall be able to teach others also." That the reference in this place is to the doctrine of faith is plain from the purpose here named for which Timothy is to commit these things. Also in 1 Tim. 6, 20: "Keep that which is committed to thy trust," the reference is to Timothy's official function as a teacher of Christianity, hence, to the doctrine, because the apostle adds the warning: "avoiding profane and vain babblings and oppositions of science falsely so-called." Finally, in 2 Tim. 1, 14: "That good thing which was committed unto thee keep by the Holy Ghost which dwelleth in us," the reference is to the doctrine and office of Timothy, as the preceding verse shows: "Hold fast the form of sound words, which thou hast heard of me in faith and love which is in Christ Jesus." The close succession in which *paratheke* in this chapter is twice used in vv. 12 and 14 might seem sufficient reason for us to assume the same meaning for it in both places. And yet, we hesitate to explain *paratheke* in v. 12 as denoting the doctrine of faith, for the following reason: In all the passages quoted, excepting our proof-text, *paratheke* is something which is committed to men, and by men, and the exhortation is virtually a reminder to be faithful to one's ordination vows as an evangelical minister. But in our text the situation is different. True, *paratheke mou*, in itself, may mean, either something that God has committed to the apostle, or something that the apostle has committed to God. However, the connection with: "I know whom I have trusted," and the fact that the apostle expects this same God to keep his *paratheke* for him, compels us to look for another meaning. The passage would, indeed, yield good meaning, if interpreted thus: "I know that my creed is correct, and that God will protect the fortunes of my doctrine and office unto the end of time." But the passage yields a still better meaning, if interpreted thus: "I know in whom I have placed my trust," i. e., I know what I may expect in the end; God has laid up for me a rich reward, and I am persuaded that He is able to keep my deposit, that which was given me along with my faith, my hope of eternal life. Salvation would not be safe in my hands; I place it, and I leave it in His almighty hands and expect to receive it from Him at the latter day. In this manner Paul speaks of eternal life to the Colossians (ch. 1, 5): "the hope which is laid up for you in heaven," *ten elpida ten apokeimenen humin en tois ouranois.* Under the adverse circumstances under which the apostle wrote these words, we hold, this is the most appropriate meaning. *Paratheke*, then, is "the end of faith, the salvation of our souls." The confidence of faith, then tends heavenward. Its goal is the life eternal. Lack of confidence, doubt, is damning.

It is to be noted, too, that Scripture predicates saving powers as well of the knowledge, as of the assent, and of the confidence of faith. (See above.) Faith is àlways a unit, but is viewed by us, now according to this, now according to that feature. Knowledge, assent, confidence are not parts of faith in the mathematical sense. Faith, saving faith, is always these three combined.

Faith is a personal affair. We can do some things through an agent, but we cannot believe thus. Hence, in confessing our faith we use the first person singular rather than the plural, which we might also do, and, in fact, are doing, e. g., when chanting the Creed at service.

Hab. 2, 4: *The just shall live by his faith.*

It is customary to emphasize the personal pronoun in this passage. There is no warrant for this in the text. It should rather be pointed out that the ultimate object of faith is life eternal. Everybody desires to go to heaven himself. *Ergo.* However, faith brings also temporal blessings.

Luke 7, 50: *Thy faith hath saved thee; go in peace.*

In our troubles we approach God in prayer. We ask others to pray for us, but we do not neglect to pray for ourselves. Our prayer is a statement of our personal wants and our personal trust that God can supply these wants. The passage adduced shows that God rewards such trust. But the folly of trusting that the religious concern of our parents, teachers, pastors for our salvation is a valid substitute for our personal faith, or that in the hour of need we can supply our lack of faith from the abundance of others, as the Roman Church teaches, is shown by the parable of the foolish virgins.

PROF. WESSEL'S EXPOSITION.

THE FIRT PERSON OF THE TRINITY IS NAMED "THE FATHER."

John 20, 17: *I ascend unto my Father, and your Father; and to my God, and your God.*

In that touching discourse with Mary Magdalene after His resurrection, Christ says among other things: "I ascend unto *my Father,* and *your Father.*" The term *Father* is here applied to the first person of the Trinity, and He is said to be the Father of Christ and the Father of Christ's disciples, the true Christians. But let us observe the peculiar wording of the text. The Lord does not say: "I ascend unto *our* Father," but, "I ascend unto *my* Father and *your* Father," indicating that though we have with Christ the same Father, yet not in the same sense. *Christ stands in a peculiar and unique relation to the Father.* God is the Father of Christ on account of the essential, most singular, and inexplicable eternal generation of the Son. Ps. 2, 7: "Thou art my Son; this day have I begotten Thee." Christ is "the Only-Begotten of the Father," John 1, 14.18; He is the essential and co-equal Son of God, being "one with the Father," John 10, 30. "He is the Son of God, not *chariti,* or by grace, but *fusei*, by nature, John 1, 14.18." (Quenstedt.)

The "brethren," however, to whom this message is to be communicated (cf. John 20, 17: "Go unto my *brethren*, and say to them"), the disciples of Christ, the true Christians, are through Him the adopted children of God, *chariti*, by grace. John 1, 12: "But as many as received Him, to them *gave* He the power to become the sons of God, even to them that believe on His name." His disciples He taught to pray: "Our Father which art in heaven."

In short, Christ born out of the essence of the Father is very God of very God; the believers, begotten "with the word of truth," James 1, 18, "born of incorruptible seed, by the Word of God," 1 Pet. 1, 23, "born of God," John 1, 13, remain men, creatures of God.

The subtile discrimination made in the text between "*my* Father and *your* Father," etc., has been observed and commented on ever since the days of the church-fathers. Augustine's terse explanation may find a place here: "Non ait, Patrem *nostrum;* aliter ergo meum, aliter vestrum; *natura* meum, *gratia* vestrum. Et, Deum meum et Deum vestrum. Neque hic dixit Deum *nostrum;* ergo at hic aliter meum, aliter vestrum. Deum meum, sub quo et Ego sum homo: Deum vestrum, inter quos et Ipsum Mediator sum." (Tract. 121. "He does not say: 'Our Father'; therefore in one sense mine, in another, yours; mine by *nature*, yours by *grace*. And, He says, '*my* God and *your* God.' Here, too, He has not said, '*our* God;' therefore also here in one sense mine, in another yours. *My* God, under whom also I am as a man; *your* God, whom I reconciled to you as the Mediator between you and Him.")

Mal. 2, 10: *Have we not all one Father? Hath not one God created us?*

In a certain sense God is the Father of all mankind. "Have we not all one *Father?*" This rhetorical question demands an answer in the affirmative. The reason for this implied assertion is given in the second interrogation which is in the nature of an explanation to the former. "Hath not one God *created* us?" Inasmuch as God *created* all mankind, He is said to be the *Father* of all.

But this universal fatherhood of God over all creatures must not be confounded with the special fatherhood over His children adopted unto Himself through Jesus Christ. As Christians we have become God's children in a sense in which not all men are His children.

If there be no other connection between God and man than the fact that God created him, this fatherhood will avail him nothing. Man, by sin, has lost the first estate into which he was created. Sin has separated him and his God. The Prodigal Son, who had wasted his substance in riotous living, full well knew that he was not worthy to be called his father's son. He was a *lost* son until he returned penitently. Cf. Luke 15, 11 sqq. The relation in which man by nature stands to God is that in which a violator of the law, convicted of, and condemned for, his crime, stands before his Sovereign. He is the object of divine displeasure. "The wrath of God abideth on him," John 3, 36. The condemnation that Christ hurls at the Jews who did not believe on Him, applies to all unbelievers: "Ye are of your *father*, the *devil*, and the lusts of your father you will do," John 8, 44. Again, in the language of Scripture: "They have corrupted themselves; their spot is not the spot of children: they are a perverse and crooked generation," Deut. 32, 5. The wicked are not spiritual children of God, but rather "children of the wicked one," Matt. 13, 38.

Who, then, are the only true children of God? Paul anwsers: "Ye are all the children of God *by faith in Christ Jesus*," Gal. 3, 26.

This distinction between the universal and the special fatherhood of God must be plainly kept in view, in order to guard against that rationalistic conception of the "all-fatherhood of God," according to which God is supposed to be a gracious God without Christ, a conception about which the lodges prate so loudly in order to mislead the unwary, and which finds expression in that meaningless jingle of phrases: "The fatherhood of God and the brotherhood of man."

Eph. 3, 14.15: *For this cause I bow my knees unto the Father of our Lord Jesus Christ, of whom the whole family in heaven and earth is named.*

In these opening words of the supplication of the Apostle Paul for the congregation at Ephesus,. the first person of the Trinity is spoken of as the Father in reference to His dear Son, Jesus Christ. Why He is so termed has been sufficiently expounded in a preceding passage. But God is also called Father on account of the *family* that is named of Him. This latter fact we shall endeavor to elucidate.

The phrase: "Of whom the whole family in heaven and earth is named," reads in the original: *ex hou pasa patria en ouranois kai epi ges onomadzetai.* The point made by the apostle in these words is somewhat obscured by the English translation. In Greek there is a play upon the words *pater* (Father) and *patria* (family) which cannot be reproduced in English. The Greek word *patria* (family) is etymologically derived from *pater* (Father.) "The relation of names expresses here a relation of facts. God is the true Father to every family, loving it and caring for it." (Voigt.) The word for *family (patria)* designates a lineage, the descendants of a common father; so a *patria* is a generation of children. Thus Joseph, Luke 2, 4, is described as being of the household and *family (patria)* of David."—"From whom," *ex hou,* obviously refers to the *"Father (patera)* of our Lord Jesus Christ." Every *patria*, says the text, receives its name from the *pater* (Father). It is so named because it stands in close relation to the Father. The term *Father* connotates the notion *child.* A person is called a *father* because he has a child or children. Now, who are they that stand in child-relation to this heavenly Father? Who are they of whom God says: These people belong to my family, they are my children? "Ye are all the *children* of God *by faith* in Christ Jesus," Gal. 3, 26. So, then, "every family" does not comprise all mankind, but only the community of God's own. This explanation is in keeping with the context and is favored by the tenor of tne whole epistle. (Cf. chap. 1, 9.10.)

From the foregoing it is already patent what the endearing appellation is that the Father has bestowed upon those constituting His family. In holy wonderment over the ineffable grace of God in Christ Jesus, St. John exclaims: "Behold, what manner of love the Father has bestowed upon us that we should be called the *sons*"—*tekna, the children*—"of God," 1 John 3, 1. Only they who have received the adoption of sons can cry: "Abba, Father!" (Cf. Gal. 4,6.)

The name *Father* calls to mind all the abundant mercy God has bestowed upon us through His dear Son, in whom He has adopted us as His children; the name *"child of God"* contains the unspeakable blessedness of a sinner saved. "And if children, then heirs; heirs of God, and joint-heirs with Christ," Rom. 8, 16.

Now, God has a family *in heaven*. The text says: *pasa patria en ouranois*—every family in heaven. This expression does not only comprise the perfected saints, but primarily the "sons of God," Job 38, 4.7, the holy angels, divided amongst themselves into various orders, such as thrones, dominions, principalities, powers, Col. 1,16, cherubim and seraphim, Is. 6, 2.—The Father has a family on *earth*: His children collected from among all nations, kindreds, and tongues. Both the children in heaven and those on earth constitute one great family, the *ecclesia una sancta* in a wider sense.

Luther's free translation: "Der der rechte Vater is ueber alles, was da Kinder heisst in Himmel und auf Erden," is at the same time a beautiful commentary of the text.

THE FATHER IS CALLED "ALMIGHTY" AND "MAKER."

Gen. 1, 1: *In the beginning God created heaven and earth.*

This statement so simple yet so sublime on account of its very simplicity, brands all the nebulous theories regarding the creation of the world of so-called scientists as falsehoods and lies.

"In the beginning *God* created heaven and earth." Incontrovertibly, then, God already existed *in* the beginning, aye, *before* the beginning of things. Besides Him there was nothing that had existence. It was He alone that inhabited eternity. "Before the mountains were brought forth, or ever Thou hadst formed the earth and the world, even from everlasting to everlasting, Thou *art* God," Ps. 90, 2.

"In the beginning God created heaven and earth." The phrase, "In the beginning," precludes the evolutionistic notion of the eternity of matter. This world of ours had a beginning. "Of old hast Thou laid the foundation of the earth: and the heavens are the work of Thy hands," Ps. 102, 25. In the light of these majestic dicta of Scripture, how absurd, nonsensical, and puerile are the vague mouthings of the evolutionists! Millions of ages ago, say they, the illimitable space was filled with nebulous matter. This indefinable something "gradually cooling and contracting, threw off, in obedience to mechanical and physical laws, successive rings of matter, from which subsequently, by the same laws, were produced the several planets, satellites, and other bodies of the solar system." Whence did this nebulous matter come? Who established these mechanical and physical laws? How did they work?—all of which questions we should not have the temerity to ask: It must suffice that science has spoken. Thus God is done away with. "The *fool* hath said in his heart, There is no God." A scientist of this stripe is a *fool*.

"In the beginning God created *heaven and earth.*" That was the actual beginning of this world's history, the beginning of all things, the beginning of time. Heaven and earth were *created*. They did not arise by a process of emanation, nor were they evolved from any pre-existent primeval material. The statement simply reads: God *created* heaven and earth in the beginning. That says, when as yet there was no material existence, God brought this world into being by His almighty creative power. "He spake, and it was done; He commanded, and it stood fast," Ps. 33, 9.

From the foregoing explanation the meaning of create becomes patent. Prior to the *beginning* of which the text speaks God only was in existence, nothing else besides Him. God called into being this universe. How? Out of nothing. Hence to *create* means *to make out of nothing.* The verb *to create* occurs about fifty times in the Old Testament and is always used in reference to God. God only can create. Everywhere it signifies a divine production, a bringing into being by God's almighty power that which had no existence before. In a few instances where *to create* is used, a material is not absolutely excluded, as for example in Gen. 1, 27, but the primary and proper signification of the term is *to produce something out of nothing,* as is evident from the passage under consideration, where the idea of pre-existent material is simply absurd. The making of heaven and earth is *a creation out of nothing.* By His creative word God called the things that were not into existence, *ta me onta: hos onta,* Rom. 4, 17. "Things which are seen were not made of things which do appear," Hebr. 11, 3. (See Is. 42, 5; 40, 26, etc.) —

Bara, to create, is also applied to the almighty work of Renovation. When David prays: "Create in me a clean heart," Ps. 51, 12, he thereby confesses his utter inability to make his heart clean. To do so is not within the power of man; it, too, is a work of divine omnipotence. This David knew from the Word of God; this he had learned by sad experience.

The Greek word corresponding to the Hebrew *bara* is *ktidza* (create), as is evident, e. g., from Col. 1, 16: "By Him were all things created" (ektisthe). Rom. 1, 25: "They worshipped and served the *creature* (te ktisei) more than Him who *created* it" (ton ktisanta). Eph. 3, 9: "God who *created* all things *(ta panta ktisanti)* by Jesus Christ." Instances might be multiplied. The term is not only used in reference to the creation of the world, but also in regard to the new-creation in Christ. Conversion of man, is, according to Scriptures, a new-creation. Eph. 2, 10: "We are His workmanship, *created (ktisthentes)* in Christ Jesus." Man, by nature, is *dead* in trespasses and sin. To bring this dead man to life spiritually is as great a miracle as to raise a dead man from the grave; it is a work requiring the same almighty creative power that produced the visible world. Conversion, too, is a *creatio ex nihilo* by the word of God.—In short, the true and original meaning of *create* in the Old and New Testaments is *to produce out of nothing by the mere power of His word.* It is a prerogative of the almighty God.

From this very passage of the Bible we learn how vain are the imaginings of those self-styled scientists who endeavor to substitute a vapory theory of evolution for the doctrine of creation; we observe furthermore how flatly Scripture denies atheism, polytheism, pantheism, and all other cognate "isms."

On the other hand, this passage affords great consolation for the Christians. This God, who has created heaven and earth, is our dear Father in Christ Jesus. He, the Almighty, can keep us in every need. With Him all things are possible. In all confidence we can trust in His divine guidance, saying with the psalmist: "I will lift up mine eyes unto the hills from whence cometh my help. My help cometh from the Lord, which made heaven and earth." Ps. 121, 1.2. And again: "Our help is in the name of the Lord, who made heaven and earth," Ps. 124, 8.

NOTE. It may not be amiss to call attention to the fact that the words "God created" in the original text read: *bara Elohim*, thus joining a verb in the singular number *(bara) with a plural noun (Elohim). This plural form of* the noun indicates plurality *in* God, but not a plurality of Gods. The verb in the singular indicates that the Creator of heaven and earth is *one* God.

Hebr. 11, 3: *Through faith we understand that the worlds were framed by the word of God, so that things which are seen were not made of things which do appear.*

In the preceding passage the *fact* of God's having created heaven and earth was stated; in this we are informed of the *manner* in which He performed the work. "The worlds were framed *rhemati theou, by the word of God.*" God said, "Let there be light!" and there was light.

Through this almighty fiat of God things that did not exist before came into being. "He spake, and it was done," Ps. 33, 9. This assertion is enforced by what follows. The "things which are seen," *ta blepomena*, "the worlds," *tous ainos*, all that exists in time, have not their being from things which appear in outward manifestation, *me ek fainomenon*. This says emphatically that there was no material present out of which the "things seen" could have been made; there were no earthly germs, substances, or cells pre-existent from which by the power of nature the world could have evolved. This latter clause says as plainly as language can put it that the creation of the world was a *creatio ex nihilo*, and thus it substantiates the former, which declares that the worlds sprang into existence by the omnipotent *word* of God. Luther's translation, "dass alles, was man siehet, *aus nichts* worden ist," though not literal, hits the nail on the head.

The doctrine of the creation of the world is an article of faith. "*Through faith* we understand that the worlds were framed by the *word* of God." But does not Rom. 1, 18-20 say that natural man can know of the existence of God by virtue of his reason, that he can know by the things that are made that there is a Creator? Is there a contradiction between these two passages? By no means. When contemplating nature the light of reason tells us that of itself, by accident, this world could not come into being. It must have had a rational, supernatural, wise, divine author. Further than this, however, reason cannot argue. *How* this universe was made reason cannot fathom. That it was made by the *word* of God reason cannot know. Reasons says: *Ex nihilo nihil fit!* There must have been a matter from which the world was made. Therefore the text says: "*Through faith* we understand that the worlds were framed *by the word of God.*" Through what faith do we understand this? Through faith in the Word of God as it is recorded in Gen. 1, Ps. 104, and other passages which treat of this matter. This word is God's word, therefore true. This we believe, upon this we rely, and are thus divinely certain as to how this world was created, all the vain babblings of science falsely so-called to the contrary notwithstanding. Scientists are fallible men; God, who speaks in the Scriptures, is infallible. He, the Creator, knows more about His handiwork than all the geologists and germ theorists put in a heap. Where the statements of scientists and those of the Bible clash, the Bible must prevail, because it is the absolute truth from Genesis to Revelation.

Ps. 115, 3: *Our God is in the heavens: He hath done whatsoever He hath pleased.*

This passage is a mighty weapon in the hands of the believers, with which to put to flight all reproaches of unbelievers, scoffers and blind reason. When questions are asked such as these: "How is it possible? How can these things be?" we answer in the words of Scripture recorded above. The text points out the omnipotence and sovereign majesty of God. "Our God is *in the heavens:*" that is the seat of

His power and glory. He is not a man-made, impotent idol (cf. context), but the *almighty* God: "He hath done whatsoever He hath pleased."

Col. 1, 16: *By Him were all things created, that are in heaven and that are in earth, visible and invisible.*

In the Creed we confess: "I believe in God the Father Almighty, *Maker of heaven and earth.*" Luther explains these words thus: "I believe that God has made me and all creatures." By the phrase: *heaven and earth* therefore we mean all creatures, visible and invisible. This truth is beautifully set forth in Col. 1, 16. "By Him were all things *(ta panta)* created." This is a sweeping assertion. "All things," whether animate or inanimate, rational or irrational, all things that have existence were produced by His creative power. The apostle specifies this comprehensive term *all* by saying: all "that are in heaven, and that are in earth." In whatsoever *place* things may exist, they have been created by Him. A further specification of "all things" is made when the apostle adds: "visible and invisible." Of whatever *nature* the things may be, they are His handiwork. He created the *visible* things, such as the earth with its flora and fauna; the luminaries of heaven: the sun, the moon, the myriads of stars, and, last but not least, man, the crown of creation. He called into being the *invisible* things, by which, according to the context, St. Paul primarily understands the heavenly world of spirits—the thrones, dominions, principalities, and powers. In short, God "created heaven, and the things that therein are, and the earth, and the things that therein are, and the sea, and the things that therein are," Rev. 10, 6. "All things were made by Him; and without Him was not anything made that was made," John 1, 2.

NOTE. The context discloses the fact that the phrase *"by Him"* in Col. 1, 16, as well as in John 1, 2, denotes Christ. So Christ is the Creator of the world. And still we confess in the Creed: "I believe in God the *Father* Almighty, Maker of heaven and earth." How is this to be understood? In the words of Dr. Graebner: "Being an *opus ad extra*, the work of creation was performed with the concurrence of the three Persons of the Godhead. It was the *Father* who made the world *by* the *Son*, Hebr. 1, 1.2, 'by whom the world was made,' John 1, 10, and all things were created, that are in heaven, and that are in earth, visible and invisible,' Col. 1, 16. By the 'Word of the Lord' were the heavens made; and all the host of them 'by the Breath of His mouth,' Ps. 33, 6, i. e., by the Spirit of God, Gen. 1, 2. But while this work is thus attributed to the three Persons in the Godhead, it is not unscriptural to ascribe it, by appropriation, to the First Person, as is done in the Apostles' Creed, since in the texts already quoted the world is said to have been made *by* the Son, *by* the Word of the Lord, and *by* the Breath of His mouth, He who by the Son and Spirit created the world being the *Father, Almighty, Maker of heaven and earth.* Acts 17, 24; coll. v. 31."

The Good Angels.

Hebr. 1, 14: *Are they not all ministering spirits, sent forth to minister for them who shall be heirs of salvation?*

This text gives occasion to speak (1) of the nature, and (2) of the ministry of the good angels.

1. *Their nature.* They are *spirits.* What is a spirit? This may be clearly seen from the record of that remarkable appearance of the risen Christ, related in Luke 24, 36 ff. When the apostles were sitting at supper, with the doors closed through fear of the Jews (John 20, 19), Jesus suddenly appeared in the midst of them, and "they were terrified and affrighted and supposed that they had seen a spirit." Allaying their fears, the Risen One says: "Behold my hands and my feet, that it is I myself: handle me and see; for *a spirit hath not flesh and bones, as ye see me have.*" Hence, the angels, being spirits *(pneumata),* are incorporeal beings. The supposition that angels possessed a subtile, celestial, material body is refuted by the passage above. Man, consisting of body and soul, is composed of a material and an immaterial element; the angels, however, are simply spirits, without a body or the attributes of material things. Nevertheless they have a personal subsistence; they are *personal* spirits. From our text this truth may be clearly perceived from the fact that they are charged to perform certain tasks —they are *sent forth to minister* unto men. Sadducees, ancient and modern, deny the personal existence of angels; our secular literature, too, is sprinkled with slurs, direct and indirect, at this doctrine; hence the necessity of stressing this truth. Being spirits, the angels are *invisible.* Col. 1, 16, they are enumerated among the *aorata,* the invisible beings, created by Christ. The fact that angels now and then assumed visible forms does not subvert this doctrine. When they were made, the Mosaic record does not say. That they were called into being within the six days of creation we know. Gen. 1, 1; 2, 2; Ex. 20, 11.

2. *The ministry of the good angels.* Our text informs us in the first place that the ministry of the good angels is by *divine appointment.* They are *"sent forth."* God sends them forth; His messengers they are. What a glorious truth to contemplate! Here is the multitude of the heavenly host, distinguished into various orders, and by various names, such as, principalities, powers, thrones, dominions, etc., standing in the the presence of that great and glorious King, whose throne is in the heavens and whose kingdom ruleth over all, ever ready, ever willing to be *sent forth* to execute His every word. Of the "ten thousand times ten thousand" (Rev. 5, 11) of angels not one is, nor would one be, exempt from the duty of serving God. They are *"all* ministering spirits."

The objects of their ministry. They "minister for them who shall be *heirs of salvation."* *"For them,"* dia *tous, on account of* those, on behalf of those, for the benefit of those, who are children of God, heirs of God,

Rom. 8, 17; 1 Pet. 1, 2.

The *diakonia*, the service, of the angels is intended especially for the pious. It is true, they are not co-workers of our salvation. It has pleased God to use the ministry of sinful men to preach the Gospel of salvation to sinful men. It was something extraordinary when God in the Holy Night and on that eventful Easter Day availed Himself of the ministrations of angels to proclaim the tidings of great joy. Still God, whose will is our salvation, sends· forth His messengers to keep and protect us, so that the heirs of salvation may reach the appointed goal.

The character of this ministry is indicated by the words "*to minister*." To minister means *to serve*. Scriptural examples of the service of angels rendered the pious are numerous. Subsequent passages will give occasion to instance a number of them.

For our *consolation* let us bear in mind that this service is being carried on today. The Greek word *apostellomena, sent forth,* is the present participle, and indicates the act designated by the verb as being permanent. The ministering servants were sent forth in olden times, they are sent forth at the present time, and they ever will be sent forth to the end of time for them who shall be heirs of salvation.

Matt. 25, 31: *When the Son of Man shall come in His glory, and all the holy angels with Him, then shall He sit upon the throne of His glory.*

When the Son of Man, the once despised Nazarene, returns visibly as the Judge of the world, "coming on the clouds of heaven with power and great glory" (Matt. 24, 30), a magnificent retinue—*all the holy angels*—will accompany Him. This sublimely beautiful text does not call for a discussion here, but the phrase "*all the holy angels*" may serve to speak (1) of the term *angel*, (2) of an attribute of the angels *(holy)*, and (3) of the number of angels *(all)*.

The Hebrew word for *angel* is *maleach;* the Greek is *angelos.* Both words etymologically mean *one who is sent, a messenger.* In the Authorized Version the one word *maleach* is rendered by two English ones, *angel* and *messenger;* the same is true of the Greek word *angelos.* According to a count made, based on Young's Analytical Concordance, the Hebrew term *maleach* is translated 98 times by the word *messenger,* and 107 times by the word *angel.* The Greek *angelos* is rendered but seven times by *messenger* (Matt. 10, 11; Mark 1, 2; Luke 7, 24; 7, 27; 9, 52; 2 Cor. 12, 7; James 2, 25); in all other cases *angel* is the word used. The general principle which the Authorized Version seems to have followed was to translate *maleach* and *angelos* by *messenger,* when the concept indicated by the English word was apparent in the original text, and to restrict the use of the word *angel* as much as possible to the *stratia ouranios,* "the heavenly host," Luke 2, 13. From the fact that each of the words, *maleach* and *angelos,* has two renderings, both in

English and German, arises the difference in the translation of some passages of the two versions. Mal. 3, 1: "I will send my *messenger.*" "Ich will meinen *Engel* senden."—"The *messenger* of the covenant." "Der *Engel* des Bundes." Mal. 2, 7: "He is a *messenger* of the Lord." "Er ist ein *Engel* des Herrn Zebaoth." Matt. 11, 10: messenger—Engel; 9, 54: messenger—Bote; 2 Cor. 12, 7: messenger—Engel; James 2, 25: messenger—Engel.

Now, as to the application of the word. No less a person than our Savior *Himself* is called "the Angel of the Covenant," Mal. 3, 1; Matt. 11, 10. He is the Angel *kat exochen,* the *uncreated* angel, the messenger sent by God to consummate and announce the covenant of grace between God and man. Besides this, which is the highest application of the word "*angel,*" we find it used of any messenger of God. *John the Baptist* was an *angel* of the Lord, Mal. 3, 1; Luke 2, 27; Mark 1, 2, because he was sent by God with a message to prepare the way of the Lord. *Prophets and preachers* are termed *angels* because of the message they have of God to proclaim to the people. 2 Chron. 36, 15; Hagg. 1, 13; Rev. 2, 1. 8. 12. 18; Mal. 2, 7. In a still wider sense, the words *Maleach* and *angelos* designate *anyone bearing a message from one to another.* Gen. 32, 3.6; Numb. 20, 14; 21, 21; 22, 5; Josh. 6, 17.25; Judges 6, 35; 7, 24; Luke 7, 24; James 2, 25, etc.

But *in its restricted sense,* as it is commonly used and commonly understood, the term *angel* denotes a specific creature, the ministering spirit of Hebr. 1, 14. In this use of the word it is also of importance to remember that the term *angel* is an official name, and indicates the purpose for which the heavenly host was destined, i. e., to be "sent forth," Hebr. 1, 14. "The name angel does not describe the nature of the being, but its office, and signifies 'one sent,' a legate, a messenger. Hence Augustine: 'Do you ask for the name of their *nature?* It is spirit. Do you inquire concerning the name of their *office?* It is angel.'" (Quenstedt.) The particular office, for example, which these heavenly messengers are to perform on that great day of which the text speaks is to "gather together His elect from the four winds, from one end of heaven to the other," Matt. 24, 31.

These angels are *holy,* says the text, that is, they are without sin. Scripture speaks of holy men and of holy women; all Christians are holy people. The distinction, however, between the holiness of the angels and that of the believers is this: Christians are holy in the sight of God on account of the righteousness and holiness of their Redeemer which they have put on by faith, Gal. 3, 2; the angels, on the other hand, are holy in themselves, having retained their concreated righteousness. Being holy, their will is conformable to the holy will of God.

"*All* the holy angels" will be with Christ at His Second Coming. How glorious a sight that will be for the believers goes beyond the powers of our imagination. But once before, on the Night of the Nativity, when the Word was made flesh, did the entire heavenly host leave its celestial home to fill the still air on the plains of -Bethlehem with a melodious symphony, such as never again was vouchsafed for men to hear; now again, at His final coming, they *all* will be with Him "with a great sound of a trumpet," Matt. 24, 31. There will be assembled the angels and the archangels, the seraphim and the cherubim, the thrones, dominions, principalities, and powers. Is. 6, 2; Gen. 3, 24; Col. 1, 16; 1 Pet. 3, 22; 1 Thess. 4, 16. A glorious host, indeed, and a great host! There is a certain, fixed number of angels. Being sexless, Matt. 22, 30, the number is not multiplied; being immortal, Luke 20, 36, the number is not decreased. How great the number is we do not know; but we do know that it is vast. "A multitude of the heavenly host" sang the first Christmas anthem, Luke 2, 13; the number of them, says Rev. 5, 11, is "ten thousand times ten thousand, and thousands of thousands." What a vast assembly! And what a glorious and mighty King must He be who is the Lord of all these hosts!

Matt. 18, 10: *In heaven their angels do always behold the face of my Father which is in heaven.*

To be admitted to the very presence of an Oriental monarch, to see him face to face, was a distinguished privilege, enjoyed by such only as had gained the special favor and confidence of the king. The Queen of Sheba, admiring the wisdom of Solomon, says, "Happy are these thy servants, which are continually before thee." Cf. 2 Kings 25, 19; Jer. 52, 25. How great, then, is the happiness of the angels, these servants of God, who behold the King of kings face to face! To see God face to face, to behold Him as He is, is salvation itself. 1 John 3, 2.

The holy angels are *"in heaven,"* where God dwells, hence they are happy, blessed. They *"always* behold the face of My Father which is in heaven," hence *they are always blessed.* This dictum of the Lord excludes the possibility of sinning on the part of the good angels; it teaches their impeccability, and presupposes their confirmation in bliss. In express words their confirmation in bliss is taught, Luke 20, 36: "Neither *can they die any more;* for they are equal *unto the angels."* Quenstedt says: "Good angels are so confirmed in the good that, as before they were only able not to sin, now they are altogether unable to sin. Matt. 18, 10; 6, 10; 1 Tim. 5, 21; Luke 20, 36; Gal. 1, 8......Those who are to be blessed in eternal life are called 'equal to the angels.' Now, *we* are sure *we* shall never lose that celestial felicity; therefore, much more are the angels thus assured, to whom we shall be like." When this confirmation took place, Scripture does not say. It suffices us to know the fact. The dogmaticians give it as their opinion that it occurred after the apostasy of the evil angels, as a reward of grace to the good angels for having remained faithful to God.

Observing the context of the present passage we may also note an *employment* of the holy angels. The text is adduced as a motive for not despising the "little ones." "Their angels," i. e., the angels of the "little ones," especially appointed to watch and protect them, "do always behold the face of my Father which is in heaven." To the tender care of such exalted beings Christ's lambs are committed. How great, therefore, is the dignity with which they are clothed, and how heinous is the sin of putting stumbling blocks in their way! How full of consolation, on the other hand, is not this text for the Christian father and mother, who, filled with anxiety for the welfare of their little ones on account of the dangers that also beset them, can calm their troubled hearts with the firm assurance, God's holy angels are with our little ones. Not a hair can fall from their heads without the will of our Father in heaven.

Ps. 103, 20.21: *Bless the Lord, ye His angels, that excel in strength, that do His commandments, hearkening unto the voice of His word. Bless ye the Lord, all ye His hosts; ye ministers of His, that do His pleasure.*

"*Bless the Lord, ye His angels;*" "*bless ye the Lord, all ye His hosts.*" Thus the choir invisible is called upon to tune their harps in melodious praise of the Lord Jehovah. We know somewhat of the raptures that encompass the soul when hymns of jubilee go heavenward in one mighty sweep, but all earthly music pales into insignificance when compared with the majestic hymn of praises of the heavenly choristers with which the dome of the Celestial City continually reverberates: "Holy, holy, holy, is the Lord of hosts: the whole earth is full of His glory," Is. 6, 3. The employment of the angels consists in praising God always. And this song service they perform gladly. Their perfect blessedness, consisting in the beatific vision of God, impels them again and again to break out in strains of music, the "Leitmotif," the theme of which is: "Amen: Blessing and glory, and wisdom, and honor, and power, and might, be unto our God forever and ever. Amen." Rev. 7, 11. 12.

When the psalmist says: "*Bless,*" i. e., praise, "*the Lord,*" that is not to be understood "as if they needed any excitement of ours to praise God, they do it continually; but thus he expresses his high thoughts of God as worthy of the adoration of the holy angels; thus he quickens himself and others to the duty, with this consideration, that it is the work of angels." (M. Henry.)

Thus the holy angels praise God continually, and we who have even greater reasons than they to sing the praises of our Lord are so prone to hang our harps upon the willows! Sursum corda! "Bless the Lord, O my soul; and all that is within me, bless His holy name. Bless the Lord, O my soul, and forget not all His benefits. Who forgiveth all thine iniquities; who healeth all thy diseases." Ps. 103, 1 sqq.

But from adoration the angels may at any time be turned to work. "*They do His commandments,*" they "*do His pleasure.*" (Cf. Hebr. 1, 14.) And there are attendants in plenty to do God's behests, there are "*hosts*" of them; and these *hosts*, these *ministers,* are "*His,*" created for

His glorification. He, God, is their Lord and Ruler; His every word they cheerfully perform.

Not only are there hosts to do God's word, but they have the ability to carry out every command, they *"excel in strength,"* literally, they are "mighty in strength," heroes in strength. The angels are created beings, hence they are not omnipotent; God alone is almighty; but their strength is vast. The great slaughter of the firstborn in Egypt, the destruction of the 185,000 of the Assyrian army, each effected by a single angel, are striking proofs of their power.

This great powerful host is pervaded by but one sentiment—to be willing servants of the Most High. *"They hearken unto the voice of His word."* They *hearken*, i. e., they listen intently to catch the first whispered indication of His will. This beautiful imagery indicates the willingness, the eagerness, and the delight with which God's ministers execute His every word. Contemplating this willing service of the angels, the sigh goes up from the believer's heart: "Thy will be done on earth, as it is in heaven!"

Ps. 34, 7: *The angel of the Lord encampeth round about them that fear Him, and delivereth them.*

The Christian's life is beset with many dangers. His enemies are powerful, Eph. 6, 12. Luther well says: "With might of ours naught can be done, soon were our loss effected." How consolatory therefore to know that "the angel of the Lord encampeth round about them that fear Him, and delivereth them." Viewing this encampment with the eyes of faith, we need not fear. The eyes of the Lord are over the righteous. Herod intended to execute Peter. Peter was put in chains and closely watched. Escape seemed impossible. But the Lord sent His angel to deliver him out of the hands of his enemies. Acts 12, 5-10. Shadrach, Meschach, and Abed-nego feared the Lord. They would not worship the image of gold set up by Nebuchadnezzar, and hence were cast into a fiery furnace. To his surprise, Nebuchadnezzar saw four men walking in the midst of the fire. The fourth was an angel sent by God to deliver "them that feared Him." Dan. 3, 6. Daniel feared the Lord. He would not turn idolater at the king's decree. Though he was cast into the lion's den, no harm came to him. The Lord sent his angel to shut the lions' mouth. 2 Kings 6, 17; cf. Gen. 32, 1. Knowing that our path, too, is encompassed with perils manifold, we do well to pray: "Let us this day, and all the remaining time of our mortal life in this vale of tears, be commended to Thy fatherly blessing and divine protection; and may Thy holy angels keep charge over us, that the wicked one may have no power over us."

Ps. 91, 11.12: *He shall give his angels charge over thee, to keep thee in all thy ways. They shall bear thee up in their hands, lest thou dash thy foot against a stone.*

From the text we observe: (1) That the ministry of the angels is by divine appointment. The text says, *"He,"* God, "shall give His angels charge over thee." This fact we noted in Ps. 103, 20.21. (2) That they are God's servants, carrying out His behests. They are *"His* angels"; cf. Ps. 103, 20.21; Hebr. 1, 14. (3) That the ministry is intended especially for the pious. The *"thee"* in the text is he who says of the Lord, "He is my refuge and my fortress: my God, in whom I trust," vv. 2.9. Cf. Hebr. 1, 14; Ps. 34, 7.

The new matter calling for consideration is the charge committed to the angels, or rather the limitation of the charge: *"To keep* thee in *all thy ways."* What does this limitation, "in all thy ways," mean? Whose ways? "Thy ways," that is, the ways of the Christian. What are his ways? Those prescribed by the Word of God. "Wherewithal shall a young man cleanse his way? By taking heed thereto according to Thy Word," Ps. 119, 9. "Thy Word is a lamp unto my feet, and a light unto my path," Ps. 119, 105. Walking on his way through the wilderness of this world, this lamp, this light of the Word, is to show the Christian the path he can safely tread. Protection through the ministry of the angels is promised him only in so far and inasmuch as he walks on this narrow path; in other words, so long as he leads a godly life. A Christian must not argue, "I am a child of God. My Father will now and then overlook my stepping aside out of the beaten, prescribed path." Forsaking the way of the Lord, he becomes ungodly. Omit the all-important phrase "in all thy ways" from the text, and the devil will quote this Scripture for his purpos , to make people enter on foolhardy enterprises. He did it when making his onslaught on Christ in the wilderness. Matt. 4, 1 sqq. The Savior tells him to expect protection where no promise is given is *tempting* God. The high-diver, the "aeronaut," the "loop-the-looper," and others of that ilk, who perform hazardous feats that tend neither to the glory of God nor to the benefit of man, simply tempt God. They have no promise of divine protection.—What a mighty incentive is this passage to take heed to our way according to God's Word! Ps. 119, 19.

The ministry of the angels is furthermore a *continuous* service. It reads, "In *all* thy ways." Sleeping or waking, at times when there is no apparent danger, or when we are conscious of being in imminent peril, this invisible guard is at our side. We also note the great *carefulness* of their service, which is expressed in the words, *"lest thou dash thy foot against a stone."* Among the many images these words call to mind is that of a fond mother carefully watching her toddling child, taking his first lessons in walking. There is a stone in the way. That is a great obstacle for the tot. Harm might come to him. That must not be; her child is in danger. So she carefully lifts him in her arms till the danger spot is passed. Thus God acts towards us. We are His children. He says to the angels: Keep them in all their ways! Help them over the difficulties; protect them from danger, and be careful about it. Truly, the eyes of the Lord are over the righteous. He careth for us.

From our past experiences can we not recall many an escape from impending danger, on land or on sea, many an unexpected assistance?

THE EVIL ANGELS.

Jude 6: *The angels which kept not their first estate, but left their own habitation, He hath reserved in everlasting chains under darkness unto the judgment of the great day.*

Their apostasy. The words: *"The angels which kept not their first estate"* clearly imply that originally all angels alike possessed a "first estate." All were created good and holy, for after the entire creation had been finished, "God saw everything that He had made,"—also the angels,—"and behold, it was very good," Gen. 1, 31. A great number, however, fell from God. Now two classes of angels exist: such as persevered in their primeval state, and such as *"kept not their first estate."* To these fallen angels, called demons, *daimones, or daimona,* Matt. 8, 31; Mark 1, 34; Luke 8, 30, Scripture refers as "angels that sinned," 2 Pet. 2, 4. Of what nature this sin was we are not definitely informed. The apostasy took place after the sixth day of creation and before the fall of man, Gen. 1, 31; 3, 1-5; 1 John 3, 8. How it was possible for such holy beings, as these angels originally were, to fall into sin, is a metaphysical problem we cannot solve. We know the fact; that must suffice us.

The text, however, emphatically affirms that their apostasy was brought on by a *voluntary* act on their part. They "kept not their first estate," as they might have done, "but left their habitation." It was *their* estate, *their* habitation. Willfully, deliberately, they deserted God. To stress this idea of guilt on the part of the evil angels, the text says that the habitation they forsook was their "own," *idion,* one which, since God had assigned it to them, belonged to them of right. "They kept not,"—"they left,"—they have themselves to blame for the awful loss entailed by the fall.

What did they forsake? *"Their first estate."* The word *arche* translated "first estate," literally means *beginning.* They were created just and holy. This beginning, this first estate, this concreated state of holiness, they kept not. They sinned.

But the meaning of the word *arche* easily slips from that of "beginning" to that of "first place," hence "rule," "magistrate," "principality." Thus we find the word *arche* used as a title of angels in such passages as Col. 1, 16; Eph. 1, 21; 3, 10; 4, 12, where it is rendered "principality." In harmony with these passages Luther translates: "Engel, die ihr *Fuerstentum* nicht behielten." The Revised Version, too, has seen fit to substitute "principality" for "first estate." These two renditions—"first estate" and "principality"—are not opposed to each other. The latter includes the former and adds a thought. It points to the dignity these fallen angels possessed. By not keeping *ten heauton urchen* and *to idion oikterion* they not only lost their original condition, their blissful state, but at the same time deprived themselves of the high rank they occupied, of their position of honor, power, and glory. What a fall this was!

Their punishment. The text reads: *eis krisin megales hemeras desmois aidiois hupo dzofon tetereken.* "*Unto the judgment of the great day in eternal bonds under darkness He has kept.*" God has kept and still keeps—that is the force of the perfect *tetereken*—them under darkness. So the punishment of the evil angels is a present one. *Dzofos, darkness*, is used here, v. 13, and in the parallel passages, 2 Pet. 2, 4.17. Its synonym is *skotos, darkness*. We find the two linked in Jude 13: *ho dzofos tou skotous*, "the blackness of darkness," to intensify the meaning, the expression being equivalent to "the densest darkness." Cf. 2 Pet. 2, 17. *Skotos, darkness*, is the emblem of grief, sorrow, misery. Its signification it derives from the context. It may mean *physical* darkness, Matt. 27, 45, *spiritual* darkness, the state of sin and unbelief, 1 Pet. 2, 9: "the outer darkness,"—*to skotos to exoteron*,—where "there shall be weeping and gnashing of teeth," the darkness of hell, Matt. 8, 12. Manifestly this last mentioned meaning of *skotos* is to be applied to its synonym *dzofos* in our text. Jude says, and there is a touch of irony in the double use of the word *terein*, "*kept*": "Angels which *kept* not their principality—He has *kept* under darkness." The implied contrast is this: These angels were angels of light once, now they are angels of darkness, of hell. Their fate is sealed. They are kept in *chains*, from which they cannot extricate themselves; there is no hope of release, the chains are *eternal*, forever they will be excluded from light, from the presence of God. .

Now already they are in hell, but worse is to come. They are kept in eternal bonds *unto the judgment of the great day.* Now, as it were, the devil finds consolation in persecuting the Christians, in seducing men into shame, misbelief, and other great vices, but on that great day, the Judgment Day, Acts 2, 20; Rev. 6, 17; 16, 14, this pernicious activity of his, too, shall cease, and he himself shall receive his final judgment and be tortured in that everlasting fire that was prepared for the devil and his angels, Matt. 25, 41.

Eph. 6, 12: *We wrestle not against flesh and blood, but against principalities, against powers, against the rulers of the darkness of this world, against spiritual wickedness in high places.*

The forces marshaled against the Christians here pass in review.

Nature and intent. Our enemies are not "*flesh and blood*," human antagonists that can be fought with carnal weapons, but our battle is "*against spiritual wickedness in high places*"; the conflict is a *spiritual* conflict. The phrase: *ta pneumatika tes ponerias*—"spirituals of wickedness," i. e., "spiritual powers of wickedness," is equivalent to "wicked spirits." Our opponents are *spirits*, hence unseen, and for that very reason all the more dangerous. No sound or footfall announces their coming. They are far superior to us in intellect and wisdom.

The Apostle characterizes them as spirits "of wickedness." The phrase "of wickedness" says much more than the simple adjective "wicked." The devils are wickedness personified; wicked are all their thoughts, wicked all their desires, wicked all their deeds—and all these thoughts, desires, and deeds are centered upon one thing—to destroy the soul of man.

Organization. These "spiritual powers of wickedness" resemble a well-organized army. The commander-in-chief is *ho diabolos,* the devil, v. 11. Under him, governing and directing the attacks of the legions of evil angels, Mark 5, 9, are the *archai*, the principalities, and the *exousiai*, the authorities, which terms evidently denote ranks and orders among the evil spirits, as the terms signify ranks and orders among the good angels, Eph. 1, 21; 3, 10.

His rule of darkness. The devil and his host are *kosmokratores tou skotous tou aionos toutou*, "world-rulers of the darkness of this age." The whole world is the field of their satanic activity; no part of it, however remote or secluded, is exempt from their rule. How vast is their dominion! They are "world-rulers *of darkness*." Darkness is the element, the means, and the result of their pernicious rule. Matt. 4, 16: "The *people* which *sat in darkness* saw great light, and to them which sat *in the region and shadow of death* light is sprung up," i. e., Christ and His Gospel. Without the Gospel, darkness prevails. Darkness is the region of spiritual death.

Paul, in speaking of his mission to the Gentiles, says that he was sent "to open their eyes, and to *turn them from darkness to light*, and *from the power of Satan unto God*," Acts 26, 18. Darkness is the state of spiritual blindness, the state of alienation from God and subjection to the power of the devil. In Col. 1, 13, the apostle exhorts the Christians to render thanksgiving to God who "hath *delivered us from the power of darkness*, and hath translated us into the kingdom of His dear Son." Darkness is the kingdom of Satan, in which all men are by nature. Here the "works of darkness," such as "rioting, drunkenness, chambering, and wantonness, and fulfilling the lusts of the flesh," hold full sway. Rom. 13, 13. Darkness is the state of sin and unbelief. Such, then, is the nature of this rule of darkness out of which we have been called into God's marvelous light, 1 Pet. 2, 9; such is, in brief outline, the gigantic opponent, with whom we Christians are to cope.

The apostle writes: *ouk estin hemin he pale pros aima kai sarka alla pros ktl.* "*The wrestling is not to us*," or "*our wrestling is not against flesh and blood, but against*," etc. The conflict is a bitter conflict, a *"wrestling-match,"* he pale, a hand-to-hand encounter, a life-and-death struggle. And when the text says: "Our wrestling *is—estin—*" etc., this indicates that it is an ever-present conflict; there is no cessation of hostilities. No one is immune against the devil's attacks, not even the great apostle himself, for when he warns the Christians against the wiles of Satan, he includes himself, saying: *"We* wrestle," etc. The repetition of the preposition "against" gives prominence, rhetorically, to each concept separately, and vividly pictures the vast and mighty forces arrayed against us. At first sight the thought: "We wrestle *not* against *flesh and blood,"* may seem strange. The truth imbedded here is this: Our contests may appear primarily as being contests against flesh and blood, but back of this flesh and blood, back of the world with its manifold enticements to sin, is the devil inciting us through these willing tools. Indeed,

> The old evil Foe
> Now means deadly woe:
>> Deep guile and great might
>> Are his dread arms in fight;
> On earth is not his equal.

How necessary, therefore, to "put on the whole armor of God, that ye may be able to stand against the wiles of the devil," vv. 11.13.

John 8, 44: *The devil was a murderer from the beginning, and abode not in the truth, because there is no truth in him. When he speaketh a lie, he speaketh of his own: for he is a liar, and the father of it.*

"Murderer," *anthropoktonos, man-slayer,* this name fully characterizes the aim and end of the devil's designs. He seduced our first parents. Thus sin and death came into the world, "and death passed upon all men, because all have sinned," Rom. 5, 12. Thus the devil was a "man-slayer." Such he was "from the beginning," not of his existence, for he, too, was created good and holy, Gen. 1, 31, but from the beginning of his apostasy from God. Here, by the way, we have the biblical solution to that vexed question of the Gnostics: *pothen to kakon;* "Whence did evil come?"

"The first estate," Jude 6, the state of concreated purity and rectitude, was *eo ipso,* a state of truth, as it is in God. Truth, absolute truth, was the element in which he stood and moved, truth, nothing but truth, governed his inner self. This state of truth he wantonly forsook when apostatizing from God. He *"abode not in the truth,"* en te aletheia. Since then there is no truth and truthfulness, *aletheia,* in him. The sphere in which he now lives and moves is the lie, *hoti pseustes estin,* "for a liar he is." *"When he speaketh a lie, he speaketh of his own."* This does not discriminate between his speaking the truth at times, at times the lie. Literally it reads: "When he speaks *the lie," to pseudos,* as is his nature, "he speaketh of his own," *ek ton idion, out of his own resources;* the well-spring of lies, falsehood, and deception is within him. He cannot do otherwise, "for a liar he is."

The devil is a *murderer* and a *liar.* The name "murderer" indicates his design; "liar," one of the methods by which he endeavors to carry out his purposes. By means of a lie he felled our first parents. God had said: Ye shall surely die! The devil is so monstrous a liar as to have the effrontery to call God a liar, saying: "Ye shall not surely die," Gen. 3, 4. The devil denies Scripture, thus he lies. It was a lie when he said to Christ: "He shall give His angels charge concerning thee: and in their hands they shall bear thee up, lest at any time thou dash thy foot against a stone," Matt. 4, 6. By omitting the phrase "in all thy ways," Ps. 91, 11, this quotation was emptied of its true meaning; it was no longer Scripture, it was a lie. False doctrines i. e., lies, "the doctrines of devils," 1 Tim. 4, 1, is one of his most efficient weapons of warfare even today. The devil is a liar, *"and the father of it."* Ananias lied, but it was Satan *who filled his heart to lie,* Acts, 5, 3. See 1 John 3, 8.

This passage teaches, (1) the personal existence of the devil, (2) his being the cause of the fall of mankind, (3) his own apostasy and (4) the depth of wickedness into which he has sunk.

1 Pet. 5, 8.9: *Be sober, be vigilant; because your adversary, the devil, as a roaring lion, walketh about, seeking whom he may devour: whom resist steadfast in the faith.*

Strictly speaking, the term *ho diabolos,* the devil, is a proper name and designates the prince of the devils, the enemy *kat exochen,* Matt. 13, 25.39. The Greek word *diabolos,* Latin, *diabolus,* from which come the English *devil* and the German *Teufel,* signifies "slanderer," "false accuser," Tit. 2, 3; 3,3, *et al.* "The accuser" (the devil, v. 9) "of our brethren is cast down, which accuseth them before God day and night," Rev. 12, 10. The equivalent in Hebrew is *Satan* (Job 1, 6 ff; 2, 1; 1 Chron. 21, 1), "adversary," "opponent." In the New Testament both terms, devil and Satan, are practically synonymous. Matt. 4, 1 has: "tempted of the *devil,*" and Mark 1, 13: "tempted of Satan." See Matt. 4, 1.10; 16, 23, and John 6, 70. The devil is the Christians' *antidikos,* says Peter. This word strictly denotes *an opponent in a court of justice;* but since there is no allusion to the divine judgment in this passage, and since the *katapinein* (to devour) is given as the aim of the devil, it is best to accept the word in its general sense—that of *"adversary."* Satan is filled with enmity against all mankind; he has no pity even for the children of disobedience in whom he has his work, Eph. 2, 2; but the true Christians, who, by the grace of God, have escaped his dominion, are the particular objects of his hatred. Hence the apostle says, speaking to Christians, he is "your adversary." His purpose is to deprive them of their faith, their salvation. He is a formidable enemy. The text compares him to a *lion,* Prov. 30, 30. The image is made more vivid and the danger stressed by the use of the adjective *roaring*. As a lion intimidates people by his roaring, so the devil seeks to terrify the Christians by persecutions, sufferings, etc. The pages of Church history treating of the satanical cruelties devised and practiced during the Christian persecutions of the first three centuries are saturated with the blood of the martyrs who would not deny their Savior. Then the devil roared most fiercely! These persecutors of the Christians were the tools of Satan. Powerful in himself, he, as "this prince" and "god of this world," John 14, 30; 16, 11; 2 Cor. 4, 4, pressed and still presses his allies, the children of disobedience in whom he works, Eph. 2, 2, into his service. He is the instigator of persecutions and afflictions visited on the Christians. Thus he manifests himself as a roaring lion.

This, however, does not exclude that these things also come from God. The apostle begins this exhortation with the words: "Humble yourselves under the *mighty hand of God*," v. 6. The devil and his host are subject to God's supreme dominion and control. God holds the reins of government in His hands. Satan can go no further than God permits. Of Job the Lord said to Satan: "Behold, all that he hath is in thy power; only upon himself put not forth thine hand," Job 1, 12. See Job 2, 6; Luke 13, 16. In persecutions, in afflictions, under the cross, the devil has evil intents, while God has good intents. And God controls the evil intents of Satan for the good of His beloved ones, Gen. 50, 20; Rom. 8, 28.

With this ferocity our adversary combines a relentless and an untiring activity in the pursuit of his prey. "He *walketh* about, *seeking* whom he may devour." He is always on the alert. "Whence comest thou?" said the Lord to Satan, when he, as the accuser of the brethren, appeared in the midst of the sons of God. Satan answered: "From the going to and from through the earth, and from walking up and down in it," Job 1, 7. He is all the more assiduous in the work of destruction, "having great wrath, because he knoweth that he hath but a short time," Rev. 12, 12. Together with his legions of devils, he keeps a sharp lookout for the Christians collectively, and for each one individually. It is to be observed that the "whom"—*tina*—is in the singular number. No Christian at any time is safe from his attacks. Peter speaks from bitter experience. The wily enemy engaged a frail maiden to fell Peter. Peter did not watch; he denied his Lord.—

LUTHER: "He is, moreover, an angry and bitter enemy to you, who have life in Christ. This he cannot endure, and seeks, and meditates only how he may again deprive you of it, and do not, by all means, think that he is far from you, or assails you at a distance; on the contrary, he is encamped as near as possible to you, and round about you; yea, in your own field, that is, in your flesh and blood, where he seeks when he may reach you, and surprise you when you are unguarded, and tries now this artifice, and then that, when he cannot overthrow you with one; now with false confidence, with doubt; then with anger, impatience, avarice, evil lusts, etc., as he sees opportunity, and finds you weak.—Therefore think not that it is a jest, and that he is playing with you, for he is furious and more hungry than any hungry lion, and aims not only at inflicting wounds upon you, nor giving you a thrust, but at devouring you wholly and entirely, so that there remain not anything of you, either as to the soul or the body." (Ep. for 3 p. Trin. New Market Ed., p. 45.)

The dangers which compass the Christians are great indeed, hence the apostle exhorts them: "Be sober, be vigilant!" "Resist steadfast in the faith." Resist *steadfast*, *stereoi*, as *firm* people. How are they such? Through *faith*. Faith relies upon God, upon Christ, and God is stronger than the devil. Faith is the victory that overcometh the world and the devil. "Resist the devil, and he will flee from you," James 4, 7; Matt. 4, 1-11.

MAN.—THE IMAGE OF GOD.

Gen. 2, 7: *And the Lord God formed man of the dust of the ground, and breathed into his nostrils the breath of life; and man became a living soul.*

Man consists of body and soul. His body was formed *of the dust of the ground.* Into man's nostrils God *breathed the breath of life,* i. e., a breath that produced life. This breathing was a creative act of God whereby He made *ex nihilo* the human soul, uniting it with the body. Thus man became a living soul. Adam, as he came from the hands of God, was at once an intelligent, moral being; a person physically mature with mental and moral endowments of a very high order both in kind and degree, as a study of the Mosaic record Gen. 1-3 reveals. Of his passing by degrees through a brute existence till he finally reached a superior state, Scripture knows nothing. Hence the theory of Evolution is wrong.

Gen. 1, 27: *God created man in His own image, in the image of God created He him; male and female created He them.*

"Another antiscriptural assumption hopelessly exploded and untenable even in the light of scientific induction is that primeval man was androgynous. Man was not created a monstrosity, but the first human being was a male person, and on the same day with the first man a second human being, a mature female person, woman, was made, Matt. 19, 4; Gen. 2, 18.21-24. The sexes are not a result of gradual differentiation, but *in the beginning,* when God made the first ancestors of our race, He *made them male and female.*" (Dr. Graebner.)

The text speaks of man's being created in the image of God. What this means the following passages will show.

Col. 3, 10: *Put on the new man, which is renewed in knowledge after the image of Him that created him.*

Eph. 4, 24; *Put on the new man, which after God is created in righteousness and true holiness.*

The context contrasts the *old man* with the *new man.* The *old man* is our sinful nature, *"corrupt according to the deceitful lusts,"* Eph. 4, 22. These deceitful lusts are the ruling principle of the old man. He manifests himself in the *"former conversation,"* in the mode of life before conversion. Such life the apostle calls the walk of the Gentiles. In this condition men have "the understanding darkened, being alienated from the life of God through the ignorance that is in them because of the blindness of their heart." It is the state of unregenerate man, who has not yet learned Christ. See Eph. 4, 17-20. Natural man is *palaios anthropos* pure and simple. The *new man*, on the other hand, is the new life, the new principle, the gifts of grace, given to man in his conversion by the Holy Ghost.

Whence is this new nature? Is it of our own procuring? No. *"The new man* ⁕ ⁕ ⁕ *is created."* The *kainos anthropos* is wrought by a creative act of God in man's conversion, Eph. 2, 10. In Christ man becomes *a new creature*, a *kaine ktisis*, 2 Cor. 5, 17; Gal. 6, 15. Before the Fall, man, made in the likeness of God, was perfectly righteous and holy; his *will* was completely in harmony with the holy will of God; he possessed a deep *knowledge—epignosis—*of God's essence and will. Through the Fall all was lost. Its sad consequences are depicted in such passages as Rom 3, 24; Eph. 5, 8; 2 Cor. 3, 5. Nothing in natural man is of the image of God. In order to restore it, a new-creation had to take place, a renewal had to be effected, hence the texts say "the new man is *renewed*," *"is created."* This is done in the Christians. The new man is created *"in righteousness* and *true holiness,"* and is "renewed in *knowledge.*" *Righteousness* over against the neighbor; *holiness*, true piety, towards God; *knowledge* of God's essence and will are the manifestations of this new life.

This new man is a reflection of the image of God. The text reads: "The new man which *after* God is created," etc., that is, as the passage in Colossians so beautifully explains: *kat eikona tou ktisantos auton, after the image of Him that created him.* Manifestly the apostle alludes to the words spoken by God at the Creation: "Let us make man in our image, after our likeness," Gen. 1, 26. God is a Spirit, hence cannot be represented by any material form. Righteousness, holiness, knowledge—the resemblance to God in these divine perfections—are constituent parts of the image of God. Righteousness, holiness, knowledge, have their seat in the will and the intellect of man. So the image of God has its seat primarily in man's *intellect* and *will.*

In these divine perfections, it is true, a *beginning* only is made in the believers in this life, as is evident also from the admonition:

"*Put on* the new man." Again and again the Christian puts on the new man; he increases in sanctification. By daily contrition and repentance the old Adam is drowned and dies with all sins and evil lusts, and again, a new man daily comes forth and arises. Thus the new man asserts himself. See Eph. 4, 23-32. But since the righteousness, holiness, and knowledge in the believers constitute the incipient restoration of the image of God, the image lost, in its perfect state, was an image of God's righteousness and holiness; the intellect of the first man was an image of the knowledge which is in God.

Luther says: "The divine image in which Adam was created was the noblest and most glorious feature, namely, that neither his reason nor his will had become tainted with the leprosy of sin * * * His intellect was pure, his memory good and fresh, his will upright and true, and, withal, he possessed a very good, pure, and calm conscience, without a single care and without the fear of death * * * Hence, I understand the image of God to have been in Adam essentially, and that by its means Adam not only knew God and believed in Him, as in a benevolent Being, but also led a wholly divine life, void of the fear of death and of every danger."

Gen. 5, 3: *Adam begat a son in his own likeness, after his image; and called him Seth.*

The close proximity in which this statement stands to Gen 5, 1: "In the day that God created man, in the *likeness of God made He him*," adds a peculiar stress to the inherent emphasis in the phrases of the present passage: *in his own* (Adam's) *likeness, after his image.* Adam had fallen into sin; the image of God was lost. Seth was not begotten in the likeness of God, but in the likeness of fallen Adam. Not the image of God was transmitted to Adam's progeny, but Adam's *own* sinful image.—In the believers a beginning is made of the renewal of God's image, as was shown in preceding passages; fully restored it will be in the life to come, as the psalmist says:

Ps. 17, 15: *I will behold Thy face in righteousness: I shall be satisfied, when I awake, with Thy likeness.*

In the name of all believing children of God, the psalmist voices his living hope of a blissful life after death and beyond the grave. —*When I awake* from the sleep of death, *I will behold Thy face: I shall see Thee, God, as Thou art, and by this beatific seeing of Thee I shall be satisfied.* Thou, God, wilt be my meat and my drink, my joy, my salvation. I shall behold Thy face *in righteousness, in perfect innocence and righteousness.* Thy image will be perfectly restored to me, for when I awake, it will be *with Thy likeness.*

What a clear testimony of the Old Testament is this as to the resurrection of the body and the renewal of the image of God! Involuntarily it reminds one of the language of St. John: "We shall be *like Him,* for *we shall see Him as He is*," 1 John 3, 3.

Ps. 139, 14: *I will praise Thee; for I am fearfully and wonderfully made: marvelous are Thy works; and that my soul knoweth right well.*

The almighty dictum of God: "Let there be!" called into existence marvelous works, Gen. 1. The crown of creation, however, is man. Contemplating his own body, this masterpiece of God's workmanship, the psalmist, touched with awe, exclaims: "I am fearfully and wonderfully made," i. e., I am made in an astonishingly wonderful manner.—On the basis of this text the catechumens should be led to see man's superiority over all other creatures of God's handiwork. This knowledge should induce them to say with the inspired singer: "I will praise Thee."

DIVINE PROVIDENCE: 1. PRESERVATION; 2. GOVERNMENT.

Acts 17, 27.28: *He is not far from every one of us: for in Him we live, and move, and have our being.*

Athens, the center of culture, art, literature, and science, knew not God. She proclaimed her ignorance loudly to all the world on one of her temples by the humiliating inscription: "To the Unknown God." Paul saw the city wholly given to idolatry, and his spirit was stirred within him. On the summit of the Areopagus Christianity and paganism met. Confronted by the adherents of the Stoic and the Epicurean systems of philosophy,—pantheists and atheists,—surrounded by temples filled and ornamented with gods and goddesses, the objects of heathen idolatry, Paul discourses on the Creation, the Preservation, and the Government of the world by this "Unknown God."

A close analysis of this speech, which the scope of this article precludes, would show how Paul fearlessly hurls blow after blow with telling effect at the philosophic systems of the day.

From this masterful oration our text is taken. Having told them "that God made the world and all things therein," v. 24, he goes on to say: *"It is He that giveth unto all life, and breath, and all things."* God created the world; it still exists. God created us; we exist. The existence of the world, our own existence, is not due to self-preservation, but to God's sustaining power. He gives to all *life— dzoen*—that is, life in itself; not only that, but He gives to all *breath— pnoe*—the continuation of life by means of breathing; not only that, but He gives to *all things—ta panta*—everything necessary to maintain this life.

The true God, says Paul furthermore, is in no way similar to your dead idols enthroned in the temple of Mars nearby or in the Parthenon below me. In temples made with hands the Deity does not dwell. "He," God, *"is not far from every one of us."* The true God is nigh us, protects us, sustains us. *"In Him we live"*—without Him we should have no life. *"In Him we move"*—without Him we could not move from place to place, we could not lift our arms or open our mouths. *"In Him we have our being"*—without Him we should have no existence at all.

This was strange doctrine to the heathen philosophers of that day; it is a matter of jest to the philosophers of our day. Worldly-wise philosophers, "men of science," as they love to style themselves, whether of the first century or of the twentieth, are but ignorant idolaters.

Hebr. 1, 3: *He upholds all things by the word of His power.*

God upholds, i. e., maintains, *all things,* the whole world. If God would withdraw His hand from this world but for a single moment, it must collapse, chaos must ensue. "God has not forsaken His work, as the architect leaves the house when it is finished, but He preserves all things and governs them by His paternal providence." (Dietrich.) Of God's government the next passage speaks.

Ps. 33, 13-15: *The Lord looketh from heaven; He beholdeth all the sons of men. From the place of His habitation He looketh upon all the inhabitants of the earth. He fashioned their hearts alike; He considereth all their works.*

This beautiful anthropomorphism, representing God as seated upon His throne of majesty, looking down upon the doings of men, forcibly teaches the great truth that God is not unconcerned about the affairs on earth. *"He looketh from heaven,"* and of all the millions of people not one escapes His all-seeing eye, for *"He beholdeth all the sons of men, He looketh upon all the inhabitants of the earth."* Nor is He an idle spectator, allowing men to do as they please, but "He fashioneth their hearts alike," i. e., He fashioneth the hearts of them all, "He considereth all their works." All things and all the affairs of men are in His hands, subject to His control and direction.

Ps. 145, 15.16: *The eyes of all wait upon Thee; and Thou givest them their meat in due season. Thou openest Thine hand, and satisfiest the desire of every living thing.*

Though God can preserve our lives without any earthly means (Moses on Mount Sinai for forty days, Ex. 34, 28), and though He can provide the necessaries of life, directly (Deut. 8, 3.4, Israel in the desert; 1 Kings 17, Elijah; the widow), still it is His good pleasure to provide for our sustenance mediately. In the sweat of our brow we are to earn our livelihood. Who will not work shall not eat, says the apostle. But it is God who preserves our strength, our skill, etc., which enable us to obtain our daily bread. It is He that promised: *"While the earth remaineth, seed time and harvest, cold and heat, and summer and winter, and day and night shall not cease,"* Gen. 8, 22. It is He that "maketh His sun to rise on the evil and on the good, and sendeth rain on the just and on the unjust," Matt. 5, 45. It is He that "giveth rain in his season; He reserveth unto us the appointed weeks of the harvest," Jer. 5, 24. The words of our text, teaching the universality of God's providence, are literally true. Our *meat*, i. e., our food, our nourishment, is a *gift* of God. "*Thou givest* them their meat in due season." And for Him it is a trifling matter to provide for the millions of His creatures. He has but to *open His hand* and they are satisfied. May God through His Word lead us to know this more and more so as to receive our daily bread with thanksgiving! Then while performing the work of our calling industriously, we will commit the success of our labor to God, and thus escape the carking cares for the morrow.

I Pet. 5, 7: *Cast all your care upon Him; for He careth for you.*

The section from which this passage is taken treats of the cross of the Christians. They are exhorted: "Humble yourselves therefore under the mighty hand of God that He may exalt you in due time," v. 6. Closely connected with this Christian humility is confidence, trust, in God. "*Casting all your care upon Him.*" Trials of faith produce cares, spiritual cares. These they are to cast upon God in fervent prayer. But Christians are also oppressed by temporal cares, cares for food, raiment, and the like. These, too, they are to cast upon God. Christians are not to bear their lot stoically, in dull resignation. Thus the children of the world suffer the sorrows that befall them. In its last analysis this sentiment is despair. In the trials of this life, both spiritual and temporal, the thought oftentimes assails the Christian: God has forsaken thee! No, says the apostle, not so. These cares, of whatever nature they may be, are not to make us doubt God's grace and mercy. Whatever may betide: *cast all your care upon Him.*" Why can the Christian cheerfully do that? "*He careth for you.*" It is not a blind fate that rules over your lives, but God, your Father, guides you, protects you, provides for you. "*He careth for you*, He is mindful of you, His fatherly eye rests upon you. He will not allow you to be tempted above that you are able to bear. Hence trust this Father in childlike confidence, and cast *all* your cares— also the temporal cares—upon Him, and rest assured: The Lord will provide.

Matt. 10, 29.30: *Are not two sparrows sold for a farthing? And one of them shall not fall on the ground without your Father. But the very hairs of your head are all numbered.*

God's government extends even to the smallest and most trifling matters. This comforting truth is most beautifully set forth here by an *argumentum a minore ad majus.*

The word *farthing, assarion*, was used among the Greeks to designate any small, insignificant amount. Its value, in our money, is about five-eights of a cent. Two sparrows sold for five-eights of a cent!

"And yet" (kai) God cares for them; *one of them shall not fall on the ground*—dead—without God's permission. To the sparrows God stands but in the relation of the Creator to the creature. To you, however, He stands in the relation of a *father* to a child. Emphatically God is called *"your Father."* The Creator who cares for the meanest of His creatures, e.g., the sparrows, will not He care for you, His child, whom He has bought with a price? Why, you are so precious in His sight that His care extends to *the very hairs of your head*—trifling matter as that may seem. Every one of them is numbered.

"Our Lord's line of argument here is precisely the contrary direction to that which men often follow on this subject. They will say that no doubt God controls great matters, but that it is questionable whether His care extends to such little things as the concerns of an individual man. Jesus says, God takes care of the smallest and most trifling things, and therefore we may be sure He cares for man, who is so much more important." (Broadus.)

Ps. 91, 10: *There shall no evil befall thee, neither shall any plague come nigh thy dwelling.*

This is said of them that have made the Most High their habitation, v. 9, that is to say, the true children of God. They have the assurance that no *evil* shall befall them, and no *plague* shall come nigh unto them. Troubles and afflictions may assail them, the cross will enter their threshold, yet there shall not be a real *evil* in all this, for it comes from the love of God and is sent not for their hurt, but for their good, as St. Paul expressly declares: "We know that *all things* work together *for good* to them that love God," Rom. 8, 28. "Now no chastening for the present seemeth to be joyous, but grievous: nevertheless, afterward it yieldeth the peaceable fruit of righteousness unto them that are exercised thereby," Hebr. 12, 11. "They that sow in tears shall reap in joy. He that goeth forth and weepeth, bearing precious seed, shall doubtless come again with rejoicing, bringing his sheaves with him," Ps. 126, 4.5.

Gen. 50, 20: *Ye thought evil against me; but God meant it unto good, to bring to pass, as it is this day, to save much people alive.*

These words Joseph spoke to his brothers when they craved his forgiveness for the evil they had done unto him. He contrasts the evil intents of men to the good intents of God, showing how God overrules the evil for good. God's government extends also to the evil. It is not his will that evil should be done, but when it is committed, He directs its consequences. Joseph was sold into slavery by his brothers. They *"thought evil against him."* Reason asks, Why did God not prevent this abominable deed? God, looking into the future, *"meant it unto good."* Not only did Joseph become a great man—thus evil turned into good for him—but God, controlling the evil for good, *"brought it to pass to save much people alive."* Among these people were the very brothers of Joseph. It was for their welfare also that God overruled their evil act. They did not deserve it, but God is kind.

Ps. 37, 5: *Commit thy way unto the Lord; trust also in Him; and he shall bring it to pass.*

The entire course of our life is pictured as a way over which we Christians travel to reach our heavenly destination. On this way there are obstructions to impede our progress—trials, cares, afflictions manifold are encountered. What are we to do in the face of such dangers? *"Commit thy way unto the Lord,"* or as St. Peter says, "Cast all your care upon Him," and then, whatever may betide, *trust in Him* as in a most faithful counselor and guide and an ever-present help in every need, *and He shall bring it to pass*, He will bring it to a good end. Appropriating the words of the psalmist, we may confidently exclaim: "Yea, though I walk through the valley of the shadow of death, I will fear no evil: for Thou art with me; Thy rod and Thy staff they comfort me," Ps. 23, 4.

Ps. 103, 13: *Like as a father pitieth his children, so the Lord pitieth them that fear Him.*

All the divine blessings spoken of in the preceding passages the Lord showers upon *"them that fear Him,"* upon the Christians. What impels Him to do it? Any merit or worthiness in us? No. God owes us nothing. "When ye shall have done all those things commanded you, say, We are unprofitable servants: we have done that which was our duty to do," Luke 17, 10. So, even though we had fulfilled all the commandments of God, the idea of merit would be excluded. Moreover, though we belong to the number of *them that fear Him*, yet we are *sinners*, and do not deserve to be helped. David's plea must ever remain ours: "Enter not into judgment with Thy servant." What, then, prompts God to bless us so abundantly? The answer is found in the text: "The Lord *pitieth* them that fear Him," or as the psalmist says in another place: *"For He is good: because His mercy endureth forever,"* Ps. 118, 1. His *pity*, i. e., His *mercy* wherewith He attends the miserable; His *goodness*, i. e., His *love* whereby He bestows blessings—these are His only motives. And God *pitieth* us *"as a father pitieth his children."* A *fatherly* pity, a *fatherly* mercy is one such as a dear father entertains and manifests towards his dear children. And since it is the *Lord* that has pity on us, this mercy is a *divine* mercy, such as only God can entertain and show, one that is altogether perfect, and one *"that endureth forever,"* Ps. 118, 1.

Now, since God does all this purely out of fatherly, divine goodness and mercy, we are constrained to confess with Jacob:

Gen. 32, 10: *I am not worthy of the least of all the mercies, and of all the truth, which Thou hast showed unto Thy servant.*

On returning home, after an absence of twenty years, Jacob reviews his past life. His heart expands with the goodness of his God, for what he beholds is all *mercy*, all *truth*. God had faithfully kept His promises, and overwhelmed him with blessings manifold as from an inexhaustible store. Though Jacob is a *servant* of the Lord, yet he knows that he has deserved none of the things bestowed upon him; they are due only to God's mercy and truth. He is *not worthy of the least of all mercies received.*

This is the sentiment of every true Christian. Hence he asks with the psalmist: "What shall I render unto the Lord for all His benefits toward me?" Ps. 116, 12. And the answer is found in Ps. 118, 1: "O give thanks unto the Lord; for He is good: because His mercy endureth forever."

THE SECOND ARTICLE

THE NAMES OF THE SAVIOR: JESUS—CHRIST—MESSIAH.

Acts 4, 12: *Neither is there salvation in any other: for there is none other name under heaven given among men whereby we must be saved.*

These words are taken from Peter's address before the Sanhedrin, when he was "examined of the good deed done the impotent man," v. 9. This man, "lame from his mother's womb," 3, 2, stood before them whole, Peter declared, "by the name of Jesus Christ of Nazareth, whom ye crucified, whom God raised from the dead," v. 10. This Jesus Christ of Nazareth is the Messiah, v. 11, in whom alone there is salvation, not only from disease and ills of the body, as in the case of this lame man, but from sin, spiritual disease, of which bodily disease is but the consequence.

"*And there is not in another the salvation,*" *kai ouk estin en allo oudeni he soteria.* The meaning of the word *salvation, soteria,* clear in itself according to New Testament usage, is enforced by the article *he, the* salvation. It is the salvation *kat exochen,* the salvation the Messiah was to bring according to prophecy, Luke 4, 18 ff. This salvation consists first and foremost in the forgiveness of sins. Zacharias, the priest, recapitulating the prophecies of the Old Testament, says in his hymn of praise concerning the Child Jesus that He should "give knowledge of *salvation* unto His people *in remission of their sins,*" *tou dounai gnosin soterias to lao autou en afesei hamartion auton,* Luke 1, 77. "Jesus shall *save* His people *from their sins,*" Matt. 1, 21. "Him," Jesus, "hath God exalted with His right hand to be a Prince and a *Savior,* for to give repentance to Israel, and *forgiveness of sins,*" Acts 5, 31.—But where there is salvation from sin, there is also deliverance from *death,* 2 Cor. 7, 10 (*soteria* opposed to *thanatos*), from *perdition,* Phil. 1, 28 (soteria opposed to apoleia), from the *wrath of God*, 1 Thess. 5, 9 (*soteria* opposed to *orge*)   This salvation we now possess by faith; the fruition thereof, full, final, complete salvation, will be ours in yonder life.   (For *soteria* thus used see 1 Pet. 1, 5; Rom. 13, 11, *et al.*)

Now this *salvation*, this deliverance·from sin, "*is not in another.*" Hence, Jesus is the *only Savior*.   It is He only that can "save that which was lost," Luke 19, 10.   The second clause: "*For there is none other name*," etc., is explanatory to the first.   The phrases: "*none other name under heaven*," and "*given among men*," emphatically insist upon the truth expressed in the preceding clause: "*there is not in another the salvation.*"   Search the broad expanse of heaven from the rising to the setting sun, inquire among the millions of men of all ages and climes for another savior, your search will be in vain. Salvation is in Jesus alone.—This name of Jesus Christ is given "*among men*," among all men; He is the Savior of all mankind, "the Savior of the world," *ho soter tou kosmou*, John 4, 42; 1 John 4, 14. This name is *given* among men.   Salvation in Christ is a free gift of God.   The plan of saving fallen mankind had its origin in God, not in the power or wisdom of men.   "God so loved the world that He gave His only-begotten Son," John 3, 16; 17, 4; 1 Cor. 3, 5; Gal. 1, 4.   Thanks be to God for His unspeakable gift! 2 Cor. 9, 15.

Matt. 1, 21: *She shall bring forth a son, and thou shalt call His name* JESUS: *for He shall save His people from their sins.*

Here we have the authentic interpretation of the name *Jesus.* The angel of the Lord appeared unto Joseph and said to him: "Thou shalt call His name Jesus."   This angel was a messenger sent by God Himself. His message is God's will.   God willed that His Son and Mary's son should be called *Jesus.*   Why was He so called?   "For"—indicates the reason for giving Him this name—"He shall *save.*"   Jesus means *Savior.*   God's names are facts.   He is called Jesus, Savior, because He is the Savior of His people.

The Hebrew equivalent for this Greek form is Joshua or Jeshua, a contraction of Jehoshua, which signifies: "Jehovah is Helper," "Jehovah is Savior."   The son of Nun, the successor of Moses, who led the Israelites into the Promised Land, was called Joshua, Josh. 1,1. Jeshua was the leader of the Jews at the time of the return from the Babylonish captivity.   Ezra 2, 2; 3, 8.   Through these Joshuas, Jehovah, the Lord, helped His people.   Both these men were types of our Savior in respect to His name and work.   Like Joshua, who led Israel into the land of promise, Canaan, so Jesus, "the Captain of our salvation," Hebr. 2, 10, delivers us from all dangers, and leads us into the heavenly Canaan.   Like Jeshua, the high-priest, who was instrumental in bringing the Jews back from captivity, so Jesus, our High-priest, delivers us from bondage of Satan.

But there is a great difference between these Joshuas and our

Lord Jesus. These Joshuas were but mere men, whom God chose as His instruments, and through whom He helped His chosen people. Jesus, indeed, is true man, but at the same time He is true God, the Jehovah Himself, who saves. Thus the name *Jesus*—Helper, Savior—applies to Him preeminently. Again, whilst these Joshuas were but "saviors" in temporal things, Jesus *saves* His people *from their sins*, the cause and source of all evil.—The majority of the Jews expected a savior from the hated rule of the Romans. Contrary to their carnal expectations, the salvation which Jesus brought was a salvation from sin. Through sin the world was lost, eternally lost. "None of them can by any means redeem his brother, nor give to God a ransom for him; for the redemption of their soul is precious, and it ceaseth forever," Ps. 49, 8.9. The only salvation is in this Jesus. Emphatically the text says: *autos gar sosei*—"*He shall save*," i. e., *He and no other* can save. Jesus is the only Savior from sin. He is to save *His people*, that is, in the first place, the lost sheep of the house of Israel, the Jews; but then also the Gentiles, who by the Gospel were to be made His people. Thus this Jesus is the true *Emmanuel*, the God-with-us, v. 23.—This passage, so sublimely simple, is a powerful weapon against the error of Pelagius of old, who taught that mankind is still after the Fall brought into the world as pure and innocent as the first pair were before the Fall, and that therefore Christ was sent into the world merely to show us by His example how to lead a virtuous life. This soul-destroying error is rampant even to-day. No, Jesus means *Savior*. —Furthermore, the supposition that Christ, even though sin had not entered into the world, would have become man, in order to provide mankind with a unifying head, is a philosophical speculation. Scripture knows nothing thereof. The question, *Cur Deus homo?* is implicitly answered in the very definition of the name Jesus: *He shall save.* Explicitly the purpose of His coming into the flesh is stated in such passages as 1 Tim. 1, 15: "Christ Jesus came into the world *to save sinners*," *hamartolous sosai.* Luke 19, 10: "The Son of Man is come *to seek and save that which was lost.*" Cf. Gal. 4, 4.5 *et al.* Hence the dictum of Augustine is scriptural: "Tolle morbos, tolle vulnera, et nulla est causa medicinae. Si homo non periisset, Filius hominis non venisset." Hollaz expresses the same thought thus: "Filius Dei non assumsisset carnem, si homo non peccasset."

Ps. 45, 7: *Thou lovest righteousness, and hatest wickedness: therefore God, Thy God, hath anointed Thee with the oil of gladness above Thy fellows.*

It is not within the province of this article to go into a detailed analysis of the Psalm. But since it is the duty of the catechetical instructor in his private study to enter upon the context, in order, among other things, to ascertain who the person addressed "Thou" and adored as "God" is; and, moreover, since a great number of commentators, influenced by the anti-Messianic school, endeavors to empty the Psalm of its true meaning, a few remarks relative to this matter may be welcomed by some of our readers.

The Psalm consists mainly of two parts, with an introduction and a conclusion. Vv. 2-9 describe the King and Bridegroom; vv. 10-17 treat of the bride. Many bewildering conjectures have been made as to who this royal bridegroom is. Some believe Solomon's marriage to an Egyptian princess to be celebrated here; others think of Ahab's nuptials to Jezebel; others again have thought of identifying the king in the Psalm with a Persian monarch; Ewald contends that it is Jeroboam II of Israel; still others, observing that "the language is a world too wide for the best and greatest of Jewish kings," have given up all hope of identification.—We shall not speak of the exegetical violence done to the text by the explanations mentioned above. For us Lutherans, who are firm believers in the inspiration of the Scriptures, the question is of easy solution. *The Epistle to the Hebrews* (1, 8-10) *refers the very words of our text to Christ.* There we read: "But unto *the Son* He saith, Thy throne, O God, is for ever and ever." Beyond the shadow of a doubt *that establishes the Messianic character* of the Psalm. Scriptura Scripturam interpretatur.

The royal bridegroom is Christ. The *King,* v. 1, is *"fairer than all the children of men,"* v. 2. The King belongs to the class called "children of men"; He is true man, but we are at once given to understand that He is not a mere man. He is at the same time very God, for of this King it is said: *"Thy throne, O God, is forever and ever,"* v. 6. This King, who is both true man and true God, is none other than Christ. And of Him who is addressed here as, "O God," the text says: *"Thou* (Christ) *lovest righteousness, and hatest wickedness: therefore, O God,* (Christ), *Thy God* (the Father) *hath anointed Thee with the oil of gladness,"* etc.

In order to do away with the clear testimony of the deity of Christ in v. 6: "Thy throne, O God, is forever and ever," three renderings have been suggested by the leaders of the anti-Messianic school: 1. "Thy throne is the throne of God," etc., a translation which the Revised Version has placed in the margin. 2. "Thy God's throne is," etc. 3. "Thy throne is God," etc. A little reflection will reveal what has inspired these impossible renderings: this buttress for the truth of the Divinity of Christ must be demolished! Aside from the clear testimony in the Epistle to the Hebrews: "But unto the *Son* he saith, *Thy* throne, O God, is for ever and ever," all three translations are not only unnatural harsh, and very questionable grammatically, but wholly untenable, as Hengstenberg has clearly shown in his *Christologie.* In the Hebrew the vocative is used: O God. So also all the older versions have correctly understood the text.—Again, in v. 7: "Therefore, O God, Thy God hath anointed Thee," etc., the Messiah, who was addressed "O God" in v. 6, is again called *God.* The *King,* who is God, is discriminated from God. Two distinct persons of the God-head are mentioned. The Messiah is God, and He who anoints Him is God. The same word—*Elohim*—is used of both; the one is God as much as the other. These considerations may suffice to show that the Psalm is Messianic. The royal bridegroom is Christ, true man and true God in one person. Of Him our text says: "Thou lovest righteousness," etc.

Now to the matter in hand. "Therefore, O God, Thy God has anointed Thee with the oil of gladness above Thy fellows." From the Hebrew word signifying *anointed* the proper noun *Messiah* has been derived. The Greek word *Christos, Christ,* from *chrio,* signifies the same thing —*anointed.* Hence our Savior is called by either name, *Messiah* or *the Christ.* After that memorable interview with our Lord, Andrew finding his brother Peter, says to him: "We have found the *Messias, ton Messian,* which is, being interpreted, the *Christ, ho Christos,*" John 1, 41. See also John 4, 24.—"Ut nomen Jesus ratione primae originis Hebraeum est, ita cognomen Christus est Graecum. Quod ergo Salvator noster Hebraea et Graeca appellatione insignitur, per illud insinuatur, quod et Judaeorum et gentium, id est, omnium omnino hominum salvator sit." Gerhard, Baier III, p. 19.—Christ was anointed above His *"fellows."* These *"fellows,"* i. e., *associates, companions,* were, first and foremost, since the Psalm speaks of the Messiah as our King, the kings of the Old Testament, but also the prophets and the high-priests. Elisha, the prophet, was anointed; Aaron, the high-priest, was anointed; David, the king, was anointed, before taking office. They were *anointed with oil,* Lev. 4, 3; 6, 20; Ex. 28, 41; 29, 7; 1 Sam, 9, 16; 15, 1; 2 Sam. 23, 1. Those thus anointed and consecrated for their work were called *the Lord's anointed,* 1 Sam, 16, 6; Ps. 84, 9; Is. 45, 1. The anointment with oil was an emblem of the unction with the Holy Ghost. As the *"fellows"* of Christ were anointed with oil, so He was anointed with oil —the *oil of gladness.* Christ's being anointed does not mean that He was literally anointed with oil, but that as these *fellows* of His were anointed for the discharge of their office as priests or prophets or kings, so Christ was set apart by God to be our Priest, Prophet, and King. Ps. 118, 4; Deut. 18, 15; Ps. 2, 72. The *oil of gladness* wherewith Christ was anointed is *the Holy Ghost.* God *anointed* Jesus of Nazareth *with the Holy Ghost,*" Acts 10, 38. "The Spirit of the Lord is upon me," says the Messiah, "because He has anointed me," Is. 61, 1. The text says: "Therefore, O God (Christ), Thy God (Father) has anointed Thee." The Father, who is God, anoints the Son, who is God. How is this to be understood? Kromayer says: *"He theotes chrisis tes anthropotetos* . . . . We thought fit to quote this dictum of the Greek fathers as an axiom to show that Christ has been anointed not according to His *divine nature,* but *according to His human nature;* that the divine nature has rather been the anointing than the anointed. For to Him who by nature possesses all things no gifts can be conferred. But when it is said in Ps. 45, 8 that God was anointed, this is an idiomatic proposition of the first genus of the *communicatio idiomatum,* in which the properties of the natures are ascribed to the person *in concreto.* In the cited passage this property is the anointment or collation of gifts, which is predicated of the person, designated in this place from the divine nature, just as I say: God has shed his own blood,' Acts 20, 28." (Baier III, p. 101.) Christ is a *born* King, John 18, 37; Is. 9, 6.7; Matt. 2, 2.11, by virtue of the personal union of the two natures.—The Spirit is called the "oil of *gladness*," because of the delight wherewith Christ was filled in carrying out His great work of redemption, and because He is a Spirit that works gladness, joy. This Spirit with whom Christ is anointed, He communicates to His subjects. Christ was anointed *above*, i. e,, *more than*, his fellows. The prophets, for example, were inspired on *particular* occasions only to deliver special messages. The source of their knowledge was *inspiration*. The Messiah, however, was *continually* filled with the Spirit of God. The source of His knowledge was not inspiration, but *incarnation*. God gave Him the Spirit *without measure, ouk ek metrou*, John 3, 34, that is, He possessed *infinite* knowledge, *infinite* wisdom, also according to His human nature. Christ is the Anointed of the Lord preeminently.

JESUS CHRIST IS TRUE GOD, 1. BECAUSE THE SCRIPTURES ASCRIBE DI-

VINE NAMES TO HIM.

1 John 5, 20 St. John writes: *And we know that the Son of God is come, and hath given us an understanding, that we may know Him that is true, and we are in Him that is true, even in His Son Jesus Christ. This is the true God and eternal life.*

Two persons of the Trinity are here discriminated: "*Him that is true*," *ton alethinon*, and "*The Son of God*," "*His Son*," i. e., the Father and the Son. The Son has given us an understanding of "Him that is true," of the Father. Christ has taught us to know the Father as the true God.

NOTE.—*Hina ginoskomen ton alethinon*—"that we might know the True One." "Him that is true" in our Bible is a translation of *ton alethinon*—"*the True One.*" What is the meaning of the word *alethinos*? It should be discriminated from *alethes*, true, truthful, faithful. *Alethinos* means *true* in the sense of *real, genuine*, as contrasted with the fictitious, Luke 16, 11; John 1, 9; with the typical, as John 6, 32. *Theos alethes* would mean, the *true*, i. e., the faithful God, who is true to His promises, who does not deceive; *theos alethinos*, however, expresses the thought that this God is the *true*, i. e., the real, the very God, in opposition to idols, to fictitious gods. Dr. Tittman says: "*alethes alethinos*. Non videntur synonyma, sed tamen distinguenda sunt. Nam *alethes* in N.T. sensu morali tantum dicitur: *theos alethes*, Joh. 3, 33. Sed *alethes* est, qui non tantum nomen habet et speciem, sed veram naturam et indolem, quae nomini conveniat. Joh. 1, 9: *fos alethinon*; 6, 32: *arton alethinon*; 17, 3: *ton monon alethinon theon*. Occurrit tantum apud Johannem et in ep. ad Hebraeos."

(The Synonyms of the New Testament, vol. II, p. 28.)

Through the Son, in whom we believe, we are in "Him that is true," we have communion with the Father. The Father is the true God. And now, who is this Son of God, this Jesus Christ, who has mediated this blissful knowledge to us? *"This"—houtos—*with emphasis at the head of the sentence, pointing back to the last words of the preceding verse: Jesus Christ—*"This"* Son, Jesus Christ, *is* Himself *the true God,* as well as the Father. This is the truth to be imparted in our text, v. 20b. The Father is God, but this Son, too, who has shown us the Father is *ho alethinos theos—"the true God,"* so that being in Christ, we in Christ already have the true God. Thus, according to the obvious connection, the expressions: "the Son of God," "His Son," are to be understood, and only then do we understand them aright, if we know and believe: "the Son of God" is "the true God." Thus only, too, is there a progress of thought in the passage.—To refer the pronoun "this"—*houtos* to "Him that is true," the Father, would destroy all thought-connection and produce a senseless, unbearable tautology. The meaning then would be: "He that is true," the Father—God—of whom the Son of God gave us an understanding, is the true God: The true God is the true God! That would be *idem per idem!* Obviously the demonstrative pronoun *houtos—*"this"—refers to "Jesus Christ," to which expression it stands in such immediate proximity, and not to "Him that is true," i. e., the Father. The clear, unmistakable thought-connection is this: "The Son of God," v. 20a, is "the true God," v. 20b.

> NOTE. "The question is whether the demonstrative pronoun *houtos,* 'this,' points back to 'Him that is true' or to 'His Son Jesus Christ.' . . . . Which relation is demanded by the usage of language? The most natural thing is to refer such a demonstrative as *houtos,* 'this,' when several persons have been mentioned before, to the one last named. Thus in John 1, 2 *houtos,* 'this'—'The same *houtos* was in the beginning with God'—refers to *ho logos,* 'the Word,' the person last named in v. 1. . . . . . Now in our passage 'His Son Jesus Christ' is not only the subject which immediately precedes the demonstrative 'this,' but it is also the emphasized subject. The apostle wishes to bring the thought into prominence that the Son of God has imparted this understanding, this knowledge of 'Him that is true' to us, and that we are in the Father because we are in the Son, that the Son has mediated the communion with the Father for us. Hence the relation of the *houtos* to Christ is linguistically the only one justifiable." (Dr. Stoeckhardt in *Lehre und Wehre,* vol. 40, p. 293.)

Additional proof that the pronoun "this" refers to "Jesus Christ" is found in the second predicate: *kai he dzoe aionios, "and the eternal life."* In St. John the thought constantly recurs that only in Christ Jesus, the Son of God, we have eternal life, that He is the eternal life. The purpose of St. John's Gospel is expressed thus: "These are written, that ye might believe that Jesus is the Christ, the Son of God, and that believing *ye might have life* through His name," John 20, 31.—"God sent His only-begotten Son into the world that *we might live* through

Him," 1 John, 4, 9. In St. John not the Father, but only the Son is called directly: *life, eternal life.* "In Him (the Logos) was *life,* and the *life* was the light of men," John 1, 4.—"Jesus said to her: I am the Resurrection and *the Life,*" John 11, 25.—"Jesus saith unto him, I am the Way, the Truth, and *the Life;* no man cometh unto the Father but by me," John 14, 6. "And this is the record that God hath given to us *eternal life,* and this life is in His Son," 1 John 5, 11.12. In John 1, 1 Christ is called *ho logos tes dzoes,* and in v. 2 He is not only called *dzoe,* but *he dzoe he aionios,* the very same appellation given Him in our text, so that the conclusion of the epistle stands in the most striking harmony with its beginning. In the beginning we read: "We have seen it and bear witness and show unto you that *eternal life,*" i. e., Jesus Christ; and in the close: "This is the true God and *the eternal life.*" Truly, St. John explains himself. Beyond the shadow of a doubt this latter designation in our text: *the eternal life,* signifies Christ. Grammar, context, *usus loquendi—all* say *una voce:* Jesus Christ is the true God!

A further remark. In the interest of the Subordination theory a great theological find is supposed to have been made by modern theology. Christ, it is said, is, indeed, called *theos* (God) in the predicate, but never *ho theos* (the God) in the subject. This discovery has been made, as Meyer would express it, to mark "the delicate line of separation between the Father and the Son." What nonsensical twaddle is this: Christ is called *theos* in the predicate, but never *ho theos* in the subject! That is learned nonsense. Is it not immaterial whether I say, "This man, who witnessed the ceremony, is President Roosevelt," or, "President Roosevelt witnessed the ceremony"? In the one case the name completes the predicate verb in the sentence, in the other it is the subject; in both, it designates the same man—Roosevelt. If Christ is called *theos* or *ho theos* anywhere, whether in the subject or in the predicate, He is *theos,* God, and all that name implies—the one true God, besides whom there is no other God. Or are the names *theos, ho theos tituli sine re?*—Again, it is said where *God* forms the subject God the Father is always meant. Is that true? No. Let us turn to Acts 20, 28: "Take heed unto yourselves . . . . . to feed the Church of *God,* which He hath purchased with His own blood." And still again, is Christ never called *ho theos,* as some of the modern theologians maintain? Is not Hebr. 1, 8.9 plain enough: "But unto the Son He saith, Thy Throne, *O God, ho theos,* is forever and ever"? Did not Thomas say to Jesus: "My Lord and *my God"—ho theos mou?* John 20, 28. Does not Paul speak of this Jesus as *"our great God* and Savior Jesus Christ" —*tou megalou theou kai soteros hemon Iesou Christou?* Tit. 2, 13. What spirit, then, actuates these modern theologians to belittle our Savior, who "is over all, God blessed for ever"? Rom. 9, 5.—Returning to our text, let us observe that Christ is not only called *theos* (God),— this would be sufficient for any Christian reader to know who Christ is,— but He is called *ho theos, the* God, and in order to assert His divinity in the strongest terms possible, the word *alethinos*, true, is added. Christ is *ho alethinos theos*. Let us ponder each word: Christ is *God;* He is *the* God; He is the *true* God.

Now, where is the "delicate line of separation between the Father and the Son"? It exists only in the minds of the modern theologians. By assuming this "delicate line of separation," they delicately, veiledly, deny the deity of Christ. This "delicate line of separation," in its last analysis, contains the same heresy that Arius indelicately, but honestly, taught. He, too, maintained, among other things, that Christ might be called *theos* and *logos*, but in an *inexact* way.—Subordinationism is but one remove from Arianism.—Deus nos impleat odio novae theologiae!

Rom. 9, 5: *"Whose are the fathers, and of whom as concerning the flesh Christ came, who is over all God, blessed for ever. Amen.*

The paragraph of which this passage forms a part enumerates the great prerogatives vouchsafed to the Jews. The apostle writes: "Who are Israelites, to whom pertaineth the adoption and the glory, and the covenants, and the giving of the Law, and the service of God, and the promises." Exalted prerogatives, indeed! The polysyndeton: and—and—and, is to arrest the attention of the readers, to cause them to ponder each prerogative separately, so that they may see, feel, realize how highly favored they are. In our text this enumeration continues: *"and whose are the fathers,"* sc., Abraham, Isaac, and Jacob. To be descended from such illustrous ancestors, from men so highly honored of God, was a great distinction. But a greater and higher advantage follows: *"and of whom"*—of the Israelites—*"Christ came."* To appreciate this prerogative duly, the apostle sets forth who Christ is. *"Concerning the flesh"*—*kata sarka*—*as to the flesh,* according to His human nature, He is a descendant of the Jews, *a true man.* Why are they to account Christ's being born among them such a great honor? The climax of the whole grand thought follows, setting forth the prerogatives of the Jews in their strongest light. This Christ, who is true man, is at the same time *"over all God,"*—*ho on epi panton theos,*—the supreme God, to whom the sacred doxology applies: *"blessed for ever."*

Here Paul directly asserts Christ to be very God. He is God, over all God, God in the fullest, highest sense of the word. This is the plain, simple meaning of this grand text, which any Christian reader, not biased by dogmatical prejudices, readily apprehends.

Were it not for the fact that so many strenuous efforts had been made, especially by such as deny the divinity of Christ, to torture the text and thus empty it of its sublime truth, our task were done so far as this passage is concerned. However, the objections raised compel us to enter somewhat more deeply into a discussion of the matter.

Let us again look at the text. It reads: *"Of whom as concerning the flesh Christ came who is—."* What is the antecedent of *who?* Obviously: *Christ*. The apostle speaks of no one else. So we read on: "*who*," *sc.*, Christ, "*is over all God.*" The plain, grammatical construction demands the "who" clause to be referred to Christ, and the sense therefore is: Christ is the supreme God.

Again, if we look at the thought-connection, the result will be the same. In the clause: "of whom as concerning the flesh Christ came," the limitation, "*as concerning the flesh*," obviously implies a contrast and demands a correlative. We naturally ask: If Christ is descended from the Jews as to the flesh, as to His human nature, what, then, is He as to His higher nature? And the answer is: He is "*over all God.*" Here is the unmistakable antithesis to *kata sarka*. Or does the *kata sarka*, as some contend, not demand an antithesis? Why, then the phrase: "as concerning the flesh," is entirely superfluous, and the apostle might have simply written: "of whom Christ came." Stuart's remark is to the point: "But if He, Christ, had no other nature, why should such a distinction as is implied by *kata sarka* be here designated? Would a sacred writer say of David, for example, that he was descended from Abraham *kata sarka*? If this should be said, it would imply that *kata pneuma* he was not descended from Abraham, but from some one else. But here, the other nature of Christ is designated by the succeeding phrase, *ho on epi panton theos.*" (Stuart, *Com. on Romans*, p 376.)

Why raise difficulties here where the text is so plain? Why willfully try to close one's eyes to the force of the passage? Unbelief is at the bottom of it all. Christ is to be dethroned. The one thing all objections have in common is this: the doxology is to be referred to the Father. Thus the great truth that Christ is called God is to be eliminated. But all such exegetical tricks are in vain. The words of Luther, uttered on another occasion, apply here also: "Der Text steht zu gewaltig da."

Which are some of the suggestions made as to another reading of the text? Some say: Place a period after the word "all." The words then read: "Of whom as concerning the flesh Christ came, who is over all. God blessed for ever." The doxology, "God blessed for ever," as has been said, is to apply to God the Father. How, we ask, is a doxology to the Father possible here? Nothing is said of the Father in the context. The subject spoken of is Christ. And where, then, is the antithesis to *kata sarka*? Furthermore, a doxology pertaining to the Father is out of place here, because it breaks the trend of thought too abruptly. The reader is in no way prepared for it, because no reason for it has been given. No, the apostle's mind is not given to such freakish, clownish jumps.—In addition to all this the thought-connection of the paragraph manifests the utter absurdity of introducing a doxology to the Father. Says *Stuart*, "There is something incongruous in a doxology here to God the Father. The apostle is here expressing the deepest and most unfeigned regret of his soul, that, notwithstanding the exalted and peculiar privileges of the Jewish nation, they had by their unbelief forfeited them all, and made themselves obnoxious to a most terrible condemnation. To break out into a doxology here would be (as Flatt suggests) like saying: 'These special privileges have, by being abused, contributed greatly to enhance the guilt and punishment of the Jewish nation; God be thanked that He has given them such privileges!' It is a duty, indeed, to be grateful for blessings which are bestowed, but— all in its proper place. Doxologies are not appropriate to paragraphs, which give an account of mercies abused, and deep guilt contracted."

But, suppose for the sake of argument, we should grant the untenable punctuation of the sentence given above, and have the text read: "Of whom concerning the flesh Christ came who is over all,"—does not the clause, *"who is over all,"* say that Christ is the supreme God, that He is, as the Epistle to the Ephesians puts it, "far above all principality, and power, and might, and dominion, and every name that is named, not only in this world, but also in that which is to come," and that all things are put under his feet? If Christ is "over all," if all things are under His feet, is He not true God? Most emphatically, yes. For to explain *"who is over all"* as meaning, who is over all the fathers, i. e., greater than all the fathers, is an exegesis so frigid and says so little in the context that it cannot be entertained for a minute. But the attempt to thus distort the text shows to what desperate straits the opponents are driven. *Hodge* pointedly remarks: " *'Over all,'* i. e., over all things, not over all persons. The *panton* is neuter, and not masculine; see Acts 10, 37; 1 Cor. 15, 28. It is supremacy over the universe which is here expressed."

But rather than concede that Christ is called God in our text, as is so plainly done, the rationalists unmercifully break its grammatical construction, violate the context, and what not. Others place a period after the term *sarka*, making the passage read thus: "Of whom Christ came as concerning the flesh." The relative clause following, which is so intimately connected with the preceding: "who is over all God blessed for ever,"—*ho on epi panton theos eulogetos eis tous aionas,*—they treat as an independent sentence embodying an entirely new thought. It has nothing whatever to do, they say, with Christ mentioned in the preceding clause. They translate: "He who is over all God blessed for ever," and contend the doxology refers to God the Father, not to Christ. The reasons urged against the false rendering noted above apply with equal force to this one: 1. Christ is the immediate subject of the discourse, not the Father. 2. A doxology to the Father is too abrupt here. 3. It is incongruous. Aside from these arguments: 4. There is no antithesis to *kata sarka.*—"If God were to be the subject of a new, independent sentence and were at the same time to be designated as the one who is over all, *ho epi panton theos* without *on* would have been the adequate expression according to the analogy of similar Greek locutions, as, for example, *ho epi ton hoplon, ho epi ton huperetikon, ho epi tes frouras, ho epi ton ergon.* With the Greek fathers the constant designation of

God is *ho epi panton theos."* (Stoeckhardt, *Roemerbrief*, p. 419.)

Thus we see it is contrary to the grammatical arrangement of the text to look upon the "who" clause as an independent sentence. On the other hand, the *ho on* in our text, that is to say, the article *ho* followed by the participle *on*, is equivalent to *hos esti, who is.* This construction is often found in the Greek language, e. *g.*, John 1, 18; 3, 13; 12, 17; 2 Cor. 11, 31. The truth of the matter is: the *ho on, who is,* is intimately connected with the principal clause. The antecedent of "who" is *Christ*, and the sentence must read: *"Christ who is .. : . . . . . blessed for ever."*

Again, if we examine the form of the doxology as proposed by the opponents, we find it to be: *theos eulogetos—God blessed.* Says *Hodge:* "No such doxology occurs in all the Bible. That is, the uniform expression is, 'Blessed be God,' and never, 'God be blessed.' The word *blessed* always stands first, and the word *God* after it with the article. . . . . . See Ps. 31, 21; 72, 18.19; 51, 13; 68, 35; 89, 52; Gen. 9, 26; Ex. 18, 10, and a multitude of other examples. In all these and similar passages, the expression is, *Blessed be God*, or *Blessed be the Lord*, and never, *God blessed*, or *Lord blessed*. This being the case, it is altogether incredible that Paul, whose ear must have been perfectly familiar with this constantly recurring formula of praise, should, in this solitary instance, have departed from the established usage. This passage, therefore, cannot be considered as a doxology, or an ascription of praise to God, and rendered *God be blessed*, but must be taken as a declaration, *who is blessed;* see chap. 1, 25: 'The Creator, who is blessed for ever.' 2 Cor. 11, 31: 'The God and Father of our Lord Jesus Christ, who is blessed for evermore.' See Matt. 21, 9; Luke 1, 68; 2 Cor. 1, 3; Eph. 1, 3; 1 Pet. 1, 3. In these and all other cases where, as here, the copula is omitted, it is *eulogetos ho theos.* Where the relative and verb are used, then it is not an exclamation but an affirmation, as Rom. 1, 25: *ton ktisanta hos estin eulogetos eis tous aionas. Amen.* 2 Cor. 11, 31: *ho theos kai pater—ho on eulogetos eis tous aionas;* and here: *Christos, ho on epi panton theos, eulogetos eis tous aionas.* To separate this passage from the class to which it obviously belongs, and to make it a solitary exception, is to do violence to the text." (Comm. on Rom., p. 474.)—We close the discussion with the words of *Bengel,* quoted in Dr. Stoeckhardt's excellent *Commentary on Romans:* "Impense laetari debemus, quod in hac solemni descriptione Christus tam aperte Deus appellatur."

John 20, 28: *Thomas answered and said unto him, My Lord and my God!*

On the evening of His resurrection, Christ appeared to His disciples. Thomas alone was absent. The disciples tell him: "We have seen the Lord." Say what they will it takes no effect. "Except I shall see in His hands the print of the nails, and put my finger into the print of the nails, and thrust my hand into His side, I will not believe." Poor

Thomas, his faith had vanished! Eight days later Christ agaih appears to His disciples, Thomas included. Overpowered by the majesty and grace of his Savior, Thomas cried out: "*My Lord and my God!*"—*ho kurios mou, kai ho theos mou.* Not only does he call *Christ* God, but *ho theos,* the one, the *true* God, like as the Father.—A clearer proof for the divinity of Christ is hardly imaginable. And yet rationalists have dared to lay violent hands even to this text. Thomas's confession, they assert, was merely an expression of surprise, an irrevelant cry of an astonished person! Is it not rather surprising what unbelievable lies unbelievers believe? These words of Thomas an expression of surprise! How unspeakably absurd! What brazen effrontery! Does not the text clearly read: "Thomas said *unto Him*"? If these words had been an exclamation of surprise, they would have been blasphemy, and Christ would not have been slow to rebuke Thomas sharply. No; Thomas speaks the truth: Christ is *ho theos.* Christ has no reproof for Thomas (cf. Acts 14, 13-15; Rev. 22, 8.9), hence He tacitly acknowledges: Thomas, thou hast spoken truly; I am God. Moreover, the Lord lauds this confession as an evidence of true faith, to which the erstwhile doubting, unbelieving disciple had now again attained. "Jesus saith unto him, Thomas, because thou hast seen me, thou hast *believed.*" Believed what? That Jesus is his Lord and his God. Christ wills His disciples to believe that He is *ho kurios kai ho theos.*—And what was St. John's purpose in recording this incident also? It was in full keeping with the object for which he wrote the whole Gospel. Only two verses further on he says: "These are written that ye might believe that Jesus is the Christ, the Son of God, and that, believing, ye might have life through His name," v. 30.

Luther's sermon on this text is grand. Two short extracts may find a place here:

"There can be no forgiveness of sins nor salvation, where this article of the resurrection of Christ is not believed, because in it lies all power of faith and of eternal life; as Paul says, 1 Cor. 15, 14.17.18: 'If Christ be not risen, then is our preaching vain, and your faith is also vain; ye are yet in your sins. Then they also which are fallen asleep in Jesus are perished.' Thither St. Thomas also wills to go, he wills not to be saved, but to be lost, because he will not believe that Christ has risen from the dead. And in such unbelief he would have been lost and damned, if Christ through manifestation of Himself had not saved him therefrom." (St. L. ed. XI, 771.)

"This is the power of the resurrection of Christ that Thomas, formerly more stubborn in unbelief than all the rest, is suddenly changed into a different man, who now frankly confesses, not only that he believes the fact of Christ's resurrection, but becomes so illumined through the power of the resurrection of Christ that he now also most firmly believes and confesses that Christ, his Lord, is true God and man, through whom, as he has now been saved from unbelief, the fountain of all sin, so he will also be raised by Him on the last day from death, and live with him in unspeakable glory and blessedness." *(Ibid.,* p. 777.)

Jer. 23, 6: *This is His name whereby He shall be called,* THE LORD, OUR RIGHTEOUSNESS.

Lord, i. e., Jehovah, is the exalted name here attributed to Christ. To see the full force of this name as applied to Christ, we must inquire into the meaning of the term Jehovah.—God, appearing to Moses in the burning bush, commissioned him to bring the children of Israel out of Egypt, to deliver them from the hands of Pharaoh, Ex. 3, 10.11. Timidly Moses asks: "Behold, when I come unto the children of Israel, and shall say unto them, The God of your fathers hath sent me unto you; and they shall say unto me, What is His name? what shall I say unto them? And God said unto Moses, I AM THAT I AM, (ehyeh asher ehyeh); and He said, Thus shalt thou say unto the children of Israel, I AM (ehyeh) hath sent me unto you."—From the same root of which Ehyeh is formed, the proper names of the Deity *Jahve* or *Jehovah* are etymologically derived. Hence, in the very next verse God says to Moses: "Thou shalt say unto the children of Israel, *Jehovah* (the Lord) . . . . . hath sent me unto you." Thus, from this revelation of Himself, we learn the authentic interpretation of the name *Jehovah* to be: "I Am That I Am," or briefly, "I Am." Jehovah is the eternal I Am; Jehovah is He that is and is and always is, He that is absolutely unchangeable, remaining through all eternity one and the same.

Whilst *Elohim*, another name of God (derived from *El*, strength, power), is found principally in such passages where God is manifested in the plenitude of His power and strength as the Creator, the Preserver, and the Governor of the world, *Jehovah* is generally used to exhibit His relation to His people as their faithful God, their *covenant God*, as the God of their salvation, Ex. 3, 15.

The use of this exalted name, Jehovah, God has expressly reserved unto Himself. Ex. 3, 15 He says: "Jehovah . . . . . this is my name for ever." Is. 42, 8. "I am *Jehovah* (the Lord): that is my name: and my glory will I not give to another." Is. 45, 5.21. "I am Jehovah (the Lord), and there is none else, there is no God beside me." Ps. 83, 18. "Thou, whose name is alone Jehovah, art the most high over all the earth." But why multiply instances? The name Jehovah, as is evident from the passages quoted, is applicable to the one true God only, beside whom there is no other God; it is a name that God has strictly forbidden another to assume.

Now, this exalted name, applicable to "the Most High" only, is ascribed in our text to Christ. *Christ is Jehovah.* "*This is His name whereby He shall be called, Jehovah.*" Christ is Jehovah, is God, in the fullest sense of the word, without any limitation or restriction. Not even the faintest trace of a "delicate line of separation between Him and the Father" is discernible. Christ Himself says: "I and my Father are one"—*hen*, John, 10, 30. "Before Abraham was, *I am*, John 8, 58. Christ is *the* "I ,Am"—*ego eimi.*—And because Christ Himself is Jehovah, He is also our Righteousness. The righteousness we have in Him is perfect, one that availeth before God. Because this Lord Jehovah takes the place of sinners, "Judah shall be saved and Israel shall dwell safely," v. 6.

Ps. 2, 7: *Thou art my Son; this day have I begotten Thee.*

The psalm speaks of the Lord and His Anointed, i. e., of the Father and the Son, v. 2. The Lord says to the Anointed: *"Thou art my Son."* Christ is the Son of God. What is the basis of this sonship? Christians, too, are called the sons of God. Is the nature of the relationship the same? No. Whilst Christians are the children of God by faith in Christ Jesus, Christ is the son of God by eternal generation of the Father. *·"Thou art my Son"* finds its explanation in the second dictum: *"I have begotten Thee."* Because I have *begotten* Thee, therefore thou art my Son. This sonship of Christ is unique. "Unto which of the angels said He at any time, Thou art my Son, this day have I begotten Thee?" Hebr. 1, 5. In an inscrutable and ineffable manner God has communicated His essence to His Son. In other words, Christ is very God of very God, "the brightness of His glory, and the express image of His person," Hebr. 1, 3.

John 3, 16: *For God so loved the world that He gave His only-begotten Son, etc.*

The magnitude of the love of God towards a world fallen into sin can, in a measure, be apprehended by the greatness of the gift made to redeem it from everlasting perdition. "He gave His only-begotten Son." *"Only-begotten, monogenes,* means, *single of its kind, only, unigenitus.* To feel the force of this word it is but necessary to read such passages as Luke 7, 12: "Now when he came nigh to the gate of the city, behold, there was a dead man carried out, the *only* son *(huios monogenes)* of his mother." Luke 8, 42: Jairus, the ruler of the synagogue, "had *one only (monogenes)* daughter." Luke 9, 38: "Master, I beseech Thee, look upon my son: for· he is mine *only (monogenes)* child." Hebr. 11, 17: "By faith Abraham, when he was tried, offered up Isaac: and he that had received the promises offered up his *only-begotten (monogene)* son."—Christ is the *monogenes,* the *only* Son of God, in a sense in which He has no brethren. He is God's Son, born of the essence of the Father, therefore true God. The word "only-begotten" marks His unique sonship from that of the "sons of God," John 1, 12, the Christians, who become such by adoption.

Rom. 8, 32: *God spared not His own Son, but delivered Him up for us all, etc.*

When St. Paul writes: *hos ge tou idiou huiou ouk efeisato*—"who indeed His own Son spared not," he lays a very strong emphasis on the word *own, idion,* thus calling attention to the exhibition of a love that

surpasses all human understanding. To save the world God spared
not His *own* Son, Him who is born from the essence of the Father, who,
therefore, is equal with the Father, who is true God. The word rendered *own (idios)* expresses a *peculiar personal Sonship, an equality of
nature with God.* That this is the force of the word becomes very patent
from one of the discourses which the Lord had with His adversaries,
the Jews. Among other things he had said: "My father worketh hitherto, and I work." For this cause, we are told, "the Jews sought the
more to kill Him, because he said *patera idion ton theon*—that God was
His *own* Father, *making Himself equal with God,*" John 5, 18. So, to
say of Christ: God is His *own* Father *means* Christ *is equal* with God.
With this compare what St. Paul says of Christ. Let us put the two statements side by side. According to the Jews, Christ maintained—and
their interpretation is correct—that "God was His *own* Father;" Paul
says Christ is God's "*own Son.*" The enemies of Christ, the Jews, were
quick to perceive that the first locution expressed *equality* with the
Father, but such as pose as His friends, aye, as pillars of His Church,
cannot, will not see that Paul's statement concerning the Savior is in
substance identically the same. Is it not sad?—Says *Plummer,* in his
Notes on St. John: "They (the Jews) fully understand the force of the
parallel statements, 'My Father is working; I am working also.' 'Behold,' says Augustine, 'the Jews understand what the Arians fail to understand.' If Arian or Unitarian views were right, would not Christ at
once have explained that what they imputed to Him as blasphemy was
not in His mind at all? But instead of explaining that He by no means
claims equality with the Father, He goes on to reaffirm this equality
from other points of view; see especially v. 23."

JESUS CHRIST IS TRUE GOD, 2. BECAUSE THE SCRIPTURES ASCRIBE DI-

VINE ATTRIBUTES TO HIM.

John 1, 1.2: *In the beginning was the Word, and the Word was
with God, and the Word was God. The same was in the beginning with
God.*

An inspection of the Prologue, vv. 1-18, clearly reveals the fact
that the *Word,* the Logos, is none else than the Son of God. In express
words we find this truth in v. 14: "The Word was made flesh and dwelt
among us, and we beheld His glory, the glory as of the Only-Begotten of
the Father, full of grace and truth."

In our text three weighty assertions, arranged in climactic order,
are made concerning this Word, the Logos, Jesus Christ. These are: 1.
The eternity of the Word; 2. the distinct personality of the Word and
His intimate communion with God; 3. the Deity of the Word.

1. *The eternity of the Word.* "In the beginning was the Word."
The meaning of the phrase: "in the beginning," depends upon the con-

text. In Gen. 1, 1 we read: *"In the beginning* God created heaven and earth," i. e., the creation of the world was the beginning of the world's history, the beginning of time. Here it says: "In the beginning *was* the Word." Before anything was formed the Word *was*. The past tense *was, en,* places the Word before the beginning of things. Gen. 1, 1 marks the first moment of time; this, eternity. It does not read *egeneto* here as in v. 14: "the Word *became* flesh," but the Word *en—was—was already in existence* in the beginning. Hence the German translation: "Im Anfang *war* das Wort;" not: "Im Anfang *ward* das Wort." So the Word is a Being existing prior to all beginning. But what was before the world and time we call eternity. *The Word,* Christ, is *eternal.* This truth, so plain in itself from this phrase, is corroborated by v. 3: *"All things were made by Him."* Since all things were made by Him, it is self-evident that He existed *before* all things. He is no creature, no part of creation, but the Creator, the *eternal* God Himself. Col. 1, 17, Ps. 2, 7.

2. *The distinct personality of the Word and His intimate communion with God.* The text says: *"And the Word was with God."* Two persons are here discriminated: the Word and God, i. e., the Son and the Father. The Word was *pros ton theon—with God.* The Word, Christ, is not an attribute or a power of God, but a person *distinct* from the Father. Luther: "John insists hard on the little word *with,* thus clearly distinguishing the Word from the person of the Father." The Son is co-existent and co-eternal with the Father. Hence Christ is true God. His being with the Father at the same time indicates the ineffable union between the two persons.

3. *The Deity of the Word,* clearly discernible from the first two members, is explicitly asserted in the third: *"The Word was God."* Christ is not an inferior God, but is God in the fullest sense of the term. They who deny the divinity of Christ concede that He is called *a* God, *theos,* but contend He is not called *the* God, *ho theos.* Of such quibblings we have spoken in a previous article. In this connection we shall merely call attention to the fact that *theos* without the article also designates the one true God, for in v. 18 we read: "No man hath seen *God, theon,* at any time; the only-begotten Son, which is in the bosom of the Father, He hath declared Him." In the present passage: *kai theos en ho logos,* "and the Word was God," *ho logos* is the subject, *theos* is the predicate, hence cannot take the article *ho.* Alford: "The article could not have been here expressed, whatever place the words might hold in the sentence. *Ho logos en ho theos* would . . . . . destroy the idea of the logos altogether. *Theos* must then be taken as implying 'GOD,' *in substance and essence,*—not *ho theos,* 'the Father,' *in Person.* It does not mean *theios,* nor is it to be rendered *a God*—but, as in *sarx egeneto, sarx* expresses that *state* into which the Divine Word entered by a definite act, so in *theos en, theos* expresses that *essence* which was His *en arche:*— that He was *very God."* (Greek Testament, vol. I, p. 615.)

The passage might be paraphrased thus: The Word existed from all eternity, distinct from, yet intimately connected with, the Father, and equal to the Father.

This single passage demolishes the Arian heresy. Arius (about A. D. 318) denied the divinity of Christ, maintaining that Christ was not from eternity. He said: *en pote hote ouk en*—"there was a time when He was not;" consequently, Christ was a creature—*ktisma ex ouk onton*—created out of nothing. St. John, however, says, "In the beginning *was* the Word."—The Semi-Arians, developing this Arian heresy, reasoned: Since Christ is a creature, He cannot be equal with the Father. They conceded: He is like the Father—*homoios, homoiousios*, but not *homoousios*. St. John says: "The Word was *God.*"

In the Oecumenical Council at Nice, summoned by Constantine in A. D. 325, this Arian heresy was condemned. Under the brave leadership of the young and eloquent Athanasius of Alexandria, the Biblical doctrine was thus formulated: "And"—I believe—"in one Lord Jesus Christ, the only-begotten Son of God, begotten of His Father, before all worlds, God of God, Light of Light, very God of very God, begotten, not made, being of one substance with the Father." (Nicene Creed, pp. 2.3.) The words that settled the controversial point read in the original: *ek tes ousias tou patros, gennethesis, ou poietheis, homoousios to patri.*—Arians of modern times are plentiful; Kahnis, Ritschl, and Harnack being among their number.

Hebr. 13, 8: *Jesus Christ the same yesterday, and to-day, and for ever.*

This is the well-known paraphrase of immutability. *Yesterday* denotes the past time: *to-day*, the present; and *for ever*, the future. God is immutable, unchangeable; Christ is unchangeable: *ergo*, Christ is true God.

Matt. 28, 18: *All power is given unto me in heaven and in earth.*

In compliance with the command of their Master, the disciples went to Galilee, to the mountain designated by Him as the place where He would meet them, v. 16. Here the Lord delivers His last Great Commission unto them, v. 19, which He introduces by the words of our proof text: "All power is given unto me in heaven and in earth." What mere human being, what angel, can truthfully utter such words? But Christ is not mere man; He is the God-man, the "over all God," Rom. 9, 5, through whose omnipotent word the world and all that is therein came into being, John 1, 3; Cor. 1, 16.17; Hebr. 1, 8. When He therefore says: "All power is *given to me,*" He refers to His human nature, which is inseparably united with the divine. The man Christ, by virtue of the personal union, possesses *all power, pasa exousia—all authority.* These words admit of no inferiority to the Father. *All authority* is omnipotence, which is an incommunicable attribute of God. *Christ*, being omnipotent, *is God.* And, as if to ward off all erroneous conceptions, He develops the thought in *"all power,"* saying: I, the Son of man, possess all power *in heaven*—angels, authorities, the cherubim and the seraphim are my willing servants; I possess all power *on earth*—all things are put under my feet," Eph. 1, 20; I Pet. 3, 22.—Then follows the Great Commission: "Go ye, therefore, and teach all nations, baptizing them in the name of the Father, and of the Son, and of the Holy Ghost: teaching them to observe all things whatsoever I have commanded you," vv. 19.20. To this He appends the promise:

Matt. 28, 20: *Lo, I am with you alway, even unto the end of the world.*

The disciples were to wage war against the formidable kingdom of Satan, destroy its bulwarks, and upon its ruins plant the cross, the emblem of the Crucified One. What a task! And was not the Master just now bidding them a solemn farewell? Well might they grieve. But no. Arresting their attention and directing it to something of great importance, the Lord says: "*Lo!*" take heed to what follows: "*I*"—*ego*—with emphasis—I, your now exalted Savior, "I am with you." Though you will no longer enjoy my *visible* presence, still *invisibly* I will be with you, "a very present help," Ps. 46,1, in putting down the strongholds of Satan. Not a day shall you be left alone, for I will be with you *alway, pasas tas hemeras*—all the days. In days of victory or seeming defeat, in days of joys or sorrow—*all the days* I am with you to guide and to protect you.—Truly, He who can speak thus must be very God. His disciples, obedient to His command, were soon to scatter in all the world, making disciples by baptizing and teaching, but still they were to know: He is with you *all the days*. His disciples were soon to multiply, but He was with them, too, *all the days*. Only God can be present at all places and at all times. This *omnipresence* is here predicated of Christ; hence Christ is true God.—And Christ is with us, His disciples, His Church, even to-day. Speaking to His disciples then the Lord does not say: I am with you "all *your* days"—thus limiting His gracious presence to the apostolic era, but He uses words of wider application: "*all the days.*" The command is: "Disciple—*mathēteusate*—all nations." The men to whom these words were originally spoken have long ago closed their eyes in death, but still the nations are being discipled by baptizing and teaching. Wherever Christ's commission (vv. 19.20) is carried out, wherever His doctrine is preached and the sacraments are administered according to his institution, there He is with us and will be with us, even "*until the completion of the age*"—the end of the world, 2 Pet. 3, 7-10.

John 21, 17: *Lord, Thou knowest all things.*

When Peter was asked the third time by his beloved Master: "Simon, son of Jonas, lovest thou me?" he answered: *su panta oidas, su ginoskeis hoti filo se*—"*Thou all things knowest; Thou knowest that I love Thee.*" The "Thou," being separately expressed, *su—su,* and at the head of the members of the sentence, is emphatic. *Thou,* being the

Lord, *all things, panta,* nothing excepted, *knowest, oidas,* by supernatural intuition. Thou art absolutely omniscient, and since nothing is secret before Thee, not even the inmost thoughts of the hearts, Thou also knowest, *ginoskeis, perceivest, seest,* that I love Thee. Thou knowest *all;* Thou knowest *me.* Absolute omniscience is here ascribed to our Lord Jesus; such omniscience as the true God only possesses. Even in His state of humiliation Christ was the Omniscient of whom the psalmist says: "O Lord, Thou hast searched me, and known me. Thou knowest my downsitting and mine uprising; Thou understandest my thought afar off," Ps. 139, 1.2. Only a Kenotist, like Meyer, whose eye is blinded as to the Divinity of Christ, can say: " 'Thou knowest,' etc., which popular and deeply emotional expression is not to be interpreted of absolute omniscience."—For other proofs of Christ's omniscience see John 1, 42.47.48; 3, 3; 4, 29; 11, 4.15, etc.

JESUS CHRIST IS TRUE GOD, 3. BECAUSE THE SCRIPTURES ASCRIBE DIVINE WORKS, DIVINE HONOR, AND DIVINE GLORY TO HIM.

John 1, 3: *All things were made by Him; and without Him was not anything made that was made.*

By appropriation the divine work of Creation is ascribed to the Father. Since, however, it is an *opus ad extra* it was performed by the Triune God. Hebr. 1, 1.2; John 1, 10; Col. 1, 16; Ps. 33, 6; Gen. 1, 2.— The present passage attributes this work to Christ. The words are too plain to require elucidation. "*All things* were made by Him," hence Christ was prior to all things. Coeternal with the Father, He, in conjunction with the Father and the Spirit of God, Ps. 33, 6, in the beginning made heaven and earth. Gen. 1, 1.—When the text adds: "And without Him was not anything made that was made," it brings out the thought most markedly by means of an antithesis: Christ is the Creator of the world; Christ is true God.

Assailants of the divinity of Christ, Gnostics and other heretics, ancient and modern, point to the preposition "*by,*" *dia,* contending that *dia, by, through,* indicates the instrument. Their argument is this: All things were made *by* Christ. Christ, therefore, was but a mere instrument in the hands of the Father, hence Christ is inferior to the Father. *Non sequitur dia* does not only indicate the *causa secunda,* but also the *causa principalis,* e. g., 1 Cor. 1, 9: "God is faithful, *by, dia,* whom ye were called." See Gal. 1, 1; Hebr. 2, 10.—The argument based upon the preposition "by" does not hold water. Moreover, the creation of the world is ascribed to Christ *directly* in Hebr. 1, 10: "And Thou, Lord, in the beginning hast laid the foundation of the earth; and the heavens are the works of Thine hands."—

Hebr. 1, 3: *He upholds all things by the word of His power.*

Christ is not only the Creator of the world, He is also its *Preserver.*

LUTHER: "This is the third time he (the writer of the epistle) declares *Christ to be God*. First he says that the worlds have been made by Him; next, that He is the brightness of God's glory and the express image of His person; now he says that *Christ upholds all things*. Since Christ upholds all things, He Himself is not upheld; He is above all things, and hence must be God. This *upholding*, however, signifies that He nourishes and preserves all things, so that all things have not only been made by him, but also that all things are preserved and maintained by Him, as St. Paul says, Col. 1, 17: "He is before all things, and by Him all things consist." (W. XII, 161.)

Matt. 9, 6: *The Son of man hath power on earth to forgive sins.*

When Jesus said to the paralytic: "Son, be of good cheer; thy sins be forgiven thee," critical auditors, "certain of the scribes," took offense at these words. Publicly they did not give vent to their feelings, but they "said within themselves," or, as Mark puts it, "they reasoned in their hearts" (Mark 2, 6): "This man blasphemeth," Matt. 9, 6. "Why does this man thus speak blasphemies? Who can forgive sins but God only," Mark 2, 7. True, God only can forgive sins. Sin is an offense against the majesty of God. So far these scribes were right; but they were totally wrong when they thought: "This man blasphemeth." For "this man," the Son of man, is at the same time true God. One proof of His divinity He furnished them immediately. They had said *"within themselves,"* "This man blasphemeth." "Jesus, knowing their thoughts, said, Wherefore think ye evil in your hearts?" "This man" was the *omniscient* God, to whom the reasoning of the hearts of the scribes was an open book.—He proceeds: "For whether (which) is easier to say, Thy sins are forgiven thee, or to say, Arise, and walk?" Which is easier? One is as difficult as the other; both require divine power. But to say, "Arise, and walk" effectively, to cure this paralytic by a mere word, was capable of investigation. If He can do that, He can do the other—forgive sins. "Arise, take up they bed, and go unto thine house," so said Jesus. And the paralytic "arose and departed to his house." We imagine the moment of suspense for the multitude, the thrill that must have passed through the crowd, as the sick of the palsy was bidden to arise, and then actually went off. How the scribes must have been abashed and confounded!—Here was proof positive, indisputable, tangible proof, that this man Jesus is almighty. Now they might know that "the Son of man hath power,"—*exousia*, authority— "on earth to forgive sins."

John 5, 27: *The Father hath given Him authority to execute judgment also, because He is the Son of man.*

Authority to execute judgment, authority to decide about life and death, is a prerogative of God. Christ possesses this prerogative. Christ is God.

But why does it read: "The Father *hath given* Him authority"?

Christ is the Theanthropos, the God-man. His divine nature is immutable; nothing can be taken away from it, nor can anything be given to it. "Thou art the same," Ps. 102, 28. But on account of the personal union the essential attributes of the divine nature are communicated to His human nature. The Scriptures ascribe divine majesty to Christ according to His human nature. Hence what is said to have been given to Christ in time cannot have been given to Him according to His divine nature, according to which He possesses all things, but to His human nature which he assumed in the fulness of time. "Authority to execute the judgment" was *given* to Christ because He is the *Son of man*, a title which describes His human nature.

John 5, 23: *All men should honor the Son, even as they honor the Father. He that honoreth not the Son honoreth not the Father which hath sent Him.*

The Son is in no whit inferior to the Father. "All men should honor the Son *even* as they honor the Father." The divine honor due the Father is also due the Son. He who withholds this divine honor from the Son declares the Son to be inferior to the Father, and so does not truly honor the Father. "Whosoever denieth the Son hath not the Father." The Jews who do not believe in Christ as the Messiah do not worship the true God, but an idol. Secret societies studiously exclude the name of the Son from their rituals, etc. Their worship is a vain worship.—

Hebr. 1, 6: *Let all the angels of God worship Him.*

Matt. 4, 10 Christ says to Satan: "It is written, Thou shalt worship the Lord, thy God, and Him only shalt thou serve." Divine adoration must be offered to the true God only. When St. John fell down before the angel in the Apocalypse to worship him, he was admonished: "See thou do it not . . . . . worship God." But of Christ Hebr. 1, 6 says: "*Let all the angels of God worship Him.*" And St. Paul, Phil. 2, 10.11: "At the name of Jesus every knee should bow, of things in heaven, and things in earth, and things under the earth, and every tongue should confess that Jesus Christ is Lord, to the glory of God the Father." When the Scriptures inculcate on all men the duty of worshiping the Savior, of *honoring Him like as* the Father, etc., they afford the strongest possible evidence of His divinity.

JESUS CHRIST IS ALSO TRUE MAN.

1 Tim. 2, 5: *There is one God, and one Mediator between God and men, the Man Christ Jesus.*

Christ is *anthropos, man,* having a perfect human body and soul. Had He not become man, He could have not effected a mediation between God and men, v. 6.—The human nature of our Savior is often prominently brought forward: 1 Cor. 8, 6; 15, 21; Phil. 2, 7.8; Hebr. 2, 14.

16.17; 4, 15. This fact has been frequently misused by heretics, who, pointing to these passages only, contended Christ was mere man. Satan is a sly trickster. Such passages do not disprove the fact that Christ is also divine. Scripture says both things; both are true. In John 1, 1; 20, 28; Rom. 9, 5; 1 John 5, 20, *et al.*, Christ is called God. For reasons which the context generally discloses, the one or the other nature of our Savior is stressed. Other passages, and not a few, combine both truths, *e. g.*, Gal. 4, 4.5: "God sent forth *His Son*" (divine nature), "*made of a woman*" (human nature), "made under the law, to *redeem* them that were under the Law." Our Redeemer is the God-man.

Luke 24, 39: *Behold my hands and my feet, that it is I myself: handle me, and see; for a spirit hath not flesh and bones, as ye see me have.*

Christ is *man*, 1 Tim. 2, 5. This says beyond the shadow of a doubt that He possesses a true, natural body and a rational soul, but, as if to cut off all subterfuges of errorists, these constituent parts of man are distinctly ascribed to Christ. Thus Luke 24, 39 affirms that He has a true natural body.—The two disciples with whom Christ held such touching converse on the way to Emmaus hastened back to Jerusalem. Here they found the others at their evening meal. Of a sudden the risen Christ is in their midst. Their hearts are filled with terror, for they believe to see a vision from the other world. To assure them that it is He Himself and no spirit, He uttered the words of our text. He has *hands* and *feet*, *flesh* and *bones*. He is so thoroughly human that He can be *handled*, touched, felt of. He invites the closest investigation: "Handle me and see!" And to give them another "infallible proof," Acts 1, 3; John 21, 12.13; Acts 10, 41, He "did *eat before them*," v. 43.

Furthermore, the genuineness of His humanity is manifested by the fact that He was born "a child;" He grew in knowledge and in stature; He ate, He drank, He slept, He wept in sympathy for the sorrows of men; He suffered hunger and thirst and pains and, finally, death. Nor had He merely a body, the divine nature, as some assert, taking the place of the human soul. "My *soul*," said He, Matt. 26, 38, "is exceedingly sorrowful, even unto death."

*   *   *

We have given the passages bearing upon Christ's humanity but a brief treatment. To some readers it may seem to be an *opus supererogationis* to do so at all. The cry round about us is: Christ is not God, but mere man! Still there was a time when even this plain truth of Scriptures—Christ's humanity—was assailed.—Manichaeism (Manes, its founder, flourished about the middle of the third century) taught that Jesus was simply clothed with the *appearance* of a body. The sufferings and death inflicted upon Him by the Prince of Darkness were only *in appearance*. Eutychianism (Eutyches, A. D. 444-451) maintained that after His incarnation Christ had but one nature, and that the body of

Christ is not of like substance with our own. Like or similar views were held by various other heretics. The devil was and is always busy to storm this citadel of the Christian religion, the Scriptural doctrine of the Person of our Savior. The primitive Church valiantly and successfully defended the truth as taught in Holy Writ. In the successive Councils of Nice, A. D. 325, Constantinople, 381, Ephesus, 431, and Chalcedon, 451, the doctrine regarding this theanthropic person—Christ—was lucidly set forth.

In this connection the language of the *Chalcedon Symbol* becomes interesting reading matter. It bears testimony to the truths laid down in the preceding passages and links well with the doctrines of texts that will soon come up for discussion. This Symbol says: "We teach that Jesus Christ is perfect as respects His divinity, and perfect as respects His humanity; that he is truly God, and truly man, consisting of a rational soul and a body; that He is consubstantial *(homoousion)* with the Father as to His divinity, and consubstantial *(homoousion)* with us as to His humanity, and like us in all respects, sin excepted. He was begotten of the Father, before the ages *(proaionon,* from eternity) as to His deity; but in these last days He was born of Mary, the mother of God *(theotokos),* as to His humanity. He is one Christ, existing in two natures, without mixture *(asunchutos),* without change *(atreptos),* without division *(adiairetos),* without separation *(achoristos),*—the diversity of the two natures not being at all destroyed by their union in the person, but the peculiar properties of each nature being preserved, and concurring to one person *(prosopon),* and one subsistence *(hupostasin)."*

The Two Natures in Christ.

2 Sam. 7, 19: *And is this the manner of the man, who is Lord God.*

The translation of the Authorized Version: "And is this the manner of man, O Lord God?" does not do justice to the Hebrew text. The interrogative form is uncalled for, and the vocative, "O Lord God," is untenable in view of the text and the context. The Revised Version reads: "And this *too* after the manner of men, O Lord God!" This makes little or no sense. The marginal note: "And is this the law of man, O Lord God?" is still less illuminating, to say the least. Luther, with keen insight into the text, translated it: *"Das ist die Weise eines Menschen, der Gott der HERR ist."* *"This is the manner of man,"* rather *"the man, who is Lord God."* This rendering is demanded by both text and context.

Examining the context briefly, we shall find that it throws a flood of light upon our present proof-passage. The salient facts of the section beginning with v. 1 are these: During David's reign the people of Israel had attained to a position of honor and power. Peace prevailed. "The Lord had given him"—David—"rest round about from all his enemies," v. 1. Then it was that David conceived the idea of building a house unto the Lord. He speaks about it to Nathan. God intervenes. Nathan is sent to David with this message: "Thus saith the Lord, Shalt thou build me an house for me to dwell in?" No.—After reviewing the earthly blessings God had vouchsafed unto David, vv. 8. 11, Nathan proceeds: "The Lord telleth thee that He will build thee a house," v. 11b. The nature of this house the subsequent verses reveal.

Now follow words of the most precious promise to David. "When thy days shall be fulfilled, and thou *shalt sleep* with thy fathers, I will set up *thy seed after thee,* which shall proceed *out of thy bowels,* and I will establish his kingdom. He shall build an house for my name, and I will establish the throne of his kingdom *for ever,*" vv. 12.13. Of whom does the text speak? Of a descendant of David. Is it Solomon? No. Solomon lived at David's time, but this king was to arise when David's days had been fulfilled, when he slept with his fathers. It was a promise looking to the future. So David himself understood the words. In his prayer he says: "Thou hast spoken also of thy servant's house *for a great while to come,*" v. 19. Furthermore, the throne of this promised kingdom is to be established *for ever,* v. 13. Neither Solomon's throne, nor that of any other great king of Israel, lasted *for ever.* Who, then, we ask, is this eternal king? Clearly he is to be David's son. David was told: "I will set up *thy* seed, which shall proceed *out of thy bowels.*" This king is to be David's son—*a true man.* And his kingdom is to last *for ever!* A unique king indeed he must be whose kingdom is to be eternal! The mystery of this person is revealed in the next verse—the climax of Nathan's speech: *"I,"* the Lord, *"will be His Father and He shall be my Son,"* v. 14. This king, David's Son, is at the same time Jehovah's Son, God of God, very God of very God. O mystery of mysteries! He by whom the throne of David is to be established forever is *God's Son* and *David's son,* is God and man in one person.

Overwhelmed by the mercy of God, "King David went in and sat before the Lord" and poured out a prayer of thanksgiving. "Who am I, O Lord God? and what is my house, that Thou hast brought me hitherto?" v. 18. Thus he speaks while thinking of the great blessings of God that Nathan had reminded him of in vv. 8-11. He proceeds: "And this was yet a small thing in Thy sight, O Lord God." Great as were these earthly blessings, still they were "a small thing" in comparison with what was promised him, vv. 12-16. "Thou hast spoken also of Thy servant's house for a great while to come." And what great thing hast Thou promised? *My* seed which shall proceed *out of my bowels, my son,* shall at the same time be *Thy Son.* "This is the manner of the man" —O miracle of miracles!—"who is Lord God," v. 19. My son, this man, is God!

To recapitulate: The Lord says to David: "I will set up thy seed after thee, which is to proceed out of thy bowels . . . . . I will be His Father, and He shall be my Son." David believes these words and in v. 19 shows us how he understands them by exclaiming in wonderment:

"This is the manner of *the man, who is* Lord *God.*"

In Christ there are two natures: the human and the divine.

John 1, 14:   *The Word was made flesh, and dwelt among us, (and we beheld His glory, the glory as of the Only-Begotten of the Father,) full of grace and truth.*

> *The Word was made flesh* (incarnation; two natures, one person), *and dwelt among us* (during the state of humiliation); *and we beheld His glory* (rays of glory in the state of humiliation), *the glory as of the Only-Begotten of the Father* (eternal generation; equality with God), *full of grace and truth* (purpose of incarnation).

Kai ho logos sarx egeneto. "And the Logos, the Word, became flesh." Who is this Word? "The Word was God," v. 1, Jesus Christ, v. 17. So the sentence is equivalent to: The Son of God became flesh. *Flesh, sarx,* by synecdoche—pars pro toto—means *man,* the *human nature.* Hence, *ho logos sarx egeneto* says: The Son of God became *man,* assumed the *human nature.* Text and context loudly proclaim this mystery, and the parallel passages substantiate this sublime fact beyond a doubt. In 1 John 4, 2; 1 Tim. 3, 16; Hebr. 2, 14 we read: the Son of God *en sarki eleluthota, is come into the flesh; efanerothe en sarki, was manifested in flesh; sarkos kai haimatos . . . . . meteschen, of flesh and blood he took part.* Four simple words: "The Word became flesh" —and yet they declare the mystery of mysteries, the cardinal fact of Christianity, the incarnation of the eternal Logos. What a contrast: *God* and *man!* The Logos assumed the impersonal human nature into His already existing divine person. This is called the *personal union.* The Son of God became a true and perfect man, uniting our human nature with His divine nature. So in Him there are two natures; but still there is but one Person—one Person who is God as well as man. This union of the two natures in Christ is one of the greatest mysteries of the Christian religion. St. Paul exclaims: "Without controversy great is the mystery of godliness: God was manifest in the flesh," 1 Tim. 3, 16.

This God-man, says St. John, "*dwelt,*" tabernacled, tented, "*among us.*" The Son of God became a man, like as we are, sin excepted. He dwelt among us, He was in our midst, we ate with Him, we conversed with Him, we went in and out with Him. He was true man. He hungered, Matt. 4, 2; He experienced thirst, John 19, 28; weary of the day's journey, He sat down on Jacob's well, John 4, 6; on the storm-tossed ship He slept, Matt. 8, 24; He wept over the death of his friend Lazarus, John 11, 35. In brief: He "was made in the likeness of men, and was found in fashion as a man," Phil 2, 7. And yet this man was unlike other men in one respect. He was "holy, harmless, undefiled, separate from sinners, and higher than the heavens." His opponents, the Jews, he met with the defiant challenge: "Which of you convinceth me of a sin?" Christ was man without sin. Outwardly, to all appearance, He was but a man; but He was a man withal that possessed divine majesty. During the time that He dwelt visibly among us, says St. John, "*we*," i. e., St. John and the other disciples of Christ, "*beheld*," *etheasametha*, we *discerned*, we saw with wonder and amazement, "*His glory.*" Glory, *doxa*, is the aggregate of all divine attributes in which God manifests Himself, such as holiness, love, truth, omniscience, omnipresence, omnipotence. This glory they beheld in Christ. It was *His* glory, not one delegated to Him by the Father. In the state of humiliation Christ was very God. Of this glory, which was His own and communicated by the divine nature to the human, Christ did not make use at all times but only when it pleased Him. In His words, in His miracles, at the Transfiguration, and in His Passion, rays of this divine glory flashed out from time to time. He *saw* the faith of the paralytic; He *saw* the evil thoughts of the Pharisees; He *saw* Nathanael under the fig tree; "He knew what was in man." At the marriage festival at Cana of Galilee He performed the miracle of changing the water into wine, and, we read, He "manifested forth His glory;" He raised the widow's son, and they beheld His glory; He stilled the angry tempest on the Galilean sea, and they beheld His glory; Lazarus was called forth out of the grave by Christ's omnipotent voice, and they beheld His glory; with the words, "It is I," He felled His captors, and manifested forth His glory. With wonder and amazement Christ's disciples saw again and again: This man Jesus is omnipresent, omnipotent, omniscient! This man is God!

Of this glory St. John says it was "*the glory as of the Only-Begotten of the Father.*" The only-begotten Son He was, and therefore of the same essence with the Father, very God of very God, and as such He needs must possess glory, full, unlimited, divine glory. The essence of God and the glory of God are inseparably united with each other.— Kenoticism is rationalism pure and simple. According to this heresy, Christ, when assuming human nature, abandoned certain divine attributes, such as omnipresence, omniscience and omnipotence. He did not only not use them, say the Kenotists, but He did not even possess them. Hofman, for example, goes so far as to say in one place: "He ceased to be God in order to become man." Thus this mystery concerning the God-man, which the Bible teaches so plainly, but which we cannot fathom, is flatly denied. Deny the omniscience of Christ, or His omnipotence, or His omnipresence, and you deny His divinity. In our text, St. John plainly teaches, though Christ became *man*, He still remained what He was before—*God*.

RESUME.—Christ is the God-man. God He is from all eternity; man He became in time. There are two natures in Him, personally united so as to constitute one person. From this personal union follows the communication of the natures and from this again the communication of attributes. Subsequent passages may lead us to enter upon the latter topics more fully.

1 Tim. 3, 16: *Without controversy great is the mystery of godli-*

758 THE SECOND ARTICLE

ness: God was manifest in the flesh.

The doctrine of the personal union of the two natures in Christ is a *"confessedly great mystery."* Paul knows it to be such, and as such he propounds it to Timothy. A mystery transcends all human comprehension. Timothy is not to endeavor to reason out this doctrine; he is simply to accept it in faith. The mystery is this: *"God was manifest in the flesh."* That says: The invisible God was visible in the flesh. Christ was God invisible from all eternity. By the assumption of the human nature God was so in Christ that He, God, became *manifest.* In the person of Jesus Christ divinity and humanity were so closely united that whosoever saw the man Jesus saw God; whosoever heard the man Jesus speak heard God speak. He was the express image of the invisible God. He Himself said: "He that hath seen me, hath seen the Father," John 14, 9. "I and my Father are one," John 10, 30. In Christ God became man. *Gerhard:* "The mode of this union is wonderfully unique and uniquely wonderful, transcending the comprehension not only of all men, but even of angels, whence it is called 'without controversy, a great mystery.'"

Though God was manifest in the flesh, though we have a clear revelation of the fact in Scriptures, still it *is* a great mystery and will continue to be such to the end of time.—But it is a blessed mystery, for it is a mystery of *godliness.* Where this mystery of the God-man, the doctrine of His person and work, is unknown or rejected, godliness cannot exist; but where it is preached and believed, true godliness is generated. "Every spirit which confesseth that Jesus Christ is come in the flesh is of God; whosoever shall confess that Jesus is the Son of God, God abideth in him, and he in God." 1 John 4, 2. 15.

Col. 2, 9: *In Him dwelleth all the fullness of the God-head bodily.*

The context shows that this passage speaks of Christ. "In Him" therefore says: in Christ, in this theanthropic person. According to what nature does it speak of Christ? This the word *dwells* indicates. "The fullness of the Godhead" would not be said to *dwell* in the Son of God as such, because the Son *is* God in the fullest sense of the term. Hence it is the Son of Man, the *human* Christ, of whom this text primarily speaks. What does it say? "The fullness of the Godhead" dwells in this *man* Jesus Christ. The *Godhead, he theotes,* that is: *the being God, the divine essence, the deity, Gottheit; (he theotes,* is to be distinguished from *he theiotes, the divine quality, divinity, Goettlichkeit.)*— So the *theotes,* the divine essence, dwells in Christ, not in part only, but the *fullness,* the plenitude of the essence of God, and as if that were not strong enough, the apostle adds: *all* the fullness of the divine essence undivided and entire dwells in the man Christ. How does it dwell in Christ? *Bodily.* The human body of Christ is the temple which "all the fullness of the Godhead" has made its dwelling-place.—"The entire fullness of the divinity dwells in Christ, not as in other holy men and angels, but bodily, as in its own body, so that, with all its majesty, power, glory, and efficacy, it shines forth in the assumed human nature of Christ, when and as, He wills, and in, with, and through it exerts its divine power, glory, and efficacy, as the soul does in the body and fire in glowing iron." *(Formula of Concord.)*

Truly, if the stupendous mystery that the man Jesus Christ is at the same time very God, "over all God" (Rom. 9, 5), can be expressed by the medium of human language, this passage, Col. 2, 9, beyond a doubt expresses it.

Is. 9, 6: *Unto us a Child is born, unto us a Son is given: and the government shall be upon His shoulder; and His name shall be called Wonderful, Counsellor, The Mighty God, The Everlasting Father, The Prince of Peace.*

"Behold, a virgin shall conceive and bear a Son, and shall call His name Immanuel," Is. 7, 14. Of this Immanuel, Christ, the present passage speaks.—The *son* of the virgin is a *child* like other children, a child with flesh and blood. And still he is unlike other children in this, that He is said not so much to be born unto his parents, but *unto us,* a son *given unto us.* This child is a gift of the Father to the world. He is a unique child, for "the government shall be upon His shoulder." What government? The *government* in its widest and fullest sense, the government of the world. This Child, from the moment of His birth, is the Ruler and the Preserver of the world. It is He to whom all power is given in heaven and in earth, Matt. 28, 18 His name is *Wonderful.* Indeed, wonderful is His person—He is man and God. Aye, directly He is called: *The Mighty God.* This child in the manger, helpless like other children, is at the same time The Mighty God! "Without controversy great is the mystery: God was manifest in the flesh."

NOTE. "The translation of this name (The Mighty God) is, as Gesenius remarks, 'almost a criterion whether the translator is a Christian or a non-Christian.' The Septuagint translates: *ischuros, exousiastes,* Aquila and Symmachus: *ischuros dunatos,* Theodoret: *ischuros dunastes.* Luther, too, who, as no other theologian, lauds and extols the Messiah of prophecy as the God of Israel, as the Lord Jehovah, has translated: "Kraft," "Held." But in 1542 he adopted the translation of the Vulgate: *Deus fortis. Deus fortis,* starker Gott, mighty God: that is the only correct rendering of this name." (Steockhardt, *Commentary on the Prophet Isaiah,* p. 120.)

Matt. 28, 18: *All power is given unto me in heaven and in earth.* Though by virtue of the personal union the two natures in Christ are inseparably united, still they are distinct. Though distinct, but being inseparably united, "each of the two natures," in the language of the Catechism, "partakes of the properties of the other."—We turn our attention, first, to Matt. 28, 18. The speaker is the visible, palpable Christ, the God-man. This person is the *"me"* of whom the text speaks.

What is the assertion made? He possesses *"all power in heaven and in earth."* "All power" clearly is omnipotence, and omnipotence is an *essential* attribute of God. This person Christ, who is man as well as God, possesses *"all power."* Manifestly He speaks by pre-eminence of His *human* nature, for He says: this power is *given* to me. "There is a unanimously received rule of the entire ancient orthodox Church, that whatever Holy Scripture testifies that Christ received in time he received not according to the divine nature,—for, according to this nature, He has everything from eternity,—but the person has received it in time, by reason of, and with respect to, the assumed human nature." *(Formula of Concord.)* So when we read of Christ: "All power is *given* unto me," this says: the *human* nature has received "all power," the *man* Christ is almighty.—The divine nature in Christ possesses omnipotence as an essential attribute, but this essential attribute, by virtue of the personal union of the two natures, becomes a *communicated* attribute of the human nature. In other words, omnipotence is and remains a property of the divine nature; it is not transferred to, or infused into, the human nature. The human nature *per se* does not become omnipotent. To say that would be tantamount to asserting that the human nature has become the divine nature; but the human nature, being united with the divine, partakes of this divine attribute. Suppose the impossible. If at any time the human nature in Christ were separated from the divine, the human nature would not possess the attribute ascribed to it in the text, *viz.,* omnipotence, because it is not endowed therewith as an attribute properly its own.

Matt 28, 20: *Lo, I am with you alway, even unto the end of the world.*

Let us again note of whom the assertion is made. The personal pronoun "I" designates the whole person. This "I" is both human and divine. Of this "I," of His whole person, Christ predicates omnipresence when He says: *"I am with you alway, even unto the end of the world."* The divine nature in Christ possesses it as an *essential* attribute; the human nature *partakes* of it in virtue of its personal union with the divine. Christ is with us according to both natures.

Acts 3, 15: *Ye killed the Prince of Life.*

Peter speaks of God's Son Jesus, the Holy One and the Just, whom the Jews had crucified. He is here named after His divine nature: *The Prince of Life.* Of this person something human is predicated: *Ye killed* Him. To be *killed,* to *die,* however, can be said of the human nature only, but it is here ascribed to the whole person. The Prince of Life, *i. e.,* God, ye killed. This is biblical language. Hence the poet's wail: "O sorrow dread, our God is dead" rests on a Scriptural basis. We do not say: the Godhead has died, or God died according to His Godhead, but this dying happened to Christ who is God as well as man. Christ was put to death after the flesh. The divine nature partakes of the property of the human nature.—"If I believe that the human nature only has suffered for me, I have a Savior of little value...It is the person that suffers and dies. Now the person is true God; therefore it is rightly said: 'The Son of God suffers.' For although the divinity does not suffer, yet the person who is God suffers in His humanity. For the person, the person, I say, was crucified in His humanity. In His own nature God cannot die; but now God and man are united in one person, so that the expression 'God's death' is correct, when the man dies wno is one thing or one person with God." *(Formula of Concord.)*

1 John 1, 7: *The blood of Jesus Christ, His Son, cleanseth us from all sin.*

Again the, person of the Savior is' named after His divine nature: *"His Son,"* God's Son. But this God's Son is at the same time *"Jesus,"* Mary's son. Mary's son has flesh and blood, but, Mary's son being God's Son, this property of having *blood* is ascribed to the whole person. And because it is God's blood, it has the power to *cleanse us from all sin.*

✲   ✲   ✲

A brief review of the doctrine of the Person of Christ seems to be in place here.—As we have seen, the Son of God assumed the impersonal human nature into His already existing divine person. "The Word became flesh," "God was manifest in the flesh"—such and other dicta of Scripture prove the *personal union.* From this personal union flows the *communication of natures, i. e.,* the interpenetration, the mutual permeation—*perichoresis*—of the natures. Glue two pieces of wood together and they may be said to be united—externally, but there is no internal, no organic union. Soul and body in man constitute the person. Where the soul is, there is also the body, and vice versa. Likewise, where the divine nature in Christ is, there is also the human, and vice versa. Owing to this personal union the so-called Personal Propositions are true: "God is man," and "Man is God," John 1, 14; 1 Tim. 3, 16, et al. Furthermore, from this personal union and the resultant communication of natures follows the *impartation of their attributes, or properties.* Each of the two natures partakes of the properties of the other. In Dogmatics this is known as the *Communicatio Idiomatum.* It is threefold: 1. *Genus idiomaticum;* 2. *Genus majestaticum;* 3. *Genus apotelesmaticum.*

1. The *Genus idiomaticum* consists in this, that the properties of the two natures are ascribed to the *whole person.* Christ is but one person—a human-divine person. The analogy of the union of soul and body may help somewhat in making the meaning clear. *Thinking* is an essential property of the soul; still one does not say: "My *soul* thinks," but *"I* think." To be hungry is an essential property of the body; but one does not say: "My body.is hungry," but *"I* am hungry." In both cases the subject is "I," which pronoun designates the *whole person.* Apply this to the two natures constituting the one person Christ. *To possess all*

power, e. g., is an essential property of the *divine* nature, hence there is no difficulty in understanding the proposition: *"The Son of God* is almighty." But this Son of God is at the same time *man;* hence the proposition is equally true: *"The Son of Mary* is almighty." *To die* is an essential attribute of the *human* nature; but since this dying happened to this person who is God as well as man, it is just as true to say: "God died," "the Prince of Life was killed," God, "the Lord of glory, was crucified," (Acts 3, 15; 1 Cor. 2, 8), as it is to say: "The son of Mary died, the son of Mary was killed, was crucified." The person remains the same, whether He is named after His divine or His human nature.— Other dicta of this genus are: "The Son of God was born of a woman;" "the son of Mary was before Abraham."

2. *Genus majestaticum.* The very name indicates this genus to be one-sided. Majesty is possessed by the divine nature only as an *essential* attribute. Hence the divine nature only can communicate majesty. The second kind of communication therefore consists therein, that *the divine nature communicates its properties to the human.* The human nature thereby does not become divine, but remains truly human, and the divine nature does not lose its attributes, but remains truly divine. The sun, by sending its rays through the universe, does not thereby lose its essence.—The *essential* attributes of the divine become *communicated* attributes of the human nature. The *Formula of Concord,* quoted above, alludes to two analogies often used by our forbears. Soul and body are intimately united and constitute one person. *Life,* an *essential* attribute of the soul, becomes a *communicated* attribute of the body. Of the whole person we say: He lives. The soul acts through the body in which it dwells. By virtue of this union the eye sees, the ear hears, the nose smells. In death the soul is separated from the body. Though still possessing eyes, ears, hands, etc., it can as little use them as could a lifelike marble statue of the person.—Again, an essential attribute of iron is that it is *heavy;* of fire, that it is *hot.* Iron in itself is not hot, nor is fire heavy, but conjoin the two, as in the case of a red-hot iron poker, and we have an interpenetration of attributes. Of this poker we may properly say that it is both hot and heavy. The essential attribute of the iron—its weight—is partaken of by this fire.—Still another analogy. Wire in itself is not electric. Connect it with a dynamo and it becomes a "live" wire; shut off the electric current and it is a "dead" wire. *"Life,"* a quality it does not possess in itself, has been communicated to the wire by means of the electric battery. Thus the human nature in Christ *per se* is not omniscient or omnipotent, but by virtue of the personal union the properties of the divine nature are imparted to it.

To the above analogies we would add the caution: *Omne simile claudicat.* In our efforts to make this doctrine somewhat apprehendable, we must never forget: it is and will remain "a confessedly great mystery," which we are simply to believe as the Scriptures declare.

3. *Genus apotelesmaticum.* The Greek word *apotelesma*, from which this genus takes its name, signifies an official act. According to this genus, Christ, in the works of His office, acts not through one nature alone, but through both natures, each nature performing what is *proper* to itself, in *communion* with the other. Passages illustrating this kind of communication may call for consideration later. (See Gal. 4, 4.5; 1 John 3, 8; Gen. 3, 15; Luke 9, 56.)   .

Matt. 18, 11: *The Son of Man is come to save that which was lost.*

In a previous article we have spoken of the personal union of the two natures in Christ. The question arises: *Cur Deus homo?* Why did God become man? Christ Himself states the purpose thus: "The Son of Man is come *to save* that which was lost." What was the cause of our lost condition? Sin. Hence Paul says: "Christ Jesus came into the world to save *sinners*," 1 Tim. 1, 15. In the present passage Jesus speaks, but He does not say: "*I* am come to save," etc., but: "The *Son of Man* is come to save," thus calling attention to the fact that it was necessary for Him to become *man* in order to carry out the plan of salvation. But why was it necessary that our Redeemer should be a true man? This the next passage tells us.

Hebr. 2, 14: *Forasmuch, then, as the children are partakers of flesh and blood, He also Himself likewise took part of the same, that through death He might destroy him that had the power of death, that is, the devil.*

The "children" are partakers of flesh and blood. These "children" had sinned. Through sin they had come into the bondage of the devil. "Through one man sin entered the world, and death by sin," Rom. 5, 12. "The wages of sin is death." How was this power to be broken? Man had sinned, and man must bear the penalty of sin; the Law was given to man, and by man it must be fulfilled. In order to become man's substitute, Christ became man. The "*children*," the sinners, were "*partakers of flesh and blood*," so Christ "*likewise took part of the same.*" Why? "*That through death He might destroy him that had the power of death, that is, the devil.*" That says, Christ became man in order to become capable of fulfilling the Law man had transgressed, to suffer and die in man's stead. "He was made like unto His brethren, that He might make reconciliation for the sins of the people," v. 17. Thus, both the fact and the purpose of Christ's incarnation are set forth in Hebr. 2, 14.—But why was it necessary that He should be true God at the same time?

Ps. 49, 7.8: *None of them can by any means redeem his brother, nor give to God a ransom for him: for the redemption of their soul is precious, and it ceaseth forever.*

To be saved man must be *redeemed*, a *ransom* must be paid, God must be reconciled. Who was to pay this redemption money? A *"brother"* for a brother? Not *"by any means"* could this be done. Why not? *"The redemption of their soul is too precious."* The *brother, i. e.,* man, any man like ourselves, cannot even redeem himself, much less "his brother." Aye, even a sinless man could have kept the Law for himself only, because it would have been his duty to do so. Among men there was no savior to be found; hence, looking for help from this quarter the *redemption must cease forever.* The sin of the whole human race had to be borne, the wrath of God must be appeased, the curse of the Law must be removed, infinite divine justice must be satisfied, death, hell, the devil must be overcome—aye, "the redemption of their soul was precious." The price with which our souls must be bought was too great for a mere man to furnish. "A high priest became us who was holy, harmless, undefiled, separate from sinners, and made higher than the heavens," Hebr. 7, 26. Our Savior must be God and man in one person. "While a mere God could not have suffered and died at all, and a mere man could not have suffered and died sufficiently, the suffering and death of the God-man was both real and sufficient; real, because of the human nature, and sufficient, because of the divine nature."

The Threefold Office Of Christ.

This wonderful Person, Christ, has performed a wonderful work, which may be expressed in that one all-comprehensive word—salvation. Comparing the Scripture passages that treat of His activity, in order to see what Christ did and does to carry out the work of salvation, we find that it is threefold. It consists in *teaching* us the way to salvation, in *reconciling* us with His heavenly Father, and in *governing* and *protecting* us. Hence we speak of a threefold office of Christ: the prophetic, the priestly, and the kingly.

GERHARD: "Christ atones God for the guilt of our sins . . . . . . which is a work peculiar to a *priest.* Christ publishes to us God's counsel concerning our redemption and salvation, which is the work of a *prophet.* Christ efficaciously applies to us the benefit of redemption and salvation, and rules us by the scepter of His Word and Holy Ghost, which is the work of a *king.*"

Christ Our Prophet.

Deut. 18, 15: *The Lord, thy God, will raise up unto thee a Prophet from the midst of thee, of thy brethren, like unto me; unto Him ye shall hearken.*

On Mount Sinai Jehovah had said to Moses: "I will raise them up a Prophet from among their brethren like unto thee; and I will put my words in His mouth, and He shall speak unto them all that I shall command Him. And it shall come to pass that whosoever will not hearken unto my words which He shall speak in my name, I will require it of him," Deut. 18, 16-19. Shortly before his death, Moses bequeathed this precious promise of the Great Prophet as a rich legacy to his people, saying, in the words of our text: *"The Lord, thy God, will raise up unto thee a Prophet,"* etc.

Who is this prophet *par excellence?* Scripture is its own interpreter. It does not leave us in doubt as to who is meant. It is Jesus of Nazareth. Peter, in his great discourse to the Jews, quotes the very words of our text and says they find their fulfillment in Jesus Christ. (Acts 3, 18-23.) Again, Philip finding Nathanael, said unto him: "We have found Him, of whom Moses in the Law, and the prophets, did write, Jesus of Nazareth, the son of Joseph," John 1, 45. Jesus Himself says to the Jews: "Think not that I will accuse you to the Father: there is one that accuseth you, even Moses, on whom ye have set your hope. For if ye believed Moses, ye would have believed me; for he wrote of me,". John 5, 45.46. And on the Mount of Transfiguration the voice of the Father was heard: "This is my beloved Son, in whom I am well pleased; *hear ye Him!"* Moses, by preeminence the great prophet of the Old Testament, speaks of Christ, the prophet *kat exochen.*

Moses says: "The Lord will raise up a *Prophet* like unto me." What is the proper meaning of the word *prophet?* We must avoid the narrow interpretation which would make this term simply to mean a fore-teller of future events. Exod. 7, 1 we read: "And the Lord said unto Moses, See, I have made thee a god to Pharaoh; and Aaron, thy brother, shall be thy *prophet."* Moses had shrunk from the commission imposed upon him by God to deliver Israel, especially because, as he said, "I am slow of speech and of a slow tongue," Exod. 4, 10. To overcome this difficulty his brother Aaron was directed to be his *prophet, i. e.,* his spokesman, his mouthpiece. "He shall be a *mouth* to thee," Exod. 4, 14-16. God says of Jeremiah the prophet: "Thou shalt be my *mouth."* A prophet is the *mouth* of God. God put His words into the prophet's mouth, and to these the prophet gave utterance. *"God spake* unto the fathers *through the prophets,"* Hebr. 1, 1. Two things therefore make up the content proper of the term *prophet:* 1. the divine revelation—"Holy men of God spake as they were moved by the Holy Ghost;" 2. the declaration to men of what the prophet had received by inspiration. Hence the formula we so frequently meet with in Scriptures, especially in Matthew: "Now all this is come to pass, that it might be fulfilled which was spoken *by* the Lord *through* the prophet," Matt. 1, 22. The Lord is the speaker; the prophet is His mouthpiece, His organ. John the Baptist, of whom we have no recorded predictions, is called a prophet, Matt. 11, 9: "But what went ye out for to see? A prophet? Yea, I say unto you, and more than a prophet." So the meaning of the term "prophet" is not chiefly a foreteller of future events, but rather a mouthpiece, a spokesman, an interpreter of God. Such was Moses, such was Christ. *"God,* who at sundry times and in divers manners *spake* in time past unto the fathers *by the prophets, hath* in these last days *spoken* unto us *by His Son,*" Hebr. 1, 1.2.

But Christ is a prophet in a much higher sense than Moses. This *Son,* of whom Hebrews speaks, is God's Son, is God Himself. In Christ God spoke and taught on earth. Moses declared unto the people: "Thus saith *the Lord;*" Christ proclaimed: "Verily, verily, *I* say unto you." Moses received his knowledge of divine things by revelation from God; Christ, the incarnate Word, was Himself the fountain of all knowledge.

Unto this Great Prophet *"ye shall hearken,"* i. e., unto Him and Him only. He is the only Teacher in the Church. "And it shall be, that every soul that shall not hearken to that prophet shall be utterly destroyed from among the people," Acts 3, 23. Therefore, "Kiss the Son, lest He be angry and ye perish in the way. Blessed are all they that take refuge in Him!" Ps. 2, 12.

Moses says: God will raise up a prophet *like unto me.* It is not within our purpose to draw all the parallel lines between Moses and Christ; moreover, too, it is self-evident that Christ is superior to Moses regarding both His person and His office. Wherein, then, does the *likeness* between Moses and Christ consist? "When Christ is called a prophet *like unto Moses,* Deut. 18, 15, the point of comparison is the mediation of a covenant. As Moses was the mediator of the old and transient covenant, so Christ is the Mediator of the new, permanent covenant, Hebr. 12, 18-28." (Dr. F. Pieper, *Die Lehre von Christi Werk,* p. 11.) "The Law was given by Moses, grace and truth came by Jesus Christ," John 1, 17.

Matt. 17, 5: *This is my beloved Son, in whom I am well pleased; hear ye Him!*

Jesus, we are told, ascended a high mountain, probably Mount Tabor. Three of His disciples, Peter, James, and John, were with Him. And He "was transfigured before them: and His face did shine as the sun, and His raiment was white as the light." Two heavenly messengers, Moses and Elias, appeared on the scene. Presently the glory of God manifested itself in a bright cloud as of old in the wilderness, Exod. 13, 21.22. The Father's voice, 2 Pet. 1, 17.18, was heard, saying: "This is my beloved Son, in whom I am well pleased; hear ye Him!" We observe: 1. The man Jesus of Nazareth is at the same time the Son of God, very God. 2. The work which the incarnate Son performs for the salvation of mankind is well-pleasing to God. God accepts the sacrifice of His Son. 3. The Father demands: "Hear ye Him!" Here is the echo of Deut. 18, 15. Him only shall we hear, in Him we shall believe. He is the true Prophet that teaches the way to God aright. And this Prophet speaks to us in the Scriptures. "Blessed are they that hear the Word of God, and keep it," Luke 11, 28.

Christ executes His prophetic office in two ways: 1. immediately, John 1, 18; 2. mediately, Luke 10, 16.

John 1, 18: *No man hath seen God at any time; the only-begotten*

Son, which is in the bosom of the Father, He hath declared Him.

The pronoun *ekeinos*, literally, *that one*, here translated *He*, in various other passages rendered *the same*, e. g., 1, 33, lends a very marked emphasis to the clause: *"He* hath declared Him." The meaning is: *He* declared Him as no other could. And *declared, exegesato*, says He acted as the Father's exegete, as His interpreter. Through Him the Father's inmost thoughts have been revealed to fallen mankind. All true knowledge of the Father is mediated by Him. And why was He so well qualified to do this? Because this *man* Christ, in the state of His humiliation, while sojourning visibly upon earth, as St. John says, *"is in* the bosom of the Father," in the most intimate and continuous communion, with the Father," and what He "saw and heard" there, John 3, 32, He communicated to us. Aye, this *man* Christ was at the same time *"the only-begotten Son"* of the Father, hence very God Himself, who in the eternal counsels of the Holy Trinity devised the plan, the ways and means, of redemption for a world lost in sin. Hence the knowledge that He communicates is a *divine* knowledge. If we would know the Father's will, the command is: "Here *ye Him!"* If any one should ask as did Philip: "Show us the Father," the answer is: "He that hath seen me hath seen the Father."

And what was the quintessence of His declaration? Let St. John answer, from whose Gospel this passage is taken and who carries out this thought from the beginning of the Prologue to the very last chapter. He says: "These have been written, that ye might believe that *Jesus is the Christ, the Son of God*, and that *believing ye might have life through* His name," John 20, 33. The prophets of old preached about Him; He preached about Himself. In the days of His visible presence here upon earth He performed this prophetic office in His own person—immediately. This His activity has ceased today. Today He performs it mediately.

Luke 10, 16: *He that heareth you heareth me; and he that despiseth you despiseth me; and he that despiseth me despiseth Him that sent me.*

At the close of the charge to His twelve disciples, Christ said: "He that receiveth you receiveth me; and he that receiveth me receiveth Him that sent me," Matt. 10, 40. Words of the same import are found in our text. They are addressed to the seventy who were to proclaim the Gospel of the kingdom of God. *"He that heareth you heareth me."* Christ today does not speak to men directly, but through human ministers. The treatment accorded to His ambassadors is accorded to Christ, to God. The Gospel is Christ's voice. Wherever it is proclaimed Christ speaks. He is the only Teacher in the Church to this day. This truth we find throughout the New Testament. Paul says, Col. 3, 16: "Let *the word of Christ* dwell in you richly in all wisdom." The Corinthians he admonishes: "Ye seek a proof *of Christ speaking in me*," etc. To the Thessalonians he writes: "From you hath sounded forth *the Word of the*

Lord," 1 Thess. 1, 8. "We waxed bold in our God to speak unto you *the Gospel of God*," 1 Thess, 2, 2. Again: "When ye received *the Word of God* which ye heard of *us*, ye received it not as the word of men, but, as it is in truth, the Word of God," 1 Thess. 2, 13. The word of *the Lord*, the Word of *God*,—these are controvertible terms,—is the only word to be preached, and nothing but this word. Hence the admonition to the preachers of the Gospel: "If any man speak, let him speak as the oracles"—the words—"of God," 1 Pet. 4, 11. Phrases such as are frequently heard in sectarian churches: "In my opinion the Lord would say;" or, "My view of this passage is this;" or, "The idea conveyed here seems to be," must not be uttered from a Lutheran pulpit. Lutheran ministers say with the apostle: "We speak that we do know." Opinions, views, conjectures, have no place in the pulpit. Throughout the sermon the Word of God, the voice of Christ, must be heard. He is the only Teacher in the Church. "One is your Master, even Christ."

CHRIST OUR HIGH PRIEST.

As our Prophet Christ *taught* the way of salvation; as our High Priest He *merited* salvation. Hence the priestly office is the foundation for the prophetic. To stand as the High Priest of the world between the holy and just God, on the one hand, and man, lost in sin, on the other, Christ must do two things: He must make *satisfaction* and *intercession* for our sins.

He must make *satisfaction* for our sins. How? 1. By rendering perfect obedience to the divine Law that man did not keep and cannot keep. This is called His *active obedience*. 2. By suffering the penalties threatened to the transgressors of that Law, and hence offering Himself a sacrifice for the sins of the world. This is known as His *passive obedience*.

Now as to the passages quoted in our Catechism. Hebr. 7, 26.27 shows us our need of a High Priest; Gal. 4, 4.5 speaks of Christ's active obedience; 1 Pet 2, 24 treats of His passive obedience, and 1 John 2, 1.2 of His intercession.

Hebr. 7, 26.27: *Such an High Priest became us, who is holy, harmless, undefiled, separate from sinners, and made higher than the heavens; who needeth not daily, as those high priests, to offer up sacrifice first for his own sins and then for the people's: for this He did once when He offered up Himself.*

The central thought of this passage is: Christ is our true High Priest who offered up Himself once for all time.—The people of the Old Testament had a great multitude of priests, chief of them being the high priest. His most important duties were: 1. the bringing of the great annual sin-offering for the atonement of the manifold transgressions of the people; 2. the intercession before God for the people. These priests and their sacrifices were but types of the Great High Priest Christ. "The law had the *shadow* of the good things to come, not the very image of the things," Hebr. 10, 1. Of the insufficiency of the Old Testament priesthood the writer of Hebrews says: "If there was perfection through the Levitical priesthood, what further need was there that another priest should arise after the order of Melchizedek?" Hebr. 7, 11. Hence the stress of the opening words of our text: *"Such an High Priest became us,"* i. e., was suitable to us, of such a one we stood in need, *"who was holy, harmless, undefiled,"* etc. The inscription on the miter of the Old Testament high priest read: "Holiness to the Lord," but he himself was a sinner, not "holy, harmless," etc., who therefore had need *"to offer up sacrifice, first for his own sins,"* before making offering for the sins of the people. Such a high priest could do us no good. We stood in need of one *"who is holy, harmless, undefiled, separate from sinners."* This High Priest is Christ Jesus. He is true man, and as such could become man's substitute; He was at the same time *"made higher than the heavens,"* i. e., true God. This High Priest could fill up the chasm between God and man.

And what was the nature of His sacrifice? The high priest of the Old Testament offered up—what? A bullock, two goats, and a ram. But such sacrifices "can never take away sins," Hebr. 10, 11. Our High Priest *"offered up Himself."* He Himself was the Lamb that took away the sins of the world. The high priest of the Old Testament offered up a thing distinct from his own person; our High Priest offered up *Himself.* Because of this fact His sin-offering has *infinite* value. *Christ is both High Priest and Sacrifice.* This sacrifice was a *vicarious* sacrifice, made *"for the people's"* sins, for our sins, in our stead; the Righteous took the place of the unrighteous, *dikaios huper adikon,* 1 Pet. 3, 18. We further note that it was a *voluntary* sacrifice. Emphatically it is said: "This He *did* once," "*He* offered up Himself." O for the great love of our Savior! And this sacrifice is complete, perfect, perpetually efficacious. This thought is made prominent. We read: "This He did *once,*" i. e., once for all time. The repetition of the sacrifices in the Old Testament was a constant reminder of the insufficiency of the Levitical priesthood, of their sinfulness and that of the people. Our High Priest offered up Himself *once.* "He offered *one* sacrifice for sins *forever.*" "By *one* offering He hath *perfected forever* them that are sanctified," Hebr. 10, 12.14. Hence, how abominable is the sacrilege and the blasphemy, of the Popish priests who pretend to offer up Christ in an unbloody manner in their unholy mass, and that not only as an expiatory sacrifice for the living, but also for the dead! (See *Concil. Trid,* sess. 6, cap. 2.—Cf. Hebr. 9, 12.24-28; 10, 10-14; Rom. 6, 10; 1 Pet. 3, 18.) By such false, pernicious doctrine the Catholic Church declares the death of our Redeemer, the *only* sacrifice for our sins, to be insufficient and ineffective. "This He did *once,*" says the text, and thereby "obtained *eternal redemption,*" Hebr. 9, 12. This offering is not to be and cannot

be repeated. It is eternally valid and efficacious.—Such, then, is briefly
1. the character of the High Priest that became us; such is 2. the nature of the sacrifice that became us.

* * *

God's justice is immutable. He demands: "Thou shalt love the
Lord, thy God, with all thy heart, and with all thy soul, and with all
thy mind. Thou shalt love thy neighbor as thyself," Matt. 22, 37.39.
But how about us? "All have sinned, and come short of the glory of
God," Rom. 3, 23. The consequence of sin Isaiah states thus: "Your
iniquities have separated between you and your God," Is. 59, 2 On
account of our sin we are enemies of God, Rom. 5, 11, and under
the curse of the Law, Gal. 3, 15. That there might be help for us
a reconciliation must be effected, divine justice must be satisfied, the
Law must be fulfilled. For this purpose, our High Priest came into the
world. He says: "I am not come to destroy the Law, but to fulfill,"
Matt. 5, 17. Of His rendering perfect obedience to this immutable Law
of God (obedientia activa) Gal. 4, 4.5 speaks.

Gal. 4, 4.5: *When the fullness of the time was come, God sent forth
His Son, made of a woman, made under the Law, to redeem them that
were under the Law, that we might receive the adoption of sons.*

"The fullness of the time," *to pleroma tou chronou,* is the time of
the New Testament which began with the appearance of Christ in the
flesh, when *God sent forth His Son.* The Greek word *exapesteilen—sent
forth*—clearly indicates the pre-existence of Christ before His incarnation. (Cf. John 1, 1.) This Son, coequal and coeternal with the Father,
God *sent forth.* How? The text answers: *made of a woman.* This
Son, very God, "was made of a woman," i. e., He became *man.* Christ,
our High Priest, is God and man in one person. The phrase "made of a
woman," moreover, points to His wonderful conception and birth. He
was conceived by the Holy Ghost, born of the *Virgin* Mary. Of this
God-man it is said that He was *"made under the Law."* We, all men,
are by nature subject to the Law of God. Not so with Christ. He,
God's Son, very God, is Himself the Lawgiver. But for our sake He
was *made* under the Law.

And what was the purpose of His incarnation ("made of a woman")
and His subjection to the Law ("made under the Law")? Answer:
"To redeem them that were under the Law." This perfectly holy life,
in full conformity with the Law, was not lived in the first place to be a
pattern for us, but to fulfill the Law perfectly, and thus *to redeem* us.
The *guilt* of having transgressed God's most holy will must be removed
ere we could find favor in His eyes. The further purpose of Christ's
obedience to the Law is stated thus: *"That we might receive the adoption of sons."* By nature we were the children of wrath. Eph. 2, 3.
But now, since the Law has been fulfilled by our High Priest in our
stead, the adoption of sonship is in store for us. "Christ is the end of

the Law for righteousness to every one that believeth," Rom. 10, 4. "As by one man's disobedience many were made sinners, so by the obedience of one shall many be righteous," Rom. 5, 19.

* * *

But our disobedience to the divine Law not only incurred the *guilt* of being sinners, but also subjected us to the *curse* of the Law. God said: "The soul that sinneth it shall die," Ezek. 18, 20. "Cursed is every one that continueth not in all things which are written in the book of the Law to do them," Gal. 3, 10. From this curse we could not free ourselves, Ps. 48, 8.9. Christ did. "Christ has redeemed us from the curse of the Law, having become a curse for us," Gal. 3, 13. How? Peter answers:—

1 Pet. 2, 24: *Christ His own self bare our sins in His own body on the tree, that we, being dead to sins, should live unto righteousness: by whose stripes ye were healed.*

"Christ His *own self* bare *our* sins." These words teach the *vicarious* sufferings of Christ. The pronouns *hemon—autos: our—He Himself,* easily overlooked, are very significant. They express two great important truths: substitution and atonement. These pronouns say, Christ took the place of the sinner. Our sins they were, which He, the Holy One, took upon Himself and atoned for.—Again, the text says: "*Who* (Christ) bare our sins." Christ is the acting subject. *He* bare our sins. So it was not a fate which He could not escape. The bearing of our sins was a *voluntary* act on His part, and because it was such a willing, patient suffering, His sacrifice is perfect and acceptable to God. Both locutions are biblical: 1. Christ imputed our sins to Himself (Eph. 5, 2), and 2. *God* imputed them to Him, as Isaiah says: "The Lord hath laid upon Him the iniquity of us all," Is. 53, 6.—And when the apostle says: "He bare our sins *in His own body,*" Christ's body appears as the vessel in which He carried our sins to the cross. Our sins, the sins of the whole world, He carried "*on the tree,*" i. e., on the cross, Acts 5, 30; 10, 39. Christ suffered the most ignominious death for our sins, the death on the cross, the death of a vile criminal. He became a *curse* for us. "Cursed is every one that hangeth on a tree!"— Having taken our sins upon Himself, Christ carried them to the cross. Upon this altar they were offered and thus blotted out, atoned for. By His stripes we were healed. This is the sacrifice of our High Priest, Christ, the God-man. "Christ hath loved us, and hath given *Himself for us* as an *offering* and a *sacrifice to God* for a sweet-smelling savor," Eph. 5, 2. "He gave *Himself for us,* that He might redeem us from all iniquity," Tit. 2, 14. By giving Himself a ransom for all, Christ, the High Priest, was the Mediator between God and men, 1 Tim. 2, 5.6.

Peter addresses Christians who know that the first and foremost purpose of Christ's sacrifice was to redeem them, Tit. 2, 14. In the present passage he describes the effect of Christ's sacrificial death thus:

"That we, being dead to sins, should live unto righteousness." Here the
state of the converted is described: they are "dead to sin." They are
transplanted from a life of sin into a new life; they are freed from the
dominion of Satan. Their new life is governed by "righteousness"; they
"live unto righteousness," earnestly striving to do the will of God. And
this, too, was one purpose of the death of Christ.

* * *

Christians, as was said, "live unto righteousness"; they are earnest
in their endeavors to avoid sin, and are continually admonished to *sin
not,* 1 John 2, 1. And still we have cause daily to pray, "Forgive us our
trespasses!" And on account of these trespasses Satan accuses us "before our God night and day," Rev. 12, 10. How consolatory therefore
to know that our High Priest, who made satisfaction for us, "hath an
unchangeable priesthood," and "is able to save to the uttermost that
come unto God by Him, seeing He ever liveth to make *intercession* for
us," Hebr. 7, 24.25. Of His intercession the last passage treats.

1 John 2, 1.2: *If any man sin, we have an Advocate. with the
Father, Jesus Christ the Righteous: and He is the propitiation for our
sins: and not for ours only, but also for the sins of the whole world.*

Jesus is our Advocate, *parakletos,* whence the transliterated English
noun Paraclete. *Parakletos* (from *parakaleo)* means *summoned, called
to one's side,* especially to one's aid; hence a *helper,* an *assistant,* a *suc-
corer,* a *pleader, legal assistant,* one who pleads another's cause, an
advocate. Here Christ is called our *Helper, parakletos,* before the throne
of the Father, hence the specific term *advocate, intercessor,* is demanded
by the context. Our Advocate is Jesus Christ *"the Righteous,"* He, who
"is the propitiation for our sins," He, who made reconciliation, atonement, for our sins. Hence the relation between Christ's intercession and
atonement is apparent. He intercedes for the sinners, by pleading His
righteousness, His merits, the propitiation made by Him.

For whom does Christ intercede? The text says: *"He is the propitiation for our sins: and not for ours only, but also for the sins of the
whole world."* He, being the propitiation for all men, makes intercession
for all, also for the ungodly. An example of this kind we find in Luke
23, 34. This is called His *general intercession* (intercessio generalis).
Of this we cannot speak here.—For whom does Christ intercede especially, and of whom especially does our text speak? Of the believers. St.
John writes: "My little children, these things write I unto you, *that
ye sin not. And if any man sin,* we have an Advocate," etc. Who are
they that sin not and yet have sin? They that sin not intentionally,
willingly, with forethought and malice; they that are "dead to sin" and
"live unto righteousness," and still must daily pray, "Forgive us our
trespasses,"—the Christians. For these Christ especially intercedes
(intercessio specialis). How great is the comfort we derive from this
doctrine! Jesus Christ, the Reconciliation for our sins, continually

makes intercession for us with the Father. So we may rest assured that our petitions to the throne of grace are not unheard, but seconded and sustained by our great High Priest in heaven. "Who is he that condemneth? It is Christ that died, yea rather, that is risen again, who is even at the right hand of God, who also maketh intercession for us."

CHRIST OUR KING.

Christ's kingship was foretold in the Old Testament. "Thou hast put all things under His feet: all sheep and oxen, yea, and the beasts of the field; the fowls of the air, and the fish of the sea, and whatsoever passeth through the paths of the seas," Ps. 8. And what Daniel saw in the night vision he thus describes: "Behold, one like the *Son of Man* came with clouds, and came to the Ancient of Days, and they brought Him near before Him. And there was given Him dominion and glory, and a *kingdom*, that all people, nations, and languages should serve Him." Dan. 7, 13.14. Christ is a king. Hence the inquiry of the wise men from the East was: "Where is He that is *born King* of the Jews?" Matt. 2, 2.

According to the various subjects and diverse modes of government Christ's kingdom is threefold: 1. The *kingdom of power*, pertaining to all creatures; 2. *The kingdom of grace*, pertaining to the Church militant; and 3. The *Kingdom of glory*, pertaining to the Church triumphant.

In that final interview with His disciples in Galilee, and as a prelude to His last Great Commission, Christ speaks of Himself as the King of the universe. He said:

Matt. 28, 18: *All power is given unto me in heaven and in earth.*

The sphere of His kingdom is indicated by the phrase: *"in heaven and in earth."* How vast is that kingdom! He possesses all power *"in heaven"*—all the holy angels, authorities, powers, the cherubim and the seraphim, are His willing servants. And *"in earth,"* too, all things are put under His feet. His kingship is world-wide, universal. A grand, a majestic truth! Christ rules and reigns over all, whatever it may be, however powerful it may be, wherever it may be, "in heaven or in earth"—all, all is in His kingdom, the heathen that rage, the kings of the earth and its rulers, aye, the very devils in hell not excepted. His is all power without any limitation. Over all He mightily rules and reigns. This is His kingdom of *power!*

And why is it so called? Because the means whereby He rules in this kingdom is, as stated in the text, *"all power." "All power,"* all *authority,* clearly is *omnipotence.* If His omnipotent word goes forth, who can withstand? And so, "why do the heathen rage, and the people imagine a vain thing? The kings of the earth set themselves and the rulers take counsel together, against the Lord and against His Anointed, saying, Let us break their bands asunder, and cast their cords from us. He that sitteth in the heavens shall laugh: the Lord shall have them in derision," Ps. 2.

Of this "all power," this omnipotence, Christ says, It is *"given to me."* The divine nature of Christ possesses omnipotence as an *essential* attribute, but this essential attribute, by virtue of the personal union, becomes a *communicated* attribute of the human nature. The man Christ is almighty. The God-man was not exalted to royal dignity and power after His resurrection or ascension, but was *born* a king, Matt. 2, 2.6; Luke 2, 11; Is. 9, 6. This "all power," given unto Him according to His humanity, He manifested before His exaltation by numerous miracles, thus proving the truth expressed in our text and in that other saying of His: "All things have been delivered unto Me of My Father," Matt. 11, 25. He rebuked the winds and the sea, and they obeyed Him, Matt. 8, 27. He walked on the sea, Matt. 14, 26. He cast out evil spirits with His word, and healed the sick, Matt. 8, 16. With a single word He felled His captors, John 18, 6. He spoke to him that was dead: "Young man, I say unto thee, arise; and he......sat up and began to speak," Luke 7, 14.15. The winds, the sea, the evil spirits, the devil, sickness, enemies, death—all are subject to His power.

This truth affords great *consolation* for us, since our King so regulates the whole universe and all things upon earth as to contribute to the glory of His divine name and to the gathering and preservation of His Church. "We believe according to the working of His *mighty power,*" Eph. 1, 19. By virtue of His omnipotence the spiritually dead Lazaruses are made spiritually alive. The Church is gathered through His almighty Word. And this His Church He protects against all enemies, aye, against the very devil himself, for as He, the King, said: "The gates of hell shall not prevail against it," Matt. 16, 18. Why, the very connection in which the words of our text stand to the Last Great Commission of our King prove the same majestic truth. "All power is given to me in heaven and in earth. Go ye *therefore* and make disciples of all the nations, baptizing them into the name of the Father, and of the Son, and of the Holy Ghost: teaching them to observe all things whatsoever I commanded you. And lo, I am with you alway, even unto the end of the world." As if to say: Ye ambassadors of mine, be not afraid! Ye are to wage war against the formidable kingdom of Satan, to destroy its bulwarks, and upon its ruins ye are to plant the cross, the emblem of the Crucified One. What a task! But fear not ye! "Go ye *therefore,*" since mine is all power, go ye therefore—and build my Church. Though you will no longer enjoy my *visible* presence, *invisibly* I will be with you, guide you, protect you in the performance of your sacred office. "Disciple the nations, baptizing them," etc., and when the last one according to God's decree has been brought into the Church, then will the end come and the scaffold of this world will be torn down, since it has served its purpose; the *una sancta,* the holy Christian Church, will be complete.

So, then, this "all power," His omnipotence, wherewith our King mightily rules over all creatures, has but one object in view—the gathering and the preservation of His Church, which is called His kingdom of *grace*.

This universal kingship of Christ is not apparent to the natural eye. As the writer of Hebrews says: "But now we see not yet all things put under Him," Hebr. 2, 8. It is an article of faith which we are to lay hold of for our consolation. In yonder life, when the mists will have been lifted from our eyes and our vision will be clear, when we no longer know in part, we shall see that this whole universe, together with its governments, rulers, and ordinances, lay in the hollow of Christ our King's hands and were made subservient to His gracious purpose—the building of the kingdom of grace. And what is this kingdom?

John 18, 37: *Pilate therefore said unto Him, Art Thou a king, then? Jesus answered, Thou sayest that I am a king. To this end was I born, and for this cause came I into the world, that I should bear witness unto the truth. Every one that is of the truth heareth My voice.*

In the trial before Pilate, Jesus had said: "My kingdom is not of this world," etc., v. 36. He spoke of His special kingdom of grace, which, though *in* the world, is "not *of* this world." Pilate asks, "Art Thou a king, then?" Jesus, asserting that He, indeed, is a king, and describing the true character of His kingdom, makes answer: I am a king; I am a *born* king; I am a king of the *truth*. Who are His subjects? *"Every one that is of the truth heareth my voice."* Every one "that is of the truth," that is born of God, whose heart has been conquered and won by the truth unto which He bears witness, belongs to this kingdom. This is a mark of the true subjects in this kingdom: they hear *His voice*. Who hear His voice? The Christians, the believers. And these, collectively, constitute His kingdom. Wherever the believer may live, to whatsoever nationality he may belong, whatsoever language he may speak—in the eyes of Christ he belongs to that "holy nation" of which Peter speaks, 1 Pet. 2, 9. This kingdom Christ rules by *His voice*, the Gospel, the Gospel of Grace. Hence it is not a worldly kingdom, but a *spiritual* kingdom. Another name for this kingdom is the Church, the communion of saints.—Of this same kingdom the following passage treats.

Matt. 21, 5: *Tell ye the daughter of Zion, Behold, Thy King cometh unto thee, meek, and sitting upon an ass, and a colt, the foal of an ass.*

The context speaks of Christ's royal entry into Jerusalem. By it, the Evangelist avers, the prophecy recorded in Zech. 9, 9, was fulfilled. Zechariah describes the New Testament kingdom of peace and grace. The King of Zion, whom, according to the context of the prophecy, the heathen also shall serve, v. 10, is the Messiah, the son of David, He, whom the multitudes pronounce to be "Jesus, the prophet of Nazareth of Galilee," Matt. 21, 11. The subjects of this kingdom are denominated "the daughter of Zion," the daughter of Jerusalem, *i. e.,* the inhabitants of Jerusalem, who represent the people of Israel. But the true, the spiritual Israel is meant, the Church of God, God's people, as contra-distinguished from the heathen world. Zech. 9, 3-8. Accordingly, when the announcement is made to the daughter of Zion: "Thy King cometh unto thee," the Christian Church is accosted, *i. e.,* the believers gathered from among Jews and Gentiles, for they are the true, spiritual Israel.

To "the daughter of Zion" Christ comes *"meek."* Thereby the Evangelist indicates the rule of this kingdom. Christ rules therein with "meekness," *i. e.,* by His grace, by His Word of grace, the Gospel of salvation. "Thy King cometh unto thee, *meek."* "Flee not, be not despond-ent! Your king does not approach you as He did Adam or Cain, or as at the time of the flood, or when He visited Babylon, or Sodom and Go-morrah. Nor does He come to you as He did to the people of Israel on Mount Sinai. He makes His advent not in anger to take you to account; wrath is laid aside, there is nothing but meekness and kindness. He purposes to treat you in such a manner that your heart may be of good cheer, love, and confidence toward Him, to cling to Him and seek shelter in Him." (Luther, Erl. ed. X, 13.)—In other words, by means of His Word Christ rules over the *hearts* of His subjects; hence this kingdom of grace is a spiritual kingdom. Of it Christ, speaking to the carnal-minded Pharisees, says, Luke 17, 20.21: "The kingdom of God cometh not by observation"—its coming cannot be observed with the bodily eyes. "Neither shall they say, Lo here! or, Lo there!"—a definite locality can-not be assigned to it,—"for, behold, the kingdom of God is within you," it is of a spiritual nature, has its seat in the heart. There the King erects His throne and fills it with joy, and grace, and comfort, and peace that surpasseth all understanding.—And when Christ's loyal subjects die, they pass out of the world, but remain in His kingdom—the kingdom of *glory.*

2 Tim. 4, 18: *The Lord shall deliver me from every evil work, and will preserve me unto His heavenly kingdom: to whom be glory for ever and ever! Amen.*

Having recounted several instances in which God preserved him, Paul concludes the letter proper with the words: *"The Lord,"* as He has so often done in the past, *"shall deliver me,"* also in the future, *"from every evil work,"* that my enemies may concoct against me. From these words we see: the kingdom of grace is at the same time a kingdom of the *cross.* But final deliverance will surely come. In spite of all trials and tribulations here below, the King guards and protects His subjects "from every evil work," and we shall and can rest assured with Paul that He *"will preserve us unto His heavenly kingdom."* From the Church militant the believers are transplanted into the Church tri-umphant, from the kingdom of grace into the *kingdom of glory.* Here "God shall wipe away all tears from their eyes; and there shall be no more death, neither sorrow, nor crying, neither shall there be any more pain: for the former things are passed away," Rev. 21, 4. Here the cross, there the crown. "Now we see through a glass, darkly; but then face to face," 1 Cor. 13, 12.

As our Prophet, Priest, and King Christ is our Redeemer. As Prophet He taught the way of salvation; as Priest He merited salvation, and as King He imparts what He has merited, governs, protects us, and leads us into His heavenly kingdom. Thus Christ is our Lord.

THE STATE OF HUMILIATION.

Phil. 2, 5-8: *Let this mind be in you, which was also in Christ Jesus, who, being in the form of God, thought it not robbery to be equal with God, but made Himself of no reputation, and took upon Him the form of a servant, and was made in the likeness of men: and being found in fashion as a man, He humbled Himself, and became obedient unto death, even the death of the cross.*

."*Let this mind be in you which was also in Christ Jesus.*" Christ is set forth as a pattern from which Christians should copy. What *mind* was in Christ? "*He humbled Himself.*" So Christ is a pattern of humility for the Christians. This is the scope of the present passage, and must not be overlooked in its interpretation. *Balduin:* "Hoc observetur tantum scopus apostoli nostri, cui propositum non est, docere, quomodo Filius Dei carnem assumserit, sed quomodo Jesus Christus in sua humanitate formam servi assumserit *et hoc ipso exemplum humilitatis suis reliquerit.*" At the same time we have in this text the *sedes doctrinae* for the state of humiliation.

1. *Who humbled Himself?* "He," "*Christ Jesus.*" Let us mark well! Christ Jesus humbled Himself, the God-man, this Person who possesses a divine and a human nature, this theanthropic person. So who is humiliated and afterwards exalted? The *person* of Christ Jesus. *Quenstedt:* "Subjectum quod est persona *tou logou*, non qua *asarkos*, et incarnanda sed qua *ensarkos* et incarnata." The entire context bears out this statement. Of the *Christos ensarkos* only the apostle can say that He "made Himself of no reputation," "He humbled Himself," and, later, that He was "exalted."

2. *According to which nature did Christ humble Himself?* According to His *human* nature. For *a priori:* the *divine* nature cannot be abased and cannot be exalted; it is immutable. *In Deum non cadit mutatio.* Again: The apostle says: "Let this mind be in you, which was also in Christ Jesus,"—be humble! According to His *divine* nature Christ would not be presented to us as an example whom we were to follow. And again: The text says: He took upon Himself the form of a servant; He was made in the likeness of men; found in fashion as a man; He died—all of which can be said of the *human* nature only.

3. *Wherein does the humiliation not consist?* Not in the assumption of the human nature. One may call that a condescension, but not humiliation in the biblical sense of the term. If His humiliation had consisted in His assumption of the human nature, His exaltation would consist in the laying aside of His human nature, and Christ would no longer be the God-man! The text does not say: "He was made *man*," but: "He was made *in the likeness* of men." Furthermore, as we have seen, the subject of the whole discourse is Christ Jesus, the God-man. This theanthropic person, possessing a divine and a human nature, "*was made* in the likeness of men," "*took upon Himself* the form of a servant." So "the form of a servant" is not equivalent to His human nature, because that He already had and hence could not "take upon Himself."

4. *What, then, is the state of humiliation?* St. Paul says: *"Christ Jesus, being"*—existing—*"in the form of God, thought it not robbery to be equal with God, but made Himself of no reputation,"* etc. What is *the form of God?* Clearly not the *divine* nature, otherwise *the form of a servant* were His *human* nature; of this *form of a servant*, however, Christ divested Himself, consequently that would be asserting that Christ is no longer true man. *Form, morfe, Gestalt*, is the external manifestation, it is that whereby one is known, is seen; *form of God* is the external manifestation of God, that whereby God is known, is seen. The *essence* of God is presupposed; only He who possesses the essence of God can exist in the *form* of God. The *form* is the manifestation of the *essence*. God only can appear in the form of God. Since Christ is in *the form of God*, He is true God. God is invisible; still a *form, Gestalt*, is predicated of Him. The *form* of God is that whereby this invisible God manifests Himself as God. The *morfe theou* is equivalent to the *doxa theou, the glory of God*, John 1, 14, *i. e.*, the aggregate of all divine attributes, especially His omnipotence, His omniscience, and His omnipresence. "The Word was made flesh," says St. John, "and dwelt among us, *and we beheld His glory*, the glory as of the Only Begotten of the Father." By the manifestation of His divine attributes, of His divine majesty, they saw this *man* Christ is almighty, this *man* is God.

"Being in the form of God," Christ was "equal with God." *En morfe theou huparchon*, "in the form of God *existing*"; *huparchon*—existing—is a very emphatic participle. It shows: (1) that Christ *did not take upon Himself* the form of God, as it is said that He "took upon Himself the form of a servant," but that *He existed in it*; (2) that with the form of God Christ is said to have possessed, at the same time, a divine essence and nature; that Christ Jesus, when He had taken upon Himself *the form of a servant*, neither laid aside the divine nature itself, nor in any way resigned the form of God. (Quenstedt.)—Christ existed in the form of God, and hence could have exercised it to its fullest extent, could have always made use of His divine majesty imparted to Him according to His human nature; He could at all times have acted as God, so that all might have seen this *morfe theou* at all times. But this he did not do. For the text reads: *"He thought it not robbery to be equal with God,"* i. e., He possessed the equality with God, but did not think this a thing of booty that should be used as a means of self-glorification. And that He did not look upon this being equal with God as robbery, as booty, may be seen from the fact that He manifested this form of God, His divine majesty, only now and then in the service of the brethren, but not for His own honor and glory.

So Christ might at all times have made use of this *form of God.* He did not—for a purpose: He wanted to become our Substitute and Savior, and so He *"made Himself of no reputation,"* etc. That is to say, as a rule, He laid aside the use of His divine majesty communicated to His human nature. He became a man like unto ourselves; He became a servant instead of a master; He humbled Himself so deeply as to die the death of a vile criminal on the cross; and all this He did for our sakes.

5. *Rays of glory.* The passages cited in the Catechism prove conclusively that Christ possessed "the form of God," divine majesty, in the state of humiliation. John 2, 11 says that by the miracle of His turning water into wine Christ "manifested forth His glory." John 11, 40 ff. speaks of the climax of Christ's miracles, the raising of Lazarus. John 18, 6 tells us that with the words, "I am He," Christ felled His captors to the ground. Aye, indeed, this man Jesus is almighty. Instances might be multiplied. Read Matt. 8, 23-27, which relates His stilling the tempest. In v. 24 we read: "He was asleep." Here we see the form of a servant: He slept. "He was made in the likeness of men;" like other men He was in need of sleep; "He was found in fashion like a man." Reading v. 26, we behold "the form of God." The danger to that frail craft was exceedingly great, but the angry waves were obedient to His will. "He rebuked the winds and the sea; and there was a great calm." Whenever it pleased Him, He could make use of His divine majesty, as here. In v. 27 the men marveling say: "What manner of man is this, that even the winds and the sea obey Him?" He is "in the likeness of men," just like other men; yet He must be something greater. He cannot be from the earth, He must be from heaven! They saw the form of God, the majesty of God. They saw He was "equal with God." And it was not robbery on the part of Christ to act as He did act, for He was God even in the state of humiliation. Or take Mark 5, 4 ff. The daughter of Jairus was dead. Christ had said: "The damsel is not dead." "They laughed Him to scorn." He was in fashion as a man; this they saw. The girl was dead; this they knew. Christ brought her to life: "Talitha cumi!" The sneers were turned into astonishment; they saw the form of God.

* * *

We append a running commentary. *"Let this mind be in you which was also in Christ Jesus,"* be humble, *"who, being"*—existing—*"in the form of God,"* having in or about Him that whereby God is known, seen, manifested as God, *"thought it not robbery to be equal with God,"* counted not the being on an equality with God a thing to be grasped, esteemed it not rapine to be equal with God. In ancient times the victors looked upon their booty as upon a means of self-glorification and so used it. Thus did Christ not look upon His being equal with God; He did not make a boast, a display, of it; He did not use it constantly and fully, *"but,"* though He could have done so, *"He made Himself of no reputation,"* He emptied Himself. What this means the preceding context reveals negatively: He did not make a boast of His equality with God. The succeeding text states the thought positively: He emptied Himself, *"taking the form of a servant."* Christ, the God-man, who also according to His human nature possessed all power in heaven and in earth; who, also according to His human nature in the state of humiliation was the Lord of lords, He, whom the heavenly hosts would gladly have served at all times, came to serve others, to serve, to redeem us. The concept *form of a servant* is developed in the next phrases: *"being made in the likeness of men, and being found in fashion as a man."* He was a man like other men, yet without sin. This "likeness" was manifested: He ate, He drank, He wept, He slept; thus He was "found in fashion as a man"; thus *"He humbled Himself."* He did it; it was an act of His; willingly He humbled Himself. Willingly, for our sakes, He forewent high stations, honors, prerogatives, which He might rightfully claim and enjoy. And when the apostle says: *"and became obedient unto death, even the death of the cross,"* he indicates the last stage of humiliation, the climax of self-humiliation. So deeply Christ humbled Himself that He died the death of a vile criminal—for us! On the cross He cried out, "It"—the work of redemption—"is finished!" That was the purpose of His humiliation—our salvation! That was the reason why He did not employ His divine majesty constantly which He at all times possessed. The purpose of His humiliation was to swallow death up into victory, that we might bless God, saying, "Thanks be to God which giveth us the victory through our Lord Jesus Christ!"

The Conception of Christ.

Luke 1, 35: *The Holy Ghost shall come upon thee, and the power of the Highest shall overshadow thee: therefore also that holy thing which shall be born of thee shall be called the Son of God.*

The angel Gabriel was sent to Mary, a descendant of David. His sudden appearance and unusual greeting amaze Mary. The angel tells her, she, the virgin, is to become the mother of a son whom God will have named Jesus, Savior. This, her son, is at the same time to be the Son of God, and is to fulfill the prophecies concerning the son of David, the eternal King of Israel. Mary asks wonderingly, "How shall this be, seeing I know not a man?" Gabriel explains matters, saying, *"The*

Holy Ghost shall come upon thee," and thus *"the power of the Highest shall overshadow thee,"* and in the power of God, the Holy Ghost, Mary shall conceive. Here, then, we have a proof passage for the words of the Creed: "Conceived by the Holy Ghost." What we are here told is wonderfully corroborated by the account of Christ's conception, Matt. 1, 18: "She (Mary) was found with child *of (ek) the Holy Ghost,"* and by the divine message of the angel to Joseph: "Fear not to take unto thee Mary, thy wife; for that which is *conceived in her is of the Holy Ghost,"* v. 20.

Her son, so Mary is told, will not owe his existence as man to a human father, but to the miraculous operation of the Holy Ghost, and hence *"also that holy thing which shall be born of thee shall be called the Son of God."* Here Christ's humanity and divinity are asserted. Mary's son is the Son of God. *"That holy thing which shall be born of thee"*: thus the child of the Virgin Mary is distinguished from all other children of men. Man, born according to the common course of nature, is sinful. What is born of the flesh is flesh. Mary's son, however, is "holy, harmless, undefiled, separate from sinners," Hebr. 7, 26; "in Him there is no sin," 1 John 3, 5; He knows of no sin, 2 Cor. 5, 21. Mary's son is the Son of God. A miraculous conception, a wonderful birth! If asked how it came to pass, we answer with the theologians of old:

> Quid sit nasci, quid processus,
> Me nescire sum professus.

THE BIRTH OF CHRIST.

Is. 9, 6: *Unto us a Child is born, unto us a Son is given.*

Seven centuries before the Christian era Isaiah prophesied of Christ's conception and birth, saying: "Behold, a virgin shall conceive and bear a son, and shall call His name Immanuel," Is. 7, 14; and again: "Unto us a Child is born, unto us a Son is given." Noting the context of the latter passage, we observe the prophet speaking of a great light shining to a people walking in darkness. The result of the illumination shed by that light is joy, great joy. Who is this great light? Immanuel. He is the cause of all this gladness. As to the structure of this passage, we notice that the prophet has employed the *parallelismus membrorum,* which abounds in Hebrew poetry. The two members virtually express the same thought, the latter enforcing the former, thus throwing more light upon it. *"A Child is born,"* a child of human flesh and blood. This Child is a *son;* Immanuel, Christ is true man. This Child is *given.* Christ here appears as a gift, a gracious gift of God. God's grace impelled Him to bestow this gift upon us. It is a wonderful Child indeed. Commonly speaking, a child is born unto his parents, but this Child is born *unto us,* is given *unto us,* unto all people. And man, walking in darkness, all his thoughts, words, and deeds being enmity against God, had and has need of this *Child,* this *Son.* Man, without Him, must be damned everlastingly. Only the true believers, however, who know what a precious gift He is, can exult with the prophet: "Unto *us* a Child is born, unto *us* a Son is given!"—And as to the fulfillment of the prophecy see Matt. 1, 21 ff.: "And she" (the Virgin Mary) "shall bring forth a *son*, and thou shalt call His name *Jesus*, for He shall save His people from their sins. Now all this was done that it might be fulfilled which was spoken of the Lord by the prophet, saying: Behold, a *virgin* shall be with *child*, and shall bring forth a *son*, and they shall call His name *Immanuel*, which being interpreted, is, "God with us." Cf. Luke 2, 41; John 1, 14; Gal. 4, 4.

The Burial of Christ.

Ps. 16, 10: *Thou wilt not suffer Thine Holy One to see corruption.*

This passage is quoted by Peter in his great discourse on the day of Pentecost, Acts 2, 27. This proves beyond doubt that Christ is God's *Holy One*. When the psalmist says of the *Holy One*, the God-man, that He is not *"to see corruption,"* he speaks of Him according to that nature according to which He had flesh and blood, and according to which He might have seen corruption had He not been the Holy One. This truth, so plainly stated in the Old Testament, finds its corroboration in the New. Christ's sacred body was laid in the sepulcher and remained there to the third day without seeing corruption.

The Purpose of Christ's Humiliation.

Christ was not compelled to undergo this humiliation, but He did it willingly, out of love to us. In this state He carried out the work of redemption. Hence, in answer to the question, "For what purpose did Christ thus humiliate Himself?" our Catechism says: "To redeem me, a lost and condemned sinner."—This topic, having frequently been dwelt upon in explanation of preceding passages, needs but brief mention here.

Rom. 3, 23: "For all have sinned, and come short of the glory of God." Since all have sinned, all men by nature are lost and condemned creatures. But "the Son of Man is come to save that which was lost," Matt. 18, 11. Since all men by nature are lost, Christ has saved all without exception. This truth Scripture reiterates again and again. "Behold the Lamb of God, which taketh away the sin of the world," John 1, 29. He taketh away the sin of the world, *i. e.*, of all men. "He is the propitiation for our sins, and not for ours only, but also for the sins of the whole world," 1 John 2, 2. Christ has even bought them that deny Him, 2 Pet. 2, 1. So whosoever is now lost is lost of his own fault. In answer to the question, "Whom has Christ redeemed?" we confess: "Me, and all lost and damned sinners." (Cf. Mezger, *Entwuerfe*, p. 136.)

The Work of Redemption.

Gal. 3, 13: *Christ has redeemed us from the curse of the Law, being made a curse for us; for it is written: Cursed is every one that hangeth on a tree.*

The Law is good and holy. It promises eternal life on condition that it be kept perfectly: "This do, and thou shalt live." This condition, however, no man can fulfill. "We are all as an unclean thing, and all our righteousnesses are as filthy rags." Hence the Law pronounces its curse upon us: "Cursed is every one that continueth not in all the things which are written in the book of the Law to do them," v. 10. We are "*under the curse of the Law.*" In ourselves there is no way of escaping this terrible curse. What we could not do Christ did for us: *He has redeemed us from this curse.* How? By "*being made a curse for us.*" Observe well the words: "*for us*"; they express the doctrine of substitution emphatically. The curse to be pronounced upon us was pronounced upon Him. He became a curse "*for us,*" in our stead. He took the sinner's place, "was made under the Law," and satisfied its every demand. Where is the curse of the Law? Taken from us and placed upon Him. A blessed truth, full of consolation, is contained in these words: "*Christ—for us.*" He hung *on a tree;* that is indubitable proof that He was accursed—for us, because it is written: "*Cursed is every one that hangeth on a tree.*" "The chastisement of our peace was upon Him," Is. 53.

Note.—Luther's famous classic on Gal. 3, 13, is worthy of prayerful meditation. Among other things he says that Christ, in our stead, is no longer "an innocent and sinless person, the son of God born of the virgin, but a sinner, who has and bears the sin of Paul, the blasphemer and persecutor, and of Peter, the denier of his Master, and of David, the adulterer and murderer: in a word, He bears and has all the sins of all men in His body. Not that He has committed these sins, but that, being committed by us, He assumed them and transferred them to His own body, in order to render satisfaction for them with His own blood. The general law of Moses, therefore, lays hold of Him, although innocent in His own person, because it finds Him among sinners and robbers, just as a magistrate holds and punishes as guilty one whom he finds among robbers, even though he had never committed anything wrong or worthy of death. Christ, however, was not only found among sinners, but even of His own accord and by the will of the Father wished to be the associate of sinners by assuming the flesh and blood of those who, as sinners and robbers, were sunk into all sins. When the Law, therefore, found Him among robbers, it condemned and killed Him as a robber. But some one may say, 'It is blasphemous to call the Son of God a sinner and a curse.' I answer, 'If you want to deny this, deny also that He suffered, was crucified, and died.' It is no less absurd to say that the Son of God was crucified than that He was a sinner. But if it is not absurd to confess and believe that Christ was crucified between thieves, it is not absurd to say the other. Certainly there is something in the words of Paul, '*Christ became a curse for us.*' '*He made Him to be sin for us, in order that we might be made the righteousness of God in Him.*' So John the Baptist calls Him the Lamb of God, bearing the sins of the world, John 1, 29. He Himself is innocent, because He is the Lamb of God without spot or blemish; but since He bears the sins of the world, His innocence is weighed down by the sins and guilt of the whole world. Whatever sins I and you have done have become the sins of Christ, as though He Himself had committed them. Is. 53, 6: 'The Lord hath laid upon Him the iniquity of us all.' These words we ought not to extenuate, but give them their proper force."

1 Pet. 1, 18.19: *Ye know that ye were not redeemed with corruptible things, as silver and gold, from your vain conversation received by tradition from your fathers, but with the precious blood of Christ, as a lamb without blemish and without spot.*

Peter here addresses especially the Gentile Christians. He reminds them of their former state in which they led "*a vain conversation received by tradition from their fathers.*" Their "*conversation,*" i. e., their manner of life, was "*vain,*" empty, purposeless; it was a walk after the flesh, Eph. 2, 1.2.17. To the Ephesians Paul writes that they should no longer walk, as the other Gentiles do, in the *vanity* of their mind, Eph. 4, 17. This vain mode of life had been "*received by tradition from their fathers.*" The parents of such men, having themselves no true knowledge of God, could impart none to the children. Sinners can rear sinners only; what is born of the flesh is flesh. This life in the lusts of the flesh held dominion over them; they were enslaved to sin. From this dominion they could not free themselves. Christ *redeemed* them therefrom. *Redeem* means to buy back, to repurchase. A price had to be paid to release them from this terrible bondage. What was it? *Silver and gold,*" which men deem so precious, and with which the value of all earthly things is measured, are but "*corruptible things.*" The ransom was infinitely more precious. On Calvary the "*blood of Christ*" was shed for our sins. Christ's blood was the only ransom that could buy us back from the power, the dominion, the slavery of sin. "*Precious*" this blood is because of the Person of Him who shed it, Christ—God! Not the quantity, but the quality of this blood imparts to it its infinite worth. The "*lamb without blemish and without spot,*" the innocent Christ, takes the place of the guilty, becomes our substitute, sheds His blood as a sacrifice, and thus atones for sin. Christians know that they were bought with a price, but they are apt to forget it, hence they must be reminded again and again: Know that ye are redeemed! He who believes that he is free from the dominion of sin, rules over sin. Know that ye are redeemed! this is the most powerful incentive for Christians to follow after sanctification.. They are under obligation to do so: Christ redeemed them; they have the power to do, so: Christ redeemed them.

Hebr. 2, 14.15: *Forasmuch, then, as the children are partakers of flesh and blood, He also Himself likewise took part of the same, that through death He might destroy him that had the power of death, that is, the devil, and deliver them who through fear of death were all their lifetime subject to bondage.*

"Flesh and blood," man as he is by nature, is in the power of "*him that had the power of death, that is, the devil*," hence he is also *in fear of death*, of temporal death, because back of it eternal death awaits him. To break this power and to deliver us from this fear of death, Christ took part of flesh and blood, became man like unto us, sin excepted. Being man, He could die and through His death sin was expiated, the devil's power over us was destroyed, the sting of death—sin—lost its poison, its killing power. Now we Christians need not fear temporal death, because it is but the entrance to. eternal life.

2 Tim. 1, 10: *Christ hath abolished death, and hath brought life and immortality to light.*

Death abolished! An astounding declaration, incomprehensible for human reason, a blessed truth which faith only can grasp! Death *abolished*, *katargesantos*, death annulled, death deprived of its power to terrify, on the one hand; on the other, "*life and immortality*," i. e., immortal life, brought to light through the Gospel. This Christ, our Savior, has accomplished by His work of redemption. Temporal death, the king of terrors, is changed into a welcome messenger from above. For the Christians, who believe the Gospel, temporal death is no longer a transition from spiritual death to eternal death, but from spiritual life to eternal life and immortality.

Gen. 3, 15: *I will put enmity between thee and the woman, and between thy seed and her seed; it shall bruise thy head, and thou shalt bruise his heel.*

Adam and Eve transgressed the commandment of God, Gen. 2, 17. Thus sin entered into the world and death by sin. "By the offense of one judgment came upon all men to condemnation," Rom. 5, 18. The victory seemingly was Satan's; all mankind was to be forever in his kingdom—lost—damned. God interposes. He announces to fallen man the Protevangel, Gen. 3, 15, promising a Redeemer. In the presence of our first parents He said to the serpent, or rather to the devil concealed in the serpent: "*I will put enmity between thee,*" the devil, "*and the woman, and between thy seed and her seed.*" A fierce warfare is to rage between the devil and the woman's seed, ending in a glorious victory for the latter and thus for fallen man. That was indeed Gospel, "good tidings," for Adam and Eve and—for us.

Who is "*the seed of the woman*" that is to bring about this victory? None else but Christ. St. Paul authoritatively settles this question, Gal.

3, 16. Our English text reads: "I will put enmity between thee and
the woman, and between thy seed and her seed," and then proceeds:
"*It* shall bruise thy head," etc. The antecedent of "it" is obvious; it is
"seed." "Seed" being of the neuter gender in English, the translators
chose the neuter pronoun "it"; since, however, "her seed" is Christ, it
is also patent who is meant by "it," *viz.*, "her seed"—Christ. But
though no mistake can be made by the thoughtful reader as to its meaning, the "it" is an inaccurate translation. The Hebrew word is a personal pronoun of the masculine gender, and should have been rendered:
"He." It may be of interest to note that whilst even the Revised Version still retains the "it," the American Standard Version correctly
translates: "*He* shall bruise thy head."

A pardonable digression.—In the interest of Mariolatry papacy has
changed this pronoun "He," meaning Christ, into "she," meaning Mary.
Says the THEOLOGICAL QUARTERLY, vol. IV, p. 418: "Contrary
to all rules of grammar and logic, and what is even worse, contrary to
the analogy of faith and to all the teachings of Holy Writ, the Catholic
Bible has rendered *she*, and the teachers of the church of Antichrist
have referred this prophecy to Mary, the mother of Christ, and claim
that Mary is the one that bruises the serpent's head. Of course, this
forgery and blasphemous perversion of God's own Word is calculated to
support their Mariolatry and to render this idolatry the more acceptable
to the sense of an ignorant and pomp-loving multitude. Many popish
churches and cathedrals have been decorated with pictures and paintings
representing Mary as the one that treads upon, and crushes, the head of
the serpent."

Returning to the matter in hand, we note first that the passage
speaks of the conqueror of Satan as being an individual person—"*He*"—
Christ. We further observe the expression "*her seed*," the seed of the
woman; Christ, the Redeemer, is to be true man. But the peculiarity
of the expression consists in this, that it speaks of "the seed *of the
woman*." Here is an intimation, as in Is. 7, 14, of the Messiah's miraculous conception and birth. Christ is the one made of a woman, born
of the Virgin Mary, having no human father, but conceived by the Holy
Ghost, Luke 1, 35. We learn still more of the person of this mighty
Victor. God says of Him: *He shall bruise*, crush, *thy*—the serpent's—
head. Since the serpent's, *i. e.*, the devil's, head is to be *crushed*, the
victory will be a complete victory; the devil will be overcome, Luke 11,
22. But to "destroy him that had the power of death, that is, the devil,"
Hebr. 2, 15, is a *divine* work. It is Scriptural to argue from the work to
the person who performs the work. He that can crush the devil's head
cannot be mere man; he must, at the same time, be true God.—How clear
the prophecy of Christ's humanity and divinity! How clear, too, the
prophecy of Christ's signal victory over Satan! Through the Messiah's
work Satan's victory shall be undone; the human race shall again be
freed from his hellish power. True, Satan will wage a furious warfare.

Satan *"shall bruise His heel."* In this mortal combat Christ receives a wound; the victory is dearly bought. Says Paul: "Ye are bought with a price." But whilst the crushing of the *head* of the serpent is fatal, the bruising of the *heel* of the Victor is not. When reading the clause· *"Thou shalt bruise His heel,"* we are especially reminded of Christ's Great Passion. He was indeed, as Isaiah says, a man of sorrows. Judas, the disciple, betrays Him; Peter, the disciple, denies Him; His own people cry: "Crucify, crucify Him!" Pilate and Caiaphas condemn the Innocent One. He is nailed to the cross. After all, the devil seems to be the victor. But no—all this is merely the bruising of Christ's heel. On the cross He cries out: "It is finished!" By His death He carried out the deadly combat to a glorious victory. (Cf. Hebr. 2, 14.15.)—"The great dragon was cast down, the *old serpent*, he that is called the devil and Satan, the deceiver of the whole world," Rev. 12. 9.—*Summary.* Gen. 3, 15 is the first Gospel message. It speaks of Christ's Person and His office. It says Christ is true man and true God. It prophesies His sufferings and His complete victory over Satan.

1 John 3, 8: *For this purpose the Son of God was manifested, that He might destroy the works of the devil.*

St. John says: "He that committeth sin" willingly, consciously, "is of the devil," is minded like the devil, the devil's sentiment is in him; "for the devil sinneth from the beginning," it was he that made the beginning of sin, he was the first sinner; now, whosoever wantonly sins follows in his footsteps, is governed by him. But Christians, purchased and won from the power of the devil, are to contemplate the purpose of Christ's coming into the world, and then they will not do the devil's bidding. *"For this purpose the Son of God was manifested, that He might destroy the works of the devil."* Christ destroyed the works of the devil, *i. e.*, sin, and now Christians should sin, wantonly sin, sin intentionally and with aforethought? Nevermore! Why, then they would build up what Christ has destroyed! They would build the devil's kingdom, and building this kingdom, they would but prove that they are in the devil's employ, that they had fallen from grace, that they had received God's grace in vain! It is a contradiction in itself to say, I am a Christian, and still to "commit sin" willingly. "He that committeth sin" is not of Christ, but "of the devil."—Christians, by God's grace, have the power to resist Satan's temptations, 1 Pet. 5, 9.

2 Cor. 5, 21: *He hath made Him to be sin for us who knew no sin, that we might be made the righteousness of God in Him.*

God is merciful; He is also just. He could not show mercy at the expense of his justice. Sin separated between us and our God. Sin is guilt, our guilt. Guilt demands penalty. This obstacle, penalty of guilt, God removed. How? Christ *"knew no sin"*; He was holy, righteous, sinless. The Holy One took the place of sinners—the unholy. Him God made to be sin *"for us," huper hemon,* in our stead. *"For us"*—that plainly, forcibly, unmistakably expresses the doctrine of substitution. This the apostle here teaches. The translation of the American Standard Version: "on our behalf," is weak and colorless. *"For us"* Christ was *"made to be sin."* That does not mean that Christ in His nature was now a sinner, or that He committed sin in thought, word, or deed; just as little does it mean this as the correlative clause: *"that we may be made the righteousness of God in Him,"* says that our sinful nature were annihilated and replaced by a divine righteous nature. As strongly as possible the assertion is made: *"He knew no sin."* The innocent Christ *"was made to be sin,"* not by a physical act, but by a judicial act of God. He was made to be sin by imputation. "The Lord hath laid on Him the iniquity of us all," Is. 53, 6. In the eyes of God Christ is the sinner, the malefactor. God punished our sin in Christ. Thus His justice is satisfied. What was God's purpose in imputing our sin to Christ? *"That we may be made the righteousness of God in Him."* Our sin has been liquidated by our substitute, Christ, satisfaction is rendered, the penalty is paid, righteousness is merited. Since He has taken our place, His righteousness is our righteousness. Our sin was imputed to Him; His righteousness is imputed to us. That, oftentimes, is very hard for us to believe. We see our sins, know the Law and our shortcomings. But the point is not, What do we think and judge concerning ourselves? but, What does God think of us? God looks upon us in Christ, who is our righteousness.

Is. 53, 4.5: *Surely He hath borne our griefs, and carried our sorrows: yet we did esteem Him stricken, smitten of God, and afflicted. But He was wounded for our transgressions, He was bruised for our iniquities: the chastisement of our peace was upon Him, and with His stripes we are healed.*

The Ethiopian eunuch, homeward bound from Jerusalem, where he had worshiped, sitting in his chariot, is reading the Prophet Isaiah. By direction of an angel, Philip goes that way, meets the eunuch, and is asked the question: "I pray thee, of whom speaketh the prophet this? of himself, or of some other?" Now the passage of Scripture which he was reading was this: "He was led as a sheep to the slaughter," etc. (Is. 53, 7 ff.) "And Philip opened his mouth, and beginning from this scripture, preached unto him Jesus," Acts 8, 26 ff. Incontrovertibly Is. 53 speaks of Jesus. Isaiah lived about 760 before Christ, but his description of the suffering Messiah is as vivid as though he had stood below the cross at Calvary.

The verses before us treat of the cause of Christ's suffering. "Surely!" The statement to follow is absolutely true, beyond the shadow of a doubt. *"Surely He hath borne our griefs,"* or sicknesses. Observe the stress here, and in the following clauses, upon the pronouns: *"He"* —*"our"*. He was not suffering for Himself, but for us. This the contrast between *"He"*—*"our"*; *"We"*—*"Him"* loudly proclaims. The doctrine of substitution and atonement cannot be more strongly expressed than it is done here, a fact which cannot be emphasized too strongly in our days. Sad to say these precious doctrines—substitution and atonement—are hushed up more and more in denominations outside the Lutheran Church, and in their place a shallow morality is taught.— "He"—"our"—the Messiah, takes our place, suffers for us. Vicarious suffering—this is the burden of the prophecy. Christ is the Righteous, the Holy One, and He suffers! So He does not suffer for His own, but for sins of others. They are *our* griefs, *our* sorrows; *we* have sinned. *Our* griefs, *our* sorrows rest as a heavy burden upon *Him*. Taken from us, they are imputed to Him. Says Peter: Christ "His own self bare our sins in His own body on the tree," 1 Pet. 2, 24. What the prophet says is truth, divine truth. Mark the emphatic assertion: *"Surely He hath borne our griefs."* And willingly, voluntarily, He became our substitute; voluntarily He took the vast burden of our sin upon Himself. The prophet says: *"He* hath borne our griefs." It was His doing, His act; His suffering and death was not a fate He could not have escaped.

To return to the main thought: Our sins were the cause of His sufferings; but what did people in general assume to be the cause? *"Yet we did esteem Him stricken, smitten of God; and afflicted."* He is a criminal, His crimes have found Him out; God has given this malefactor over to inexorable justice—so men thought then, so now. Blind reason cannot understand the cause of Christ's suffering. What, says the prophet, the Holy Ghost, was the cause? *"But He was wounded for our transgressions, He was bruised for our iniquities."* Transgression, iniquity, is sin, is rebellion against the majestic God, and deserves punishment, damnation. The vials of God's wrath should have been poured upon our guilty heads, but He took our—the criminals'—place, and so they were emptied upon Him. And why did He make this vicarious sacrifice? To redeem us. "The chastisement of our peace"—so that we might have peace—*"was upon Him."* Sin separated between us and our God. This enmity Christ abolished. "Christ is our peace," Eph. 2, 14. How? By bearing the *chastisement,* the punishment, such as God inflicts for sin. Thus our transgressions and iniquities have been atoned for; the penalty is paid. "Who is he that condemneth? It is Christ that died, yea, rather, that is risen again," Rom. 8, 34.

Rev. 5, 9: *Thou wast slain, and hast redeemed us to God by Thy blood.*

Thou, Christ, *wast slain* as the only offering well pleasing to God. Thus we were *redeemed,* bought back from the slavery of sin and iniquity, from the servitude of Satan, and became Christ's own, Eph. 5, 2; Hebr. 9, 14. Thou hast given *Thy blood* as the redemption-money, as a ransom, to the Judge, and it had the power to quench God's wrath. For Thy blood is God's blood, Acts 20, 28.—Indeed, we

are bought with a price, 1 Cor. 6, 19.   Now by right of purchase we
Christians are Christ's own, and He is our Lord.

Is. 53, 11:   *He shall see of the travail of His soul, and shall be
satisfied: by His knowledge shall my righteous Servant justify many;
for He shall bear their iniquities.*

This passage speaks of the redemptive work of Christ.   "*He
shall see of the travail of His soul.*"   Christ suffered not only in
His body, but also in His soul.   His *soul*, too, was *in travail*.   The
work is accomplished.   Now He shall see the fruits of this travail.
As v. 10 expresses it: "He shall see His seed"—the *ecclesia*—"and
shall be satisfied."   (Acts 20, 28.)   He has bought the Church of God
with His own blood.   The Gospel is preached.   Sinners, who have caused
the travail of His soul, are won thereby.   They acclaim Him their King.
This the exalted Christ views with satisfaction.   He took away the
sins of the world, John 1, 29;   He is the propitiation for the sins
of the whole world, 1 John 2, 2.   He bought even them that deny Him,
2 Pet. 2, 1.   He would have all men to be saved, but, alas! of many
He must weepingly complain: "Ye would not."   But still there are some
who receive Him, believe in Him.   These constitute the Church.   As these
believers are added to the Church, either one by one, or in great num-
bers, Christ sees of the travail of His soul, and views it with great
satisfaction.   His work bears results.   "*He shall see and be satisfied
with the travail of His soul.*"   "*By His knowledge shall my righteous
Servant justify many.*"   Christ, the righteous Servant, shall *justify*
many, shall make many righteous.   He is not only righteous in Himself,
but also the one who makes others—sinners—righteous, righteous before God.   The means with which He accomplishes this is expressed in
the phrase: "*by His knowledge,*" or as it may be translated: "*by the
knowledge of Himself.*"   Both renditions say the same thing essentially.
"By the knowledge of Himself" says that the many shall know Him—
believe in Him.   The former, "by His knowledge," says: Christ possesses
this knowledge.   This knowledge He imparts to others.   The contents of
this knowledge are essentially Christ's sufferings and death, their
purpose and effect, in short, the Gospel of our salvation.   Through it
Christ imparts knowledge, knowledge of Himself as the Savior, implants
faith in the heart.   Thus the righteousness merited by Him is applied
to the many—they are justified, made righteous before God.   Thus the
many are robed in Christ's righteousness.   This Christ sees, and is
satisfied with the travail of His soul.

An outflow of this righteousness of faith is the righteousness
of life.   Before God the believers are holy, but their life is still imperfect.   Iniquities—sins—are still to be found on account of the weakness of the flesh.   We need consolation therefor.   It is this: "*For (and)
He shall bear their iniquities.*"   By one offering Christ has perfected
forever them that are sanctified.   But this offering, this propitiation, has

continuous power. The exalted Christ is our Advocate with the Father; the righteousness which He, the sin-bearer, merited for us, 1 John 1, 1.2, He makes His plea. Thus our sins of weakness cannot subvert our state of righteousness before God.

STATE OF EXALTATION.

Phil. 2, 9-11: *Wherefore God also hath highly exalted Him, and given Him a name which is above every name: that at the name of Jesus every knee should bow, of things in heaven, and things in earth, and things under the earth; and that every tongue should confess that Jesus Christ is Lord, to the glory of God the Father.*

Treating of Christ's state of humiliation, we have seen that divine majesty was communicated to His human nature in virtue of the personal union, but that, though He possessed it, He did not make use of it constantly and fully.

The present passage speaks of Christ's exaltation. Wherein does it consist? The text says: *"Wherefore God hath also highly exalted Him."* In the previous paragraph we were told what Christ had done; in this we are informed what God did. God exalted Christ. *Wherefore?* Because this mind was in Christt, v. 5, because He humiliated Himself so deeply. This was so well pleasing to God that He exalted Christ. According to Scripture, God exalted Christ, and Christ exalted Himself, Hebr. 1, 3. The one dictum does not exclude the other. Here it is predicated of God. God did this—exalted Christ. That does not argue for subordination, does not say that Christ is inferior to God the Father. Whom did God exalt? The *man* Christ. Christ is true God. According to His divine nature He could not be exalted. He is "over all God." But according to His human nature He could be and was exalted. In the state of humiliation the Savior took upon Himself the form of a servant, v. 7. In the state of exaltation this form of a servant was discarded. In the former state He did not fully and constantly use the divine majesty imparted to His human nature; now He does. Observe the adverb "highly." He is *highly exalted, huperupsosen,* that is, He is exalted above *all things.* He is the Lord of all, and mightily rules and reigns over all things also according to His human nature— rules, as the context manifests, mightily in the kingdom of glory, in the kingdom of grace, in the kingdom of power. He has *"a name above all names"*—none is higher, greater than His. Christ is God like unto the Father. The man Christ is the most high God. "Exaltation" signifies a change of Christ's state, not a change of His essence. The incarnate *logos* was always the same, only His mode of existence was different; hence we speak of His two states, the state of humiliation and the state of exaltation.

God gave *"Him a name which is above every name,"* sc., the name Jesus. And what was the purpose of His exaltation? *"That at the name of Jesus every knee should bow,"* etc. That clearly says, as Paul expresses it: "He is far above all principality, and power, and might, and dominion, and every name that is named, not only in this world, but also in that which is to come," Eph. 1, 20-22. *At the name of Jesus every knee should bow*—so highly God exalted Him. Divine honor is to be accorded to this name. At the name of Jesus *every knee should bow,* that is, acknowledge Him as Lord. Jesus, the man Jesus, is thus to be honored. Three classes of creatures are mentioned that should thus accord divine honor to His name: *"things in heaven"*—angels and saints; *"things in earth"*—all mankind; *"things under the earth"*—Satan and his hellish cohorts. For a time He had become lower than the angels, Hebr. 2, 7. Voluntarily He had taken upon Himself the form of a servant—to serve, to save man. Voluntarily He had subjected Himself to the power of the Evil One. But after that cry on the cross, "It is finished!" all pain, poverty, subjection had come to an end. Now, in the state of exaltation, all creatures, whatsoever name they may have, wherever they may be, how great soever their power may be, are subjected to Him, bow and must bow their knees to Him, acknowledge Him as Lord of all. The angels in heaven do it willingly, likewise the believers on earth, and the unbelievers must do so, though unwillingly. Secretly, in their heart of hearts, they are forced to confess that He is Lord. Even the very devils in hell must acknowledge Christ's lordship, even they, albeit with gnashing of teeth, must concede that they cannot hinder His will.

Highly God exalted Christ. How highly? He has a name above every name; every knee must bow before Him; every tongue must confess Him Lord. Verily, this man Jesus is "God over all!" "Thou madest Him a little lower than the angels; Thou crownedst Him with glory and honor, and didst set Him over the works of Thy hands: Thou hast put all things in subjection under His feet. For in that He put all in subjection under Him, He left nothing that is not put under Him," Hebr. 2, 7.8.

And this was done, says our text, *"to the glory of God the Father."* God's decree from eternity was to save man through His Son. This decree has been carried out. "All glory be to God on high." All enemies are subdued. God's power, holiness, righteousness, wisdom, love, mercy, His truth and faithfulness, have become manifest in Christ's redemptive work.

DESCENT INTO HELL.

1 Pet. 3, 18. 19: *Christ was put to death in the flesh, but quickened by the Spirit: by which also He went and preached unto the spirits in prison.*

1. Who descended into hell? *"For Christ also hath once suffered for sins * * * being put to death in the flesh, but quickened by the Spirit * * * went."* Christ went. This person, who is at once true man and true God, went; the whole person, with body and soul, went. It is the same person that afterwards, as the subsequent context shows, ascended into heaven. So it is wrong to say, as some do, that this descent took place while Christ's body lay in the grave, and that He performed this work according to His soul only. Let us observe the text closely: *"For Christ"*—that is, the God-man, the whole person, *"being put to death in the flesh"*—Christ died according to His human nature, *"but"*—He did not remain in death—*"but quickened by the Spirit,"* i. e., made alive by virtue of His divine nature, as He said, speaking of His death: *"Break this temple,"* meaning His body, *"and in three days I will raise it up."* So Christ, who suffered and died for us, was quickened, vivified, made alive; body and soul were reunited. This same Christ, now in a glorified state, went.

2. According to what nature did He go? According to His human nature, for as God He is omnipresent and cannot be said to go anywhere. On account of the personal union of the natures in Christ, this going to a certain place, which is a property of the one nature only, is predicated of the whole person. So Christ, the God-man, went to this place designated *"prison."*

3. Now what are we to understand by this term? Light is shed upon the nature of this place by the text itself. It reads: Christ *"went and preached to the spirits in prison."* What spirits? To the spirits *"which sometime were disobedient."* *Disobedient* to what? To the Word of God. The Gospel had been preached to them, but they turned a deaf ear to it, just as so many do to-day. *"In the days of Noah"* people were *"disobedient,"* they *believed not.* These people perished in the Flood. And these disobedient people, dying in unbelief, are now in *prison.* Whither do unbelieving people go? To hell. This prison is hell. "He that believeth not shall be damned." "Prison" is the abode of the damned—hell. According to all the teachings of Scriptures there are but two places hereafter, heaven and hell. To designate this latter place—hell—the New Testament employs three words: Hell, Hades, Prison. All three denote the same place—hell. This place is called "hell" on account of the *fiery* tortures there to be endured. The same place is called "Hades"—"the realm of the dead"—in reference to the *eternal death.* Once in Hades, death is everlasting. Hades is hell, aye, "Hades" is a direct synonym for "hell" in the New Testament, all the vain mouthings of the modern theologians to the contrary notwithstanding. It does not take great acumen of mind to see this. Luke 16, 23.24 speaks of the rich man in hell. Our King James' Version correctly and plainly renders the text thus: "And in *hell* he (the rich man) lift up his eyes." The Revised Version says: "And in *Hades* he lift up his eyes." Hades, the modern theologians would have

us believe, is a sort of quiet anteroom to heaven, a waiting-room, and, withal, a pretty comfortable place. All this is mere twaddle. Judge for yourselves! Take the text of the Revised Version: "And in *Hades* he lift up his eyes, *being in torments.*" So Hades is a place of torments, of excruciating pain. Hades is hell. We read on: "And seeth Abraham afar off, and Lazarus in His bosom." Abraham and Lazarus were in heaven; the rich man *afar off* in that other place—hell. "And he cried out and said, Father Abraham, have mercy on me!" The rich man, being in Hades, was in a place where no mercy is shown. Hades is hell. Proceed with the text: "And send Lazarus that he may dip the tip of his finger in water and cool my tongue." Hades is a place of such a nature that, being granted one drop of water to alleviate the terrible torments there endured for the hundredth part of a second, this is looked upon as great mercy. Hades is hell. The rich man continues: "For I am tormented in this flame." Hades is a place where the inmates are tormented in the *flame*—in fire. Hades is hell.—The translation of the King James' Version is true; so is Luther's: "Als er in der *Hoelle* und in der Qual war."

The third word the New Testament employs to describe "hell" is the one in our text—*prison.* Prison this place of torment is called to indicate its *purpose.* Hell is a prison from which there is no escape. Matt. 5, 26 our Lord Himself speaks of this prison, saying of such as enter it: "Verily, I say unto thee, thou shalt by no means come out thence till thou hast paid the uttermost farthing." When will that be? Never.—Thus "hell," "Hades," "prison," all denote one and the same place, "that place which is prepared for the devil and his angels," that place of which, in reference to the unbelievers, it is said: "Their worm shall not die, neither their fire be quenched; and they shall be an abhorring to all flesh." To this place Christ went.

4. When did He go? That question is easily answered by consulting the text. V. 18 speaks of Christ's suffering, death, and quickening; v. 19, of *His descent into hell;* v. 21, of His resurrection; v. 22, of His ascent into heaven and His sitting at the right hand of God; chap. 4, 5, of His return to judgment. Thus the time is clearly marked. It was after His quickening and before His resurrection. In that interval, perhaps in a moment of time, the now glorified Christ appeared in the nether world.

5. What was His purpose in going there? The text answers: "*to preach.*" Despite this plain, unmistakable assertion, there are such as teach that Christ descended to hell to suffer the torments of hell for us. This is absolutely false. It does not only do violence to this text, but it is contrary to the words of our Savior uttered on the cross: "It is finished."—Nor was it His purpose in going there to release the Old Testament saints from prison *(limbus patrum),* as the papists aver. He went there *to preach.*

6. What did He preach? There are such as say that He preached
the Gospel in order to give those who had no opportunity to hear the
Gospel in this life another chance to hear of, and accept, the merits
of Christ and thus be saved. This is absolutely false again, for the
text plainly says that Christ preached to such as were "sometime disobedient," who would not believe. This thought, that the Gospel was
preached in hell, is furthermore expanded, and the possibility of conversion after death for all is taught by most modern theologians.
This dogma, which is but the doctrine of purgatory of the Catholics,
furbished and polished up somewhat, has no foundation in Scripture,
as even some noted leaders who promulgate it honestly concede; but the
thought is fascinating to them, and thus they teach "commandments",
or rather figments, "of men as doctrines of God." It is a soul-destroying doctrine, which fosters carnal security. It is a religion of the
flesh. People are led to think: "Well and good, it matters not how I
live or die here on earth, after death I'll have another chance, and
I'll be sure to embrace it." Oh, how much these seducers of souls
will have to answer for on that Great Day, for it is written: "It is
appointed unto men once to die, but thereafter"—what? a millenium?
a state of second probation? a possibility of conversion? No, a thousand times no!—"but thereafter the judgment." There is no conversion
after death. "He that believeth and is baptized shall be saved, but
he that believeth not shall be damned." And what does the text of the
rich man and Lazarus teach? "The rich man died and was buried." And
the very next thing? "And in hell he lift up his eyes," etc., Luke
16, 19. No conversion after death! "He that believeth not is condemned
already because he hath not believed in the name of the only-begotten
Son of God," John 3, 18 ff.—All Scripture is against this false tenet,
and they that hold it get no consolation from our text. For nowhere
does it say here that Christ preached the Gospel. It simply says:
Christ *preached*. The word in the original is a word of neutral meaning, which, translated, means *to preach, to proclaim, to publish as a
herald.* This is conceded by all conversant with the matter. How, then,
do we know what Christ did preach? The context must give us a key
to that. And the context is plain, forceful, cogent, so that any one
open to conviction, any one who investigates it with an unbiased mind,
without preconceived opinions, cannot be left in doubt as to its meaning. Christ preached the Law, the damning Law; He told them in effect:
"You are justly damned." Let us see that! *"Christ preached to the
spirits in prison which sometime were disobedient when once the long-
suffering of God waited in the days of Noah, while the ark was a-pre-
paring."* What does the text say? 1. These people were *disobedient*.
The Gospel had been preached to them during their lifetime. They
despised it. "He that believeth not shall be damned." This Christ
preached to them. "You have despised me, spurned my Gospel message; your lot is just." 2. God was *long-suffering once*. But now
His long-suffering had come to an end; *once*—during their lifetime;

now—no more. 3. God *waited*. He had waited 120 years! God had given them a long time to repent; He had done all to save them. 4. God had sent them the preacher of righteousness, Noah, to warn them of the impending doom if they should not repent. 5. The building of the ark itself was an object sermon. They despised Noah, and ridiculed the building of the ark. Thus we see the *guilt, the damning guilt,* of these people is stressed. And the correlative of guilt is punishment. 6. If the modern theologians were in the right, who maintain that the Gospel was here preached by Christ, we should at least expect to hear of a mitigating circumstance, an excuse for the disobedience of the spirits in prison. But no, nothing of the kind. *Their guilt is emphasized, and guilt demands punishment.* Whosoever despises the grace of God must be punished. The doctrine taught here is: *"Unbelief is a cause of damnation."* So, then, it was not the Gospel that Christ preached, but the Law, the judgment.

The exact words of this sermon are not given, but the import of it was: "You have despised me, whom you now see to be the victor over death, and hell, and sin; you are justly damned." Thus "Christ, having been quickened in His grave, exhibited Himself to hell as its conqueror, and triumphed over all His infernal enemies." He has, as we read in Col. 2, 15, "spoiled principalities and powers, He made a show of them openly, triumphed over them in it."

THE RESURRECTION OF CHRIST.

Rom. 1, 4: *Jesus Christ, our Lord, which was made of the seed of David according to the flesh, and declared to be the Son of God with power, according to the spirit of holiness by the resurrection from the dead.*

"Spirit of holiness," *pneuma hagiosunes*, is a rare expression in the New Testament. Does it here designate the third person of the Trinity, the Holy Spirit? No. "Holy Spirit" would be expressed by *pneuma hagion*. Studiously, as it were, the apostle avoids this latter expression, and uses the designation "spirit of holiness," to indicate that it is not to be understood of the Holy Spirit.—What, then, does "spirit of holiness" mean? Let us observe the text! "Christ was made of the seed of David *according to the flesh*," *kata sarka*. "According to the flesh" obviously means: according to His human nature. Christ was a descendant of David, and as such true man. But this same Christ also possessed a higher nature, a divine nature. This is expressed by *kata pneuma, according to the spirit,* according to His divine nature. (Cf. 1 Pet. 3, 18.) Since "according to the spirit" is an antithesis to "according to the flesh," and "according to the flesh" means His *human nature,* "according to the spirit" can designate nothing else than His *divine nature.* This the antithesis demands. *Pneuma* is *nomen essentiae.* John 4, 24; 2 Cor. 3, 17. Jesus Christ is true man and true God, the Son of God.—This divine nature is *pneuma hagiosunes,* spirit of *holiness;* i. e., it is absolutely holy. And this holy divine nature of the Son of God permeates, fills, as it were, the human nature of the Son of David.

Now, says Paul, this Person, Jesus Christ, who was not only true man, a seed of David, but also true God, was *declared,* marked off, determined, to be such—God, Son of God. How? *"By the resurrection from the dead."* The incontrovertible fact of His resurrection proves His divine Sonship beyond the shadow of a doubt. The studious change of the language should be noted: Christ was *made* of the seed of David, but He was *not* made, but only declared *to be the* Son of God. (See John 1, 1.14)—Christ was the Son of God before the foundation of the world, Col. 1, 15. In the state of humiliation He proved Himself to be the Son of God by His many miracles. Nowhere else, however, have we such conclusive evidence of His being what He claimed to be— Son of God—as in His resurrection from the dead.—The emphatic statement: "He was declared to be the *Son of God in power"—huios theou en dunamei, i. e.,* the powerful, the almighty, the majestic Son of God, moreover, adds an important thought. In the state of humiliation Christ always was the almighty God, but He did not always appear as such; He did not always use His divine majesty and power, communicated to His human nature by virtue of the personal union; now, however, by and since His resurrection, He is declared to be Son of God *in power;* now, in the state of exaltation, He fully and constantly uses the divine majesty communicated to His human nature also according to this His human nature.

John 2, 19: *Destroy this temple, and in three days I will raise it up.*

One day the Jews demanded a special sign of Christ as a proof for His Messiahship. *"Destroy this temple,"* said He, meaning *His body,* v. 21, *"and in three days I will raise it up."* What a stupendous assertion to make! For ages and ages generations had come and gone, but from the grave not a single person had returned. And here stands this man Jesus before the Jews and says: "You will kill me, but I shall return from the grave, and I shall rise by my own power. I am the Conqueror of death." What happens? He was crucified, dead, and buried, but on the third day, according to His prediction, He arose again. He spoke truly when He said: I will raise my body up; He spoke truly when He said on another occasion: "I have power to lay it (my life) down, and I have power to take it again," John 10, 18. None but God is the lord over death. Christ conquered death. He rose *of His own power;* Christ is God.—

But there is another truth in this passage pertinent to the matter in hand. The words, John 2, 19, are a prophecy. Christ prophesied His *death:* "Destroy this temple, my body." He foreknew what the Jews would do with His body: they would "destroy it"—kill Him; and

He plainly tells them so. He prophesied concerning His *resurrection:* "In three days I will raise it up." Both prophecies came true. Christ is a true prophet; His doctrine is the truth.—The resurrection of Christ provides us with a solid foundation for our faith in the divinity of Christ, and gives us absolute assurance of the reliability of His doctrine.

1 Cor. 15, 17: *If Christ be not raised, your faith is vain; ye are yet in your sins. Then they also which are fallen asleep in Christ are perished.*

The resurrection of Jesus Christ from the dead is the cornerstone of our Christian faith. Disprove it, and the Christian religion collapses. Sad, beyond expression sad, were our lot if Christ were not risen. St. Paul draws this gloomy picture: 1. "If Christ be not raised, *vain is your faith.*" Vain, *mataia,* is put in an emphatic position. *Mataia*—vain, fruitless, hence without power and effect, futile. "Vain is your faith;" your faith has no ground on which to stand, no truth on which to rely. 2. *"Ye are yet in your sins."* If Christ is not risen, reconciliation with God is not effected, His wrath abideth on you, you have no forgiveness of sin, you are not redeemed. 3. *"Then they also which are fallen asleep in Christ are perished."* These deceased Christians died in the faith of Christ as their Savior; they believed their death to be but a sleep after which there would be a joyful awakening—but lo! if Christ be not raised, they were deluded—they died without expiation of their sins and are accordingly lost, damned. Aye, indeed, "if in this life only we have hope in Christ, we are of all men most miserable. But," the apostle proceeds, "now is Christ risen from the dead." Hence it follows: 1. that our faith is not vain, not groundless, but rests upon a firm foundation; 2. that our sins are atoned for; 3. that when we fall asleep in Christ, we, too, shall rise and live with Him eternally.—Christ's resurrection is proof positive for the completeness and the sufficiency of our redemption, and it gives us full assurance of the truth of His doctrine.

Rom. 4, 25: *Who (Christ) was delivered for our offenses, and was raised again for our justification.*

Christ was our Substitute. This well-known truth of Scriptures is obvious in our text also, if we but observe the pronouns "who—our." The Just takes the place of the unjust, and the Just, Christ, "was delivered," was given up, *viz.,* to death, *dia ta paraptomata hemon,* on account of our trespasses. God delivered Him into death on account of our sins. Rom. 8, 32; Gal. 1, 3. The Just died for the unjust in order to expiate their trespasses. And willingly "Christ gave Himself for us, that He might redeem us all from iniquity." Tit. 2, 14. On the cross at Calvary our Substitute expired with the words on His lips: "It is finished." Atonement for our sins was made. But the anxious question remained, "Will God accept this atonement?" A dead

Savior can avail us nothing. Where is the proof that God is satisfied with the work of His Son? Triumphantly Christ rises from the grave on the third day. *"He was raised for our justification."* Here is proof, positive proof, that His death had been accepted as an expiation for our sins. In order to justify us, God raised Christ from the dead. We look to Calvary and we know: "Christ was delivered for our offenses." We look into the empty grave of Christ and are assured: "He was raised for our justification." God the Father has accepted the sacrifice of His Son for the reconciliation of the world.

John 14, 19: *Because I live, ye shall also live.*

John 11, 25.26: *I am the Resurrection and the Life: he that believeth in me, though he were dead, yet shall he live; and whosoever liveth and believeth in me shall never die.*

In a little Christian family, in the small village at Bethany, there is deep sorrow. Martha and Mary mourn over the death of their brother Lazarus. Jesus comes that way, and in the course of the conversation He consoles Martha by saying: "Thy brother shall rise again." Martha believes that. She says: I know he shall rise again in the resurrection at the last day." Then Jesus utters the mighty words of our text. In the fullness of emphasis he says: *"I am"*—*Ego eimi*—*"the Resurrection,"* and hence the whole power to effect it is mine. In me the resurrection is absolutely certain. I am *"the Life."* I have immortality, imperishable, unchanging life, in myself (John 1, 4), and can impart it to others, so that they need not and cannot die. *"He that believeth in me, though he were dead, yet shall he live."* Belief in me, faith in me, so intimately unites the believer with with me that as certainly as I live the believer shall also live.—John 14, 19: *"Because I live, ye shall also live."* True; the Christians, too, must die. But in the light of Scriptures, what is temporal death for the Christians? A sleep. Says Paul: "If we believe that Jesus died and rose again, even so *them also which sleep in Jesus* will God bring with Him," 1 Thess. 4, 14. And Jesus says: "Verily, verily, I say unto you, If a man keep my saying, *he shall never see death,"* John 8, 51. The bitterness of death the Christian will not taste. Death to him is but a sleep after which there is a blissful awakening. Death has been swallowed up of life. Temporal death of Christians is so little to be looked upon as death that Christ says: *"And whosoever liveth and believeth in me shall never die."* Temporal death to the Christians is but an entrance to eternal life.—Thus the resurrection of Christ from the dead makes us absolutely certain of a blessed life beyond the grave.

CHRIST'S ASCENSION.

Ps. 68, 18: *Thou hast ascended on high, Thou hast led captivity captive; Thou hast received gifts for men, yea, for the rebellious also.*

Forty days after His resurrection, Christ ascended into heaven visibly, according to His human nature, as narrated in the Gospels and the Acts. In the night when He was betrayed, He said to His disciples: "In my Father's house are many mansions * * * I go to prepare a place *for you*," John 14, 3. Christ ascended into heaven *for us, for our benefit.* Hence this doctrine, too, is full of strong consolation for His servants.—This His ascension was foretold in the Old Testament. Ps. 68 is a Messianic psalm. Paul quotes it Eph. 4, 8 as speaking of Christ. Christ is the Lord Jehovah extolled in the psalm. After a long and fierce warfare with His enemies, Christ·remains the Victor. His and our enemies have been overcome. The work of redemption being completed, He *"ascended on high,"* i. e., into heaven. He despoiled principalities and powers, Col. 2, 15; He *"led captivity captive,"* He *"led away captives"* (S. A. V.), i. e., Satan and all his hellish cohorts, making a show of them openly in a triumphal procession. Our enemies are vanquished. Not only that. This exalted Christ who ascended into heaven has not only *"led away captives,"* but He also "received gifts for men," or rather, He "received gifts *among men*," that is to say, the "men" are the gifts, "men" He has received; men, who are now His own, believe in Him and serve Him. He "received gifts among men *so that rebellious also dwell with the Lord God."* (Stoeckhardt.) The Standard American Version translates thus, the sense remaining essentially the same as the one here given: "Thou hast received gifts among men, yea, among the rebellious also, that Jehovah God might dwell with them." *Rebellious,* too, i. e., men who at one time opposed the Lord, turn to the Lord, lay down their rebel arms, and by His grace live with Him in His kingdom. To such rebellious people whom the Lord draws to Himself belong the heathen, such as the Ethiopians and the Egyptians, of whom the psalm speaks. (Cf. Stoeckhardt, *Epheserbrief,* p. 190.)

Eph. 4, 10: *He that descended is the same also that ascended far above all heavens, that He might fill all things.*

St. Paul, quoting Ps. 68, 18, goes on to say: "Now that He ascended, what is·it but that He also descended first into the lower parts of the earth?" Then follows our text. *"He that descended,"* the very same, just He, and no one else, He precisely, *"is the same also that ascended."* His ascent corresponds to His descent. *"He that descended"* —whither did He descend? "Into the lower parts of the earth," says v. 9. This is a fitting description of His *descensio ad inferos.* (Cf. 1 Pet. 3, 19.) As Victor He descended into hell. Having descended into the *utmost depth,* He, after a brief sojourn here on earth, ascended to the *utmost height;* He *"ascended far above all heavens,"* above all created heavens, to sit at the right hand of God the Father, Eph. 1, 20. The purpose of His ascension the apostle expresses thus: *"that He might fill all things."* After His exaltation and ascension Christ fills "all things" with His efficacious presence, also according to His glorified human nature, and from this omnipresence flows His special gracious presence with His Church, as the apostle shows further on.

John 12, 26: *Where I am, there shall also my servant be.*

Speaking of His approaching death, Jesus had said: "The hour" decreed in the eternal counsel "is come that the Son of Man should be glorified." By His passion and death, through which He must pass, He was to enter into the glory of the Father. Pursuing this thought, He thinks of His own. *"Where I am"* in this my kingdom, *"there shall also my servant be."* Christ and His servants shall be together always. He has ascended to prepare a place for us.

CHRIST'S SITTING AT THE RIGHT HAND OF GOD.

Ps. 110, 1: *The Lord said unto my Lord, Sit Thou at my right hand, until I make Thine enemies Thy footstool.*

The *right hand of God*, what is it? God is a spirit, hence has neither a right hand nor a left hand. The expression is an anthropomorphism. What does it signify? To the people of Israel, Moses said: "And thou shalt remember that thou wast a servant in the land of Egypt, and Jehovah, thy God, brought thee out thence by a *mighty hand* and by an *outstretched arm*," Deut. 5, 15. Clearly God's *hand* and *arm* here indicate His *great power*. "Thou hast a mighty arm," says the Psalmist; "strong is Thy *hand,* and high is Thy *right hand*," Ps. 89, 13. Obviously again, *hand, right hand*, bespeaks God's almighty power. Hence in the trial before the Sanhedrin, Jesus, speaking of His exaltation, says: "Henceforth ye shall see the Son of Man sitting at the *right hand of power.*"

As the expression "right hand of God" is figurative, so is the phrase: *"Sitting* at the right hand of God." What does it mean? The mother of the sons of Zebedee asks Jesus: "Command that these my two sons may sit one on Thy right hand and one on Thy left hand, in Thy kingdom," Matt. 20, 21. Jesus understands this request as meaning that the sons should be allowed to *share in the rule of His kingdom;* cf. v. 25. The locution: to sit at the right hand of a ruler, therefore, conveys the idea of *participating in the rule.*

Now as to our text. Ps. 110 is a Messianic psalm. This we have on no less an authority than Christ's Himself. One day, when the Pharisees were gathered together, Jesus propounded the question, "What think ye of Christ? Whose Son is He?" They answered, "The *Son of David.*" Then followed the perplexing question, "How, then, doth David in Spirit call Him *Lord,* saying, The Lord said unto my Lord," etc. Matt. 22, 41 ff. David's Lord is none other than Christ. Christ, the Messiah, is true God and true man in one person. This the blind Pharisees could not see. Cf. also Mark 12, 35 ff.; Luke 20, 41 ff.; 1 Cor. 15, 25; Hebr. 1, 13.

David begins his comforting psalm thus: *"The Lord* (the Father) *said unto my Lord* (Christ)*."* Two persons are here discriminated: the speaker and the one spoken to; but both are called "Lord." The Father is Lord; Christ is Lord. Christ is equal with the Father; Christ is God. But David's Lord is also David's son, true man. As the God-man He has been sent forth to redeem them that were under the law. Even in this state of humiliation David's son was "God over all," Rom. 9,5, "the mighty God," Is. 9, 6; "our great God," Tit. 2, 13. But in that state the Messiah did not constantly use the divine majesty communicated to His human nature. David "in Spirit," *i. e.*, by divine inspiration, sees the work of redemption completed, sees the state of humiliation of his son come to an end. Now the Father says to David's son: *"Sit Thou at my right hand,"* i. e., share in my rule; rule with me with divine power and majesty. God exalted the man Christ. According to Christ's divine nature, He could not be exalted; in reference to it the Father could not and would not say: *"Sit* at my right hand." The very word "sit" indicates that these words were said to Him according to His human nature. Now, in the state of exaltation, Christ, *also according to His human nature,* rules all things with divine power and majesty. That is the significance of His *sessio ad dexteram.* Hence we read in v. 2: "Rule Thou (Christ) in the midst of Thine enemies," which enemies are made His "footstool," v. 1.

Eph. 1, 20-23: *God set Him (Christ) at His own right hand in the heavenly places, far above all principality, and power, and might, and dominion, and every name that is named, not only in this world, but also in that which is to come: and hath put all things under His feet, and gave Him to be the Head over all things to the Church, which is His body, the fullness of Him that filleth all in all.*

The paragraph, Eph. 1, 15-23, of which the foregoing text forms the close, contains a supplication of St. Paul for the Christians at Ephesus. It is replete with consolation and encouragement for the Christians and the Christian Church. Our text speaks of the Church, of its security. We often tremble for its welfare. We observe the high winds and the angry waves of adversity coming threateningly upon the ship of the Church, and forget the nearness of the Lord. A thorough knowledge of what this means: Christ sits at the right hand of God, and a childlike faith in that truth, will dispel our fears. Instead of crying out in consternation with the disciples on the tempest-tossed Galilean sea: "Lord, save; we perish!" we will become emboldened triumphantly and defiantly to challenge all adversaries with Paul: "If God be for us, who can be against us?" Rom. 8, 31.

St. Paul prays God that the Ephesian Christians may have the eyes of their heart enlightened so that they may know, among other things, also this, what is the power of Him who sitteth at the right hand of God, and what is His relation to the Church.

God set Him (Christ) at His own right hand." God's right hand is the hand of *His power* (Matt. 24, 64), the right hand of *His majesty* (Hebr. 1, 3). Here God *set* Christ. Christ is God, and the divine government belonged to Him from all eternity. According to His divine nature, Christ could not be said to be *set* at God's right hand. The very word "set" indicates that this was done according to His *human* nature. The context, too, speaks of Him that was raised from the dead, v. 20a., of the man Christ. The man Christ was exalted to an unceasing participation in the divine government. (See exposition of Ps. 110, 1.) *"In the heavenly places."* This phrase does not denote a certain locality, which, by the way, would militate against God's spirituality and would disrupt the natures in Christ, but it designates the sphere of majesty and glory in which our Lord and God lives and reigns. In the succeeding phrases and clauses the meaning of that grand thought: "Christ sits at the right hand of God in heavenly places," is most sublimely unfolded. In virtue of this participation in the divine government, Christ is *"far above all principality, and power, and might, and dominion."* "That these names denote angels, angels of light, is now most generally acknowledged, likewise also, that these synonymous designations do not point to an order or rank within the *hierarchia coelestis* * * * , but to the superhuman power and might of the heavenly spirits." (Stoeckhardt.) Observe the polysyndeton: "principality *and* power *and* might *and* dominion." That serves to make the thought emphatic. The reader is invited to ponder each concept separately in order to become all the more impressed with the marvelous power of these holy angels. However powerful they may be, aye, though all their power and might be combined, yet there is one who possesses far greater power; for *"far above"* them all is He that sits at the right hand of God, Christ, and majestically rules over them. Christ, our Brother, is on the throne of majesty. "Why, then, are ye fearful, O ye of little faith?"

The circle of Christ's dominion widens: He is far above "every *name that is named, not only in this world, but also in that which is to come."* That says: Christ rules over all, whatever it may be, howsoever great and powerful it may be, wherever it may be found, here in time or in eternity. Let the heathen rage and the kings of the earth set themselves, and the rulers take counsel together, against the Lord and against His Anointed—no power on earth can shake His throne.—And as if to round off his majestic thought and guard against all misconception as to what the rule of Christ, who is at the right hand of God, comprises, the apostle sweepingly asserts: *"and hath put"* in subjection, lastingly, permanently, *"all things under His feet,"* so that Christ exercises absolute sovereignty over *all things,* all creatures whatsoever, the very devils in hell not excepted. Heaven, earth, hell— all under His feet! What a mighty Ruler this man Christ is! And this God-man is our Savior. What a sweet consolation! In the days of His flesh He said: "All power is given to me in heaven and in earth." He proved His assertion to be true. He rebuked the winds and the waves, and there was a great calm. He cast out evil spirits with His word. The leper is cleansed of his leprosy; the centurion's petition in behalf of his dying servant is answered. The young man at Nain is called to life; at His word, Lazarus comes from the grave. Rays of divine glory these—in the state of humiliation. Now He, the glorified Christ, is in the state of exaltation, and now He has come into the unceasing use, also according to His human nature, of the divine majesty that was always His. And He is the same Savior to-day that He was then, with the same merciful heart. Will He not guard and protect us and His Church against all enemies?

But the majestic thought of the apostle reaches its climax in the last clause: *"and gave Him to be the Head over all things to the Church, which is His body."* In this translation the peculiar emphasis imparted by the Greek to the pronoun "Him" is lost. The original reads: *kai auton edoke kefalen huper panta te ekklesia, hetis esti to soma autou*—"and *Him* He ,gave as Head over all things to the Church, which is His body." Him—this glorious majestic Ruler just described; Him—who is equal with God; Him—to whom all, heaven, earth, and hell, is made subject: *Him God gave as Head of the Church, i. e.,* the communion of saints, *which*—Church—*is His body.* He that is Head over all things as Ruler and Sovereign, Col. 2, 10, is at the same time the Head of the Church. But the headship, the rule, over the Church is entirely different from His headship over all creatures. In the kingdom of power He rules by means of His omnipotence; in the kingdom of grace He rules with His gracious Word. In the true sense of the word, as head that possesses a body, Christ is Head of His Church only, Col. 1, 18. The unbelievers are not members of His spiritual body. "If any man hath not the Spirit of Christ, he is none of His," Rom. 8, 9. How great the dignity of the Church: Christ is the Head; the believers are the members of this spiritual body. As intimately as the head is connected with the body, so intimately is Christ connected with the Church. As the head governs the body, so this Head governs His body, the Church. The Church hears the Word of Truth, the Gospel of salvation, v. 13. That is Christ's voice; by it the body, the Church, is governed. Whatsoever the Head, Christ, wills, the body, the Church, executes. "One is your Master, even Christ."

But another incomparable prerogative of the Church comes out in the last phrase: the Church is *"the fullness of Him that filleth all in all."* *Pleroma*—fullness, is a rare expression. The preponderance of usage gives it the meaning "that which fills," not "that which is filled;" not the receptacle, but that which fills the receptacle. (See Stoeckhardt, *Epheserbrief.)* So the text says: The Church is *"the fullness* of Him," i. e., the fullness of Christ; the Church is in full possession of the gifts of Christ. From Him, the exalted Head, the plenitude of spiritual, heavenly blessings are communicated to His body, the Church.—Note the distinction clearly marked in the text: the Church is the *"fullness of Him that filleth all in all."* He that is *far above* all things also *fills all things.*—In passing we remark that the context speaks of Christ who died and rose again; hence the omnipresence of Christ's human nature finds expression here. Col. 1,17.— The text says: He *that filleth all in all*—all things, also fills the Church. Christ fills all things with His efficacious presence, and from this omnipresence flows His special gracious presence with His Church.

And now, let us again ponder the emphasis in the clause: "And *Him* He gave as Head over all things to the Church, which is His body." What does this unmistakably peculiar stress say? He that is so intimately connected with His Church, He that has given His heart's blood for it as the purchase price, He is at the same time the Ruler of the universe—heaven, earth, and hell being made subject to Him, *and He will, therefore, rule and govern all things for the benefit of the Church.* True, "now we *see* not yet all things put under His feet," Hebr. 2, 8; it is an article of faith. Though now we do not *see* all things put under His feet, yet the fact remains. The whole course of this world is shaped for the benefit of the Church. When a building is completed, the scaffold is taken away. When the last elect has been gathered into the fold, or, to change the figure, when the last stone has been placed in God's temple, the Church, Eph. 2, 19 ff., the scaffold of this world will be destroyed. So the whole world still stands to-day for the benefit of the Church.—When, at the time of Christ, the then known world was brought under one rule—that of the Roman emperor—highroads were built connecting the entire vast domain, commerce was established along these routes, intercourse was made comparatively easy, one language was understood by all—the Greek. These self-same means of communication the apostles used. Along these highroads they travelled, publishing the Gospel of the Kingdom in Greek, thus building the Church. —About the time of the Reformation, the invention of printing books by movable type was made—for the benefit of the Church. The Bible, Luther's translation, could be easily and cheaply procured, and the Gospel could be widely spread. And the discovery of America—we see it *a posteriori*—was for the benefit of the Church. Here, under the providence of God, the principle of separation of Church and State became an established fact—for the benefit of the Church. Just now there are dark clouds looming up on the horizon. The elevation of three archbishops of the Catholic hierarchy to the cardinalate forebodes nothing good, neither for the Church nor for the State. But Christ sits at the right hand of God and is the Head of the Church. This is our consolation.—Even the persecutions of the Church, in the last analysis, served for the benefit of the Church. (Acts 17, 1 ff.)

In yonder life, when the mists will have lifted and our vision will have become clear, we shall see that this whole universe, the governments, the rulers, "every name that is named," lay in the hollow of His hand who sitteth at the right hand of the Father, and that all and everything was made subservient to the building of His kingdom, the Church.

CHRIST'S RETURN TO JUDGMENT.

Acts 1, 11: *This same Jesus which is taken up from you into heaven shall so come in like manner as ye have seen Him go into heaven.*

To His disciples Christ "showed Himself alive after His passion by many infallible proofs, *being seen of them forty days*, and speaking of the things pertaining to the kingdom of God," Acts 1, 3.   At the completion of these forty days His ascension took place from Mount Olivet, v. 12, about two miles distant from Jerusalem.   The narrative lays all stress upon the fact that Christ's ascension was a *visible* ascension and not a sudden disappearance.   "And when He had spoken these things, *while they beheld*, He was taken up," v. 9.   In full view of the disciples He went up gradually, and as He did so, He blessed them, Luke 24, 50.51. He ascended higher and higher until "a cloud received Him out of their sight," v. 9.   The disciples "looked steadfastly toward heaven as He went up," v. 10; they "gazed up into heaven," v. 11, following Him with their eager eyes with mixed feelings of rapt astonishment and saddened hearts.—Whither He went, the "two men that stood by them in white apparel," angels in human form, told them: "He is taken up from you into heaven," v. 11.   Thus all stress is laid upon His *visible* ascension. His *visible* presence they should no longer enjoy, though *invisibly* He, the God-man, was always with them as He is still with us, according to His promise: "Where two or three are gathered together in my name, there am I in the midst of them," Matt. 18, 20, and: "Lo, I am with you alway, even unto the end of the world," Matt. 28, 20.—But there will be a time when He will return *visibly*.   For so say these "two men": *"This same Jesus which is taken up from you into heaven shall so come in like manner as ye have seen Him go into heaven."*   As in the preceding verses we have a studied account of His *visible* ascension, so we have here a studied declaration of His *visible* return.—Who will return? *Houtos ho Iesous.   This* Jesus, *this same Jesus* who was born in Bethlehem, who suffered, was crucified and died; the same Jesus who was raised again on the third day, who was seen by them for forty days after His resurrection; the same Jesus who had just spoken to them the things pertaining to the kingdom of God, and who now visibly departed from them, this same Jesus, God's son and Mary's son, shall come again.   How?   He "shall *so* come," visibly, *"in like manner as ye have seen* Him go," visibly, gloriously, "into heaven."   Cf. Matt. 26, 64; 24, 30; Rev. 1, 7; Matt. 25, 32.

For what purpose He will return we are told in

Acts 10, 42:   *He (Christ) is ordained of God to be the Judge of of quick and dead.*

Christ's own words furnish a commentary to this passage. To the Jews He had said: "For the Father judgeth no man," immediately, "but hath committed all judgment unto the Son," John 5, 25, "and hath given Him authority to execute judgment also, because He is the Son of man," v. 27.

Acts 17, 31: *God hath appointed a day in the which He will judge the world in righteousness by that Man whom He hath ordained.*

This text is taken from St. Paul's speech at Athens on The Unknown God.—The following obvious points may be noted: 1. The certainty of Judgment Day. "God hath appointed a *day*" of judgment. And not only has a certain, definite *day* been decreed in the eternal counsels of God, but also the very *hour* in which the judgment is to take place. See Mat. 24, 36.42 and Mark 13, 32: "that *day*," "that *hour*." This day is called "the last day," John 12, 48; "the day of the Lord," 2 Pet. 3, 10, *et al.*—2. Christ will be the Judge. "He (God) will judge . . . . . .by that Man whom He hath ordained," *i. e.*, Christ. (Cf. Acts 10, 42; Matt. 25, 31.)—3. It will be a judgment of the whole world. "He will judge the *world*," the "quick and dead," Acts 10, 42; "all nations," Matt. 25, 32; "all," 2 Cor. 5, 10.—4. It will be a righteous judgment. "He will judge . . . . . .in righteousness." St. Paul calls Judgment Day "the day of wrath and revelation of the *righteous judgment* (dikaiokrisias) of God," Rom. 2, 5. In this judgment there will be "no respect of persons with God," Rom. 2, 11; 1 Pet. 1, 17.

2 Pet. 3, 10: *But the day of the Lord will come as a thief in the night; in the which the heavens shall pass away with a great noise, and the elements shall melt with fervent heat, the earth also and the works that are therein shall be burned up.*

Speaking of "the day of the Lord," St. Peter directs our attention to three things: 1. The certainty of its coming; 2. the manner of its coming; 3. the terrors attending that day.

Hexei de he hemera—"Come will, however, the day." The verb *hexei*—"come will" is very emphatic, being placed at the head of the sentence, thus calling attention to the absolute certainty of this event. Why this stress? Because "there shall come in the last days scoffers, walking after their own lusts, and saying, Where is the promise of His coming? For since the fathers fell asleep, all things continue as they were from the beginning of creation," vv. 3.4. "All things continue"— that was the argument of the scoffers in Peter's days. Though Peter in the succeeding verses, in masterful fashion, has put the quietus on the cavilings of these despicable lustful fellows, the cry to-day remains the same: "All things continue!" In stentorian voice the watchman on Zion's walls, therefore, must call out again and again: "*Come will the day!*" Do not lull yourselves into security. The promise of His coming will not fall to the ground; *come* will the day!—This day will come "*as a thief in the night.*" The point of comparison is the sudden, unexpected advent. (Cf. Matt. 24, 27.43; 1 Thess. 5, 2; Rev. 3, 3; 16, 15.) As a thief steals upon men at an hour when they least expect it, so "this day" will come suddenly, unexpectedly, and find most men wrapped in spiritual sleep.—When this day will come, what will happen? *"The heavens shall pass away with a great noise."* "All things continue," say the scoffers; "the heavens shall pass away," says Peter. "To describe the dread process, he has a striking word, which, like so many of the Apostle's expressions, is used nowhere else in the New Testament, 'With a great noise,' *horidzedon.* It is applied to many signs of terror: to the hurtling of weapons as they fly through the air; to the sound of a lash as it is brought down for the blow; to the rushing of waters; to the hissing of serpents. He has chosen it as if by it he would unite many horrors into one." (Lumby.) Next follows the thought of nature's dissolution: *"the elements shall melt with fervent heat."* "Elements," *stoicheia,* is a difficult concept. Some commentators believe that, since "elements" are mentioned after "the heavens," the sun, the moon, and the stars are designated by that word; others again—Luther, Wahl, *et al.*—understand *stoicheia* to mean the *component materials* of the world. These will "melt," be dissolved, by that fervent heat. *"The earth also and the works that are therein,"* works of nature, of art, of science, etc., *"shall be burned up."* An irresistible fire, indeed!—The text is a warning against carnal security. "Let your loins be girded about, and your lamps burning, and ye yourselves like unto men looking for their lord," Luke 12, 35.

Mark 13, 32: *Of that day and that hour knoweth no man, no, not the angels which are in heaven, neither the Son, but the Father.*

What is the precise time of Christ's coming? It is a profound mystery. Observe the climax! No *man* knows, not even the *holy angels* know, yea, not even the *Son,* during the state of humiliation according to His human nature, knew of "that day and that hour."—What is the lesson contained herein for us? The Lord Himself gives it: "Take ye heed, *watch and pray;* for ye know not when the time is," v. 33. *"Watch* therefore," v. 35. "And what I say unto you I say unto all, *Watch!"* v. 36.—*Notes:* 1. How futile and foolish are the attempts of those wiseacres who, with pencil and pad in hand, endeavor to compute "that day and that hour." 2. Of Christ, the God-man, we read, Matt. 9, 4: Jesus *knew* their *thoughts;* John says (2, 25): "He needed not that any one should bear witness concerning man; for He Himself *knew what was in man."* Christ is omniscient. Now if the question be asked, How is it possible that not even the Son in the state of humiliation knew of "that hour"? we answer, We don't know. It is a mystery. Scripture, the Son of God Himself, states it as a fact; by that we abide.

1 Pet. 4, 7: *The end of all things is at hand.*

These words were written well-nigh two thousand years ago. Was it a mistaken utterance? St. Paul admonishes the Philippians: "The

Lord is at hand," Phil. 4, 5. St. John beseechingly warns the Christians: "Little children, it is the last hour," 1 John 2, 18. Have Peter, Paul, and John erred? Let Dr. Walther answer: "We durst not imagine that the holy apostles have erred here; they cried out: 'The Lord is at hand!' and still they knew full well that millenniums might pass before the Lord's return. For example, when St. Peter had spoken of the nearness of Christ's Second Advent, he added: 'But be not ignorant of this one thing, that one day is with the Lord as a thousand years, and a thousand years as one day.' And St. Paul, after proclaiming the nearness of the last day, nevertheless adds: 'Let no man deceive you by any means; for that day shall not come, except there come a falling away first, and that man of sin be revealed, the son of perdition.' But ....why, notwithstanding, could the apostles speak so clearly concerning the nearness of the end of the world? Because they did not speak man's language, but God's language; before God the end is *at hand* even though millenniums must still pass by." (Ep. Post. p. 255.)

2 Cor. 5, 10: *We must all appear before the judgment seat of Christ, that every one may receive the things done in his body, according to that he hath done, whether it be good or bad.*

"*We must all,*" none excepted, "*appear,*" rather, "*be manifested, be made manifest,*" appear in our true character, before the judgment-seat of Christ. Why? In the sight of God we all are at all times manifest; He need not institute this judgment for His sake to find out where we stand. In that great panorama of the Last Day unrolled before our eyes in Matt. 25, the separation between the sheep and the goats is made *before* the sentence is pronounced. This judgment is to be a public judgment to vindicate God's righteousness, to prove that "He judgeth the world in righteousness," Acts 17, 31. Unerring justice will be meted out on that day. The very damned themselves, conscience-smitten, must concede: My damnation is just.—How will that be effected? The judgment will be based upon the works of man, "*according to that he hath done, whether it be good or bad.*" "God will render to every man *according to his dues,*" Rom. 2, 6. God, "without respect of persons, judgeth *according to every man's work,*" 1 Pet. 1, 17. The outward semblance of having been a Christian will not save; hypocrisy will be no cloak here. The works are manifest proofs of man's sentiment, whether he was for Christ or against Christ. The good works of the believers will be produced in evidence of their faith; the evil works of the unbelievers, in evidence of their unbelief. Thus the doctrine: Through grace by faith in Christ are ye saved, is not subverted, does not clash with this or similar passages.—But will the evil works of Christians also be brought to light on that great day? No. In that sublime account of the final judgment, Matt. 25, the Lord speaks of the *good* works only of those on His right hand, thus proving their relation to Him, showing that their faith bore fruits. (See Ezek. 33, 13; Is. 43, 25; Jer. 31, 34; Hebr. 10, 17; Is. 38, 17.)—In passing, may it be said that these good works of the

Christians are in no way to be looked upon as being meritorious. Before praising the good works of those on His right, the Lord does not say: "Come, for ye have *merited* the kingdom," but His words are: "Come, ye blessed of my Father, *inherit* the kingdom prepared for you from the foundation of the world," Matt. 25, 34. So, then, the good works of the children of God are considered only as fruits and proofs of faith which can be recognized also by men. "In this the children of God *are manifest*, and the children of the devil: whosoever doeth not righteousness is not of God, neither he that loveth not his brother," 1 John 3, 10.

John 12, 48: *The word that I have spoken, the same shall judge him in the last day.*

This is the rule of judgment: Christ's Word. This same Word that we now hear, read, study, this same Word "shall judge him" who despises Christ "in the last day." What is that rule stated in other words? "He that believeth and is baptized shall be saved; but he that believeth not shall be damned," Mark. 16, 16. Or, to quote another passage: "He that believeth on Him (Christ) is not condemned; but he that believeth not is condemned already, because he hath not believed in the name of the only-begotten Son of God," John 3, 18.

Luke 1, 74.75: *That we, being delivered out of the hand of our enemies, might serve Him without fear, in holiness and righteousness before Him, all the days of our life.*

The *Song of Zacharias*, Luke 1, 68-79, is commonly called the *Benedictus*, because in the Latin version the first word of the hymn, *Eulotegos*, is rendered *benedictus*—blessed, praised. The *Benedictus* is a prophecy inspired by the Holy Ghost, v. 67. The first part, vv. 68-75, contains a praise unto God for the salvation prepared by the Messiah as foretold by the holy prophets of the Old Testament, v. 70. The Deliverer is at hand, but Zacharias with prophetic foresight views all the precious promises made to the fathers and to be fulfilled in Him as already completed. He speaks in the past tense: "Blessed be the Lord, God of Israel, because He *looked upon* and *wrought redemption, epoiesen ultrosin,* for His people."

"*Our enemies,*" devil, sin, death, in whose hands we were, held us fast with a relentless grip. Slaves we were to these masters, Eph. 2, 1; and the wages? That of enemies bent on our destruction: death, damnation! And from this awful servitude we could not free ourselves. This the Messiah did. He *"delivered us out of their hand."* This work of deliverance, this work of *salvation,* vv. 69.71, was also one of *redemption,* v. 68. A price was paid. Which? "The Son of Man came.........to give *His life* a ransom, *lutron,* for many," Matt. 20, 28. We were bought with a price; thus we were saved. Now He is our Lord, and we are His own and live under Him in His kingdom. O the blessed change! Formerly we lived in Satan's kingdom, now we live in Christ's kingdom, in the kingdom of grace, endowed with spiritual life here, and life eternal to come. This is the first and foremost fruit of Christ's redemptive work—salvation. But as subjects in His blessed kingdom it behooves us to *serve* our God and King. This is also a fruit of His work. And liberated slaves of that hard taskmaster, the devil, that we are, how gladly, how joyously should we not serve our Liberator! 1. As to the *manner* of this service: *"without fear we should serve Him,"* our Lord and God. *"Without fear"* from our former masters and tyrants; they are vanquished, they can harm us none. In the daily walks of our life, whether we be father, mother, daughter, son, master, servant, we are to perform the works of our calling "not with eye-service, as men-pleasers, but as the servants of Christ, doing the will of God from the heart," Eph. 6, 6.—2. As to its *nature:* we are to serve God *in holiness and righteousness* (cf Eph. 4, 24). Clothed in the garb of Christ's holiness and righteousness, we Christians are holy and righteous in God's sight, and as such the new man in us is to assert himself more and more in our conversation towards God and our fellow-men. 3. As to its *duration:* it is to be a constant, persevering service; it is to last *"all the days of our life."*

2 Cor. 5, 15: *He died for all, that they which live should not henceforth live unto themselves, but unto Him which died for them and rose again.*

"He (Christ) *died for all."* *"For all"*—*in the place of, in the stead of,* is the only correct translation of the phrase *huper panton,* the *huper* being synonymous with *anti,* since text and context manifestly proclaim the truth of Christ's death being a substitutionary death.—*"Christ died for all."* What sentiment does this knowledge of Christ's vicarious substitution generate in the hearts of the believers? Under what obligation are they? *"That (hina) they who live should not henceforth live unto themselves,"* live for selfish ends, but they should dedicate their whole life to the service of Him *"who died for them and rose again."*

THE THIRD ARTICLE.

THE PERSON OF THE HOLY GHOST.

Divine names, divine attributes, divine worship, divine works, are ascribed to the Holy Ghost; hence He is true God.

Matt. 28, 19: *Go ye, therefore, and teach all nations, baptizing them in the name of the Father, and of the Son, and of the Holy Ghost.*

This text, which is a conclusive proof for the doctrine of the Trinity in Unity, is for that very reason a decisive proof for the Holy Ghost's being a person distinct from the Father and the Son. The command reads: *"Baptizing them in the name of the Father, and of the Son, and of the Holy Ghost."* Observe the singular noun: *name, eis to onoma, not eis ta onomata.* By Father, Son, and Holy Ghost but *one* God is named; there is but *one* essence, undivided, indivisible, but in three *distinct* Persons. The Holy Ghost is not, as some heretics taught and still teach, simply a divine power, a divine energy, but a *distinct* person, the Third Person in the Holy Trinity.—Another lucid text is John 14, 16.17, where our Savior says: *"And I (Christ) will pray the Father* (i. e., a different person from Himself, the Son), *"and He shall give you another Comforter"* (i. e., God the Holy Ghost, another, different person), *"that He may be with you forever, even the Spirit of Truth, whom the world cannot receive,"* etc. This text, too, clearly teaches that the Holy Ghost is a person distinct from the Father and the Son, and applies the personal pronoun "He" to Him.—The Unitarians will not see this; their high intellectual culture does not admit of such an unintelligent belief! They follow their blind reason; we "bring into captivity every thought unto the obedience of Christ," 2 Cor. 10, 5.

1 Cor. 3, 16: *Know ye not that ye are the temple of God, and that the Spirit of God dwelleth in you?*

The *"and"* connecting the two clauses is the so-called explanatory *"and,"* equivalent in meaning to "because." The rhetorical question, *"Know ye not,"* etc., appeals forcibly to the Christian consciousness of the Corinthians, and reminds them of an important truth they had been taught, but which, as their conduct implied, they had ignored, forgotten. Which is that truth? Christians, *"ye are the temple,"* the sanctuary, *"of God."* Why? Because *"the·Spirit of God,"* i. e., the Holy Spirit, *"dwelleth in you."* The indwelling of the *Holy Spirit* made them a temple of God. Clearly the indwelling of the Holy Spirit and that of God is one; the two names are used interchangeably: *the Holy Spirit is God.*—That is the important truth taught here directly. But observe also the implied truths pertinent to the matter in hand. *"To dwell"* is an act attributable to a person only; hence the Holy Spirit is a *person.* Again, His indwelling converts man into *"a temple of God."* This suggests His work of sanctification and renovation.

Acts 5, 3.4: *Peter said, Ananias, why hath Satan filled thine heart to lie to the Holy Ghost? Thou hast not lied unto men, but unto God.*

Ananias's heart was not right before God. He cared neither for the good pleasure of God nor for the welfare of the poor. As Barnabas had laid the full price of the field at the apostles' feet for the benefit of the poor, so Ananias pretended to do the same. He craved honor before men, but sordidly stingy as he was, he kept back part of the money received for the possession, simulating that he had given all. Ananias was a hypocrite and a liar. Satan was his master. Peter discloses his grievous sin to him, saying: Thou hast *lied to the Holy Ghost* and thereby *thou hast lied unto God.*—The Holy Ghost is God.—This passage also teaches that the Holy Ghost is a *person*. You cannot lie to an "energy" or to a "power," but to a person only. Ananias is said to have *lied to* the Holy Ghost, hence the Holy Ghost is a person.

Ps. 33, 6: *By the word of the Lord were the heavens made, and all the host of them by the breath* (Spirit) *of His mouth.*

By appropriation the work of creation is ascribed to God the Father, but being an *opus ad extra*, an external work, all three persons of the Godhead concurred in it.—In our passage, creation is ascribed to the Holy Ghost, thus proving that He is God.

"By the word of the Lord," the only-begotten Son of the Father, Eph. 3, 9; Col. 1, 15.16; Hebr. 1, 2, *"were the heavens made; and all the host of them,"* the sun, the moon, the myriads of stars, *"by the breath of His mouth,"* by the Holy Spirit.—Gen. 1, 2 we read: "And the Spirit of God moved upon the face of the waters," and Job 33, 4 we read: "The Spirit of God hath made me, and the breath of the Almighty hath given me life."

Ps. 139, 7-10: *Whither shall I go from Thy Spirit? or whither shall I flee from Thy presence? If I ascend up into heaven, Thou art there; if I make my bed in hell, behold, Thou art there. If I take the wings of the morning, and dwell in the uttermost parts of the sea, even there shall Thy hand lead me, and Thy right hand shall hold me.*

Omnipresence is an essential attribute of God. Whosoever is omnipresent is God. The text teaches the omnipresence of the Holy Spirit, *ergo* He is God.

The two members of the topic sentence are substantially parallel in thought and have the force of rhetorical interrogations: *"Whither shall I go from Thy Spirit? or whither shall I flee from Thy presence?"* The answer is obvious. No flight can remove me from Thy presence; Thou art everywhere. Personally, the psalmist has no desire to flee from the presence of God. Thrilled by that majestic attribute, his purpose is rather to magnify God the Holy Spirit's omnipresence. Vivid, striking pictures set forth the utter impossibility of escape, thus bringing the thought into bold relief: "Thou (whole and entire) art there!" He imagines himself taking a flight into heaven, of making his bed in hell; he thinks of passing through the universe from the extreme east to the extreme west with the swiftness of the morning ray, yet: "Thou art there!" "Thy hand leads me;" "Thy right hand holds me." Heaven, hell, earth—all filled by the presence of the Holy Spirit.

1 Cor. 2, 10: *The Spirit searcheth all things, yea, the deep things of God.*

Omnipresence and omniscience are closely interrelated. 1 Cor. 2, 10 teaches the *omniscience* of the Holy Spirit.

The apostle speaks of "the wisdom of God in a mystery," v. 7, of the mystery that "eye hath not seen, nor ear heard, neither have entered into the heart of man, the things which God hath prepared for them that love Him," v. 9, *i. e.*, the glad Gospel tidings. This hidden wisdom "God ordained before the world unto our glory," v. 7, a mystery "which none of the princes of this world knew," v. 8. No creature knew it, could know it; it was a knowledge only God possessed. To come into possession of this mystery God must reveal it to us. This He did. How? "By His Spirit." "Holy men of God spake as they were moved by the Holy Ghost," 2 Pet. 1, 21. So the Spirit knows the mysteries God only knows. His knowledge and God's knowledge are identical; the Spirit is omniscient, is God. Why does the Spirit know these things? "The Spirit searcheth *all* things;" He is all-knowing; nothing is hidden from Him. Yea, He searcheth "the deep things of God," the inmost things, the infinite depths of the mysteries of God. The next verse, by an *argumentum a minore ad majus*, emphasizes this same truth—the omniscience of the Holy Spirit—and proves His Godhead: "For which man knoweth the things of a man, save the spirit of man which is in Him? Even so the things of God knoweth no man but the Spirit of God."

Is. 6, 3: *Holy, holy, holy, is the Lord of hosts: the whole earth is full of His glory.*

"The service of the seraphs is now more closely described. Above all, their service consists in praising and glorifying God. Arranged in two choirs, the seraphs hover around the throne of God, and the two choirs chant in antiphon. The prophet hears them cry to each other: 'Holy, holy, holy, is the Lord of hosts.' This is a true service of God, so well-pleasing in His sight; this, indeed, is praising God, when the creatures acknowledge and confess with a loud voice that God is God, that God is holy, etc. The heavenly hosts praise and glorify the Lord Sabaoth, the Lord of hosts, the Creator of the spirits, the Creator and Ruler of all things. The holy angels confess that the Lord is holy, holy in an infinitely higher degree and sense than that in which they themselves are holy. God is holy, set apart, put at a distance from, infinitely exalted not only above the sin of men, but above all creatures. The thrice-repeated Holy, the Trisagion, not only reinforces the concept holiness, but suggests, as modern exegetes also acknowledge, the mystery of the Holy Trinity. In God there are three persons, and the one person is God, is holy, in the same measure as are the others. In this song of the seraphs the Church has at all times recognized a *hymnus trinitatis.*" (Stoeckhardt, *Jesaias.*)

1 Cor. 6, 11: *But ye are washed, but ye are sanctified, but ye are justified in the name of the Lord Jesus and by the Spirit of our God.*

In the preceding verse, the apostle had enumerated a horrible catalogue of vices practiced in that godless city of Corinth. He proceeds: *kai tauta tines ete*—"And these things"—"such a set," "such stuff" (Meyer) *"some of you were."* You *were*, i. e, it is a thing of the past;

thank God, a change has been wrought in you. To accentuate this wonderful change and to bring the great contrast between them and now into strong relief, the apostle emphatically repeats the "but" three times. *"But ye are washed," apelousasthe.* The prefix *apo, off,* intensifies the idea of the verb, hence the meaning is: ye are *thoroughly* washed, ye are washed *clean.* Through the forgiveness obtained in baptism, "the washing of regeneration," you have been washed clean from the filth of sin, for Christ has cleansed the Church "with the washing of water by the Word," Eph. 5, 26. Being thus cleansed from sin, ye are put in intimate relation with God, *"ye are sanctified,"* i. e., separated from the world, taken out of the *massa perditionis,* and consecrated to God. *"Ye are justified."* Your guilt of sin has been removed, by imputation of the merits of Christ, apprehended by faith, you are declared righteous before God. Thus the state of grace of the Corinthian Christians is described.

How was this change effected? *"In the name of the Lord Jesus."* The ground of their being washed clean by baptism, of their justification and sanctification, is the redemptive work of Christ. The name *Jesus* means Savior. In Him they believe, and thus He is their *Lord,* He having bought them with a price. Thus they were saved; for there is no other name under heaven given among men whereby we must be saved but that of Jesus. But who brought them to this faith? The Holy Spirit. Hence the last phrase reads: *"and by the Spirit of our God."* It is He who through the Gospel applies, imparts, communicates to individuals all that is implied in that blessed name—Jesus, Savior. It was the Holy Spirit that brought both the apostle and the Corinthian Christians to faith so that the apostle can write: "and the Spirit of *our* God."

*   *   *

Attention is called to the admirable climactic arrangement of the proof-texts. 1 Cor. 2, 14 proves that man by nature is *blind* spiritually; Eph. 2, 1 that he is spiritually *dead;* Rom. 8, 7 that he is an *enemy* of God. His conversion, therefore, is solely the work of God the Holy Ghost, 1 Cor. 12, 3.

1 Cor. 2, 14: *The natural man receiveth not the things of the Spirit of God, for they are foolishness unto him; neither can he know them, because they are spiritually discerned.*

Throughout this second chapter the apostle contrasts the Wisdom of God manifested in the Gospel, and the wisdom of man that cannot apprehend the wisdom of God. Furthermore, there is a contrast between the spiritual and the natural man. The spiritual man has saving knowledge, the natural man has not. In the course of the development of this thought the apostle says: *"The natural man receiveth not the things of the Spirit of God; for they are foolishness unto him; neither can he know them, because they are spiritually discerned."* To grasp the meaning easily let us clear up an expression or two.

1. Whom does the apostle designate by *"the natural man"?* The "natural man," *psuchikos anthropos,* is contrasted with the "spiritual," *pneumatikos,* v. 15. The "spiritual man" is one who has received the Holy Spirit. "We have received the Spirit—so that we might know the things," etc., v. 12. So only the "spiritual man" can know these things; only he can judge of these things, v. 15. The spiritual man is one who is enlightened by the Holy Spirit, one who is converted. The "natural man," on the other hand, is man as he is by nature, *"unspiritual,"* as the Greek word may be rendered, not having received the Spirit, not yet born again, converted, not enlightened by the Spirit, or, as Jude 19 puts it, *psuchikoi, pneuma me echontes,* literally: *"psychical, not having the Spirit."* Hence Luther says: "The natural man is man as he is *apart from grace,* albeit decked out as bravely as he may be with all the reason, skill, sense, and faculty in the world."

2. The expression: *"The things of the Spirit of God"* taken out of its environment may seem difficult of understanding at first sight, but when viewed in the connection in which it stands, it becomes perfectly simple. I quote from the chapter. The apostle says: "We speak —not the wisdom of this world, but the wisdom of God"—"the hidden wisdom which God ordained before the world unto our glory." What is that? *The plan of salvation through Jesus Christ, the Gospel.* Again he says: "As it is written: Eye hath not seen, nor ear heard, neither have entered into the hearts of men the things which God prepared for them that love Him"—again, this is the plan of salvation, of our redemption, *the Gospel of Jesus Christ.* How did we learn of these things? "God hath revealed them to us by His Spirit, for the Spirit searcheth the deep things of God. Now we have received the Spirit that we might know the things,"—the Gospel-tidings of Jesus Christ,—"which things also we speak in words which the Holy Ghost teacheth." "But the natural man receiveth not the things of the Spirit of God." Now, plainly, what are *"the things of the Spirit of God"?* Primarily, the Gospel of Jesus Christ.

Now we are ready to see what the text says: "The natural man receiveth not the things of the Spirit of God"—*The natural man receiveth not the Gospel.* Natural man, man as he is by nature, *receives* not, *i. e.,* he cannot apprehend, cannot understand the Gospel. First and foremost the apostle speaks of natural man's *intellect* here. He says: *"he receives not,"* ou dechetai, *"er vernimmt nichts,"* as Luther has so aptly translated; he cannot *"know,"* he cannot *"discern,"* i. e., judge spiritual things. Paul speaks of natural man's receptive, knowing, judging faculties—of his reason, his intellect. Natural man's intellect is *blind* in spiritual matters. However keen his mind may be in matters mundane, however great things he may accomplish in the various branches of knowledge and science,—marvelous to behold,—still of the

gospel, though it be preached to him ever so plainly, he understands—
nothing. And this the apostle predicates of *every* natural man. However powerful, moral, intelligent, learned man may be, if he is still in
his natural condition, he understands just as little about spiritual things
as the illiterate ditch-digger who is still unconverted. The learned has
no advantage over the unlearned; the one understands just as much
about it as the other, namely—nothing. That is what the apostle says:
"The natural man receiveth not the things of the Spirit of God." He
does not say: Natural man's intellect is *weak* in spiritual matters; he
says, he *receives nothing;* his intellect is blind. There are blind minds
as well as blind eyes.

The second statement is even stronger. The text says with emphasis: *kai ou dunatai gnonai*—"and *not can* he know them." It is utterly impossible for him to understand spiritual things; he has absolutely
no capacity for them. To illustrate: Given the best teacher, the most
approved methods, and yet Darwin's most highly developed ape cannot
grasp a mathematical problem, say that of Pythagoras. While following the demonstration on the blackboard, the ape may put on a wise
face, but he is a brute, and a brute has no capacity for mathematics.
He cannot understand it. So with the natural man in spiritual matters
—he has no capacity for them. Why this utter inability? *"For they
are spiritually discerned."* Natural man is unspiritual, the things are
spiritual. A blind man can know nothing of colors; a deaf man can
know nothing of music; an unspiritual man can know nothing of spiritual things. Natural man is not like another Hercules at the parting of
the ways; he is not a free agency here so that he could either accept or
reject the Gospel. He can do but one thing: reject it. Natural man's
condition is deplorable indeed. Note what the apostle furthermore says.
When the Gospel is preached to natural man, he not only does not receive it, does not understand it, but—how great is that blindness!—does
not even recognize the fact that these things are too deep for him, beyond
his comprehension, and hence does not say: "I don't understand them;
they may be true, but I can't judge of them." No, he acts as though
he were perfectly competent to sit in judgment on divine matters. What
is his judgment? *"Foolishness!"* *"They are foolishness unto him."*
When a philosopher discourses on the system of his philosophy, let us
say, to a body of wise doctors of medicine, the doctors will say as rational men, "Mr. Philosopher, your talk was very interesting, but beyond
our grasp. What you said may be true, we shall not contradict you, but
it was beyond our ken. Medicine is our sphere of knowledge; philosophy
is yours." The next day the philosopher takes sick; he goes to the doctor, saying, "I understand philosophy, but not medicine. What ails me?
Prescribe for me!" Each is wise enough to remain in his own distinct
sphere of knowledge.—Again, you hold up a color-plate to a blind man
and say, "Describe the colors!" "How absurd," says he, "I cannot; I
am blind!"—But here is a blind man—natural man—who has not even

sense enough to know that he is blind in spiritual matters. Here is a man—natural man—who has absolutely no knowledge of, and no capacity for, spiritual things, and still he dares sit in judgment on divine things and pronounce them foolishness! How forcibly are we not here reminded of that deep saying of our Lord, Matt. 6, 23: "If the light that is in thee be darkness, how great is that darkness!" The sweet Gospel of Christ is preached, and natural man says, "Foolishness!" He is told, Christ is both God and man in one person, and he says, "Foolishness!" He is told this God-man would be your Savior also, and he says, "Foolishness!" He is told, Accept the Gospel and be eternally happy! "Accept the Gospel," says he, "accept foolishness! No, I reject it, I spurn it, I ridicule it—away with it!" Such is the attitude of natural man towards the only hope of his salvation. The wisdom of God he adjudges foolishness. His *intellect* is blind; he cannot know spiritual things. He accounts them "foolishness!" hence he *will* not have them. His *will* is entirely perverted. "We preach Christ crucified, unto the Jews a stumbling-block and unto the Greeks foolishness," 1 Cor. 1, 23.

The chief purpose of this text, 1 Cor. 2, 14, in the Catechism is to prove that man by nature is spiritually blind. The text furthermore makes it very plain: 1. that it is absurd to ascribe spiritual powers to natural man; 2. that man cannot co-operate towards his conversion; 3. that reason has absolutely no authority in spiritual matters, and when it does essay to speak of them, it talks about things of which it knows nothing.

> The *Formula of Concord* says: "In the first place, although human reason, or the natural understanding of man, may have a feeble spark of the knowledge of the existence of God, and also of the Law, Rom. 1, 19; 2, 15; still, it is so ignorant, blind, and perverted, that, *even when the most ingenious and learned persons* on earth read or hear the Gospel concerning the Son of God and the promise of everlasting salvation, they are nevertheless unable by their own powers to perceive, or to comprehend, or to understand, or to believe these things, and to hold them as truth, but rather, the *greater* diligence and assiduity they employ in this respect to comprehend these spiritual things with their reason, *the less* they understand or believe; and they regard all as mere foolishness or fables before they are illuminated and taught by the Holy Spirit. 1 Cor. 2, 14: 'The natural man receiveth not the things of the Spirit of God,' etc." *(Sol. Decl.*, Art. II. *Of Free Will*, p. 611. New Market Ed.)

Eph. 2, 1: *Ye were dead in trespasses and sins.*

Man by nature is not only spiritually blind, he is also spiritually *dead*. *"Ye were dead in trespasses and sins,"* St. Paul writes to the ᴌphesian Christians. The meaning of *"dead"* is clear from the text. The apostle writes in the past tense: "Ye *were* dead," i. e., now you are dead no longer, you are spiritually alive; but formerly you were spiritually dead. In v. 5 the apostle repeats the same idea emphatically: "But God......even when we *were dead in sins*, hath quickened us together with Christ." Formerly, before their conversion, they were dead, not physically, but morally, spiritually; now, they are quickened, alive with Christ.—Before conversion man is dead, spiritually dead. "Verily, verily, I say unto you, The hour cometh, and now is, when the *dead* shall hear the voice of the Son of God; and they that hear shall *live*," John 5, 25. Hence the apostle admonishes the Christians: "Neither present your members unto sin as instruments of unrighteousness, but present yourselves unto God, as *alive from the dead*, and your members as instruments of righteousness unto God," Rom. 6, 13.—*"Dead"*—that word adequately describes the lamentable condition of man as he is by nature: he is *dead*, there is no spiritual life in him, not a spark of it.— "Ye were dead *in trespasses and sins*." This life "in trespasses and sins" resulted from their spiritual condition. The sphere in which they lived and moved in the sight of God was "trespasses and sins." Nothing that they did or could do was pleasing to God; they were *"by nature the children of wrath."* Such was natural man then, such he is now. How is this dead man to come to life? By his own powers? Absurd question; he is dead; he has no powers. Can natural man co-operate towards his conversion? Absurd question again: *he is dead!*

"Now, as a man who is physically dead cannot by his own powers fit or prepare himself so as to obtain temporal life again, so a man who is spiritually dead in sins cannot by his own powers adapt or prepare himself for the attainment of spiritual and heavenly righteousness and life, if he be not made free from the death of sin and made alive by the Son of God." *(Formula of Concord*, p. 611.) Again: "In spiritual and divine things the understanding, the heart, and the will of unregenerate man are unable, by their own natural powers, to understand, to believe, to accept, to think, to will, to begin, to accomplish, to do, to perform, or to co-operate in anything whatever, but are wholly and entirely corrupted, and dead to everything good, so that in the nature of man, since the fall, and prior to·his regeneration, *not a spark of spiritual power remains or exists* by which he can prepare himself for the grace of God, or accept the offered grace, or ·be capable thereof, or apply himself, or accommodate himself to it, of and by himself. Nor is he. able by his own powers to help, to·do, to perform, or ·to co-operate in anything towards his conversion, either as to the whole of it or any part, *even in the least or most insignificant part;* but he is the servant of sin, John 8, 34, and the captive of Satan, by whom he is led, Eph. 2, 2; 2 Tim, 2, 26. Hence the natural free will, according to its perverted nature and character, is efficient and active in that alone which displeases God and is opposed to Him." *(Formula of Concord,* p. 610.)

Rom. 8, 7: *The carnal mind is enmity against God.*

The paragraph, vv. 5-11, contrasts the carnally minded and the spiritually minded. The former are *"they that are after the flesh,"* v. 5, governed by the flesh; the latter, *"they that are after the Spirit,"* born again by the Spirit, hence governed by the Spirit, the spiritual, John 3, 6. The former *"mind the things of the flesh;"* their thoughts, desires, pursuits are centered on things of the flesh; on these their hearts are set, to these their lives are devoted. These "things of the flesh" are the "works of the flesh," as enumerated, *e. g.,* Gal. 5, 19. The latter *"mind the things of the Spirit,"* i. e., the works, the fruits of the Spirit, Gal. 5, 22. This sinful, carnal state of mind of the former class is death. The apostle says: *"For to be carnally minded is death."* The English translation "to be carnally minded" covers the idea expressed in the Greek. "To be carnally minded" expresses the *state of being,* not so much the acts flowing from that state. This being carnally minded, this carnal state of man is death. Of course, this state manifests itself in acts. As the spring, so the water. But that is not the point here. The point is that man who is in this state is dead, spiritually dead. Says Hodge: "The phrase *fronema tes sarkos* (the mind of the flesh) is substantially of the same import with *fronein ta tes sarkos,* the minding of the things of the flesh. It is thus active in its signification. It is, however, more in accordance with the proper signification of the word to understand it as expressing a state of mind. This is implied in the English version, *to be carnally minded.* The idea is not merely that the actual seeking the things of the flesh leads to death, but that a carnal state of mind, which reveals itself in the desire and pursuit of carnal objects, is death. And by death is, of course, meant spiritual death, the absence and the opposite of spiritual life. It includes alienation from God, unholiness, and misery. On the other hand, the *fronema tou pneumatos* (the mind of the Spirit) is that state of mind which is produced by the Spirit, and which reveals itself in the desire and pursuit of the things of the Spirit. This state of mind is life and peace. Therein consists the true life and blessedness of the soul." *(On Romans,* p. 402.)

And why is to be carnally minded death? *"Because the carnal mind is enmity against God."* In its very nature it is opposed to God, inimical to God. "The carnal mind is enmity against God, *for* it is not subject to the Law of God." The Law of God is the revelation of His will. Whosoever opposes this holy Law is an enemy of God. Man by nature is not only not subject to the Law of God, but *"he cannot be,"* v. 7. He has no ability to change himself, he lies in spiritual *death.* "It is precisely because of this utter impotency of the carnal mind, or unrenewed heart, to change its own nature, that it involves the hopelessness which the word death implies." (Hodge.)

Natural man, who is spiritually *blind* and spiritually *dead,* in another sense is very much alive, active; alive in his *enmity* and hatred against God. His *will* is opposed to the will of God. There is nothing but malice and hatred in his heart against God. When the Law of God is preached to natural man, he cannot but acquiesce that the demands made therein are right and just, for the Law is inscribed in his heart. But he hates God for having given the Ten Commandments, and to God's "Thou shalt!" he opposes his "I will not!" Hence Scripture says: "The Law worketh wrath," Rom. 4, 15. And when the Gospel is preached to him, his enmity oftentimes knows no bounds. St. Paul was stoned for preaching Christ crucified. Thus the enmity of the carnal mind manifested itself then. To-day the enmity is just as great, though it dare not manifest itself so violently. To be saved by Christ, by a foreign righteousness—never! Natural man will be his own Savior; he will be able to answer God on Judgment Day, so he imagines. Having lost the image of God, fallen away from original righteousness, man by nature is now wholly defiled in all the faculties of both body and soul. His life is a life of opposition and rebellion against God.

"This verse," says Philippi, "is a strong argument against the doctrine of the so-called *liberum arbitrium* of the natural man. For this carnal state of mind, which cannot subject itself to the will of God, is not produced by any act of man's will, nor can it be removed by any such act; it constitutes, according to the apostle's doctrine, the original nature of man in its present or fallen state."

> "In the second place, the Word of God testifies that in divine things the understanding, heart, and will of the unregenerate man are not only wholly alienated from God, but adverse to Him, inclined to all evil, and perverted. Again, man is not only weak, impotent, without ability, and dead to that which is good, but so miserably perverted, poisoned, and corrupted by original sin that by nature and character *he is altogether evil, stubborn, and inimical to God, actively, eagerly, and energetically engaged in doing everything that is displeasing and opposed to God.* Gen. 8, 21: 'The imagination of man's heart is evil from his youth,' etc." *(Formula of Concord, S. D., Art. II, p. 613.)*

1 Cor. 12, 3: *No man can say that Jesus is the Lord but by the Holy Ghost.*

Here we have the answer to the question, How is this dead man— man as he is by nature—to be brought to life? How are his blind eyes to be opened? This is solely the work of the Holy Ghost; for *"no man can say that Jesus is the Lord but by the Holy Ghost."* Of course, this does not mean that no one can utter these words, "Jesus is the Lord," except under special divine influence, but rather that no one can *believe* in Jesus as his Savior unless he is enlightened by the Spirit. For what does that mean: *Jesus is the Lord? "Jesus"* designates the Savior after His human nature; "Jesus" is the name of Mary's son—true man. *"The Lord"* designates the Savior after His divine nature—true God. So to say that "Jesus is the Lord" is to say that Mary's son, this true man, is at the same time the Lord, the very God; it is to confess that Christ is both true man and true God in one person; it is to confess the mystery of mysteries: "God is manifest in the flesh;" it is to confess that

Jesus is He at whose name "every knee should bow, of things in heaven, of things in earth, and things under the earth; and that every tongue should confess that Jesus Christ is Lord, to the glory of God the Father," Phi. 2, 10.11. And he who says, confesses, that at the same time believes that Jesus is his Lord who has purchased and won him by His bitter sufferings and death from the power of sin, death, and the devil. And this confession, this faith, is possible only by the power of the Holy Spirit. What did the Lord Himself say when Peter confessed Him to be the Son of God? "Blessed art thou, Simon Barjona; for flesh and blood hath not revealed it unto thee, but my Father who is in heaven," Matt. 16, 17.—Hence we confess with Luther: "I believe that I cannot by my own reason or strength believe in Jesus Christ, my Lord, or come to Him, *but the Holy Ghost has called me* by the Gospel."

*   *   *

In the words, "But the Holy Ghost has called me by the Gospel, enlightened me with His gifts, sanctified and kept me in the true faith," we confess that sanctification is solely the work of the Holy Ghost. This truth we considered in a recent article.

Four distinct acts are ascribed to the Holy Spirit: (1) The call; (2) enlightening; (3) sanctification in the narrower sense; (4) preservation. The phrase "by the Gospel" qualifies the verbs *called, enlightened, sanctified,* and *kept.* And when we confess, "The Holy Ghost has called me *by the Gospel,*" etc., we give utterance to the distinctive Lutheran, *i. e.,* Biblical, doctrine, that the Holy Ghost never works without means, the means of grace, and thereby we reject the doctrine of the sects, that the grace of God and His Spirit are communicated by an *immediate* and *secret* operation, by an inner light, etc. "Faith cometh by hearing, and hearing by the Word of God." Rom. 10, 17. The Gospel is the word of the *grace of God,* Acts 20, 24.32; it *ministereth the Spirit,* Gal. 3, 5. This Gospel, since it is the Word of God, is "quick and powerful," Hebr. 4, 12; and it is the *power of God* unto salvation," Rom. 1, 16. Paul explicitly writes to the Thessalonians: "He *called you by our Gospel,*" 2 Thess. 2, 14. Christians are born again *by the Word of God,* 1 Pet. 1, 23; they *grow thereby,* 1 Pet. 2, 2; this Word is the seed and the nourishment of the new life.

> "We must, therefore, constantly maintain that God will confer with us in no other way than through His external Word and sacraments. And all that is boasted of independent of such Word and sacraments as being the Spirit, is the very devil himself." *(Smalcald Articles,* Art. VIII., p. 322.)

Luke 14, 17:   *Come; for all things are now ready.*

The process of *calling* is beautifully illustrated in the parable of the Great Supper. God has prepared salvation for all, *"all things are now ready"*; and He earnestly and urgently calls, *"Come!"* This is the Gospel call.

2 Tim. 1, 9: *God hath saved us and called us with an holy calling, not according to our works, but according to His own purpose and grace, which was given us in Christ Jesus before the world began.*

Paul exhorts Timothy: "Be not ashamed of the testimony of our Lord, nor of me, His prisoner; but suffer hardships with the Gospel according to the power of God; who saved *us*," etc. Paul speaks of himself and Timothy, and what applies to them applies to all Christians. "Be not ashamed," Timothy, "suffer hardships with the Gospel"; for remember what great things God has done by you and me: He *"saved us and called us."* The statement *"God saved us"* is followed by the manner in which He saved us: *"He called us."* We were called, and thus we were saved. God called us, and thus we came to Him. He called us *"with a holy calling."* The call proceeded from the *holy God,* and it was a call to *holiness.* Our salvation *in toto* we owe to God. *Expressis verbis* the apostle denies that there was a ground or cause in us that impelled Him to "save and call us," when he says: *"not according to our works."* Next, he positively asserts the only reason for His act: *"but according to His own purpose and grace"*; the reason was *His own purpose* which was founded on His *grace,* i. e., upon His gracious purpose. The two words, "purpose and grace," emphatically say: it was a *gracious purpose.* Paul proceeds: *"which was given us in Christ Jesus before the world began."* So the call is referred back to eternity; we did not then exist, hence could not impel God in any way. It was *given us;* hence it is pure grace. It was given us *in Christ;* hence it is a grace not without Christ, but in Christ.—*"Not according to our works, but according to His own purpose and grace."* Works and grace are opposed to each other; the one excludes the other. Studiously the passage inculcates the blessed truth: nothing in us, not our good works, good conduct, or anything else in us, caused God to call us. It was a call of pure grace.

1 Pet. 2, 9: *Ye are a chosen generation, a royal priesthood, an holy nation, a peculiar people, that ye should show forth the praises of Him who hath called you out of darkness into His marvelous light.*

Who are they of whom Peter speaks in such eulogistic terms? They are they who have been begotten again unto a lively hope according to the abundant mercy of God, chap. 1, 3; they who are born again, not of corruptible seed, but of incorruptible, by the Word of God, which liveth and abideth forever, 1, 23; they who are admonished: "Desire the sincere milk of the Word, that ye may grow thereby," 2, 2; they who are built up a spiritual house on the living stone, Christ. 2, 5; the believers, 2, 7. These same people, in contradistinction to the unbelievers, are now addressed: *"But ye are a chosen generation,"* chosen out of the *massa perditionis; "a royal priesthood."* Priests they are who through Christ have access to God, and they are *royal priests,* kings, who rule over their spiritual enemies. *"An holy nation,"* a *nation* whose king is Christ; a *holy* nation because of faith in Christ, and who from faith lead a holy life. *"A peculiar people,"* literally, *"a people for a possession,"* for God's possession, who will not allow them to be plucked out of His hand. What purpose has the apostle in view in thus enumerating the high prerogatives of the Christians? *"That ye should show forth the praises of Him who hath called you."* So we have an exhortation to sanctification. Here, by the way, is a valuable lesson for theological students, future ministers, as well as for ministers in active service. When exhorting Christians to do good works, let us learn from the apostle to build a solid substructure, to exhort them "by the mercies of God"; let us not hammer down upon them with the Law, "Thou shalt!" "Thou shalt not!" Let us remember that truly good works flow out of gratitude to God; furthermore, good works, as we may see from a close inspection of this text, do not and cannot flow out of our natural powers, but from the spiritual powers given us in conversion.

When the apostle admonishes the Christians to show forth the praises of God, he adds: *"Who hath called you out of darkness into His marvelous light."* The call obligates them to a life in sanctification, and through the call they have received power to live such a life.

As Paul, in the preceding passage, spoke of the call, so does Peter in the present. By reminding the Christians of the *call,* he reminds them of their entrance into Christianity. Let us observe what he says: He "hath called you out of *darkness."* *Darkness, skotos,* is the total absence of light. Clearly, *before* the call they were in *darkness.* What state does that signify? Peter in the context answers: "In time past ye were *not a people";* "which had *not obtained mercy."* What state is designated by *"light"* into which they were translated by the call? Again the context answers: "but are *now* a people of God," "but *now* have obtained mercy." And now observe the prepositions *ek—eis, out of —into.* *Out of* darkness—*terminus a quo: into* light—*terminus ad quem.* How was this entrance *into* light effected? By any act of theirs? No. If left to themselves, they would have remained in darkness. How did the blessed change come about? God *called* them *out of—into.* By and through the call they were transferred from *darkness* to *light.* It was an *efficacious* call. *God* called. Through the *call* they became what they now are—Christians. The call included the effect; it was an *effective call.* At the same time it was a *gracious* call. They were in darkness and loved darkness. Nothing *a parte hominis* impelled God to extend the call. God called them *into light.* The spiritual darkness vanished, their dark minds became illumined. The sinner who is thus called is at that same moment illumined; he sees Jesus as his Savior, trusts, believes, rejoices, and takes comfort in Him.

2 Cor. 4, 6: *For God, who commanded the light to shine out of darkness, hath shined in our hearts to give the light of the knowledge of the glory of God in the face of Jesus Christ.*

This brilliant passage is the standard text for the doctrine of illumination. In his defense over against the accusations of certain detractors of his apostleship, Paul had spoken of people "in whom the god of this world," the devil, "hath blinded the minds of the unbelieving, that the light," the illumination, "of the Gospel of the glory of Christ, who is the image of God, should not shine unto them," v. 4. Speaking for himself and the other preachers of the Gospel, the apostle says their blindness is not the fault of the Gospel, for that is a powerful light, v. 4, nor is it their fault, "for we preach not ourselves," we have no self-seeking aims, "but" we preach "Christ Jesus the Lord, and ourselves your servants for Jesus' sake," v. 5. Continuing his argument, he avers that it was God Himself who bestowed such knowledge upon them which qualified them to preach Christ Jesus by enlightening them, and that for the purpose of enlightening others. *"God it is who shined in our hearts"*; thus our hearts, dark in themselves by nature, became illumined. God "shined in our hearts" by manifesting unto us Christ Jesus as Lord, our Savior. Thus we received this light, this illumination. And why did God do this? *"To give the light of the knowledge of the glory of God in the face of Jesus Christ."* This we do; "we preach Christ Jesus the Lord," v. 5. This is the sum and substance of the Gospel; and this Gospel is a light that shines, v. 4. Stating the purpose for which they had been illumined, the apostle writes: *pros fortismon tes gnoseos*, etc. We may translate: God shined in our hearts *"for the enlightening of the knowledge of the glory of God,"* or: God shined in our hearts *"to give the light,"* the illumination, *"of the knowledge of the glory of God."* In either case *"the knowledge of the glory of God"* is "the light," the illumination, which God Himself has kindled through the Gospel, v. 4. None but God could do this. This truth is impressively set forth by the comparison of the creation of light on the first day of creation and the creation of this spiritual light in the heart. "God, *who commanded the light to shine out of darkness,* shined in our hearts." In the beginning, darkness covered the earth. God said, "Let there be light!" and there was light. Through this creative word it sprang into existence. No power inferior to the omnipotence of God could produce it. The same power, God's Word, is necessary to dispel spiritual darkness in natural man. Cf. 1 Cor. 2, 14; Eph. 2, 1. Where and how does God today say, "Let there be light!"? In the Word, by the preaching of the Gospel, v. 5. This is God's voice. "The light of the Gospel of the glory of Christ," v. 4, is put on the candlestick, and through its illuminating power the darkness of the heart is dispelled; it becomes enlightened. And whosoever is enlightened sees *"the glory of God."* The glory, *doxa*, of God is the sum total of all divine attributes whereby God manifests Himself as God. Such attributes are His holiness, love, mercy, justice, grace, omniscience, omnipotence, etc.—Where do we see "the glory of God"? The text answers: *"in the face of Jesus Christ."* What does that say? "The light of the Gospel," says v. 4, reveals "the glory of *Christ*," and Christ *"is the image of God."* The *"glory of Christ,"* v. 4, and *"the glory of God,"* v. 6, are identically the same, John 1, 14. Now, who sees Christ, "the image of God," sees the Father, John 14, 9. So by beholding the glory of Christ in the Gospel, we have a knowledge of the glory of God. Which of the various attributes constituting the "glory" of God are meant in a given passage, the context reveals. Now since the context speaks of the Gospel, v. 3, of "the light of the glorious Gospel of Christ," v. 4, of preaching "Christ Jesus the Lord," v. 5, the grace, mercy, and love of God, which He manifested by sending His Son as the Redeemer of the world, Tit. 3, 4, *et al.*, are primarily to be thought of.

Jer. 31, 18: *Turn Thou me, and I shall be turned; for Thou art the Lord, my God.*

In the Scriptures the bestowal of faith is denoted by various terms such as call, enlightenment, regeneration, conversion, etc. The same event is looked at from a different view-point. The sinner who is effectually called is at the same moment enlightened, regenerated, converted, etc.—Our Catechism mentions *conversion* and *regeneration*. The sinner who is called is said to be *converted* because he is turned from sin to God; he is said to be *regenerated* because he is placed in a new life.

Jer. 31, 18 speaks of conversion. Ephraim prays: *"Turn Thou me, and I shall be turned."* The English word *turn* gives rise to a striking and truthful picture. Natural man is going in the wrong direction, away from God. Of himself he cannot turn and come to God. *"Turn Thou me,"* Thou alone canst do it, *"and I shall be turned."* The reason follows: *"for Thou art the Lord, my God."* God manifests His divine power by turning man, who flees from Him into destruction, and changing his mind so that he bids farewell to sin, the world, and Satan, and turns to God.—God is *subjectum convertens*, and man is simply *subjectum convertendum*.

But is this not a prayer of the converted Ephraim? Whosoever can and does pray, "Turn Thou me," is already converted. True. Far from subverting the point made, this objection simply strengthens the position taken. Ephraim, who is already turned, prays to be turned. What does this prove? That conversion here is to be understood in the wider sense, of the daily turning to God, the daily conversion, that conversion which is to last through life. Now, since even this daily conversion is a work of God, how much more is not the first conversion, conversion in its narrower sense, a work of God! And Ephraim expressly says, "After I was turned, I repented," v. 19.

1 Thess. 4, 3: *This is the will of God, your sanctification.*

When Paul came to Thessalonica, he preached the Gospel of Christ first and foremost. He "reasoned with them out of the Scriptures, opening and alleging that Christ must needs have suffered and risen again from the dead; and that this Jesus, whom I preach unto you is Christ," Acts 17, 3. Through this Gospel the Thessalonians came to faith. But Paul did not only preach redemption and justification, but also *"how"* they *ought* to walk and to please God," 1 Thess. 4, 1; in other words, he also preached sanctification. He showed them not only the necessity *(dei)* of walking in the newness of life, but also the "how" *(pos)*, the manner of this walk, to please God. He exhorted them to "walk worthy of God, who hath *called* you unto His kingdom and glory," 1 Thess. 2, 12. The call obligated them thereto, and gave them power so to walk. And in the present chapter he tells the "brethren," v. 1, why he so earnestly beseeches and exhorts them to "abound more and more" in sanctification: *"This—your sanctification—is the will of God."* God's good and gracious will is, first of all, their salvation by faith in Christ Jesus. But this is also His will that Christians, being called out of darkness into His marvelous light, should show forth the praises of Him that called them, 1 Pet. 2, 9; that, being "light in the Lord," they should "walk as children of light," Eph. 5, 8; that, to quote St. Peter again, "as He which hath *called* you is holy, so be ye holy in all manner of conversation," 1 Pet. 1, 15.

"This," namely, "your sanctification," "is the will, *thelema*, of God." The apostle does not use the article before *thelema*; he does not say: *to thelema*, but simply *thelema*, which indicates that he does not mean to say: this—your sanctification—is the whole will of God, this exhausts His will concerning you, but the construction says: this also belongs to the will of God—your sanctification. And the word for "sanctification" is *hagiasmos*, not *hagiosune*. *Hagiasmos* has an *active* sense, *Heiligung*; whilst *hagiosune* has a *passive* meaning, *Heiligkeit*. Hence the exhortation is: sanctify yourselves, flee sin, get rid of sin more and more; cf. v. 1. This is God's will, just as much His divine commandment as, "Thou shalt not steal;" "thou shalt not kill," etc. And "brethren," v. 1, who are besought and exhorted "by the Lord Jesus," v. 1, will willingly give heed to such exhortations, will gladly run the way of God's commandments.—From the Law, though it cannot give spiritual life, they learn God's holy will, and the power to put off the old man daily they obtain from the Gospel, Rom. 12, 1.2.

Eph. 2, 10: *For we are His workmanship, created in Christ Jesus unto good works, which God hath before ordained that we should walk in them.*

The peculiar emphasis on the first words of our text: *Autou gar esmen poiema*—"for *His* workmanship we are," finds its explanation in the preceding context. By nature we were dead in trespasses and sins, v. 1; but God, who is rich in mercy, even when we were dead in sins, hath quickened us, made us alive, together with Christ, vv. 4. 5. So it is plain: "by grace ye are saved," v. 5. This thought is resumed in v. 8 and amplified by the phrase: "through faith"—"by grace are ye saved through faith." God's grace impelled Him to kindle faith in our spiritually dead hearts, faith in Christ Jesus, and thus we are saved by grace. Grace excludes all merit on our part. To make this thought outstanding, the apostle continues: *"and that not of yourselves."* Spiritual vivification, quickening from spiritual death, vv. 2.5, is a *gift*, and it is a "gift *of God*," v. 8. It is "*not of yourselves*," hence "*not of works*," v. 9. Our conversion is in no way a work of our own, else man might boast, v. 9. But it is "by grace," "through faith," that no man should boast. Conversion is God's work *in toto;* to Him belongs all glory.—All boasting on the part of man is excluded; "*for*," as shown in the foregoing verses, "*His workmanship we are.*" We, we as Christians, our Christianity— all is "a thing of His making," *poiema*. This is further explained and emphasized: We are "*created in Christ Jesus,*" we are new-created. "Therefore, if any man be in Christ, he is a new creature," 2 Cor. 5, 17. Thus "*His* workmanship we are." And now the apostle says: We are created in Christ Jesus *unto good works, which God hath before ordained, prepared, that we should walk in them.* Good works cannot be performed until we are new-*created unto* them. In other words: Christians only *can* do good works; but, on the other hand, Christians must know that they "*should* walk in them." Good works do not save, do not justify, but the justified, the saved Christians should be zealous of good works. Tit. 2, 14; Gal. 5, 22-25.—But what does the apostle mean when he says: We are created unto *good works, which God hath before ordained,* prepared? The words yield no other sense than this, that God has made ready, prepared, beforehand those good works in which the Christians should walk. And when we ask where we are to find them, the context answers: in Christ Jesus, in whom we have been created. "Our walk in Him (Christ) is a walk in them (the good works)." Our being and life in Christ includes the walk in good work , so that we walk as He has walked.—Thus all self-glorification is barred. A true Christian does not boast of his truly good works that flow from faith. All glory and honor for what we Christians are and do as Christians belongs to God. (Cf. Stoeckhardt, *Epheserbrief.*)

Good Works.

Advisedly the Catechism asks: "What is a good work *in God's sight?*" Works that appear great and good in the sight of men, in the sight of God may be nothing but "shining vices." Such are all so-called good works of unbelievers, Hebr. 11, 6; Rom. 14, 23. Augustine's dictum: "*Omnis infidelium vita peccatum est,*" expresses a deep theological truth.

The Catechism answers the question: "What is a good work in the sight of God?" thus: 1. The *subject* of good works is *a child* of God, John 15, 5. 2. The *source* is *faith,* John 15, 5. 3. The *rule* is the *Ten Commandments,* Matt. 15, 9. 4. The *purpose* or *aim:* (a) *the glory of God,* 1 Cor. 10, 31; (b) *the benefit of the neighbor,* 1 Pet. 4, 10.

John 15, 5: *I am the Vine, ye are the branches: He that abideth in me, and I in him, the same bringeth forth much fruit; for without me ye can do nothing.*

The purpose of this text is to prove that only *"a child of God"* can do good works.—The passage is taken from our Lord's Farewell Address. He speaks to His *disciples,* to Christians: *"I am the Vine, ye are the branches."* Between them and Him there is a relation as intimate as that between the vine and its branches. A striking similitude this, since Palestine abounded in vineyards, a similitude that frequently occurs in the Old Testament (Is. 5, 1-7; Ps. 80, 8-16; Jer. 2, 21, *et al.),* hence was familiar to Jewish people, the new application of which would readily find lodgment in the minds of His disciples.

In order to get the full force of v. 5, the preceding verses, 1-4, should be read. "I am the *true* Vine," *he ampelos he alethine, i. e.,* I am the *real,* the *genuine* Vine. I really and truly give what is emblematically represented by a vine. As the vine imparts life and nourishment to all the branches, large and small, so you, my disciples, have received, and still receive, life from me. How did this intimate relation come about? The husbandman, my Father, v. 1, has grafted you in me. By what means? Through the Word: "Now ye are clean *through the Word* which I have spoken unto you," v. 3. Through the Word ye have come to faith in me, through it ye are cleansed, ye have forgiveness of sins, 1 John 1, 7. Ye are in me, now *"abide* in me," v. 4. Remain united to me by a living faith, and ye can and will bring forth "fruit," v. 2, "more fruit," v. 2, "much fruit," v. 5.

In v. 5 the Lord emphatically repeats the thoughts of the preceding paragraph. *"I am the Vine, ye are the branches."* What follows from this? *"He that abideth in me, and I in him, the same"*—*houtos*—he and no other—*"bringeth forth much fruit."* The branch, cut from the vine, is severed from the source of its strength and nourishment; it must die. Just so only he who is united by a living faith to Christ can bear fruit, can be productive of good works. "As the branch cannot bear fruit of itself, except it abide in the vine, no more can ye, except ye abide in me," v. 4. *"Without me,"* choris emou, separate from me, *"ye,"* my disciples, *"can do nothing,"* absolutely nothing that is pleasing to God. Capacity, capability, to perform good works comes from Christ.

The text is rich in truths pertinent to the *locus* in hand. We shall tabulate the most important.

1. *Christians only can do good works.* This is shown above. They only are "His workmanship created in Christ Jesus unto good works," Eph. 2, 10.

2. *Christians do good works,* they bring forth "fruit," "more fruit," "much fruit," vv. 1-5. The righteous is like a tree planted by the rivers of water that bringeth forth his fruit in his season, Ps. 1, 3; cf. Acts 9, 36; Rom. 16, 12; Mat. 25, 35 ff.; John 5, 28.29.

3. *Good works flow from faith as their source.* *"The same,"*

houtos, he and no other, sc., "that abideth in me, and I in him, bringeth forth much fruit." Only they "which have *believed* in God" are and can be exhorted to be "careful to maintain good works," Tit. 3, 8; 1 Pet. 2, 12; 1 Thess. 4, 3; Eph. 2, 10.

4. *Good works are performed only in the power of Christ, of God.* "Abide in me"—"the same"—"without me ye can do nothing." Christ, God, is the Author of good works; the Christians are but the instruments through which He performs them. "It is God that worketh in you both to will and to do according to His good pleasure," Phil. 2, 13; cf. Rom. 16, 12; 15, 19; 2 Cor. 3, 5.—The Christian is not a clock, which, if wound up, runs for a certain length of time. He is rather an electric light, which shines so long as the power is turned on. Shut it off, and all is darkness. The "power" of the Christian life is Christ, faith in Christ, abiding in Him. *"Without me,"* separated from me, and the result is? "Ye," *my disciples*, "can do—nothing." Hence, all honor and praise for these good works belong to Christ.

5. *Good works are not laborious productions, but "fruits."* As it is natural for a good tree to bring forth good fruits, so it is self-evident that a Christian through his intimate connection with Christ should produce "fruit." Cf. Gal. 5, 22; Matt. 13, 8.23.—But we must observe that the Catechism says a good work in the sight of God is "whatever a child of God does, speaks, or thinks *in faith*," etc. The Christian is, as it were, a composite being, part spirit, part flesh. And "the flesh lusteth against the spirit, and the spirit against the flesh; and these are contrary, the one to the other, so that ye cannot do the things that ye would," Gal. 5, 17. To the Romans, St. Paul writes: "I know that in me (that is, in my flesh,) dwelleth no good thing." Hence it comes about that "the good that I would I do not, but the evil which I would not, that I do." But the Christian can say: "It is no more I that do it, but sin that dwelleth in me." Cf. Rom. 7, 17-19. Whatever comes from the flesh is sinful. Perfect sinlessness is unattainable in this life, 1 John 1, 8. In the Christian there is a constant warfare between the flesh and the spirit; but the spirit dominates in him, Gal. 5, 24.

6. *The means through which God operates in the Christians is the "living Word,"* 1 Pet. 1, 23. This truth can be gathered from our text also. The exhortation is: "Abide in me." When do we abide in Him? "If ye abide in me, and *my words* abide in you," etc., v. 7. Tit. 2, 11.14.

7. Since only *"the same"* who abide in Christ Jesus can do good works, since *"without me,"* as Christ says, even *"ye,"* my disciples, *"can do nothing,"* v. 5, and since persons must be *"created* in Christ Jesus unto good works," Eph. 2, 10, it is plain that *unbelievers cannot do good works.* The apparently good works of unbelievers are comparable to the wriggling of a dead frog whose body is connected with an electric battery. The frog goes through all the motions of one seemingly alive, but still he is nothing but a dead frog. *Fiat applicatio.* The so-called

good works of unbelievers are but caricatures of the truly good works of Christians.

"Although nature is able in some sort to do the outward work (for it is able to keep the hands from theft and murder), yet it cannot work the inward motions, such as the fear of God, trust in God, chastity, patience," etc. *(Augsburg Conf.,* Art. 28.)

Matt. 15, 9: *In vain they do worship me, teaching for doctrines the commandments of men.*

The *"commandments of men"* to which the Lord here refers are *"the traditions of the elders,"* v. 1. These consisted of explanations, applications, and additions to the law of God made by learned expounders of the Scriptures among the Jewish people. Begun at about the time of Ezra, they accumulated as the years went by. Transmitted at first by word of mouth from generation to generation, they were finally collected in what is known as the Jewish Talmud. These "traditions of the elders," man-made precepts, the scribes and Pharisees taught, must be punctiliously observed, being equal in authority with the Law of God itself; aye, if the traditions and the written Word of God clashed, these traditions took precedence of the Word of God: the traditions must be kept, the Word of God disregarded.

Christ tells these blind leaders of the blind that their traditions were but *"commandments of men"* which His disciples must not keep (cf. vv. 1.9); that because of the traditions of *men* they transgressed the commandment of *God,* v. 3, hence sinned against God. By means of a concrete example, the Fourth Commandment, He proves that their traditions made "the commandment of God of none effect," null and void, vv. 4-6. Hence, their whole religion—what was it?—hypocrisy.

With words of stinging rebuke borrowed from the prophet Isaiah, the Lord deals a crushing blow to the hypocritical traditionalists of that day and ours: "Ye hypocrites, well did Esaias prophesy of you, saying: This people draweth nigh unto me with their mouth, and honoreth me with their lips; but their heart is far from me. *But in vain they do worship me, teaching for doctrines the commandments of men."* Teaching commandments of men as binding as the doctrines of God is a lip and mouth service, a vain worship.

How strongly the Lord expresses the truth: the only works that please Him are such as He Himself has commanded! The only rule of works pleasing in His sight is the Decalogue.

The Pharisee was the Roman Catholic of that time. The Roman Catholic church today makes the Word of God of none effect by her numberless traditions respecting fasts, holidays, pilgrimages, legends of saints, etc.

1 Cor. 10, 31: *Whether, therefore, ye eat, or drink, or whatsoever ye do, do all to the glory of God.*

Good works, this passage teaches, should have for their aim the glory of God. A Christian serves the Lord also when he eats and drinks and rests. He lives unto the Lord and dies unto the Lord. Sanctification includes the entire life of a Christian.—*"Magnum axioma!"* says Bengel of the present passage. Indeed, a great axiom this: Do all to the glory of God.—See Matt. 5, 16.

1 Pet. 4, 10: *As every man hath received the gift, even so minister the same one to another as good stewards of the manifold grace of God.*

In the section from which this text is taken, Peter admonishes the members of the congregation to be faithful in the discharge of their duties. The various gifts which God has distributed among the Christians shall be used *for the benefit of each other and one another.*—The translation: "As every man hath received *the* gift" is inadequate since the definite article "the" is wanting in the original. The apostle says: *"As every one has received a gift." Gift, charisma,* is a gift of grace, a gift of the Spirit. "As every one has received *the* gift" might give rise to the thought that there is but one certain, definite gift intended here which all Christians share alike. What the apostle does say is this: The grace of God is manifold; all Christians have gifts; gifts of grace; each Christian has a special gift. The one can teach, the other exhort, a third, rule, etc. Cf. Rom. 12, 6-9. Again in the congregation there are various offices for which certain members have been elected on account of their fitness. These gifts which the Christians have received they are to use for the benefit of all. The special gift which one Christian has received before others he is not to put in a napkin. He is to remember: it is a *gift;* God has given it to him for a special purpose. He is to use it, not for his own person only, but for the good of others, for the benefit of the whole congregation.—The *truth* expressed by the apostle is: You have received a gift; the *exhortation* is: "Minister the same," the gift, "one to another." Upon this thought all stress lies here: Be faithful in the use of the gift you have received, so that others may be benefited thereby and the congregation be edified.—The next clause intensifies this thought. "Minister the gift one to another," says the apostle, *"as good stewards of the manifold grace of God."* The emphasis lies on the word *"good."* God is the Lord, the Christians are but "stewards." The Lord will one day, "at the end of all things," v. 7, demand: "Render account of thy stewardship," Luke 16. This the Christians are to bear in mind and be *good, i. e.,* faithful stewards of the manifold grace of God.—Next, the apostle enumerates two gifts: 1. "If any man *"speak"*; 2. "if any man *minister,"* and again inculcates faithfulness in speaking and in ministering, v. 11a. Then he adduces the ultimate end of his exhortation: *"That God* in all things *may be glorified* through Jesus Christ," etc., v. 11b. Thus the text yields two points relevant to the doctrine under discussion: Good works should be performed (a) for the benefit of the neighbor, (b) for the glory of God.

PRESERVATION IN FAITH.

1 Pet. 1, 5: *Ye are kept by the power of God through faith unto salvation.*

The First Epistle of St. Peter is written to Christians who "now for a season, if need be, are in heaviness through manifold temptations," v. 6. One should think that the first words of the Epistle would be words of sympathy with their present sad lot. But no; Peter, or rather the Holy Ghost, has a better means of lifting them above trials and troubles. He begins the body of the letter with a fervent thanksgiving: "Blessed be the God and Father of our Lord Jesus Christ, which according to His abundant mercy hath begotten us again." *Sursum corda!* Think of the wonderful thing God has done by you: He has *begotten you again.* What impelled Him? Nothing of merit or worthiness in you; it was His grace, pure grace, His *abundant mercy.* And the purpose He had in view? You are begotten again *"unto a lively,"* i. e., a living, *"hope,"* a hope sure to attain its end. It is not a Fata Morganà. The firm basis of this "living hope" is "the resurrection of Jesus Christ from the dead." Cf. 1 Cor. 15, 17.18. "Jesus, my Redeemer, lives, I to life shall also waken."— What is the object of that hoped-for treasure? It is an *inheritance* of incomparable beauty, an inheritance "incorruptible, and undefiled, and that fadeth not away." Language is inadequate to express its gloriousness; we can speak of it in negatives only. And this inheritance is secure: it is "reserved in heaven for you." This "inheritance" is life eternal, life in the kingdom of glory. What a consolation for the suffering Christians to know: your "inheritance is reserved in heaven for you." In heaven are no enemies of the Christians, hence no danger of its being lost. Well and good; but, the Christian might falteringly ask, what of me? I am still a pilgrim here below in the enemy's territory; the end of my journey is not at hand as yet; shall I not fall into the hands of spiritual robbers and murderers on the way? Shall I be preserved for this inheritance? Most assuredly. Fear not; *"ye are kept unto salvation."* Ye are *kept,* literally, *guarded,* unto salvation. The apostle would say: I know you have powerful enemies, devil, world, and your own flesh, to contend with, but take heart: ye are *guarded.* "With might of yours naught can be done," but ye are *guarded.* How? Ye are *"kept guarded, through faith,"* *frouroumenous dia pisteos,* through faith in Christ Jesus. But how do I know that I shall be kept in faith? The apostle answers: *"By the power of God* ye are kept through faith unto salvation." Therein the power of God manifests itself that He preserves faith in us and through this faith keeps us unto salvation. What a sweet, strong consolation for the suffering Christian who is anxious about his soul's salvation! It is a consolation that has inherent power to strengthen the weak faith of the Christian, and to cause him to rejoice when he looks forward to that time when this salvation shall be revealed, v. 5b.

Phil. 1, 6: *Being confident of this very thing, that He which hath begun a good work in you will perform it until the day of Jesus Christ.*

Paul begins his thanksgiving for the Philippians thus: "I thank my God upon every remembrance of you, always in every prayer of mine for you all making request with joy."

Why does he thank God? "For your *fellowship in the Gospel* from the first day until now." He thanked God because the Philippians had become partakers in the Gospel, that by God's grace they had received it in faith, and lived in faith of their Savior Jesus Christ. For this he thanks God. God "had begun this good work" in them. When man comes to faith, all thanks therefor are due to God, and to Him only. Co-operation on the part of man is totally excluded. The apostle proceeds: "I thank my God........*being confident of this very thing that He which hath begun a good work in you will perform it.*" God "*had begun a good work*" in the Philippians, had brought them to faith by the Gospel, and the apostle is *confident, pepoithos,* has the firm conviction, is absolutely certain, that He will surely finish it, complete it, until the day of Jesus Christ. Not the Philippians themselves can or will do this, but God, and He only. He will keep them in the fellowship of the Gospel; He will keep them in faith and strengthen their faith. The warrant for Paul's firm confidence is the fact that it was *God* who began this work. His beginning the work is a pledge of its being completed, perfected. In spite of all our spiritual enemies we shall attain the end of our faith, our souls' salvation. Of such precious promises we should boldly lay hold, and be certain that neither death nor life shall be able to separate us from the love of God which is in Christ Jesus, our Lord, Rom. 8, 38.39.

The Cause of Unbelief.

Ezek. 33, 11: *As I live, saith the Lord God, I have no pleasure in the death of the wicked, but that the wicked turn from his way and live.*

The *wicked* are they who must confess: "Our transgressions and our sins are upon us, and we pine away in them," v. 10. The wicked are they whose sins are not forgiven. When they ask, "How should we then live?" v. 10, the answer is, The wicked as wicked cannot live. Their lot is death, *the death of the wicked,* eternal damnation. Their death is just. "The wages of sin is death." Whose fault is it if they die this death? Their own. They will not *turn from their wicked way.*

Or is it perhaps God's fault? The Lord God declares: "*I have no pleasure*" in their death; my pleasure is for them to *live.* This is God's good and gracious will towards the wicked, though they have richly deserved death. This His gracious will is an *earnest* will. He declares: "I have *no pleasure*" in their death; that should suffice us. But to make assurance doubly sure, God confirms this declaration with the oath:

"As I live!" His earnest will is their salvation, hence He lovingly implores them: *"Turn ye, turn ye, from your evil ways."* God has done all to save them. If they despise His call, they die of their own fault; they *will* to die. Hence God can say: "Why *will ye* die, O house of Israel?" v. 11b. God's will to save man is an *earnest* will; His grace, a *universal* grace. Whosoever knows that he belongs to "the wicked" and comes to a knowledge of his sins and transgressions, shall also know and firmly believe that for him, too, there is grace in store. Rom. 5, 6; Is. 53, 12; Matt. 9, 13; Luke 15, 2.

1 Tim. 2, 4: *God will have all men to be saved, and to come unto the knowledge of the truth.*

The cause why so many men are eternally lost does not lie in God. *"God will have all men to be saved."* God's will is an *earnest* will; this the verb *thelei* expresses. It comprises *"all men";* according to God's gracious will not a single soul is destined to damnation. How are "all men" to be saved? By *"coming unto the knowledge of the truth."* This is God's gracious, earnest will. What is meant by "the truth" through the knowledge of which "all men" are to be saved? Christ says: *"I am the Way, the Truth, and the Life."* So to know Christ is to know the truth, the way to salvation. And of this *truth* we are to have a deep knowledge, an *epignosis.* The head-knowledge does not save, but the deep knowledge of the heart that "Christ is the Way, the Truth, the Life," that "no one cometh to the Father but by Him." We are to know that we, "all men," are by nature unsaved, lost; that our sin separates us from God, but also that this barrier has been removed by Christ. He came into the world to save sinners. To this knowledge "all men" are to come and thus be saved. This is God's earnest will, and hence He has the Gospel preached, the sun and center of which is faith in Christ Jesus; and this "Gospel is the power of God unto salvation to every one that believeth," Rom. 1, 16.

2 Pet. 3, 9: *The Lord is not willing that any should perish, but that all should come to repentance.*

In the preceding paragraph the apostle had administered a stinging rebuke to the scoffers who ridicule the idea of Christ's return to judgment. They rest their argument on the proposition: "All things continue as they were from the beginning of the creation," v. 4. In masterful fashion Peter turns their own weapon against these mockers, proving conclusively that they are willful ignoramuses, vv. 1-4.

In the present paragraph he addresses the Christians. Among other things he says: "The Lord is not slack concerning His promise." Why, then, does He delay His second coming? "He is long-suffering to us-ward," *makrothumei eis humas.* Men have sinned and still sin. God might justly punish, but He stays His blow. Why this patience, this long-suffering? Because *"He is not willing that any should perish, but that all should come to repentance."* **God's great love to all mankind is**

the ground of His long-suffering. The word translated *"willing,"* *boulo-
menos*, implies deliberate consent. The Lord does *not will*, does *not wish*,
the death of any sinner. If any perish, it is not because God so willed,
so desired, so wished, so decreed. He did not, as Calvin teaches, pre-
destine some people to eternal damnation for the glorification of His
sovereign majesty. Negatively and positively His gracious will toward
all mankind is here set forth: *"Not any* should *perish, but all* should
come to repentance." Language can devise no stronger way to express
the thought: God's earnest, gracious will is the salvation of all mankind. More emphatically than is done here this truth cannot be expressed: There is no predestination to damnation.

"God will have all men to be saved." "The Son of Man is come
to save that which was lost," Matt. 18, 11. And He, "the Lamb of God,
taketh away the sin *of the world,"* John 1, 29. "He is the propitiation
for our sins; and not for ours only, but also for the sins of *the whole
world,"* 1 John 2, 2. All things are ready. And now God wills, earnestly
wills, *"that all should come to repentance,"* that all should come to a
knowledge of their sin, come to know that by virtue of their sin they
deserved to "perish" eternally, come to know that in Christ Jesus there
is salvation, firmly believe in Him and His merits, and thus escape perdition, and enter into everlasting life. So God is minded towards all.
His grace is *universal.* And because He is so minded towards us, He is
long-suffering. He will give to all time and opportunity to come to repentance, v. 9a.

Matt. 22, 14: *Many are called, but few are chosen.*

This passage has been the subject of much discussion. The controversy centers on the word "called," *kletoi*. The *tertium comparationis*
of text and context is lost sight of, hence the confusion. In his latest
book, *Conversion and Election, a Plea for a United Lutheranism
in America*, Dr. F. Pieper gives a very lucid explanation of Matt. 22, 14.
We take great pleasure in quoting it, the more so because much there
said is pertinent to the matter treated of in this article. We read, pp.
123 ff.:

> Without question, "calling" is used in a twofold sense
> in Scripture. Rom. 1, 6 "the called of Jesus Christ,"
> *kletoi Iesou Christou*, are the converted of Jesus Christ,
> those actually received into the kingdom of God, the *Chris-
> tians*. Being called is here identical with being converted
> or becoming a believer. And this is certainly the meaning
> of the term in the great majority of passages in the epis-
> tles. On the other hand, Matt. 22, 14: "Many are called,
> but few are chosen," *polloi gar eisin kletoi, oligoi, de
> eklektoi, distinguishes* the called from the elect. According
> to the context the called are persons toward whom God has
> omitted no effort, as regards their being invited, with
> earnest and urgent pleading, to the kingdom of God. But
> God has expended His efforts upon them in vain. The great
> majority of them do not obey the call. They are not trans-

lated from the world to the Church; they remain *extra ecclesiam*. In this passage of Holy Writ "call" and "conversion" are not identical in meaning. The call, in this sentence, is a person's *invitation* to the kingdom of God, without including his conversion. The same meaning appears in two more passages, Matt. 20, 16; Luke 14, 24.

Next, Calvin's argument, who would determine the character of the call by reference to the *result*, is refuted:—

Over against this it should be maintained: The call is a divine quantity *in itself*, regardless of the *result*. This is most powerfully exhibited Matt. 22. The king's benevolence, evidenced by the gracious terms of his invitation to the supper he has prepared, as well as his anger, enkindled by the contempt with which his invitation is received, demonstrate the intense divine earnestness of the calling even in the case of the *ineffectual* call. Matt. 22 is in subject-matter a parallel of Is. 5, 4: "What could have been done more to my vineyard that I have not done to it?" and of Matt. 23, 37: "I would have gathered you— and ye would not." Hence it is quite proper to say that all who live under the sound of the Gospel *may* be converted and saved, as was shown in the preceding chapter. Hence, too, our Confession treats of the call which God directs to all hearers of the Word in such terms as these: "This call of God, which is made through the preaching of the Word, we should not regard as being a mere delusion *(non existimemus esse simulatam et fucatam vocationem)*, but know that God thereby *reveals His will*, that He would *work* by His Word, in those called in such manner, that they might become enlightened, converted, and saved. For the Word by which we are called is 'a ministration of the Spirit,' giving the Spirit, or by means of which the Spirit is given, 2 Cor. 3, and 'a power of God unto salvation,' Rom. 1. And since the Holy Spirit would, through the Word, be active, strengthen, and give power and ability, it is God's *will* that we should receive and believe the Word and be obedient to it." Also the calling which remains ineffectual has behind it the gracious workings of divine omnipotence and the omnipotent workings of divine grace. There are *motus inevitables*. Our Confession says of the called who do not come: *Veritati AGNITAE perseverantes repugnant*, they offer constant resistance to the truth *which they have recognized*. The reason why men *are able to resist* the call: "Come unto me, all ye that labor and are heavy-laden, and I will give you rest," while they cannot resist the call of doom which summons them before the judgment-seat of Christ, is, because in His call of grace in time God works through means, while on Judgment Day He operates in glory *unveiled, en te doxe autou*. Not only in the latter, but in the former instance as well, the operative power is a divine and omnipotent power. "We *believe* according to the working of His mighty power which He wrought in Christ when He raised Him from the dead." But the operations of God through means have the property of being resistible. God working without means, in majesty unveiled, cannot be resisted, as is evident from Matt.

25, 31 sqq., and as is shown at length by Luther in *De Servo Arbitrio.* To say that "the *result* is the interpretation of the purpose of God" is the smart talk of a would-be wise person.

Matt. 23, 37: *O Jerusalem, Jerusalem, thou that killest the prophets, and stonest them which are sent unto thee, how often would I have gathered thy children together, even as a hen gathereth her chickens under her wings, and ye would not.*

This "cry of the mother-heart for its perverted and lost child" Jesus utters at the end of His prophetic career, on the last day of His public preaching in the Temple.—*"How often would I"*—*"and ye would not!"* How sharp the antithesis between the "I" and the "ye," between Christ's gracious will and the perverted will of the Jews!

Christ first says that *He* willed. This His will He had manifested by His deeds, and it was known to the people of Jerusalem. With the words, "How often would I," etc., Jesus points back to all those signs and wonders which He had performed in Jerusalem, and to all those sayings which the children of Jerusalem had heard out of His mouth. The Lord had often called the inhabitants of Jerusalem to repentance; with word and deed He had manifested Himself as their Savior and Redeemer; with great and precious promises He had lovingly invited them to come to Him. Back of all these admonitions and pleadings was the *will* of Jesus, the earnest will, to gather them to Himself, "even as a hen gathereth her chickens under her wings," to gather them to Himself, *episunagagein*, to convert them so that they might find rest for their souls. "*And ye would not.*" Herewith Jesus reminds the children of Jerusalem how they had conducted themselves over against Him from the very beginning; He reminds them of their conduct as it was patent then and there. Jerusalem had stoned and killed the prophets, and when Christ had come into His own, His own received Him not. They had remained aloof from Him, had not become His disciples, had contradicted His teachings, had blasphemed His great signs and wonders; often they had tried to apprehend Him in order to kill Him. Back of this evil conduct of theirs was their *perverted will.* "*And ye would not.*" Thus the Searcher of hearts lays bare the evil counsel of their hearts.— These exhortations and enticements of Jesus had affected the heart and the will of the Jews; they had felt how He was minded towards them; but they opposed their perverted will to His gracious will, and thus hindered the earnest gracious will of Christ: their conversion and salvation. (Cf. *Lehre u. Wehre,* Vol. 43, 200.)

Acts 7, 51: *Ye stiff-necked and uncircumcised in heart and ears, ye do always resist the Holy Ghost: as your fathers did, so do ye.*

These are words of Stephen, the first Christian martyr. In his address he had recounted all the benefits God vouchsafed to His disobedient people. God had left nothing undone to save them. Oftentimes

He had called them to repentance by the prophets. But what had they done? Moses the fathers had refused, v. 35; the prophets they had persecuted, v. 52. By refusing Moses and persecuting the prophets, they had despised the *Word, God's Word,* that Moses and the prophets spoke; they despised, *resisted, the Holy Ghost,* who spoke through Moses and the prophets. Thus did "the fathers, and *"as your fathers did, so do ye."* The "ye," the children, had betrayed and murdered the Just One, Jesus, v. 52. Him and His Word they rejected. And now they were resisting the preaching of the apostles, who testified that in Jesus alone there is salvation, and by resisting the word of the inspired apostles, they resisted the Holy Ghost, who is in and with the Word, Luke 10, 16. Thus they manifested their stiff-neckedness and their being uncircumcised in heart and ears. They closed their ears to the Gospel of Christ and their hearts to the Holy Ghost, who spoke through this Gospel.— Unbelief resists the Holy Ghost. Man hears the Word of God, and in, by, and through the Word the Holy Ghost wills, earnestly wills, to convert man; but man resists the operation of the Spirit in the Word and is thus lost. Whose fault is it? His own, not God's.

The word used for *"resist," antipiptete,* is a very strong one. It means: Ye *fall against* Him, i. e., the Holy Ghost. The Holy Ghost endeavors, earnestly endeavors, to convert them through the Word, and they experience that power from above, but they "fall against" Him, they resist with might and main. The Holy Ghost, as it were, tried to storm the citadel of the hearts of the unbelieving Jews, but this earnest will and purpose to take them captive was frustrated by their own obstinate resistance.

Hos. 13, 9: *O Israel, thou hast destroyed thyself; but in me is thine help.*

From the study of the preceding passages we have learned that God's gracious will to save mankind is *universal:* "God will have all men to be saved," 1 Tim. 2, 4; Ezek. 33, 11; 2 Pet. 3, 9.—This His will to save man is an *earnest and sincere* will. Besides the emphatic assertions making this truth plain, 1 Tim. 2, 4; 2 Pet. 3, 9, we have the oath of God, "As I live," Ezek. 33, 11, the positive statement of the Savior, "How often would I," etc., and His mournful lamentation over Jerusalem, Matt. 23, 37. With emphasis it is said that it is God's earnest, sincere will that "the wicked turn from his way and live," Ezek. 33, 11; "that all should come to repentance," 2 Pet. 3, 9. To accomplish that end God sent prophets, His mouthpieces, to proclaim His good and gracious will; to that end Christ Himself, the exegete of the Father, John 1, 18, revealed the Father's gracious will in order to gather men unto Himself, Matt. 23, 37; to that end the apostles, men sent by God, preached the Gospel, the power of God unto salvation, Acts 7, 51; Rom. 1, 16. And through this efficacious Word men are brought to faith and thus are saved. Rom. 10, 17; 2 Cor. 4, 6; Eph. 1, 17.20.—

Why, then, do not all that hear the Gospel come to faith? Because they resist God's earnest, sincere, and gracious will, and thus *prevent* their coming to faith. "Ye would not," Mat. 23, 37; "Ye do always resist the Holy Ghost," Acts 7, 51. This is the Scriptural answer to the question, Why are most men lost? Hence our Catechism says: "Most men obstinately resist the Word and Spirit of God, and are thus lost by their own fault."

These two truths so pointedly set forth in the foregoing passages are summed up and placed side by side in that dictum of Hosea, so often quoted by our Confessions: *"O Israel, thou hast destroyed thyself,"*—non-conversion depends entirely on man's evil conduct; *"but in me is thy help"*—conversion depends solely on the grace of God.

But here reason immediately interposes: All men by nature are *equally guilty* before God and *dead* in sins, 1 Cor. 2, 14; Eph. 2, 1; aye, the carnal mind is *enmity* against God, Rom. 8, 7; hence, man's coming to faith, or his conversion, is solely and only the work of God. True. Scripture declares: "Ye are risen with Him through *the faith of the operation of God*, who hath raised Him (Christ) from the dead; and you, being dead in your sins and the uncircumcision of your flesh, hath He quickened together with Him, having forgiven you all trespasses," Col. 2, 12.13. But why, then,—since all by nature are equally guilty and dead in sin,—does not God, whose will to save man is universal, whose grace is free, earnest, sincere, efficacious, grant faith to all? Why is a Saul converted into a Paul, and why is Caiaphas not converted? Why does Peter rise from his deep fall, and why does Judas fall into despair? In other words, why is it that some persons *in preference to others*, come to repentance and are saved?

We do not know. Scripture is silent on this point, so we must be silent. What we do know is this: If man comes to faith, this faith is of the operation of God through the means of grace, Col. 2, 12. "We *believe* according to the working of His mighty power which He wrought in Christ when He raised Him from the dead," Eph. 1, 19.20. If man does not come to faith, but remains in his unbelief, it is because, as Christ says, "ye would not," or, as Stephen words it, "ye do always resist the Holy Ghost." Doubting questions of reason must be fought down with the Spirit's weapon: "It is written!" In the school of theology here below the axiom applies: *Quod non est biblicum, non est theologicum;* in the school of theology up above where "we shall see Him as He is," 1 John 3, 2, we shall clearly understand the truth of God's Word uttered by His prophet Hosea: "O Israel, thou hast destroyed thyself; but in me is thine help."

OF THE CHURCH.

The Church is "properly *nothing else* than the congregation of all believers and saints." *(Augsb. Conf.,* Art. VIII.)

Eph. 2, 19-22: *Now, therefore, ye are no more strangers and for-eigners, but fellow-citizens with the saints and of the household of God, and are built upon the foundation of the apostles and prophets, Jesus Christ Himself being the chief corner-stone; in whom all the building, fitly framed together, groweth unto an holy temple in the Lord; in whom ye also are builded together for an habitation of God through the Spirit.*

The apostle addresses the Christians at Ephesus, who had been "Gentiles in the flesh," v. 11. In their lives there is a marked distinction between "once," vv. 1 ff., and "now," vv. 13.19 ff. "Once" they "walked according to the course of this world," v. 2; "once" they "were far off," "separate from Christ, alienated from the commonwealth of Israel, and strangers from the covenants of promise, having no hope, without God in the world," v. 12. Once they had been *strangers, foreigners, xenoi,* aliens, not citizens in the city of God, without any privileges in the commonwealth of the true Israel; they had been "sojourners," like unto people who have their abode in a family, but who do not belong to it, are not children, members of the household. A most deplorable condition!

Now, however, they have access to the "Father," v. 18, hence are children of God. How did the change come about? Christ came and preached peace to them, etc., v. 17.

"*Now, therefore*"—"so, then"—an inference from the foregoing sec-tions—"*ye are no more,*" as ye have been, "*strangers and foreigners.*" What are ye? "*Fellow-citizens with the saints.*" Who are "saints"? Sanctification, *hagiasmos,* is an act of God in virtue of which He sets apart certain people for Himself, separates them from the world, *i. e.,* through the Spirit, by the Word, makes them Christians, who are dedi-cated to Him. They are believers, *hoi hagioi tou theou,* "the saints of God," Acts 9, 13. And all believers, saints, in the imagery of the text, form a vast city in the eyes of God, the city, the commonwealth of God. These Ephesians, having been converted, *eo ipso* are *fellow-citizens,* have all the rights and privileges in this city. Who only are citizens in this city? The believers.

The image changes. These Ephesian Christians are "*of the house-hold of God,*" they belong to God's family, hence are His children. He is their Father, v. 18. Who only are children of God? The believers. Gal. 3, 26.

Again the image changes. The Ephesians—once heathen, now Chris-tians—are not only citizens in the city of God, not only are they members of the family of God, but, viewed from another aspect, they themselves are the stones, "living stones," 1 Pet. 1, composing the temple of God. They are "*built upon the foundation of the apostles and prophets, Jesus Christ Himself being the chief corner-stone.*" How beautiful, how grand the conception of this temple! Apostles and prophets the foundation, Christ the corner-stone, the believers the "living stones," and the temple still "growing," v. 21.

So, apostles and prophets are the foundation of this building. The apostles and prophets, though dead, still live and work through their writings. Whosoever comes to faith, does so by their writings—the Word of God. Who are built on this foundation? The believers. But the sun and center of this Word is Christ. John 5, 39. They who come to faith are built upon the word of the apostles and prophets, and *ergo* upon Christ, the Alpha and Omega of this Word. Who are living stones in this temple? Believers in Christ, and they only.

These beautiful images picture the *una sancta*, the Church. The Church is comparable to a commonwealth, a household, a temple. Who belongs to the Church in the proper sense of the word? They only who belong to this commonwealth, this household, this temple. Who are they? The believers. What is the Church? The sum total of all believers. What is the all-deciding factor of church-membership? Faith.

And faith intimately binds the Christians together. *"In whom,"* Christ, *"all the building, fitly framed together, groweth unto an holy temple in the Lord."* Stone is placed upon stone; the mortar holding them together is faith, faith in Christ. This *one* building is at the same time a harmonious, symmetrical building. It is not a chaos of stones, lying about higgeldy-piggledy. The stones are *fitly* framed together. In the eyes of God all Christians constitute *one* building, with *one* corner-stone, *one* foundation. The Church is *one*. As yet the temple is not completed. "It groweth." More and more stones are added, more and more people are brought to faith by the Spirit through the Word, and all these are "fitly framed together" unto this holy temple. Thus it had been with the Ephesian Christians. Of them it is said: "In whom *ye* also are builded together for an habitation of God through the Spirit." This will continue till the number of elect is complete. Then the last stone will have been laid, and the scaffold, this world, will be torn down, and this grand edifice, built by the Triune God, will stand forth in all its incomparable beauty on the last day.

We observe, too, that this temple is a *holy* temple. Christ, the corner-stone and foundation, is holy, and from Him the "living stones" receive their character. The blood of Christ cleansed them from all sin, thus they are holy. And Christ, the Holy One, at the same time dwells in this temple founded upon Himself. The believers are a holy temple in the Lord, a habitation of God through the Spirit. The Church is a habitation of the Triune God.

The text is too rich to do ample justice to it here. We must content ourselves with the main thoughts under discussion. We have seen, 1. what the Church is: the sum total of all believers. We have also noted 2. some properties of the Church. It is invisible, one, holy, Christian, apostolic.

2 Tim. 2, 19: *The foundation of God standeth sure, having this seal, The Lord knoweth them that are His.*

The conception underlying this passage is that of the Church, the Church of God. The foundation is mentioned by way of synecdoche for the entire building. *"The foundation standeth sure,"* it is firm; hence, the Church built upon it is firm and cannot be subverted. The seal this structure bears, reads: *"The Lord knoweth them that are His." "Them that are His"* are built on this firm foundation composing the Church. *"Them that are His,"* God's people, are the believers. We cannot look into the hearts of men, to see and know who believe, and who do not. *"God knoweth them."* To Him the Church is visible, to us it is *invisible.* Hence we confess: "I *believe* in the Holy Christian Church." The Church is the whole number of all believers. Believers are persons. Believers, Christians, confess their faith with word and deed. True, but then these things may deceive, may be hypocrisy. So we cannot positively say who is a member of the Church proper, who not. We cannot take a census of the true Christians, as the government does of its citizens, but "the Lord knoweth them."

Luke 17, 20.21: *The kingdom of God comet. not with observation; neither shall they, Lo here! or, Lo there! for, behold, the kingdom of God is within you.*

The Pharisees asked the Lord when the kingdom of God would come. The motive of the question is not assigned. To Luke this was of little moment; the Lord's reply was the important thing. When the Pharisees asked, "When cometh the kingdom?" they had in mind a great earthly kingdom in which they fancied to enjoy high stations, privileged positions. It was a kingdom that would come *"with observation,"* as the Lord's answer suggests. What does Jesus reply? *"The kingdom of God cometh not with observation,"* meta paratereseos. Its coming cannot be observed, seen, with the natural eye, so that a specific locality could be assigned to it and one could say: *"Lo here! or, Lo there!"* Behold, in this place or in that place is the kingdom apparent to observation. Why not? *"For, behold, the kingdom of God is within you."* This kingdom is not an earthly kingdom, but it is of a spiritual nature. It has its abode *"within you,"* in the heart, hence cannot be observed with bodily eyes.— The contrast lies in the phrases *"not by observation"* and *"within you."* It is not a visible, but an *invisible* kingdom; it is not an earthly, but a *spiritual* kingdom. The kingdom of God is the one which God established by sending the Christ, the promised Messiah, in whom people should find rest for their souls by accepting Him in faith.

Matt. 16, 18: *Thou art Peter, and upon this rock I will build my Church; and the gates of hell shall not prevail against it.*

On this passage the enormous, preposterous pretensions of the archenemy of the Church and the State, the Pope, mainly rest, claiming that Christ here constituted Peter the visible head of the Church, the first Pope, the rock of central authority in the Church. Naturally, we feel tempted to write a lengthy essay on the subject. But it must not be; we shall endeavor to stick to our text.

We are told "when Jesus came into the coasts of Caesarea Philippi, He asked *His disciples*, 'Whom do men say that I, the Son of Man, am?'" The question is directed to *all* His disciples. "And *they* said, 'Some say that Thou art John the Baptist; some, Elias; and others, Jeremias or one of the prophets.'" The disciples say: There are various opinions afloat about Thee. "He saith *unto them*," to His disciples, "But who say *ye* that I am?" You have recorded the opinions of others regarding me, now what is *your* belief? "And Simon Peter answered and said," in the name of those addressed *ye*, in the name of *all* disciples: *"Thou art the Christ, the Son of the living God."* That was Peter's faith; that was the disciples' faith. That this was the other disciples' belief also is plain from the fact that they utter no word of dissent or contradiction; it is plain from the words of Jesus in v. 20, where "He charged His *disciples* that *they* should tell no man that *He was Jesus the Christ.*"

Hence, what follows applies to *all* His disciples, though naturally Christ addresses Peter, since he had been the spokesman. Christ says: "Blessed art thou, Simon Bar-jona; for *flesh and blood* hath not revealed it unto thee, but my Father which is in heaven." What had *flesh and blood* not revealed unto Peter? To know and believe the mystery of mysteries he confessed: the *"Son of Man,"* Mary's son, true man, is at the same time *"the Christ,"* the promised Messiah, *"the Son of the living God,"* true God. To "flesh and blood," to natural man, this blessed truth: Christ, true man and true God, is foolishness. 1 Cor. 2, 14: "No one can say that Jesus is the Lord but by the Holy Ghost." This knowledge must be *revealed* to man by the Father through the Spirit. It is *divine knowledge*, not human knowledge.

In the name of the disciples and in his own name Peter had made a great confession of Christ. The Lord shows him the origin of that faith, and then proceeds: "And I say also unto thee that *thou art Peter.*" Peter means rock-man. *"Thou art Peter,"* thou art a rock-man. You have based your faith upon rock—solid, safe, unshakable. This rock is expressed in your confession: *"The Son of Man is the Christ, the Son of the living God,"* "and *on this rock*, on Myself, I will build my Church." Christ is the rock on which the Church is built. All who confess with Peter: "Thou art Christ, the Son of the living God," are founded on this rock, Christ, are His disciples, belong to the Church.

NOTE. There is a paranomasia, a play upon the words *Petros* and *petra* in the phrases *su ei Petros, kai epi taute te petra* which cannot be reproduced in English. *"Petros* and *petra* are not absolutely identical. Not the mere, bare human individual Peter, but the characteristic quality in the individual Peter which deserves to be designated as *petra* is the subject of the remark *epi taute ktl.* 'Jesus says: *Epi taute te petra*, plainly referring to the name of Peter. But by using the feminine *petra* for the masculine *petros,* and by placing *taute* alongside of it, Matthew effects a distinction between the person of the apostle and that which makes the apostle a rock, and the latter element is credited to that knowledge which he had received by revelation. It was because this distinction had to be made that the Lord did not simply say *epi sou.* Besides, the express statement that this knowledge had not sprung from his *sarx kai haima* declares that it was not his personality that made Peter a rock-man (a fact which the history of his life clearly corroborates), but something that had been implanted in him by God.' " (See Prof. Dau's Article: Theol. Quart., Vol. XIII, p 109.)

Christ is the impregnable Rock upon which the Church is built— this is the plain meaning of the text. And, with it the other Scriptures agree. The Church is "built upon the foundation of the apostles and prophets, *Jesus Christ* Himself being the chief *corner-stone,*" Eph. 2, 19. So says Paul. Again Paul says: "For other *foundation* can no man lay than that is laid, which is *Jesus Christ,*" 1 Cor. 3, 11.—This sure Foundation was predicted hundreds of years before the Christian era. In Is. 28, 16 we read: "Thus saith the Lord God, Behold, I lay in Zion for a foundation a stone, a tried stone, a precious corner-stone, a sure foundation: he that believeth shall not make haste." This is said of Christ. Cf. Rom. 9, 33.

And now let us call upon Peter himself to give testimony. "Peter, the Pope says, you are his man, you are the rock of central authority in the Church, you are the visible head of the Church, you are the first Pope. Now, Peter, what say you?" "This"—Jesus Christ of Nazareth— "is *the stone* which was set at naught of you builders, which is become *the head of corner.* Neither is there salvation in any other; for there is none other name under heaven given among men whereby we must be saved," Acts 4, 11.12. Peter's testimony is clear. Again he writes: "To whom"—Christ—"coming, as unto a *living stone,* disallowed indeed of men, but chosen of God, and precious, *ye* also, as lively stones, *are built up* a spiritual house," 1 Pet. 2, 3.4. The testimony is plain. Hear him once more. Addressing the pastors, he says: "The *elders* which are among you, *I* exhort, who *also am an elder,*" etc., 1 Pet. 5, 1. Again the testimony is clear. Peter arrogates no superiority, no supremacy, to himself. He is simply "a fellow-elder," on a level with the rest.

Clarke has some pointed remarks on this text. Says he: "Had he, Peter, been what the Popes of Rome says he was, the Prince of the Apostles and head of the Church, and what they affect to be, mighty secular lords, binding the kings of the earth in chains, could he have spoken of himself as he here does? It is true that each of the Roman pontiffs, in all their bulls, style themselves *'Servus servorum Dei,'* servant of the servants of God, while each affects to be *'Rex regum,'* king of kings and vicar of Christ. But the popes and Scripture never agree."

But let us return to the main thought of the text. The Church has a firm foundation—Christ, a glorious head—Christ. *"The gates of hell shall not prevail against it."* What does this say? Briefly this. Oriental cities were enclosed by strong walls as a protection against sudden invasions of enemies. The gates were the most strongly fortified places. Gen. 22, 17; Ps. 127, 5. Here, too the garrisons gathered. Out of the gates the soldiers marched in attack of the enemy. So the expression "gates of hell" represents hell as a strong, well-fortified city with walls and gates. Hell's intent is, of course, to destroy the city of God, the Church, but "the gates of hell shall not prevail against it"; *the Church shall not be overcome by its power, she shall not cease to exist,* the Church shall last to the end of time.

There have been times of oppression in the Church, but not of total suppression, extinction. Elijah thought and said: "I, even *I only,* am left." Jehovah answered him consolingly: "Yet will I leave me *seven thousand* in Israel, all the knees which have not bowed unto Baal, and every mouth which hath not kissed him," 1 Kings 19, 8-18.

The main point taught here is: "There *always will be* one holy Church." (*Augsb. Conf.,* Art. VII.)—Implied points: Believers *only* are members of the Church proper; only they can confess with Peter: "Thou art Christ," etc. The Church is *one.* Christ speaks of "my *Church*" in the singular. It is Christian; Christ says: *"my Church"; "I* will build."

Eph. 4, 3-6: *Endeavoring to keep the unity of the Spirit in the bond of peace. There is one body and one Spirit, even as ye are called in one hope of your calling; one Lord, one faith, one baptism, one God and Father of all, who is above all and through all and in you all.*

St. Paul exhorts the Christians to lead a godly life. The admonition is of a general character: "I, therefore, the prisoner of the Lord, beseech you that ye walk worthy of the vocation wherewith ye are called," v. 1. Once ye were "Gentiles in the flesh," now ye are Christians, having been called by the preaching of Christ. Once "ye were far off," now "ye are fellow-citizens with the saints and of the household of God"; hence it behooves you to walk as saints, to conduct yourselves as becomes members of this household. Walk worthily of your high calling. This walk is now defined; walk "with all *lowliness,*" i. e., with all *humility,* subordinating yourselves to the brethren; walk "with *meekness,*" gladly serving one another, "with *long-suffering,*" not easily becoming embittered by the frailties and shortcomings of the fellow-Christians, but "bearing with one another *in love,*" loving them, forgiving them their faults, or overlooking them, if possible.

"Endeavoring to keep the unity of the Spirit in the bond of peace." The unity of the Spirit is not established by the conduct of the Christions, but it is a unity that is produced, effected, by the Spirit. *Tou pneumatos* is genitivus *autoris.* Being produced by the Spirit, this unity is spiritual. This unity they are to *keep,* to maintain. How? *"In the*

bond of peace." "Of peace," *tes eirenes,* is genetive of apposition. Keep this unity in the bond of peace, therefore says: Peace is the bond that should knit the brethren together. Keep peace amongst yourselves, and the unity of the Spirit will be preserved. And how is this peace kept? By practicing the virtues, v. 2: humility, meekness, long-suffering, love. "Big heads," egoists, do incalculable harm to the congregation, and, if they be in high positions, to the Church at large.

In the next verse the concept "unity of the Spirit" is further unfolded. What the Christians really are, what they actually possess, we are here told, not what they shall become. Because the Christians are *one* body, have *one* Spirit, etc., they are to keep this unity by striving after the virtues enumerated in v. 2.

"There is *one* body;" all Christians are closely united with one another as the members of "one body." What links them together? The one Spirit who lives in them. He is, as it were, the soul of this body, the Christian Church. By this one Spirit the Christians are led and governed, and by this Spirit they all strive after one goal, "*even as ye are called in one hope of your calling*"—which is the hope of eternal life. What furthermore binds the Christians together, and what all possess in common, is: "*one Lord, on faith, one baptism.*" The *one Lord* is Christ, who has bought them with a price, in whom they believe, in whom they were baptized. The climax of the paragraph follows: "*one God and Father of all, who is above all and through all and in you all.*" Through Christ *God* has become our *Father.* He is *above* us all; He protects and governs us, and causes all things to work together for good for His children. He works *through* the Christians; the good the Christians do God works in and through them. And, finally, He lives *in* the Christians; we are His temple.—The three main concepts of the passage are: "*one Spirit,*" "*one Lord,*" "*one God and Father.*" To these the rest are linked and subordinated. In this Triune God the Christians are united with one another. By the one Spirit and in the one Spirit they are at the same time united with the one Lord and the one God and Father. Knowing this, they should walk worthy of their vocation.

Eph. 4, 4-6 is a *locus classicus* for the doctrine of the Church.—We learn, 1. what the Church is. The text says: There is one body, one Spirit, one Lord, one faith, one God and Father. So all who have one and the same Spirit and faith, all who call upon one and the same Lord and God, constitute *one* body, this spiritual body, the Church. The Church is the aggregate of all believers, the communion of saints. Hypocrits, sham Christians, do not belong to the Church. 2. Since only believers constitute the Church, she is *invisible.* 3. Though invisible, the Church has certain *marks* whereby we know with absolute certainty where the Church is. The believers have one hope of calling. But they were called by the Gospel. The Gospel produces faith. Where the Gospel is preached, there are believers, there is the Church. (Cf. Stoeckhardt, *Epheserbrief*, in loco.)

Eph. 5, 25-27: *Christ also loved the Church, and gave Himself for it, that He might cleanse and sanctify it with the washing of water by the word, that He might present it to Himself a glorious Church, not having spot or wrinkle, or any such thing, but that it should be holy and without blemish.*

"The Church, the Bride of Christ," is a fitting caption for this paragraph.—"*Christ also loved the Church.*" He proved His love: "*He gave Himself*" unto death "*for it,*" thus acquiring for it the forgiveness of sins, the righteousness that availeth before God. The aim Christ had in view in His sacrificial death was also this: "*that He might sanctify it,*" by His Word and Spirit purify it more and more of spots and wrinkles and blemishes, and adorn it with all Christian virtues, "*having cleansed it by the washing of water with the word,*" i. e., by Baptism, the washing of regeneration. Baptism works forgiveness of sins; by baptism new spiritual powers are implanted, sanctification begins and is to continue through life. The love spoken of here Christ manifests to each one of His believers. He sanctifies and purifies them by His Word and Spirit. But all believers collectively make up the Church. Just here that which Christ does to every one of His members the apostle predicates of the communion of saints, the Church. All saints are a unit in the eyes of the Lord. This Christian Church Christ sanctifies and cleanses again and again of all impurities, spots, and blemishes.—The final aim of Christ's giving Himself for the Church is that at the consummation of the world "*He might present it to Himself a glorious Church, not having spot or wrinkle, or any such thing, but that it should be holy and without blemish.*" On the last day, when Christ will appear in all His glory, He, the Bridegroom, will place by His side His bride, the Church, in all her spotless splendor.

In the words of *Hodge:* "Christ presents the Church to Himself, *autos beauto,* He and no other, to Himself. He does it. He gave Himself for it. He sanctifies it. He, before the assembled universe, places by His side the bride purchased with His blood. He presents it to Himself a glorious Church. That is glorious which excites admiration. The Church is to be an object of admiration to all intelligent beings, because of its freedom from all defect and because of its absolute perfection. . . . . The figure is preserved in the description here given of the glory of the consummated Church. It is to be as a faultless bride, perfect in beauty and splendidly adorned. She is to be without spot or wrinkle, or any such thing, i. e., without anything to mar her beauty, free from every indication of age, faultless and immortal. What is thus expressed figuratively is expressed literally in the last clause of the verse, that it should be holy and without blame, *hagia kai amomos.*"

The purpose for which this passage is adduced in the Catechism is to show that all the members of the Church are holy by faith in Christ, and that they are to serve God with *holy* works; hence the Church is *holy*.

1 Pet. 2, 5: *Ye also, as lively stones, are built up a spiritual house, an holy priesthood, to offer up spiritual sacrifices, acceptable to God by Jesus Christ.*

In the preceding sections the Christians were addressed as individuals. Beginning with v. 4, a new thought is introduced. The Christians are spoken of as a spiritual house, a temple. So the congregation of Christians is addressed. The main thought is: Build yourselves up on Christ, and manifest your Christian character by serving God with "spiritual sacrifices," with holy works. Peter writes: *"To whom coming, as unto a living stone, disallowed indeed of men, but chosen of God and precious, ye also, as lively stones, are built up a spiritual house."* Christ is the "living stone" pre-eminently. He is so called here to emphasize the thought that in Him there is life. Coming into contact with this stone, life is imparted. An impulse goes forth from this stone to those placed upon it. An illustration is the magnet. Iron, steel, coming into contact with it, becomes magnetic; disconnected, the magnetic power is lost. In order to be "built up," the Christians must daily come to this "living stone," Christ; daily, by contrition and faith, they must renew the connection, daily they must dedicate themselves to God.

True, Christ is *"disallowed of men"*; He is rejected by humanity in general. But this is not to deter the Christians' coming to Him. They are to remember that, though He is dishonored, rejected, by the world, He is highly honored of God, He is *"chosen of God and precious."* Chosen, for what purpose? To be the "chief corner-stone in Zion," v. 6, to be the foundation of this "spiritual house," the Church.

Christians are to know and to remember: *"To Him coming . . . . . ye also, as lively stones are built up a spiritual house."* Christians, too, are "lively stones," having received their life from Christ, John 14, 6. But this life must be nourished. And this is done by coming to Him again and again in true faith. Thus the connection with the living stone is maintained. Only in this manner can they be *"built up a spiritual house,"* i. e., a house filled by the Spirit, the Spirit of Christ. Only in this way the life received in conversion is augmented and strengthened— the "lively stones" must come again and again to the "living stone," the foundation and corner-stone of this spiritual house, this temple.

Christians are living stones in this temple, but, changing the figure, they are, at the same time, priests in this temple. They are *"an holy priesthood,"* says Peter. Priests in the Old Testament had access to God, offered sacrifices to God. In the New Testament all Christians are priests. They should be true to their priestly character. The purpose of their having been made priests is: *"to offer up spiritual sacrifices acceptable to God by Jesus Christ."* Priests and sacrifices go together. So in the Old Testament, so in the New. But in the New Testament the offerings are not to consist of sacrifices of animals, etc., as in the Old, but they are to be *spiritual*. Christians are a *spiritual house*, hence the offerings in this temple are to be spiritual, *i. e.*, such as are wrought in them and through them by the Spirit, who dwells in this sanctuary. In short, the spiritual sacrifices are the good works of the Christians. Of these sacrifices Hebr. 13, 15.16 speaks: "By Him, therefore, let us offer the sacrifice of praise to God continually, that is, the fruit of our lips, giving thanks to His name. But to do good and to communicate forget not; for with such sacrifices God is well pleased." Hence, in the New Testament there are especially two classes of sacrifices: 1. sacrifices of the lips, 2. sacrifices of the hands.

> NOTES.—The conception of the Church here is similar to that in Eph. 2, 19 ff. Christ is the corner-stone laid in Zion; the Christians are the "lively stones" composing the temple. It is *one* building: the Church is *one*. *Christians only* belong to the Church; there are no "dead" stones in this building. This Church is *holy:* it is Christ's, God's sanctuary, the workshop of the Holy Spirit. It is *holy* because the members of this Church serve God with *holy* works, "spiritual sacrifices." The Church is *Christian:* it is built on Christ.

MARKS OF THE CHURCH.

Is. 55, 11: *My Word shall not return unto Me void, but it shall accomplish that which I please, and it shall prosper in the thing whereto I sent it.*

Believers only constitute the Church; but faith, which makes a person a member of the Church, is invisible, and so, too, the Church is invisible. Where, then is the Christian Church to be found? Faith is generated by the preaching of the Gospel. Hence the Church exists where the Gospel of Christ is in use, and there only, since faith cannot be produced by any other means. Rom. 10, 17; 1 Pet. 1, 23.25. So *the Word is the only mark* of the Church. This statement does not exclude the Sacraments, the *visible* Word, because they receive their power and efficacy from the Word of God.

Of this Word the Lord says: *"It shall not return unto Me void."* He sends it for a purpose, *viz.*, to work faith, to preserve faith, and to save by faith. This Word, being God's Word, goes forth with divine power. Wherever it is preached, the Lord's promise holds good: *"It shall accomplish that which I please, and it shall prosper in the thing whereto I sent it."* The Word always bears some fruit, though rejected by many. Where the Word is, there is the Church. Luther's dictum, "'God's people cannot be without God's Word, nor can God's Word be without a people,'" is Scriptural.—Rome enumerates fifteen marks of the Church, such as its name, Catholic; its antiquity; its succession of bishops; its doctrinal agreement with the ancient Church, *et al.*, none of which has a foundation in Scripture. The one indispensable mark of the Church is the Word—the *audible* and the *visible* Word.

What *consolation*, by the way, this beautiful passage affords the faithful pastor! Often all seems to be topsy-turvy in the congregation; the devil seems to be getting the upper hand. How downcast the pastor then becomes! Cheer up, brother, "preach the Word!" Cling to this faithful promise: "My Word shall not return unto Me void."

GENERAL REMARK. The Church proper, the *una sancta*, is invisible. Still we sometimes speak of the visible Church. What do we mean by that? We see people gathering about the means of grace, the Word. This Word produces faith; *ergo* there is the Church. However, we cannot see into the hearts of our fellow-men to ascertain in whose heart faith has been produced. We consider all such as gather about the Word, profess the Christian faith, and do not contradict such profession by an ungodly life, Christians, believers. These professing Christians we can see, hence we speak of a *visible* Church. So the Church is *visible* inasmuch as we see people flocking to hear the Word of God; *invisible*, inasmuch as we cannot tell which of these that gather about the means of grace believe. Still we do not establish *two* churches. The Biblical definition of the Church—the Church is nothing else than the congregation of saints—remains intact. For the visible Church is, and is called, a church only on account *of the true believers in it.* *A potiori parti fit denominatio.* A gold ring is a gold ring though the gold is mixed with alloy. A manufacturing city is such though private dwellings and stores are within its confines. A wheat-field has tares in it, still it is a wheat-field. When the Church is said to be visible, this is done by the well-known figure of synecdoche. In 3 John 10 and Rev. 2, 14 ff. we read of *churches* though there was Diotrephes in one, and Balaamites in the other. Hypocrits were *intermingled* with the believers. So it is still to-day. This truth the Lord teaches in the parable of the tares among the wheat, Matt. 13, 24-26, and in that of the net that gathered fish of every kind, Matt. 13, 47.48.

Matt. 28, 20: *Teaching them to observe all things whatsoever I have commanded you.*

We have no pet doctrines. We preach all doctrines of the Bible. There are none superfluous, none unimportant. According to our Lord's command in His Final Commission His disciples were to be taught "to observe *all things whatsoever*" He had commanded. This the Lutheran Church does. She teaches the entire doctrine of the Word of God in all its purity, or, in the words of St. Paul, Acts 20, 27, she declares "*all the* counsel of God," and administers the Sacraments according to Christ's institution. By God's grace, despite the wild onslaughts of erroneous doctrines, she continues in Christ's Word, John 8, 31.32. The Evangelical Lutheran Church, therefore, is to-day the *true* visible Church.

THE PROPER USE OF THIS DOCTRINE.

2 Cor. 13, 5: *Examine yourselves, whether ye be in the faith; prove your own selves.*

Believers only belong to the invisible Church, the *una sancta.* The outward semblance of being a Christian does not suffice; the mere external membership in the Church of the pure doctrine cannot deceive God. Our chief concern must be to be and remain members of the invisible Church. And to this end we ought frequently to examine ourselves. "*Examine yourselves*"; "*prove your own selves,*" so St. Paul exhorts the Corinthian Christians. The repetition of the same thought shows how dangerous self-deception is. What is the examination to reveal to them? "Whether ye be *in the faith.*" How can they tell? "If Jesus Christ is in you"—you are in the faith, says the context, v. 5b. True faith is not a matter of the intellect and the mouth, but a heavenly gift, by which man is united with Christ, and his heart becomes a habitation of Christ. Christ dwells in man when he has the Spirit of Christ, as the apostle elsewhere says: "If any man have not the Spirit of Christ he is none of His." But whosoever has the Spirit of Christ loves Christ, hates sin, and follows after sanctification.—Let us take heed to be and remain members of the invisible Church.

John 8, 31.32: *If ye continue in My Word, then are ye My disciples indeed; and ye shall know the truth, and the truth shall make you free.*

Christ had discoursed on Himself as being the Light of the world. His words had made a deep impression on many of His opponents, the Jews, so much so that they believed on Him. "Then said Jesus to those Jews who believed on Him: *If ye continue in My Word, then truly*"— *alethos,* emphatically put at the head of the phrase—"*My disciples ye are.*" His true disciples are such, He says, as continue, abide in His Word. Now, what is Christ's Word? Self-evidently not only the few words He here spoke to those Jews, but all the words that are recorded of Him in the Scripture. Only these? No. Christ is God; the whole Bible is given by inspiration of God. The whole Bible is God's, Christ's, Word. 2 Pet, 1, 21; 2 Tim. 3, 15-17.—As we read the Scripture, we find that the writers everywhere speak of the Word of God and the Word of Christ as interchangeable terms, as being one and the same thing; cf. 1 Thess. 2; Col. 3, 16, *et al.* In short, God's Word is Christ's Word; to abide by God's Word is to abide by Christ's Word, *et vice versa.*

Who is a *disciple* of Christ? A disciple of Christ is one who learns of Christ, an adherent of, and believer in, Christ, a follower of Christ. As such they are characterized throughout the entire New Testament. In Jerusalem, in Antioch, in Ephesus, we find "disciples," believers in Christ. Who are Christ's *true* disciples? He says: Such as "continue in My Word," abide by My Word, adhere to My every word, accept it just as it reads. A disciple is a learner; Christ is the Master. A disciple, being a learner, does not criticize His Master, doubt His Word, or set it aside. Doing that, he is no longer a disciple, but a master in his own conceit. He virtually says: Though the Master says so and so, I'll not accept it; I cannot understand it, hence it is wrong! A true disciple says: "One is my Master, even Christ"; in His Word I'll continue. This is the correct attitude of a disciple, a believer in Christ, knowing that this Master is not a fallible man, but "God over all," "the Mighty God." And this humble attitude—to bow before His every word —Christ demands.

And now note the glorious assurance these true disciples are given: "*Ye shall know the truth.*" In this age of doubt, of unrest, of skepticism, where round about us Pilate's cynic question, "What is truth?" is bandied about as the acme of intellectual wisdom, Christ's true disciples possess *truth, the truth*—absolute truth. Take My Word, says Christ, read it, understand it just as it reads, adhere to, continue in this Word believe it, and you shall know—what? *Ten aletheian,* the truth. He does not say: If you do not understand this or that, try to harmonize My Word, endeavor to make it acceptable to human reason; if you do not understand the how and the wherefore, reject it. Nothing of the kind. Christ says of Himself: "I am the Truth." He cannot err; if we continue in His Word, we have the truth, we cannot be in error. Are all opposing doctrines wrong? Yes. Why? There is but *one* truth. "What arrogance of the Lutheran Church!" we hear some one say; "other denominations are more liberal; they modestly say, 'This is *our* view of this doctrine'; 'Jesus here *seems* to teach'; 'in *my opinion* the apostle would say.'" Is that teaching the *truth*? Is it not rather teaching doubts? Is it honoring Christ? He says: "Continue in My Word, and *ye shall know the truth.*" Here is the one infallible rule to arrive at the truth according to the promise of our Lord. And what is not the truth is a lie. Sad to say, such a simple, self-evident statement finds little favor in our times of wishy-washy theology. Said a noted English divine a few years ago:

> "People look at you with amazement if you suggest that there is such a thing as a fixed truth; and they eye you with supreme contempt if you dare hint that the opposite of truth must be a lie. You must be some old fogy or antedeluvian, or you would never make such an observation. The sooner you are back in Noah's ark the better. A man says that black is white, and I say that it is not so. But it is not kind to say, 'It is not so,' you should say, 'Perhaps you are right, dear brother, though I hardly think so.'"

Brethren, let us thank God that without any merit or worthiness in us He has given us *the truth.*

This truth, Christ says, "*shall make you free.*" Of which freedom does Christ speak? The explanation follows in the text: "If the Son shall make you free, ye shall be free indeed." It is the freedom the Son of God has merited by His sufferings and death, and which they possess who believe in Him: the freedom from the dominion of sin, from the accusation of the devil, the freedom from death and its terrors and from the tortures of hell. This heavenly, spiritual freedom he attains who possesses the truth.

Our Lord does not countenance such phrases as these: It is immaterial to which church you belong; one church is as good as the other. Again and again we are bidden to avoid false prophets, and to shun false doctrines. It is our bounden duty to adhere to the truth, to the Church of the pure Word and confession, and in our times this is the Evangelical Lutheran Church.

1 Cor. 9, 14: *The Lord ordained that they which preach the Gospel should live of the Gospel.*

In vv. 3-14 Paul claims the right of getting the means of sustenance from those to whom he preaches the Gospel, and adduces various interesting and striking arguments in proof thereof, the culmination of which we find in v. 14. *"The Lord," ho kurios,* that is, Christ, *"ordained that they which preach the Gospel should live of the Gospel."* It is the duty of the congregation to supply the minister's temporal wants. His salary, often meager indeed, is not an alms, but money earned by hard, honest, unselfish labor. Aye, the money-remuneration can never be an equivalent for the faithful pastor's services. *"If we have sown unto you spiritual things, is it a great thing if we shall reap your carnal things?"* V. 11. Emphatically, no. Let it be impressed upon the hearts and minds of our parishioners that ministers *"should live of the Gospel."* Thus the Lord ordained. "The workman is worthy of his meat," Christ says, Matt. 10, 10, and Luke 10, 7: "The laborer is worthy of his hire." (Cf. Gal. 6, 6; 1 Tim. 5, 17.18; 1 Thess. 5, 12.) It is the Christians' bounden duty,—aye, rather call it their blessed privilege,—to contribute to the maintenance of the church.

Matt. 28, 19: *Go ye, therefore, and teach all nations, baptizing them in the name of the Father and of the Son and of the Holy Ghost.*

These well-known words are taken from Christ's Final Commission. *"Go ye,"* My disciples, "therefore," since "all power is given to Me in heaven and in earth," v. 18, since "I am with you alway," v. 20, to guide, protect, and assist you, *"and teach," matheteusate, i. e.,* make disciples of, *"all nations."* Here is the divine command to do mission work. The Gospel is for all nations. "Preach the Gospel to every creature," *pase te ktisei.* "He that believeth and is baptized shall be saved." Mark 16, 15.16. The Gospel is for "every creature," *i. e.,* of course, for such creatures as can believe, for men, all men, all nations. *"Ge ye, make disciples."* How? *"Baptizing them....teaching them...."* Vv. 19.20. Thus His disciples are to "make disciples" by propagating the Gospel of salvation.

Matt. 7, 15: *Beware of false prophets, which come to you in sheep's clothing; but inwardly they are ravening wolves.*

We find this solemn warning towards the close of Christ's wonderful Sermon on the Mount.—Having entered the strait gate and walking on the narrow way, Christians must know of the dangers besetting their path. One is mentioned in the text.

"Beware!" That certainly is a danger signal. For the protection of unwary and unsophisticated strangers signs are often posted in public places in our large cities, reading: "Danger!" or "'Beware of pickpockets!" Thus they are put on their guard.

"Beware of false prophets"—thus the Savior's voice of warning puts the disciples on their guard. You are on the narrow way, "which leadeth to life"; but *beware!*—there is danger of your being misled into walking the broad way, "that leadeth to destruction." Whence this danger? *"Beware of false prophets."* Who is a prophet? A spokesman of God, God's mouthpiece, one who speaks for God, one who teaches the Word of God. So the Lord speaks of the preachers of the Word. His note of warning is sounded against *false* prophets. Who are they? Prophets, preachers, who pretend to proclaim the Word of God, but who pervert it, do not give the true meaning to all the Word of God, but a false one. The false prophets are those "that use *their* tongues and say, '*"He"*— the Lord"—"saith," Jer. 23, 31. They are deceivers, falsifiers, liars.

Now as to their outward appearance. *"They come to you in sheep's clothing."* This is emblematic of the external appearance of innocence, gentleness, and harmlessness. A wolf in sheep's clothing does not look dangerous; to all appearances he is a sheep. So with the false prophets. What is his sheep's clothing? He is a prophet, he holds the office of a preacher of the Gospel. He claims that God has sent him. He says: "Lord, Lord," vv. 21.22. i. e., he frequently uses the name of the Lord, speaks of Him as reverently as do the true prophets. They *"come to you,"* unbidden, as prophets; they show a great concern about your soul's welfare; they, perhaps, make house-to-house visits to gain proselytes, as do the Mormon apostles; they may distribute tracts and pamphlets galore, as do the Russellites. They employ "enticing words," Col. 2, 4; "feigned words," 2 Pet. 2, 3; "good words and fair speeches," Rom. 16, 18, and make "a show of wisdom," Col. 2, 23. That is their stock in trade—their sheep's clothing.

But as to their true inward character,—*"inwardly they are ravening wolves."* Image the picture of a ravening wolf in sheep's clothing among a flock of guileless sheep. Such is the true inward character of a false prophet—he is a *wolf*; such is the danger threatening the sheep of Christ—he is a *ravening* wolf.

What does a wolf do among a flock of sheep? He kills, devours, the sheep. And the false prophet in sheep's clothing kills, destroys, the souls of the sheep of Christ. How? Why, he is a *false* prophet; he *perverts* the word of God, *misconstrues, misinterprets* it, and thus "uses his own tongue," and still says: "He"—the Lord—"saith." False doctrine leads to destruction. A poisonous fluid poured into wholesome water changes the pure water into poison. A little pin-prick has often caused blood-poisoning. Error mixed with truth does not make error truth, but the truth, error. "A little leaven leaveneth the whole lump," Gal. 5, 9, How necessary the exhortation, *"Beware of false prophets!"*

Paul's farewell words to the Ephesian elders are very illuminating and instructive in this connection. We offer them without further comment. Observe that the "grievous wolves" either come from without, they *"enter* in among you," or they arise from within, *"of your own selves shall men arise."*—We read: "For I know this, that after my departing shall grievous wolves *enter in* among you, not sparing the flock. Also of *your own* selves *shall* men *arise,* speaking perverse things to draw away disciples after them. Therefore watch, and remember that by the space of three years I ceased not to warn every one night and day with tears," Acts 20, 29-31.

1 John 4, 1: *Beloved, believe not every spirit, but try the spirits whether they are of God; because many false prophets are gone out into the world.*

The "spirits" mentioned in our text are men of flesh and bone, *prophets,* as the context discloses. Some "spirits" "are of God," and hence are to be believed; others, and there are *many* of them, "are not of God," v. 3, and are to be shunned. *"Beloved,"*—love for your immortal souls impels me to warn you,—*"believe not every spirit."* These spirits, prophets, manifest their wisdom by preaching, and demand *belief,* acceptance. But be on your guard. The very doctrine they preach manifests their spirit. *"Try the spirits";* there is great danger: *"many false prophets are gone out into the world."* Try them, *"whether they are of God,"* or whether they breathe the spirit of Antichrist, v. 3. How are you to know whether they are "of God"? This is the test: "Hereby know ye the Spirit of God: Every spirit that confesseth that Jesus Christ is come in the flesh is of God," v. 2. If these spirits publish a wisdom contrary to "the wisdom of God," 1 Cor. 2, they are not of God, not actuated by His Spirit. They are false prophets. Beloved, believe them not!

In 1529, at Marburg, Luther was face to face with such a false prophet—Zwingli. Despite the grave differences between his doctrine of the Lord's Supper and that of the Bible, which Luther upheld, Zwingli offered Luther the right hand of fellowship. Luther refused, saying, "God's Word and His truth are dearer to me than the friendship of the whole world. You have a different spirit from ours."

Indirectly there is a *consolation* contained in the present passage.

If the apostle in his days saw the necessity of warning the Christians against *"many* false prophets," need we marvel that we must combat with so many today? Moreover, does not our Lord say of these last sad times: "For there shall arise false Christs and false prophets, and shall show great signs and wonders, inasmuch that, if it were possible, they shall deceive the very elect. Behold, I have told you before"? Mat. 24, 24.25.

Rom. 16, 17: *Now I beseech you, brethren, mark them which cause divisions and offenses contrary to the doctrine which ye have learned, and avoid them.*

Who causes "divisions and offenses" in the Church? St. Paul says they are caused by men that teach things *"contrary to the doctrine which ye have learned.* "From whom had the Christians at Rome learned *the doctrine?* From Paul the Apostle. From whom had he received it? He says to the Galatians: "I certify you, brethren, that the Gospel which was preached of me is not after man. For I neither received it of man, neither was I taught it, but by the revelation of Jesus Christ," Gal. 1, 11-12. When, therefore, the apostle writes to the Romans of *"the doctrine which ye have learned,"* that doctrine was the doctrine of Jesus Christ, "the truth," in which we are to continue, according to the exhortation of our Lord, John 8, 31.32. It is the Word of God, of which Peter says: "If any man speak, let him speak as of the oracles of God," 1 Pet. 4, 11. This Word of Truth does not cause divisions and offenses; it unifies. By the devil's deceit and craftiness, however, men arise and teach *contrary to* the true doctrine. Arius denied the deity of Christ, and thus caused divisions in the Church and *offenses,* that is, causes for stumbling, so that people departed from the Truth. Pelagius denied the doctrine of original sin, and thus caused divisions and offenses. Thus Nestorius, Zwingli, Calvin, and a host of others taught *"contrary to the doctrine,"* thus "divisions and offenses" were caused.

The text says the false teachers teach "contrary to" the doctrine. The translation is good; Luther's translation *"neben der Lehre,"* is better. The Greek text reads: *para ten didachen*—"beside the doctrine which ye have learned." This closer translation of *para—beside,* gives us an insight into the method of the false teachers by which they endeavor to gain adherents for their false doctrines. They do not say: "Scripture teaches this and this doctrine, but we teach *contrary to* the explicit words of Scripture." No, the method of causing divisions and offenses is a subtle one. The false doctrines are taught *beside* the true doctrines. Apparently the false teachers adhere to the Word of God; they use the words of Scripture; but *beside,* under cover of, the Scripture they smuggle in their erroneous doctrines. In 2 Pet. 2, 1 we read of false prophets *hoitines pareisaxousin haireseis apoleias,* "who privily," stealthily, "will bring in damnable heresies." The word "privily," is to translate the *para* in the composite word *pareisaxousin.* With keen insight

into the text Luther happily translates thus: "Sie werden. *neben*
einfuehren verderbliche Sekten." In Galatia the perverters of the
Gospel of Christ, to gain a hearing, and to make converts to their
views, taught that the doctrine of justification as taught by St. Paul
was good. Justification by faith in Christ Jesus—why, sure, that is a
good doctrine, as far as it goes, but it doesn't go far enough. In order
·to be saved, you must also be circumcised, you must "observe days and
months and times and years." Thus, "beside the doctrine" the Galatians
had learned, these perverters taught their own perverse things: Justification by faith *and* circumcision; justification by faith *and* observing
of days and months. By teaching this "beside"-doctrine, they mixed error
with truth. And the result? The truth was destroyed. What does Paul
say to this plus annexed to the doctrine of justification? "I marvel that ye
are so soon *removed from Him* that called you into the grace of Christ
unto another gospel, which is *not another,*" i. e., which is not Gospel
at all, Gal. 1, 6. "If any man preach any other gospel unto you than
ye have received, let him be accursed," v. 9. Again: "Christ is become
of none affect unto you whosoever of you are justified by the Law; *ye
are fallen from grace,*" Gal. 5, 4.

The Pope hypocritically avows full acceptance of the Scriptures as
the Word of God, but *beside* this statement he places that other one:
The traditions are of equal authority with the Bible, thus making the
Word of God of none effect. And when the synergists say that conversion and salvation indeed depend on the grace of God, but to some extent
also on the conduct of man, the latter assertion is an assertion *beside* the
doctrine, and annuls the former.—Let these instances suffice.

Now, when we observe such deviations from the truth, what are we
to do? Are we to view them with indifference? No. The apostle is
very earnest in his appeal: *"I beseech you, brethren,"* for there is great
danger for your souls' salvation; *"mark them"*—consider attentively
them—*"which cause divisions and offenses."* For what purpose? *"Avoid
them,"* ekklinate ap' auton, i. e., turn away from them, give them no
hearing.

In the light of this passage judge of the union services as practiced by various denominations. Observe, too, how strongly it condemns
pulpit-fellowship and altar-fellowship with errorists.

It pains us, it is true, to keep aloof from all other denominations,
but here is the command of God: "Avoid them!" This command is
clear; we cannot refuse obedience to God.

2 Cor. 6, 14-16: *Be ye not unequally yoked together with unbelievers; for what fellowship hath righteousness with unrighteousness?
And what communion hath light with darkness? And what concord hath
Christ with Belial? Or what part hath he that believeth with an infidel? And what agreement hath the temple of God with idols? For ye
are the temple of the living God, as God hath said, I will dwell in them*

and walk in them; and I will be their God, and they shall be My people. Wherefore come out from among them, and be ye separate, saith the Lord, and touch not the unclean thing; and I will receive you, and will be a Father unto you, and ye shall be My sons and daughters, saith the Lord Almighty.

It required a great deal of self-denial on the part of the Corinthian Christians to sever all fellowship with those former friends and associates who had remained unbelievers. This the apostle knew; but it must be done.—In order to gain a favorable hearing, he assures them of his love, vv. 11-13. He speaks to them as to "his children." Children will listen to the warning of a loving father. And warn them he must— their salvation was at stake.

The *warning* reads: "Be ye not unequally yoked together with unbelievers." The *reasons* for this warning follow in five rhetorical questions, which appeal to their Christian consciousness, and admit of but one answer. We observe that the idea "yoked together" in the topic sentence is developed by the words: fellowship, communion, concord, what part, agreement. The accumulated contrasts in the questions are most impressive, and were to convince the Corinthians of the fact: it is wrong to be "unequally yoked together with unbelievers"; hence the *demand* is made: "Wherefore come out from among them, and be ye separate."

"Be ye not unequally yoked together with unbelievers." Paul has in mind the yoking together of an ox and an ass, of a clean and unclean animal, in violation of the Law, Deut. 22, 9.10. An apt portrayal, indeed, of a Christian having fellowship with an unbeliever. The two are too unlike to be put under one yoke.

Why should the Corinthian Christians not be yoked together with unbelievers? *"For what fellowship hath righteousness with unrighteousness?"* None. The one is the very opposite of the other. The believer, doing righteousness, running the way of God's commandments, cannot, at the same time, "walk in the counsel of the ungodly, nor stand in the way of sinners, nor sit in the seat of the scornful," Ps. 1.—*"What communion hath light with darkness?"* Light and darkness exclude each other. The believers are the children of light, the light of the world, John 12, 36; Eph. 5, 8.9; Matt. 5, 14; the unbelievers are darkness, love darkness, walk in darkness, and hate the light, John 3, 19.20. What communion between the two? None. How unreasonable, therefore, for Christians to be yoked together with them! How unreasonable, for example, for a Christian to belong to the godless lodge!—*"What concord hath Christ with Belial?"* Is a greater contrast imaginable—Belial, the devil, the father of lies, the murderer of men's souls, and Christ, the Truth, the Life, the Savior? You cannot serve two masters. Like master, like servant. Hence ye Christians, the redeemed of Christ, be ye not unequally yoked together with the slaves and tools of Satan.—

"What part hath he that believeth with an infidel?" To the believer the Gospel is "the wisdom of God," to the unbeliever "the things of the Spirit," the Gospel, are foolishness, 1 Cor. 2. What have the two in common? Nothing. Hence, be ye not unequally yoked together with unbelievers.—*"What agreement hath the temple of God with idols? For ye are the temple of the living God."* Idols are *dead* things,— these the unbelievers serve, to such they offer their sacrifices. You Christians serve the *living God;* He dwells in you, walks in you, He is your God, and you are His people. And you, "the temple of the living God," would be yoked together with unbelievers, the habitation of Belial? Impossible! Since you are *internally* separate from them, you should and must be *externally* separate. A fellowship, a communion, a concord, an agreement, with them is out of the question. There is but one course to take: *"Come out from among them, and be ye separate."* This is the Lord's command. (Cf. Eph. 5, 11.)

What holds good concerning our attitude over against unbelievers holds good also towards those of a false faith. They are simply unbelievers regarding those doctrines in which they differ from the Bible. Methodists, Baptists, et al. do not believe, *e. g.*, the words of Christ: "This is My body." Hence, in so far and inasmuch as they do not believe these and other words of Scripture, they are *unbelievers.* "Be not unequally yoked together with them." All false doctrine comes from Belial, not from Christ; false doctrine is darkness, sound doctrine is light from above. True doctrine and false doctrine are separated from each other as far as are heaven and earth, Christ and Belial. Hence, be separate, go out from among them, do not participate in their services; in church-affairs have nothing in common with them. (Cf. *Smalcald Articles*, p. 337. Study 1 Cor. 5, 9.10.)

THE FORGIVENESS OF SIN.

"This article concerning justification by faith is, as the *Apology* declares, the leading article of the whole Christian doctrine, without which a disturbed conscience can have no sure consolation, or rightly conceive the riches of the grace of Christ; as Dr. Luther has written: If this article remains pure, the whole Christian community will also remain pure and harmonious and without any factions; but if it remain not pure, it is impossible to resist any error or fanatical spirit," *(Formula of Concord,* Sol. Decl., III. 630.)

"It is the only key to the whole Bible." *(Apology,* III, 156.)

"In my heart dwelleth alone, and shall there dwell, this only article, to wit, faith in my dear Lord Jesus Christ, which is the sole beginning, middle, and end of all my spiritual and divine thoughts which I happen to entertain at any time, whether by day or by night." (Dr. Luther.) —It is the *"articulus stantis et cadentis ecclesiae,"* the article with which the Church stands or falls.

Mark 2, 7: *Who can forgive sins but God only?*

Sin is the transgression of God's law, 1 John 3, 4, and as such rebellion against the majesty of God. And the result? "Your iniquities have *separated* between you and your God," Is. 59, 2. God pronounces a curse upon every sinner: "Cursed is every one that continueth not in all things which are written in the book of the Law to do them." Gal. 3, 10; Deut. 27, 26. "The wages of sin is death," Rom. 6, 23. There is but one way to escape this curse, this death: by an act of forgiveness on the part of the Lawgiver.

The paralytic, borne by four, was brought to Jesus. Seeing their faith, Jesus said to the sick of the palsy, "Son, thy sins be forgiven thee." Critical scribes, "reasoning in their hearts," said, "Who can forgive sins but God only?" That argument was valid: *God only can forgive sins.* When they, however, thought, "Why doth this man"— Jesus—"thus speak blasphemies?" they were in the wrong, because this man Jesus is also true God, and, by forgiving sins, proved Himself God. (Cf. Ps. 32, 6; 51, 1.) —

This passage simply states the fact that only God can forgive sins. That He does it by grace, for Christ's sake, through the Gospel, other Bible-texts reveal. The doctrine of the forgiveness of sin is an article of faith. It is not implanted in our heart. "By the Law is the *knowledge* of sin," but not of the *forgiveness* of sin. This is a matter of revelation.—

Ps. 130, 3.4: *If Thou, Lord, shouldest mark iniquities, O Lord, who shall stand? But there is forgiveness with Thee, that thou mayest be feared.*

Ps. 130 is one of the fifteen Songs of Ascents (Ps. 120-134). Why these are so called remains a matter of conjecture. Happily it is of no importance to know for their interpretation.—From the abyss of dejection on account of his sinfulness David rises to the height of peaceful assurance of the Lord's forgiveness. The psalm falls into two parts, of four verses each, of which the first part (vv. 1-4) breathes the supplication of one who has experienced the thunders from Sinai, and the second (vv. 5-8) gives expression to full redemption from all iniquities.

"Out of the depths have I cried unto Thee, O Jehovah.
Lord, hear my voice!
Let Thine ears be attentive
To the voice of my supplications." (vv. 1.2.)

The psalmist is in great distress; his is the "voice of supplications," the voice of one who is on his knees, imploring mercy. And this pleading cry comes "out of the depths," and ascends to the throne of Jehovah. None else can help him. Into what depths has David fallen from which this suppliant voice comes like a faint call?

"If Thou, Jehovah, shouldest mark iniquities,

O Lord, who could stand?"

In the flash-light of the Law David beholds his iniquities. "Iniquity," *avon*, is sin viewed as a debt, an unpaid debt. The Law is not a dead letter. It requires strict obedience. If transgressed, there is a debt accumulated, the payment of which the Lawgiver, the Judge, can and will exact. (Cf. Matt. 18, 23 ff.) These iniquities accuse him before the holy God, who has a right to *mark* them i. e., to keep, to watch, to take account of them, to retain them in remembrance, in order to punish him who has contracted them. For God is the *Lord, Adonai, i. e., the Master*, who has a right to demand implicit and perfect obedience of His servants, of all men. What if God should do that? *"O Lord, Adonai, who could stand?"* No one, not even a David. His conscience, his sense of guilt, puts him to confusion in the presence of the holy God. Guilty, lost, damned, because of numberless iniquities. "The soul that sinneth, it shall die." (Ezek. 18, 20.) And God is just. What, then, makes David bold to cry "out of the depths" of his iniquities? God is not only *Adonai*, the Omnipotent God and Master, who demands perfect obedience, but He has also revealed Himself as *Jehovah*, who has made a covenant with the fathers to be merciful for the Messiah's sake. Hence the cry "out of the depths" with the "voice of supplication" unto Jehovah for mercy. *"If Thou, Jehovah, shouldest mark iniquities,"*—woe unto all who know not this God as Jehovah, the covenant God! To all such He is *Adonai*, a consuming fire. There is but one way to escape this righteous wrath over iniquities, sin,—David's way,—to acknowledge one's sinfulness with a contrite heart, to acknowledge God's justice in marking iniquities, and with the voice of supplication plead for mercy. This David does:

"For (but) there is forgiveness with Thee."

Jehovah, Thou merciful God, do not *mark* iniquities, but *forgive* them, cancel the debit side in the account of Thy unfaithful servant. This is the only way I can stand before Thee, the holy God.—But how can God forgive sins? He is just. True, but David says: "With Thee *is* forgiveness," aye, *"the* forgiveness"; forgiveness of sins is acquired for sinners. "Behold," says Luther, "the true Master and Doctor of Holy Scriptures. He understood what these words meant: 'The Seed of the woman shall crush the serpent's head,' Gen. 3, 15, and these: 'In thy seed shall all the families of the earth be blessed,' Gen. 12, 3, 22, 18." God is just, but He is also merciful. He found a way to reconcile His mercy with His justice. This David knew. He says: "For with Jehovah there is mercy," v. 7. How so? "With Him is plenteous redemption," v. 8. The justice of God must be satisfied; His Law must be fulfilled. It was. By whom? "This is His name whereby He (Christ) shall be called, The Lord—Jehovah—our Righteousness," Jer. 23, 6. Christ is Jehovah, and this Jehovah is our Righteousness. Christ has fulfilled the Law for us. Now, since Jehovah has satisfied Jehovah's demands, there is redemption, "plenteous redemption." Without violating His justice, God can and does forgive sins on account of this storehouse of plenteous redemption procured by the Messiah. And all who cry with David with the voice of supplication for mercy to Jehovah receive forgiveness.— This is David's consolation. Whence did he derive this knowledge and this confidence? He answers: "In His Word do I hope," v. 5. What had God said? "Though your sins be as scarlet, they shall be as white as snow; though they be red like crimson, they shall be as wool." Is. 1, 18; Jer. 31, 34; Ex. 34, 6.7. Now, sin is not forgiven that more sin shall be committed. The repentant and pardoned sinner is filled with a holy awe of the holy God, whom he has offended; hence his purpose to fear God: "*that Thou mayest be feared.*" The pardoned sinner and God stand in the relation of Father and child. Hence his fear is not that of a slave, but that of a loving child. Out of gratitude he runs the ways of God's commandments.—

Resume: Only God can forgive sins. He does it by grace for Christ's sake, so the Scriptures declare. Sanctification follows justification.

Ps. 103, 2.3: *Bless the Lord, O my soul, and forget not all His benefits: who forgiveth all thine iniquities; who healeth all thy diseases.*

Unspeakably great and manifold are the "benefits" God extended to the psalmist, but the foremost, the greatest of all the mercies enumerated in this hymn of thanksgiving is the forgiveness of sin. The royal singer, David, had committed "'iniquities," and they were many; he was guilty, so he confesses. Instead of inflicting punishment, God, Jehovah, the covenant God, forgave them all. Previous to this pardoning act of Jehovah, the psalmist's soul was sick, sin-sick; now, however, it is "healed"; it has recovered as from a disease. This unfathomable grace of the Lord deserves not to be forgotten, but to be glorified in hymns of praise.—Justification, forgiveness of sin, brings peace of mind, joy of heart, and union of the soul with God.

Eph. 1, 7: *In Christ we have redemption through His blood, the forgiveness of sins, according to the riches of His grace.*

"Blessed be the God and Father of our Lord Jesus Christ, who hath blessed us with all spiritual blessings in heavenly places in Christ." So Paul writes, v. 3. Next, he enumerates the blessings bestowed upon them before the foundation of the world. In the paragraph beginning at v. 6b he unfolds the blessings flowing from election which we Christians have received in time. "He hath made us accepted in the Beloved," Eph. 1, 6. All eternal and temporal blessings have this one source, grace, which favor of God towards unworthy sinners is mediated through the Beloved, His Son. The principal gift of grace is mentioned in our text— the forgiveness of sin. By nature we are carnal, *sold* under sin, Rom. 7, 14. To be saved, we needs must be redeemed. This Christ did. *"In whom we have redemption."* Redemption, *apolutrosis,* signifies to *buy back, to redeem from bondage* by paying the ransom, *lutron.* What was the purchase price? "Redemption *through His blood.*" Ponder the price

Of your redemption from sin! Christ Himself says: "The Son of Man came—to give His life a ransom—lutron— for many," Matt. 20, 28. Paul writes to Timothy: "Christ gave *Himself* a ransom for all," 1 Tim. 2, 6; and to Titus: "Christ gave *Himself* for us, that He might *redeem* us from all iniquity," Tit. 2, 14. Truly, we are "bought with a price," 1 Cor. 6, 20; 7, 23; Gal. 3, 13.—"Redemption through His blood" was an act accomplished once for all times; but the apostle here represents it as a permanent possession, an ever-present treasure: we *have* redemption and through and with it "*the forgiveness of sins.*" "Forgiveness of sins" is in apposition to "the redemption through His blood," the former explaining the latter; both are practically identical. The redemption made, prompts God to forgive sin. We *have* redemption through His blood; we *have* forgiveness of sin, always, continually. The apostle employs the present tense, *echomen*, which expresses a present and a still continuing state. God daily and richly forgives sin. To whom? "In Christ we have" this great treasure, so long as we remain in Him, in faith. By faith Christ is ours, and all He merited. God does not forgive sin by an act of His sovereign majesty, but for Christ's sake. Without Christ there is no justification. And what impelled God to send Christ into the world for our liberation? The apostle answers· He did it "*according to the riches of His grace.*"—

God forgives sin: 1. to believers, 2. for Christ's sake. 3 by grace.— The efficient cause: His grace; the meritorious cause: redemption through His blood.—The foundation of justification is the atonement of Christ This justification is constant and enduring.

Rom. 3, 28: *Therefore we conclude that a man is justified by faith, without the deeds of the Law.*

In chapter 1 of Romans Paul had proved that the heathen are sinners; in chapter 2, that the Jews are sinners; in chapter 3 he had instituted a comparison between the two, but, though the Jews had certain advantages over the Gentiles, he draws the conclusion: in one respect they are both on a level: "There is no difference; all"—Jews and Gentiles —"have sinned, and come short of the glory of God," and hence cannot be justified by the Law. But still there is a justification, apart from the Law, by grace. In verses 21-27 we have the *locus classicus* of the doctrine of justification, followed by our text, which obviously is a brief summary of the preceding paragraph.—There are but two ways to be justified before God, either by works or by faith. *Tertium non datur.* By works it is impossible; by faith is the only way.—"*Therefore,*" from all that has been said in the previous sections about the sinner's justification, "*we conclude that a man,*" any man, Jew or Gentile, "*is justified by faith.*" The Greek lays all possible stress on the word faith, to emphasize the truth that justification is by faith, and by faith only, which truth is further made prominent by the phrase: "*without,*" apart from, "*the deeds of the Law.*" Luther, seeing that text and context loudly proclaimed this truth, brought out the thought demanded by the idiom of the German language by translating thus: "So halten wir es nun, dass der Mensch gerecht werde ohne des Gesetzes Werke, *allein* durch den Glauben."—

There are two new terms in this passage pertaining to the doctrine of the forgiveness of sin that need consideration. The one is *to justify*, *dikaioun*. This verb occurs about thirty-eight times in the New Testament, and in every instance it denotes a forensic, a judicial, act of God, and means *to declare righteous*. (Cf. Matt. 11, 19; 12, 37; Luke 7, 29.35; 10, 29; 16, 15; Acts 13, 39; Rom. 2, 13, *et al.*) In all these and other passages it does not and cannot mean: *to make righteous* by removing sin, or to infuse righteousness into one, but *to declare, to hold one righteous*. Take but one illustration, Luke 7, 29. We there read: "The publicans justified God." To interpret this: the publicans "made God just," or the publicans "infused righteousness into" God, would be the height of absurdity. The obvious meaning is: they declared God to be a just, a righteous God. Luther translates it nicely by: "Sie gaben Gott recht." Again, the opposites used in some passages with the verb justify bear out the same exegesis, but of these, perhaps, anon. So, substituting these words, the text reads: "We conclude that a man is *declared righteous* by faith." "*Faith*" is another term the meaning of which requires notice. How is this to be understood: We are declared righteous *by faith (dia pisteos*, Rom. 3, 22.25.30; *ek pisteos*, Rom. 1, 7; *pistei*, Rom. 3, 28)? Does faith justify because in the eyes of God it is such a great virtue, on account of which He were impelled to declare us righteous? No. Observe the text: "A man is justified by faith, *without* the deeds of the Law." This contrast says: Faith and works are opposites, and hence exclude each other; faith must not be viewed as a work, a virtue, owing to which God were gracious to the sinner. Were it so viewed, it would be tantamount to saying: A man is justified by this work, *sc.* faith.

How, then, is faith to be viewed in this article of justification? Says Paul: "Knowing that a man is not justified by the works of the Law, but by the faith of Jesus Christ, even we have believed in Jesus Christ, that we might *be justified by the faith of Christ* and not by the works of the Law," Gal. 2, 16. Note the sharp antithesis between works and faith. Faith is not to be considered in any way as a work, as anything that man does on account of which God looks with favor upon him. But let us read on: "But if, while we seek to be *justified by Christ*," etc., Gal. 2, 17. Verse 16 speaks of *being justified by the faith* of Christ; v. 17 speaks of *being justified by Christ (en Christo*—in Christ). So to be justified *by* the *faith* of Christ and to be justified *by Christ* is one and the same thing. And just this shows how little faith is to be considered as a work in this doctrine. All depends upon the object of this faith— Christ. Faith apprehends Christ and His merits, and because of this we are justified. Christ and His work, Christ's blood alone, has cleansing power, and Christ can be grasped by faith only; and this is the sole reason why faith justifies. And when the apostle in our text simply says: "*A man is justified by faith,*" it is plain from the context, vv. 21-26, that the basis of this justification is the meritorious work of the Savior. So it is not any kind of faith that justifies, but a very specific faith, faith in Christ Jesus. And this faith is of the operation of God; and so viewed, this faith, too, is of grace. In plain words Paul expresses this truth, Rom. 4, 16: "Therefore it (the righteousness) is *of faith* that it might be *of grace.*" Since righteousness is of faith, the apostle argues, this is proof positive that it is by grace. Faith *in articulo justificationis* is not to be regarded as a meritorious cause or a ground of justification, but merely as the beggar's hand that grasps salvation, the means of acceptance, the *medium leptikon.*— "*Sola fide; sola gratia!*" *Soli Deo gloria!*

2 Cor. 5, 21: *For He hath made Him to be sin for us who knew no sin, that we might be made the righteousness of God in Him.*

How does God forgive sins? This question our text answers. "*Christ knew no sin,*" sin was altogether foreign to Him; He is the absolutely Sinless One, *ton me gnonta hamartian.* The writer to the Hebrews extols Him as "holy, harmless, undefiled, separate from sinners"; Peter declares: "He did no sin, neither was guile found in His mouth"; St. John affirms: "In Him is no sin." Of this impeccable Christ—"*who knew no sin*"—Paul says: "*God hath made Him to be sin.*" He knew no sin, and yet He had sin, aye, all sins, the sins of the whole world. How? By imputation. God imputed our sins to the sinless Christ. This plainly is the meaning of the sharp antithesis: Christ "*knew no sin*"—God "*hath made Him to be sin,*" a meaning which is furthermore demanded by the second clause: "*that we might be made the righteousness of God in Him.*"

The sinless Christ was made sin "for us," in our place, as our Substitute. We had sin, we were the guilty; the guiltless Christ takes the place of the guilty sinners. Christ "for us," our Substitute! Oh, blessed truth: Christ "for us"! Our sins taken from us and laid upon Him! "He bare our sins," says Peter, and Isaiah exclaims: "The Lord laid the iniquity of us all upon Him." Christ was the one great universal sinner in the eyes of God, and was dealt with accordingly. (Is. 53, 4.5; Gal. 3, 15; Rom.) God did this; God made Christ to be sin for us. What was His purpose? The text answers: "*that we might be made the righteousness of God in Him.*" It was done for us. We are the sinners, and as such must needs be damned. But God's gracious will is not that we should die in our sins, but, rather, that we should live. God's gracious purpose was and is that we should possess "righteousness," so that we may be looked upon as having done all that God demands in His holy Ten Commandments, that we possess the "righteousness *of God,*" one that is valid before Him. Back of the imputation of our sins to Christ is God's gracious purpose expressed by the "that" clause. God's mercy to us impelled Him to impute our sins to the sinless Christ, so that He might impute the perfect righteousness acquired by Christ through His suffering and death to us. The "righteousness of God," perfect, complete to the last jot and tittle, the righteousness that God demands, is found in Christ. Nothing more is to be. done.—How does it become ours? We are *"made the righteousness of God in Him."* Christ's righteousness, acquired for us, is imputed to us. As God looked upon, and dealt with, the sinless Christ as the sinner, aye, as sin, so He now looks upon us, the sinful and unrighteous, as righteous, as such as possess all righteousness.—This is the blessed mystery expressed by those wee words: "He—for us"—*peccatum imputatum;* "we in Him"—*justitia imputata.*

Rom. 8, 33: *Who shall lay anything to the charge of God's elect? It is God that justifieth.*

The rhetorical question: *"Who shall lay anything to the charge of God's elect?"* or, in other words: "Who shall bring *an accusation* against the elect of God?" implies an emphatic denial. The fact of being God's elect precludes all possibility of *laying a charge,* or bringing *an accusation,* against them. God's elect, the true believers, are not criminals in God's sight. Sin may accuse them, Satan may accuse them, the Law and their own conscience may accuse them, but God says: Not guilty! *"It is God that justifieth,"* says the apostle, laying great stress upon the word "God." Now if God justifies, "if God be for us, who can be against us?" (V. 31.) *"Is is God that justifieth."* God says: There are no charges against My people, no accusations can be brought against them; they are not guilty. I *justify* them, *I declare them righteous.* They cannot be condemned. Why not? "It is Christ that died, yea, rather, that is risen again, who is even at the right hand of God, who also maketh intercession for us." (V. 34.)—The foundation of justification is the redemptive work of Christ.

2 Cor. 5, 19: *God was in Christ, reconciling the world unto Himself, not imputing their trespasses unto them; and hath committed unto us the word of reconciliation.*

"God was in Christ" essentially. "In Him dwelleth the fullness of the Godhead bodily." Christ's work was God's work. What did He do? He *"reconciled the world unto Himself."* Why was a reconciliation necessary? On account of the "trespasses" of the world. When was this reconciliation of the world effected? More than 1900 years ago, when Christ expired on the cross, crying out: "It is finished!" and, in proof of His redemptive work being complete, triumphantly rose from the dead. What does *"to be reconciled with one"* mean? All hatred, grudge, wrath, ill-feeling is banished; former enemies have become friends. So with God. God made friends of His enemies—in Christ. He is reconciled with *the world,* with all men. No one must do or suffer anything in order to appease the wrath of God on account of the trespasses committed. In Christ God now looks upon man as though man had never

offended against Him. Clearly, here is taught the so-called objective justification. For since God *is reconciled* with the world, since He has nothing against man, He has absolved man of his sin, He looks upon man, upon the world, as righteous for Christ's sake. In plain words this justification, this absolution from sin, is expressed in the text thus: *"not imputing their trespasses unto them."* Not to *impute trespasses,* however, is equivalent to *justify,* to *declare righteous,* as is patent from Rom. 4, 6-8.—The cardinal Gospel truth is this: "'We were reconciled to God by the death of His Son." (Rom. 5, 10.) Christ is "the propitiation for the sins of the whole world." (1 John 2, 2.)—Thus, according to Scripture, there exists a reconciliation with God before the faith of the individual sinner. Now, in order that the sinner should know of this salvation, come into actual possession of it, God established "a ministry of reconciliation" (2 Cor. 5, 18), and committed unto His ambassadors *"the word of reconciliation."* What is the quintessence of their proclamation? God is reconciled with you; "be *ye* reconciled with God." (V. 20) Do not reject the amnesty which is in the heart of God. There is righteousness in store for you in Christ. What must I do to be saved? *"Believe* on the Lord Jesus Christ." "Whosoever *believeth* in Him shall *receive* remission of sins." (Acts 10, 43.) Thus man, by "the word of reconciliation." by the Gospel, comes into actual possession of the full pardon proclaimed to the world by the resurrection of Jesus Christ from the dead. Thus man is justified by faith. This is called subjective justification.

Gen. 15, 6: *Abram believed the Lord; and He counted it to him for righteousness.*

We are told: "Abram believed the Lord." What had Abraham believed? God had promised him that his seed should be innumerable as the stars of heaven, and, most important of all, that from this seed should come One in whom all the families of the earth should be blessed. This promise of the Lord Abraham *believed,* on this he relied, on it he rested all his hope. From this promised Seed righteousness, salvation, would come. And this *belief* in the Promised One was *"counted* to him *for righteousness."* Abraham had no righteousness of his own with which he might be pleasing to God. Righteousness was to be found only in the Promised One. That righteousness became his. How? Abraham *believed* the Lord. And this belief, this faith in God's promise, in Christ, was *counted,* was reckoned, was imputed, to him for righteousness. Faith grasped the promise and, with it, the promised Seed and His meritorious work. Thus by faith Abraham came into possession of righteousness that availeth before God.

Rom. 4, 5: *To Him that worketh not, but believeth on Him that justifieth the ungodly, his faith is counted for righteousness.*

This passage is the New Testament parallel to the preceding text. Having spoken of Abraham in the words of Gen. 15, 16, Paul continues his argument on justification thus: "Now to him that worketh is the reward not reckoned of grace, but of debt." (V. 4.) This is the statement of a maxim that holds good in every case. Work deserves reward, pay. And if by works one could earn salvation, salvation would not be of grace, but a debt which God, in justice bound, owed to the worker. Paul uses this impossible case for the sake of illustration. He goes on to say: *"But to him that worketh not, but believeth on Him that justifieth the ungodly, his faith is counted for righteousness."* The contrast says: This righteousness cannot be merited, cannot be acquired by works. There is but one way to come into possession of it—by faith. And again, this faith is not to be viewed as a good deed, an act on account of which God is prompted to grant this righteousness. Observe the sharp antithesis between *"worketh not"*—*"but believeth,"* excluding all idea of merit being attached to the act of believing. This truth is furthermore emphasized by the assertion that God *"justifies the ungodly."* The person justified is said to be *ungodly, ton asebe, i. e.,* a wicked person, one who not only has violated God's commandments, but who also dishonors God, is inimical to Him. Hence God sees nothing in the sinner whom He justifies but ungodliness, guilt. And this ungodly, this guilty person He justifies, declares him to be not guilty. Every man, such as he is by nature, is such an "ungodly" person. What does he deserve? Damnation. But what does God do? He justifies him, declares him righteous, guiltless. Whom does He so look upon? *"To him that worketh not, but believeth on Him."* The foundation of this justifying sentence is Christ and His work. This self-evident Bible truth the apostle had previously carried out. The point here is: God justifies the ungodly. This justification is ready now, was ready in the Old Testament, aye, was ready in the decree of redemption before the world began, which decree was carried out in time, and completed when Christ expired on the cross for the sins of the ungodly. This fact is published in the Gospel, and whosoever comes to faith simply accepts, receives, from the storehouse of God's justifying grace this blessed assurance: You, too, the ungodly, God justifies.

2 Tim. 1, 12: *I know whom I have believed, and am persuaded that He is able to keep that which I have committed unto Him against that day.*

When viewing "that day," the well-known day of the Lord, Paul is calm; there is no fear for "that day" in his heart. Writing to Timothy, who, like the apostle, is called upon to suffer affliction for the Gospel's sake, Paul confidently assures him: *"God is able to keep that which I have committed unto Him against that day."* What does the apostle mean by *"that which I have committed unto Him"*? This clause translates the Greek word *paratheke*, which Luther renders *"Beilage,"* and for which the English equivalent is *deposit,* a deposit for safe-keeping. Now, what was this deposit? Paul says: "I know whom I have believed." What did he believe, when, by God's grace, he put his trust in

Christ? That his sins were forgiven, that he was a child of God and an heir of salvation; that God, who began the good work in him, would also perform it unto the day of Jesus Christ. (Phil. 1, 6.) That was his *paratheke*. This he committed unto God, and he knows that God is able to keep it. The apostle is weak in himself; afflictions there are many, temptations are great to cast aside faith, and thus to lose salvation. But God is able, powerful, strong. And He is perfectly assured that God will *keep* it, *fuloxai, i. e.*, guard it over against all enemies who would wrest it from him. Paul is certain of his salvation. "*I know,*" he says, I have personal knowledge of, I am fully assured of, "*whom I have believed.*" My Savior will not fail me. Upon His Word I can safely rely. "*I am persuaded,*" I confidently know, I am divinely assured, that my "deposit" is secure in spite of all spiritual enemies who would deprive me of it. Paul's certainty of salvation rests upon God's promise of preserving him in grace.—A thought similar to this one St. Peter expresses when he consoles the Christians in Asia Minor who were afflicted with the cross. He writes: "Blessed be the God and Father of our Lord Jesus Christ, which according to His abundant mercy hath begotten us again unto a lively hope........to an inheritance........ *reserved* in heaven for you, who are kept by the power of God through faith unto salvation." (1 Pet. 1, 3-6. Cf. Theol. Quart. X, 231 ff.)

Rom. 8, 38.39: *I am persuaded that neither death, nor life, nor angels, nor principalities, nor powers, nor things present, nor things to come, nor height, nor depth, nor any other creature, shall be able to separate us from the love of God which is in Christ Jesus, our Lord.*

In the second half of this chapter the Apostle Paul treats of the cross of the Christians. Intoning a sublime hymn of triumph, he consoles them in all their afflictions by assuring them that no cross, however great it may be, can separate them from their God and their Savior. Boldly he confronts all enemies of salvation with this defiant challenge: "If God be for us, who can be against us?" (V. 31.) Again: "Who shall lay anything to the charge of God's elect?" (V. 33.) Again: "Who is he that condemneth?" (V. 34.) And again: "Who shall separate us from the love of Christ?" (V. 35) These rhetorical questions imply a strong denial. In vv. 38.39 Paul reaches the climax of his *hymnus consolationis:* "*I am persuaded,*" he says; and he uses the word *pepeismai,* which expresses full assurance. There is no uncertainty about this in his mind, no doubt whatever. And when he says: "*I am persuaded,*" I am fully assured, he does not speak in his own name merely, but in the name of all believing Christians, as is evident from the preceding context, where he employs the plural pronoun "*us*"; likewise in the succeeding context, v. 39, the same form of the pronoun occurs. Of what is the apostle persuaded? In v. 35 he had asked rhetorically: "Who shall *separate* us from the love of Christ?" Here he picks up that word *separate* and says: "I am persuaded that neither death," etc., "shall be able to *separate* us from the love of God which is in Christ Jesus, our

Lord." *Separate, choridzein,* presupposes being *linked* together, *fastened* to some one or some thing; it presupposes *connection.* With whom are we Christians linked together, connected? With "the love of God which is in Christ Jesus, our Lord." How? By faith. This connection no one, nothing, shall be able to sever. The great danger in affliction is that it may make us uncertain of the love of God. This idea the apostle opposes, powerfully consoling the suffering Christians. Forces there are at work in plenty that endeavor to cause a separation between us and our merciful God, to break the connection with our Savior. Which are they? *Death* with its terrors; this *life* with its many dangers and temptations; *angels and principalities,* the spirits of iniquity; *things present,* afflictions which bear heavily upon us; *things to come,* trials and unknown vicissitudes of life in days and years to come; *height and depth,* crosses sent from above to test our faith, powers from the depth of hell to cause our fall. The outlook is truly appalling. But what says the apostle? "I am persuaded" that all these, including "any other creature," cannot separate us. The love of God which is in Christ Jesus, our Lord, guarantees that.—Our Savior has said: "My sheep hear My voice, and I know them, and they follow Me; and I give unto them eternal life; and they shall never perish, neither shall any man pluck them out of My hand." (John 10, 27.28.) And St. Paul writes to the Philippians: "Being confident of this very thing that He which hath begun the good work in you will perform it until the day of Jesus Christ." (Phil. 1, 6.) On these and similar promises, not on any strength of their own, believers rest the assurance that they will reach the end of their faith, life everlasting.

THE RESURRECTION OF THE BODY.

John 5, 28.29: *The hour is coming in which all that are in the graves shall hear His voice, and shall come forth: they that have done good unto the resurrection of life, and they that have done evil unto the resurrection of damnation.*

The Lord speaks of two resurrections: the spiritual, here in time (vv. 24-27), and the bodily resurrection at the last day (vv. 28-29). Of the latter we treat.

The passage is so clear as to need little comment. It will suffice to indicate the statements made. "*The hour is coming* in which all......shall come forth." Not only the day (Acts 17, 31; 2 Pet. 3, 10), but the very *hour* of this event is fixed, and this hour *is coming,* surely, certainly, inevitably. This resurrection of the dead is a *universal* resurrection: "*All......*shall come forth." In the same hour, simultaneously, *all* will arise. There will be no interval of a thousand years between the raising of the just and that of the unjust. They that espouse the latter opinion, the Chiliasts, the Millennialists, give Christ the lie. Christ says: "*All* shall come forth" in that "*hour.*" (Cf. Matt. 24, 27-39; 25, 21-32.)—

"All that are *in the graves*......shall come forth," *i. e.*, the dead bodies. The identical bodies that were separated from the soul in death, and lowered into the grave with many a tear, shall be restored to their senses, to life, so much so, as the text says, that, *e. g.*, they *hear*. They shall hear *His*, *i. e.*, Christ's voice, v. 27. Christ's voice will call them forth. Christ's voice is God's voice; this almighty voice can and will do that. (Rom. 4, 17.)—The passage divides the "all that are in the graves" into two classes: *"they that have done good,"* the believers; and *"they that have done evil,"* the unbelievers. Believers and unbelievers are described according to their works, since the Judgment is to be a public judgment of the whole world. (2 Cor. 5, 10; Acts, 17, 31.) The good works will be produced in evidence of faith, the evil works in evidence of unbelief. (Matt. 25, 31-46.) The doctrine, "By grace are ye saved through faith," is hereby in no wise subverted or called into question.—As there are but two classes of people, believers and unbelievers, so there are but two places hereafter, *life* and *damnation*. The genetives, *dzoes, of life,* and *kriseos, of judgment,* express purpose. The one class is raised for the purpose of inheriting eternal *life;* the other, for the purpose of being cast into *damnation.*—There are only *two* places hereafter, heaven and hell. The Catholic purgatory is a figment; Russell's theory of the annihilation of the bodies of the ungodly is a lie.— God grant that we belong to them "that have done good," and are called forth "unto the resurrection of life."

Dan. 12, 2: *Many of them that sleep in the dust of the earth shall awake, some to everlasting life and some to shame and everlasting contempt.*

The confession of the Christian Church, "He will at the *last day* raise up me and all the dead," is the doctrine of the Old Testament as well as that of the New.—God says to Daniel, the prophet: "But go thou thy way till the end be; for thou shalt rest, and stand in thy lot *at the end of the days,"* i. e., the Last Great Day.—In the verse preceding our text, Daniel prophesies of "the time of trouble" that shall come at the end. Many shall be slain for their faith in Jehovah. But the slain and their slayers shall rise again, and these will be *many, "rabbim,"* a great multitude, namely, when all shall rise. Of the *"many"* of whom the prophet speaks, *"some,"* i. e., they who suffered death for their faith, shall awake "to everlasting life" to suffer no more; *"and some,"* i. e., the persecutors of the believers, the infidels, shall awake *"to shame and everlasting contempt."* *Shame*, reproach, will be their lot for their wicked folly of rejecting the only means of salvation. They will be objects of *contempt*, of abhorrence, of loathing. And this fate will be *everlasting*, endless; it will continue throughout eternity.—Blessed the lot of them that awake on that day to *life everlasting*.

Job 19, 25-27: *I know that my Redeemer liveth, and that He shall stand at the latter day upon the earth; and though after my skin worms destroy this body, yet in my flesh I shall see God, whom I shall see for myself, and mine eyes shall behold, and not another.*

Truly, this text is one of the most brilliant gems among the many of the Old Testament. How clearly it speaks of the Redeemer's work, of the resurrection of the body, and of life everlasting! Not knowing this author, one might think it to be culled from the sayings of some New Testament writer. Small wonder the enemies of the Bible and its Christ have busied themselves again and again to becloud its glorious, heavenly rays.

It is a text replete with consolation. Let us briefly bring to our minds the dark background of the text by means of the context. Job is sorely afflicted; humanly speaking, a cure of his disease is out of the question; he is soon to die. His brothers, his kinfolk, his servants, his friends, are estranged from him; even his own wife has turned against him (vv. 13-19). His "consolers" have no sympathy, no word of consolation for him. He is smitten of God for his wickedness; this they give him to understand (chap. 18). They "break him in pieces with words" (19,1-5). Yea, God Himself seems to be his enemy (v. 21). Yet he knows his accusers are doing him injustice.

And out of the depth of this great misery rises this joyful hymn of triumph and faith. Job looks beyond the grave and decay and death, and there beholds the Redeemer and His work, beholds the day of the resurrection of the body and of eternal bliss. Conscious of the depth of the utterances he is about to make, he sorrowfully exclaims: "Oh, that my words were now written! Oh, that they were printed in a book, that they were graven with an iron pen and lead in the rock forever!" Condemned and forsaken by his contemporaries as a wicked person, posterity at least then would know of his justification in the sight of God.

Amid all this earthly misery, what is his consolation? *"But,"* over against all that my "friends" may say to the contrary, *"I know,"* I have positive knowledge, I am divinely assured of a certain fact. And the contents of this knowledge? *"My Redeemer,"* my Goel, *"liveth."* Who is this *Goel?* Not the Triune God is meant here as, for example, in Is. 41, 14; 43, 1, but the second person of the Trinity. (Gen. 48,16.) How do we know? The context says that this Goel will raise Job from the dead,— this is a work of the Son of Man, John 6, 40; 5, 22. It says that this Goel will lead Job to a beatific vision of God,—this is a work of the Savior. Hence the Hebrew *Goel* is properly translated by *"Redeemer."* What does Job confess of Him? "My Redeemer *liveth.*" Satan, sin, death, have assaulted Job; but Satan, sin, death, will be overcome by Job's Goel. He will redeem Job from their clutches. Satan, sin, death, will assail Christ; and Christ, too, Job's Goel, must die. But death cannot retain Him; for He is the Prince of Life. (Acts 3, 15; John 17, 25.) The Redeemer *lives.* "Through death He destroyed him that had the power of death, that is, the devil." (Hebr. 2, 14.15.) The redemption-money was paid, and now He lives and lives, and will forever live. Of this living Redeemer Job confidently asserts: He is *my* Redeemer. The ransom was paid for *me;* I shall not die, but live. In New Testament diction Job's Redeemer is He who said to His disciples: *"Because I live, ye shall also live."* (John 14, 19.) In this lifegiving Redeemer Job puts his trust. His body may decay, still eternal life will be his.—With the children of the New Testament he sang:

> Jesus, my Redeemer, lives!
> I, too, unto life must waken;
> Endless joys my Savior gives;
> Shall my courage, then, be shaken?
> Shall I fear? Or could the Head
> Rise and leave His members dead?

What follows in the context confirms and develops this thought. Job proceeds: *"And as the Last One He shall stand upon the earth,"* or, *the grave.* The whole earth—this is the sublime conception—is one vast sepulcher, in which the dead rest. Job views himself as being dead and bedded in the earth, the grave. But on this earth, on this dust of his, the Redeemer *stands* in all His glory, power, majesty, and He will manifest His power; he will prove Himself to be Job's Goel. When will this be? When He shall stand as the *Last One* on the earth, and shall destroy the last enemy, death (1 Cor. 15, 26), *i. e.*, on "the day of the Lord," on Judgment Day.—What will this mighty and gracious Redeemer do for Job? *"And though after my skin worms destroy this body, yet in my flesh shall I see God."* Though in the original the words "worms" and "body" are wanting, still the sense of the Hebrew text is clearly brought out. Luther's translation: *"Und werde danach mit dieser meiner Haut umgeben werden,"* is more faithful to the original. Job says: My skin will be destroyed, my body will turn to dust and ashes in the grave, but there will be a resurrection day, when my body will again be clothed with the selfsame skin I now possess. "I believe in the resurrection of the body."

> I am only flesh and blood,
> And on this *corruption* seizeth;
> But I know my Lord and God
> From the grave my *body* raiseth.

And after the resurrection, what? *"In my flesh shall I see God."* My flesh, my body, will be restored, and in this restored body, the organ of the soul, *I shall see God*, and this beatific seeing of God will make me eternally happy. (Cf. Ps. 17, 15; 1 John 3, 2.) This my Redeemer that liveth will do for me.—What a contrast; Job in his suffering state now; in his blissful state then! This happy prospect causes Job to dwell upon, and to unfold, this blessed truth. He heaps words upon words to make his *knowledge*, his belief, clear; his belief in the resurrection of the body and life everlasting. *"And mine eyes shall behold."* The eyes he now possesses shall be restored to him, and with these identical eyes he shall behold God. And as if to make the meaning still plainer, he adds: *"and not another,"* which says emphatically: I shall be the same Ego that I now am, the same person with the same eyes, the same body. I shall come forth out of the grave with body and soul reunited, and enter eternal bliss, everlastingly seeing God. This *"I know,"* of this I am absolutely sure, because *"my Redeemer liveth."* (Cf. 2 Tim. 1, 12.)

> Note.—The words of our text: *"In my flesh shall I see God,"* correctly translated, the Standard American Version renders: "Then *without* my flesh I shall see God," the purpose being, of course, to do away with the clear declaration of the resurrection of the *body.* Aside from linguistical reasons, text and context, even in their English dress, loudly protest against this mistranslation. The same S. A. V. translates v. 27 correctly (the text here being so very clear): "And *mine eyes* shall behold." Query: How can Job's eyes behold *without* his flesh? Ought not these contradictory translations: *"Without* my flesh I shall see God," and still: *"Mine* eyes shall behold," bring the flush of shame to their faces?—To do them justice, we shall add that in a foot-note we find the alternative rendition: "Yet *from* my flesh shall I see God."

Phil. 3, 20: *For our conversation is in heaven, from whence also we look for the Savior, the Lord Jesus Christ: who shall change our vile body that it may be fashioned like unto His glorious body, according to the working whereby He is able even to subdue all things unto Himself.*

The resurrection-body will be the *same* body, in all its parts, that we possessed in this life; but it will be *changed, glorified.* This we learn from the present text.

The apostle had spoken of "the enemies of the cross of Christ: whose end is destruction, whose God is their belly, and whose glory is in their shame, who mind earthly things" (v. 19). They live but for this life; their heaven they seek here on earth. With these infidels he contrasts the Christians. *"Our conversation,"* that is, *our commonwealth, our citizenship, politeuma,* "is in heaven." The citizenship of the unbelievers is on earth; ours, in heaven; they mind earthly things; we, on the contrary, are heavenly minded. Heaven is our true home. Here we are but sojourners, pilgrims, wandering through this City of Destruction to the Celestial City. Our attitude is this: *"from whence* (heaven) *we look for,"* we are awaiting, *"the Savior, the Lord Jesus Christ."* He may come at any time. When that event occurs, He will effect a glorious change in our bodies. What will be the nature thereof? The apostle says: *"Christ shall change our vile body that it may be fashioned like unto His glorious body."* Two bodies are here contrasted, our body and Christ's body. Our body is *vile,* Christ's is *glorious.* Now, what is said? Our vile body shall be *changed.* The word rendered "changed," *metaschematisei,* means *transform, change into another form, umgestalten, in eine andere Gestalt verwandeln,* so that the essence of the thing remains, but other properties are given. Now, when the apostle asserts that Christ will "change," transform, our vile body, that says: The *same* body will remain, but this body will be endowed with new attributes, adapted to the nature of the circumstances then existing. What transformation will take place? Our *vile* body will be changed into a *glorious* body. The *vileness* will be taken away from it, and *glory* will take its place. To be somewhat plainer,—what is here nicely translated by *vile body* the apostle calls a *"body of humiliation," to soma tes tapeinoseos,* a sinful, frail, corruptible, mortal body, a body subject to all sorts of humiliation. This "vileness" will be a thing of the past when the change spoken of in the text takes place, and "gloriousness," like unto that possessed by Christ's body, will be ours. How is this done? We do not know. But take an illustration. Here is a glass, say, of "vile," filthy water. Filter it. What is the result? It is the same water, to be sure, but in a "glorious" condition; it is clear as crystal. The "vileness," the filth, has been separated from it. *Fiat applicatio.*

Let us proceed. Christ will transform *"our body of humiliation that it may be fashioned like unto the body of His glory."* "That it may be *fashioned* like unto," that is to say, "that it may become *conformed* to the body of His glory." The glory of our bodies will be the same in kind as the glory of Christ's body, though not of the same degree.—In order to better apprehend the meaning of the apostle's dictum: "Christ shall change our vile body that it may be fashioned like unto His glorious body," let us contemplate the *glorified* body of Christ. When the Lord rose from the dead, He did not have a new body, but the one taken from the essence of the Virgin Mary. His disciples knew Him: they saw the selfsame Master; they heard the selfsame voice. To assure them that He was not a spirit, He showed them His wounds. "A spirit hath not flesh and bones, as ye see Me have," He said to them. (Luke 24, 39.) When they still doubted, He ate and drank with them. But His body had new qualities, new endowments. He did not come and go now, after the resurrection, as He had been wont to do, after the manner of men. He appeared to the disciples of Emmaus and—vanished. Suddenly He is amongst His disciples,—they knew not whence He came; just as suddenly He departs, they know not whither. Barred doors are no hindrance to Him. He was no longer limited by time or space. Christ's glorified body was a *spiritual* body. It is called a spiritual body, not because Christ no longer had flesh and blood, and had been changed into a spirit, but because, although the body remained the same as to its essence, it possessed the properties of a spirit. Which are some of the properties of a spirit? Invisibility, no necessity of progressing successively from one place to another, no need of meat and drink, etc. But we cannot enumerate all the properties of the glorified bodies in heaven; space forbids.—The resurrection-body of our Lord is a type of the bodies of the believers that will be theirs at the resurrection day.

What a glorious thing this is that we have contemplated! Who can understand it? How can it be? Does this question come to your minds? Paul has answered it. He says: Let the Lord attend to that He will and can do it *"according to the working whereby He is able even to subdue all things unto Himself."* This believe.

> Note.—The Catechism cites 1 Cor. 15, 51-52 with the remark: "Transmutation of the living." The persons living at Christ's second advent will experience this same transformation spoken of in Phil. 3. The process will be instantaneous. Paul says: "Behold, I show you a mystery; we shall not all sleep, but we shall all be changed *in a moment, in the twinkling of an eye,* at the last trumpet."

Luke 16, 23-24: *And in hell he lift up his eyes, being in torments, and seeth Abraham afar off, and Lazarus in his bosom. And he cried and said, Father Abraham, have mercy on me, and send Lazarus that he may dip the tip of his finger in water, and cool my tongue; for I am tormented in this flame.*

The believers will rise with glorified bodies to everlasting life. The unbelievers will rise to eternal death. Of the unbelievers' awful fate we must now treat.

Our text is taken from the well-known narrative of the rich man and Lazarus. Of the rich man we are told that he died and was buried. And the very next thing we read of him is this: *"And in hell he lift up his eyes,"* etc. There is no room here for a Catholic purgatory, no room here for an intermediate state, call it what you will, a state of probation, a modern Hades, or what not. All such opinions are anti-Scriptural and soul-destroying. But, say some, consult the Greek of this text; there it says of the rich man: "And in *Hades* he lift up his eyes." So there is such a place as Hades. Good, let us inquire into the nature of this place called Hades. The rich man—in Hades—is "in torments"; he cries pitifully for "mercy," but no mercy is shown him; he is "tormented in this flame," in hell-fire; even the drop of water that might adhere to the tip of a finger is denied him; he finds no alleviation, no cessation of this excruciating pain. He suffers both in body and soul. Such is the description of this Hades. Hades is hell.—There are but two places hereafter: Abraham's bosom and hell. "Abraham's bosom" is a figurative expression, picturesquely designating heaven. In the Scriptures Abraham is called the father of all believers; by faith they are closely connected with him; they are his spiritual children, who rest in his bosom, enjoy what he enjoys: heavenly rest, security, heavenly bliss. (Rom. 4, 1. 11. 12. 16. 17. Cf. Matt. 8, 11.)

Into hell the rich man must go, and all they who are like-minded. The rich man went there, not because he was rich, but because during his lifetime he despised Moses and the prophets, *i. e.,* because of his unbelief. In hell the rich man turns to spiritualism: he requests Abraham to send Lazarus to testify to his five brothers, "lest they also come into this place of torment." (v. 28.) In hell there is remorse, but no repentance. Abraham says, No. The rich man insists, "Nay, Father Abraham, but if one went unto them from the dead, they will repent." Abraham makes answer, "If they hear not Moses and the prophets, neither will they be persuaded though one rose from the dead." Spiritualism is not based on "Moses and the prophets"; spiritualism is a hellish doctrine, a snare of the devil. The time deciding man's eternal fate is on this side the grave. Nothing in heaven and on earth can and will save him, who will not believingly hear Moses and the prophets!

Matt. 10, 28: *Fear not them which kill the body, but are not able to kill the soul; but rather fear Him which is able to destroy both soul and body in hell.*

When the Lord sent out His twelve disciples to preach the Gospel, He gave them special instructions for their work. In the course of this beautiful address He forewarned them of the hardships and persecutions awaiting them in the faithful discharge of their duties. Steadfastly they are to confess Him before men. Publicly, from the housetops, they are to preach the saving Gospel. What would come to pass? Cruel persecutions, even death. But, says the Lord encouragingly: the worst your enemies can do is to *"kill the body"*; they *"are not able to kill the soul."* Hence, *"Fear them not."* Do not shirk your duty,—maintain silence, abjure your faith,—and thus sin against God, *"who is able to destroy both soul and body in hell."* So much as to the text in its context.

Now as to the doctrine pertinent to our *locus.* The text expressly says: The *body* can be killed, but not the *soul.* The soul is immortal. But, say the Adventists and the Russellites, the second member of the passage says that both body and *soul* may be *destroyed* in hell; and destruction is annihilation. *Non sequitur.* Destruction is not annihilation. Again, the statement here is not simply: Body and soul of the unbeliever will be destroyed, but: They will be destroyed *in hell.* What is the Biblical meaning of being *destroyed in hell?* For an answer see what is said about the rich man: his body and soul were destroyed in hell, and are continually being destroyed. In hell, "the lake of fire and brimstone," the godless "shall be tormented day and night forever and ever." (Rev. 20, 10.) Would you know what "destruction in hell" means, turn to 2 Thess. 1, 9. Of the ungodly the apostle there says: "Who shall be punished with *everlasting* destruction from the presence of the Lord and from the glory of His power."

Is. 66, 24: *Their worm shall not die, neither shall their fire be quenched; and they shall be an abhorring to all flesh.*

This passage describes the inexpressible torments of the damned in hell. We know this from the authoritative interpretation of our Lord Himself, Mark 9, 43-48. In the most solemn manner He repeatedly warns against hell, a place in which the "fire shall never be quenched," and three times He repeats these words from Isaiah: *"Where their worm dieth not, and the fire is not quenched."*—Isaiah speaks of the Great Judgment Day, in which the world will be "judged in righteousness." (Acts 17, 31; 2 Cor. 5, 10.) In hell the unbelievers will writhe in unspeakable agony forever and ever. *"Their worm,"* their guilty conscience, will gnaw at them into all eternity by accusing them of the fact: You are damned, and justly so; you rejected and despised the grace in Christ that was offered you. Aye, indeed, hell is "the furnace of fire," where "there shall be weeping and gnashing of teeth." (Matt. 8, 12; 22, 13; 13, 41, *et al.*) What unutterable, endless sufferings of body and soul in hell! How great the torment,—this accusing conscience acting like the *undying* worm! And what objects of abhorrence, terrible to look upon, the inmates of hell will be! *"They shall be an abhorring to all flesh."*—From this fate preserve us, heavenly Father, for Christ's sake!

Matt. 7, 13: *Enter ye in at the strait gate; for wide is the gate and broad is the way that leadeth to destruction; and many there be which go in thereat.*

We find this exhortation towards the close of the Sermon on the Mount. In striking imagery the Lord pictures man's journey into eternity. There are two roads. Many walk on the "broad way," few on the "narrow way"; the former leads to "destruction," the latter to "life." At the beginning of the narrow way is the *"strait,"* i. e., *narrow,* gate. This "strait gate," is conversion by means of contrition and repentance. By regeneration, conversion, one enters on the "narrow way," a way full of self-denial, beset by temptations to sin, etc., a way that requires wary walking. The meaning, of course, is not that we Christians merit eternal life by the careful walk on the narrow way. No. Faith alone saves; but faith manifests itself in a Christian walk, in good works. Faith without works is dead. The "wide gate" and the "broad way" are the image of an unbridled life, a life of sin. By nature man is on the broad way, and—if no change of heart occurs—his end is "destruction."—The passage speaks of but *two* gates, of *two* ways, of *two* destinations, of *two* classes of people. There is *no third* way, a way leading to an intermediate state between heaven and hell, leading, *e. g.,* to Hades, to a *Mittelort zur Selbstentscheidung,* or to purgatory.

OF ETERNAL LIFE.

Luke 23, 43: *Verily I say unto thee, To-day shalt thou be with Me in Paradise.*

"Lord, remember me when Thou comest into Thy kingdom." Who knows them not, these words of the repentant malefactor!—"This was a case of repentance in the last hour, the trying hour of death; and it has been remarked that *one* was brought to repentance there, to show that no one should *despair* on a dying bed; and but *one,* that none should be presumptuous and *delay* repentance to that awful moment." (Barnes.) The criminal dying on the cross recognized the crucified Savior as the "*Lord,*" *i. e.,* God, Jehovah. This bleeding, dying Jesus, moreover, he knew to be a king, who rules over a kingdom,—not, indeed, a kingdom of this world (John 18, 36), but a heavenly, supernatural kingdom. This prayer of faith the Lord answers immediately, saying, "*Verily I say unto thee, To-day shalt thou be with Me in Paradise.*" Christ's kingdom is Paradise. "Paradise," we are told, is a word of Persian origin, signifying a magnificent garden, a garden of pleasure. Whatever its etymological meaning may be, in its New Testament usage it is a synonym for heaven, connoting heavenly bliss and glory; it is the abode of the blessed. (2 Cor. 12, 4; 1 Cor. 2, 9; Rev. 2, 9.) Into this heavenly glory I shall enter, says Christ to this criminal, and thou shalt be with Me.—When was that happy event to take place? "*To-day.*" Whilst his body would still be on the cross or consigned to the grave, his *soul* would be with Jesus, would exist separately from the body. This is the plain meaning of the text, and the truth to be pointed out in reference to the thesis in the Catechism, which says: "All believers, when they die, are, according to the *soul, at once present with Christ.*"

But, sad to say, even this plain passage has been tortured, *e. g.,* by the Adventists, who deny the immortality of the soul. To cloak their antiscriptural doctrine, they punctuate Christ's answer thus: "Verily, I say unto thee to-day, thou shalt be with Me in Paradise." How absurd this procedure is becomes apparent at once when we observe the idea contrasted. The dying thief had said, "Remember me when Thou comest into Thy kingdom," the petition implying that he thought of some *future* time when the Lord should remember him. Emphatically Jesus places the word *to-day* in opposition to this erroneous notion, saying, *To-day,*— not in the distant future,—but *to-day,* this very day, thou shalt be with Me.—Again, looked at from another viewpoint, how utterly nonsensical the sense: "I say unto thee to-day, Thou shalt," etc.! The culprit well knew that Jesus did not speak these words yesterday or tomorrow! But observe the audacity of the tactics of the errorists: contrary to text and context, contrary to even the elementary rules of exegesis, they boldly put their gross perversions in cold print, relying on the old dictum: *Semper aliquid haeret.*

And now as to the Catholics. If any one needed a cleansing according to papal doctrine, surely this thief stood in need of it. Jesus says nothing of a purgatory. The pope and Scriptures never agree.

Finally, we must pay our respects to the modern theologians. We ask, Where is their Sheol or Hades in the light of this passage? As is well known, they have gone the Catholics one better. The Catholics dream of three places in the hereafter: heaven, hell, and purgatory; the modern theologians, of four: heaven, hell, and Hades with two apartments—Paradise and a place of preliminary torture. Now, where did the repentant criminal go? To this third place, **Apartment I of the** modern theological construction? No. He was *with Jesus:* "Thou shalt be *with Me* in Paradise." Not even modern theologians have the temerity to assert that Jesus was in their self-constructed Hades. This miracle of God's grace, the repentant thief, was *with Jesus.* To be *with Jesus* is the chief glory of eternal life. St. Paul, filled with longing for this blessed state, declares: "I desire to depart and *to be with Christ.*" (Phil. 1, 23; cf. Rev. 21, 23.) This was the bliss granted this penitent criminal: "Thou shalt be *with Me.*"

Rev. 14, 13: *Blessed are the dead which die in the Lord from henceforth.*

According to the text in its context, to *"die in the Lord"* means to die professing the Lord, to die because one is a Christian, to die for faith's sake. Such, *e. g.,* was the death of the martyrs. Deny the Lord, they were told, and you live; confess Him, and you die. They preferred death to denial; they "died in the Lord" to live with Him eternally. "To die in the Lord," therefore, in general means to believe steadfastly in Him despite all trials and tribulations of this present time, till death calls us hence.—Now, what is predicated of such as "die in the Lord"? They are *blessed, i. e.,* eternal bliss is theirs. (Cf. Matt. 5, 8 ff.) They are *in* the Lord, closely united to Him by faith, and death does not and cannot sever this union, but, dying *"in* the Lord," they are forever with Him—*blessed.*—When does this glorious state begin? *"From henceforth," aparti, forthwith,* from the moment the soul departs from the body.

Again we call attention to the fact that this passage, too, deals a death blow both to the purgatory of the Catholics and the Hades of the modern theologians. They that "die in the Lord" are blessed *forthwith;* they need no purgatory-cleansing; they have been cleansed from all sin by the blood of Jesus Christ. (1 John 1, 7.)

John 10, 27.28: *My sheep hear My voice, and I know them, and they follow Me: and I give unto them eternal life.*

A gracious promise, indeed, it is the Lord Jesus here makes to them that are His.—It was at the Feast of Dedication that His opponents, the Jews, who reproached Him for holding them in suspense as to whether He were the promised Messiah, were flatly told by Jesus: "Ye are not of My sheep." (v. 26.) He goes on to describe His sheep, showing that they have certain characteristics.—We ask, Who are His sheep? *"My sheep," ta probata ta ema, the sheep that belong to Me,* says Jesus, have this mark,—they "hear My voice," that is to say, they hear My voice not externally only, as you, My enemies, do, but they hear it *believingly,* trustingly *(akouein c. Gen).* They know My voice to be the voice of the Good Shepherd, whose leadership they can implicitly follow. This they do: *"They follow Me,"*—That is another mark of "the sheep *that belong to Me."* They are absolutely assured of the fact that I will lead them to green pastures and beside the still waters.—The Good Shepherd's voice is heard today. He assures us: "Who heareth you heareth Me." The Gospel is Christ's voice. His sheep, the Christians, hear and read this Gospel. In it Christ speaks to them, exhorts them. They know it to be His voice and put their hearts' confidence in it. Gladly, too, they follow Him whither He leads them. They know Him.—*"And I know them,"* Christ says. *"I know them,"* ginosko, says more than, I know of them, I have a knowledge of them, I know who they are, and how many there are of them, I know all their trials, difficulties, etc. All this is true. But this saying, "I know them," goes deeper; it means, I know them *with love and affection*, I know them *as My own*. And to all these He makes this promise: *"I give unto them eternal life."* "I give" is present tense; eternal life is theirs now already. Man, by nature, is spiritually dead. Unbelievers are walking and breathing corpses. Life, true life, they have not. The sheep of Christ, the Christians, of whom Jesus speaks, have life through Him who is Life. He knew them, foreknew them, and this is the reason why they possess life. It was a gift of His. This true life manifests itself: they "hear His voice" believingly; they "follow Him" trustingly. This is proof positive that they possess life, true life. Believers, "born of God" (John 1, 13), possess true life now in time, life of God, life in God, life with God. Temporal death does not destroy this life, but, on the contrary, brings about a full, perfect fruition of this life with God, with Christ, never to cease— *eternal* life. And all sheep that are His receive this gift; not one shall be lost; no one shall be plucked out of His hand. Said Jesus to Martha: "He that believeth in Me, though he were dead, yet shall he live; and whosoever liveth and believeth in Me shall never die." (John 11, 25, 26.)

1 John 3, 2: *Beloved, now are we the sons of God, and it doth not yet appear what we shall be; but we know that, when He shall appear, we shall be like Him; for we shall see Him as He is.*

There is a peculiar emphasis upon the word "are" in this text: "Now *are* we the sons of God." The reason thereof becomes evident from the preceding verse. There the statement is made: "We are the sons of God," and the thought is added that to the eyes of the world this great blessedness is not apparent. "The world knoweth us not"; the world looks upon us Christians as being of all men most miserable, and the faith that we profess of being God's own it sneers at as a delusion. But what of it? The *fact* remains: "Now *are* we the sons of God." Our sonship is a reality; great is our present blessed condition, but far greater things are in store for us. This sonship, hidden now, will one day be revealed. *"It is not yet manifest what we shall be."* What great blessedness awaits us even we Christians cannot apprehend. But some things we do know because revealed in Scriptures, and among these is: *"We know that we shall be like Him."* "We know,"—it is not fiction fancy of the mind; we *know*,—here is absolute knowledge. What do we know? One day *"He, Christ, shall appear"* in great glory with all His holy angels and with the trump of God. (1 Thess. 4, 16.) Then all that are in the graves shall come forth; we Christians, the sons of God, will meet the Lord in the air. In the twinkling of an eye we shall be changed. (1 Cor. 15, 51.) Our bodies will be like unto Christ's glorious body. (Phil. 3, 21.) *We know we shall be like Him.* The image of God, lost through the Fall, and renewed according to the beginning in this life, in yonder life will be fully restored. (Ps. 17, 15.) *We shall be like, homoioi, Him.* We do not become gods; we remain "children of God," but children, sons of God, glorified. This *we know* to be true. Why? *"For"*—reason why we know it to be so—*"we shall see Him as He is."* With the eyes of our glorified body we shall see Him, Jesus, Lord, Jehovah, *"as He is"*; we shall see Him as to His essence and as to His properties. All the glory of yonder life St. John compresses into this one clause: *"We shall see Him as He is."* We shall know and see, e. g., the mystery of the Trinity in unity, the mystery of the incarnation of Christ, *et al.* How do we know? "For we shall see Him *as* He is." And His ways, so often past finding out here below, will be manifest to us. Here the questions often occur to us: Why must I go through this suffering? Why did this calamity befall me? But there is no answer. Then, however, we shall know and see, what we here believed, "that all things work together for good to them that love God" (Rom. 8, 28); "for we shall see Him *as He is.*" "Now," says the apostle, 1 Cor. 13, "we see through a glass, darkly, but then face to face. Now I know in part, but then I shall know according as also I am known." In yonder life soul and body will be reunited and live with Christ in eternal joy and glory. And this beatific seeing of Him *"as He is"* will be the acme of heavenly bliss.

Ps. 16, 11: *"In Thy presence is fullness of joy; at Thy right hand there are pleasures forevermore.*

Ps. 16 is a Messianic psalm. (Cf. Acts 2, 25-28; 13, 35-37.) The words of v. 11 are words of the suffering Savior. And the believers in Christ repeat these words after Him, and console themselves therewith. Language is inadequate to express the blessedness awaiting us in yonder life. *"Fullness* of joy," "pleasures *forevermore,"*—such and similar expressions, indicating the abundant quantity and the endless duration of the joys of heaven, must suffice us here below. And when we consider that these joys and pleasures are in God's *"presence,"* "at His right hand," we know that the splendor and glory awaiting us will far surpass all our fondest anticipations, and we confidently say with the Psalmist: "I shall be satisfied when I awake with Thy likeness." (Ps. 17, 15.)

John 17, 24: *Father, I will that they also whom Thou hast given Me be with Me where I am; that they may behold My glory which Thou hast given Me.*

John 17 comprises the high-priestly prayer of Christ. It was uttered

previous to the journey to the Garden of Gethsemane, in the presence
of the eleven disciples, Judas having left the company to carry out his
dark design of betraying his Master. In this intercessory prayer Christ
views His work of redemption as an accomplished fact. "I have finished
the work which Thou gavest Me to do," He says, v. 4. On the basis of
this finished work He prays.

An analysis of the prayer reveals three distinct parts: Christ prays
for Himself (vv. 1-5); for His disciples (vv. 6-19); for all who through
the apostles' word—His Word—shall believe on Him (vv. 20-26).

In v. 26 the intercession reaches its culmination point. *"Father,*
Thou lovedst Me before the foundation of the world," v. 24. Thou art a
"righteous Father" (v. 25); I am Thy beloved Son, and as Thy Son, to
whom Thou hast made promises, I express My just demands: *"Father,
I will,"* thelo, I demand. What is it that He wills? *"That they be with
Me where I am,"* in life eternal. Who are they that are to participate
in this blessedness? *"They whom Thou hast given Me."* "I have mani-
fested Thy name unto the men which Thou gavest Me out of the world.
Thine they were, and Thou gavest them Me; and they have kept Thy
Word" (v. 6). These *"I will that they be with Me where I am"*; they
have received Thy words, "and have known surely that I came out from
Thee; and they have believed that Thou didst send Me" (v. 8). These,
and all these that believe on Me, the entire body of believers, the Holy
Christian Church on earth, with regard to these *"I will* that they be with
Me where I am." In the decree of foreordination Thou hast given them
to Me as the fruit of My labors; Thou hast promised that I "shall see
of the travail of My soul, and shall be satisfied" (Is. 53, 11); Thou hast
said: "Ask of Me, and I shall give Thee the heathen for Thine inheritance" (Ps. 2, 8); and now with regard to these, and *all* these that believe on Me through Thy word, *"I will that they be with Me where I
am,"* and, being with Me, *"that they may behold My glory,* the glory that
belongs to Me, *"which Thou hast given me."* "My glory," My divine
majesty, communicated to My human nature, the fulness of the Godhead
that dwells in Me bodily, and glimpses of which I now and then vouchsafed My disciples to behold (John 1, 14) in My state of humiliation,—
I will *that they shall behold* uninterruptedly, wonderingly, and admir-
ingly.

Being with the Lord (2 Cor. 5, 8), enjoying His presence, beholding
His glory, seeing Him "as He is,"—this is the principal constituent part
of heavenly glory.

But what a consoling "I will" this is! The Christian in death's last
struggle looks up to his Savior in faith, knowing that this "I will" of
the Savior's intercessory prayer embraces him also, and that he, the
servant, will be where the Master is, according to His promise: "Where
I am, there shall also My servant be." (John 12, 26.)

Rom. 8, 18: *I reckon that the sufferings of this present time are not worthy to be compared with the glory which shall be revealed in us.*

In the preceding section Paul had spoken of the afflictions that befall Christians. He had shown the necessity of conformity to Christ in suffering. Christians must undergo the refining process of tribulation. (1 Pet. 1, 6, 7.) "If children, then heirs, heirs of God, and joint-heirs with Christ; if so be that we suffer with Him, that we may be also glorified," so says the apostle v. 17. Christians should suffer willingly, gladly, with Christ; it is a mark of their Christianity, not a ground for their participation of Christ's glory. But it is a hard lesson to learn; hence Christians need encouragement, consolation, under the cross. The passage before us is one for cross-bearers.

"*I reckon,*" *logidzomai,* I conclude, says Paul. He has made calculations, has weighed certain things in the balance, and now renders his judgment. He has placed "*the sufferings of this present time*" on the one scale, and on the other "*the glory which shall be revealed in us,*" and his verdict is: no comparison possible between the two. And Paul, let us remember, knows by experience whereof he speaks. (Read 2 Cor. 11, 16 ff.) Christians must suffer; true, that is the *via dolorosa* along which they must wander. Like Master, like subject. "If any man will come after Me, let him deny himself, and take up his cross, and follow Me." (Matt. 16, 24.) But though they are "*sufferings*" that smart and burn, they are but temporary, sufferings "*of this present time.*" *Kairos* is a fixed time, or season, and but of short duration; hence the sufferings *of this time* are comparatively insignificant, they last but for a season. That is one consolation. (1 Pet. 1, 6.) But the principal consolation is this: "*the glory to be revealed in us,*" which is certain and near, is eternal. Set over against the coming glory, the sufferings of this time, this short life, dwindle into insignificance. The sufferings of this present time are "*not worthy of,*" *ouk axia,* are not of like weight with, the coming glory, are not weighty in comparison with the glory to be revealed. "As the glory so outweighs the suffering, the idea of merit, whether of condignity or of congruity, is of necessity excluded. It is altogether foreign to the context. For it is not the ground on which eternal life is bestowed, but the greatness of the glory that the saints are to inherit, which the apostle designs to illustrate." *(Hodge.)*

This glory is ours now already by faith; as yet it is hidden (1 John 3, 2); but one day, the last day, it shall be *revealed in us;* we Christians shall be glorified with Christ. *Sursum corda!*

John 3, 16: *For God so loved the world that He gave His only-begotten Son, that whosoever believeth in Him should not perish, but have everlasting life.*

This text has been fitly called "the Gospel in a nutshell." It is needless to give its setting. Everybody knows that these words were spoken by Christ to Nicodemus, who needed instruction on the way to life.

Houtos gar egapesen ho theos ton kosmon—"*For God so loved the world,*" the original Greek reads, throwing emphasis on every word, and thus manifesting the profundity of God's love to the world. *Houtos*— So greatly, so deeply, so intensely God loved. The fact that God at all loved the world is *remarkable*. This thought is brought out by the position of the verb "loved," it being placed before the subject: so loved God. Remarkable, indeed, this love; for what is the object of God's love? "So loved God *the world*," *ton kosmon*, i. e., fallen, sinful mankind. What a contrast! God and the world! The holy God loved this unholy world! Love longs for union and communion with the object of its love. God loved the world! He hates sin, but He loves the sinner. This world, sinful mankind, had rebelled and deserved to die, "to perish." (John 6, 33.) But God willed not its death. "*Not perish, but have everlasting life*"—this was and is His earnest, sincere, gracious will towards the rebelling world. To carry it out, the world must be redeemed from sin, and so "*He gave His only-begotten Son*" into suffering and death. The Son "tasted death for every man" (Hebr. 2, 9); He "died for all" (2 Cor. 5, 15); "He is the propitiation for the sins of the whole world" (1 John 2, 2). Thus God manifested His love towards the world, and the fact that it was His *only-begotten* Son (John 1, 14) shows the depth of the love of God still more. This was a free and unmerited gift; nothing impelled God to do it but His great love. Sin being atoned for, God's love and justice could be reconciled. God's justice demanded: "The world" must "perish"; His love said: The world shall have "everlasting life," and so He gave His Son. Now there is a way of escape from perdition. Which? "*Whosoever believeth* in Him shall have everlasting life."

John 3, 36: *He that believeth on the Son hath everlasting life; and he that believeth not the Son shall not see life, but the wrath of God abideth on him.*

"*The wrath of God abideth on him*" that believeth not the Son. Man, as he is by nature, is under the wrath of God (Eph. 2, 3), and this wrath *abideth*, continues to remain, on him so long as he is without Christ. Oh, miserable condition of him who believeth not the Son! There is but one way of escaping this wrath, but one way of obtaining everlasting life,—by believing the Son. This truth, all-important, is set forth both positively and negatively.

Now, what does "*to believe on the Son*" say and imply? It implies that you are unable to appease God, that so far as you are concerned the wrath of God for sin must abide on you forever; it furthermore implies that the Son has effected a removal of God's wrath, has brought about a reconciliation with God for man, so that now there is an open sesame to everlasting life; to believe on the Son says that you rest your heart's confidence in Him, on what He has done for you, as upon an impregnable rock, where you are safe from the wrath of God. To believe on the Son says that your faith has a firm foundation to stand. on, forgiveness of sin is yours; and where there is forgiveness of sin, there is life everlasting; and of this life eternal you *now* already have a foretaste, for "he that believeth on the Son *hath* everlasting life," the full fruition thereof to come in the life hereafter.

The passage before us says emphatically: There is salvation in one name, one name, and one alone—the Son, Jesus, the Savior.

The second part of the text enforces the truth of the first. "*He that believeth not the Son*," i. e., he that does not believe what the Son says, what He teaches in reference to His redemptive work, "*shall not see life.*" No other faith can save. One may, for instance, loudly proclaim that Christ is the Great Teacher, or that He is the highest moral example to follow, etc.,—all such faith cannot save. But one faith saves, faith in Christ, the Savior from sin. Where this faith is wanting, man is under God's wrath, "*the wrath of God abideth on him.*" (Eph. 2, 3.)

Matt. 24, 13: *But he that shall endure unto the end, the same shall be saved.*

Christ had spoken of the terrible dangers threatening the Christians in the last times. Among other things He had told His disciples of severe persecutions that were to come upon them because of their faith in Him; of the rise of false prophets disseminating soul-destroying errors; of the multiplication of iniquity and the waxing cold of the love of many in consequence thereof. Hereto He annexes the solemn warning: "*But he that shall endure unto the end, the same shall be saved.*" "*The same,*" *houtos,* reverts to the pronoun "he" of the main clause, stressing the truth that *he, and he only, and no other,* shall be saved. Steadfastness in faith *unto the end* is inculcated in the text. Similar exhortations abound in the Scriptures, *e. g.,* Rev. 2, 10: "Be thou faithful *unto death,* and I will give thee a crown of life."

What did it avail Lot's wife to leave Sodom? She looked back, and was turned into a pillar of salt. It availed Judas nothing to have been at one time a disciple of the Lord. He did not watch and pray, avarice took possession of his heart, he betrayed his Master, and "went to his place." Demas, an associate of Paul, became a backslider. Paul mournfully writes of him: "Demas hath forsaken me, having loved this present world."—From such fate preserve us, heavenly Father!

Per contra. Paul at the end of his life exultingly exclaims: "I have fought a good fight; I have finished my course, I have kept the faith." Stephen, the martyr, endured to the end, dying, amidst a hail of stones, with the prayer on his lips: "Lord Jesus, receive my spirit."

Let us pray: Heavenly Father, grant that we may serve Thee with steadfast faith, and continue in the confession of Thy name *unto our end,* through Jesus Christ, Thy beloved Son, our Lord. Amen.

Eph. 1,3-6: *Blessed be the God and Father of our Lord Jesus Christ, who hath blessed us with all spiritual blessings in heavenly places in Christ: according as He hath chosen us in Him before the foundation of the world, that we should be holy and without blame before Him in love: having predestinated us unto the adoption of children by Jesus Christ to Himself, according to the good pleasure of His will, to the praise of the glory of His grace, wherein He hath made us accepted in the Beloved.*

Eph. 1, 3-6 and Rom. 8, 28-30 are universally recognized as the principal seats of the doctrine of Election. They are placed here at the conclusion of the Third Article to teach the comforting truth that a believer can and should be sure of his final salvation.

Let us briefly analyze Eph. 1, 3-6. We have, 1. An *exhortation* to praise God: "Blessed be the God and Father of our Lord Jesus Christ"; 2. the *reason* therefor: "who hath blessed us with all spiritual blessings in heavenly places in Christ"; 3. the *source* of these blessings —election: "according as He hath chosen us in Him before the foundation of the world"; 4. the *purpose* and *aim* of election: "that we should be holy and without blame before Him in love: having predestinated us unto the adoption of children by Jesus Christ to Himself"; 5. the *motive* of election: "according to the good pleasure of His will, to the praise of the glory of His grace."

Now we are ready for a more detailed explanation of the text. *"Blessed be the God and Father of our Lord Jesus Christ."* At first sight the word "blessed" in this connection: "Blessed be God" may seem peculiar to English readers; but familiarity with New Testament diction teaches them to interpret it by "praised." This is correct. The Greek word *eulogein*, with God as its object, means: to praise God. So we render the phrase: *"Praised be God."* In what respect God is to be praised is indicated by the addition: Praised be "the God *and Father of our Lord Jesus Christ."* God, as the *Father* of our Lord Jesus Christ, is the God who has sent His Son into the world for our salvation. The God who did this, this *gracious* God, is to be praised. Paul addresses these words to Christians, who joyously confess: *"I believe that Jesus Christ,* true God, begotten of the Father from eternity, and also true man, born of the Virgin Mary, *is my Lord,* who has redeemed me," etc. By faith in Him, the Redeemer, He has become *"our Lord Jesus Christ,"* and God has become our Father. Paul praises God for the riches of His grace; not only he, however, is to do this, but all the Ephesian Christians, as is clearly indicated by the use of the pronouns "us" and "we" going through the whole paragraph, and with the Ephesian Christians all believers everywhere should unite in praising God.—The reason why we should praise God, the apostle puts thus: "Praised be the God and Father of our Lord Jesus Christ, *who hath blessed us with all spiritual blessings in heavenly places in Christ."*

Which are such "spiritual blessings"? If we run our eye along the following context, we immediately perceive that amongst them are: "the adoption of children," "the redemption through His (Christ's) blood, the forgiveness of sins," *et al.* Now, in time, we Christians possess *"all spiritual blessings."* Our present blissful state of faith is thus briefly outlined. And to show us whence these "spiritual blessings" were bestowed the apostle says: they are "spiritual blessings *in heavenly places," i. e., in what is heavenly:* not from the earth did they come, but from heaven. And these spiritual blessings—*all* of them are given us *in Christ.* By Him they were merited; by Him they were mediated (vv. 6.13.20, *et al.*). No spiritual blessings without Christ! No praise of God for gracious gifts possible without Christ!

Having thus stated the reason that should impel us to unite with him in eulogy of God's grace, the apostle traces these spiritual blessings to their source and begins to enumerate them. "Praised be God— who blessed us—in Christ, *according (kathos) as He hath chosen us in Him (in Christ) before the foundation of the world."* "He *hath blessed us* with all spiritual blessings *in Christ*—these we possess now, here in time—*according as He hath chosen us in Christ* before the foundation of the world." The choice in Christ *precedes* the blessings in Christ. The choice in Christ dates back to *all eternity;* the blessings in Christ we receive *in time.* Clearly, the nexus of these two statements is this: Since God has chosen us in Christ before the foundation of the world, we now are blessed with all spiritual blessings. The former is the cause; the latter the effect. This decree of God, His eternal election, has been manifest in us in the very blessings we now enjoy. Now as to the statement itself: "He hath chosen us in Him," *i. e.,* in Christ. "He hath chosen," *exelexato,* from *eklegomai,* in the medial form, means: *to single out for one's self, to choose to make one's own;* and the prefix *ex, ek,* indicates the choosing of some objects *from,* or *out of,* a number; it refers to the *massa perdita* out of *(ex)* which the elect have been taken. The object of the verb "chosen" is "us." Paul speaks of himself and the Ephesian Christians when he says· "He hath chosen *us."* These same people he had designated in v. 1 as "the saints which are at Ephesus," the faithful "in Christ Jesus." These Christians are to consider themselves the chosen of God: "He hath chosen *us."*—As he had just said: "He hath *blessed us in Christ,"* so now he says: "He hath *chosen us in Christ."* Thus it is patent that before the foundation of the world, the decree of redemption was prior to the decree of election, for the decree of election is *based* on the decree of redemption: "He hath *chosen* us *in Christ!"* Election is founded on Christ, the foreordained Redeemer of the world. Hence it is an election of *grace,* as the apostle subsequently states, and as we read *expressis verbis* in Rom. 11, 5.

Says Dr. Graebner (Theol. Quart., Vol. V, p. 31): "This, then, was the order of the divine decrees of redemp-

tion and of predestination. Having foreseen the fall of
man, which He had not purposed and decreed, God foreordained Christ before the foundation of the world, 1 Pet. 1,
20; Acts 2, 23; 4, 28, to be the Redeemer of the fallen race.
Then, in Christ, the Prophet, Priest, and King, in consideration of His ordained work for man's salvation, and in every
way determined by Christ, God furthermore, also *pro kata-
boles kosmou*, chose unto Himself by another eternal decree, an election of grace in Christ Jesus, all those who in
time, as a chosen generation, a royal priesthood, a holy
nation, a peculiar people, show forth the praises of Him
who has called them out of darkness unto His marvelous
light. (1 Pet. 2, 9.) It is a perversion of this order and
of the nature of these decrees when Calvinists teach an absolute decree of election, not in every way or any way
determined by Christ, and a subsequent decree of redemption conceived as a measure for the execution of the decree
of election and restricted to the elect. In this as in other
points of doctrine the difference between Calvinism and
Lutheranism is fundamental. They differ in their material
principles. In Calvinism the cardinal and ruling doctrine,
the doctrine which forms the base of all other doctrines,
the central doctrine from which all other doctrines radiate,
and to, which they all converge, is the doctrine of the sovereign majesty of God. In Lutheran theology, the theology
of St. Paul and all the Scriptures, the center is Christ,
our Righteousness, to whom all the prophets give witness,
that through His name, whosoever believeth in Him, shall
receive remission of sins. (Acts 10, 43.)

　　"On the other hand, Lutheran theology with St. Paul
also excludes all manner of synergism. While its *Soli Deo
Gloria!* is not chiefly and primarily a praise of the sovereign majesty of God, but a praise of God's grace in
Christ Jesus, and its *Sola gratia* is nowhere a grace of God
without Christ, it also emphasizes the *Soli* and *Sola*, and
rejects everything which would in any way or measure
make man a determining factor in his salvation. This applies also to the doctrine of election and predestination.
It was not our holiness or anything in our conduct which
determined God in His election of grace. The nexus of
cause and effect is not such as to place the cause in us and
the effect in God, but the reverse."

　　The text proceeds: "He hath chosen us in Him before the foundation of the world, *that we should be holy and without blame before
Him.*" The "that" clause, in Greek, the infinitive: *einai hemas hagious ktl.*, states the purpose for which God has chosen us. When God
in eternity chose us to be His own, He did it with the purpose that
by virtue of this choice, this election, we, in time, "should be holy
and blameless before Him." Our "being holy and blameless before
Him" is an outflow of election. In time God wrought faith in our
hearts through the Gospel, faith in Christ. By faith in Christ we are
"holy and blameless before Him." (Eph. 5, 26.27.) Thus God's election
in eternity was realized in time.

　　There is a question about the phrase "in love." Does it go with

v. 4, or does it modify the verb "predestinated" in v. 5, so as to make it read: *"in love having predestinated us unto the adoption of children by Jesus Christ"?* Dr. Graebner answers the question thus: "The phrase, *en agape,* is, in the English Bible, connected with the preceding verse. This connection is based upon the supposition that the holiness and blamelessness spoken of in v. 4 is a Christian's walk in newness of live, sanctification, the fruit of faith which worketh by love. (Gal. 5, 6.) Remembering, however, that the keynote of the entire context is a eulogy of the goodness of God, who has blessed us with all manner of spiritual blessing, and that the words, *hagious kai amomous katenopion autou,* would seem to refer to the holiness and blamelessness of justification rather than to sanctification, the mention of *our* love would seem to introduce a notion foreign to, and out of keeping with, the context. For the same reasons, the connection of *en agape* with *proorisas* seems in every way preferable. Thus referred, the love here mentioned is the love of God, that everlasting love wherewith He from eternity longed for union and communion with the objects of His holy desire, and which prompted Him to choose them unto Himself, and to predestinate them to eternal bliss and glory."

"He hath chosen us in Him before the foundation of the world, that we should be holy and without blame before Him, in love having predestinated us *unto, eis,* the adoption of children by Jesus Christ to Himself." That says that at the same time when God *chose us,* He also *predestinated* us, *proorisas hemas,* determined beforehand, predestined our status—we should become His children. How? *"By Jesus Christ."* Plainly, faith in Christ is an outflow of election. For "we are all *children* of God *by faith* in Christ Jesus." (Gal. 3, 26; 4,4.5.) To maintain that we are elected in view of faith, *intuitu fidei,* manifestly militates against this *clara Scriptura:* God "predestinated us *unto the adoption* of children by Jesus Christ." Since we are predestinated unto the *adoption of children,* we are *eo ipso* predestinated to faith. Clear as this thought is in itself, it becomes still more evident by the addition: *"unto Himself,"* which shows the close relation in which we stand to Him: we are His children. In the decree of election faith was *included,* not presupposed. We believe because we are elected.

What moved God to choose us in Christ, and to predestinate us unto the adoption of children? The apostle answers: He did it *"according to, kata, the good pleasure of His will";* kata, according to, expresses the motive that prompted the act. What moved God to do as He did? *"His will."* Why did He so will it? Because it was His *good pleasure.* Was there anything in man that God foresaw, and that would make Him inclined to act as He did? No, Paul knows nothing thereof. He did it "according to the good pleasure of His will."

And so the decree of election and predestination redounds *to the praise of the glory of His grace,"* eis epainon doxes tes charitos autou.

An emphatic statement, indeed! Separating the thought into its elements so as to show the emphasis, we might say: it all redounds "to the praise of His grace."—Thus God's *love* to us, which in reference to *sinners* manifests itself as *grace*, would already be highly glorified, but in order to emphasize this idea of grace still more, the apostle says: "to the praise of the *glory* of His grace." It is a glorious grace; but how weak is the thought: "to the praise of His *glorious* grace" when contrasted with the literal rendering of the text: "to the praise of *the glory* of His grace"! The greatness, the richness, of this grace is thus prominently brought to the fore. "He hath chosen us in Christ" —that is grace; "He hath predestinated us unto the adoption of children by Jesus Christ"—that is grace; ."He hath blessed us with all spiritual blessings in Christ"—that is grace. The aim of election is to magnify and glorify the riches of His grace toward us miserable sinners, who deserved nothing but punishment.

The apostle proceeds to show the execution of this gracious decree of eternity in time. He continues: "to the praise of the glory of His grace, *wherein He hath made us accepted in the Beloved,*" i. e., in Christ. (Cf. context; also Col. 1, 13; Matt. 3, 17; John 17, 23-26, *et al.*) In the fulness of time God sent forth His Son to redeem mankind. And how great is God's love for us, since He gave His *"Beloved"* into death for us, that we might *be made accepted in Him,* that God might be able to grant us grace! In the course of man's life the Gospel of salvation is preached to him, and God carries out His eternal decree of mercy regarding the sinner. We, whom God has called from darkness to light, and thus *"made* accepted in Christ," shall thereby know that God had from eternity embraced us in His eternal decree of election, and that "He that began the good work in us will also fulfill it unto the day of Jesus Christ." We, who with the Ephesians are "blessed with all spiritual blessings in Christ," are thereby to know and confidently to believe that we are numbered among the elect. This is the only way according to the Scriptures by which we can ascertain this blessed truth. (1 Thess. 1, 4 ff.; 2 Thess. 2, 13 ff.; Rom. 8,28 ff.)

We tabulate some of the important truths gained from the passage.

1. There is a decree of election and predestination unto salvation: "He hath chosen us in Him before the foundation of the world."

2. This decree embraces certain persons: *exelexato*—"He hath chosen out of to Himself." An election of *all* is a contradiction in itself. "He hath chosen *us.*"

3. There are but two causes of election: 1. *God's grace;* His "good pleasure"; "to the praise of the glory of His grace." 2. *Christ's merit:* "He hath chosen us *in Him*"; "He hath made us accepted in the *Beloved.*"

4. Logically considered, the decree of redemption is prior to the **decree** of election: "He hath chosen us *in Christ.*"

5. In the decree of election and predestination the *faith* of the elect is not presupposed, but it is *included:* "He predestinated us *unto, eis,* the adoption of children by Jesus Christ." Faith flows out of election as its source.—In fact, all spiritual blessings bestowed upon the Christians in time flow out of their election in eternity as their cause. This is evident from the entire text and its context: He "hath blessed us with all spiritual blessings in heavenly places in Christ— *according as* He hath chosen us in Him."

6. All Christians are to consider themselves the elect of God. From the fact that the Ephesian Christians had been blessed in time with all spiritual blessings, they should know: God has chosen you before the foundation of the world. So we. We possess the *result;* we know the *cause.*

7. The blessings of the eternal election rest on an immovable foundation: God's grace in Christ. What great *comfort* for the Christians! This doctrine—which is Gospel throughout—is one for which Christians should feel impelled to unite with the apostle in thanksgiving: "*Praised* be God and the Father of our Lord Jesus Christ," etc.

※   ※   ※

Is there a predestination unto death? No. This *sedes doctrinae* of election knows nothing thereof, neither does any other passage of Scripture teach it. Calvin's "*horribile decretum,*" thank God, has no foundation in Scripture. It is a figment of reason

Is synergism Scriptural, according to which God, foreseeing man's faith, man's good conduct towards grace, elected him? No. This text knows nothing thereof, neither do other texts treating of this matter. On the contrary, this text teaches that faith is an outflow of election. Because we are elected, we believe. (Cf. 2 Tim. 1, 9; John 15, 16; Rom. 8, 28-30.)

Are there mysteries in this doctrine? Yes. What are we to do in view of them? We are to take our reason captive under the obedience of Christ, and wait for a solution of the mysteries in the school of theology up above. Meanwhile, while wandering in this vale of tears, we are to offer God thanks for His great mercy toward us, saying: "Praised be the God and Father of our Lord Jesus Christ," etc.

Rom. 8, 28-30: *And we know that all things work together for good to them that love God, to them who are called according to His purpose. For whom He did foreknow, He also did predestinate to be conformed to the image of His Son, that He might be the First-born among many brethren. Moreover, whom He did predestinate, them He also called: and whom He called, them He also justified: and whom He justified, them He also glorified.*

The purpose of St. Paul in the second half of chapter 8 is to comfort the Christians under the cross, and to assure them of their future glory. In this environment we find vv. 28-30.

In v. 28 the comforting assurance is made: "We know that all things work together for good to them that love God"; 28b adduces the reason for the certainty of this statement: they that love God "are the called according to purpose." In v. 29 the phrase "called according to purpose" is resumed and explained, and v. 30 describes the realization of this eternal purpose: it is carried out in time, and again reaches into eternity. In one mighty sweep past eternity is linked with future eternity. The entire paragraph carries out the topic: "All things must work together for good to them that love God."

"We *know*," *oidamen*. No guesswork this, no loose conjecture, but knowledge, absolute knowledge, of a comforting truth. "*We* know" —I, Paul, know and the Christians know or should know, and believe, "*that all things*," also "the sufferings of this present time," v. 18, *all* trials and sorrows, which seem so hard to bear, "*work together*," co-operate, mutually contribute, "*for good*"; they are no hurt, no harm, but a blessing; they do not and cannot hinder the attainment of salvation, but rather are *viae regni*. They work for good "*to them that love God*," *i. e.*, to the true Christians, for of these text and context speak. (Cf. Eph. 6, 24; 1 Cor. 2, 9.) Truly, this is rich consolation under the cross. We Christians love God; He is our Father by faith in Christ Jesus; we are His true children. All that befalls us, cross, affliction, etc., comes from the hand of the loving Father; all is under His guidance and control, and must work together for good.

Is this consoling assurance well founded? Indeed, yes. The apostle asserts this by way of an appositive clause: "*to them who are the called according to purpose*." "They that love God" are "*the called*." God called them "from darkness to His marvelous light." (Cf. 1 Pet. 2, 9.) It is an effectual call Paul speaks of, as the whole tenor of the paragraph manifests. And this call has for its goal—eternal glory. "God hath called us unto His *eternal glory* by *Jesus Christ*." (1 Pet. 5, 9.) Of this glory our text, too, speaks, as the sequel will show. (Cf. 2 Thess. 2, 14.) God's call will not fail. When God called us, He said: Eternal glory is yours. Now cross, sorrows, etc.,—this is the thought expressed by the apostle,—cannot hinder, but "must work for good" to attain the end. Paul's consolation has a firm foundation: God's call. But still firmer, as it were, his declaration is made by saying: We are "the called *according to purpose*," *kata prothesin*. God's *prothesis*, purpose, is simply what the English word says. God *purposed* to do something. What He purposed to do becomes evident from the text. Here He speaks of "the called according to purpose." He *purposed to call* them. So the call was not due to any merits on their part, but to God's *purpose*. In 2 Tim. 1, 9 the term *purpose* is linked with the word *grace:* "God called us according to His *own purpose and grace*." "They who love God" are "the called." The call was owing to God's *purpose*, and this was *grace;* it was a gracious purpose.

In our text all stress is placed on the word *purpose*, on the fact that the Christians are—to imitate the original diction somewhat— "*according to purpose the called.*" This purpose is a *prothesis ton aionon*, an *eternal purpose* (Eph. 3, 11); a *prothesis * * * pro chronon aionion*, a purpose *before the world began* (2 Tim. 1, 9). So God's *purpose* dates back into eternity (Eph. 1, 9); the *call* is executed in time. When God *called* them in time, this was no child's play, but a realization of what He had *purposed* to do in eternity. The call was a result, an effect, of this eternal purpose. And this truth, that we are called according to His purpose, is a powerful reason why "all things work together for good" to the Christians.

"They that love God," "the called according to the purpose"— these clauses are now explained. "*For whom He did foreknow* He also did predestinate." To understand "foreknow" in its primary sense, "to know beforehand," is too trivial to require an extended refutation. God is omniscient; He knows all mankind beforehand; hence, according to this sense of the word, *all* men would be predestinated to eternal life, which, of course, is not true. What, then, does the clause "whom He did *foreknow*" mean? Does it mean: whom God did *foreknow would believe?* Impossible! Plainly that would be an addition to the words of Scripture, an interpolation, an alteration of the text. Instead of reading: "*whom* He did foreknow," the text would be made to say: "whose *belief, faith,* He did foreknow." The object of the verb foreknow would be changed from "whom" to "faith," a word not in the text. Instead of foreknowing *certain people, hous*—"*whom,*" as the text plainly says, this interpolation would make the text speak of foreknowing the *faith* of these people. Such procedure does not *explain* the text, but imports a *foreign thought* into it; it is not *exegesis*, but a plain case of *eisegesis*. Besides, this interpolation, that God foreknew those who "*would believe,*" destroys the whole tenor of the text, which is *consolation* for the suffering Christians, and it moreover militates against the very words preceding this clause, *viz.*, "who are the called *according to* His *purpose.*" So this cannot be the sense. What, then, do the words "for whom He did foreknow" say? It is an irrefutable fact that the verb "foreknow," *proginoskein*, according to the *usus loquendi* of Scripture, when used of God, is a synonym for *foreordain, preordain, elect*. It is not within the sphere of this commentary to enter into a disquisition of all the pertinent passages to establish this Biblical usage. That has been done time and again in our various periodicals during the last thirty years. For our purpose it may suffice to adduce just one passage, the cogency of which will be immediately seen also by readers of the English version of the Bible only. Peter says: "Christ verily *was foreordained* before the foundation of the world, but was *manifest* in these last times for you" (1, 20). Now, if we consult the Greek text, we shall find that the word translated "*foreordained*" is *proginoskein*, the very same word that is employed in our passage, (Rom. 8, 29), and is translated here and elsewhere by *foreknow.* Why, then, we ask, did not the translators of our English Bible so render the verb in 1 Pet. 1,20? Why does the passage not read: "Christ verily *was foreknown* before the foundation of the world, but *was manifest* in these last times for you"? Because such rendition would not do justice to this powerful and plain text. Two acts of God are described, one taking place "before the foundation of the world,"—that act was to *"foreknow," i. e.,* to *foreordain,"* Christ as the Redeemer of the world; the other act, the execution of this eternal decree, taking place "in these last times," was to *manifest* Christ as the Redeemer. This is the thought the sharp antithesis of the two Greek verbs—*proegnosmenou*—was foreordained; *fanerothentos*—was manifest—loudly demands. To read the text: "Christ verily was *foreknown* before the foundation of the world" and to understand "foreknow" in its primary sense: God *"knew beforehand,* before the foundation of the world," that Christ would be the Redeemer of the world, and therefore manifested Him as such, says next to nothing. Only foreordination, predestination, and manifestation, not a mere mental knowing beforehand and manifestation, does justice to the two verbs that are so strongly set over against each other. So the translators of our English version, knowing the *usus loquendi* of *proginosko,* to *foreordain, preordain, elect,* observing furthermore the strong contrast between the two Geek verbs: *proegnosmenou* and *fanerothentos,* the one, as afore said, describing a decree of God in eternity, the other telling of the realization of that decree in time, rendered the passage admirably thus: "Christ, who verily *was foreordained* before the foundation of the world but *was manifest* in these last times for you." Christ was *foreordained, preordained* as the Redeemer from all eternity; in time this decree was carried out: He was *manifested* as such. Thus it is evident that the meaning of *foreknow, proginosko,* in this passage, is *foreordain, preordain, choose beforehand* unto Himself. The same holds true of other passages in which this verb *proginoskein* is used of God. (Cf. Acts 2, 23; Rom. 11, 2; Pet. 1, 2.) So also of our passage. The apostle had spoken of those "who love God" as being "the called according to His purpose." The latter phrase he now resumes and explains. "For whom He did *foreknow," foreordain, choose unto Himself,*—and these are "the called *according to purpose,"*—"He also did predestinate." So God from eternity foreordained, chose, certain persons unto Himself to be His own. The text does not give the *reason* why God did this; it simply states the mere *fact that He did so.*

We proceed with the text. These persons whom God *foreknew,* preordained unto Himself, chose for His possession, "He also did *predestinate.*" Both expressions: *proegno,* foreordain, and *proorise,* predestinate, describe one and the same eternal counsel of God, but from different view-points. The former has reference to the individuals that God foreordained, chose unto Himself; the latter looks to the end, the goal, for which they have been elected.

Now, what is the purpose for which God predestined those whom He chose? *"To be conformed to the image of His Son."* That says: In eternity, when God elected those persons of whom the text speaks, He at the same time decreed that once, in spite of the power of Satan and his hellish cohorts, they should bear the image of His Son in everlasting righteousness, innocence, and blessedness. Heavenly glory should be theirs (1 Cor. 15, 49). Their "vile body," the body of humiliation, "shall be changed, transformed, that it may be conformed to the body of His glory" (Phil. 3, 21). That this is the meaning of the text the context proves, for the apostle proceeds: *"that He might be the First-born among many brethren."* In yonder life, in the *status gloriae,* there will be "many brethren," a great family of children of God, and among these Christ, our Brother, will hold the rank of the First-born, the Leader, the Captain of our salvation, who brings many sons to glory (Hebr. 2, 10). That high-priestly prayer will be answered: (John 17, 24) "Father, I will that they also whom Thou hast given Me *be with Me where I am, that they may behold My glory* which Thou hast given Me." From eternity God has foreknown, *i. e.,* chosen us unto Himself to be His own, and predestinated us to eternal glory. This His firm purpose cannot fail. How great is the comfort for suffering Christians contained in this text! The attainment of the goal, eternal glory, is certain. They may rest assured that the sufferings of this present time, indeed, "that *all* things must work together for good."

Thus far the apostle had spoken of God's eternal decree of election. What God has purposed to do in eternity He unfailingly carries out in time. Of this Paul now speaks. *"But whom He did predestinate, them He also called."* God has not only set the goal, eternal glory, He has also provided ways and means for us to reach it. The way to eternal glory leads through the Kingdom of Grace. He sends His messengers into the highways and byways with the glorious Gospel of our salvation. This Gospel, the glad tidings of the free grace of God by faith in Christ Jesus, is "the power of God unto salvation to every one that believeth." God *calls* us through the Gospel, brings us to Christ, to faith in Him, and *justifies* us, declares us righteous in His sight. And He that has begun the good work in us will also perform it (Phil. 1, 6). Of this the apostle is so certain that he speaks of the glorification to come in yonder life as being completed now already, saying: *"and whom He justified, them He also glorified."* And now let hell and Satan rage against us, let afflictions, sorrows, pile themselves up mountain high, let the waves of adversity threaten to overwhelm us, all can harm us none, for "we know that all things work together for our good;" we are Christ's, and no one, yea, nothing, shall pluck us out of His hands.

SOLI DEO GLORIA!

The

Proof Texts of the Catechism

with a

Practical Commentary

By

LOUIS WESSEL, D. D.

Professor at Concordia Theological Seminary
Springfield, Ill.

NOTE.—Since this edition is a photographic reproduction of the original one, which was published in two separate volumes, the pagination is not continuous.
Concordia Publishing House

VOLUME II.

containing the

III, IV, V, and VI Chief Parts

PRINTED IN U. S. A.

PART III.

THE LORD'S PRAYER

OF PRAYER IN GENERAL

What Is Prayer?

Ps. 19, 14. *Let the words of my mouth and the meditation of my heart be acceptable in Thy sight, O Lord, my Strength and my Redeemer.*

This verse forms the conclusion of the psalm. What words did the psalmist's mouth utter? Words composing a noble hymn of praise for the glorious Gospel, interwoven with some petitions, vv. 12.13. These *"words of his mouth"* are but an expression of *"the meditation of his heart."* God is worshipped by hymns of praise, thanksgiving, and by petitions. This is prayer. The "words of the mouth," however, to be a true prayer, must come from the heart, must be a "meditation of the heart," otherwise the "words of the mouth" are but lip-service. —Prayer need not always be formulated in words, it may be simply "a meditation of the heart." God understands our thoughts afar off.

In this act of worship—prayer—we Christians must remember that, coming from sinful beings, it is not perfect, faultless *per se.* "Let the words (the meditation) be acceptable in Thy sight," says the psalmist. The pious Israelites, when offering sacrifices to God, prayed: "Let them meet with favor in Thy sight"; and so pious Christians, when offering the sacrifices of their hearts and lips, pray: "Let them be acceptable in Thy sight." And the Old Testament believer was assured that his sacrifices were acceptable since they were offered to Him who is *Lord, i. e., Jehovah,* the covenant God, who looked with favor upon the pious Israelites and their sacrifices for the Messiah's sake. To the same Lord, Jehovah, the New Testament believers direct the meditations of their hearts, and they, too, know that for the Redeemer's sake they are graciously heard. Only in His name dare we approach Jehovah's throne in hymns of praise or in prayers of supplication; but in His, our Advocate's, name they are acceptable and heard.

Ps. 10, 17. *Lord, Thou hast heard the desire of the humble: Thou wilt prepare their heart, Thou wilt cause Thine ear to hear.*

The topic of this psalm we find in verses 1 and 2: "Why standest Thou afar off, O Lord? Why hidest Thou Thyself in times of trouble? The wicked in his pride doth persecute the poor: let them be taken in the devices that they have imagined."—The character and conduct of the wicked, the "times of trouble" caused by the "wicked," the enemies of the afflicted pious Israelites, are, as it were, photographed from life vv. 3-11. Next follows a prayer of deliverance, ending with a strong consolation.

The believing Israelites do not and cannot cry in vain. It is to the *"Lord,"* i. e., *Jehovah,* their Helper, to whom they have lifted up their voice. *"Thou hast heard"*—this is their heart's confidence, and so their troubled soul is calmed; the peace of God that passeth all understanding quiets their hearts. And though their prayer be but a *"desire,"* a longing, an unspoken thought, of the soul, *"the humble,"* the meek, the faithful, know: *"Jehovah, Thou hast heard."*—What great comfort for believers: God hears even the *desires* of our heart! *"Thou wilt prepare,"* establish, *"their heart,"* make it firm, Ps. 51, 12, in the assurance that *"Thou hast heard,"* either by answering their prayer, or by a firm, unwavering reliance of the heart upon the gracious promises of Thy word, Rom. 8, 26; I John 3, 19-22, *"that Thou wilt cause Thine ear to hear,"* and that Thou carest for them that cast their cares upon Thee. I Pet. 5, 7.

Is. 65, 24. *And it shall come to pass that, before they call, I will answer; and while they are yet speaking, I will hear.*

"Before they call, I will answer." How consolatory this truth! The heavenly Father often anticipates the prayers of His children. The Christians frequently receive blessings, help, comfort, for which they have not asked. Our Father knows our every need long before we realize it, and He is willing to meet it. When the three women, Mary Magdalene, Mary, the mother of James, and Salome, went to the grave of our Savior on that Easter morning to anoint the body of Him whom they loved, they had forgotten all about the great stone that was to guard the sepulcher. On their journey thither this thought of a sudden comes to them: "Who shall roll us away the stone from the door of the sepulcher?" But "when they looked, they saw that the stone was rolled away." So it is in our lives. Obstacles in our path, dangers that encompass us, are removed oftentimes ere we are aware of them.— Words full of cheer, these: *"Before they call, I will answer."* How many a blessing we now enjoy we should lack if every one were conditioned upon a knowledge of the need thereof, and our actual petition therefor!—Again: *"While they are yet speaking,"* before the prayer has been fully uttered, *"I will hear."* (Ex. 14, 15.)—God's readiness to hear prayer, which this text twice so emphatically asserts, should urge His children cheerfully to lay their wants and necessities before their dear Father in childlike faith with the full assurance that He "will answer," that He "will hear."

Matt. 6, 7. *When ye pray, use not vain repetitions, as the heathen do; for they think that they shall be heard for their much speaking.*

"Vain repetitions" is the translation of the Greek word, *battologesete*, "a word probably without any further derivation than an imitation of the sounds uttered by stammerers, who repeat their words often without meaning." (Alford). Luther translated it felicitously with "viel Plappern," and Tyndale rendered it "babble not much," both excellent translations. The transliterated word battology—a needless repetition of words—has found a place in our English speech.

The heathen, not knowing the true God, made of prayer an *opus operatum*. The greater the *opus*, the greater the reward; the longer the prayer, the more certain the answer. They employed battology, "vain repetitions," *i. e.*, repeating the same or similar words again and again for the purpose of lengthening prayer. Length, verbosity, *"much speaking,"* was, according to their notion, an essential, a meritorious requisite of prayer. On account of their *"much speaking,"* this laborious work, this mouth-work, they expected to be heard. And oh, how this battology appeals to the people of poor spiritual discernment! This or that revivalist prays a long prayer, and on his knees at that; *ergo*, no matter as to its contents, it is a "powerful" prayer and an unassailable evidence of his being highly spiritual. In Colonial times preachers often prayed for one whole hour, measured by the hour-glass. We are told that on one occasion, when a young minister could not offer a long prayer, an older, more experienced brother got down upon his knees and asked the Lord, "Lord, open Thou this dumb dog's mouth,"— "After a Mohammedan funeral, in some countries, devout men assemble and repeat, *Allah el Allah*, 'God is God,' three thousand times. A traveler in Persia tells of a man who prayed so loud and so long that he lost his voice, and then groaned out, in voiceless accents, the name of God fifty times,"—(Broadus.)—The priests of Baal continued from morning until noon to cry: "O Baal, hear us!" 1 Kings, 18, 26.— Roman Catholics practice battology, "vain repetitions," by their frequent repititions of the *Ave Maria* (Hail, Mary), and the *Pater Noster* (Our Father), reeled off by means of the beads of the rosary. Thus the very prayer—Pater Noster—our Savior set in contrast to such evil practices is so misused by them. God does not measure prayer with a yard-stick—so many yards of prayers, so much grace.

But just what does the Lord censure in our text? Let us observe that it is not *much praying* that is condemned, but *"much speaking."* This thought is heathenish: that for making *"vain repetitions,"* "for much speaking," for performing this laborious work, for this *opus operatum*, "much babbling," God will reward them.

Is a long prayer *eo ipso* improper? No. Our Lord Himself often spent whole nights in prayer. Luke 6, 12. Is it wrong *eo ipso* to repeat the same words? No. In Gethsemane Jesus "prayed a third time, saying again the same words." Matt. 26, 44.—What, then, is forbidden? The making a certain length a point of observance; "imagining that prayer will be heard, not because it is the genuine expression of the desire of faith, but because it is of such a length, has been such a number of times repeated." (Alford).

But *cave!* Vain repetitions! Who of us has not been guilty of it? Who has not in chapel service, in church, in the family circle, repeated the well-known words of a familiar prayer, such as the greatest of all, the Lord's Prayer, without devotion? Was it not Luther who for this very reason said that the Lord's Prayer is "the greatest martyr?"— Lord, teach us how to pray!

What Shoud Induce Us to Pray?

Ps. 27, 8. *When Thou saidst, Seek ye My face, my heart said unto Thee, Thy face, Lord, will I seek.*

A closer rendering of the text shows that Luther's translation surpasses that of the Authorized Version in that it hits the sense of the original admirably. Luther: "Mein Herz haelt dir vor dein Wort: Ihr sollt mein Antlitz suchen. Darum such ich auch, Herr, dein Antlitz." The order of the Hebrew is: "To Thee hath my heart said (when Thou saidst), 'Seek ye My face;' Thy face, Jehovah, will I seek." The parenthetical clause, "when Thou saidst," is not in the original, but it helps to make the meaning clear.

"Seek the Lord and His strength, seek His face continually"—this was the command given by David to his people, when he set up the ark in the holy Mount of Zion. 1 Chron. 16, 11. The figurative expression, "Seek ye My face," was God's command to come into His presence to get audience with Him, to commune with Him, to pray to Him. Ps. 91, 15. This command, "Seek ye My face," gave David courage to supplicate God in the hour of distress. In times of affliction and despondency, when the Evil One, in order to cast us into deeper gloom and finally into despair, assails us with thougths of our unworthiness to seek God's face in prayer, we should plead this command, "Seek ye My face," in spite of the devil, as our warrant for coming to Him.—This David did. Circumscribed, the text says: Because Thou, Jehovah, who hast made a covenant of grace with Thy people, hast said: "Seek ye My face," therefore, I, David, will overcome all fears and doubts arising in my heart, and make bold to come into Thy presence. Thou hast commanded me to pray to Thee. To Thee I will pray, "Thy face, Jehovah," Thou gracious God, "will I seek."

Matt. 7, 7-8. *Ask, and it shall be given you; seek, and ye shall find; knock, and it shall be opened unto you: for every one that asketh receiveth; and he that seeketh findeth; and to him that knocketh it shall be opened.*

God only can give the gifts we need for body and soul, but He wants to be asked for them in prayer. Knowing how timid we oftentimes are to ask boldly, our Savior takes great pains to encourage us to pray. He condescends to make gracious invitations and precious promises. Such we find our text.

Ask—seek—knock! "Each of these terms presents what we desire of God in a different light. We *ask* for what we *wish;* we *seek* for what we *miss;* we *knock* for that from which we feel ourselves *shut out.* Answering to this threefold representation is the triple assurance of success to our believing prayer. (J. F. and B. Com)—We observe that the promises are here unqualified: "Ask, *and it shall be given you,*" etc. But we must remember the Lord instructs His disciples, Christians. It is, therefore, presumed that they ask aright—in faith, according to God's will. 1 John 5, 14.

Ask—seek—knock! Sometimes, for reasons known to Him only, our Father does not answer our prayer immediately. What are we to do? *Ask—seek—knock!* The fervor of our prayer must grow more and more intense—this is implied by the climax: ask— seek—knock. The woman of Canaan, Matt. 15, 23 ff., understood this art. She was in great distress owing to her daughter's being possessed with a devil. She cries unto the Lord for mercy. He answers her not a word. His disciples intercede for her—without avail. She renews her prayer, "Lord, help me." She is repulsed brusquely: the children's bread must not be cast to a dog such as she is. Her faith is sorely tried. Nothing daunted, she turns the tables on the Lord, as it were, saying: I grant I am a dog, on a dog's right I insist—to eat the crumbs which fall from the Master's table. Jesus is conquered by that importunate asking, seeking, knocking, flowing from faith in His mercy, and he exclaims in wonderment: "O woman, great is thy faith; be it unto thee even as thou wilt." "And her daughter was made whole from that very hour."

> Have we trials and temptations?
> Is there trouble anywhere?
> We should never be discouraged,
> Take it to the Lord in prayer.

Ps. 145, 18, 19. *The Lord is nigh unto all them that call upon Him, to all that call upon Him in truth. He will fulfill the desire of them that fear Him; He also will hear their cry, and will save them.*

What a strong encouragement to prayer this beautiful passage affords! Four times—in climacteric order—the assurance of divine help is made to Christian cross-bearers who cast their care upon the Lord.

The Christians' needs are many. God is their helper; "they call upon Him," they pour out a prayer into His ears. They call upon Him *"in truth,"* i. e., sincerely, with confidence that He will hear; for the *Lord* unto whom they pray is Jehovah, who has made a covenant of grace with them. The Christians who thus call upon the Lord also "fear Him;" they approach the throne of grace not only with confidence, but also with a filial fear, with profound reverence; their prayer, both as to form and contents, moves within the confines of the Word of God. Such are the suppliants; such is the nature of their supplication.—They are to know and firmly to believe: 1. *"The Lord is nigh unto them"* with His gracious presence. 2. *"He will fulfill their desire"* since they pray according to His will. 3. *"He will hear their cry."* The prayer of the children of God in which they lay their needs, their wants and necessities, before Him in childlike faith, assumes the character of a loud cry in the ears of Jehovah. This He cannot and will not overhear. He will answer it. 4. *"He will save them,"* succor them. Though help may sometimes be delayed, come it will. Here is His fourfold promise. Though the answer may not be exactly as we expected it to be, still answer our prayer He will when His time has come, and in a way far superior to our thinking, in a way that is for our good.

Ps. 50, 15. *Call upon Me in the day of trouble: I will deliver thee, and thou shalt glorify Me.*

Daily Christians call upon the Lord. But in the Christians' life there oftentimes dark days, *"days of trouble,"* in which the waves of adversity and calamity rise to such a height as to threaten to engulf them. At such times the devil suggests: Don't pray; it is useless. God has become your enemy; He will not hear you. The devil is a liar. God says: *"Call upon Me* in just such days of trouble." He promises: *"I will deliver thee."* What an incentive to cry unto Him from the depths of our hearts! And when divine help has come, as it surely will come in one form or another, let us not forget to *glorify* His holy name.

"Call upon Me"—this is the divine *command;* "I will deliver thee"—this is the divine *promise;* "thou shalt glorify Me"—this is the Christian's *duty* and *privilege.*

To Whom Shall We Pray.

Matt. 4, 10. *Thou shalt worship the Lord, thy God, and Him only shalt thou serve.*

This passage recalls the temptation of Jesus. The Prince of Peace and "the Prince of the World," John 12, 31, are in battle array. The Savior is tempted to doubt the Word of God, v. 3. Satan is baffled by an "It is written." Next, the Lord is to be tripped into disobedience by a misquoted passage of Scripture. The Tempter's lie is laid bare by another "It is written." Finally, Jesus is to reject the Scripture. By diabolical art "all the kingdoms of the world and the glory of them" are shown the Lord, and the promise is made: "All these things will I give Thee" on this condition: "If Thou wilt fall down and worship me." The Savior immediately recognizes the device of the devil to lure Him from the path of humiliation. With disgust He says: "Get thee hence!" Begone! Now you are showing your true colors. Your name is *Satan*, Adversary; you would thwart my plan, God's plan, for the salvation of sinful man. Worship thee! Such a demand is truly satanical. Worship is due to God only. "*Thou shalt worship the Lord, thy God, and Him only shalt thou serve.*" Get thee hence! Thus the Lord Jesus repels His adversary, fighting as man in man's stead by appealing to the Scriptures, the weapon all Christians should continually use in their spiritual battles. The quotation is from Deut. 6, 13: "Thou shalt fear the Lord, thy God, and serve Him, and shalt swear by His name." The emphasis indicated by text and context in the Hebrew, Deut. 6, 13, is brought out by our Lord's free quotation in introducing the word "only"—"Him *only* shalt thou serve,"—and by substituting the specific word "worship" for the general term "fear." Thus the intent of Deut. 6, 13, that "the Lord," *i. e.*, Jehovah, the true God only is to be worshipped, is made apparent. To Him alone such honor is due.

Ps. 65, 2. *O Thou that hearest prayer, unto Thee shall all flesh come.*

The first strophe of Ps. 65 deals with the great blessings of the man dwelling in God's courts, that approaches Him in prayer. "*O Thou that hearest prayer,*" *i. e.*, it is an attribute of God to hear prayer; He is, if we translate the participle more closely, "the Hearer of prayer." That is God's characteristic. He is willing, always ready, to hear prayer; and only He is able to do so. Hence: "*unto Thee,*" —not to idols, not to Mary nor to the saints, —"*unto Thee* shall *all flesh,*" —all men, not only Israel, but "*all flesh,*" —you and I, and all that are in weariness, necessities, and sorrows,—"*come.*" Only the true God, Father, Son, and Holy Ghost, is able and willing to hear our prayer.

Is. 63, 16. *Doubtless Thou art our Father, though Abraham be ignorant of us, and Israel acknowledge us not. Thou, O Lord, art our Father, our Redeemer; Thy name is from everlasting.*

This passage is part of a most beautiful prayer. Here the reason is given why Jehovah is entreated to look down upon Israel with favor and to manifest His love towards them. "Doubtless," according to the Hebrew, might have been rendered simply by "*for.*" "For Thou art our

Father." The contrast in the text brings out the thought: Thou, Jehovah, art our *true* Father. Abraham and Israel, *i. e.*, Jacob, are
fathers, it is true, and great men they were, great was their authority,
great is the honor to be descended from them; but still they were but
men. "Abraham is ignorant of us" now; he is dead; Jacob, Israel, acknowledges us not, *i. e.*, he has no knowledge of us, knows us not; he,
too, is dead. Both are incapable of hearing prayer, much less, of answering it. *"Thou, O Lord, Jehovah, art our Father."* Jehovah is Thy
covenant name. In the Messiah, the Redeemer, Thou hast covenanted
to be our *Father;* we are Thy children for the Messiah's sake. This
Messiah will redeem, aye, in Thy sight has already redeemed, Israel
from all sin. To Him we take refuge; our sins are covered before Thy
face. The barrier between Thee and us—sin—has been removed. Thou
art our loving Father, who wilt hear when Thy children cry unto Thee.
How can it be otherwise? *"Our Redeemer, from everlasting is Thy
name";* and as Thy name is, so wilt Thou deal with us.

Isaiah deals the Catholic saint-worship a mighty blow. Saint-worship is gross idolatry. Abraham and Jacob, both saints, cannot hear
prayers. "Abraham is ignorant of us, and Israel acknowledges us not."
Saint-worship has no command, no promise of being heard, and no example in the Scripture.

What Should We Ask In Our Prayers?

Phil. 4, 6. *Be careful for nothing, but in everything, by prayer and
supplication with thanksgiving, let your requests be made known unto
God.*

What should we ask of God in our prayers? Phil. 4, 6. gives the
answer: *"Be careful for nothing,"* meden merimnate. Similar to this
is Matt. 6, 25; *"Take no thought"*==be not careful, me merimnate, "as
to your life," etc. "Be careful for nothing," does not argue for care-
lessness; but what St. Paul does wish the Philippian Christians to cultivate is the virtue of casting all their cares upon God, to cut loose from
the anxious, carking, harassing-cares for the things of this life, which
are so apt to smother the thoughts pertaining to yonder life and to
hinder the growth in sanctification. *"Be careful for nothing,"* entertain
no overanxious cares, but "cast all your care, ten merimnan, upon Him;
for he careth for you." 1 Pet. 5, 7.

But cares, both temporal and spiritual, will crowd upon the Christians. What are they to do? Bring them to the Lord in prayer; *"let
your requests be made known unto God,"* pros ton Theon==before God;

lay the matter before Him. For means to help will fail Him never.

What requests are we to make known to God? All, both spiritual and temporal. There is no limitation whatever. "In everything" let your requests be made known to God; be the matter great or small, pray. Cultivate the habit of bringing all that troubles you to your God in prayer. He knows your frame and understands your cares. What an encouragement to pour out our hearts to God!

> What a privilege to carry
> Everything to God in prayer!
> Oh, what peace we often forfeit,
> Oh, what needless pain we bear,
> All because we do not carry
> Everything to God in prayer.

How should we make our requests known to God? *"By prayer and supplication with thanksgiving."* Says *Lightfoot*: "While *proseuche* prayer, is the general offering up of the wishes and desires to God, *deesis*, supplication, implies special petition for the supply of wants. Thus *proseuche*, prayer, points to the frame of mind of the petitioner, *deesis*, supplication, to the act of solicitation. The two occur together also in Eph. 6, 18; 1 Tim. 2, 1; 5, 5. In *aitemata*, requests, again the *several objects* of *deesis are implied."*—"Great stress is laid on the duty of *eucharistia*, thanksgiving, by St. Paul; e. g., Rom. 1, 21; 16, 6; 2 Cor. 1, 11; 4, 15; 9, 11. 12; Eph. 5, 20; Col. 2, 7; 3, 17; 1 Thess. 5, 18; 1 Tim. 2, 1. All his own letters to the churches, with the sole exception of the Epistle to the Galatians, commence with an emphatic thanksgiving. In this epistle the injunction is in harmony with the repeated exhortations to cheerfulness, *chara*, which it contains."

Pray, offer up your requests *"in everything;"* send them to the throne of grace. *Supplicate*, lay this special trial, this special distress, this special trouble before Him, and do not neglect, thou child of God, *to thank* Him for His manifold blessings which He daily and richly showers upon you. Is it a *spiritual* gift you crave for, observe the prayer of the publican, Luke 18, 13. Is it a *temporal* thing you desire, follow the example of the woman of Canaan, Matt. 15, 22, 28. In childlike confidence say, "Abba, Father."

What Distinction Should We Observe in Our Prayer?

For spiritual things pray unconditionally, Luke 11, 13; for temporal blessings pray conditionally, Luke 22, 42; Matt. 8, 2; 1 John 5, 14; in both cases "with all boldness and confidence ask Him as dear children ask their dear Father."

Luke 11, 13. *If ye, then, being evil, know how to give good gifts unto your children, how much more shall your heavenly Father give the Holy Spirit to them that ask Him!*

Let us not overlook the *"then," oun,* in our text. Clearly it marks an inference drawn from the preceding context. The inference is based on a *contrast* between a human *father* and our *heavenly Father,* and by means of the rhetorical figure *a minore ad majus* the truth is forcefully brought home by our Savior: Since what I say holds good in the minor case, in that of the human father, *how much more* will it not hold good in the major case—in that of our heavenly Father?

"If ye, then, being evil, know how to give good gifts unto your children." A human father, though*"evil,"* sinful, can and does discriminate between good and bad gifts for his children, and gives them the good gifts only. (See vv. 11, 12.) Should the wisdom and love of God, our heavenly Father, *ho pater ho ex ouranou,* "the *Father who is of heaven,"* who is altogether good, be less than that of an earthly father? Impossible! Our heavenly Father *"knows how to give good gifts unto His children."* Hence, ask, seek, knock! v. 9. Our heavenly Father loves us, His children, much more than a human father can love his. Ask, seek, knock!—But oftentimes we ask, and do receive what we asked for! What is the reason? Our heavenly Father will give us gifts if we ask for them, that is His promise, but they must be *"good gifts"* we *ask* for. In our short-sightedness we often ask for things not good for our spiritual welfare; we imagine we are asking for bread, but in reality it is a stone we are petitioning for; or we imagine we are requesting fish or eggs, but in truth we are demanding a serpent or a scorpion. (See vv. 11, 12.) Such bad gifts our Father will not bestow upon us. His wisdom, looking to our eternal welfare, forbids it; His love towards His children will not allow it. "Ye . . . know how to give *good* gifts unto your children, *how much more* shall your Father which is in heaven give *good* things to them that ask Him." Matt. 7, 11. Not only will God give us *"good things,"* both spiritual and temporal, but he will give the best of all gifts, *"the Holy Ghost,* to them that ask Him." Bread, fish, eggs, ordinary articles of food, necessities of life, a father gladly gives to his children; likewise our heavenly Father lovingly bestows upon us "good things," Matt. 7, 11, the necessities of life, if we ask Him. But the one indispensably necessary gift unto salvation is *the Holy Ghost.* The Father wills our salvation. Hence ask Him for His Holy Spirit, and your prayer will be granted. This is His promise. Ask the Father *unconditionally* for this precious gift, because you know you are asking according to His will. "If we ask anything according to His will, He heareth us," 1 John 5, 14. Hence we pray:

Come, Holy Spirit, heavenly Dove, ,
With all Thy quickening powers;
Come, shed abroad a Saviour's love,
And that shall kindle ours.

Luke 22, 42. *Father, if Thou be willing, remove this cup from Me;
nevertheless, not My will, but Thine, be done.*

The indescribable agony of the God-man had begun. The full moon
cast her mellow beams on the sad scene in the Garden. Jesus "was
withdrawn" from His disciples "about a stone's cast," "He was taken
away," He tore Himself away reluctantly from the companionship of
His disciples. Through this dark hour He must go alone. He "kneeled
down," the posture corresponding to the intense agony of His heart.
Next, as Matthew informs us, He "fell on His face," prostrating Himself before His heavenly Father, and prayed: *"Remove this cup from
Me."* In Oriental countries the master of a feast presents a *cup* to the
guests. The Father here extends to the Son a *cup;* however, *not* a cup
of joy, but one brimful of sorrowful affliction. John 18, 11. (Cf. Matt.
26, 39; Is. 51, 17, 22; Ps. 73, 10; 75, 8.)

"What is the *poterion* (the cup) of which our Lord here prays that
it may pass by? Certainly not the mere present feebleness and prostra-
tion of the bodily frame, not any mere section of His sufferings, but *the
whole* —the betrayal, the trial, the mocking, the scourging, the cross,
the grave, and all besides which our thoughts cannot reach." (*Alford,*
ad Matt. 26, 37.)

Oh, the deep agony of our Saviour in this hour! Who can fathom
it? It is true what Luther remarks upon this *text:* "We men, conceived
and born in sin, have an impure, hard flesh that is not quick to feel.
The fresher, the sounder the man, the more he feels what is contrary to
him. Because Christ's body was pure and without sin, and our body is
impure, we scarcely feel the terrors of death in two degrees where
Christ felt them in ten, since He is to be the greatest martyr and to feel
the utmost terrors of death."

Now, in a measure, we are in a position to apprehend faintly the
prayers our sins have pressed forth from our Substitute's heart.

"Father," hear the supplication of Thy Child, *"Father, if Thou be
willing,"* if it be possible, Matt. 26, 37; and if it is possible, Thou wilt
be willing to remove this cup from Me. Father, the cup is bitter. Is
drinking it the only way of gaining the end in view —the salvation of
the sin-stricken world? Hast Thou in Thy unlimited wisdom and power
no other means than the cross to save mankind? *"Father, if Thou be
willing,"* if another course is consistent with Thy counsel, if the world
can be redeemed by other means *"remove this cup from me."* —Who can

understand the reluctance, the shrinking of the sinless Son of God, who, as the *man Jesus*, prays to be spared to go through the depths of God's justice and Satan's hate?

But let us inspect the wording of the prayer more closely: *"Pater, ei boulei, parenegke touto to poterion ap' emou; plen me to thelema mou, alla to son ginestho."* Father, if Thou be willing to take away this cup from Me —but not My will, but Thine, be done." Note the break in the thought after the first clause indicated by the dash. The sentence is not complete, the afterthought is suppressed, an abrupt change to a new thought is made. This suppression of words after the dash—a figure of speech called aposiopesis —indicates the thought flashing through the mind of the agonized Jesus: "If Thou be willing," —but no, it cannot be done, this cup cannot be removed, the *via dolorosa* is the only way to save mankind, —then, Father, *"not My will, but Thine, be done."*

The Savior here has given us a model prayer. In time of calamity, of sickness, of affliction, it is proper to ask the Father for deliverance. This is the child's privilege. This the Saviour did. But let us not overlook the "if": *"If* Thou be willing." When we have no definite promise of the Father in His Word as to this or that petition which we may utter; when we pray for earthly things, for the removal of a burden, which may seem to us greater than we can bear, let us pray to the Father but let us not omit the "if." *We* do not know whether the answer to our prayer for things mundane will accrue to our Father's glory and our own welfare.

Though "this cup" was not and could not be removed from the lips of Jesus, —He had to drink the contents to its very dregs, —still His prayer was answered: *"And there appeared an angel from heaven, strengthening Him."* And thus *strengthened* He went forth to do His Father's will.

The Lord hearkens to the prayer of His children in earthly matters, in which they submit their will to His by a confident "If Thou art willing"; "If it be possible"; and if in His wisdom He sees that we pray amiss, He answers our prayer in a way that makes for our salvation and His glory.

Matt. 8, 2. *And, behold, there came a leper and worshipped Him, saying, Lord, if Thou wilt, Thou canst make me clean.*

A person in great bodily distress, a leper, comes to Jesus. Leprosy baffled and still baffles the skill of the physicians —it is an incurable disease. This the leper knew. But he also knew that what is impossible with men is possible with Jesus. Jesus is man and God, He is almighty, He can cure even leprosy. The leper is a believer, a Christian. He evidences this by his coming to Christ; by his action; *"he worshipped Him,"* bowed down unto Him as unto God in his prayer. —Afflictions, great afflictions, befall also the Christians. What are they to do? Do as the leper did—go to Jesus. Said the leper, *"If Thou wilt, Thou canst make me clean."* He knows that Jesus *can* heal him, so he places his case before Him, but resigns himself entirely to Jesus' will. Jesus knows best. Great faith is here coupled with entire dependence on the *will* of Jesus: *"If Thou wilt."* Observe the "if," the restriction. In asking for *spiritual* blessings, which are necessary for our salvation, there is no place for an "if" in our petitions. We know the Father's heart, we know He wills our salvation. He wills to give us the blessings necessary to reach the end. For these blessings we have His divine assurance, Luke 11, 13. Not so in earthly matters. Here we should pray *conditionally*: "If Thou wilt," If it be possible," that God would grant them to us if they tend to His glory and our welfare. But, Christian friend, go to Jesus even in temporal matters, *go* confidently, *go* with the "If Thou wilt," and you will oftentimes experience that in these matters, too, the Lord does according to your prayer. He frequently says to us as He did to the leper, "I will." v. 3.

1 John 5, 14. *This is the confidence that we have in Him, that, if we ask anything according to His will, He heareth us.*

This passage is to engender *confidence, parrhesia, boldness,* bold confidence, in prayer. How timid we oftentimes are to approach God! Why do we not, as Luther so often did, speak to Him confidently, boldly confident of His hearing our prayer? We "believe on the name of the Son of God"; "we know that we have eternal life," cf. v. 13. God is our Father, we are His children. Hence "with all boldness and confidence we should ask Him as dear children ask their dear father." (Luther) Belonging to God's family by faith in Christ God does not look upon us as a stern Judge, but as a kind Father, who gladly, attentively, listens to what we say, and cheerfully grants our requests. This is what the words *"He heareth us"* say. "He heareth us" does not merely mean: He hears our prayers in a general way, He knows what we say. God is omniscient; so that is self-evident. The construction in Greek is not *akouein hemas* (*akouein* with the objective case), but *akouei hemon* (genitive). That says: "He hears us" and grants our petition. So, child of God, make use of a child's privilege; knowing the heart of your God to be a merciful, loving Father's heart, approach the Father in bold confidence.

What may you ask of Him? *"Anything,"* be it of a temporal or a spiritual nature —*anything;* be it great or small —*anything*. We sinful fathers, though we love our children, often become irritated when Ruth or Adele bother us too frequently with their trivial, childish grievances. Not so God, for *"He heareth us."* Is there *anything* that grieves you?

Bring it to the Lord in prayer. You are a child of God and hence will ask *"according to His will."* For spiritual blessings pray boldly, with-out condition: "Father, Thou must give me this or that." For temporal blessings pray boldly, but insert the "If Thou wilt." In both cases you know that you are praying according to His will, and you know you have the assurance: *"He heareth us."*

If we ask *"according to His will,* He heareth us." "God's will is infinitely wiser than ours. And our faith in Him will lead us to offer our petitions subject to His will. "God hears the prayer, but answers it according to His infinite wisdom, rather than according to our limited foresight." "God, in His love, buries our own mistakes in prayer, and gives us just what we should most desire, could we see as He sees." (Pulpit Commentary.)

How Should We Pray?

John 16, 23. *Verily, verily, I say unto you, Whatsoever ye shall ask the Father in My name, He will give it you.*

When you address God in prayer, says Christ to His disciples, you speak to the *Father;* you are His children. How did you become such? Through Me. So, when praying, say: This do, Father, for Thy Son's sake, in whom we are made acceptable in Thy sight. Ask Him *"in My name,"* not in your own; go to Him relying on My merits, not on your own, and He cannot and will not refuse you.—To pray in Jesus' name means to pray in faith and firm confidence in Christ's merits. And go to Him for *"whatsoever"* it may be. There is no burden too great, no burden too small that you may not bring to the Lord in prayer. "Cast *all* your cares upon Him," says Peter. In order to make us bold to let our requests be known to God, the Lord not only promises that the Father will grant our petition, but He confirms the promise with an oath: *"Verily, verily."* And if the Lord delays in answering our prayers for a merciful purpose, let us remember that at Cana He said: "Mine hour has not yet come." "Not yet" —but come it will.

Matt. 21, 22: *All things, whatsoever ye shall ask in prayer, be-lieving, ye shall receive.*

The all-embracing promise, *"All things, whatsoever ye shall ask,"* we considered in the previous text. The new element upon which all stress is to be here laid is *"believing."*

We pray to "Him that is able to do exceeding abundantly above all that we ask or think," Eph. 3, 20, to the *almighty* God, to whom we have access through our Lord Jesus Christ, Rom. 5, 1, whose *sons* we are, John 1, 12, who *promises* with an oath that He will hear us, John 16, 23. Why, then, not banish all doubts from our minds and pray *believingly?* Why not fight down all doubts and obstacles which would interpose and cry out, "I believe, help Thou mine unbelief?" Doing this, we even in this day may hear the encouraging words, Man, woman, "great is *thy* faith; be. it done unto thee as thou wilt."

For Whom Should We Pray?

1 Tim. 2, 1: *I exhort therefore that, first of all, supplications, prayers, intercessions, and giving of thanks be made for all men.*

With apostolic authority St. Paul exhorts (parakalo) Timothy that prayers *"be made for all men."* Timothy is pastor at Ephesus. He is to teach his congregation this virtue and duty to make a practice of intercessory prayers *"for all men,"* hyper—in behalf of, in the interest of *"all men,"* for the world. Where there is life, there is breath; where there is faith, there is prayer. We pray in our own behalf,—sometimes through the devil's deceit and craftiness even this is neglected,—but to intercede before the throne of grace *"for all men,"* how little is that done, except in taking part, oftentimes in a lukewarm way, in the General Prayer pronounced from the pulpit of a Sunday! How necessary, therefore, to heed the exhortation of the Apostle!

To what does he exhort? That *"supplications,"* etc., be made *"for all men."* It is somewhat difficult to make a cleancut distinction between and among these terms.. The accumulation of the various terms designating prayer is undoubtedly made for the purpose of impressing us Christians with the great and various needs *"all men"* have for our prayers, and the plural forms of the nouns are to instigate us to pray much and fervently *"for all men."*

But let us attempt to discriminate between the more or less synonymous terms. *Supplications* (deeseis) are prayers that flow from the consciousness of a special need; they are prayers in which we petition God for this or that. *Prayers* (proseuchas) indicate prayers of a general character. The term *proseuche* expresses an act of adoration, an address to God made in reverential fear, coupled with childlike confidence. *Enteuxeis*, translated by "intercessions," sometimes has a wider application but generally is best rendered as here by "intercessions." *Eucharistias*, thanksgiving, denotes the prayers in which thanks are offered to God for benefits received, for evils averted, for divine protection bestowed during the day, etc. (See Morning and Evening Prayers.)

So the passage may be paraphrased. Christians, intercessory prayers are of utmost importance; therefore pray much and often *"for all men."* Offer supplications "for all men" for their bodily and spiritual needs; specify these needs according to the times and circumstances; pray "for all men" in reverential fear, but in childlike boldness; intercede "for all men" before the throne of grace, for friend and foe; "give thanks" "for all men" for the benefits showered upon them by a gracious God.

This *"I exhort first of all,"* says Paul. Not as though the intercessory prayer of believers were the thing of primary importance in their lives, but the words *"first of all"* say that this arrangement of universal church-prayers is the first part of that charge or administration which was now committed unto Timothy.—Fellow-Christians, since "the effectual fervent prayer of a righteous man availeth much,"—ponder the thought,—what a stream of blessings would be poured out upon our congregations, upon the world, if all Christians would heed the apostle's exhortation to pray much, to pray fervently "for all men!" If ever there was a time when the world needed these prayers of the Christians, that time is now.

This exhortation of the apostle finds its exemplification in our Bidding Prayer, pronounced from the pulpit Sunday after Sunday, in which, besides praying for the Church, we pray for "the President and Congress of the United States and all others in authority," for all sorts and conditions of men, "for all that travel by land and sea, for all that are in peril or need, for the afflicted in mind, body, or estate," etc.

What an exhortation, too, this text is to shake off all lukewarmness when the Bidding Prayer is said, and not to go through it, as is so often done, in a perfunctory manner!

Matt. 5, 44. *Pray for them which despitefully use you, and persecute you.*

In the Sermon on the Mount Jesus also speaks of the proper conduct of His disciples toward their enemies, and among other things says: *"Pray for them."* So the passage is put here to show that Christians are to pray even for their enemies. The full import of the text becomes apparent from the context. Jesus says: "Ye have heard that it hath been said, Thou shalt love thy neighbor and hate thine enemy. But I say unto you, Love your enemies, bless them that curse you, do good to them that hate you, and *pray for them which despitefully use you and persecute you."*

"Thou shalt love thy neighbor," was and is a precept of the moral law. Thou shalt "hate thine enemy" was an addition to, and hence a perversion of the Law by the scribes and the Pharisees. Nowhere in the

Old Testament is there a command or even a permission to hate our enemies.

Authoritatively Christ opposes this perversion of God's holy Law. "But I say," over against what "ye have heard that it hath been said," I say unto you: *"Love your enemies."* Thus Christ explains the term "neighbor." "Neighbor" includes one who is your enemy. Even he is to be the object of your love. In Luke 10, 29, a certain lawyer asks Jesus, "Who is my *neighbor?*" In the story of the Good Samaritan he receives the answer: Even your bitter enemy.

Now as to the passage itself. *"Love your enemies"* may be looked upon as the topic-sentence. The following phrases explain and develop the concepts: "love" and "enemies," exhibiting the great contrast between love and hate.

How may your "neighbors" manifest their *enmity?* They may "curse you," "hate you," "despitefully use you, and persecute you." How are you to manifest your *love?* "Bless them" —say loving words; "do good to them" —perform loving deeds; *"pray for them,"* the climax of the manifestation of love, *"pray for them"* —thus showing love of the *heart,* from which source "blessing them" and "doing good to them" flows. The climactic way in which, the concepts "love" and "enemies" are unfolded, and the juxtaposition of the thoughts: *"Bless* them that *curse* you, *do good* to them that *hate* you, *pray* for them which *despitefully use* you, and *persecute* you" go to show that the greater the manifestation of hatred of our "neighbor" is, the greater should be our manifestation of love. This is not the conduct of natural man, but that of a child of God. Thus you, My disciples, says Christ, prove, thus it becomes apparent by your works, that you have received a mind from your *Father.* In the words of Jesus: "That ye may be the *children* of your *Father* which is in heaven."—We sigh: Lord Jesus, teach us so to pray and so to act!

Heb. 9, 27: *It is appointed unto men once to die, but after this the judgment.*

Are prayers for the dead justifiable? No. Scripture knows nothing whatsoever thereof. The question, however, requires an answer because of the Roman Catholic and the Greek Churches in which prayers for the dead are offered in their so-called *mass,* according to which Christ is offered still today as a bloodless sacrifice for the sins of the living, and for the dead who swelter in purgatory. Both, the mass as well as purgatory, are unscriptural, hence godless inventions of the papists. According to the Council of Trent, "the holy Synod" teaches that "not only for the sins, punishments, satisfactions, and other necessities of the faithful who here are living, but also for those who are departed in Christ, and who are not as yet fully purified, it (the mass) is rightly offered, agreeably to a tradition of the apostles."

What monstrous doctrine—"departed in Christ," and still "not as
yet fully purified!" But it is founded on *"tradition,"* and tradition is
not Scripture. When scribes and Pharisees propounded the question
to Jesus: "Why do Thy disciples transgress the *tradition* of the elders?"
He answered by a slashing counter-question: "Why do ye transgress
the commandment of *God* by your *tradition?*" Matt. 15, 3. Indeed, it
is true: "In *vain* do they worship Me, teaching for doctrines the *commandments of men."* Matt. 15, 9.

Is there any ground in the Bible for prayers for the dead? The
one simple passage quoted in our Catechism is all-sufficient and plain:
"It is appointed unto men once to die." What next? After this a
purgatory, or a hades, or an intermediate state in which there is
another chance for the ungodly, or where prayer for such as are there
detained might avail? Nothing of the kind. After death, what? *"But
after this the Judgment."* Further comment is unnecessary.

Or take Prov. 11, 7: *"When a wicked man dieth, his expectation
shall perish; and the hope of unjust men perisheth."* Prayers for the
wicked dead avail naught, and prayers for the faithful dead are unnecessary, for they live in bliss: "Blessed are the dead which die in
the Lord from henceforth." Rev. 14, 13.

Where should we pray? Everywhere, 1 Tim. 2, 8; in private, Matt.
6, 6; in Church, Psalm 26, 12.

1 Tim. 2, 8: *I will therefore that men pray everywhere, lifting up
holy hands, without wrath and doubting.*

In chapter 2, St. Paul instructs Timothy on congregational prayer.
In vv. 1-7 we are informed for whom a Christian congregation should
pray; in vv 8-15 we are told *who* is to pray publicly.

"Lifting up hands" was the Oriental fashion when addressing God;
today the custom of folding hands in prayer predominates. The
former posture is expressive of the truth that all blessings must come
from heaven, from God, Ps. 28, 2; 63, 5; the latter, indicates submission to, and trust in, God's will.—*"The men"* are to lift up *"holy
hands."* The men are Christian men, believers, saints, *holy* men, whose
imperfections are covered by Christ's blood and righteousness. Christians, holy men, engage in work becoming Christians. Their handiwork
tends to the welfare of the neighbor and to the glory of God. No tainted
money, no grafted coin, no profiteering, soils the hands of "holy" men.

A hypocrite may assume the posture of prayer as well as the true Christian, but a hypocrite cannot "lift up" or fold "holy" hands. Besides being cautioned to lift up "holy hands," the men are also reminded to pray *"without wrath or doubting."* *Men,* moving about among men, meet with more occasions and temptations than women do, to be offended by this act or that word of their fellow-men, to resent it, and to harbor *wrath* in their soul against their fellow-men. Men, moving among men, coming in contact with unbelievers, cannot avoid hearing scurrilous remarks and taunts about, and gibes at, religion and religious practices. Such poisonous remarks, often clothed in witticism, may cause them to *doubt* this or that truth of the Word. Against these two sins—wrath and doubting—to which men especially are exposed, they are to be on their guard; against these especially they are to fight in the armor of God, to vanquish them, and so in the proper frame of mind to address God. See Jas. 1, 6, 7.

Now to the point of the passage *in loco.* "I will," says the apostle, *"that men pray everywhere"*—in every place, not only at home, in the family circle, but also (see context) in public worship. Here, if circumstances so demand, Christian *men,* (tous andras), not *women,* should pray, and men should not be ashamed to pray.

But observe the *"everywhere"*—*"in any place."* Prayer is not confined to a certain locality or place, but *everywhere* the Father may be "worshiped in spirit and in truth;" everywhere—in the lions' den, as did Daniel; in the fiery furnace, as did Shadrach, Meshach, and Abednego; in the mountain, in the garden, as did our Savior.

Matt. 6, 6: *Thou, when thou prayest, enter into thy closet, and when thou hast shut thy door, pray to thy Father which is in secret and thy Father which seeth in secret shall reward thee openly.*

Again we are taken to the Sermon on the Mount. Treating of prayer, our Savior gives two cautions: 1. When praying avoid ostentations; 2. Guard against the superstition as though "vain repetitions," "much speaking," made the prayer effectual. The first is a Pharisaic practice, the second heathenish. Our passage argues against the malpractice of the scribes and Pharisees.

"The hypocrites," scribes and Pharisees, says Jesus, "Love to pray standing in the synagogs and in the corners of the streets, *that they may be seen of men."* Prayer offered in this spirit and with this purpose in view is an abomination in the sight of God. To show the true spirit in which prayer is to be offered, the Lord employs beautiful striking imagery. "But *thou,* when *thou* prayest," act not as did the Pharisees; "enter into thy closet." This generally was an upper room in the Oriental house, called the oratory—the prayer-room. Here, the Lord would say, you are apart from men, in the privacy of your own home. "Shut the door," secure the utmost privacy, avoid all possible opportunity for ostentation. When a boy, the writer was permitted to visit a convent at a stated hour—the hour of convent prayer. Passing along the corridor, room after room, or rather cell after cell, stood wide open; the occupant, a nun, on her knees praying ostentatiously, "to be seen of men."—"Shut the door!"—"Pray to thy Father." You and your Father are alone. "Thy Father seeth in secret," He is with you, hears your petitions, and answers them. Prayer is a matter between you and Him. It is an affair of the heart. While praying, think of nothing else but your prayer; give your heart up to the Father.

Observe the occasion which called forth this declaration of our Lord, and all thoughts as though prayer in public were displeasing to God are dispelled.— Moreover, the text—and this is the purpose for which our Catechism quotes it—establishes the fact that prayer may be, should be offered also in the privacy of our "upper chamber." God grant that every Christian home may know of an oratory!

As to the propriety of prayer in *public* worship, it will suffice to quote a few self-explanatory passages from the hymn-book of the Old Testament believers, the Psalms. David says, Ps. 26, 12: "In the *congregations* will I bless the Lord." Ps. 27, 6, we read: "And now shall mine head be lifted up above mine enemies round about me: therefore will I offer *in this tabernacle* sacrifices of joy; I will sing, yea, I will sing praises unto the Lord." Again, Ps. 22, 25: "My praise shall be of Thee in the great *congregation;* I will pay my vows before them that fear Him."

Finally, When Should We Pray?

---

1 Thess. 5, 17: *Pray without ceasing.*

Does this say that we are to walk about continually with folded hands, mumbling words of prayer? Are we not to sleep? to work? "Study to be quiet, and to do your own business, and to *work* with your own hands, even as we charged you." 1 Thess., 4, 11. "We commanded you, if any will not work, neither let him eat." 2 Thess. 3, 10. Never was there a more industrious Christian worker than St. Paul himself, who admonishes the Thessalonians: "Pray without ceasing." But during all the busy hours of each day, his thoughts were turned heavenward, awaiting "that blessed hope." His frame of mind was such as to be able at any time to call upon God, to pray, praise, and give thanks. "Prayer is to be the accompaniment of our whole life—a stream ever flowing, now within sight and hearing, now disappearing from view, forming the under-current of all our thoughts, and giving to them its own character and tone." (Findlay.) Cf. Eph. 6, 18; Luke 18, 1-7.

Is 26, 16: *Lord in trouble have they visited Thee; they poured out a prayer when Thy chastening was upon them.*

It is a sad fact that in days of sunshine and prosperity our prayers are often half-hearted, weak, faint. So the Lord in His wisdom sends us "trouble" for our good; He "chastens" us. He would thereby draw us nigh unto Him. "In trouble" the Christians are stirred up to prayer, to earnest, fervent prayer. In trouble we "visit" Him; look to Him for help. We remember that He is the Lord, Jehovah, our covenant God; we flee to His covenant of mercy; implore Him for forgiveness of our sins by which we have merited "trouble" and "chastening" a thousand-fold, and we "pour out a prayer" from an overflowing, burdened heart for deliverance. "Before, prayer came drop by drop, but now they pour out a prayer; it comes now like water from a fountain, not like water from a still." (M. Henry.) In affliction those will seek God early who before sought Him slowly Hos. 5, 15. This is one of the chief purposes of "trouble" and "chastening"—to "visit" Him, and to "pour out a prayer" to Jehovah, the God of mercy.

THE LORD'S PRAYER.

THE INTRODUCTION.

The Introduction to the Lord's Prayer reads: *"Our Father who art in heaven."*

Why Do We Address God as "Father?"

1 John 3, 1: *"Behold, what manner of love the Father hath bestowed upon us that we should be called the sons of God!*

What Christian can read this marvelous passage without experiencing a thrill of joy? *"Behold,"* look well, pay strict attention to this remarkable exhibition of God's *love*: He calls us His *sons*. And as if that "behold" were not enough to arouse our minds to be on the alert as to the wonderful thing he has to disclose, the apostle says: "Behold, what *manner* of love" (*potapen agapen*), of what *amazing* quality, of what surpassing excellence, the love is that *"the Father hath bestowed upon us!"* And this *"manner"* of love—how did it manifest itself? The *Father* bestowed upon us a glorious title: "sons," *"children"* (*tekna*) *of God!* God's titles are not *tituli sine re;* God's names are facts; when God calls us *tekna*, "children," "sons," we *are* His children indeed. But, how amazing the fact: *we*, sinners, by nature children of wrath, nevertheless *children of God!* Can there be any nearer and dearer relationship than that of father and child? And how did this relationship between us and God come about? God's *love* to us impelled Him to declare us His "sons." "God so *loved* the world that He gave His only-begotten Son, that whosoever *believeth* in Him should not perish, but have everlasting life."—"In this was manifested the *love* of God toward us, because that God sent His only-begotten Son into the world that we might live through Him." 1 John 4, 9. And this *child*-relationship—how was it effected? Paul tells us: "Ye are all the *children* of God *by faith* in Christ Jesus." Gal. 3, 26. Christians *only* are children, "sons," of God, and Christians are *nothing less* than children of God. This title was *bestowed* upon them, *dedoken, given* them out of *love, i. e.,* by grace.—Well may St. John exclaim: "*Behold, what manner of love,*" what amazing, astonishing *love* of the *Father!*

And when Jesus teaches His disciples to pray, He tells them: When you address the Thrice Holy call Him—*Father.* Why this endearing address? He knoweth our frame. Although by faith we are God's children, still, because of our innate sinful nature, we are prone to doubt; we oftentimes cannot muster up courage to pray as we should; especially is this true in times of affliction when we need it most. Says Jesus: Go to God; call Him *Father*—that He is. What child fears to tell his loving father of his troubles? Satan, get thee hence with all kinds of doubts thou wouldst instill in me as though God would not hear my prayer! God Himself has declared me His *child* in His Son; He is my *loving* Father; hence I shall cry even out of the depths, in spite of devil, world, and flesh that endeavor to dissuade me: *Father,* dear Father, hear Thy *child!*

Rom. 8, 15: *For ye have not received the spirit of bondage again to fear; but ye have received the spirit of adoption, whereby we cry, Abba, Father!*

"For as many as are led by the Spirit of God, they are the *sons* of God." V. 14. This assertion is proved by the experience of the Roman Christians: they are led by the Spirit: they live and act as children of God. This is proof of their child-relation to God. "*For,*" at the time of your conversion, "*ye did not receive the spirit of bondage,*" *i. e., of slavery (douleias),* "*unto fear,*" so that you live in constant *fear* and trembling as slaves do in anticipation of the dreaded severity of their masters, who may punish, aye, kill them at their pleasure. At the time of your conversion "*ye received the Spirit of adoption*" (*hyiothesias*) of *child-relationship:* you received a *filial* spirit, so that you may approach God *without fear,* with love and confidence.—The unbelievers lead a life of fear; "Through fear of death they are all their lifetime subject to bondage," Heb. 2, 15; not so the Christians. We are delivered from this "bondage," Heb. 2, 14, by our Savior. Through Him we have become children of God. Under the promptings of the Holy Spirit, who assures us through the Word of our *filial* relation to God, from our hearts rises again and again that *"cry,"* that sweetest of all appellations, *"Abba, Father!"* And our Elder Brother, Jesus, who so teaches us to pray, did He not in His great agony in the Garden cry, *"Abba, Father!"?*. And so, even if our Jesus should take us, as He did His disciples, into the garden of adversities, let us cry boldly, confidently, *"Abba, Father!"* "This is a noble and comforting text, worthy of being written in letters of gold." (Luther.)

NOTE—*Abba*, we are told, is the Syriac term for "father." *"Ho pater"* (Father) is the Greek translation, added by Mark by way of explanation, because he primarily wrote for Gentile Christians, to whom the *Abba* would be unintelligible. Later, the two terms were closely linked together as *one* endearing appellation of God.

Eph. 3, 14, 15: *For this cause I bow my knees unto the Father of our Lord Jesus Christ, of whom the whole family in heaven and earth is named.*

From a point of view different from, though related to, those mentioned in the preceding texts, we here again have a mighty incentive to humble, but bold and confident prayer.

In the Greek there is a play upon the words *"pater"* (Father) and *"patria"* (family). The word for *family (patria)* designates a lineage, the descendants of a common father; so a *patria* (family) is a generation of children. Joseph, Luke 2, 4, is described as "being of the household and family *(patria)* of David." So, says our text, *"the whole family in heaven and earth is named" "of the Father."* The name He bestowed upon us is *"children,"* 1 John 3, 1. After the *"Father of our Lord Jesus Christ"* this *family* is named. Christ is God's unique Child; we are Christ's—Christians, bought by Him with a price; thus He became "our Lord," and so we also belong to the Father as His dear children. Gal. 3, 26.

The *Father* has a family *in heaven*: the "sons of God," Job 38, 4, 7, the holy angels, and the perfected saints. The *Father* has a family *on earth*: His children from among all nations, kindreds, and tongues. Both, the family in heaven and the family on earth, constitute *one* great family—the *ecclesia una sancta* in a wider sense.

The text speaks of Paul as *bowing his knees* in humble prayer unto the Father, supplicating Him in Christ's name for the bestowal of precious gifts upon one part of this family named after Him, for His children "on earth." The "family" in heaven is well provided for—it is the family *triumphant*. But the family *militant* also needs be provided for. And great are the gifts which he asks of the Father, cf. 15 ff. But Paul, who *humbly* bows his knees before God, at the same time prays *boldly, confidently,* knowing that the Father *can* and *will* do what he asks of Him; and hence he concludes his supplication with a triumphant doxology: "To Him be glory," etc.

What a grand conception this: "a family in heaven," "a family on earth"! You belong to the latter as yet. God is the *Father* thereof. Will He not hear His *children's* cry? Truly, God would by this winning name "Father" encourage us to pray without fear or doubt, in all boldness and confidence.

Why do we pray: *"Our* Father who art in heaven"?

Eph. 4, 6: *One God and Father of all, who is above all, and through all, and in you all.*

This text forms the close of the *locus classicus* for the doctrine of the Church—the sum total of all believers. It reads: "Endeavoring to keep the unity of the Spirit in the bond of peace. There is one body and one Spirit, even as ye are called in one hope of your calling; one Lord, one faith, one Baptism, *one God and Father of all, who is above all, and through all, and in you all."*

Through Christ God has become our *Father.* He is *above* all; He protects and governs us, and causes all things to work together for good to His children. He works *through* the Christians; the good the Christians do, God works in and through them. Finally, He lives *in* the Christians; we are His temple. The three main concepts are: *one Spirit, one Lord, one God and Father.* In this Triune God the Christians are united with one another. By the one Spirit and in the one Spirit they are at the same time united with the one Lord and the one God and Father. Knowing this, they should walk worthy of their high calling: this is the trend of the Apostle's thought.

But since there is *one* God and Father of *all,* since all that have one and the same Spirit and faith constitute *one* body,—this spiritual body, the Church,—what a strong incentive for the *members* of this *body,* or, to go back to the picture portrayed in Eph. 3, 14. 15, for the *children* of this *family,* to pray for and with one another! And does not Paul, in the passage considered before, Rom. 8, 15, say, studiously changing from the second person in which he had addressed the Romans to the first person, *"we* cry, Abba, Father," suggesting that all *children* should pray together and for one another? To teach us this lesson, Jesus said to His disciples: "When ye pray, say, *Our* Father," etc.

And what a consolation to know: we do not pray alone; the whole family of God's children bows its knees before the throne of grace intoning that sublime prayer: *"Our* Father who art in heaven."

Why do we add, *"Who art in heaven"?*

Eph. 3, 20. 21: *Now unto Him that is able to do exceeding abundantly above all that we ask or think, according to the power that worketh in us, unto Him be glory in the Church by Christ Jesus throughout all ages, world without end.*

The Apostle bows his knees unto the Father, v. 14, imploring to grant to the Ephesian Christians growth of the new spiritual life implanted in them, cf. vv. 16—19; he knows that the Father "is able to do" what he asks, v. 20; he is confident that the Father will do it, v. 21.

Earthly fathers must sometimes shake their heads in answer to petitions from their children, saying, "Child, what you ask exceeds my ability." Need God's children entertain any fears as to the heavenly Father's ability to grant their petitions? *"He is able to do exceeding abundantly above all that we ask or think."* Why this impressive accumulation of words? Would it not have been sufficient to say: *"He is able to do what we ask"?* Observe the addition: "He is able to do *above all* that we ask or—think." Thought oftentimes cannot find adequate expression in speech, in prayer. God *is able to do* not only *above* all that we *ask, but* even *above all* that we *think!* And still the Apostle has not exhausted the definition of God's ability to answer our prayer. He says: God "is able to do *exceeding abundantly* above all that we ask or think." It is as if he were struggling to find words to make us feel, realize, God's infinite, limitless resources of power to grant our petitions, and to assure us that He can and will hear us if we ask Him as dear children ask their dear fathers.—God's name is Omnipotence. This is the meaning of that phrase: *"who art in heaven."* Expressed in words of the psalmist: "Our God is *in the heavens"*—He is not an "idol of silver and gold, the work of men's hands"—"He hath done *whatsoever He hath pleased."* Ps. 115, 3. 4; cf. Eph. 1, 20—22.

We have considered the Introduction to the Lord's Prayer. "Our Father who art in heaven." What does this mean? Can a better answer be given than that of Dr. Luther? He says: "God would by these words tenderly invite us to believe that He is our true Father, and that we are His true children, so that we may with all boldness and confidence ask Him as dear children ask their dear Father."

Our Father, Thou in heav'n above,
Who biddest us to dwell in love
As brothers of one family,
And cry for all we need to Thee:
Teach us to mean the words we say,
And from the inmost heart to pray.

(Hymn 396, 1.)

The First Petition.

Hallowed Be Thy Name.

What is the name by which God wills to be known among us? "Our Father,—hallowed be Thy *name*," so Jesus taught His disciples to pray. As *Father* God has revealed Himself to us in Jesus. If we know Jesus aright, we know the *Father* aright.—"*Hallowed* be Thy name." God is holy, so is His name; we cannot render it more holy. "*Hallowed* be Thy name" means that it be *hallowed*, be holy, kept sacred, receive the honor due it, among us. This is done, says Luther, by pure doctrine and holy life. How true this answer is we shall see from a consideration of the following passages.

John 17, 17: *Sanctify them through Thy truth: Thy Word is truth.*

The sublime High-priestly Prayer, whence our text is taken, contains three parts: Christ prays for Himself, vv. 1—5; for His disciples, vv. 6—19; and for the Church, vv. 20—26.

"*Sanctify them through Thy truth,*" so Jesus prays in the hearing of the Eleven as He is about to leave them in the world. What a solemn hour, this, for the disciples! *Sanctify, hagiazein,* signifies to separate from the world and to dedicate to God, to set apart for God, to *consecrate* to God. "Sanctify them *in Thy truth.*" These disciples were "*in the truth.*" Jesus says they are "*in* the world," v. 11, but "not *of* the world," v. 14; "they have kept Thy Word," v. 6, "and have known surely that I came out from Thee, and they have believed that Thou didst send Me," v. 8. So these Eleven had been *sanctified, consecrated,* to God; but they were still to remain in this world for some time to do very important mission-work. But "the world hath hated them, because they are not of the world," v. 14; so they must be kept "from the evil," v 15.—"Holy Father," v. 11, "*sanctify* them," set them apart for Thee more and more, *consecrate* them to Thee more and more to do Thy will; keep them and confirm them in the true faith.

How is this to be done? "Sanctify them *in Thy truth.*" The Greek preposition *en=in,* is frequently used in an instrumental sense= *by* or *through.* And naturally we look for the agency or the means by which Christ's disciples are to be sanctified when we read: "Sanctify them"—how? "*Through* Thy truth." Thus the sense of the original text is given by the Authorized Version. But, taking the usual translation of *en = in,* nothing of the instrumental force of *en* is lost, but it is rather augmented by the addition of another, a deeper truth. Luther translates: "Heilige sie *in* deiner Wahrheit!" These disciples had already been sanctified *by* the truth: they believed the Word of God given them by Christ, v. 14; they were "in the truth." "Sanctify them *in* Thy truth," speaks of the truth as being the sphere *in* which alone sanctification can take place, and presupposes that it can be done only *by* the truth. Or expressed differently: *en aletheia* says not only that the truth is the *means* whereby, but also that the truth is the *sphere* in which, sanctification takes place. To illustrate: If one lives *in* a healthful climate, one's health is promoted *by* the climate *in* which one lives.

The sanctification of the disciples *by* the truth is to continue, to be carried on and out "*in* the truth," the only means by which it can be done. "Sanctify them in Thy *truth*" = the truth only *can* sanctify. Which is this only sanctifying truth? *Thy Word is truth.*"

Some MSS., and hence some translations, omit "*Thy*" and read: "Sanctify them in *the* truth." But this omission does not alter one iota of the sense of the passage. There is but *one* such definite truth as "*the*" truth, *i. e.*, divine truth, God's truth. Not speculations, fictions, fancies of men, can sanctify, but only "*the* truth," pure and unadulterated. How true this is we see from the corroboration by the next member of the sentence: "Sanctify them in Thy truth: *Thy Word is truth.*" Literally translated: *Ho logos ho sos*="The Word *the Thine is* truth"=The word *that is Thine* is truth. All possible stress, as we see, is laid upon the fact that the *truth* that is to *sanctify* them is "*Thy Word*," God's Word, and His Word only. Hence in reading our good English translation, all emphasis is to be put on the word *Thy*: "*Thy* Word is truth."

Observing the two members of our text, it is plain that it is one and the same to say: Sanctify them in *Thy truth*, or: Sanctify them in *Thy Word.*

And lest we lose sight of the main thought, let it be repeated: "*The Truth*," "*Thy Word*," without any admixture of human ideas, views, fancies, the *pure* truth, pure doctrine, is the only *means* of sanctification, Acts 20, 42. Impure truth, false doctrine, in the last analysis, is not truth at all, but a lie. Impure food is not wholesome, neither is impure truth, untruth. False doctrine cannot sanctify, at most it can produce but a caricature of sanctification.

But what has all this to do with the petition, "Hallowed be Thy name?" God's name can be kept holy among us only in so far as His Word is taught in its truth and purity. If this is not done, the honor due Him, the glorification He should receive is detracted from. To illustrate: "The Truth," His Word, teaches that we are saved by grace, for Christ's sake, by faith. Thus *all* glory is given to God; but where this Word is adulterated and men are taught that salvation depends in part on their own merit and works, Christ's and God's glory is diminished. God would have us praise Him: "*All* glory be to God on high" who has made us accepted in the Beloved.—From glorification of God by *pure doctrine* flows glorification of His name by *holy life.*

Matt. 5, 16: *Let your light so shine before men that they may see your good works, and glorify your Father which is in heaven.*

"Ye are the light of the world," says Christ to His disciples, v. 14. Christ is the *lumen illuminans;* His disciples are *lumina illuminata.* His illuminated followers are to illuminate others. The world is enveloped in spiritual darkness; Christ's disciples are the light to dispel this darkness. What high dignity they possess! Do not put your light under a bushel! Do not hide it! Put it on a candlestick! This is the drift of the exhortation: *"So let your light shine before men."* Possessing the light, you have a solemn duty to perform over against "men." "Men" in contrast to disciples are the unbelievers, the people that are still in spiritual darkness. They are to *"glorify your Father;"* *doxazoosin ton Patera,* to *glorify,* to give Him the honor due Him. Which is this honor? They are to glorify your *Father;* they, too, are to know Him as *Father* and sing His praises. This can be done only by His *children,* and such "men" become only by faith in Christ Jesus. Gal. 4—So these "men" are to be brought from spiritual darkness to spiritual light. How is this to be accomplished? By *"seeing your good works."* Your good works are the beams of your light shining before "men," by which these are attracted to the light and are thus enlightened. In other words: your good, *kala, i. e.,* laudable works, speak a loud language. The "men" know that you profess faith in Christ. *Let your light shine.* Let them see that your life is in conformity with that profession, let them see that you are faithful and honest in your daily vocation, that you do not recompense evil with evil, that you live soberly, righteously, and justly in this evil world, etc. This is a powerful object sermon on faith in Christ. When disciples so live, God's name is hallowed; the Father is glorified. "Men" see, feel, realize, that a higher power is at work in Christ's disciples, enabling them so to live. And "men" that see these *good,* laudable, works may be led to enquire for the power, the source, and thus they may come under the influence of the mighty Word of God, which is able to call also these "men" from "darkness to His marvelous light," and then they, too, show forth the praises of Him that called them. Thus "men" may come to a knowledge that "in time past they were not a people, but are now the people of God" by faith in Christ Jesus. 1 Pet. 3, 9 ff.

"So," disciples of Christ, *"let your light shine"*—this is your duty and your privilege—and then the *end* ("so that") will be attained with some "men:" they will "glorify your Father which is in heaven."

St. Peter couches the same thought in this language: "Dearly beloved, . . . having your conversation honest," laudable, right, "among the Gentiles, that . . . they may be your good works which they shall behold glorify God in the day of visitation." 1 Pet. 2, 11, 12.

That is what we pray for in the First Petition: "Hallowed be Thy name."—"Sanctify them through Thy Word," so Jesus prays for His disciples, and these sanctified disciples are admonished: "So let your light shine before men," etc.—By pure doctrine (John 17, 17) and holy life flowing therefrom, "hallowed be Thy name."

For instructive examples, showing that the good works of Christ actuated the people to praise God, see Matt. 9, 8; 15, 31, et al.

NOTE.—The hypocrites do good (?) works "that *they* may have glory *of men*," "that *they* may be seen *of men*" (Matt. 6, 2, 5); the disciples do good works that the "men," the unbelievers, may see them and "glorify *your Father*." The hypocrites perform works for the glorification of self; the disciples, for the glorification of God. The source of the former is sin; of the latter, faith.

Ezek. 22, 26: *Her priests have violated My Law, and have profaned Mine holy things.*

Among the thousands carried into captivity at Babylon by Nebuchadnezzar, 577 B. C., was Ezekiel. His duty, as God's prophet, was to endeavor to convince the captive Jews of the certainty of the destruction of Jerusalem—a judgment brought upon the city by the faithlessness of the people. These prophecies we find in chapters 1—24.—Our text is taken from a fearful indictment of all classes of people: prophets, priests, princes, people. Their moral deterioration is shown; all have departed from God. "I sought for a man among them," says God, "that should make up the hedge, and stand in the gap before Me for the land that I should not destroy it; but I found none," v. 30. (Read vv. 23—31.)

Arraigning the *priests*, Ezekiel says: "*Her priests*," i. e., the land's, Jerusalem's priests, "*have violated*"—rather: *have done violence to*—"*My law, and have profaned Mine holy things.*"

The priests, bound by their order to observe every ordinance of God's Law, not only did not keep it, but, on the contrary, *violated*, did *violence to, the Law. i. e.*, they misinterpreted it (Luther: "sie verkehren mein Gesetz freventlich"), so as to make their violation, their transgression, of the Law seem laudable and in conformity with the Law. *Ut rex, ita grex!* "Like priests, like people!" From laxity in doctrine flows laxity in life; from false doctrine flows ungodly life. "*The priests have profaned Mine holy things.*" The text unfolds this thought: "They have made no distinction between the holy and the common, neither have they caused men to discern between the unclean and the clean, and have hid their eyes from My sabbaths, and I am profaned among them."

"It was the special office of the priests to keep up the distinction between holy and unholy, between clean and unclean, consecrated and common things. Lev. 10, 10; 22, 1—13. They should have instructed the people what meats were lawful for them, what not; what sacrifices were fit to be brought to the Lord, and what not; who were worthy, and who not, to eat the holy things and to approach unto the holy God. But this they had not done. The law of the Sabbath, as Hengstenberg remarks, is given as an example. This they rob of its deep spiritual character, and limit it to the external rest, as if it were given to animals, and not to men who are to serve God in spirit; cf. v. 8. By these things they profaned God Himself."   *—Pulpit Commentary.*

And today the *Bible* is profaned by treating it as a man-made book; the *Gospel* is profaned by the many Christless sermons resounding throughout the land from "modern" pulpits; *Baptism* and the *Lord's Supper* are profaned by representing them to be merely signs or symbols, thus emptying them of their meaning as means of grace; the *holyday* is profaned by neglecting to hear the Word of God, etc. From false doctrine flows unholy life; by both God's name is profaned. From this preserve us, dear heavenly Father!

Rom. 2, 23, 24: *Thou that makest thy boast of the Law, through breaking the law, dishonorest thou God. For the name of God is blasphemed among the Gentiles through you.*

The English version has an interrogation point after v. 23, making the sentence read as a question. Consulting text and context, we prefer with Luther to place the period. V. 23 is an awful impeachment of the Jews based on the preceding accusations (vv. 21, 22) of gross violations of the Law. This grammatical construction of v. 23 is supported by v. 24: *"For* the name of God", etc.

After several specific charges of Law-violation, put interrogatively, vv. 21, 22, challenging denial, if they dare, the apostle flings the indictment into the face of the Jews: *"Thou that makest thy boast of the Law, through breaking the Law, dishonorest thou God."* Paul's thought is this: God had given His holy Law to the Jews. That was a high prerogative; cf. Rom. 9, 4. And the Jews prided themselves thereon; they made a *boast of it.* "Sons of the Thorah" (the Law) was a title they loved to bear. This *boast* of theirs was well known by the Gentiles. But the latter not only had a fine ear to hear the boast, but also sharp eyes to watch their conduct. What did they observe? The Jews stole, committed adultery, committed sacrilege, vv. 21, 22. They *broke* God's Law. Their conversation did not tally with their profession. The *Gentiles* made conclusions from the immoral practices of the Jews to the Lawgiver. If the "Sons of the Thorah," who proudly *boasted* of being the possessors of God's Law, lead such an unholy life, then, they inferred, the God of the Jews, who gave this Law according to which His people were supposed to live, must be an unholy God. Thus, declares St. Paul, *"through you,"* through your immoral conduct, God is *"dishonored,"* *"the name of God is blasphemed among the Gentiles."*—Are applications of this text to present-day conditions necessary? Alas! they readily come to mind. One Judas casts reproach upon the Eleven; one Christian, who goes astray, causes the unbelievers to jeer and laugh at Christ and the Christian religion.—"The greatest obstructors of the success of the Word, are those whose bad lives contradict their good doctrine; who, in the pulpit preach so well that it is a pity they should ever come out; and out of the pulpit live so ill that it is a pity they should ever come in." (Henry.)—Let us pray:

Thy name be hallowed! Help us, Lord,
To keep in purity Thy word,
And lead according to Thy name
A holy life, untouched by blame.
Let no false teachings do us hurt,
All poor deluded souls convert.

THE SECOND PETITION.

Thy Kingdom Come.

John 3, 5: *Except a man be born of water and of the Spirit, he cannot enter into the kingdom of God.*

John 3 is the celebrated Nicodemus chapter. Nicodemus was "a ruler of the Jews," *i. e.*, a member of the Sanhedrin, the highest church council at Jerusalem. This Pharisee, a rationalist of the first water, had been profoundly impressed by the activity of Jesus. He came to Jesus with an important question on his mind. From the answer of Jesus, the searcher of hearts, rather than from the polite address of Nicodemus, v. 2, we infer what he was in quest of. Was Jesus about to establish a kingdom of God on earth, that kingdom which was so anxiously expected by the Jews?

"Verily, verily, I say unto thee,"—these are the words of Jesus to Nicodemus,—"Except a man *be born again*, he cannot *see the kingdom of God*," v. 3. The "ruler of the Jews" knows nothing about a new birth: *"How* can a man be born when he is old?" V. 4. It cannot be done, so Nicodemus imagines. Now Jesus not only repeats his assertion of v. 3, but develops that truth by adducing the manner in which this new birth is ordinarily effected. He says: *"Verily, verily, I say unto thee, except a man be born of water and of the Spirit"*—lit.: of water and Spirit), *"he cannot enter into the kingdom of God.* That which is born of the flesh is flesh, and that which is born of the Spirit is spirit."

Now, of which *kingdom* does Jesus here speak? The text is plain. In order to *see* this kingdom, v. 3, to *enter* this kingdom, v. 5, it is absolutely necessary that a man be *born again*, vv. 3, 5, be born a second time. A man born into this world is thereby not born into this kingdom. Being born into this world, man is a child of wrath; he is born into the kingdom of Satan. So by nature none are in this *kingdom of God.* To belong to this kingdom man must be born *again;* and when he *is* born again, he *is* in this kingdom of God. Only the *new-born*, the believers, the Christians, belong to this kingdom; only they belong to this kingdom who can pray: *"Our Father—Thy kingdom come."* In this peculiar *kingdom* the King—God—is known, honored, and adored as *Father* by His subjects. And wherever in this wide world hands are folded and the prayer goes heavenward: "Our *Father*—Thy *kingdom* come," there are the subjects, the citizens, in this kingdom. And in *this* kingdom the Ruler, God, deals with His subjects as their *Father*, rules them with His love and His *grace..* So this kingdom—God's kingdom and Christ's—is "not of this world," "not from hence," John 18, 36, it is the kingdom of "truth," John 18, 37, of the Gospel, and "every one that is of the truth heareth my (Christ's) voice," the Gospel, and is a citizen of this *Kingdom of Grace."*

How is the entrance to this kingdom effected? The text says: *"Except a man be born of water and of the Spirit* he cannot," etc. The second birth is a *spiritual* birth, effected by God the Holy Spirit, and hence this kingdom of grace is a *spiritual* kingdom, not, as Nicodemus thought, an earthly one. But this Spirit does not work without means to bring about the new birth. And the ordinary means ordained by God Himself is water, the water of Baptism. Cf. 1, 33; Titus 3, 4ff.; 1 Pet. 1, 23.

The *blessings* we enjoy in this Kingdom of Grace are beautifully and tersely stated in Rom. 14, 17: "The kingdom of God is not eating and drinking, but *righteousness*" before God through faith in Christ, *"and peace"* of conscience with God, *"and joy in the Holy Ghost."*

By the new birth, by faith in Christ, one becomes and remains a citizen in this kingdom of God, for which we pray in the Second Petition, and by living the spiritual life generated by the Spirit one proves himself a member thereof. In answer to the question, "How does this kingdom come?" Luther therefore says: "When our heavenly Father gives us His Holy Spirit, so that by His grace we believe His holy Word, and lead a godly life, here in time, and hereafter in eternity."—"Thy kingdom come," we pray, that is: "God graciously grant *us* true faith and godly life." (Luther.)

Matt. 9, 38: *Pray ye therefore the Lord of the harvest that He will send forth laborers into His harvest.*

"Thy kingdom come"—this means, secondly, that God "would graciously extend His Kingdom of Grace on earth." Cf. Catechism, Qu. 235.

Making a circuit in Galilee, Jesus saw the deplorable spiritual condition of the people. The scribes and Pharisees of His time were blind leaders of the blind, and so the multitudes were without competent spiritual leaders and teachers. His Savior's heart yearned for their salvation. His divine compassion found utterance in the well-known words: *"The harvest truly is plenteous; the laborers few,"* etc.

As then, so now. The harvest-field, this wide world, contains untold multitudes of souls to be garnered in: *"The harvest truly is plenteous."* What is to be done? Laborers, harvesters, are wanted; preachers, teachers, missionaries, are needed to sow the seed of the Gospel and later on to bring in the sheaves. Where the seed, the Gospel, is sown, there, without fail, will be a harvest—men will come to faith. Is 55, 11. Thus the kingdom of God is extended.—How are the laborers to be obtained? The disciples must see to that. Jesus addresses His *disciples*, not the multitude. Disciples, believers, have somewhat of the compassion of their Lord with the spiritually destitute. What are they to do? *"Pray ye the Lord of the harvest,"* etc. Disciples, believers only, can pray. And when do they pray earnestly, fervently? When they feel, realize their need or that of others. Disciples are to feel the need of the lost multitudes as their own, and with a heart full of compassion for their eternal welfare they are to pray: "Lord, send *laborers!* Send *laborers*, not drones, into Thy harvest-field." The disciples are to "pray *to the Lord of the harvest*" for laborers. Only He can qualify preachers, missionaries, for this high calling; only He can imbue them with the true spirit to carry out this work, to preach Christ and Him crucified with burning lips to dying souls.—We are Christ's disciples. To us He says: *"Pray ye,"* etc. Doing this, young men forsake all, flock to our seminaries to become preachers, missionaries, teachers. Through their labors God's kingdom is enlarged. But still the laborers are few: we do not pray enough—hence the lack of laborers. *"Pray ye therefore:"* "Thy kingdom come! Lord, send laborers into Thy harvest-field." And Jesus, having said this to His disciples, continues the good work of preaching the kingdom of God. And in the very next chapter we read that these selfsame disciples whom Jesus so earnestly exhorted: "Pray ye," etc., are themselves sent out into the field and they go. *Fiat applicatio.*

Luke 12, 32: *Fear not, little flock; for it is your Father's good pleasure to give you the kingdom.*

Briefly stated, the context of this passage is this: The Lord took occasion to warn His disciples against covetousness (v.13 ff.). To make the folly of this sin stand out all the more, He appended the parable of the Rich Fool (vv.16—21). Worldly cares are closely connected with covetousness and so Jesus raises His voice of exhortation against these, too.

Since "man's life consisteth not in the abundance of the things which he possesseth" (v. 15), it is evidently folly to be anxiously concerned about "what ye shall eat, what ye shall put on" (v. 22.) "All these things do the nations of the world seek after" (v. 30.) His disiples should not be so minded. Why not? "Your Father knoweth that ye have need of these things" (v. 31). But His disciples have flesh and blood and hence they need such warnings; but they also need *consolation*, and so the Lord says encouragingly: *"Fear not, little flock."* Over against the number of such as center their thoughts in the things of this life, His disciples then and now are but a *"little flock."* But being a *flock*, His flock, they have a good Shepherd and shall not want; hence they need not fear. Having Jesus as their Shepherd, God is their *Father;* they are His children. "Fear not; for it is your Father's *good pleasure to give you the kingdom."* Since the Father *"takes pleasure* in giving you the kingdom with all its spiritual blessings" which you now possess by faith and the fruition whereof you will enjoy in yonder life, surely "these things," your earthly wants and necessities, will be added to you. Hence use your earthly possessions so as to be benefited by them eternally (v. 33; Matt. 19, 21).

"How sublime and touching a contrast between this tender and pitying appellation, 'little flock' and the 'good pleasure' of the Father to give them the kingdom; the one recalling the insignificance and the helplessness of that then literal handful of disciples, the other holding up to their view the eternal love that encircled them, the everlasting arms that were underneath them, and the high inheritance awaiting them! Well might He say, 'Fear not!' " (J. F. and B. Com.)

The point of the passage here is: "the little flock" by God's "good pleasure" now possesses "the kingdom." It is in the *Kingdom of Grace* and will enter the *Kingdom of Glory*. And for this kingdom of glory the "little flock" prays: Lord Jesus, come quickly.—"Thy kingdom come" means thirdly that God would "hasten the advent of His kingdom of glory." (Cf. *Catechism*, Qu. 235.)

> "Blest river of salvation,
> Pursue thy onward way;
> Flow thou to every nation,
> Nor in thy riches stay;
> Stay not till all the lowly
> Triumphant reach their home;
> Stay not till all the holy
> Proclaim, the Lord is come."

THE THIRD PETITION:

Thy will be done on earth, as it is in heaven.

The Lord teaches us to pray: *"Our Father*, who art in heaven, *Thy will be done on earth."*.."Our *Father's* will *is* His *good* and *gracious* will in Christ Jesus." "Hallowed be Thy name;" "Thy Kingdom come"—This is the Father's will to "be done among us also." Opposed to this good and gracious will of God is the evil counsel and will of the unholy trinity: the devil, the world, and our own flesh. *"Thy will be done"* says: God, break such evil counsel and will of our spiritual adversaries, strengthen and preserve us steadfast in faith unto our end.

Of the evil counsel and will opposed to God's gracious will the following two passages speak.

1 Pet. 5, 8: *The devil, as a roaring lion, walketh about, seeking whom he may devour.*

The paragraph, beginning at v. 6, treats of the Christians' conduct under the cross. The apostle exhorts the suffering Christians *to humility:* "Humble yourselves under the mighty hand of God;" to *confidence in God:* "Casting all your care upon Him;" to *staunch resistance* to the devil: "Be sober, be vigilant; resist (the devil) steadfast in the faith."

"Be" spiritually *"sober,"* fellow-Christians; *"be vigilant,"* be wide-awake soldiers on guard duty, lest you be taken captive unawares *"because your adversary the devil seeks whom he may devour."* His is an evil counsel and will. The devil is your *adversary, antidikos;* he is not an ordinary enemy, but one who endeavors to accuse you as an ad-adversary, an opponent, does in court. Be watchful! "Watch and pray, that ye enter not into temptation." (Mark 14, 37, 38). The devil is the *adversary* of mankind in general, but especially of the Christians. He is *your* adversary, says Peter. By God's grace you have been delivered from his kingdom; into it he would fain lead you again. And he is a *mighty* adversary: he is a *lion.* The lion is the king of brutes; the devil is a mighty, powerful prince. As a lion intimidates people by his *roaring,* so the devil seeks to terrify the Christians by persecutions, sufferings, manifold temptations. Yea, suffering comes also from the devil (cf. Job 2, 6, 7). The persecutors of the Christians in the first three centuries, in all centuries, were and are in the service of Satan. He is a cause of evil that befalls Christians. This, however, does not exclude that these things come also from God. The apostle began the exhortation thus: "Humble yourselves under the mighty *hand of God."* God holds the reins of government in His

hands; when Satan *roars*, i. e., intimidates the Christians by his *roaring*, God has allowed him to do so. The cross of the Christian comes from God. Cross is sent not for our hurt but for our *gain*. God has good intents; His will under the cross is a good and gracious will; the devil, however, too, is active, and he has an evil counsel and will. His will is to *devour*. And to gain his end he never tires: *he walketh about;* he makes the rounds among the Christians: *he seeketh* as one seeks who has lost a precious treasure; he watches his chances; he watches *every single* individual Christian: "seeking *whom, tina,* he may devour." The *"whom," tina,* is in the singular number. Not *one* is immune from his assaults. The means by which he tries to gain his end is persecution, the lust of the world, the lust of the flesh, the pride of life. Peter knows whereof he speaks; he experienced the intimidation of the roaring lion; in an unguarded hour he denied his Master.

And now, can we withstand this evil counsel and will? Peter answers: "whom resist steadfast *in the faith.*"

Be steadfast. *stereoi*, people. How? "With the might of our naught can be done." Resist as firm people *through faith.* Faith in the Christian resists the assaults of Satan; faith relies upon God, upon Jesus, and God is stronger than Satan. "Resist the devil and he will flee from you," James 4, 7. Not in our own power can we break and hinder the devil's evil counsel and will, but only in God's power, by God's grace. This the apostle clearly says in this same connection, when he proceeds, v. 10: "But the God of all grace, who hath called us unto His eternal glory by Christ Jesus, after that ye have suffered a (little) while, will make you perfect, stablish, strengthen, settle you. To *Him* be glory and dominion for ever and ever. Amen."

Resume: This passage teaches, 1, God's will is the salvation of man; 2, Opposed to this is the devil's evil counsel and will to "devour" the Christians—to cause them to fall from grace; 3, God breaks and hinders such evil counsel and will, and strengthens and preserves us steadfast in His word and faith, so that we do His will and in all sufferings remain patient unto the end. Cf. Cat. Ques. 240, 241.

1 John 2, 15-17. *Love not the world, neither the things that are in the world. If any man love the world, the love of the Father is not in him. For all that is in the world, the lust of the flesh, and the lust of the eyes, and the pride of life, is not of the Father, but is of the world. And the world passes away, and the lust thereof: but he that doeth the will of God abideth forever.*

The term "world," *kosmos,* as used in the New Testament has various significations. *Kesmos* may mean, 1, the universe, Rom. 1, 20; 2. the earth, 1 John 2, 9; Matt. 4, 8, 3.; the inhabitants of the earth, v. 29; 4, 42; 4. the unbelieving world, Matt. 12, 31; et al. Text and context disclose which meaning is intended in the single case.—In the present text the apostle, contrasting the "children," *i. e.*, the Christians, with "the world," has in mind *the unbelieving world, men elienated from God*

Furthermore, the contrast *in thought*, expressed in the text should be remembered. "If any man love the *world*, the love of the *Father* is not in him." Again, "*The world* passeth away . . . but he that doeth *the will of God* abideth forever." "The world" and "the Father;" "the world" and "God" are opposites.

Now let us consider the passage. The key-sentence of the paragraph is: "*Love not the world.*" This warning is based on the preceding verses, 12-14. The apostle speaks to "children," v. 12, to Christians, who "know the Father," v. 13, "who have overcome the wicked one," v. 14.—"Love not the world," the godless world. "The world" knows not the Father, does not stand in child-relation to Him, but is ruled and governed by "the wicked one," the devil. "*Love . . . neither the things that are in the world.*" "The world" and "the things that are in the world" are inseparable. They are "the things" with which the godless people occupy themselves, and which manifest their true sentiments, showing that they are altogether alienated from God. "The things that are in the world" are specified: "the lust of the flesh, and the lust of the eyes, and the pride of life." This is the atmosphere in which "the world" breathes, moves, lives.

"*If any man should love* (ean tis agapa) *the world*," it is absolutely patent that "*the love of the Father is not in him.*" "The world" and "the Father" are opposites; the love to the one excludes the love to the other; a compromise between the two is impossible. V. 16 enforces the command of v. 15: "*Love not the world*," and explains why love for "the things in the world" is incompatible with the love of the Father: "For all that is in the world, the lust of the flesh, and the lust of the eyes, and the pride of life, is not of the Father," (*ek tou patros*=out of the Father, has as its source (ek) not the Father, but the world). Worldliness, the carnal spirit and its manifestitations—these wicked things—have their source "of the world" in the sinful lust of ungodly men, aye, in the "wicked one." Lust—lust—lust is the governing principle of the wordly-minded.

And now as to the carnal spirit of the world. It is described thus: "The lust of the flesh," etc. "The lust *of the flesh*," he epithymia tes sarkos. Every evil sentiment of the heart is "*lust of the flesh*," has its seat in the flesh (Gal. 5, 16; Eph. 2, 3). And so considered *tes sarkos*= "of the flesh" would be a subjective genetive, but since "lust of the flesh" is placed aside of "lust of the eyes," the one is discriminated from the other, so as to designate *species* of lust; hence it is preferable to consider "of the flesh" to be an objective genetive: the lust which depraved nature feels, the carnal appetites, which it longs to gratify, such as adultery, fornication, the modern dance and theatre. *"The lust of the eyes,"* says Luther, "is nothing else than avarice, a vice now so prevalent that it is almost in vain to preach against it." Prov. 23, 5. "The lust of the eyes," in general, manifests itself in seeing, in looking at the sinful things of the world and finding pleasure therein.

"The pride," the vaunting, the vain-glory, *"of life"* is the lust of shining, and making a boastful display of one's possessions, "the effort to outshine our neighbors in our mode of life." This threefold lust "is not of the Father, but of the world." It is contrary to "the will of God." Since this is true, how obvious that "if any should love the world, the love of the Father is not in him!" The love of the world drives out the love to God. Thus v. 16 is proof of v. 15.

And now another reason is adduced for the prohibition: "Love not the world." *"The world,"* the unchristian, godless world *"passeth away,"* *paragetai,* passes by, like a passing tinseled, glittering show. The world "passes away" and goes to its place where there is wailing and gnashing of teeth. Is. 14, 11. And the threefold "lust thereof" likewise comes to an end; it is transitory, evanescent, and so the person that puts his affection on it has wasted his life and destroyed his soul. *"But he that doeth the will of God abideth forever."* Christians have a sentiment different from that of the world. They are "children" of God whose "sins are forgiven for His Name's sake." V. 12. They are minded "to do the will *of God;"* their purpose and aim in life is to please the Father. They are born again *unto* a lively hope for an inheritance, salvation, in heaven. 1 Pet. 1, 3 ff. Of it John writes: "Beloved, now are we the sons of God, and it doth not yet appear what we shall be: but we know that when he shall appear, we shall be like him; for we shall see him as he is."

"Thy will be done." Opposed to this will of God is the godless *world,* back of which stands the "wicked one," the *devil.* We Christians are "of the Father," thanks to His mercy, but we, too, still have *"the flesh."* And this flesh of ours is not one whit better than that of the world. How necessary therefore the exhortation again and again: "Love not the world;" ye are "children whose sins are forgiven for His, Jesus' Name's sake." v. 12. Cf. Math. 16, 26; Heb. 11, 24-26. The passage contains two lines of thought: 1. The exhortation: Love not the world; 2. The reasons for this earnest admonition.—Its purpose is to show that the evil counsel and will of the devil, the world, and our own flesh is opposed to the good and gracious will of God. Cf. Catechism, Ques. 240.

Theme: Love not the world: 1. Love of the world excludes love to the Father: 2. Love of the world leads to destruction.

Rom. 16, 20: *The God of peace shall bruise Satan under your feet shortly.*

"Our Father who art in heaven," hear thy children's cry: "Thy will be done," that is, adapting Luther's language: "Break and hinder every evil counsel and will which would not let us hallow Thy name nor let Thy Kingdom come, such as the will of the devil, the world, and our flesh; strengthen and preserve us steadfast in Thy word and faith unto our end." And our petition is Yea and Amen in Him. This we know for the Lord Jesus has taught us so to pray.

But passages like the present make assurance doubly sure. In the last chapters of Romans, St. Paul warned the Christians against dangers threatening their soul's salvation. In the present chapter, v. 16 ff.. he cautions them to beware of false teachers and teachings. "The errorists who cause divisions and dissensions by their false doctrines are not servants of Christ, but are in the service of Satan who through them would rob the Christians of faith and salvation. And so the apostle calls attention to this archenemy, but at the same time assures his brethren that God who has called them into His peace will not permit Satan to annihilate the good work begun in them."—*The God of peace shall bruise Satan under your feet shortly.* "The day is not far hence in which the Lord will totally *'bruise'*, crush, Satan and deliver His own from all evil, from all machinations of the old bitter foe." Stoeckhardt, *Roemerbrief.* The language of our text: "The God of peace shall *bruise Satan under your feet,"* recalls to our mind the very first promise of redemption made in the Garden of Eden, Gen. 3, 15. Hence Phillippi says: "The promise of the first Gospel, of the Protevangel, has been fulfilled objectively, once for all time by the crucifixion of Christ; but it is subjectively realized again and again within the Church of Christ by every victory which faith in the atoning sacrifice of Christ gains over Satan, who has already been judged and defeated by Christ."

I Pet. 1, 5: *You are kept by the power of God through faith unto salvation.*

Phil. 1, 6: *He which hath begun a good work in you will perform it until the day of Jesus Christ.*

For exposition of these passages, treated under question 181 of the Catechism, consult Vol. I. pp. 233, 234.

The thought to be stressed here is, in the language of the Small Catechism, that God must "strengthen and preserve us in. His word and faith unto our end."

THE FOURTH PETITION

"Our Father, who art in heaven—give us this day our daily bread."

Matt. 5, 45: *"He maketh His sun to rise on the evil and on the good, and sendeth rain on the just and on the unjust."*

This text is taken from an exhortation of our Master in which He bids us: "Love your enemies." We are God's children and hence should prove ourselves to be such by our deeds. Impartially God bestows His benefits on the just and the unjust. This the text proves by saying: *"He maketh His sun to rise on the evil and on the good, and sendeth rain on the just and on the unjust."*

Now for our purpose—what truth is there in this text? Two classes of people are mentioned. On the one hand are "the evil"— *poneroi*—who are such in God's sight, measured by His holy Law; "the unjust"—*adikoi*—who are known as such by their dealings with men, measured by the norm of human justice. On the other hand the text speaks of *"the good,"* the *agathoi*, who are such in God's sight and who prove by their walk in life that they are *just, dikaioi*. These latter terms describe the God-fearing people.

Now, says the text, over both, believers and unbelievers, God maketh His *sun* to rise; to both He sends *rain*. Sunshine and rain are the two main sources of maintenance. God's love to both classes of people is impartial. The field of "the evil," "the unjust," bears fruit just as well as that of "the good," "the just." The former class, however, ignores the fact that it is *God* who maketh His sun to rise; that it is *God* who sends rain in due season. This relation of cause and effect the ungodly does not acknowledge. The truth is: God provides for all. Luther expresses it thus: "God gives daily bread indeed without our prayer, also to all the wicked." *Why, then, pray for daily bread?* Luther says: "We pray in this petition that He would lead us to *know* it, and to receive our daily bread with thanksgiving." So the psalmist was minded who speaks in our next text.

Ps. 145, 15, 16. *The eyes of all wait upon Thee; and Thou givest them their meat in due season. Thou openest Thine hand and satisfiest the desire of every living thing.*

The psalmist knows that our *meat, i. e.,* our food, our nourishment is a *gift* of God. He knows that *"every living thing,"* the unbeliever and the brute included, must be satisfied by the *cornu copia* in His hand, though the irrational brute *cannot* see it and the rational unbeliever *will* not see it. Brutes and unbelievers know not God. Christians do, and so with the psalmist they intone a hymn of praise in honor of God's providence, saying: "The eyes of all," etc. (See the same text, p. 127, Vol. I.

2 Thess. 3, 10-12. *If any would not work, neither should he eat. For we hear that there are some which walk among you disorderly, working not at all, but are busybodies. Now them that are such we command and exhort by our Lord Jesus Christ that with quietness*

they work and eat their own bread.

We pray: *"Give us—our bread."* Is this a contradiction in itself? The passage bearing on this question is both interesting and instructive.—During that brief stay of three sabbath days when the church at Thessalonica was established, even then already *"when we were with you, this we commanded you"*—an emphatic statement—*"that if any would not work, neither should he eat."* In his *first* letter St. Paul had found it needful to beseech the brethren "that ye study to be quiet, and to do your own business, and to work with your own hands." 1 Thess. 4, 10. Not having the desired effect, this admonition is repeated with great emphasis in this *second* letter.

What, then, was the situation in Thessalonica? Some members supposed that the Last Day was imminent. "Why then still follow worldly occupations? Be idle; prepare for the Lord's coming—this is the business to be concerned about." So they fancied, so they acted. Some members *"would not work;"* they positively refused to work. Not living according to God's order and commandment, they *"walked disorderly"* and became mischief-makers. "Working not at all" they turned "busybodies:" *"ouk ergazomenoi alla periergazomenoi,"* as the Greek has it; not minding their own business, they became busy in minding everybody else's business. This evil had grown to large proportions. Paul uses straight, blunt language: *"If any man will not work, neither let him eat."* He speaks of such as *will* not work, not of such as *cannot* work. If you *will* not work, starve. Aut—aut! Again he exhorts them to "work with quietness, and eat their *own* bread"— bread honestly come by. He appeals to these idle busybodies, who through their conduct became a burden and a scandal to the congregation, in the name of the highest authority for a Christian: *"We command and exhort by our Lord Jesus Christ."*

The apostle's charge: "If any one will not work, neither shall he eat" has its foundation in Gen. 3, 19: "In the sweat of thy face shalt thou eat bread." Work, labor, is an ordinance of God. God is the Giver of "daily bread," *i. e.,* "of all that we need to support this body and life," but He has ordered that man should engage in useful occupation and so eat his own bread, not that of charity, or slothfulness. "The idle soul shall suffer hunger and drowsiness shall cover a man with rags." Prov. 23, 21.

Is. 58, 7. *Deal thy bread to the hungry.*

We say *"our bread"* in the Fourth petition also for this reason because we should pray for our neighbor and communicate to him. This we are told by the prophet in Is. 58, 7. For exposition of this passage see page 47, Vol. I.

Prov. 30, 7, 9. *Two things have I required of Thee; deny me them not before I die: Remove far from me vanity and lies; give me neither poverty nor riches; feed me with food convenient for me, lest I be full, and deny Thee, and say, Who is the Lord? or lest I be poor, and steal, and take the name of my God in vain.*

The two things the supplicant asks for are: 1. *"Remove far from me vanity,"* falsehood, deceit, *"and lies."* By Thy grace grant me ever a truthful and sincere spirit toward Thee and my fellow-man. "Sanctify me through Thy truth: Thy word is truth." Joh. 17. 17. So this part of the prayer relates to spiritual blessings.

2. *"Give me neither poverty nor riches."* Here the supplication turns to temporal matters and applies to the subject-matter in hand: "Give us this day our *daily* bread." Of two extremes the petitioner begs to be spared: poverty on the one hand, riches on the other. Both conditions in life are fraught with grave temptations. Riches may lead to a frame of mind described thus: *"Lest I be full,"* have a superabundance, which may mislead me to *"deny Thee, and say"* in self-confidence,*"Who is the Lord?"* The haughty rich are prone to ask scornfully as did rich, proud Pharaoh: "Who is the Lord that I should obey Him?" (Ex. 2, 5; Dt. 8, 12 ff; Ps. 14, 1.) Poverty's temptations are set forth thus: *"Lest I be poor,"* in needy circumstances, *"and steal, and take the name of my God in vain,"* i. e., use the name of God profanely by murmuring against my fate or even by blaspheming out of impatience and want of resignation to His will. The happy mean between these two extremes—poverty and riches—finds expression in these words: *"Feed me with food convenient for me."* Literally: "Give me to eat the bread of *my portion."* The Lord, this is the petition, is to portion the bread out to him. And so this prayer comports with the Fourth Petition: "Give us *today* our *daily* bread." *Daily* bread, that is, that bread which is needed to supply our wants and necessities each day. Thus the passage teaches contentment. St. Paul voices the same truth thus: "Having food and raiment, let us therewith be content." 1 Tim. 6, 8.

1 Tim. 6, 8. *"Having food and raiment, let us be therewith content."*

See Proof Texts, Vol. I, p. 68. The lack of contentment, says Paul, is foolish, heathenish. It is the vice of covetousness.

Matt. 6, 33, 34. *Seek ye first the kingdom of God and His righteousness, and all these things shall be added unto you. Take therefore no thought for the morrow; for the morrow shall take thought for the things of itself. Sufficient unto the day is the evil thereof.*

For the proper understanding of this text it is needful to remember that it is taken from Christ's Sermon on the Mount, in which He describes the external appearance of the children of God in contradistinction to what is in their hearts—faith. The Christians are depicted according to their works, internal and external.

Even a slight inspection of text and context in the present paragraph reveals the fact that the people addressed *"ye"* are Christ's disciples, Christians, cf. v. 32. They belong to "the kingdom of God" hence have already obtained "the *righteousness* that availeth before God" by faith in Christ, who, as the apostle declares, "is the end of the law *for righteousness* to every one that believeth." So the term "righteousness" in our text does not mean the righteousness *of faith*, but the righteousness *of life*, the doing right in the sight of God according to His divine Law.

The "kingdom of God," the well-known concept occurring so frequently in St. Matthew, denotes that kingdom which Jesus established on earth, the holy Christian Church. Now let us follow the text.

"But," in contrast to the Gentiles, v. 32, *"seek ye,"* my disciples, *"first the kingdom of God."* The Gentiles who know not God continually ask: "What shall we eat? What shall we drink?" etc., (cf. v. 31), but *ye* not so. "Your heavenly Father knoweth that ye have need of all these things," v. 32. "Seek *ye* first the kingdom of God," be ye anxiously concerned about the establishment of God's kingdom in the hearts of men, take ye thought first and foremost to extend the Church of God by spreading the knowledge of Him who is your *Father* in Christ; *"seek His righteousness,"* earnestly strive to live a righteous life in conformity with the true knowledge of God. Let this be your first concern, your highest interest in life to serve God by holy living; prove by your walk that you are children of the Father, and this Father promises: *"all these things"* about which the Gentiles are so anxiously concerned—eating, drinking, clothing—v. 32, *"shall be added unto you."* An earthly father cheerfully supports his children, your *heavenly* Father, who is the Lord of all, surely will not allow you to want. So, away with these carking, heathenish cares. Since you have this promise of your Father, *"take no thought,"* be not anxiously concerned *"for the morrow."* Do the work of your calling faithfully, the success leave to God. "He careth for you." Don't borrow trouble, don't cross the stream until you arrive at it: *"the morrow shall take thought for the things of itself.* Sufficient unto the day is the evil thereof." Don't increase the real evil of the day by unnecessary care for the morrow.

Luther: "It is to His liking that we ask things of Him, and He is pleased to give them. Since He gladly gives great things, He will not stint the small things, but will throw them into the bargain. God has often caused many pious people who have helped in building God's kingdom, have served the Church and furthered God's Word, to ex-

perience this. God has richly blessed them with goods and honor.
This is evidenced not only by the examples of the Scriptures, but also
by the history of some of our pious kings and princes, who, having
liberally given for the ministry and schools, have not become poorer,
but were more richly blessed of God and have reigned in peace, in
victory and good fortune."

NOTE—A beautiful corroboration of v. 33 we find in Mark 8, 1 ff.
Read and ponder.

Ps. 127, 2. *It is vain for you to rise up early, to sit up late, to eat
the bread of sorrows; for so He giveth His beloved sleep.*

The implied contrast between God's *beloved*, the Christians, and
the un-Christians must be observed for the proper understanding of
the text. Both work, but in an altogether different spirit. *"It is vain
for you to rise early, to sit up late, to eat the bread of sorrows."* Rising
up early to work is laudable, sitting up late at one's task may often
be necessary. But the one that makes the early rising and the late
hours the sole point of success in his work, who leans to his own understanding, believing that the entire success of his toil depends upon his
planning and scheming and fretting and worrying will find that *"he
eats the bread of sorrows."* "Carking cares for the future beset him
in the morning, carking cares are his companions during the day, and
these same cares disturb his slumber and sleep at night, and, after all,
like the builders of the tower at Babel, he must often experience—all
was in vain. The best laid plans fail unless God crowns them with
success. This God's beloved know. They, too, rise up early, sit up late;
they eat their bread "in the sweat of their face," but they sleep soundly,
care-free, since they cast all their care upon God, knowing that the
success of their handiwork depends upon His blessing.—His *beloved* are
thus described in the next psalm: "Blessed is every one that feareth
the Lord, that walketh in His ways." And the blessing? "Thou shalt
eat the labor of thy hands. Happy shalt thou be, and it shall be well
with thee." Ps. 128, 1. And His beloved may well sing:

> "He who hitherto hath fed me,
> And to many a joy hath led me,
>   Is and shall be ever mine;
> He who did so gently school me,
> He who still doth guide and rule me,
>   Will not leave me now to pine."

> —Hymn 363, 2.

"There is no preaching of laziness masquerading as religicus trust.
The psalmist insists on one side of the truth. Not work, but self-tor-
turing care and work, without seeking God's blessing, are pronounced
vanity."

"The lesson of the psalm is one that needs to be ever repeated. It is so obvious that it is unseen by many, and apt to be unnoticed by all. There are two ways of going to work in reference to earthly good. One is that of struggling and toiling, pushing and snatching, fighting and envying, and that way comes to no successful issue; for if it gets what it has wriggled and wrestled for, it generally gets it in some way or other with an incapacity to enjoy the good won, which makes it far less than the good pursued. The other way is the way of looking to God and doing the appointed tasks with quiet dependence on Him, and that way always succeeds; for, with its modest or large outward results, there is given likewise a quiet heart set on God, and therefore capable of finding water in the desert and extracting honey from the rock." —MacLaren.

THE FIFTH PETITION:

And forgive us our trespasses, as we forgive those who trespass against us.

This petition contains: 1. An acknowledgement of our guilt before God; 2. a supplication for forgiveness; 3. a promise heartily to forgive those that sin against us.

1. We pray: "Forgive us *our trespasses.*" Matt. 6, 12, reads: "Forgive us *our debts,*" ta ofeilemata hemon.. Luke 11, 4, says: "Forgive us *our sins,*" tas hamartias hemon." "Our debts"="our sins." Sin is an offence against the holy God, a *debt* incurred demanding payment, reparation. Cf. 5, 25, 26; Luke 7, 41 ff.; 18, 23 ff. The same idea is represented by *trespasses,* ta paraptomata, Matt. 6, 14. *Trespasses,* literally, *transgressions,* interprets the word "debts" in v. 12. Because the word "trespasses" was supposed to be more readily understood it was substituted in our English form of the Lord's Prayer. 2. In conformity with this idea of "debts" is that of "forgiveness." We cannot pay the debt; we ask God to *forgive* the debts, *i. e.,* as Luther explains the phrase, "not to look upon our sins," or, to retain the figure of debt, to wipe out or to cancel from His "book of remembrance" all entries against us. 3. "*As* we forgive," etc., "*hos,*" etc. Not: "*For* we also forgive," but rather "*like* as we also forgive," implying similarity in the two actions, of kind, but no comparison of degree." Alford. In Matt. 6, 12, we should observe that *aphekamen*=forgive—is the aorist and is to be translated: "as *we* also *have forgiven.*" The forgiving our debtors is a proof that God's mercy in forgiving our trespasses has wrought in us a merciful heart to forgive those that trespass against us. Our Lord does not teach here that our act of forgiveing others precedes His, or that it is the reason and the proper ground

of His forgiveness. Christ's whole doctrine—the doctrine of all Scripture—is the reverse of this. Our forgiveness is rather a *fruit* and *consequence* of God's forgiveness. Gal. 5, 6; Matt. 18, 27 ff.; Luke 6, 36; Col. 3, 13: "Forbearing one another and forgiving one another, if any man have a quarrel against any: even as Christ *forgave* you, so also do ye." Eph. 4, 32: "Be ye kind one to another, tender-hearted, forgiving one another, even as God for Christ's sake *hath* forgiven you."

Luke 15, 21. *Father, I have sinned against heaven and in Thy sight, and am no more worthy to be called Thy son.*

"The crown and pearl" of Christ's parables is that of the Prodigal Son. Having come to a consciousness of his depraved condition, he resolves to make humble confession of his guilt to his highly offended father. The confession expresses deep contrition in the face of the enormity of his sin. All hope of being forgiven on account of any good in himself is abandoned, but the whole tenor of the prayer breathes a trusting confidence of his father's readiness to forgive him.

"*Father*"—though I have forfeited my sonship, still you are my *father*. In this appeal to the father's heart is the note of trust and confidence. "*I have sinned against heaven*"—the seat of God's majesty. I have rebelled against God. This is the root of my guilt—defection from God, ignoring His commands. "*I have sinned against thee*"—"in thy sight" (Greek) *i. e.*, in relation to thee, my Father; I have trampled the Fourth Commandment under foot; your authority and your love I have spurned. "I am no more worthy to be called thy son." This filial relation I have wantonly severed; all rights and privileges of a son I have forfeited. "Non in aetatem, non in malos consultatores culpam rejicit, sed nudam parat sine excusatione confessionem." Grotius. "He does not lay his fault to his age, nor to evil counsellors, but makes a confession without excuse." David's language furnishes a touching comment: "I acknowledge my sin unto Thee, and mine iniquity have I not hid. I said, I will confess my transgressions unto the Lord, and Thou forgavest the iniquity of my sin." Ps. 32, 5.

Luther: "Such lovely parables and pictures and such sweet and comforting words we ought to consider diligently, in order to comfort ourselves thereby against a bad conscience and against sin."—In our daily prayer: "Our Father—forgive us our trespasses" we, like the Prodigal, confess our guilt, for "we daily sin much," and ask His gracious pardon.

Ps. 19, 12. *Who can understand his errors? Cleanse Thou me from secret faults.*

The psalmist has sung the praise of "the law of the Lord" (cf. vv. 7ff.), as prophet by inspiration of the Spirit he has preached concerning the incomparable worth and powerful, salutary effect of the divine

Word. But as servant of the Lord he speaks at the same time in the name of all servants of God, from the experience of all believers. For his own person he has experienced the consolation and the power of the divine Word. He lives wholly in this word and meditates on it day and night. And the result of this meditation is the sigh: *"Who can understand his errors?"* Literally: *"As for errors, who can mark them?"* and the prayer: *"Cleanse thou me from secret faults,"* or literally: *"Clear Thou me from hidden faults."* The Hebrew word for *errors* comprises all *involuntary* sins, sins of *ignorance* and sins of infirmity—all sins of weakness that adhere to the believer till he draws his last breath. The query: *"As for errors, who can mark them?"* implies that errors are so manifold that one cannot count them and that they are so subtle as to escape the eye of man, as also one's own observation. For this reason the psalmist calls these errors *"hidden faults."* Though the servant of the Lord proves and searches his own heart again and again according to the law of God, much remains covered, hidden, that is wrong, sinful, in the sight of God. The deeper he looks into the bright, spotless mirror of the law of God, the deeper becomes his insight into his own hereditary depravity; but he can never penetrate the inmost workings of his ungodly thoughts, wishes, and desires. The contemplation of the law leads him to a knowledge of his sins and finally to the knowledge and the confession, that the dark spots in his heart and his life are so plentiful that he is not able to see and to mark them all, that his self-knowledge, and his knowledge of his own sin is and remains limited. But, on the other hand, he also knows that though sin abounds, grace does still more abound. Through meditation of the promises of the Scripture, of the Gospel, he learns to understand the bottomless and unfathomable grace and mercy of the Lord, and therefore prays with all confidence: *"Clear Thou me from hidden faults."* The Hebrew verb for *"cleanse,"*—*"clear,"* is like the Greek *dikaioun* a judicial term, and always means: to declare just, to declare innocent. The hidden, secret, unknown sins cannot possibly be eradicated out of the heart, but they can be forgiven. And actually God *daily* forgives the sins of His servants, who daily sin much, but who cling to His promise of grace. Daily and richly He forgives all their errors and declares them to be free and "clear" of the guilt of original sin which is inseparably grown together with their nature, and from which all unconscious and conscious sins flow. (cf. Stoeckhardt, Ausgewaehlte Psalmen, pp. 15, 16.)

Matt. 5, 23-26. *Therefore, if thou bring thy gift to the altar, and there rememberest that thy brother hath aught against thee, leave there thy gift before the altar and go thy way; first be reconciled to thy brother, and then come and offer thy gift. Agree with thine adversary quickly, whilst thou art in the way with him, lest at any time the adversary deliver thee to the judge, and the judge deliver thee to the officer, and thou be cast into prison. Verily, I say unto thee, Thou shalt by no means come out thence till thou hast paid the uttermost farthing.*

For the proper understanding of the text we must observe that our Lord instructs His disciples concerning New Testament things in Old Testament diction, which every Jew readily understood. He speaks of "bringing," *i. e..* "offering a gift." Offerings, sacrifices, were commanded by God Himself. To "offer a gift," that is, any kind of bloody or unbloody sacrifice, was the best, the holiest act of worship in the Old Testament dispensation. The offering was brought into the Temple *to the* altar; the officiating priest laid it on the altar. Jesus pictures a Jew in this act of worship.

But, since the offering was the principal part of divine worship in the Old Testament, the service itself was also called a sacrifice. Ps. 50, 14, 23. Thanksgiving and praise to God are designated offerings. See also Ps. 107, 22.

The New Testament sacrifices are of a *"spiritual"* nature. 1 Pet. 2, 5. Which are they? "By Him therefore let us offer the sacrifice of praise to God continually, that is, the fruit of our lips giving thanks to His name. But to do good and communicate forget not: for with such sacrifices God is well pleased." Heb. 13, 15, 16

Now let us consider the text. The context begins with v. 20. Verses 20 and 21, for the exposition of which see p. 45, Vol. I, illustrate and explain v. 20. The *"therefore"* of v. 23 makes an inference from the foregoing text, in which Christ, the expounder of the Law, had authoritatively stated that anger in the heart is a violation of the Fifth Commandment, is murder in the sight of God. This and the succeeding verses go on to show how sinful anger is before God.

"Therefore," since anger against the brother subjects to God's punishment—*"if thou bring* (offer) *thy gift to the altar,"* if you are already in the sanctuary of the Most High, having approached the altar to offer your gift to the priest, *"and there rememberest that thy brother hath aught against thee,"* that your brother is at variance with you, having a just cause for complaint, on account of which a reconciliation is necessary, *"leave there thy gift before the altar;"* don't take it away; don't postpone this act of worship indefinitely but set matters aright immediately, *"go -thy way: first"*—before sacrificing—*"be reconciled to thy brother,* and then come and offer thy gift." Reconciliation before sacrifice! Sacrifice, this act of worship, instituted by God Himself, is not acceptable to Him if made by one who is at enmity with his brother. Anger against the brother is a transgression of the Fifth Commandment, is murder in the sight of God. A murderer offering a sacrifice in God's holy presence! As if the good work could cover up murder! Impossible! *"First be reconciled to thy brother."* The Lord has had compassion on you! What does Christ say of the

Unmerciful Servant? "O thou wicked servant, I forgave thee all that debt, because thou desirest me. Shouldest not thou also have had compassion on thy fellow servant even as I had pity on thee?" Matt. 18, 32 ff.—Our text proceeds: *"Agree with thine adversary,"* thy offended brother, *"quickly, whilst thou art in the way with him."* The imagery is that of two people on the way to the courtroom where this difficulty is to be adjudged by the judge. *"Whilst thou art in the way with him,"* the matter may still be amicably settled without court proceedings; do it *quickly "lest at any time the adversary deliver thee to the judge."* When matters have been allowed to go too far, justice takes its course, *"the judge will deliver thee to the officer,"* the sheriff, *"and thou be cast into prison."* Once in prison there is no possibility of escape. *"Verily,"* the Lord affirms His statement with an oath, *"I say unto thee, Thou shalt by no means come out thence, till thou hast paid the uttermost farthing."*—And now as to the lesson the Lord inculcates by employing this illustration from everyday life. Without reconciliation neither the sacrifice nor the one that sacrifices is acceptable to God. So long as reconciliation does not take place, the irreconciled is in danger of being cast into the prison of hell, where payment of debt is out of question.

From the very beginning the Christian Church has applied the above passage especially to the Lord's Supper.. In the Lord's Supper we enter into the closest communion with our Savior by partaking of His body and blood under the bread and wine. Approaching the Lord's Table, knowing that a brother hath "aught," a real cause of complaint against us, can but *call* down damnation upon ourselves. "First be reconciled to thy brother."

Note: As to how to deal with a brother who will not conform with the Lord's injunction, see Dr. C. F. W. Walther's *Pastorale*, p. 194.

Mark, 11, 25, 26. *When ye stand praying, forgive if ye have aught against any, that your Father also which is in heaven may forgive you your trespasses. But if ye do not forgive, neither will your Father which is in heaven forgive your trespasses.*

Here we have the same thought as in the preceding passage. The point of difference is this: In Matt. 5, 23, we read: "If thou rememberest that thy brother hath aught *against three*"; here the converse is presented. "If *ye have* aught against any."

The question may arise: Is our forgiving our brother's trespasses against us perhaps a *ground* of God's forgiving our sins? No. We pray: "Forgive us our trespasses *as we forgive those who trespass* against us." Luther explains this admirably thus: "We pray in this petition that our Father in heaven would not look on our sins, nor on their account deny our prayer; for we are worthy of none of the things for which we pray, neither have we deserved them; but that He would grant them all to us by grace;—*so will we also heartily forgive and readily do good to those who sin against us.*" Our forgiveness is not a ground of God's forgiveness. God's forgiveness is the force impelling us to forgive others. We promise earnestly and sincerely because of God's grace toward us to forgive others if they trespass against us; we promise them a cordial treatment. Rom. 12, 20.

In the text, Mark 11, 25, 26, the Christians are represented as pray-ing to their "*Father*" which is in heaven." So we are His *children.* How did we become such? "Ye are all the *children* of God *by faith* in Christ Jesus." Faith apprehends and appropriates the merits of Christ— for-giveness of sins, first of all. Faith, however, worketh by love. Love is a fruit of faith. If this fruit of faith—love—in this case manifest-ing itself by forgiving one another's faults—is absent, faith does not function; in other words, it is dead. Such as call upon the Father, His children, Christians, have the Spirit of Christ, who said: "Father, forgive them, for they know not what they do." If "*when ye stand praying*" and then and there should remember "*that ye have aught against any*" and should refuse to forgive, your unforgiving attitude would erect an insurmountable barrier between you and your God, it would shut you out of God's mercy and render your prayer of none effect.—Listen to St. John: "Beloved, if God so loved us, we ought also to love one another. If any man say, I love God, and hateth his brother, he is a liar: for he that loveth not his brother whom he hath seen, how can he love God whom he hath not seen?" 1 John 4, 11, 19. See also Matt. 18, 28-35. Read Matt. 18, 23-35, treating of the wicked serv-ant.

THE SIXTH PETITION.

And lead us not into temptation.

The English word, "tempt" according to its primary classical sense means to offer an inducement to somebody to do wrong; to entice to evil—seduce. In the New Testament the word "*tempt*", a translation of the Greek *peirazo* signifies *to try, to prove, to test.* The motive may be either good or bad.—Satan's very name is "The Tempter"; his work is to *tempt* to evil, to sin, to cause to fall from grace. 1 Thess. 3, 5 the apostle writes to the Thessalonian Christians: "lest by some means *the tempter* (peirazon, Satan) *have tempted* (epeirazen) you, and our labor be in vain." Satan's design in tempting is plain. cf. 1 Cor. 7, 5. In Matt. 4, 1 we are told that the devil *tempted* Jesus. Again, his mo-tive is clear.

When "tempt" is used of God it is *to try, to prove, to test* us for our good. In "temptations" the devil's designs are evil; God's designs

are good. Frequently our New Testament translates the Greek word
(peirazein) *to tempt* by *try, prove, examine,* thus giving a commentary
to the Greek word for English readers. Instances of this kind we
find in John 6, 6 (peirazon)—to *tempt*—translated by "prove";
2 Cor. 13, 5: (peirazete)—*tempt* yourselves, translated: "*Examine*
yourselves whether ye be in faith." In a number of places the Greek
verb is rendered simply by "tempt", the noun *peirasmos* by "temptation", and text and context must give us the key as to the intended meaning. cf. Matt. 4, 1; 16, 1; 19, 3; Mark 10, 2; 1 Cor. 10, 13; Gal.
6, 1; et al

John 6, 5, 6. *Jesus saith unto Philip, Whence shall we buy bread
that these may eat? And this He said to prove him; for He himself
knew what he would do.*

Here was a crowd of five thousand men, not counting the women
and the children. They had followed Jesus, fascinated by His Gospel
preaching. Provision for food had not been thought of by the multitude. They must be fed. "*Jesus Himself knew what He would do.*"
Nevertheless he puts the question to one of His disciples, Philip:
"*Whence shall we buy bread that these may eat?*" This question was
for the disciple's good. We read: "And this he said to *tempt, peirazon,*
him." What is the meaning of "tempt" here? The English Bible has
properly translated it by "*prove*". "This he said *to prove* him." Here
was Jesus, the Saviour, dealing with a disciple, a believer. Though
Philip had witnessed many of Christ's miracles, Jesus knew *his faith
needed strengthening.* Hence the question: "Whence shall we buy
bread that these may eat?" Philip is a good mathematician. He says:
"It can't be done." "Two hundred pennyworth of bread is not sufficient for them that every one may take a little." He should have said:
"Lord, Thou knowest best; for means it fails thee never."

Let us not cast a stone on Philip, nor on Andrew, another ready
reckoner, cf. v. 8. When in straits, Christ's disciples to-day ask the same
question, born of little faith. When Jesus performed the miracle of
feeding the five thousand with five loaves and two small fishes, Philip
was among those that distributed the bread, so was Andrew. Philip's
little faith had been *proved;* it was purified and strengthened. This
is God's purpose in "*tempting*", i. e., in *proving* us. In Genesis 22, 1-19,
treating of the offering of Isaac, we read vv. 1, 2, "that God did *tempt*
Abraham", saying, "Take now thy son, thine only son, Isaac—and offer
him for a burnt-offering" etc. His purpose in so doing is disclosed
in v. 12 where God says to Abraham: "Lay not thine hand upon the
lad, neither do thou anything to him: *for now I know that thou fearest
God,*" etc. God tries His children for their own good. See also the
story of Jesus and the Syrophenecian woman, Mark 7, 25-30.—Of such
"temptations", trials, we learn that "Blessed is the man that endureth
temptation; for when he is tried, he shall receive the crown of life,

which the Lord hath promised to them that love Him." Of such trials for good this petition does not speak. Of such trials David says, Ps. 139, 23. 24: "Search me, O God, and know my heart: *try me*, and know my thoughts: and see if there be any wicked way in me, and lead me in the way everlasting."

The petition reads: "Lead us not into temptation, *but* deliver us from *evil*." This contrast introduced by *but* in the Seventh Petition —"*but* deliver us from evil" shows manifestly that the *temptation* spoken of in the Sixth Petition is a temptation *for evil*. Of such temptations this petition treats; of temptation to evil the next passage treats.

James 1, 13, 14. *Let no man say when he is tempted, I am tempted of God; for God cannot be tempted with evil, neither tempteth He any man; but every man is tempted when he is drawn away of his own lust and enticed.*

"Lead us not into temptation" does not say that God is or may be the cause of our being tempted to evil. St. James uses very strong language to oppose this evil thought that may at times arise even in the heart of a Christian. He speaks of temptation *to evil* in this passage. We see this because it stands in contrast to v. 2. There he had spoken of temptations *to good.* "My brethren", says he, "count it all joy when ye fall into diverse *temptations;* knowing this, that the *trying of your faith* worketh *patience.*" In vv. 13. 14, he speaks of a man being tempted, "*of his own lust and enticed.*"

Now let us follow the apostle's trend of thought. Literally it reads: "*Let no one say, being tempted: 'From God I am tempted'.*" Observe the emphasis in the phrase: "From God" at the head of the sentence. This says: "Let the thought be far removed from you: this temptation to evil comes *from God.*" Man is prone so to think. Adam thought so and spoke so. Gen. 3, 12. Two reasons are adduced proving that such a thought should be unthinkable: 1. "For God is *un*temptable, *apeirastos, by evils.*" It is contrary to His essence, contrary to His holiness. To tempt others to sin and wickedness, to stir up man's *own* sinful *lust* to entice, to seduce him, He would have to be temptable Himself. But the true God—*ho theos*—is "untemptable," 2. "God Himself"—notice the emphasis again—"*tempts no one*", to evil. This statement of fact flows from the foregoing. The holy God tempts no one to unholiness. This being true, the question arises: Whence does temptation to evil come? "*But each one is tempted by his own lust, being drawn away and being enticed.*" The tempter is in man's depraved nature; his *own* lust tempts him, and Satan uses this *lust* to draw and drag him into sin, and to allure him to commit shame and vice. Rom. 7, 7-13; 2 Pet. 3, 17. And the result? Lust brings forth *sin*, and sin brings forth *death*, v. 15. Is God the cause of *sin* and *death?* Let no man say: "I am tempted of God."

But since "we pray in this petition that God would guard and keep us, so that the devil, the world, and our flesh may not deceive us, nor seduce us into misbelief, despair and other great shame and vice," we should not do as Peter did, Luke 22, 54-55, warm ourselves at the fire of coals kindled by the enemies of Christ

1 Pet. 5, 8. 9. *Be sober, be vigilant; because your adversary, the devil, as a roaring lion, walketh about, seeking whom he may devour: whom resist steadfast in the faith.*

For exposition of this text consult p. 121, Vol. I. The preceding text taught us that our own *flesh* would deceive and seduce us into sin; this text teaches that the *devil* is the prime instigator of temptation to evil.

What then does: "Lead us not into temptation" mean? Luther: "We pray in this petition that God would guard and keep us, so that the devil, the world, and our flesh may not deceive us, nor seduce us into misbelief, despair, or other great shame and vice; and though we be assailed by them, that still we may finally overcome, and obtain the victory."

Matt. 18, 6. 7. *Whoso shall offend one of these little ones which believe in Me, it were better for him that a millstone were hanged about his neck, and that he were drowned in the depth of the sea. Woe unto the world because of offences! For it must needs be that offences come; but woe to that man by whom the offence cometh!*

"*Offend*", in the English of today, means to affront, to make angry, to displease. This, however, is not its signification in the diction of the New Testament. The Greek word, here rendered "offend" is *skandalizo*, which is best translated by "to cause to stumble." *Skandalon*, from which the verb is derived, means a *stumbling block*, or a *stone* placed in the way, over which one might stumble or fall. It also denotes the trapstick of a net against which the game strikes, the trap falls, and the game is ensnared. Hence, in its figurative use it means *to cause to stumble*, to give occasion *to be ensnared in sin.* cf. Matt. 13, 41; 18, 7; Luke 17, 1; Rom. 14, 13, 21; 1 John 2, 10; 1 Cor. 1, 23; 1 Pet. 2, 8; 1 Cor. 8, 13 et al. The Lord says: "Whoso shall *offend* one of these little ones *which believe in me*," i. e., whosoever shall *cause* one of them *to stumble, to fall into sin.* For what purpose these "*offenses*", these stumbling blocks, are laid in the way of God's children by worldlings the phrase. "*which believe in me*" discloses. *Pisteuein eis eme*="*to believe in me*" in the N. T. always expresses saving faith in Christ. Now, these stumbling blocks are laid in the way of Christians to cause them to fall into sin, to fall from grace, to rob them of their faith. False teachings, unholy lives of so-called Christians, coarse jokes of the newspapers against godliness, immoral pictures and stories, and indecent dresses are but a few of the skandala of our days.

"Woe unto the world because of offences!" Christ exclaims pitifully. The offences will be the cause of great woe and suffering. *"It must needs be"* because of man's depraved nature *"that offences come."* "Such is the depravity of man," to quote Barnes, "that there will be always some who are attempting to make others sin; some men of wickedness endeavoring to lead Christians astray, and rejoicing when they have succeeded in causing them to fall." *"Woe unto that man by whom the offence cometh."* He who leads others to sin by threats, by bad example, by persuasion, by picturing sin in alluring colors, etc.—woe to him!

Purpose of text: The temptation to evil consists also in this that the world would seduce us into misbelief, shame, and vice. We pray that the Lord might guard and keep us.

Prov. 1. 10. *My son, if sinners entice thee, consent thou not.*

For exposition see p. 56, Vol. I.

1 Cor. 10, 13. *God is faithful, who will not suffer you to be tempted above that ye are able, but will with the temptation also make a way to escape, that ye may be able to bear it.*

Mighty forces of evil are arrayed against the Christians. There is the devil, 1 Pet. 5, 8. 9; the world, Matt. 18, 6. 7.; Prov. 1, 10; and alas! "his own lust," James 1, 13. 14.—all intent upon deceiving and seducing us into misbelief, despair, and other great shame and vice. "The old Evil Foe now means deadly woe: Deep guile and great might are his dread arms in fight, on earth is not his equal." Truly, "Let him that thinketh he standeth take heed lest he fall." 1 Cor. 10, ·12, "With might of ours naught can be done, soon were our loss effected."

In this warfare over against our spiritual enemies we need consolation. This the apostle supplies in our present text. He says: In the temptation God will make His promises good to sustain you: He is faithful. He will make a way to escape. The text reads: *"God is faithful, who will not suffer you to be tempted above that ye are able."*

Temptations, incitements to sin, will assail the Christians; if not withstood, they will bring about his fall, cf. v. 10. But the Christian well knows that he is not to lean on his own strength. God has given him precious promises in His word. He "knows how to deliver the godly out of temptations," 2 Pet. 2, 9. He "will keep thee from all evil." 2 Thess. 3, 3. These promises he is to seize, to rely on, thus he relies on His Savior's strength. One little word can overthrow the Evil Foe. And God is *faithful*, He will keep His promises. This the Christians shall know and believe. God has called them to salvation.

God will carry out His purpose, in spite of all spiritual foes, He is faithful; He cannot deny Himself. And so with the eye of faith on this faithful God the temptation will be bearable. There is another promise: *"but will with the temptation also make a way to escape, that ye may be able to bear it."* *Were there not a way of escape* (ekbasis), the temptation would be too heavy, unbearable. But the faithful God who allows the "temptation" to assail His children for their good, at the same time supplies the means for *escape*. And *that God would sustain them in temptations—this is the prayer of the Christians.*

So, what does: "Lead us not into temptation" mean? Not that God tempts us to evil, James 1, 13. 14, but that, when temptations, of which we cannot be spared, since they are for good, come upon us, He would keep His promise, manifest his faithfulness, strengthen and preserve us, so that we may find a *way* of *escape*, overcome the temptation and obtain the victory.

Eph. 6, 13. *Take unto you the whole armor of God, that ye may be able to withstand in the evil day, and, having done all, to stand.*

The preceding passage gave us the assuring consolation: "God is faithful." He keeps His promises; He will guard and protect us in all temptations that assail us, but He will not do so without means. This means is His word. His Word we shall and must use in our spiritual warfare. His Word is the armory from which to procure weapons of offence and defence against our foe. The foe is formidable and wily; we are weak in ourselves, but equipped with the weapons God supplies we are "strong in the Lord, and in the strength of His Might," v. 10. Hence we are admonished: "Put on the whole armor of God, that ye may be able to withstand in the evil day." In the next verse the apostle vividly portrays the fierce "wrestling match" between the believer and the spiritual host of wickedness, v. 12. (For exposition of v. 12 see page 118, Vol. I.) And again the apostle comes back to the admonition given in v. 10. *"Wherefore,"* since the foe is so mighty, *"take unto you the whole armor of God":* the girdle of truth (of moral purity and uprightness, 4, 21), the breastplate of righteousness (of life), the gospel of peace, (to proclaim the glad tidings that produce peace with God), the shield of faith (in Christ Jesus), the helmet of salvation (the certainty of final deliverance), the sword of the Spirit (the Word of God), prayer and supplication. vv. 14-18. Thus accoutred and equipped as true soldiers under the Captain of our salvation, we shall be *"able to withstand in the evil day"*, when the devil assails us with his wiles, v. 11.

The Christian must always be on his guard, because his adversary the devil goes about seeking whom he may devour. But in the life of a Christian there are certain *"evil days"*, critical days, in which temptations to sin are especially strong, and which therefore call for the full concentration of all spiritual powers at his command, which demand the use of the "whole armor." *"Having done all,"* the apostle continues, having fought the fight to a finish in this invulnerable armor, we shall be able *"to stand"* unvanquished victors, with our foe on his knees. Of course, the Christian must not forget that the foe, once overpowered, does not give up the battle. The "evil day" returns. The Christian's life is a continual warfare Finally, however, the time for the last "wrestling match" arrives, and in this, too, clad in the armor of God, the Christian by God's grace overcomes and receives the crown of victory from the hands of his Lord with the words: "Well done!"

THE SEVENTH PETITION.

And deliver us from evil.

"Deliver us from evil." The Greek has the article before "evil" =the evil. Greek *"apo tou ponerou"*, and so it is translated in the R. V. thus: "Deliver us from the evil one," that is Satan Satan is called the Evil One, Matt. 13, 19; 1 John 2, 13. 14; 3, 12. Luther, too, using the phrase *apo tou ponerou* in the *masculine* sense, writes: "The verselet reads in the Greek: Deliver or preserve us from evil or the Wicked One; and it appears even as if He wished to comprehend all in one mass, so that the whole sum of all our prayers may be directed against our chief enemy. For he it is who impedes all that we pray for. For the devil seeks continually after our lives and wreaks his anger to bring us into misfortune and injuries."

But "apo tou ponerou" may also be the *neuter* gender="from evil," meaning evil in the abstract. cf. Luk. 6, 45; Rom. 12, 6 ; 1 Thess. 5, 22, et al.—Essentially there is no great difference whether we pray: "Deliver us from the Evil One", or "Deliver us from evil", for as Luther says: "It is the devil who impedes all that we pray for" etc. Being delivered from him, we are delivered from his power, his snares, his temptations, in short — "from evil." But the question is, which sense is demanded here, the masculine or the neuter? Nowhere in text and context do we find a reference or an allusion to Satan; moreover, in ch. 5, 37. 39, the word is used in the neuter sense, and so Luther's translation is preferable: "Deliver us from evil." "Deliver"—*"rusai"*—*break* the chains, *loose* the bands, *pluck* us away *from evil.*—"We pray in this petition that our Father—when our last hour has come, grant us a blessed end; and graciously take us from this vale of tears to Himself in heaven."

The deliverance prayed for is complete removal from this evil world. In this the prayer culminates, but so long as we are still in this vale of tears it includes deliverance of all and every evil which would hinder this final goal to be reached. Hence our ·Catechism says, in developing Luther's explanation, that the petition means: 1. that God would entirely spare us from many evils of body and soul, though we have richly deserved them; 2. that he would take the cross away from us, if such be His gracious will; or, 3. that He would help us to bear it, and turn it to our benefit; 4. that He finally would grant us a blessed end and thus wholly deliver us from all evil .

Ps. 91, 10. *There shall no evil befall thee, neither shall any plague come nigh thy dwelling.*

For exposition see p. 129, vol. I.

Note: If we think of the various diseases often prevalent in city and country, of the plagues that have visited our land—pestilence and "the flu"—which did not "come nigh our dwelling," we realize that God literally fulfilled the promise in Ps. 91, 10; He spared us from many evils.

Acts 14, 22. *We must through much tribulation enter into the kingdom of God.*

At Iconium and Antioch the apostles Paul and Barnabas preached the Gospel. Persecuted, they went to Lystra. Hostile Jews came down all the way from Iconium and Antioch to turn the people against the missionaries. Paul was stoned. The disciples thought he was dead. But the Lord watched over this servant. The next day he preached the Gospel in Derbe, making many disciples, v. 21. Undaunted by the hostile attacks, the apostles revisit Lystra, Iconium, Antioch. What might happen to them here, they know not. The congregations founded there were persecuted on account of their faith. They needed strengthening. We read: "They confirmed the souls of the disciples, exhorting them to *continue* in the faith," to hold fast to their faith, "and that *we must through much tribulation enter into the kingdom of God.'*" Tribulation, suffering, often causes one to doubt the mercy and goodness of God. Tribulation, however, is not a sign of God's disfavor. Look to the goal—the kingdom of God. The way to it leads through tribulations many and manifold. If they do come over us, we should remember there is a divine, Fatherly "must" back of it which is not for our hurt but for our benefit. These tribulations *a parte Dei* are to keep us on the way that leads to eternal glory. One thesis of God's pedagogy reads: "*We must through much tribulation enter into the kingdom of God.*" Again: "All that will live godly in Christ Jesus shall suffer persecution." Paul, who so lovingly seeks the spiritual welfare of these young converts, knows whereof he speaks. cf. 2 Cor. 11, 23-27. Through cross to crown! "Beloved, think it not

strange concerning the fiery trial which is to try you, as though some
strange thing happened unto you." 1 Pet. 4, 12.

Hebrews 12, 6. *Whom the Lord loveth He chasteneth, and scourgeth every son whom He receiveth.*

In view of the glorious instances of world-conquering faith—"a
great cloud of witnesses" for Christ—depicted in glowing terms in ch.
XI, we are admonished "to run with patience the race that is set
before us," obtaining grace and strength thereto by "looking unto
Jesus, the author and finisher of our faith," vv. 1-3. Ye have striven
against sin, it is true, the writer to the Hebrews says to his readers,
but ye have not yet resisted unto blood," v. 4; none of you had to die
a martyr's death as did some of the elders spoken of in the previous
chapter. The sufferings that have befallen you are comparatively
light. "Ye have forgotten the exhortation," which virtually is
a touching appeal: "My son, despise not the chastening of our Lord, nor
faint when thou art rebuked of Him." When chastenings do come,
avoid two extremes: On the one hand *despise* them *not*, do not regard
them indifferently, stoically, or make light of them; on the other
hand *"do not faint,"* do not become downcast, discouraged, "when you
are rebuked of Him." Remember they come *from the Lord,* your merciful Father, and are sent for a gracious purpose. Afflictions, whatever
their external cause may be, are a token not of God's wrath but of
His love; under affliction you are still His *son.* *"For"*—proof of the foregoing—*"whom the Lord loveth He chasteneth, and scourgeth"*—chas-
tiseth—i. e., applies the rod of love to *"every son whom He receiveth."*
This is the Father's invariable rule for *"every son."* Is there a loving father who does not correct his son? v. 7. Even so your Heavenly Father deals with you. "If ye be without chastisement, whereof
all are partakers," as shown in Ch. XI, "then are ye bastards and not
sons." v. 8.

Knowing that our Father has wise purposes in view in sending afflictions or allowing them to come upon us, we pray: "Deliver us from
evil," i. e., "either take the cross from us, or help us to bear it, and turn
it to our benefit," and so there will be no real evil in the affliction for
us, but only good.

Job 5, 19. *He shall deliver thee in six troubles; yea, in seven
there shall no evil touch thee.*

Thus Eliphas, Job's friend, says of the righteous. "To the number six, seven is added in order to remove the definiteness of the
former, and to make prominent only the general idea of multiplicity."
Compare Amos 1, 3; 6, 9; 11, 13. "There shall no evil touch thee;"
i. e., no *real* evil, nothing calculated to do thee *real* hurt. All affliction is "for the present grievous"; but if it "afterward yieldeth the

peaceable fruit of righteousness unto them that are exerçised thereby, Heb. 11, 11, it does not do us harm, but good." Pulpit Com.

2 Tim. 4, 18. *The Lord shall deliver me from every evil work, and will preserve me unto His heavenly kingdom.*

For exposition see p. 176, Vol. I.

Luke 2, 29-32. *Lord, now lettest Thou Thy servant depart in peace, according to Thy word; for mine eyes have seen Thy salvation which Thou hast prepared before the face of all people, a light to lighten the Gentiles, and the glory of Thy people Israel.*

To Simeon "it was revealed by the Holy Ghost that he should not see death before he had seen the Lord's Christ." v. 26. Now this happy time had come. We find Simeon in the Temple, the Christ-Child in his arms, intoning his joyful "Nunc Dimittis."

"Now"—emphatically put at the head of the sentence—now, since I embrace this Child Wonderful, the Prince of Peace, "now lettest Thou Thy servant *depart in peace.*" To Simeon death has lost its terrors; he need not fear judgment; his conscience is completely at ease; through this Christ-Child he is at *peace* with God. His death is but a *"departure."* "With the world it is usually so that when death comes, there is no joy, but unrest, anxiety, distress, fear, terror and weeping" (Luther), not so with Simeon. The reason? *"For mine eyes have seen Thy salvation,"* "to soterion sou," that salvation and that Savior whom God Himself had appointed and ordained to be a Savior from sin, death and hell. "We must not imagine, however, that Simeon had an advantage over us, because he had seen the child Jesus with bodily eyes and taken it into his arms; for such bodily seeing did not help him. The other Jews also saw the Child, and went to the devil. But this helped Simeon, that he believed this Child was the Savior." (Luther.)

Whether young or old, seeing this "salvation" with the eyes of faith, we are ready to depart in peace, for through this Prince of Peace we are at one with God, the barrier of enmity between us and God—sin—is broken down. Devil, world, and flesh can harm us none. Death is a "departure in peace," delivering us from all evil. Thus the culmination of the Lord's prayer is realized. This salvation is for believing Simeon; not for him only, however, but for *"all people",* for the Gentiles as well as for *"thy people Israel."* John 4, 22; Eph. 2, 12; Is. 9, 2; 46, 6. 7; Rom. 9, 4; Rom. 3, 2.

Phil. 1, 23. *I have a desire to depart and to be with Christ, which is far better.*

"What I shall choose I wot not." v. 22. The apostle is in a dilemma. "I am in a strait betwixt two:" "to depart" or "to abide in the flesh." The former is my desire; the latter is more necessary for your sake, vv. 23. 24. Of the first alternative he says: "I have a desire," *epithumia,* a longing "to depart," *eis to analusai.* The verb *analuein* means *to loosen, to break up.* The metaphor *to depart* this life is taken from tent-life. A tent is but a temporary abode, so is life. The apostle has a longing to pull up stakes and journey towards his real home. The verb is also used of breaking up an encampment, and of loosening a ship from her moorings ready to depart. The metaphor and its application to spirutal life is easily discernible.—Death, so horrible to natural man, has no terror for Paul. "For me to die *is gain,*" says he, v. 21. Death to him is but the taking down of a tent, or the weighing of an anchor to depart for his heavenly home. But, and this must not be overlooked, this longing to depart, is not because Paul is weary and tired of life, because he has experienced "all is vanity." Paul does not desire death *per se.*—The miserable sometimes long for death, because, as they assume, death ends all their troubles. They have become weary of life. Perhaps they are satiated and surfeited with the pleasures of this world or through a sinful life have become incapable of enjoying the things of the world; or, again, they may have become despondent, and hence are anxious to die. The frequent suicides we read of are not signs of longing to die, but rather a token of despair.—Such was not the longing of the apostle. "I have a desire to depart and *to be with Christ.*" Upon this latter thought all emphasis lies—"to be with Christ."—The departure from this life would be but an entrance into yonder life where he would be with Christ, his Savior, whom he loves, who has redeemed him, to be with Him and see Him face to face, to be with Him in His kingdom and to serve Him in everlasting righteousness, innocence, and blessedness

This is Paul's heartfelt desire. And of this life with Christ Paul affirms: *"which is far better."* In Greek there is a triple comparaaive: *"pollo mallon kreisson"* — "which is by much very far better." "Word is piled upon word to express the blessedness awaiting him with Christ; but language is too feeble an instrument to express the sentiment of joy and pleasure welling up in his heart at the prospect of being with Christ. When people have been absent from home for a long time, they feel a tugging at their heart-strings—they long to return." "There's no place like home." "Homesickness" some call it. That word is too blunt; it doesn't cover the sentiment. "Heimweh," the Germans call it. That's better: "Heimweh" for the true fatherland. "Our Father in heaven—deliver us from evil;" "when our last hour has come, grant us a blessed end" and then we'll be with Christ which is far better.

THE CONCLUSION.

For Thine is the Kingdom, and the power, and the glory for ever and ever, Amen.

The conclusion adduces the reason why we may pray with all boldness and confidence, knowing that our petitions are acceptable to our Father, and heard.

His is *the kingdom.* "For all that is in the heaven and in the earth is thine; thine is the kingdom, O Lord, and thou art exalted as head above all." 1 Chron. 29, 11. We are His subjects whom He can and will protect.—His is *the power.* His name is Omnipotence. Great are the gifts, temporal and spiritual, we ask of Him, but His is *the power* "to do exceeding abundantly above all that we ask or think," Eph. 3. 20.—His is *the glory,* "who will help us for the glory of His name's sake." Ps. 79, 9. *"Forever and ever."* "Lord thou hast been our dwelling place in all generations. Before the mountains were brought forth, or ever thou hast formed the earth and the world, even from everlasting to everlasting, thou art God." Ps. 90, 12.—*Amen.* "This is most certainly true." His whose is *the kingdom,* and *the power,* and *the glory* will hear and grant our prayers, for, 1, He has *commanded* us to pray; 2, He has *promised* to hear our prayers. Amen.

Praise God, from whom all blessings flow;
Praise Him all creatures here below;
Praise Him above, ye heavenly host;
Praise Father, Son, and Holy Ghost.

Note: On the authenticity of the doxology of the Lord's prayer, see Lehre and Wehre, 1918, pp. 408, 409; Hom. Magazine, 1919, Dec. 567,568.

Whence is it, our Catechism asks, that many complain of their prayers being unheard?—We have touched upon this topic in the explanation of preceding passages; here Matt. 20, 20-23 is adduced. That God does hear every proper prayer, we have already learned, e. g. in 1 John 5, 14. 2 Cor. 12, 9; John 2, 4; Is. 54, 7, 8, corroborate this precious truth.

Matt. 20. 20-23. *Then came to Him the mother of Zebedee's children with her sons, worshipping Him, and desiring a certain thing of Him. And He said unto her, What wilt thou? She saith unto Him, Grant that these my two sons may sit, the one on the right hand, and the other on the left, in Thy kingdom. But Jesus answered and said, Ye know not what ye ask. Are ye able to drink of the cup that I shall drink of, and to be baptized with the baptizm that I am baptized with? They say unto Him, We are able. And He saith unto them, Ye shall drink indeed of My cup, and be baptized with the baptism that I am baptized with; but to sit on My right hand, and on My left, is not Mine to give, but it shall be given to them for whom it is prepared of My Father.*

In the preceding paragraph Jesus had forboded His death and resurrection for the third time, beginning with the familiar words: "Behold, we go up to Jerusalem" etc. Closely upon this prediction followed the ambitious request of the mother of James and John. Ill-timed, indeed, was this selfish request. We read:

"Then came to Him the mother of Zebedee's children with her sons." In all likelihood this was Salome and her sons, James and John. cf. Mark 15, 40 with Matt. 27, 56. In Mark (10, 35 ff.) James and John are represented as making this request themselves. Their wish was in full accord with that of their mother. Either both the mother and the sons preferred the request, or the mother was the mouthpiece of the sons. Matt. 8, 5. Mark adds that James and John made the presumptuous demand: "Master, we would that Thou shouldest do for us *whatsoever* we shall ask of Thee." Were they perhaps conscious of the impropriety of their ambition? *"And He said unto her,"* i. e., to Salome, as the intercessor for her sons, *"What wilt thou?" She saith unto Him, "grant that these my two sons may sit, the one on Thy right hand, and the other on the left, in Thy kingdom."* (Mark: "in Thy glory.") Salome's ambition soars high. She asks for nothing less than the highest places of honor which at the same time included special authority in ruling and reigning in the kingdom, as is indicated by our Lord's answer. Mark 10, 42. See also Ps. 16, 11; 45, 9; 110, 1; Mark 14. 52; et al. *"But Jesus answered and said, Ye know not what ye ask."* Your petition is based on ignorance. Observe the "ye", addressed to James and John, showing that they were in full accord with their mother, aye, had most likely induced her to make the request.

"Ye know not what ye ask...Are ye able to drink of the cup that I shall drink of, and to be baptized with the baptism that I am baptized with?" Your ignorance consists in this: to ask to reign with me includes to suffer with me. 2 Tim. 2, 12; Rom. 8, 17. "Are ye able" to go the same way of suffering that I must go, "to drink the cup that I shall drink" in order to enter into my glory? Matt. 26, 29. 42. *"They say unto Him, We are able."* "You know not what ye ask." Ignorant of the contents of "the cup" of suffering, still they answer self-confidently: "We are able." And still these "Sons of Thunder", courageous as they were, forsook Jesus and fled, when He was drinking "the cup". Mark 14, 50. Were they able? Were they able to be baptized with the baptism Jesus was baptized with in His un-

speakable sufferings with which He earned our salvation? No man is sufficient unto this.

"*And He saith unto them, Ye shall drink indeed of my cup, and be baptized with the baptism that I am baptized with.*" Jesus deals kindly with James and John; they are His disciples; they believe in Him. They need correction. This Jesus administers. "Ye shall drink indeed of my cup"; ye shall become partakers of my sufferings, 1 Pet. 4, 13. "Remember the word that I said unto you. The servant is not greater than His Lord. If they have persecuted me, they will also persecute you." John 15, 20. And James and John, as their later story proves, richly partook of Christ's sufferings. In the Master's service and by His grace James was able to become a martyr for the faith, Acts 12, 2, and John's long life was filled with sore troubles and trials.

But what of the high stations they had coveted? "*But to sit on my right hand, and on my left, is not mine to give, but it shall be given to them for whom it is prepared of my Father.*" Luther: "So He declares *as man*, that He has no authority, that He is a servant, and answers the disciples according to their view of Him." These places are already assigned, reserved by my Father. To whom, Christ does not say. In due time we shall know. What we do know is this: "He which soweth sparingly shall reap also sparingly; and he which soweth bountifully shall also reap bountifully." 2 Cor. 9, 6. See Dan. 12, 3; 1 Cor. 15, 41.

"*Ye know not what ye ask.*" These words of Christ are the central thought for us in the application to the teaching of the Catechism. James and John's petition was born of ignorance; hence it was a foolish request. Such prayers the Lord does not answer. But even such faulty prayers He mercifully hears, corrects, and gives His disciples grace to see the error of their way and to remain with Him. Let us see to it that we pray in subordination to God's will. 1 John 5, 14 f.

Salome, by the way, was and remained a pious adherent of her beloved Savior; she was with Him under the cross, and undoubtedly too was amongst the women that came early on Easter morning to anoint His body. James and John, the disciples of our Lord, later became His apostles. Luke 5, 10.

Salome lays her petition before Jesus; she worshipped Him. In true reverential fear we should ask in Jesus' name. Jesus says: "What wilt thou?" Though the omniscient Jesus knew her foolish thoughts, he does not deal harshly with her, but rather encourages her to pray. "The bruised reed He will not break." He listens friendly to our petitions, though through our ignorance they may often be foolish, and the things for which we ask if granted be hurtful to us. When

our prayers are not answered as we desire, here ofttimes is the key—
they are foolish prayers.

2 Cor. 12, 9. *And He said unto me, My grace is sufficient for thee;
for My strength is made perfect in weakness.*

This is the divine answer to Paul's thrice repeated prayer for
deliverance from the "thorn to the flesh," by which he was afflicted of
God "lest he should be exalted above measure through the abundance of the revelations" graciously vouchsafed him.   Here is an instance of divine pedagogy.   God grants Paul wonderful "visions
and revelations" of Himself, v. 1, but lest he become puffed up spiritually, God allows a "messenger of Satan to buffet him" by this "thorn
to the flesh." v. 7. "And must this mighty apostle, O merciful God,
be subject to trials lest he exalt himself because of his great revelations?   Then how should others, how should such infirm beings as we,
be free from self-exaltation?" Luther. "For this thing," i. e., concerning this affliction he prayed to the Lord in all humility and earnestness once, but there was no answer. He prayed again, and still no
answer.   He pleaded with the Lord a third time to relieve him of "this
thorn", and the Lord answered, but not by taking the affliction from
him—God saw it was necessary for Paul's spiritual welfare to be so
tormented—but by strengthening his faith and causing him to bow
his will to God's will.

What did God say to Paul? *"sufficient for thee is my grace."* This
affliction I have sent thee for a purpose; I can and will not take it
away from thee.   You possess my *grace*, you know that through Christ
Jesus I am your *gracious* Father and you are my dear child.   This
grace is sufficient for you.   You know therefore that my reason in not
answering your prayer according to your wish, does not proceed from
wrath on my part, but that it is an emanation of my love. *"For my
strength,"* my power, *"is made perfect in weakness."*   Cheerfully, so
says the divine voice, you may let this my grace suffice thee, for I
am not only a gracious but also a powerful Savior, and "my power
in weakness is perfected", *teleioutai*, has its most perfect manifestation.   Paul, possessing my grace, relying entirely on it, you are
strong in my strength.   "Man's extremity is God's opportunity; man's
security is Satan's opportunity."

Was Paul's prayer answered?   Yes.   True, not by doing according to Paul's desire—if God had done so; perhaps we would know of no
great Apostle Paul today—but by strengthening his faith, by showing
him the reason why the affliction could not be removed and thus
granting Paul grace to submit to God's will.   So God deals with
us to-day.   In trouble let us visit Him, pour out a prayer to Him
again and again, knowing that God hears our prayers and answers
them in His own manner.   And if He does not take us out of the

trial, let us rest assured that His grace is sufficient for us, giving us strength to bear the cross. Ps. 88, 7; John 17, 15. God grant that we may learn to say with Paul v. 10: "Therefore I take pleasure in infirmities, in reproaches, in necessities, in persecutions, in distresses, for Christ's sake: for when I am weak, then am I strong."

John 2, 4. *Mine hour is not yet come.*

At the wedding at Cana the young couple were sorely embarrassed—the wine had given out. The mother of Jesus laid the need before Him in these simple words: "They have no wine." That was a true prayer. God's children may simply state their needs and necessities; He sees the spirit and the motive back of it. Mary looked for relief immediately. "They have no wine," you can and will supply it. *"Not yet is come my hour."*. . This answer must suffice his mother. It does. *"Not yet"* with emphasis at the head of the sentence, *"Not yet* is come mine. hour", but come it will. This is the implied promise. I have a certain *"hour"*, a certain time to help. This hour is *mine*. When it arrives, I'll help.

Also our bodily needs we should cheerfully carry to the Lord in prayer, but let us beware of fixing time or manner in which He is to manifest His help. These things belong to Him. He ofttimes defers His help for a purpose—to *"manifest His glory"* and to strengthen the faith of His disciples, v. 11. Mary was satisfied with her Son's answer. "Whatsoever He saith unto you, do it"—this is her direction to the expectant servants. And wonderful was the manifestation of His glory.

"Our prayers for temporal things are not orders which we write to a bank where we have a deposit and which must be promptly honored by the teller, but they are beggar's petitions which are subject to rejection or revision at the Lord's pleasure. He hears them in a far grander way than we can imagine if we leave time and manner of fulfillment all to Him." (Dau.)

Is. 54, 7. 8. *For a small moment have I forsaken thee; but with great mercies I will gather thee. In a little wrath I hid My face from thee for a moment; but with everlasting kindness will I have mercy on thee, saith the Lord, thy Redeemer.*

"I have forsaken thee;" "I have hidden my face from thee." How frequently this seems to be God's mode of dealing with the believer when in trials and sufferings. It seems as though God had forgotten all His gracious promises, as though He were dealing with us in His wrath. The words of our agonized Savior come to our lips: "My God, my God, why hast Thou forsaken me?" But His chastisements· are but temporary, aye, *momentary.* The *"little wrath"* we experience is set off by His *"great mercies,"* by His *"everlasting kindness."* So says the Lord our Redeemer. "The mountains may depart, and the hills be removed; but my loving kindness shall not depart from thee, neither shall my covenant of peace be removed, saith Jehovah that hath mercy on thee." v. 10.   Upon this immovable rock of God's promise let us ever and again build our faith.   Jehovah is our *Redeemer* that hath mercy on us. Ps. 30, 5: "His anger endureth but a moment; in His favor is life; weeping may endure for a night, but joy cometh in the morning." God's promise is the one thing in life that *cannot fail.*

Lord, teach us to pray boldly! Lord, teach us to resign ourselves confidently to Thy will.

Let us pray:

"Thy way, not mine, O Lord,
However dark it be,
Oh, lead me by Thine own right hand,
Choose out the path for me!
Smooth let it be or rough,
It will be still the best,
Winding or straight, it matters not,
It leads me to Thy rest. **Amen.**"

PART IV.

THE SACRAMENT OF HOLY BAPTISM.

First, what Baptism is.

Matt. 28, 18-20: *And Jesus came and spake unto them, saying. All power is given unto me in heaven and in earth. Go ye therefore, and teach all nations, baptizing them in the name of the Father, and of the son, and of the Holy Ghost: teaching them to observe all things whatsoever I have commanded you: and, lo, I am with you alway, even unto the end of the world.*

This passage, so rich in doctrine and consolation, has been used repeatedly in our Catechism as a proof text. See "Proof Texts," Vol. I, pp. 148, 159, 173, 92, 211, 254, 149, 160, 251.—here it is adduced to answer the question: *Who instituted holy Baptism?* Aside from this we shall use it in elucidating other topics relating to baptism, since the passage contains all the essentials of this sacrament.

In compliance with the command of their Master, the disciples went
to Galilee to a mountain designated by Him as a meeting place. (Matt.
28, 16.) Here the Lord delivered this last Great Commission, v.
19, which He introduces with these words: "All power is given unto Me
in heaven and in earth." He proceeds: "Go ye *therefore*," because I,
the God-man, possess *all authority in heaven*—the angels, authorities,
the cherubim and the seraphim being my willing servants; because I
possess *ail authority* in *earth*—all things being put under my feet—
"go ye *therefore*, and teach all nations," etc. To this commission He
appends the comforting promise: "*Lo, I am with you alway.*" So it is
plain: *the institutor of the sacrament of holy baptism is* Christ,
the exalted Christ, omnipotent and omnipresent also according to
His human nature.

True, John the Baptist baptized before this general command was
given. Of whom did he derive his authority? St. Luke, 3, 2-3,
informs us that "the word of God came unto John in the wilderness."
What was the import of this "word of God"?

We read: "John came into all the country about Jordan, preaching the baptism of repentance for the remission of sins." And John
himself says in that great testimony of his regarding the Christ:
"He," God, "sent me to baptize with water." The Baptist derived
his authority to baptize from God. Between the baptism of John and
that of Christ there is no essential difference: John baptized unto
Him that was to come; Christian baptism is unto Him that has come.
Baptism is a divine institution.

Who is to administer Baptism?

Matt. 28. 18-20   *Go ye, therefore, and disciple all nations, bap-*
tizing them, .   *teaching them.*"

To whom does Christ say: "*Go ye*"? To His disciples. Only
disciples can make disciples. How many were there to whom He
spoke? Eleven, for Judas, the traitor, had gone to his place. Were
these the only ones for whom this solemn charge was intended? No.
All disciples of Christ are so commissioned. How do we know? The
Master said: "*Lo, I am with you alway, even unto the end of the
world.*" Baptism was thus made a permanent institution of the Church
to the end of the days. These Eleven died, but the charge to make
disciples is valid even today.

Who is to carry out this command of the Master? His disciples.
By His grace we are His disciples. We have the privilege and the
power to administer Baptism. Every Christian congregation and every member of such congregation possesses this power. Why, then,

do not the individual Christians baptize their children? Because God is a God of order. The rule to obtain in the Church is: "Let all things be done decently and in order." The Christian congregations have called ministers of Christ to whom they have delegated this power to perform Baptism in their name. As Paul says: "Let a man so account of us as of the ministers of Christ and stewards of the mysteries of God." 1 Cor. 4, 1.

But in case of extreme necessity, when it is impossible to summon the minister, or when there is danger that the child may die before his arrival, any Christian has the right to administer Baptism, and hence, in your hymn-books you will find a formula for that very purpose. The minister, later on, makes inquiry how such emergency Baptism was performed, and duly records it, so that the child in after years may rest assured of his having been validly baptized.

1 Cor. 4, 1: *Let a man so account of us, as of the ministers of Christ, and stewards of the mysteries of God.*

There were factions in the Corinthian church. One said: "I am of Paul;" another, "I am of Apollos"; and a third, "I am of Cephas." One demanded a mighty orator; another, an eloquent speaker; a third, a nice dialectician. So the Corinthians had wrong notions concerning the ministers of the Gospel. St. Paul here instructs them in what light they are to view their pastors.

Paul, Apollos, Cephas are *ministers;* elsewhere Paul speaks of himself and the ministers as *servants.* A servant is in the employ of someone else. His time, his talents, his energy are at the disposal of his Master. In this case the Master is *Christ.* A high honor and a great responsibility are theirs. *So* account of us, says Paul: we are ministers, servants. of Christ, not of men. Our instructions we take from the Master. Another comparison: Pastors are *stewards.* The imagery is drawn from a large Roman estate over which the owner had set a steward to manage its affairs. The steward was charged with the special duty of regularly supplying all the domestics of the household with food, "to give them their meat in due season." (Matt. 24, 45.)—The goods over which the Lord Jesus has set His stewards are designated *mysteries of God.* What are they? Things known to God only; things that would have remained mysteries if God had not revealed them to us through His word and Spirit. They are, in short, the glad tidings of the glorious Gospel of Christ—the audible and the visible Word—baptism and the Lord's Supper.—Ministers, being called by the congregations, are ministers *of Christ,* stewards of the mysteries *of God.* They, ordinarily, are to administer these "mysteries."

"No man should publicly in the Church teach, or administer the Sacraments, except he be rightly called." Augs. Conf. Art XLV.) —"Let everything be done decently and in order."

The Meaning of the Word "Baptize."

Mark 7, 4: *"And when they come from the market, except they wash, they eat not. And many other things there be, which they have received to hold, as the washing of cups, and pots, and brazen vessels, and of tables."*

The Pharisees and scribes were ever on the alert to find fault with our Master and His disciples. This tribe hasn't died out yet. Here they had seen that "some of His disciples ate their bread with defiled, that is, unwashed hands," v. 2, "they ask Him, why walk not Thy disciples according to the tradition of the elders, but eat their bread with defiled hands?" v. 5. To the Jew this language was at once intelligible; not so to a Gentile Christian. Hence Mark explains this "tradition of the elders"—eating bread with unwashed hands, saying: "For the Pharisees and all the Jews, except they wash their hands oft, eat not, holding the tradition of the elders." v. 3. For example, "when they come from the market place, unless they *baptize* themselves—i. e., *wash* themselves, they eat not: and many other things there be, which they have received to hold, as the *baptizings*, i. e., *washings* of cups, and pots, and brazen vessels, and tables" (couches). v. 4.

The point at issue is: What does the Greek word *"baptizein"* mean? The Baptists say it means *immerse;* we contend that this Greek term has a wider usage—that it means applying water by washing, pouring, sprinkling, or immersing. The present passage clearly proves this wider usage. It speaks obviously of the religious, *ceremonial washings* observed by the Jews. In the market, possibly they might have come in contact with an unclean thing—a dead animal or the corpse of a person—or they might in some other manner have rendered themselves ceremonially unclean. On coming home they *"baptized"* themselves. *"Baptizontai"* is the Greek word used, which our English Bible translates: "they *wash* themselves," thus giving a commentary to the otherwise unintelligible word "baptize." But to see the force of the word "baptizein," reread the passage, substituting the original "baptize" for "wash," and it becomes very plain that to *baptize* means to *wash* or to *sprinkle*, or to *pour water* upon a person, for so these ceremonial purifications were performed and not by immersing the whole body into a tank of water, or by ducking cups, and pots, and brazen vessels, and tables under water—by immersing them.—The word "baptizein," *baptize* in the Lord's Commission does not prescribe any particular mode of baptism as essential. But it is generally so with errorists: the form is elevated; the essential is neglected.

Note: It may be of interest in this connection to know more about the ceremonial "baptisms," referred to in our text. Says Dr. Graebner in Theol. Quarterly, Vol. V, p. 1:

"Ritual applications of water to purify persons and things were common among the Jews, and these purifications were called baptisms, *baptismoi*, in the idiom employed in the New Testament. The epistle to the Hebrews refers to these various baptisms, diaphorois baptismois, Hebr. 9, 10, and St. Mark speaks of the Pharisees and their habit of baptizing themselves before eating, and of their *baptisms* of *cups* and *pots, brazen vessels*, and of *tables*, Mark 7, 4. Of such applications of water the Mosaic law said: *This is the law, when a man dieth in a tent: all that come into the tent, and all that is in the tent, shall be unclean seven days. And every open vessel which hath no covering bound upon it, is unclean. And whosoever toucheth one that is slain with a sword in the open fields, or a dead body, or a bone of a man, or a grave, shall be unclean seven days. And for an unclean person they shall take of the ashes of the burnt heifer of purification for sin, and running water shall be put thereto in a vessel; and a clean person shall take hyssop and dip it in the water, and sprinkle it upon the tent, and upon all the vessels, and upon the persons that were there, and upon him that touched a bone, or one slain, or one dead, or a grave: and the clean person shall sprinkle upon the unclean on the third day, and on the seventh day: and on the seventh day he shall purify himself, and wash his clothes, and bathe himself in water, and shall be clean at even.* Numb. 19, 14-19.

And of the purification of the Levites we read: *Thus shalt thou do unto them, to cleanse them: Sprinkle water of purifying upon them, and let them shave all their flesh, and let them wash their clothes, and so make themselves clean.* Numb. 8, 7. Such, then, were the *baptisms* practiced from the days of Moses among the people to whom Christ came in the fullness of time. They were *diaphoroi baptismoi, various baptisms*, not only because of the variety of objects thus to be purified, but also inasmuch as the purifying water was applied in various ways, by sprinkling, washing, and bathing.

These various baptisms, as all the rites of the Mosaic ceremonial, were symbolic in their nature, emblematic of the spiritual cleansing of the hearts and souls of men defiled with sin. Hereof the prophet says: *Then will I sprinkle clean water upon you, and ye shall be clean: from all your filthiness, and from all your idols, will I cleanse you. A new heart also will I give you, and a new spirit will I put within you: and I will take away the stony heart out of your flesh, and I will give an heart of flesh.* Ezek. 36, 25 f.

But the rites of the old covenant were not only emblematic as they represented what pertained to the soul and to spiritual life by visible and material things applied to the body and other material objects; they were also types and shadows of things to come under a new dispensation, and the waters of purifying sprinkled and poured upon the defiled children of the old covenant found their various antitypes when the fullness of the time was come. Then it was fulfilled what the prophet had spoken: *It shall come to pass afterward, that. I will pour out my spirit upon all flesh,* Joel 2, 28. Of this outpouring of the Spirit the first preacher of the new covenant spoke, saying: *He that cometh after me is mightier than I, whose shoes I am not worthy to bear: he shall baptize you with the Holy Ghost, and with fire,* Matt. 3, 11.

And, furthermore, the preacher who spoke these words, was John the Baptist. Matt. 3, 1; 11, 12. et al. His baptism, too, though he baptized with water, was a baptism of a higher order than the various baptisms, which the Jews had practiced and still practice according to law and 'tradition.' John's baptism also was a rite of purification, and, like the baptism of Jesus and his disciples, was looked upon as such by the Jews, among whom these baptisms occasioned a controversy *peri katharismou.* (John 3, 25 ff., coll. vv. 22 f. and *oun,* v. 25, which indicates a nexus of cause and effect.) John the Baptist also baptized with water. John 1, 31; Matt. 3, 11; Mark 1, 8; Luke 3, 16. But his baptism was not according to the Mosaic law, or to Jewish traditions, but pursuant to a special commission, a word of God, *rema theou,* which came to him at a certain time, the fifteenth year of Tiberius, Luke 3, 1 f., and by which he was sent to baptise with water. John 1, 33. In compliance with this word of divine command and commission, he came into all the country about Jordan, preaching the baptism of repentance for the remission of sins. Luke 3, 3, coll. v. 2. Mark 1, 4. That is to say, he publicly and by divine authority exhorted his hearers to be baptized with water, saying unto the people that they should believe on Him which should come after him, that is on Christ Jesus, Acts 19, 4, and. by such baptism, to be converted and to receive the remission of sins. And when they heard this, they were baptized in the name of the Lord Jesus, Acts 19, 5, confessing their sins, Mark 1, 5, and receiving the remission of sins. That this was not the traditional baptism practised by the Jews, but a new rite of a higher order, was apparent to the ritualists of those days, the Pharisees of Jerusalem, by whose order the question was put to John: Why baptizest thou then, if thou be not that Christ, nor Elias, neither that prophet? John 1, 25. Among the diaphoroi baptismoi with which they had previously been familiar there was no baptism for the remission of sins, no sacramental washing of water with the word whereby sinners might be sanctified and cleansed from spiritual defilement as by a means of divine grace which, to be valid and efficacious, must have been instituted by divine authority, inasmuch as God only can forgive sins. Mark 2, 7. Luke 5, 21.

"The *precise manner* in which the application of the baptismal water was performed by John the Baptist does not appear from the description given in the gospels. It is certain, however, that *baptizein* in the mouth of the Baptist cannot *vi vocis* mean *to immerse*, when he says: *I indeed baptize you with water unto repentance: but he that cometh after me is mightier than I, whose shoes I am not worthy to bear: he shall baptize you with the Holy Ghost, and with fire.* For when this word was fulfilled, it was at the same time a fulfillment of the prophecy of Joel, *I will POUR OUT my spirit upon all flesh*, and not by an immersion in a flood of fire, but by a distribution of fiery tongues upon the disciples were they baptized with fire, Acts 2, 3. Of this fulfillment of the prophecy and of the prediction of the Baptist we hear Peter say, Therefore being by the right hand of God exalted, and having received of the Father the promise of the Holy Ghost, he hath shed forth, *exegeen, poured out*, this which ye now see and hear, Acts 2, 33. In all this there is nowhere an immersion, but everywhere an outpouring or sprinkling in what must be looked upon as answering to the *baptizing* with the Spirit and with fire predicted by St. John. Hence his own *baptizein* is so far from being, in his own mind, immersion or submersion in water, that, if anything at all concerning his mode of applying the baptismal water can be collected from his words and the gospel narratives, it is that he baptized by pouring or sprinkling water upon the persons whom he baptized. The gospels say that he baptized *in the Jordan*, Mark 1, 5, into (eis) the Jordan, Mark 1, 9, with water, Mark 1. 8, and in (with) water, Matt. 3, 11; John 1. 26; 31. 33. All these expressions in the Greek do not necessitate the assumption of immersion. The number of applicants for baptism being very great, Matt. 3, 5 f, and water being plentiful, John 3. 23, the most decorous, expeditious, and cleanly way of administering the sacred rite may have been this, that John stood in the river, *en to Jordane*, the people, one by one, came near him, also in the river, and the Baptist, lifting water from the river, poured it upon the person before him, so that the water with which he baptized *(hydati or en hydati)* would run back into the river, *eis ton Jordanen*, as the water lifted from the baptismal font and poured upon the head of a child held over the font runs again into the font whence it was taken. After baptism, the person thus baptized, though not immersed in or submerged under the water, would "come out of the water," in which he had stood, making room for others to be baptized in like manner." Theol. Quart. Vol. V. p. 4 f.

Acts 22, 16: *"Arise, and be baptized, and wash away thy sins."*
These are words of Ananias to Paul. Obviously *to baptize* and to *wash away* are identical in meaning. To "wash away" is ordinarily not done by immersing, hence to *baptize* does not necessarily mean or imply in New Testament diction to immerse. There are not two things to be done: 1. be baptized, and 2. wash away. The *and* is epexegetical, i. e., explanatory: Be baptized and *thus* wash away your sins. Baptism is the cause, washing away of sins is the effect. This terse passage at the same time shows the glorious benefit of bap-

tism—it works forgiveness of sins, hence it is a means of grace.

Matt 3, 11 *"He shall baptize you with the Holy Ghost, and with fire.'*

Here we have an unmistakable reference to Acts 2, 16. 17. In his Pentecostal sermon Peter explains the miraculous outpouring of the Holy Spirit upon the disciples, saying amongst other things: "But this is that which was spoken by the prophet Joel; and it shall come to pass in the last days, saith God, I will *pour out* my Spirit upon all flesh," etc cf v. 33. John the Baptist employs the word *baptize, baptizo;* Peter, *pour out, ekcheo.* This is another strong proof that to baptize does not mean to immerse. (See the preceding article from the Theological Quarterly.)

What is baptizing "in the name of the Father, and of the Son, and of the Holy Ghost?" Qu. 277

These words contain a confession of faith. Observe that the foundation text, Matt. 28, 18-20, says "Baptize them into the name," not "baptize them into the *names* of the Father," etc. That means that there is but *one* name, *one* essence in God; there is but *one* God, but three distinct Persons. Father, Son, and Holy Ghost. Our God is the Triune God. In the name and by authority of this Triune God Baptism is to be performed

The command reads "Baptize them *into* the name of the Father," etc. This phrase *"into* the name" has a deep significance. It does not merely mean Baptize them by authority of the Triune God, but *"into"* denotes entrance. it denotes coming into fellowship with the Triune God. "Baptize *into* the name" makes the promise and gives the assurance that the person who before baptism was without God now, by baptism, has entered into relationship with God, has become a child of God. Is that true? Christ says so. He says: *Disciple the nations, baptizing them."* How does one become a disciple of Christ? By Baptism. Who is a disciple of Christ? One who is an adherent, a follower of Christ, a believer in Christ. *"Disciple* the nations, *baptizing* them," means that Baptism generates faith in the person baptized; for without faith no one can be a disciple of Christ.

Who is to be baptized? Qu. 278

Matt 28, 18. *"Go ye, therefore, and disciple all nations, baptizing them." "Nations"* are made up of men, women, and children These are to be baptized, and these only. It is a sacrilege practised by the Roman Catholic Church to baptize bells; it is a travesty upon this sacred act to "baptize" ships with wine.

Is Baptism to be administered indiscriminately, to old and young alike? **Qu. 279.**

The text, Matt. 28, 18-20. says: *"Go ye, therefore, and disciple all nations, baptizing them,   teaching them."*

The charge is: *"Make disciples* of all nations." How many means are there of making disciples? Two. Which? By *baptizing* them and by *teaching* them. The text does not say: First baptize, then teach. Christ says both should be done, each at the proper time. How did the disciples understand the Master's injunction? The hearers at Pentecost were first taught by Peter, and "having gladly received the Word, were baptized." Lydia was first instructed, then baptized; the keeper of the prison at Philippi likewise. So this was the practise of the Church in regard to adults. Thus the command of the Master was understood and carried out by His disciples.

Now as to children. They, too, are to be made disciples. They cannot be taught. But they are flesh born of the flesh, and stand in need of regeneration. They are to be made disciples by the only means of regeneration applicable to them—Baptism. The objection so often heard: Can children believe? is clearly met by the positive declaration of our Lord Himself, who speaks of "these little ones which believe in Me." How their faith is constituted is none of our business.

Hence our practise is founded on the teaching of our Lord and His disciples. Little children are baptized and thus regenerated; adults we first instruct, and when they profess faith, begotten by the Word, we baptize them in accordance with the dictum of our Lord: "He that believeth and is baptized shall be saved." To adults, Baptism is a seal of their covenant relation with God, greatly strengthening their faith.

Mark 16, 15-16. *And he said unto them, Go ye into all the world, and preach the gospel to every creature. He that believeth and is baptized shall be saved.*

The crucified and now risen Christ says to His disciples, "Go ye into all the world and preach," *keruxate,* i. e., proclaim as heralds "the Gospel," the glad tidings of the forgiveness of sins through Me the Risen Lord "to every creature," lit. to "all the creation," *pase te ktisei,* to all men, not to Jews only, or to Samaritans only, but to Gentiles likewise, none excepted. "He that believeth and is baptized shall be saved." Mark says: Preach the Gospel "to all the creation"; Matthew: Teach "all nations," *panta ta ethne.* The idea in both is the same: only human beings can *believe,* only to such baptism is to be applied.—Teach "all nations"; proclaim the Gospel, "to all the creation." The Gospel is for *all* men; Christ desires that men—all men—believe in Him, believe the Gospel, i. e., accept it with firm confidence of the heart, and be baptized as a seal and confirmation of their faith. As the Gospel is for all, so baptism is for all. Being baptized is here taught as a proof of a person's faith in the Gospel of the crucified and risen Christ. So when people are capable of receiving instructions in the Christian doctrine, we do so and then administer baptism. But baptism is for children as well as for adults. The Scriptural proof for baptizing children will be produced in the following passages.

Infant Baptism.

Matt. 28, 19. 20. *Go ye therefore and disciple all nations, baptizing them.*

That men and women are to be baptized is generally conceded. The question is: Should *children* be baptized? Children belong to a nation, aye, they make up the greater part of a nation; hence, as long as this general command, "Baptize all nations," holds good, so long, we maintain, children are to be baptized. This command, being general, is proof, positive, incontrovertible proof for the baptism of infants. We need no other. But corroboration of this truth we find amply in the Scriptures. After Peter's great Pentecostal sermon the hearers "were pricked in their hearts, and said unto Peter and the rest of the apostles, 'Men and brethren, what shall we do?" Peter answered: "Repent, and be baptized every one of you, in the name of Jesus Christ for the remission of sins, and ye shall receive the gift of the Holy Ghost. For the promise is to you *and your children.*"—The household baptisms recorded in the New Testament prove the same thing. Paul "baptized Lydia," a seller of purple, "and *her household.*" The keeper of the prison at Philippi was "*baptized,* and *all his.*" Paul baptized the *household* of Stephanas. Is it not plain as can be that such expressions as "household" and "all his" are specially used to include the little ones of the family circle?

Mark 10, 13-16: "*And they brought young children to Him, that he should touch them: and His disciples rebuked those that brought them. But when Jesus saw it, He was much displeased, and said unto them, Suffer the little children to come unto me, and forbid them not: for of such is the kingdom of God. Verily I say unto you, Whosoever shall not receive the kingdom of God as a little child, he shall not enter therein. And He took them up in His arms, put His hands upon them, and blessed them.*"

The subject of this paragraph is the familiar and touching story of Chist's Blessing Little Children. Matthew and Luke also relate it, but Mark's account is the fullest and most striking. We are told that

"they", the parents, most probably the mothers, "brought young children" to Jesus. Mark says they were *paidia*—little children; Luke
calls them *brephe*—babes, infants. What was their purpose in so doing? "That He should *touch them*." Matthew explains this by saying: that He should *"lay His hands on them and pray."* These parents
knew and believed that by Christ's touching, i. e., *by His laying hands
on them and praying*, a blessing would be conferred upon them. They
knew, their children, though infants, needed Christ's blessing. What
happened? "His disciples rebuked those that brought them." Christ's
diciples were over-officious in this instance. Without inquiring for the
Master's will, they took matters into their own hands. They reasoned
most likely thus: Why trouble the hardworked Master with such trivial
affairs, and so they rebuked the parents.

Wherein the rebuke consisted we know not. The word rendered
rebuked is *epetimon*, i. e., they intimidated, terrified, threatened them
in order to *hinder* (koluete) them from bringing the children to Jesus. Their action was ill-advised; it brought the displeasure of the
Master upon them: "When Jesus saw it, He was much displeased."
He was indignant at this rebuke and most likely His countenance
showed it. Christ loves little children, (Mark 9, 36-37.) This His
disciples knew and now they try to hinder parents to bring them
to Him! "Suffer the little children to come unto me," He says to
His disciples: *"forbid them not—hinder* (koluete) them not." The
reason our Lord adduces is this: "for of such is the kingdom of God."
He does not say: "of these," but "of such" (toiouton), of this kind
is the kingdom of God. "Of such," "of this kind" that are brought
to Him, that come to Him. They are to "come to Him" in order to
be "in His kingdom," i. e., His kingdom of grace, the Holy Christian
Church.

In other words, children by merely being children are not *therefore*
in the kingdom of God. In order to be in this kingdom, they must
be brought to Him, or as He says: "Come to Him" to receive His
divine blessing. Children are born of the flesh and hence are flesh
(John 3, 5.), sinful. By nature they are. not fit for the kingodm—
this must be maintained over against such as deny *original sin*—but they
are made fit by Jesus. Children, too, cannot *eo ipso*, enter into the kingdom; they must be born again. This passage proves that "little
children," "babes," infants, sucklings can believe, "for of such is the
kingdom of God," but no one is in this Kingdom that does not believe.

Caution. This passage does not teach ex professo, directly, that
children are to be baptized. "Suffer little children to come unto me,"
etc., does not say: Baptize little children. What it does say is this.
Christ loves little children; He wills that they should come to Him,
He wills to bless them, He wills to impart His grace to them. He says
that even they—*little* children, *babes, infants,* who as yet cannot reason,

cannot be instructed in divine matters, are to be made partakers of all the blessings of His kingdom of grace: forgiveness of sin, righteousness, et al. (Romans 14, 17.) This the text says explicitly. For this purpose it is here adduced. When, however, the further question is asked, How to-day these blessings are imparted to them by Jesus, the answer is found in Matthew 28, 18: "Baptize all *nations.*" Here is the *clara Scriptura* commanding also children to be baptized and thus "making disciples" of them.

John 3, 5. 6. *Except a man be born of water and of the Spirit, he cannot enter into the kingdom of God. That which is born of the flesh is flesh.*

"That which is born of the flesh is flesh," says Jesus to Nicodemus, and hence unfit to enter the kingdom of God. Children are *"flesh born of the flesh";* they stand in need of regeneration. We are "by nature the children of wrath."

How is the entrance into the kingdom of God effected? "Except a man be born of water and the Spirit he cannot enter this kingdom." This second birth is a *spiritual* birth, effected by the Holy Spirit. But the Spirit does not work without means to bring about the new birth. And the ordinary means ordained by God Himself is baptism. John 1, 33; Titus 3, 4 ff.; 1 Pet. 1, 23. For supplementary exposition of this passage, see p. 81, Vol. I. and sub The Second Petition.

Matthew 18, 6: *"But whoso shall offend one of these little ones which believe in me, it were better for him that a millstone were hanged about his neck, and that he were drowned in the depth of the sea."*

Speaking of infant baptism, one of the first arguments adduced against it is: "How can little children believe?" This is often said in such a tone of conviction as if the mere statement of the question were equivalent to clinching the argument. Broadus, a Baptist commentator says *in loco*: "Comparatively young children are sometimes believers, but infants cannot be." Christ says they can be. He speaks of *"these little ones which believe in me."* That is final. How that can be is not for us to solve. God will see to that. In Mark 10, 15 Christ emphatically states: *"for of such (little children*—paidia) *is the kingdom of God."* And again: "Verily I say unto you, Whosoever shall not receive the kingdom of God as a little child (paidion), he shall not enter therein." Without faith, however, it is impossible to please God. So the children belonging to the kingdom have faith.

When Christ in our text says "these little ones *which believe in me,*" *pisteuein eis eme,* he uses the strongest possible language to describe this faith as a true faith, trusting and reposing in Him, the Savior. This is the force of the phrase: *pisteuein eis eme.*

To explain the clause. "these little ones which believe in me"
as designating childlike believing grown-ups is to say the least, a
forced interpretation of the simple text. The discourse, beginning at
Ch. 18, v. 1, treats of *little children—paidia*. Four times the Lord mentions them, vv. 2, 3, 4, 5, and in verse 6 He proceeds: "But whoso
shall offend one of these *little ones,*" *hoi mikroi,* etc. Most naturally
the "little ones"—*hoi mikroi*—of v. 6 are the "little children"—*paidia*—
spoken of in the immediately preceding context.

But if for the sake of argument we should concede "the little
ones" of v. 6 to include childlike believers in general, no sane exegesis can exclude "the little ones"—*paidia*—vv. 2-5, from those of whom
the Lord says: *"they believe in me."* So the point of the passage remains.

In addition to these clear Scriptural passages take the practice of
the apostles. In Acts 16, 16 we read of "Lydia and *her household*" being baptized; in Acts 16, 33 of the keeper of the prison "and *all his.*"
What constitutes a household? Does this concept *exclude children?*
Does it not rather *include* children? Again, the general expression
"all his," does it *exclude* children? By no means. Vain are all attempts to deny baptism to children on Scriptural grounds

"But," we are asked, "where is the passage that *demands* in express words: Baptize children?" "Where is the passage," we retort,
"that *forbids* children to be baptized?" There is none. Should *women* be baptized? Certainly But where is the passage that specifically mentions women?

The passage of Scripture demanding children to be baptized is
this: "Disciple all *nations,* baptizing them," etc. Do children belong
to a *nation?* Ask the census-takers whether they include children
in their reports or not

If children are not to be baptized, the Bible must state this
somewhere or else Scripture is misleading. The command to baptize
(Matthew 28) is general and no exception is made

Why Have Sponsors?

Matt. 18, 16. *In the mouth of two or three witnesses every word
may be established.*

The context treats of church discipline, of efforts Christians are
to make to win back a sinning brother. What has been said and done
in private interview by the offending brother may later, if necessary,
be established by the mouth of two or three witnesses.

Deut. 19, 15, teaches us that in case of litigation the Jewish laws demanded the evidence "at the mouth of two witnesses, or at the mouth of three witnesses." Cf. also John 8, 17; 2 Cor. 3, 1.

Let us apply this dictum of our Lord (Matt. 18, 16) to sponsorship. Baptism is so important an act that no doubt as to its validity should be entertained in later years by anyone. Hence the desirability of sponsors. They will be ready to testify that the person in childhood has been properly baptized. This is one reason for sponsorship. There are others. As, according to a wise custom of the church, the sponsors are to pray for the child, and, in case of death of the parents, to see to his proper Christian training, it is self-evident that sponsors should be of the Lutheran faith. Though we have no command and no example of sponsors in Scripture and so the question of sponsorship is a matter of Christian liberty, still the conscientious pastor will not treat this matter lightly. "Lutheran sponsors for Lutheran children" is a very good maxim.

Secondly, what Baptism gives or profits.

Gal. 3, 26. 27. *Ye are all the children of God by faith in Christ Jesus. For as many of you as have been baptized into Christ have put on Christ.*

St. Paul addresses the Galatian Christians, assuring them of their blissful state. "All ye are the children of God by faith in Christ Jesus." Children of God belong to God's family. Whence this high prerogative? *By faith,* not by works. Nor is it any kind of faith by which this sonship was attained, but it is a very specific faith—*faith in Christ Jesus.* How did they become children of God? *"For as* many of you as have been baptized *into Christ have put on Christ.* Through baptism they entered into most intimate union and communion with Christ. How intimate that relation is we see from the phrase following: "baptized into Christ, *ye have put on Christ."* As one puts on a garment to hide one's nakedness or uncleanness, so they in Baptism *put on Christ.* Thus they were clothed with His righteousness and purity, merited through His suffering and death. Righteousness and sin are opposites. Where there is Christ's righteousness, there is *forgiveness of sin.* Baptized into Christ they have forgiveness of sin. Thus baptism "works forgiveness of sin."

Note: According to Scriptural diction, there is a twofold putting on of Christ: 1. Putting on Christ *according to the Law.* Rom. 13, 14: "Put on the Lord Jesus Christ." Text and context say this means: Follow in Christ's footsteps, follow Him as an example in your daily life. In Gal. 3, 26. 27 a putting on of Christ *according to the Gospel* is spoken of. By faith we are clothed in Christ's righteousness, so that God does not look upon our sin, but sees nothing but Christ's spotless robe of righteousness.

Acts 2, 38. *Repent, and be baptized every one of you in the name of Jesus Christ for the remission of sins.*

The Pentecost sermon of Peter touched his audience to the quick. Conscience-smitten they cry out: "Men and brethren, what shall we do? For people so asking there is help in store. *"Repent,"* says Peter, Repent truly and sincerely, realize keenly the awfulness of sin, admit your deep guilt remorsefully before your God, *"and be baptized every one of you in the name of Jesus Christ for the remission of sin."* Jesus Christ, the Savior, has fully atoned for sin. His merits He has put into Baptism Be baptized and you receive *the remission of sin.*

Baptism is not a mere sign, a symbol, or a ceremony which one must make, receive, or go through in order to become a full-fledged Christian, or a member of the Church in good standing. On becoming a member of a lodge, we are told, one must go through certain initiation ceremonies. So, some imagine, in order to become a member in good standing in the church, one must go through this ceremony—be baptized. No, not so. Baptism is a means of grace; it conveys and appropriates to the baptized person *forgiveness of sin.* The water in baptism is so powerful because "it is the water comprehended in God's command and connected with God's word." And here again let it be said in passing the promise of the forgiveness of sin conveyed by Baptism is not for adults only. The children, too, are included. Peter expressly says in this selfsame connection, v. 39: "For the promise is unto you and *your children".*

1 Cor. 15, 55-57. *O death, where is thy sting?—O grave, where is thy victory? The sting of death is sin, and the strength of sin. is the Law. But thanks be to God which giveth us the victory through our Lord Jesus Christ.*

In enumerating the blessings of Baptism, Luther says: 1. It works *forgiveness of sin.* Gal. 3, 26. 27; Acts 2, 28.—But where there is forgiveness of sin, death and the devil no longer have any power over us. Hence Luther proceeds: 2. It *delivers from death and the devil.*—1 Cor. 15, 55-57, contains no direct reference to baptism, but still the passage is very pertinent.

Christ's resurrection, our resurrection! This is Paul's great theme in this grand chapter. Die we must, but our death is really no death, it is but a sleep. "But now is Christ risen from the dead, and become the first—fruits of them that *slept!* v. 20. "Death is swallowed up," consumed, done away with, "in victory", Paul triumphantly

announces. "O death, where is thy sting." There is none. The sting
has been taken out of death. "O grave,"—the better reading here for
"grave" is "death"—"Oh, death, where is thy victory?" Victory
there is none, death has suffered a defeat. After this apostrophe
of exultation over the defeat of Death, Paul continues: "The
sting of death is sin, and the strength of sin is the *law*." But
sin is atoned for, so death has lost its sting; the *law* has been fulfilled so *sin* has lost its power to condemn us. Glorious message!
Whom have we to thank therefor? *"But thanks be to God, which giveth us the victory through our Lord Jesus Christ."* In Romans, St.
Paul tells us: "Christ is the end of the *law* for righteousness to
every one that believeth." The law is fulfilled. In Hebrews we read:
"Forasmuch then as the children are partakers of flesh and blood,
Christ also Himself likewise took part of the same, that through death
He might destroy him that had the power of death, that is, the devil,"
—the devil has lost his power over us—"and deliver them who *through
fear of death* were all their lifetime subject to bondage." Death has
lost its sting for the Christians.

"Thanks be to Go who *giveth* us the victory." Giveth—the present
tense—denotes a continued action. Again and again we are assured of
this victory over our arch-enemies by our Lord Jesus Christ in the
Gospel and in the Lord's Supper. And since Baptism works forgiveness of sin, as we have learned, by baptism we have been delivered
also from death and damnation. On this power of baptism the preacher will dwell especially at the funeral of infants.

Colossians 1, 12-14: *"Giving thanks unto the Father, which hath
made us meet to be partakers of the inheritance of the saints in light:
Who hath delivered us from the power of darkness, and hath translated us into the kingdom of His dear Son: In whom we have redemption through his blood, even the forgiveness of sins."*

"Give thanks to the Father," sc. the Father of Jesus Christ, and
hence your Father also, so the Colossians are joyfully exhorted. What
reason does the Apostle adduce as a ground for rendering thanksgiving? *"He hath made us meet,"* i. e., competent, fit, capable, *"for
the share of inheritance of the saints in the light."* How precious this
truth! A good reason cheerfully to thank God. *Saints* are sinners,
separated from the world and dedicated to God. Saints *in the light*
they are because God called them by the Gospel from darkness into
His marvelous light. (1. Pet. 2, 9.) "Christ is the Light; through
Him they have come into the light, have become *'children of the light*,"
(Eph. 5. 8; 1 Thess. 5, 5.), they no longer walk in darkness, but in
the light.

By nature they were not entitled to this inheritance. The Father
"hath made them meet," competent, fit, thereto. All merit on their
part "for a share" in the riches of this glorious state is excluded. It is

an *inheritance*. The apostle precisely elucidates the thought of their being "made meet to be partakers of the inheritance of the saints in light," by saying: "who hath *delivered* us *from the power of darkness*, and hath *translated* us *into* the kingdom of His dear Son," lit., of the Son of His love. Christ has a realm among men; Satan has a realm among men. To the latter the Colossians belonged before their conversion.

Formerly they were in *darkness;* now they are in *light,* in the *kingdom* of Jesus. *Darkness* held them in bondage, they were under *its power, exousia,* under its authority. The *power of darkness,* since it is placed in contrast to Christ's kingdom, describes Satan's domain. Satan ruled them; his was the rightful authority over them. Now— blessed transition!—they are in the *kingdom* of His dear Son. Jesus now is their Ruler and Lord. How did this change from one master to another take place? The text says: The Father hath *delivered,* *"errusato,"* plucked us, rescued us "out of the power of the darkness" into which we had hopelessly fallen, and by so doing He at the same time "translated us into the kingdom of His dear Son." By such *translation, metestesen,* we received legal standing in this spiritual kingdom. The kingdom is Christ's; we are Christ's. Christ is the "Son of His love," through Him we are God's beloved children. How was this brought about? He *"delivered"* us, *plucked us* out of Satan's kingdom. True. But "darkness" personified, Satan, had *authority,* exousia, over us. How was the devil's authority annulled, how were the shackles of bondage broken?

The answer follows: "*In whom we have redemption through His blood, even the forgiveness of sin.*" Through sin we had come into "the power of darkness." "We were by nature the children of wrath," we "walked according to the prince of the power of the air, the spirit that now worketh in the children of disobedience," Eph. 2, 2. 4. How get out of this bondage? There was but one way: By *redemption.* This *we* could not bring about. Redemption was possible only through Christ Jesus. This He did. He *redeemed,* i. e., brought us back, paid the redemption money, the ransom price. Only thus could the *exousia,* the authority of darkness be annulled   And the ransom price? "*His blood.*" Consider the price of your redemption from sin! See Matt. 20, 28; 1 Tim. 2, 6; Titus 2, 14. Christians, "ye are bought with a price!" I Cor. 6, 20; 7, 23; Gal. 3, 13. This "*redemption through His blood,*" that of the "Son of His love," brought about "*the forgiveness of sin.*" Who possesses it? "*In whom we* have the redemption," etc. All they that are *in Christ Jesus.* He alone paid the price; in Him alone is it to be had. "There is salvation in none other." Without Christ there is no justification. Embracing Christ as our Savior by God's grace—what a blessed state—we *have* forgiveness of sin, now, always, continually, as long as we remain "*in Him.*"

Let us again briefly ponder the thoughts culled from the text.

Sin brought us into the power of darkness. The redemption from sin was made by our Savior, thus we were delivered from Satan's power and translated into Christ's kingdom, thus we became partakers of the inheritance of the saints in light. By nature we were not "meet" to share therein. God made us meet. He called us by the Gospel; thus we came to faith in Christ; "in Him" we are "in the light," In Him "we belong to that blessed company, whom the apostle addresses in the salutation of the epistle "as saints and faithful brethren in Christ." Reasons plentiful, indeed, to "give thanks to the Father."

Applying this passage to baptism, we ask: When were the Colossian Christians "made meet to be partakers," etc? In the moment they were in Him, "in whom we *have* forgiveness of sin," i. e., when they believed and embraced this forgiveness and were baptized into this faith. Their children received the transfer in baptism. Since baptism works forgiveness of sin, it at the same time delivers from the "power of darkness."

Before baptizing a child, the Lutheran pastor asks the sponsors "in the name and in the stead of the child"—Dost thou renounce the devil, and all his works, and all his ways? Next follow questions relating to the confession of faith: "Dost thou believe in God the Father," etc.—thus giving clear expression to the faith that is in us, that in the sacred act of baptism the baptized child is delivered from the dominion of Satan and translated into the kingdom of "the Son of His love."

NOTE: Eph. 1, 7 is a parallel passage to Col. 1, 14. For exposition of Eph. 1, 7, see Vol. I. p. 263.

1 Pet. 3, 20. 21. *The long-suffering of God waited in the days of Noah, while the ark was a preparing· wherein few, that is, eight souls, were saved by water. The like figure whereunto even Baptism doth also now save us (not the putting away of the filth of the flesh but the answer of a good conscience toward God) by the resurrection of Jesus Christ.*

"Baptism doth also now save us." The statement is so plain; any child can understand it. So we might let it go at that and say: Quod erat demonstrandum: *baptism doth save us.* The text so lucid in itself, stands out in even greater clarity if we allow the light of the context, of the environment, to play upon it. The apostle speaks of the Flood in the days of Noah. "The long-suffering of God waited in the days of Noah while the ark was a preparing." The ark finished, Noah's family of eight entered. The Flood came. It lasted 40 days and 40 nights. The ungodly world perished; Noah and his family were "*saved by water.*" Now the text goes on: "The like figure whereunto even baptism doth also now save us." The phrase:"*The like ,figure whereunto*" is rather stiff. A smoother translation is: Noah and his family were "saved through water; which also after a true likeness doth now save us, even baptism." Luther, as usual, hits the nail on the head. He translates the thought beautifully thus: "Acht Seelen wurden behalten durchs Wasser; welches nun auch uns selig macht in der Taufe, *die durch jenes bedeutet ist*." A literal translation, though not making smooth English, will serve to make the meaning clear: The apostle. had said: "Eight souls were saved by water." He proceeds: "Which also us as antitype now saves, baptism." The relative "which"—*ho*—clearly refers to "water," so the sense is: "which" water, namely "baptism", now also saves us. The point of comparison is this: the water of the Flood appears as *saving water*: "Eight souls were *saved* by water." The water of baptism is *saving* water.

"*Eight souls were saved*"—*dia*—by means of, through, "*water*." Water, this is the point, was *the means of saving* Noah and all his. This is the tertium comparationis. Observe the words following: "Eight souls were saved by means of water, which *also* doth now save us." Clearly the antecedent of the relative "which" is "water", "which" water *also* saves us. Water saved them, water saves us. The water of the Flood saved Noah. Which water saves us? Take the literal translation: "which (water) also as antitype now saves us, even *baptism*." Which water saves us, we ask again? Answer: baptismal water. The water of the Flood is a type of the water of baptism. The water of the Flood and that in baptism correspond in this one point: both are *saving waters*. Baptismal water is saving water.

A few parallel thoughts: The water of the Deluge carried the eight souls into a new world; so baptismal water carries us into the kingdom of God. The water of the Flood separated the eight souls from the lost and saved them, so baptism separates us from the *massa perditionis* and saves us.

To return to the text: The apostle says: "*Baptism doth also now save us.*" By way of appositional phrases he tells us first, negatively, how baptismal water does *not* save us, how it is not to be viewed, then, positively, what this baptismal water is, what it bestows, *how* it saves us.

First, then, he says: "*Not the putting away of the filth of the flesh*"; baptismal water is not an outward purifier of the flesh, nor is it a ceremonial washing. Its purpose is not to cleanse the flesh from filth, but it is to cleanse the conscience from sin. Observe the adversative *but* in the next phrase, thus putting this thought in strong contrast to the former: "*but it is the answer of a good conscience toward God.*" "*Answer*", eperotema, in legal parlance signifies *compact*. Luther's translation Bund, i. e., covenant, is very good. Peter loves brevity of diction. The latter clause contains two thoughts: 1. Baptism is a *compact* with God; 2. Through this compact we receive *a good conscience.* The compact *effects* a good conscience. This good conscience does not exist *before* baptism, but is received *in*, and effected *by* baptism. When a compact with God is made, why, then, is God our Father: where a *good conscience* exists, there sins are forgiven. Thus baptism now saves us. Baptism is a means of grace. On the basis of this passage we speak of our baptismal covenant with God.

Whence has Baptism this power? The text says: *"Baptism does also now save us—by the resurrection of Jesus Christ."* How does the resurrection of Jesus serve to effect a good conscience by baptism? Reflect. What does the resurrection of Christ stand for? By the *death* of Christ forgiveness of sins was merited; by His *resurrection* the seal of God's approval was imprinted on the redemptive work of Christ. This forgiveness of sin, effected by the death of Christ, and sealed by His resurrection, is *applied* to the individual sinner by this means of grace, *baptism.* "So it is not a salvation without Christ. Salvation by baptism, is salvation by faith; by baptism, which offers, by faith, which accepts salvation as a gift of God."

Luther: Baptism works forgiveness of sins, (Gal. 3, 26. 27; Acts 2, 38) delivers from death and the devil, (I Cor. 15, 55-57; Col. 1. 12-14.) and gives *eternal salvation* to all who believe this, as the words and promises of God declare. (1. Pet. 3, 20. 21.) Mark 16, 16.

1 Cor. 6. 11. *But ye are washed, but ye are sanctified, but ye are justified in the name of the Lord Jesus, and by the Spirit of our God.*

See exposition, p. 214, Vol. I.

Mark 16, 15. 16. *Go ye into all the world, and preach the gospel to every creature. He that believeth, and is baptized shall be saved: but he that believeth not, shall be damned.* (See Qu. 287.)

"Preach the Gospel; he that believeth shall be saved."..What is the Gospel? The glad tidings of Jesus Christ, the Son of God, Mark 1, 1. Rom. 1, 1. 2. It proclaims that Jesus "died for our sins'- and that He rose again the third day." 1 Cor. 15, 1. 3. 4. The Gospel is "the word of His grace." Act 20, 3. It is "the Gospel of the grace of God." Act 20, 24. "Repentance and remission of sin should be preached in His name among all nations." Luke 24, 47. Where there is forgiveness of sin, there is life and salvation. It is "the Gospel of our salvation", Eph. 1, 13. It is this Gospel the Lord commands to be preached. "God was in Christ, reconciling the world unto Himself," 2 Cor. 5, 19; Christ is the propitiation for the whole world, 1 Joh. 2, 2; and "God will have all men to be saved and come to a knowledge of the truth," 1 Tim. 2, 2. These glad tidings we are to believe. *"Preach the Gospel, he that believeth shall be saved."*

To the words "he that believeth" the Lord appends the words: *"and is baptized."* The Lord joins the two. Baptism for adults is the seal of God's grace. Baptism is necessary to salvation. But does not the Lord in the second clause omit the words: "and is baptized?" True, Jesus does not say: "He that believeth not *and is not baptized* shall be damned." What does this prove? Faith is *absolutely* necessary to salvation, baptism, however, not likewise.

Although the Lutheran Church asserts the necessity of baptism unto salvation, still she does not make the rash and hasty conclusion as does the Catholic Church that all unbaptized persons, as, for example, children who die before baptism are damned. We must distinguish between something being *absolutely* necessary, and something being *not* necessary. To say, baptism is *absolutely* necessary to salvation, is wrong; to say baptism is *not* necessary, is wrong again. Baptism is not *absolutely* necessary for salvation, for the Bible teaches: By faith in Christ only are ye saved. Baptism is the *ordinary* means of regeneration, to which God has bound us, but He has not bound Himself thereto. When we say, baptism is necessary, we do not thereby imply that God cannot save him who is is not baptized. "The impossibility of being saved without *faith* is one thing; the impossibility of being saved without *baptism* is an altogether different thing." Carpzov. The words of Jesus: "He that believeth and is baptized shall be saved, but he that believeth not shall be damned, teach incontrovertibly that *unbelief* is really the only damnable sin. There is a remedy for sin: God's grace in Christ Jesus. Despise the remedy and death, eternal death, results. But people who have come to faith by "the Word of His grace" sometimes cannot be baptized owing to circumstances. The malefactor on the cross died in faith of his Savior, yet he died unbaptized. Many martyrs of the primitive Church had no opportunity to be baptized.

Saving faith may exist in one who is *deprived* of baptism, but it cannot exist with the *contempt* of Baptism. Hence the theological axiom: "Not the privation but the contempt of the sacrament is damnable." Mark 16. 16.

Luke 7, 30: *"But the Pharisees and lawyers rejected the counsel of God against themselves, being not baptized of Him."*

Speaking of the office of John the Baptist, we read that "all the people that heard Him," (Jesus) "and the publicans, justified God," *i. e.*, they declared God to be just who called them sinners that needed forgiveness of sin "being baptized with the baptism of John." In glaring contrast to this attitude of the people and the publicans stood that of the Pharisees. Of them it is said: *"But the Pharisees and lawyers rejected,"* i. e., set aside, nullified *"the counsel of God against themselves,"* *eis heauton,* in reference to themselves. The *"counsel"—boule—* "of God" in relation also to them was their salvation, 1 Tim. 2, 4, but they *rejected*, frustrated this gracious counsel of God. How did they exhibit their animosity? By *"not being baptized of Him."* In this baptism there was a gracious counsel, or will, of God exhibited to them. They *despised baptism* and thus they *despised* God's *gracious will*. And this contempt of baptism rendered them culpable.

Thirdly, What the Power of Baptism Is.

How Can Water Do Such Great Things?

Common water can never take away the filth of the soul; baptismal water, however, is "not simple water only, but water connected with the word of God." Baptism is, as St. Paul says, "the washing of water by the word." It is water "in conjunction with" the word of God. This word of God makes baptismal water so powerful. Matthew explicitly gives the *commandment* of Christ: "Baptize them;" and the *promise* of grace is implied in the words: *"Disciple* the nations, *baptizing* them." Elsewhere the promise is explicitly stated thus: "He that believeth and is baptized shall be saved." So the word of God, His command and His promise, communicates such great power to Baptism.

To illustrate. The water of the Jordan had no power in itself to cleanse from leprosy, but when Naaman, the leper, was bidden by the Lord through the mouth of His prophet Elisha to wash in the Jordan seven times, and he did so, he was cleansed of his leprosy. Why? Because the word of God imparted that power to the water. When Christ said to the lepers, "Be clean!" they were cleansed. Why? Because of the powerful word of God. Again, Gideon, in the name of the Lord, conquered the hosts of the Midianites with three hundred men armed with pitchers, torches, and trumpets. Why? Because of the command of God. *So all depends on the word of God.* Why does the earth bring forth grass to this day? Because of God's blessing: "Let the earth bring forth grass." The water in baptism does such great things because God's word is connected therewith. This word we believe. "Reason," says Luther, "can never understand how Baptism is a washing of regeneration, but *what God says is true,* whether my senses corroborate it or not. He is omnipotent and can and does fulfill His Word."

Titus 3, 4-6: *"But after that the kindness and love of God our Savior toward man appeared, not by works of righteousness which we have done, but according to His mercy he saved us, by the washing of regeneration, and renewing of the Holy Ghost; which He shed on us abundantly through Jesus Christ our Savior; that being justified by His grace, we should be made heirs according to the hope of eternal life. This is a faithful saying.*

"God saved us." This is the principal thought of the paragraph. Salvation is a *work of God* and God only. "But after that the *kindness* and *love* of God our Savior toward man appeared—He saved us." Salvation is a work of *God's grace.* Through the redemptive work of Christ salvation was merited. This salvation, wrought by Christ, is offered, conveyed, and sealed to the individuals also in Baptism: *"He saved us by the washing of regeneration."*

Let us consider the text. *"God saved us."* In carrying out this topic sentence the apostle says with extreme emphasis, both negatively and positively, that salvation is in no way dependent on man's work, or on his co-operation, but that it is solely a work due to His grace. "He saved us—*not by works of righteousness which we have done.*" A detailed exegesis of this clause would lead us too far afield from our subject proper. Plain as plain can be it says that God was not impelled by works of ours to save us. What was the impelling cause? "He saved us *according to His mercy.*" Observe the contrast between the: "not *we*" and the "but *He;*" between *"our works"* and *"His grace."* The impelling force was not in us, but in Him, in "His grace," in His divine compassion with our deplorable condition. This precious truth: "Saved by grace alone" is brought out in bold relief in the Greek by placing the pronoun *His* emphatically between the definite article and the noun: *"ton autou eleon."* Salvation is a work of God's grace solely and only.

Next we are told *how* God saved us. "He saved us *by the washing of regeneration and renewing of the Holy Ghost."* Text and context, likewise New Testament usage, speak loudly for the fact that this "washing of regeneration" designates baptism. Eph. 5, 26; 1 Cor. 6, 11; John 3, 5.—God saved us *"by,"* dia, *"through the washing of regeneration," "dia loutrou paliggenesias,"* i. e., "through the laver of regeneration," or in plain, homely Anglo Saxon: "through the bath of the rebirth." This baptism, this "washing" plainly was a *means* in God's hands to save us. It is a "washing *of regeneration,*" one that brings about, *effects* regeneration. Thus God saved us; He baptized us, through baptism we were regenerated, born again, faith was implanted in our hearts.—The Reformed idea: baptism is merely a symbol of regeneration is not exegesis but eisegesis; not exposition, but imposition. We are not saved by a symbol.

Baptism is said to be not only a "washing of regeneration" but also *"a renewing."* The word "renewing" is not governed by the preposition *"by."* This would make the text say: God saved us by two means: 1. *by* the washing of regeneration; 2. by the renewing of the Holy Ghost. The word "renewing" unfolds, develops the concept "washing of regeneration," the "and" connecting the two words being the explanatory "and." "God saved us by the washing of regeneration *and* renewing." The washing of regeneration is at the same time a

washing of renewing. Through baptism we are born again, we are
put into a new life. This new birth manifests itself; in Christ we are
new creatures, who walk in the newness of life.—Whosoever is born
again, is renewed, is saved. God saved us. His means: baptism.

Whence has baptism this great power? Baptism is "a washing of
regeneration and renewing *of the Holy Ghost.*" (Genetive of author.)
Baptismal water receives its great power from the Holy Ghost. Simple
water cannot do these great things. We are not saved by water-power.
In and with the water the Holy Ghost is shed on us richly. Through
this water, by means of this water "comprehended in God's command,
connected with God's word" the Holy Spirit works regeneration and
renewal in the heart of sinful man. The Holy Spirit is the Spirit of
Christ. He proceeds from Christ, is sent by Christ, our Savior. Hence
we read: "By the washing—of the Holy Ghost *whom* He (God) *shed
on us abundantly through Jesus Christ.*" The Spirit, sent by Christ,
brings Christ the Savior and with Him His salvation into the hearts
of men by regenerating and renewing them. Thus, too, Christ proves
to be *our Savior.*

And now the glorious purpose of it all: "*that,* being justified by
His grace, *we should be made heirs of eternal life.*" Having faith
kindled in our hearts through baptism, being regenerated, we are justified, *i. e.,* declared righteous, just before God. God sees nothing to
condemn in us; He is our Father, we are His children, and if children
then *heirs.*

To recapitulate: By baptism we are born again, by baptism we
are renewed, by baptism we are justified, by baptism we become heirs
of life eternal.—The main thought of the paragraph runs thus: "God
saved us . . . by the washing of regeneration .   that we . .
should be made heirs of eternal life."

As through the Gospel in general, so through baptism specifically
forgiveness of sin, redemption, is applied to the individual sinner.
As in the preaching of the Gospel God says to all that hear the glad
tidings: Your sins are forgiven you through Jesus, so in Baptism he
says to the individual: "Thy sins are forgiven thee." And he who
believes such words of God has what the words say: forgiveness of sin.

It is refreshing to read what a non-Lutheran, one who simply
follows the words of the text, has to say on this text. Plummer in his
Pastoral Epistles, p. 288, writes thus:

"We are fully justified by his language here in asserting that it
is *by means of the* baptismal washing that the regeneration takes
place; for he asserts that God 'saved us *through* the washing of regeneration.' The laver or bath of regeneration is the instrument or *means*
by which God saved us. Such is the natural, and almost the necessary
meaning of the Greek construction (*dia* with the genitive). Nor is

this an audacious erection of a comprehensive and momentous doctrine upon the narrow basis of a single preposition. Even if this passage stood alone, it would still be our duty to find a meaning for the Apostle's Greek: and it may be seriously doubted whether any more reasonable meaning than that which is here put forward can be found: But the passage does not stand alone, as has just been shown."

Ephesians 5, 25-26: *"Husbands, love your wives, even as Christ also loved the church, and gave Himself for it; that He might sanctify and cleanse it with the washing of water by the word."*

Baptism is described as *"the washing of water with word,"* en *remati.* Water and word go together to make baptism a gracious water of life. Let us hear Dr. Graebner's explanation of this phrase. He writes, Theological Quarterly, Vol. 5, pp. 9-10:

"But the sacred act which constitutes sacramental Baptism comprises more than a mere application of water. St. Paul describes Baptism as *to loutron tou hudatos en remati,* 'the washing of the water with word.'

That he speaks of a particular washing is indicated by the article before *loutron* in the text, and the only washing to which his description answers is Baptism. By *tou hydatos* it is described as a washing of water, water not used as a drink, but applied externally. But this water is *en remati, together with or accompanied by the word.* The preposition *en* is here as elsewhere employed to indicate *concomitance,* introducing that with which the water is bound up or intimately connected."

(The Greek preposition *en,* generally translated *"in," "by,"* in certain passages means: "together with" or "accompanied by," as in the present text. See 2 Cor. 10, 14; Rom. 15, 29; Luke 14, 31; Eph. 4, 4; 1 Pet. 4, 19.)

"The words, "the washing of water *en remati"*—*"in* word," together with the word, describe a certain institution known to Paul and his readers, in which the *water* as the prescribed element, is statedly connected with *rema, word.* There is one institution, and one only, with which this description tallies, and that perfectly. This is Baptism. Here we have water as the prescribed element, the *water,* and *word,* the word of divine institution whereby this water, in its prescribed use as a washing or baptizing is constituted a sacrament, a means whereby men are made disciples of Christ, Matt. 28, 19, sanctified and cleansed by Him who has redeemed them, giving Himself as a ransom for all. Eph. 5, 25 f. It was by virtue of the *rema theou*—the word of God—that the Baptism of John was "a baptism of repentance for the forgiveness of sin." Luke 3, 2 f. It is by virtue of Christ's *rema,* His word of institution, that Christian Baptism is a sacrament, a means of making disciples of Christ among all nations." Matt. 28, 19.

Fourthly, What Baptism Signifies.

Romans 6, 1-4: *"What shall we say then? Shall we continue in sin, that grace may abound? God forbid. How shall we, that are dead to sin, live any longer therein? Know ye not, that so many of us as were baptized into Jesus Christ were baptized into His death? Therefore we are buried with Him by baptism into death: that like as Christ was raised up from the dead by the glory of the Father, even so we also should walk in newness of life."*

"Where sin abounded, there grace did much more abound," so the apostle had said in the preceding chapter. (5, 20.)   What follows from this doctrine of grace as set forth by Paul?   "Shall we continue in sin, that grace may abound?"   (6, 1.)   "God forbid."   (v. 2.)   Justification must be followed by sanctification.   This is the topic the apostle now carries out.   "How shall we, that are *dead* to sin, *live* any longer therein?"   Impossible!   To be *dead* to sin and still to *live* in sin is a contradiction in itself.   We are "dead to sin," *i. e.*, we are redeemed not only from the penalty, but also from the power and the dominion of sin.   "We are dead to sin;" what follows from this?   Surely not to *live* in sin.   I appeal to your knowledge, says Paul.   "We were baptized into Christ," (John 3, 5; Matt. 28, 19).   In baptism God imputed to us the righteousness of His Son.   Christ died for our sins and thus destroyed the power of the devil over us, Heb. 2, 14.   When "we were baptized into Christ we were baptized into His death."   He freed us from the penalty and guilt of sin; not only that; He redeemed us from its dominion.   Sin is no longer our lord and master—"we are dead to sin."   "Therefore"—since we have died with Christ—"we are buried with Him by baptism into death: *that* like as Christ was raised up from the dead by the glory of the Father, *even so we should walk in newness of life.*"   Christ died for our sins.   His burial was proof of His death.   "By the glory," *doxa*—here His omnipotence—"of the Father" He was raised from the dead.   Sin was atoned for; He no longer had anything to do with sin; He entered *into a new life.*   We are His.   *"Even so we should walk in newness of life."*   This is the point of comparison here: *"like as He"*—*"even so we."*   Not are we to "live in sin," to "continue in sin," (v. 1, 2), but "to walk in newness of life." (v. 4.)   This new life, begun in baptism, must become manifest in our daily walk.   As baptism is the means and source of our *justification,* so it is likewise the source of our *sanctification.*   And to this latter fact especially the apostle here refers.

NOTE 1.   This passage speaks of the *effect* of Baptism.   Again we have seen the truth of Titus 3, 5:   Baptism is "the washing of regeneration and *renewing* of the Holy Ghost."   But it also signifies what it effects.   As the mode of sprinkling or pouring water upon the person baptized *also signifies* the cleansing from sin, Hebr. 10, 22; Hes.

36, 25; so the being "buried with Him by baptism into death" and the "walk in the newness of life," signify "that the old Adam, by daily contrition and repentance, be drowned and die with all sins and evil lusts and, again, a new man daily come forth and arise, who shall live before God in righteousness and purity forever."

NOTE 2. "It is not necessary to assume that there is any reference here to immersion of the body in baptism, as though it were a burial. No such allusion can be supposed in the next verse, where we are said *to be planted* with him. The reference is not to the *mode* of baptism, but *to its effect.* Our baptism unites us to Christ, so that we died with Him, and rose with Him. As He died to sin, so do we; as He rose to righteousness and glory, so do we. The same doctrine concerning baptism, and of the nature of union with Christ, therein expressed, is taught in Gal. iii, 27, and Col. ii, 12." cf. Hodge, Romans, p. 305.

Eph. 4, 22: *Put off concerning the former conversation the old man, which is corrupt according to the deceitful lusts.*

For explanation see Vol. I, p. 124.

Gal. 5, 24: *"And they that are Christ's have crucified the flesh with the affections and lusts."*

"Walk in the spirit, and ye shall not fulfill the lust of the flesh." v. 16. This is the basic sentence of the entire paragraph. Verses 17-23 develope the exhortation by adducing reasons. Verse 24 is in the nature of a summary sentence and shows that a Christian cannot but "walk in the spirit."

"Walk in the spirit." A better rendition of the Dative *pneumati* is "by the spirit." "Walk by the spirit" is equivalent to "walk *after* the spirit," *kata pneuma*, Romans 8, 1, which says that the spirit is to be the governing, actuating influence of this walk. What then is meant by "spirit" in our text? The term "flesh" is put in opposition to it. "Walk by the *spirit,* and ye shall not fulfill the lust of the *flesh."* When the two concepts are thus contrasted, "spirit" is the "new man," wrought by the Holy Spirit through the Gospel, and "flesh" is the "old man," our corrupted, sinful nature. The meaning of these words is plain when we consider what our Lord said to Nicodemus, John 3, 6: "That which is born of the flesh is *flesh;* and that which is born of the Spirit is *spirit."* So the exhortation is this: Christians, see to it that the "spirit" in you, the new man, governs, directs, actuates your walk, then the *"flesh,"* the old man, cannot and will not have its way. The "flesh" will try to assert itself, but the "spirit" will restrain the "flesh;" the "new man" will keep the "old man" in check so that he cannot *fulfill* his desires. Constant vigilance is necessary, "for the flesh lusteth against the spirit, and the spirit against the flesh," v. 17. There is a constant strife between the spirit and the flesh in the Christian. This struggle is a characteristic of the Christian, and hence a consolation for him. So long as he notices this fight going on, so long he knows that his "spirit" is not dead. Where there is no strife, there the "flesh" has gained the ascendency. "Walk by the spirit," Christians, *"be led of the spirit,"* v. 18.—This thought is further developed by showing the "works of the flesh," vv. 19-21, and "the fruit of the spirit," vv. 22, 23.

Now the Apostle proceeds: *"And they that are Christ's, hoi tou Christou,* they that belong to Christ, they that are His possession, "bought with a price" and brought to faith in Him, *"have crucified the flesh.* The apostle says: They *"have* crucified," the flesh. Who did? "they that are Christ's." When? In the moment they became Christ's own. "We reckon ourselves dead unto sin and living unto God *in Christ Jesus,"* says the apostle in another place. As Christ, their Savior, was crucified for them and thus redeemed them from sin, so the Christians out of gratitude have crucified their flesh, and daily crucify it by not "fulfilling the lust of the flesh," v. 16. Similarly the apostle writes: "Knowing this that our old man is crucified with Him (Christ), so that the body of sin might be destroyed, that henceforth we should not serve sin." This crucifixion hurts, smarts. To nail "the old man" on the cross daily is hard work. The "old man" will not have it so; he struggles and fights to come down from the cross. Speaking without figure the flesh gives sad evidences of life, as was the case with the Galatians. And since the flesh remains with us till death, this warfare goes on, must go on till death. In view of this fact, how necessary the exhortations: "Walk by the spirit;" "be led by the spirit!" What an incentive to maintain this spiritual warfare, when we read: "They that are Christ's have crucified the flesh with the affections and lusts."

Of this conflict between the "spirit" and the "flesh," Luther says in his Small Catechism: "The old Adam in us should by daily contrition and repentance, be drowned and die with all sins and evil lusts and, again, a new man daily come forth and arise, who shall live before God in righteousness and purity forever."

2 Cor. 5, 17. *If any man be in Christ, he is a new creature.*

Gal. 3, 26. 27. We Christians are said to be "baptized into Christ." How intimately baptism connects us with Christ! Here we are told the Christians are *"in Christ."* The former may be viewed as the cause, the latter as the effect.—*"If any man be in Christ,"* has his being in Him, lives and moves in Him, justified by faith, *"he is a new creature,"* kaine ktisis, *a new creation.* "We are His workmanship, *created* in Christ Jesus," Eph. 2. 10. Man is an altogether different person from what he was before. The "new creature" manifests itself in the every-day walk of the Christian. Baptism, which has put us into Christ, is to remind us ever and again that we should daily walk in "newness of life."

Osiander comprehensively observes: "All that man had and purposed before he knew Christ, while he was out of Christ, and when he was not born of the Spirit, all that seemed valuable to him in his natural state completely lost its influence and authority over him as soon as he believed on Christ, and gave way to the overpowering energy of a new, better, and permanent spirit." Lange's Commentary *in loco.*

Eph. 4, 24. *Put on the new man, which after God is created in righteousness and true holiness.*

For exposition see Vol. I. p. 124.

PART V.

THE OFFICE OF THE KEYS.

Rome today as stoutly as ever boasts of being the sole possessor of the power of the keys. She maintains as arrogantly as ever that the so-called "Holy Father" is the visible head of the Church, from whom, as Christ's vicar on earth, all power in the Church emanates. Again and again Rome declaims: Christ said to Peter: "I will give unto thee the keys of the kingdom of heaven"; Peter was thus made the head of the Church, the Pope is his successor, *ergo*, the Pope possesses the keys of heaven exclusively; the Roman Catholic Church is the only saving Church. *In ecclesia salus; extra ecclesiam nulla salus!* All other Churches are synagogs of Satan; with but few exceptions all non-Catholics are forever lost. Such are the exalted, but vain claims of Antichrist.

Again, *Absolution*, based on the Scriptural doctrine of the Office of the Keys, is anathematized by Rome, grossly misunderstood and severely criticised by non-Lutherans. Both doctrines, however, that of *Absolution* as well as that of the *Office of the Keys* being a "peculiar Church-power," are founded on the impregnable Rock of Scriptures; both are noble heritages of the Reformation; both are distinctive doctrines of the Lutheran Church.

Now, what answer does our Church make over against the vaunting pretensions of Antichrist? To whom do the keys of the kingdom

Note: The passages sub paragraph 302 in the Catechism: Matt. 16, 19; Matt. 18, 18; John 20, 21-23; 1 Pet. 2, 9 are treated in the present article: "The Office of the Keys." For 1 Pet. 2, 9 see also detailed exposition on pp. 223, 224, Vol. I.

For Matt. 28, 18-20 sub paragraph 303, see explanations Vol I, pp. 148, 149, 173, 251, 254. et al.

originally and immediately belong? Clear and unmistakable are the words of the *Smalcald Articles:* "But over and above all this we are to confess that the keys belong and have been given not to one man alone, but *to the whole Church,* as this can be clearly and satisfactorily proved. *For just as the promise of the Gospel belongs to the whole Church, originally and immediately, so also do the keys belong to the whole Church immediately; for the keys are nothing else than the office through which those promises are communicated to everyone who desires them.* It is evident, then, that the *Church,* in effect, has the power to appoint her ministers. And Christ in these words: 'Whatsoever ye shall bind,' etc., clearly indicates *to whom* He has given the keys, namely, *to the whole Church,* when He says: 'Wheresoever two or three are gathered together in My name, there am I in the midst of them.'· Matt. 18. 20.

So our Church teaches that Christ gave the power of the keys *immediately and originally* — not to Peter exclusively, much less to the Pope, — not to the ministers of the Gospel, through whom this power would then *mediately* pass into the possession of the Church; but, on the contrary, *immediately* this power is given to the *Church,* the believers, through whom the ministers receive this high office.

In complete harmony with the declaration of the *Smalcald Articles,* our Catechism puts this deep doctrine into these simple words: "The Office of the Keys is the peculiar *Church-power* which Christ has *given to His Church* on earth to forgive the sins of penitent sinners unto them, but to retain the sins of the impenitent, as long as they do not repent." Qu. 300.

Now the question arises: What say the Scriptures? The seats of doctrine are: Matt. 16, 19: "And I will give unto thee the keys of the kingdom of heaven: and whatsoever thou shalt bind on earth shall be bound in heaven: and whatsoever thou shalt loose on earth shall be loosed in heaven."; *Matt.* 18, 18: "Verily I say unto you, whatsoever ye shall bind on earth shall be bound in heaven; and whatsoever ye shall loose on earth shall be loosed in heaven."; *John* 20, 23: "*Whosesoever* sins ye remit, they are remitted unto them; and whosesoever sins ye retain, they are retained."

Matt. 16, 19, the Lord, addressing Peter, says: *"And I will give unto thee the keys of the kingdom of heaven: and whatsoever thou shalt bind on earth shall be bound in heaven: and whatsoever thou shalt loose on earth shall be loosed in heaven."*

This is the Pope's stronghold. We do not intend to investigate his threadbare arguments. The Pope was never known to care for a text of Scripture, except as a pretext *ad majorem papae gloriam.* Be it said, however, that this very text, like a thunderbolt from heaven, demolishes all his preposterous pretensions. Briefly, what is the import of this passage?

Jesus had asked His *disciples*, "Who do men say that I the Son of Man am?" The question was directed to *all* His disciples. "And *they* said, Some say that Thou art John the Baptist; some, Elias; and others, Jeremias, or one of the prophets." So there were various opinions afloat. "He saith unto *them*" (to His disciples), "But who say *ye* that I am?" What is your belief? "And Simon Peter answered and said," in the name of those addressed. "*ye*". in the name of all *disciples*: "*Thou art the Christ, the Son of the living God.*" That was Peter's faith, that was the *disciples*' faith. This is plain from the words of Jesus, v. 20, where He charged His *disciples*, not Peter alone, "that *they* should tell no man that He was Jesus the Christ." Hence what follows applies to *all* His disciples, though naturally Christ addresses Peter, the spokesman: "*Blessed* art thou, Simon Barjona, for flesh and blood hath not revealed it unto thee, but my Father which is in heaven." To know and to believe the mystery of mysteries which he confessed: the *Son of Man*, Mary's son, is at the same time "the Christ," the promised Messiah, "*the Son of the living God*," is divine, not human knowledge. Peter had made a great *confession* in his own name and that of the disciples. The Lord shows him the origin of that faith, and then proceeds: "And I say also unto thee that *thou art Peter*." Peter means rock-man; "Thou art Peter"—thou art a rock-man. You have based your faith upon rock—solid, safe, unshakable. This rock is expressed in your confession: "*The Son of Man is the Christ, the Son of the living God*"; and "*on this Rock*," on *Myself*, "I will build My church."

Now, what does it mean when Christ, continuing, says to Peter: "And I will give unto thee the keys of the kingdom of heaven"? Beyond the shadow of a doubt this: You are *blessed* on account of *your faith;* you are a rock-man on account of *your faith;* on account of *your faith* I will give unto you the keys of the kingdom of heaven. Peter possesses the keys because he is a *believer*, and all who confess with Peter: Thou art Christ, the Son of the living God, are founded on the Rock, Christ, are His disciples, belong to the Church, possess the keys of the kingdom. Luther correctly declares: "We are all Peters if we believe like Peter." This is the only admissible meaning according to text and context, and Matt. 18, 18, the parrallel passage, emphasizes this truth. Having spoken of excommunication by the *Church*, Christ adds: "Verily, I say unto you, Whatsoever *ye* shall bind on earth shall be bound in heaven; and whatsoever *ye* shall loose on earth shall be loosed in heaven." Not Peter alone, but all the disciples of Christ, "*ye*", *the Church*, and if there be but "two or three gathered together in His name,"*possess the power of the keys.* "O that this passage were not in the Gospel!" Luther exclaims ironically. "What a fine thing that would be for the Pope!" For here Christ gives the keys to the *whole Church* and not to St. Peter. And here belongs also the same saying, Matt. 16, 18-19, where he gives the keys to Peter on behalf of the *whole Church.* For in this 18th chapter the Lord makes a gloss upon His own words, showing to whom He had previously (Matt. 16) given the keys in the person of St. Peter. They are given to *all Christians,* and not to the person, St. Peter." *(Buechlein von der Beichte, Erl.)* 27, 363.

Again, after His resurrection, Christ repeated, corroborated, this authority given to his disciples:

John 20, 23: *Whose soever sins ye remit, they are remitted unto them; and whose soever sins ye retain, they are retained."* But before doing so, He says: *"Peace be unto you; as My Father hath sent Me, even so send I you. And when He had said this, He breathed on them and saith unto them, Receive ye the Holy Ghost."* Thus He manifested unmistakably that the keys of the kingdom are a gift to such as have *received the Holy Ghost,* to true believers, to the Church. "The keys are not the Pope's (as he falsely claims)," says Luther, "but the Church's; that is, they belong to the people of Christ, the people of God, or the holy Christian people all the world over, or wherever there are Christians. . . Just as Baptism, the Sacraments, God's Word, are not the Pope's, but belong to the people of Christ, so the keys are, and are called, claves ecclesiae, not claves papae." *(Schrift von Konzilien und Kirchen, St. Louis Ed. XVI.* 2279.) See Cat. Qu. 301.

Wherein does this peculiar Church-power consist? According to Matt. 16 in "to bind" and "to loose"; Matt. 18 speaks of "trespasses," "faults," that are to be bound or to be loosed, and John 20 says in plain words that this binding and loosing is "to remit sins" and "to retain sins." *Luther:* "Christ, our Lord, has said to His *disciples* and to the *whole Church:* I command you to forgive and to retain sin." (St. Louis Ed. XI, 763.)

Hence, Peter, extolling the high dignity of Christians, writes:

1. Pet. 2, 9: *"Ye are a chosen generation, a royal priesthood, an holy nation, a peculiar people; that ye should shew forth the praises of Him who hath called you out of darkness into his marvellous light."*

"To show forth the praises of God," to preach the Gospel is the duty, the privilege, of all Christians. This is the Office of the Keys in the wider sense. From it flows the power to forgive and to retain sins. "There is no dfference here, except that the same Word which in the preaching of the Gospel is usually everywhere publicly and generally proclaimed to every one is in private absolution declared privately to one or more who desire it." *(Luther,* St. Louis Ed. XI, 721.)

Since, then, all believing Christians have the power of the keys, who is to exercise this office *publicly?* All? Luther, having been charged by Emser with teaching that the general priesthood made all to be preachers, replied: "You lie when you say I have made all lay-men bishops, priests, and ecclesiastics, so that they may at once, *un-called*, assume the office; you do not add, pious as you are, that I also wrote: *Only extreme necessity* can justify one in doing that to which he has not been regularly called." (Walch XVII, 1597.)

Chemnitz (Examen Conc. Trid., cap. 85 p. 1687) relates that at his time the Jesuits ridiculed the Lutherans thus: "Then cobblers and tailors, cooks and day-laborers, have the power of the keys, and thus you build your own Babel and introduce endless confusions." He re-plied: "Who will deny that '*in case of need every believer may bap-tize,*' etc.? And this case of extreme necessity the Church has always made an exception, as Jerome testified against the Luciferians, and Augustine against Fortunatus. But, except in case of necessity, this is allowed to no one, unless he be a regularly called and appointed servant of the Church. For this would be to violate the divine rule: 'How can they preach except they be sent?' Rom. 10, 15. Again, 'They ran, and I did not send them.' "—

Who is to exercise the office *publicly?* Luther says, if every one would preach, who would constitute the hearers? If all would preach, there would be utter confusion and babble like that of frogs in a pond.— God is a God of order. In the Church there is a special office of the ministry. The incumbents called by the congregations are delegated to perform this Office of the Keys publicly. In Acts, 20, 28 they are designated "overseers," and their duty is "to feed the Church of God, which He hath purchased with His own blood." In 1 Cor. 4, 1 they are styled "stewards of the mysteries of God" and "ministers of Christ." In 2 Cor. 2, 5 Paul speaks of them as "your servants for Jesus' sake." So there is a "flock," and there are "overseers"; there are "servants" who preach, and people to whom they preach; there are "ministers of Christ," and such as they minister unto. The Bible and Luther teach that every congregation possesses the power of the keys, and that all believing Christians are priests and called to show forth the praises of God; but this priesthood does not involve the right of every Christian to preach and teach *publicly.* Hence the *Augsburg Confession* declares: "No one dare publicly teach or preach, or ad-minister the Sacraments, unless he be rightly called." (Art. XIV.)

Nor does this establish a superiority of the ministry over the laity. "One is your Master, even Christ; but ye are all brethren." *Luther:* "There is in reality no difference between the bishops, elders, and priests, and the laity, no one being distinguished from other Chris-tians, *except that he has an office*, which is committed to him to preach the Word of God and to administer the Sacraments; just as a mayor or a judge is in no wise distinguished from other citizens, except that the government of the city is entrusted to him." (Walch XIX, 1340.)

The congregation of *believers*—not the Pope, not the bishops, not the ministry—originally and immediately possesses the keys of the kingdom of heaven (Matt. 16, 19; 18, 18; John 20, 23); *the congregation of believers is originally and immediately commissioned to preach the Gospel* to every creature and to administer the Sacraments; *the congregation of believers is the body to whom all spiritual power originally and immediately belongs; the congregation of believers is entrusted with the power* of appointing "overseers over the flock," "stewards of the mysteries of God," pastors, ministers, who in their name preach, baptize, administer the Lord's Supper, absolve; *the congregation of believers constitutes a true spiritual democracy.*

ABSOLUTION.

The power of the keys as involved in this whole discussion refers principally to the power to forgive sins, commonly called absolution.

In perfect agreement with the doctrine briefly stated in the foregoing pages the Lutheran pastor, after a short confessional service, says to penitent sinners:

"Upon this, your confession, I, by virtue of my office, as a called and ordained servant of the Word, announce the grace of God unto all of you, and in the stead and by the command of my Lord Jesus Christ I forgive you all your sins, in the name of God the Father, God the Son, and God the Holy Ghost. Amen."

The minister says to penitent sinners: "I forgive you all your sins." Does he forgive sins by virtue of a peculiar power dwelling in him? No. He does it "by virtue of his office, as a called and ordained servant of the Word." The power is not in him, but in the *Word.* Does he forgive sin of his own authority? No, but "in the stead and by the command of my Lord Jesus Christ." Who is it, then, that forgives sin? The Lord Jesus Christ through His servant. Is there anything wrong about this? No; St. Paul did the very same thing. As a minister of Christ he forgave the sins of the man who on account of the sin of incest had been expelled from the Church of Corinth, but who had repented of his error. In reference hereto Paul writes: "If I forgave anything, to whom I forgave it, for your sakes *forgave I it in the person of Christ.*" 2 Cor. 2. 10.

The words of Jesus, spoken to His disciples, are plain as plain can be: "Then said Jesus to them again, Peace be unto you: as My Father hath sent Me, even so send *I* you. And when He had said this, He breathed on them, and said unto them, Receive ye the Holy Ghost: whose soever sins ye remit, they are remitted unto them, and whose soever sins ye retain, they are retained." *John* 20, 21-23. Again: "Verily I say unto you, whatsoever ye shall bind on earth shall be bound in heaven: and whatsoever ye shall loose on earth shall be loosed in heaven." *Matt.* 18, 18.

But, still, notwithstanding Scripture is so clear regarding absolution, this ministerial absolution is a stumbling-block for many, and the doctrine, so full of comfort for the terrified consciences, is viewed with suspicious even by some Lutherans.

All objections to this doctrine, however, find their cause in the ignorance of the Gospel of Christ, in the ignorance of the atonement of Christ, which the Gospel proclaims; in the ignorance of the means of grace, which impart the atonement to the sinner.

Absolution is firmly based on two indisputable facts: 1. God is perfectly reconciled through Christ to every sinner; 2. God has commanded this reconciliation to be preached to every sinner, to every penitent sinner, who longs for the sweet consolation of the Gospel.

When the truth of that wonderful Pauline passage, "The just shall live by faith," flashed upon Luther's mind, the cardinal principle of Christianity had been discovered. It was in defense of this doctrine— justification, forgiveness of sins, by faith alone, "the principal article of the Christian faith," "the only key to the whole Bible," "the article with which the Church stands and falls"—that Luther nailed the Ninety-five Theses to the door of the Castle Church at Wittenberg on that ever memorable October 31, 1517.

Forgiveness of sins! Three small words, and yet how much they imply!—"Sin is the transgression of the Law." 1 John 3, 4. *All* men are sinners. "There is no difference; *all have sinned,* and come short of the glory of God." Rom. 3. And the result? "Your sins have *separated* between you and your God." Is. 59, 2. God pronounces a *curse* upon every sinner: "Cursed is every one that continueth not in *all* things which are written in the book of the Law to *do* them." Gal. 3. To be a sinner means to be a "child of wrath," Eph. 2, a damned person. Is there a way of escape? None that man can devise. What man, however, could not do, God in His mercy has done. What did He do? Beautifully this is set forth in 2 Cor. 5, 19-21: *"God was in Christ, reconciling the world unto Himself, not imputing their trespasses unto them; and hath committed unto us the word of reconciliation. Now, then, we are ambassadors for Christ, as though God did beseech you by us; we pray in Christ's stead, Be ye reconciled to God. For He hath made Him to be sin for us who knew no sin; that we might be made the righteousness of God in Him."*

Here are the contents of the Gospel in small compass. The world was at enmity with God. A reconciliation must be effected. Man could not bring it about. God's love to the world, lost in sin, prompted Him to do it. "God was *in Christ,* reconciling the world unto Himself." "God sent forth His Son, made of a woman, made under the Law, to *redeem* them that were under the Law." Gal. 4. His purpose of coming into the world "to *save* sinners," 1 Tim. 1, 15, Christ achieved: "Christ *hath redeemed* us *from the curse of the Law.*" Gal 3. How? He "who knew no sin was made sin for us." "The Lord laid on Him the iniquity of us all." Is. 53, 6. "God was in Christ, reconciling the world unto Himself." When Christ, expiring on the cross, more than 1900 years ago, cried out, "It is finished!" *God reconciled the world* unto Himself for Christ's sake. And in proof of the fact that this redemptive work was complete, God raised Christ from the dead. So God *is* reconciled with the whole world. No one need do or suffer anything to appease the wrath of God on account of the trespasses committed. In Christ, God now looks upon man as though he had never offended Him. In plain words this truth is expressed thus: "Not imputing their trespasses unto them," *i. e., to the world.* In corroboration of this glorious fact St. John writes: "Christ is the propitiation for our sins, and not for ours only, but also for the sins of *the whole world.*" 1 John 2. 2.

To summarize the truths unfolded thus far: 1. God is *angry* at the sin of man; sin separates between Him and man. Is. 59, 2; Gal. 3. 2. "When we were enemies, we were reconciled to God by the death of His Son." Rom. 5, 10.

The fact is accomplished — God *is* reconciled. But God's love prompted him to do still more. In order that the sinner should know of this fact,—reconciliation completed,—aye that the sinner should come into actual possession of it, God committed unto His ambassadors *"the word of reconciliation."* They are to cry out to a rebellious world, "God is reconciled!" God beseeches you by us: "we pray you in Christ's stead, Be ye reconciled to God." Believe this *word;* accept the reconciliation, and the deed is done. This is the Gospel-message. "Preach the *Gospel* to every creature," says Christ in His last Great Commission. What does that say? Bring the Gospel, i. e., the glad tidings of the gracious forgiveness of sin, the glad tidings of pardon, to the world, and whosoever believes this Gospel is saved, his sins are forgiven.

But God's love even went beyond this. Knowing how slow of heart man is to believe, Christ not only commanded His disciples to publish these glad tidings in a general way, but He commissioned them to announce the reconciliation made by Him in particular to individuals. "Peace be unto you," (John 20, 23) Christ said after His resurrection to His disciples; *"as My Father hath sent Me, even so send I you."* And breathing on them, He said, "Receive ye the Holy Ghost: whose soever sins ye remit, they are remitted unto them." Christ's whole work of redemption had but one purpose in view: to bring peace, forgiveness of sin, reconciliation, to a sin-stricken world. To the multitudes He preached the Gospel of the kingdom; to individuals He said, "Peace be unto you." "Son, be of good cheer, thy sins be forgiven thee." This power to forgive sins to penitent sinners Christ delegated to His disciples: "As *My* Father hath sent Me, *even so* send I you. *Whose soever* sins ye remit, they are remitted unto them." Thus Christ instituted the Office of the Keys, commonly called Absolution. What, then, is absolution? It is the *Gospel*, the glad tidings of the forgiveness of sins, peace with God, the reconciliation with God, *applied to individuals.*

True to their commission the apostles preached repentance and forgiveness of sins among all nations and forgave sins to individuals. The apostles possessed this power and exercised it—that is indisputable. The power was not granted to the apostles, however, in their capacity of *apostles,* but as *believers,* as *disciples.* It is a peculiar *Church*-power —the ambassadors of Christ acting in the name and by authority of the Church.

Now, what objections can be raised to absolution in view of the facts that God *is* reconciled with the world, and that God *commands* that this "word of reconciliation" be preached? What is there to prevent a Christian brother from saying to another, distressed on account of his sins: God is reconciled with the *world* by His Son, you belong to the *world,* and therefore He is reconciled with *you?* What valid objection can be made to the called minister's saying to penitent sinners: "Be assured, Christ is the Physician of the sick, the sin-sick; your sins are blotted out by His blood; "by His stripes ye were healed"?

Popery! A rag of popery! cry some. — These people know not whereof they speak. The Biblical doctrine of absolution has nothing in common with the blasphemous auricular confession of Rome. Why, it was against this very abuse of the Catholic Church that Luther was impelled to nail his famous Ninety-five Theses to the door of the Castle Church at Wittenberg.

Rome has limited the power of absolution to its priesthood. The priest is the *judge* of man's sins. At his will he pardons or condemns. Sins not confessed to the priest cannot be forgiven. What says Scripture? "Who can understand his errors? Cleanse Thou me from secret faults." Ps. 19, 12.

From another quarter comes a voice reiterating the objection of the Pharisee: *"Who can forgive sins but God only?"* True. In the Lord's Prayer we ask God: "Forgive us our trespasses." The psalmist exults: "Bless the Lord, O my soul, and forget not all His benefits; who forgiveth all Thine inquities." Ps. 103, 2, 3. If God does not forgive our sins, we remain under its burden though man absolve us a thousand times. God only can forgive sins. But the question is: How does God forgive sins? Immediately perhaps, by a voice from heaven or by an inner voice in the heart? Luther met such enthusiasts. He writes: "If you do not seek forgiveness of sins in the *Word,* you will gape to heaven in vain for grace, or, as they say, for the inward forgiveness." (Von den Schluesseln. St. L. XIX, 1174.) "We should and must firmly maintain that God will not deal with us frail beings except through His external Word and Sacraments. And all that is boasted of independent of such Word and Sacraments (as being the Spirit) is the very devil himself." (Smalcald Articles, Art. VIII.)

God forgives sins through the Gospel. Herein the power lies, not in man. "God hath committed unto *us* the word of reconciliation," says Paul. This Gospel has been entrusted to *us* — to *men*, to the Church. "Go ye, preach *the Gospel* says Christ to *men*. Whosoever believes this Gospel preached by men *has* forgiveness of sins, absolution. To *men* Christ said: *"Whose soever* sins ye remit, they are remitted unto them." God forgives sins through the Gospel entrusted to *men*, who are to proclaim: God is reconciled! If it be said man may come to a full assurance of the forgiveness of his sins by the reading of the Word, the answer still is: he received this assurance through *men*, through the Word of the apostles and prophets, not by a voice coming from the skies, nor by an inner revelation. It remains forever true: God, having entrusted "the word of reconciliation" to the Church, thereby has enjoined upon her the duty of forgiving sins.

But still *another objection* is made by the opposition: *To forgive sins man must be omniscient;* he must be able to see the state of another man's heart to know infallibly whether a person desiring forgiveness is worthy thereof. We answer: This is a false assumption. Absolution does not pass judgment on the condition of *man's* heart, but it declares the condition of God's heart, and this we know: God *is* reconciled. Since God is reconciled with the whole world, there is not a single man on earth to whom the sweet message cannot be brought: God is reconciled also with you. This declaration is valid. God says so. He has given us the"*word* of reconciliation." This *word* man should accept, believe; if man rejects it, that is his fault. "Many do not believe the Gospel, but the Gospel does not lie or fail on that account. *A king gives you a castle;* if you do not accept the gift, the king has not on this account lied nor failed, but you have deceived yourself, and it is your own fault; the king did certainly give it." (Luther, St. L. XIX, 946.)

Finally, in the last analysis, which is the root of all errors with reference to absolution? Says Dr. F. Pieper in *Distinctive Doctrines and Usages:* "*The main reason why so many Christians take offense at the practice of absolution is to be found* in their inadequate ideas as to what the Gospel of Christ properly is. Their conceptions of the *vicarious work of Christ*, and consequently of the *Gospel* also, fail to come up to the Biblical standard. They think that Christ has brought about so much for us that *we* now, by our conversion, faith, and prayers, render God fully propitious, and thus obtain forgiveness of sins. *Hence* they conceive the Gospel to be the declaration of certain *conditions* on which God would forgive sins. With many Christians and teachers the Gospel is a mere *plan* to save sinners, Christ having caused in the heart of God a certain *tendency* to forgive sin, men com· *pleting* the change in the heart of God by their being sorry for their sins, by their praying to God for forgiveness, by their earnest endeavors to lead a better life, etc. But these conceptions both of the work of Christ and the Gospel are altogether wrong. Christ has already perfectly and completely reconciled the whole world unto God, and the Gospel, being the message of what Christ has done for mankind, is the 'word of reconciliation,' viz., the word stating that God *is* reconciled — *perfectly* and *completely* reconciled — through Christ to the whole world and every individual sinner. The Gospel is not a word which teaches how *men* might by their own exertions render God fully propitious, but a word which assures us that God *has been* reconciled to all men through the vicarious sacrifice of Christ. Therefore, to preach the Gospel does not mean to lay before men a mere *plan* of salvation, or to declare the *conditions* of forgiveness, but preaching the Gospel is preaching pardon itself, salvation itself, 'remission of sins' itself. Luke 24, 47. The Gospel is 'nothing else than a great letter of pardon directed to the whole world.' Hence it is that Luther frequently says: 'A minister preaching the Gospel cannot open his mouth without constantly remitting sin.' Wherever the Gospel is proclaimed, there absolution is pronounced. It *is from this conception of the Gospel that the Lutheran practice of absolution is to be judged and understood.* It should be borne in mind also that God has already *absolved* the whole world in laying the sins of the whole world on Christ and in raising up Christ from the dead. With *our* sins upon Him Christ entered into the prison-house of death; absolved from *our* sins He was set free in His resurrection. Hence it is seen that the resurrection of Christ actually involves an absolution of the whole world, and *the absolution we pronounce is nothing but a repetition or echo of what God has long since pronounced.*"

"In short," says Dr. C. F. W. Walther, the American Luther, "the Gospel is a universal absolution, brought from heaven to the whole world by men, sealed with the blood and death of Christ, and confirmed by God Himself most grandly and solemnly in the glorious resurrection of our Savior. And just because the Gospel is an absolution of all men, on account of the perfect redemption of the world, which is already accomplished, therefore also a minister of the Gospel may and shall, in the name of God, assure each and every man, who, as a poor sinner, desires forgiveness, of the remission of sins. Denying the minister this prerogative is denying him the power of proclaiming the Gospel in its *entirety* and completeness. For whosoever believes with all his heart that Christ has blotted out the sins of all men, how can he take exception to Christ's ministers saying to a man who professes to believe in Christ, Thy sins are forgiven thee!"

As to the great *comfort* afforded by absolution we quote from the *Augsburg Confession*, Article 25: "The people are diligently instructed with regard to the comfort given by the word of *absolution*, and the high and great estimation in which it is to be held; for it is not the word or voice of the individual present, but *it is the Word of God*, who here forgives sins; for it is spoken in God's stead and by His command. Concerning this command and power of the keys, it is taught with the greatest assiduity how comforting, how useful they are to terrified consciences, and, besides, how God requires confidence in this absolution, no less than if the voice of God were heard from heaven; and by this we comfort ourselves, and know that through such faith we obtain the remission of sins."

Finally, if the question be asked, Why is the same grace of God offered and sealed in *several ways*—in the Gospel, in the Lord's Supper, in Baptism, in Absolution? we answer with gratitude towards God in the words of our Confession: "The Gospel affords us more than one means, one counsel and assistance, in opposition to sin; for God is *superabundantly rich in His grace.*"

Whose Sins Are To Be Remitted?   Qu. 305.

Acts 3, 19. Repent ye therefore, and be converted, that your sins may be blotted out.

Peter had healed the lame man, vv. 1-10. A great crowd assembled marveling at the miracle and eyeing Peter and John as wonder-workers. This was Peter's opportunity to testify for Jesus. He reproaches the people saying: "Why look ye so earnestly at us as though by our power we had made this man to walk?" No, not so. "The God of Abraham, Isaac, and Jacob, the God of our fathers" has performed this miracle "to glorify His son Jesus." v. 13. We were only the instruments working the cure. Next, Peter brings their great sin home to them. This Jesus of Nazareth, God's Son, sent to you to be your Savior "ye delivered up and denied in the presence of Pilate," v. 14. The heathen judge was ready to release him, saying: "I find no fault in this man;" but ye raised the terrible cry: "Crucify, crucify him!" Foully ye have murdered the innocent Jesus. Do you know what ye have done? "Ye killed the Prince of Life!" This Jesus was not only true man but at the same time *very* God. What a terrible crime ye have committed! But this Jesus is no longer dead; He lives; God raised Him up from the dead. We are witnesses thereof. The healing of this lame man is but one of the many proofs of this fact. What terrible punishment awaits you, the murderers of the Prince of Life, if you do not repent!

Thus Peter preaches the Law to the multitude to bring them to a conviction of their sin. True, you killed Jesus "through ignorance"; you did not recognize in Him your Savior. This ignorance was your fault; you are not innocent; you are guilty of murder in the sight of God. But there is a way open for you; your sins may be blotted out. How? *"Repent"*—*metanoesate*—"change your mind," your heart. Ye believe that by doing the works of Moses ye are saved. *Repent!* Change your mind! See the wickedness of your self-righteousness that led you so far astray as to kill Jesus, your Savior. How often did He not call unto you: "Come unto Me," but "ye would not." "Search the Scripture," as Jesus Himself told you, "for in them ye think ye have eternal life"—and this thought is correct, but not by Moses can you attain eternal life—"for they", the Scriptures, "are they that testify *of Me*" as "the Way, the Truth, and the Life." *Repent!* change your mind! If you do not believe that it is He, you will die in your sins. *Repent!* feel sorry for your sins, and see in Jesus your only Savior; *be converted*—*epistrepsate*—turn back to Him whom you have rejected, approach Him with a contrite heart, acknowledge your *sins*, believe His promises of forgiveness. In this way your sins will be *blotted out*.

Through the Law the sinner is brought to a knowledge of his sinfulness; through the Gospel faith in Jesus is kindled in his heart; he is *converted*.

Ps. 51, 17. *The sacrifices of God are a broken spirit; a broken and a contrite heart, O God, Thou wilt not despise.*

In this well-known penitential psalm David expresses deep contrition on account of his great sin against Bathsheba and Uriah and implores God's forgiveness. Throughout the psalm we find contrition and faith side by side in David's heart.

The awfulness of his crime, revealed through the holy Law of God is ever before him, v. 3. He acknowledges his deed to be iniquity, sin, transgression. "Wash me," he pleads, "thoroughly from my *iniquity;* cleanse me from my *sin.* For I know my *transgression;* and my *sin* is ever before me. Against thee, thee only have I *sinned.*" vv. 2-4. He knows that God has a right to cast him away from His presence. v. 11. His *spirit* that rose in rebellion against God and sinned, is now broken; the heart that, self-willed, set aside God's command is broken, *contrite* —*crushed.* In David's heart there is true contrition.

Against God he has sinned; God's mercy alone can save him. "Have *mercy* upon me, O God, according to thy *loving kindness;* according to the multitude of thy *tender mercies* blot out my transgressions." v. 1. Thus he pleads out of the depth of his "broken spirit," his "contrite heart", knowing that God will not despise such "sacrifices," coming from a heart that is crushed on account of its sins and that pleads for His *mercy,* His *loving kindness,* His tender mercies to blot out his,

David's, transgressions for the Messiah's sake.

A penitent sinner. is one in whose heart there is contrition and faith. Such was the state of David's soul. An echo, as it were, of this penitent pleading we find in the New Testament. The publican prays: "God, be merciful to me, a sinner." And the publican went down justified to his house. Luke 18, 13. The prodigal son, returning to his father, confessed: "Father, I have sinned against heaven and in thy sight, and am no more worthy to be called thy son." Luke 15, 21.

And as for David — he confessed unto Nathan: "I have sinned against the Lord. And Nathan said unto David, The Lord also hath put away thy sin."

Acts 16, 31. *Believe on the Lord Jesus Christ, and thou shalt be saved, and thy house.*

In the city of Philippi lived a. slave girl, "possessed with a spirit of divination;" through the power of some evil spirit she could tell hidden things; she was a fortune-teller, a spiritistic medium. As to-day, so then this was profitable business. For driving this evil spirit out of the girl, Paul and Silas were seized by the enraged masters and finally brought before the magistrates, where they were falsely accused. The judges sent Paul and Silas to prison, "charging the jailer to keep them safely." Instead of complaining, the apostles "prayed and sang praises unto God" who had accounted them worthy to suffer for His name's sake, "and the prisoners heard them", no doubt, with wonder and amazement. Curses, imprecations, in this dark prison had been plentiful, but prayers and praises—how extraordinary!

The Lord knows how to protect His servants, and even if it be by means of an earthquake. Awakened by the earthquake, the jailer, seeing the prison doors ajar, despaired of his own life. To allow prisoners to escape meant capital punishment for him. "He drew his sword and would have killed himself." In that moment, Paul cried with a loud voice: "Do thyself no harm; for we are all here.' Then occurred a wonderful thing: The jailer "fell down before Paul and Silas, and brought them out and said: *Sirs, what must I do to be saved?*" The scales had fallen from his eyes. Terror and despair because of his sins had seized him. He knew he was a lost and condemned sinner. "What must I do?" He knew here were men that could answer this all-important question. Most probably he had heard Paul and Silas preaching "that way", but not until now had despair on account of sin taken hold of him. What would the apostles say to him? Would they say: Yours is a desperate case; you are a murderer in the sight of God; to-morrow evening we'll have a revival meeting at such and such a place. Come, and we'll pray over you and sing for you, and when you feel like exclaiming: Gloria Hallelujah! why then you're through and there is hope for you." Nothing of the sort. *"Believe on the Lord Jesus Christ, and thou shalt be saved, and thy house."* Thus they immediately apply the full consolation of the Gospel to him. To the terrified sinner the Gospel must be preached. So did Paul, so should we. The jailer asks: "What must I *do?" Do?* What could he *do* towards his salvation? Nothing. He was a blind heathen who had no knowledge of, nor love to, God. The apostles answer: *"Believe"*—put your trust in Jesus the Savior from sin. He can save and He alone.

But is not: "Believe" a command? Did the jailer have the power to comply with that command? Heathen that he was, he was *dead* in trespasses and sins. Eph 2, 1. No man can say that Jesus is the Lord but by the Holy Ghost. 1 Cor. 12, 3. But the jailer did believe. How did it come about?

When Jesus said to the dead young man at Nain: "I say unto thee, arise", the young man arose. Did he do this of his own power? Jesus said to Lazarus: "Come forth!" and Lazarus came forth. Did Lazarus do this of his own power? No. How were the young man and Lazarus restored to life? By the powerful voice of Jesus. How did the jailer come to faith? By the powerful word of God: *"Believe on the Lord Jesus."* This was Gospel. Through this Gospel the Holy Ghost wrought faith in his heart. The same night the apostles further instructed him in the Word of God and "he was baptized, he and all his, straightway . . . and he rejoiced believing in God with all his house." v. 33.

How does the church exercise this power publicly? Qu. 306.

I Cor. 4, 1. *Let a man so account of us as of the ministers of Christ and stewards of the mysteries of God.*

See exposition sub Qu. 275.

2 Cor. 2, 10. *If I forgave anything, to whom I forgave it, for your sakes forgave I it in the person of Christ.*

For exposition see sub Qu. 311, where the passage is treated in its context.

Acts 20, 28. *Take heed therefore unto yourselves and to all the flock over which the Holy Ghost hath made you overseers to feed the church of God, which he hath purchased with His own blood.*

This text is taken from St. Paul's touching farewell address to the Ephesian elders. In this section, v. 28-31, he admonishes the elders to be faithful in the discharge of their high office. Consider the honor: you are overseers over the *"church* of God." The church is composed of believers, believers are God's children; they belong to His family. Over such He has made you overseers. A high honor! A great responsibility! It is the church *of God;* it belongs to Him by right of purchase. And the price he paid? "His own blood." Christ's blood,

God's blood, the ransom price! Immortal souls, purchased by the blood of the Lamb, He has entrusted to your care. *"The Holy Ghost has made you overseers," episcopei,* i. e. bishops. The bishops, overseers, are none other than the elders, v. 7, who were elected by *cheirotonia,* i. e., by the raising of hands of the members of the congregation. Acts 14, 23. In Titus, 1, 5 and 7 we find the same truth. The elders, presbyters, v. 5, are the same men that are denominated bishops in verse 7. In apostolic times presbyters, elders, bishops, designated one and the same office. The hierarchy in the church is not of God's command.

To return to the text. The mediate call of the overseers by the congregations was a divine call, as we see from our text. The overseers shall know the Holy Ghost has put them into office. Owing to these considerations how faithfully should they not fulfill their duties! "Take heed therefore unto yourselves," first and foremost watch over yourselves closely, you belong to the flock and you are prominent members of that flock. "Be ensamples to the flock." Be able to say with the apostle, "Be ye followers of me." Then you will be in the proper position to take heed *"of all the flock,"* young and old, rich and poor. And what is your main duty as overseers? "To feed the flock, the church of God." To *feed, poimainein,* to *shepherd* the flock." You are spiritual shepherds. The spiritual food is the Gospel. Preach the Gospel. Rightly divide the Word of Truth.

Preach the Word in season and out of season. You, the shepherds, are *overseers* of the flock. Watch for their souls.

The flock, the congregation, should always bear in mind that the pastors receive their high office from the Lord Himself through the medium of the Christian congregation. The congregation should further remember that the minister, called by them, exercises the functions of his office in their name.

Note: This passage gives a clear testimony of Christ in the words: "The church of God, which He hath purchased with His own blood." Let us hear Luther: "This is surely a clear text, from which follows without all contradiction that Christ, our Lord, through whose blood the Church was purchased, is God, to whom the Church belongs. For he says clearly: It is God, who through His blood has won the Church and whose own the Church is. Since now, as we have heard, the persons are distinct, and it still is written here that God Himself through His blood has purchased the Church, therefore the conclusion comes with great force that God has His own blood which He has shed for His Church, that is, that Christ, our Savior, is true God, born of the Father from eternity, thereafter also by the Virgin Mary in time has become a man and was born." Quoted in Popular Commentary, Kretzmann, vol. 1, p. 639.

Excommunication.—Grades of Admonition.

Matt. 18, 15-18. *Moreover, if thy brother shall trespass against thee, go and tell him his fault between thee and him alone. If he shall hear thee, thou hast gained thy brother But if he will not hear thee, then take with thee one or two more, that in the mouth of two or three witnesses every word may be established. And if he shall neglect to hear them, tell it unto the church, but if he neglect to hear the church, let him be unto thee as an heathen man and a publican. Verily, I say unto you, Whatsoever ye shall bind on earth shall be bound in heaven, and whatsoever ye shall loose on earth shall be loosed in heaven.*

A Christian duty, only too often neglected, is that of brotherly admonition. What do we understand by brotherly admonition? If one knows his brother to be living in sin, it is the manifest duty of the Christian to try to reclaim his brother from damnation by showing him from the Word of God, the gravity, the damnableness of his sin. An immortal soul, bought by the blood of Christ, is in danger of being lost!

And this duty of endeavoring to save a brother's soul is often neglected? Sorry to say, yes. You see a brother venturing into a treacherous stream; you warn him. Why? He may lose his life. You see him handling a gun recklessly; you warn him. Why? He may lose his life. You see him nearing a dangerous precipice; you warn him. Why? He may lose his life. And you see him sinning: you know that he is in danger of losing life eternal, and you will not warn him? Is that acting brotherly towards him? "No, it is not," you admit. But is not eternal life worth infinitely more than this temporal life? "True," you answer; "but the common experience is this. Whereas I gain the gratitude of the brother whom I have warned against losing his life by entering the treacherous stream, by handling the gun carelessly, etc., I generally incur his bitter hatred by admonishing him of his sin." Very true; flesh and blood is so perverse. But does this fact do away with your Christian duty?

The Lord says: *"Tell him his fault."* And the purpose? How glorious! — to *gain* the brother.

Before examining the text, we shall ask a few preliminary questions.

To whom does the Lord speak? To the brethren of a trespassing brother. *Who are "brethren"?* All that belong to the church, the local congregation, all that partake of the Lord's Supper with us—men, women, youths, maidens.

What is the *nature of the sin* that is subject to church-discipline? "If thy brother shall trespass against thee." Trespass is sin. Now, is every sin of the brother the object of brotherly admonition? No. By trespass is not meant any and every sin that is inevitable even with the best Christian, owing to the sinful flesh that adheres to him even unto death. The admonition has its purpose to gain the brother, hence the "trespass against thee," the sin on account of which he is to be admonished, has caused him to fall from grace. If repentance does not follow, the brother is lost. It is a sin on account of which we ultimately, if the brother is not "gained," must look upon him as "an heathen man and a publican." St. Paul writes to the Corinthians: "I have written unto you not to keep company if any man that is called a brother be a fornicator, or covetous, or an idolator, or a railer, or a drunkard, or an extortioner; with such a one no not to eat." (1 Cor. 5, 11.) This, of course, does not exhaust the list of sins that subjects to church-discipline. That cannot be done. Any sin which may finally cause the brother to lose his soul is a "trespass against thee."

But how am I to understand this phrase, *"trespass against thee"?* That does not say that you must be the direct object of this sin, that wrong must have been done you personally, but a sin "against thee" is one that is secret as yet, but of which you have knowledge. The brother is living in a sin that actually in God's sight puts him on a level with "an heathen man and a publican." You know of it. A sin known "between you and him alone," which puts the brother's soul in jeopardy, is a sin "against thee."

Now we are ready to consider the text.

"If thy brother shall trespass against thee," what are you to do? Pay no heed to it? No. "Go and tell him his fault." In what spirit should you go? Why, in the spirit of a brother. Love for his immortal soul should impel you to go and tell him his fault. With what end in view should this brotherly admonition be carried out? To gain the brother. *"Thou hast gained thy brother"*—this thought dominates the *entire instruction of our Lord.* The brother is in danger of losing his soul eternally; reclaim him from destruction; "gain thy brother." Love for the sinning brother is to be the only motive and guide in dealing with him. The love of Christ, who shed His blood also for this erring brother, is to impel you to convince him of the error of his way. In the preceding context the Lord speaks of His seeking love towards sinners. And how great is His joy when the lost sheep is found! This is the sentiment that should govern you, govern us all, when administering brotherly admonition. "Go and tell him his fault between thee and him alone." As yet the sin is not public. Only you and he know about it. Hence let the admonition be "between thee and him alone." Love does not delight in spreading the brother's misdeeds; love delights in gaining the brother. "Tell him his fault" in brotherly love; call the fault a fault, sin; show the gravity thereof by the Word of God; tell him of his Savior, whose will is not that he should perish, but that he should come to repentance. The motive to gain the brother, the impelling motive, love towards the erring brother, will by God's grace prompt the proper words to reach the sinner's heart.

If you succeed, what? "Thou hast gained thy brother." Rejoice thank and praise God, because an immortal soul has been wrested from Satan's clutches. But otherwise the whole matter is to be buried, the object has been attained; your lips must be sealed; not a word about the matter is to be ever whispered to a third person.

But if you do not succeed, love to your brother impels you to go further. The text says: "But if he will not hear thee, then take with thee one or two more, that in the mouth of two or three witnesses every word may be established." The Lord says: "If, after repeated efforts on your part to convince the brother of his fault, you are, nevertheless, unsuccessful, then take one or two other brethren of the congregation with thee to speak with the erring brother. The brother's sin is not to receive undue publicity; only one or two are to be told thereof. Whom are you to select? Not men whom he may imagine to have a grudge against him. That very fact would close his heart against all admonition. Wisdom, love, dictates that friends of his should be selected. And these friends are not only to be reliable witnesses of what is said and done, but they too, should add their earnest exhortations and entreaties. This, if anything, should open the sinner's eyes to the gravity of the situation. If his friends, his best friends, warn him of the wrath of God; if they, bound by the love of God, impelled by the love for his soul, must tell him that, if he persists in his sin, they can no longer look upon him as a brother, as a child of God, but as a victim of Satan,— this, if anything, should melt his hardened heart and lead him to repentance and amendment of life.

This effort, if futile, should be repeated so long as there is hope of gaining the brother. If successful, well and good—"thou hast gained thy brother." Drop the matter, seal your lips, praise God. There is joy in heaven over one sinner that repenteth.

If this second grade of admonition should prove a failure, love constrains you to go still further, to take the last available means to save the brother's soul from damnation—you must bring the matter before the congregation.

The text reads: "And if he shall neglect to hear them, tell it unto the church." The "church" here comprises those that "assemble in His name," v. 20; hence it is the local congregation. This is the highest court of appeal. Here, again, every effort possible to gain the brother is to be made. What an impression the united entreaties and exhortations must make upon the sinner! How hardened the heart of such a one must be if the exhortation of the entire congregation should not cause him to repent of his sin. Thanks be to God, many and many a lost sheep has thus been brought back again into the arms of the Savior!

But even this brotherly admonition of the entire congregation may fail. What then is to be done?

"But if he neglect to hear the church, let him be unto thee as an heathen man and a publican." In other words, such a one is no longer to be looked upon as a brother, but is to be expelled from the Christian congregation. St. Paul says: "Put away from among yourselves that wicked person." (1 Cor. 5, 13.) Where the church thus pronounces the ban, she is in fact doing nothing else than pronouncing the sentence that God had long before pronounced against him because of his sin. "Let him be unto thee as an heathen man and a publican." Before God he was such long ago.

This expulsion from the congregation has for its object not so much to get rid of the person fallen into grievous sin, but in the last analysis, this, too, is an act of love; it is the last resort to open the sinner's eyes to the abyss of his guilt in order to gain him. St. Paul says, 1 Cor. 5, 5, regarding the fornicator, that the congregation should "deliver such an one unto Satan for the destruction of the flesh, that the spirit may be saved in the day of the Lord Jesus Christ." But in like manner as he had demanded the expulsion of the sinner from the congregation, so earnestly he also demanded his readmittance when the ban had had the desired result, the brother having repented of his sin and thus having been gained. (2 Cor. 2, 5-11.)

Alarmed by the earnestness of his former brethren, who must go so far as to sever all churchly connection with him,—because of love for his immortal soul, because of due regard to Christ's command, and for a testimony to them without,—the erring brother may penitently return to Christ and the church. And what the church thus does in Christ's name is valid before our Father in heaven. Christ assures us in the continuation of our text: "Verily, I say unto you, Whatsoever ye shall bind on earth shall be bound in heaven; and whatsoever ye shall loose on earth shall be loosed in heaven."

In conclusion let it be repeated that the object of church-discipline is to gain the brother. If this be kept in view, we shall readily see that the Lord speaks of three kinds of admonition. We are not to hurry from one grade to the other; we are not to put the erring brother under the auctioneer's hammer—one, two, three! The various grades of brotherly admonition are to be repeated so long as there is hope that he may be gained thereby, or till it becomes manifest that he obstinately refuses to heed the Word of God.

Because the object of church-discipline is to gain the brother, we should go to him at an opportune time. When we observe that the brother whom we are to admonish is ruffled, irritated, when matters have gone wrong in his family or in his business, it is not time to "tell him his fault"; let us bide our time. When Adam sinned, God waited. He came to him in the cool of the evening.

The object is to gain the brother. Let us go to him, therefore, in the proper attitude of mind. In our closets let us first humble ourselves before our God, look upon ourselves in the light of the law, see our own great sins and the greater Savior. Thus we shall go to the erring brother as redeemed sinners, filled with the love of Christ, seeking to save that which is lost.

God grant that the testimony of Paul to the Roman Christians may apply to us: "I am persuaded of you, my brethren, that ye also are full of goodness, filled with all knowledge, able also to admonish one another." Amen.

How to deal with the excommunicated but penitent person. Qu. 311.

2 Cor. 2, 6-10. *Sufficient to such a man is this punishment, which was inflicted of many. So that contrariwise ye ought rather to forgive him, and comfort him, lest perhaps such a one should be swallowed up with overmuch sorrow. Wherefore I beseech you that ye would confirm your love toward him. For to this end also did I write, that I might know the proof of you, whether ye be obedient in all things. To whom ye forgive anything, I forgive also: for if I forgave anything, to whom I forgave it, for your sakes forgave I it in the person of Christ.*

Church discipline is the burden of this text. It teaches us how to deal with the repentant sinner. In 1 Cor. V, 1 ff. we are told of a man that had married his step-mother, hence was guilty of incest. The apostle writes: "It is reported commonly that there is fornication among you, and such fornication as is not so much as named among the Gentiles, *that one should have his father's wife.*" The Corinthian congregation should have taken steps to have had him "taken away from among them", i. e., out of their midst, no longer to have had fellowship with him. He exhorts the congregation to meet, "to gather together" in order to excommunicate this impenitent adulterer, "to deliver such a one to Satan." The purpose to be attained by such disciplinary proceedings was "for the destruction of the flesh, that the spirit may be *saved* in the day of the Lord Jesus." The aim of church discipline was to save this person's immortal soul. cf. 1 Cor. 5, 1 ff.

What did the Corinthian Christians do? Aroused by the apostle's earnest exhortation, many brethren reproved the erring brother for his sin. He was expelled from the congregation. What happened? The fornicator came to a knowledge of his sin, was heartily sorry for it, and acknowledged his guilt — he came to repentance, cf. v. 7. Now what was the duty of the church? To forgive the offender. "Sufficient to such a man, *to toiouto, "for such a one,"* who has such a contrite spirit as the offender now manifests "*is this punishment, which was inflicted of many.*" Observe the forbearing manner in which the apostle refers to this incestuous Corinthian. Delicately and tactfully he avoids mentioning his name and his horrible offense. The "punishment" has had its salutary effect: the person experienced sorrow for his sin. There was no need to bring the blush of shame needlessly to his face whose heart was lacerated by grief. *"Sufficient* is the punishment,"* says the apostle with great emphasis. What course was now to be pursued? *"Sufficient* is the punishment .... so that contrariwise ye ought rather *to forgive* him and to *comfort him."* No further need of *punishment,* but contrariwise *forgiveness, comfort* are in place now. "I beseech you to confirm your *love* towards him," says the apostle. The motive of the severe censure applied to the erring brother was to *save* him. (1 Cor. 5, 1 ff.) Love for his immortal soul prompted the church proceedings. Since the aim had been attained: *Sufficient* is the punishment, and now the necessary result is — *so that* ye forgive him, comfort him, show him your love. This Christian attitude Paul describes thus in Ephesians 4, 32: "Be ye kind one to another, tenderhearted, forgiving one another, even as God for Christ's sake hath forgiven you." cf. Col. 3, 13.

If this Christian spirit be not shown, what may happen? The offender spoken of in our text was in danger of being *"swallowed up with overmuch sorrow"* on account of his sin; he was in danger of being driven to *despair* by his sadness, of losing all hope of salvation. "Such a one" is an object of Christian sympathy; he needs comfort, the *consolatio fratrum,* the assurance of *forgiveness* on the part of the brethren, he needs *love,* kindness, shown him. To this the apostle exhorts: "Wherefore" — lest he be swallowed up with overmuch sorrow — *I beseech you that you would confirm your love toward him."* It is your Christian duty to *forgive* him, to *comfort* him, to make good your *love* toward him. The erring brother has been *gained* (Matt. 18, 15.), *saved,* 1 Cor. 5, 1 ff., hence he is to be restored to the communion of the church. *"To whom ye forgive anything, I forgive also."* Your forgiveness insures my forgiveness. This assertion Paul strengthens by the causal sentence: *"for if I forgave anything,"* to this excommunicated but now repentant sinner, *"for your sakes forgave I it."* The breach in the congregation is healed, its honor is vindicated, the purpose of church discipline has been attained, peace and unity are restored, and you have learned to act in such a case. And I know *"I forgave in the person of Christ."* Christ receives the repentant sinner, so should we. Of His approval of our forgiving the offender I am certain. "It is as valid and certain in heaven also, as if Christ, our dear Lord, dealt with us Himself." cf. Qu. 307.

Confession.

1 John 1, 8-9: *"If we say that we have no sin, we deceive ourselves, and the truth is not in us. If we confess our sins, he is faithful and just to forgive us our sins, and to cleanse us from all unrighteousness."*

"God is light and in Him there is no darkness at all. If we *say* we have fellowship with Him, and *walk* in darkness we lie"; we are hypocrites; our actions give us the lie. "But if we walk in the light as He is in the light," we have fellowship with God, v. 6, and resultant therefrom "we have fellowship one with another," since all true Christians walk in the same sphere of light.

Christians "walk in the light." This truth, however, must not be misconstrued as though Christians were perfectly holy in their walk in the light. The sun is not spotless; the Christians are not stainless. Christians remain sinners and need continuous cleansing from sin, hence the apostle places this second truth side by side with the first: "and the blood of Jesus Christ, His Son, cleanseth us from all sin." Cleansing power this blood possesses because, as the apostle emphatically says, it is the blood of *"His"*—God's "Son." It is God's blood.

This latter thought: "The blood of Jesus Christ, His Son, cleanseth us from all sin" is developed in verses 8-10. Antithetically St. John continues: *"If we say we have no sin."* The present tense *"we have"* shows that the daily sins of those walking in the light are meant. We daily sin much. Daily we pray: "Forgive us our trespasses." The psalmist says: "Who can understand his errors? Cleanse Thou me from *secret* faults," Ps. 19, 12. Now *"if we should say, sin we have not, ourselves we deceive."* Deceive, *planan,* means to err from the right way, to lead astray, Matt. 24, 4; John 7, 12, et al.; we fall into a fundamental error; we stray from the truth, *"and the truth is not in us."* The truth, *he aletheia,* is the truth absolutely—the truth of the Gospel. *The truth* is this: "The blood of Jesus Christ cleanseth us from all sin." If we say we have no sin, we say that we have no need of the cleansing blood of Jesus. The purpose of Christ's coming into the world was to *save* sinners; for this purpose He shed His precious blood: If we say we have no sin, this truth: "In Him we *have* redemption through His blood", the heart of the Gospel message, justification by faith, *"is not in us"*, i. e., has no lodgment in our hearts.—A terrible deception to say: *"Sin we have not!"*

"If we confess our sins, He is faithful and just to forgive us our sins and to cleanse us from all unrighteousness." Confession is not the condition of our being forgiven, as though this act of ours merited forgiveness. No, whosoever confesses, admits his sins and his innate sinfulness, thereby acknowledges his being a sinner, a damned creature by nature. If we confess with a contrite heart: "I am a sinner, daily I sin much and deserve nothing but punishment; I have violated the majesty of God's Law; "the flesh lusteth against the spirit, and the spirit against the flesh," Gal. 5, 17; I daily need the Savior's blood to cleanse me; nothing else will suffice; "God, be merciful to me a sinner,"— *"He is faithful,"* He keeps His promises of mercy, *"and just,"* dikaios, righteous. He pays heed to the pleading of our *righteous* advocate, Jesus Christ, who is the propitiation for our sins (Ch. 2, 2.) It is

God's nature to be faithful and righteous and He exhibits these attributes towards us. He deals with us according to the norm He has established. The contents of this norm, His faithfulness and righteousness, the "that" clause discloses: "*hina aphe hemin tas hamartias*," etc., *that he forgives us our sins*, etc. In our English Version this is rendered smoothly by an infinitive phrase: "to forgive us our sins and to cleanse us from all unrighteousness." The terms: sins and unrighteousness are synonymous; "unrighteousness" is sin with the connotation of being a violation of divine Law. The two concepts describe the totality of sin. Whosoever penitently confesses his sin receives a perfect forgiveness, i. e., forgiveness for *all* sins.

Note 1. The text and the context: "We deceive *ourselves*" and "He (God) is faithful and just" show that the passage speaks of the confession at the bar of conscience and of God. In it the two essential parts of confession are contained: one is that we confess our sins; the other, that we receive absolution or forgiveness. These are the two essential parts of confession, whether made before God, or before men. St. John says: "If we *confess our sins*, He is faithful and just *to forgive us our sins*," etc. At every celebration of the Lord's Supper, the Lutheran Church manifests how thoroughly she enters into the spirit of this text.

Note 2. In reading the Epistle of St. John two truths in respect to the Christian's life must be closely noted: 1. A Christian still *has* sin. St. John says: "*If we say we have no sin, we deceive ourselves.*" We have need to pray daily: "Forgive us our trespasses." 2. St. John says Ch. 3, 9: "Whosoever is born of God *doth not commit sin; for his seed remaineth in him: and he cannot sin* because he is born of God." There is a great difference between *having sin* and *committing sin*, doing sin wilfully, with aforethought and malice. The solution between the two locutions of St. John is this: A Christian does not sin and cannot sin so that sin becomes the *governing principle* in him. The flesh lusteth against the spirit, hence there is constant strife between the two and the Christian must *crucify* the flesh together with its evil lusts. Cf. Gal. 5, 16-24. Rom. 7, 14-25. Read Smalcald Articles, Part 3, Art. 3. p. 319, Mueller ed.

Ps. 19, 12. *Who can understand his errors? Cleanse Thou me from secret faults.*

For explanation see sub Qu. 251.

Prov. 28, 13. *He that covereth his sins shall not prosper; but whoso confesseth and forsaketh them shall have mercy.*

To forgive the sins of the impenitent would be on a level with casting pearls before swine. The impenitent experience no contrition of heart for their sins, they are not minded to forsake them, for the treasure of the forgiveness of sin they care not. Of such the text speaks. The word *cover* stands in contrast to the word *confess*, likewise the idea *not prosper* to *have mercy*. He that *covereth* his sin is not minded to confess them; he denies, excuses, or minimizes them. Such a one shall not *prosper*, that is, he shall not *have mercy.* By covering his sin, his guilty conscience does not come to rest. Says the psalmist: "When I kept silence, my bones waxed old through my roaring all the day long. For day and night thy hand was heavy upon me." Ps. 32, 3. 4.

James 5, 16. *Confess your faults one to another, and pray one for another, that ye may be healed.*

"A Christian is to confess his faults (sins) to another and a Christian is to pray for the other, in order that they, the Christians, may be healed, be healed spiritually (Heb. 12, 13), be healed from their sins (1 Pet. 2, 24), that they may receive the true and only help (Matt. 13, 15; John 12, 40; Acts 28, 27.) from the true and only Helper. To make this truth clear we shall adduce an example from experience. One evening a young Christian came to a friend and said: "Please put out the light. I have something to tell you. This will be easier for me if you cannot see me." The light was extinguished. Then the visitor confessed a sin that burdened his conscience terribly. Having made a confession of his sin, he said: "Now speak to me." The friend spoke to him of the Lord Jesus. Then the visitor said: "Now let us kneel and you pray." Both kneeled and the friend prayed for him. Light was restored and it illumined two glad and happy Christian faces. "Confess your faults one to another", does not by any means say, that a Christian should confess all his sins to another Christian. Neither does the text speak of confessing the sins to another whereby one Christian has sinned against another. This rather is included in the admonition to be reconciled with the offended brother. Matt 5, 23, 24. "Confess your faults one to another says — as shown in the above example from life — when the heart of a Christian is burdened by a sin, and he is downcast on account of it, why, let him go to a tried Christian and confess his sin to him. Then should follow prayer which "heals", which seeks and obtains consolation, joyfulness of faith and power for amendment of life from the Lord." Cf. Zorn: Der Brief des Jacobus.

Matt. 5, 23. 24. *If thou bring thy gift to the altar, and there rememberest that thy brother hath aught against thee; leave there thy gift before the altar, and go thy way; first be reconciled to thy brother, and then come and offer thy gift.*

For exposition see sub Qu. 252 and 350.

Private Confession.

Private Confession has nothing to do with the Auricular Confession as practiced in the Roman Catholic Church which requires the penitent to enumerate every particular sin. By private confession we understand a confession of a penitent sinner of such particular sins as may above others weigh upon his heart and burden the conscience. Now what about private confession? It is neither commanded nor forbidden in the Scriptures, hence it is an Adiaphoron.

In private confession the main purpose is not the confessing of the sin that burdens the alarmed conscience but the chief purpose is to bring *comfort* and *consolation* to the alarmed heart by the Word of God. The Theological Faculty of Wittenburg gave the following "Opinion": "Private Confession is of great advantage and a special comfort to the believer, and should, therefore, be encouraged in the churches. It is such a benefit to the believer, who is thus enabled to unburden his heart more fully than he could do in a general confession. It was an advantage for David to speak personally to Nathan, and for the Prodigal Son to say: "Father, I have sinned against heaven and in thy sight." Such confession enables the penitent the opportunity of expressing the fullness of his heart in his own words and of specifying any particular sin that may trouble him above others. The experiences of all Christians are not alike, and for that reason a general confession alone will not suffice under all circumstances. The advantage also consists in this, that the penitent is enabled to have the forgiving words of the Lord applied to him in person and to the individual case in hand, which personal application is a source of great comfort (Cf. Matt. ix. 2; Luke vii. 48.)

How highly Luther esteemed private confession is well known. He writes: "I will permit no one to take from me private confession and would not give it up for all the treasures of the world. No one knows the possibilities of private confession except those who most frequently battle with Satan. I would long since have been conquered and destroyed by the devil, if this private confession had not sustained me."

Though there is no command of God in the Bible making private confession obligatory, still there are various *examples* of private confession and private absolution, e. g., that of the man sick of the palsy, Matt. 9, 1-8; that of David in 2 Sam 12, 1-14; and that of the Prodigal Son, Luke 15, 18-19.

Matt. 9, 2. *Son, be of good cheer; thy sins be forgiven thee.*

We are told of the healing of a paralytic man. "Behold, they brought unto Him a man sick of the palsy, lying on a bed; and Jesus, seeing their faith, said unto the sick of the palsy, *Son, be of good cheer; thy sins be forgiven thee.*"

"A notable point: The Lord looks, above all, for faith. In this case He found *their* faith, that of the paralytic as well as that of his friends, by virtue of His omniscience. So satisfied was He with the result of His scrutiny that He addresses words of comfort to the sick man. The Savior's intuition read in his eye the need of an assurance involving more than mere bodily recovery. The consolation of the soul was what he aspired for; the despondence, due probably to a bad conscience, must be removed. An infinite tenderness in Christ's words. Take courage, cheer up, son! There is no reason to fear that the heavenly Father and I, His Representative, will condemn. He deals first with the disease of the soul, announcing, with absolute authority, the fact of the forgiveness of sins, applying it to this individual man. As sin is the greatest evil on earth and draws after it all the other evils, that flesh is heir to, so forgiveness, pardon, is the greatest good that God can give to man. Ps. 103, 3." Kretzmann, Com.

2 Sam. 12, 13. *And David said unto Nathan, I have sinned against the Lord. And Nathan said unto David, The Lord also hath put away thy sin; thou shalt not die.*

Nathan fearlessly tells David of his horrible crime: "Thou hast killed Uriah the Hittite with the sword, and hast taken his wife to be thy wife, and hast slain him with the sword of the children of Ammon." v. 9—Read vv. 1-12. Thereupon David made confession to Nathan: "*I have sinned against the Lord.*" Nathan pronounces God's absolution to him: "*The Lord also hath put away thy sin.*" This dictum is equivalent to the New Testament mode of expressing the same truth: "Thy sins be forgiven thee."

Matt. 3, 5-6. *Then went out to him Jerusalem, and all Judea, and all the region round about Jordan, and were baptized of him in Jordan, confessing their sins.*

John the Baptist's appearance in the wilderness of Judea as the prophesied forerunner of Christ resulted in a vast outpouring of people to hear this great preacher of repentance. They came from Jerusalem, the capital of the nation; the country folk of Judea and all the region round about the river Jordan followed. Pharisees and Sadducees, priests and scribes, publicans and soldiers—all came to hear the eloquent preacher in the wilderness. John preached the Law of God in all its severity: "Repent, for the kingdom of God is at hand." He spared not the Pharisees and Sadducees. These self-styled "children of Abraham" he addressed: "O generation of vipers." John preached the Gospel in all its sweetness: "Behold the Lamb of God that taketh away the sin of the world." Many were converted by his preaching. In true repentance they *confessed* their sins; through the Law they had come to a deep conviction of their sinfulness; through the Gospel they had learned to look to the Messiah, Jesus of Nazareth, now in their midst as their Savior. Upon such confession they were baptized for the remission of sin.

PART VI.

THE SACRAMENT OF THE ALTAR.

Various Names of this Sacrament.

1 Cor. 10, 21. *Ye cannot be partakers of the Lord's table, and of the table of devils.*

The Lord's table—"trapedza kyriou"—designates the Lord's supper, as is manifest from the context.

Acts 2, 42. *They continued steadfastly in the apostles' doctrine, and fellowship, and in breaking of bread, and in prayers.*

For an exposition of this beautiful text see page 30, Vol. I. All that remains to be said here is as to the phrase the "breaking of the bread"— *he klasis tou artou.* The definite article, which our English version does not reproduce, must not be overlooked. It indicates that the concept with which it goes—"The breaking of the bread"—is one familiar to readers. In this case the apostle speaks of the breaking of the bread for sacramental use. That the "breaking of *the* bread" here spoken of denotes the Lord's Supper by the figure of speech called synecdoche —pars pro toto—a part of the whole, is plain from the text and the context. The term is derived from Christ's breaking the bread at the institution of this Last Supper in that upper chamber in Jerusalem. Cakes of unleavened bread were used in the early Christian Church. These had to be broken into convenient parts for the purpose of distribution. Hence the name.

1 Cor. 11, 20. *When ye come together therefore into one place, this is not to eat the Lord's Supper.*

This passage is so plain as to need no comment. In the time of St. Paul the sacrament was well known as *"the Lord's supper."* The name, of course, recalls the memorable scene in that upper chamber in the night when he was betrayed. Then it was "that our Lord Jesus Christ took bread," etc., Matt. 26; Mark 14; Luke 22; 1 Cor. 11.—During the celebration of the Lord's Supper, the lighted candles on the altar in church are to recall to our minds the time in which and the circumstances under which this holy sacrament was instituted.

1 Cor. 10. 10, 17. *For we being many are one bread, and one body: for we are all partakers of that one bread.*

The apostle had asked rhetorically: "The Cup of blessing which we bless is it not the communion of the blood of Christ? The bread which we break, is it not the communion of the body of Christ?" v. 16. Now he proceeds, translating the text literally: "For one bread, one body, the many we are, for all of the one bread we partake." "The communion, the oneness, of the believers with Christ, through the Eucharist, is brought out. For one bread, one body, we many are, for of the one bread we partake. It is the very closest relationship, the most vital fellowship which Paul here states to be existing. All communicants partake of that one bread which is the communion of the body of Christ, but also with one another; the fellowship of the believers is brought out with the greatest emphasis by the words of Paul" cf. Th. Qu. p. 67. Kretzman Com., p. 136, Vol. II.

The Four Records.

Read and compare the four records of the institution of the Lord's Supper: Matt. 26, 26-29; Mark 14, 22-24; Luke 22, 19, 20; 1 Cor. 11, 21-25.

The sainted Dr. A. Graebner has penned a fine study on these four records in the Theological Quarterly, Vol. V., pp. 65-90. We take pleasure in reproducing the major part of it here for prayerful and thoughtful study:

"What the Lord has made His Supper and would have it be for all time, we can learn only from the Lord himself and from those who "have received of the Lord that which also they delivered unto us." Of the institution of the Lord's supper we have four narratives, one in each of the synoptic gospels, and one by St. Paul in his first epistle to the Corinthians. (Matt. 26, 26-28; Mark 14, 22-24; Luke 22, 19. 20. 1 Cor. 11, 23-25.) All these narratives agree in all points common to all, and supplement each other in details. The text followed by the English Bible are critically attested in a way that no established reading creates any exegetical difficulty; only in 1 Cor. 11, 24, *klomenon, broken* is to be eliminated as spurious according to all the best manuscripts and versions.

According to the gospel narratives, the occasion of the institution of this sacrament was the last celebration of the Old Testament sacrament of the Passover in which Jesus united with His disciples; "the same night in which He was betrayed." This Old Testament *palaia diatheke,* was about to be abrogated. The paschal lamb of the New Testament was about to be led to the slaughter, *Christ our passover sacrificed for us.* (1 Cor. 5, 7. Cf. Is. 53, 7. Acts 8, 32ff.) The flesh of the lamb made ready for Jesus and his disciples had been eaten, and the cup of benediction had been passed and divided among the twelve. (Luke 22, 15-17). The table was not yet cleared. There was still some of the unleavened bread, *arton,* at hand. Another cup of wine, probably the customary fourth cup, the after-supper-cup, *meta to deipnesai,* (Luke 22, 20), was in readiness. And now, before the meal was fully over *esthionton auton,* (Matt. 26, 26. Mark 14, 22), *Jesus took bread.* (Matt. 26, 26. Mark 14, 22. Luke 20. 19. 1 Cor. 11, 23). All the four narratives mention this. Paul, who does not mention the passover in his account, makes this his opening statement. (1 Cor. 11, 23). It was the beginning of the solemn act he would here describe. What Jesus took was simply bread, as simple as it can be made, baked of flour and water. But He who took this bread was the *Lord Jesus,* Jesus, the Son of Mary, but at the same time the Lord, the Son of God. It was not the first time that Jesus took bread. When by the sea of Tiberias, "Jesus took the loaves," He fed five thousand men, and twelve baskets of fragments remained. (John 6, 10-13). Thus here, too, it was *the Lord* who took into His almighty hand the bread of the passover. And it is a remarkable coincidence that in all instances recorded in the gospels where Jesus "took bread" He revealed Himself and manifested His goodness and power, though in various ways. (Matt. 14, 19 f; 15, 36 ff. Mark 6, 41 ff.; 8, 6 ff. Luke 24, 30 ff. John 6, 10 ff.; 21, 13 ff.)

The next statement of the four narratives is couched in an aoristic participle, *eulogesas* in Matthew and Mark, *eucharistesas* in Luke and St. Paul. *Eulogesas, having blessed,* and *eucharistesas, having thanked,* are synonymous terms. Thus the same act is elsewhere described by *blepsas eis ton ouranon eulogesen,* (Matt. 14, 19. Mark 6, 41). and by *eucharistesas* (John 6, 10. cf. Matt. 15, 36. Mark 8, 6.) As when He took the loaves to feed the multitudes, so when He took bread to feed the little flock, Jesus spoke words of blessing, praise, and thanksgiving. What these words were, we are told neither here nor there, and the various opinions expressed by the various expositors are nothing to us either here or there, when the question is what the text says. Being words of blessing, praise, and thanksgiving, they were certainly words whereby God was acknowledged as the giver of every good gift and every perfect gift, and especially of the gift about to be dispensed as by the host to His guests or by the house-father to the members of the household.'

The next statement of the text is *eklasen, He brake it,* (1 Cor. 11, 24), or *eklasen kai edoken autois* (Mark 14, 22. Luke 22, 19,) *tois mathetais* (Matt. 26, 26), *He brake it and gave it unto them, unto His disciples.* Of Christ feeding the multitudes, it is likewise said: *klasas edoken, breaking He gave* (Matt. 14, 19), or *eklasen kai edoken* (Matt. 15, 36),*eklasen kai edidou* (Mark 8, 6), *kateklasen kai edidou* (Mark 6, 41), *He brake and gave,* or simply *diedoken, He divided, distributed.* (John 6, 10). These words are descriptive of one act, the act of distribution. When Christ *distributed, diedoken,* the five loaves, He did so by breaking and giving them, *klasas edoken, or eklasen..........* *kai edidou* (John 6, 10; coll. Matt. 14, 19. Mark 6, 41). And the bread of the passover being likewise baked in loaves or cakes of some size, Jesus distributed it by breaking it into smaller pieces and giving each disciple a piece. Thus also when at Emmaus He supped with the two pilgrims, He took bread, blessed and distributed it, *klasas epedidou autois, He brake and gave to them*. (Luke 24, 30). In all these instances, at the lakeshore, at Jerusalem, at Emmaus, the *klasis* in the narrower sense, the breaking into fragments, as distinguished from the *dosis*, the giving of the fragments, has no particular or independent signifiance, as the spurious reading in 1 Cor. 11 would indicate. (See above). The act described by both terms is the act of distribution, *diadosis*. He who gave was Jesus. They to whom He gave were His disciples. What He gave was bread.

But not bread only. The word came to the element. Jesus said: *labete, phagete, take, eat*. (Matt. 26, 26). These words are not recorded by Luke and Paul, according to the manuscripts. Mark has only *labete, take*. This does not mean that the words were not spoken as recorded by Matthew. But what the omissions do show is that the words omitted are not in themselves essential to the sacramental act. They are implied in the *dosis*. When Jesus *gave* to His disciples, He, as a matter of course, meant that the disciples should take. And giving them at the supper table from what was on the table to be eaten, *bread*, an article of food, He, again as a matter of course, meant that they should *eat*. Still it is of importance that according to the records of two evangelists Jesus also expressly *said* what His act indicated. Mark records the word, *labete, take*, which, under the circumstances, implied *phagete, eat*. When a physician or a nurse *gives* a patient a dose of medicine, that implies that the patient is to take it, and take it as medicine is taken. And when the act of giving medicine is accompanied by the word, *take*, that word means that the patient is to *take medicine*, that is, to take it into his mouth and swallow it. And now we learn from Matthew that Jesus also expressly said what He meant by *giving* the bread and by saying, *take;* He said *phagete, eat*.

The ommission of the word, *phagete*, and of *labete, phagete*, by Luke and Paul, is, however, of significance in view of the fact that the following words, *touto estin to soma mou* (Matt. 26, 26. Mark 14, 22. Luke 22, 19), or, as Paul has them, *touto mou estin to soma* (1 Cor. 11, 24), *this is my body*, are found in *all* the narratives. This statement was certainly not implied in the act of giving bread, nor in the words, *take, eat*. Without these words, *take, eat*, the disciples to whom Jesus gave bread from and at the supper table might and must have known that He would have them take and eat what He gave them. And they certainly would have taken and eaten, as the thousands in the desert took and ate when Jesus gave and what He gave, *bread*. But here in the upper room as there in the desert Jesus would give and did give more than He had taken, not according to the nature of the bread, but according to the will of the Giver, who *knew "what He was about to do"* (John 6, 6), and was able to do what He purposed to do. According to His divine will expressed by His divine word and by virtue of such word He now gave unto His disciples His own body. What He gave them was certainly bread; for the text says that it was, the bread which Jesus took and brake and gave, that they should take and eat. But what He gave, that they should take and eat, was just as certainly more than bread; for the words say so, *Touto estin to soma mou, This is my body*. The statement is very plain and simple. The sentence consists of a subject, *touto*, and a predicate, *to soma mou*, connected by the copula, *estin*. *Touto, this*, the neutral demonstrative pronoun, points to what Jesus gave and of which He·said, *take, eat.* The predicate, *to soma mou, my body*, in the proper sense of the words, denotes the material part of His human nature, as distinguished from His soul or spirit, *psyche or pneuma*, the immaterial part of His human nature. When, in the house of Simon the leper, a woman poured precious ointment on His head, Jesus said: *She is come aforehand to anoint My body, mou to soma* (Mark 14, 8), and no one doubted what He meant. And when He had commended His spirit into His Father's hands and given up the ghost (Luke 23, 46: cf. Matt. 27, 50. Mark 15, 37), Joseph begged *the body of Jesus* (Matt. 27, 58. Luke 23, 52), and Pilate knew at once what he wanted, and commanded it to be delivered, and the women of Galilee followed it to the sepulchre and beheld *how the body was laid* (Luke 24, 55). And when Jesus said, *This is my body*, His body was precisely what it was before and after the night in which He was betrayed, and what He and His friends and His enemies alike understood when His body was mentioned. The Greek form *to soma mou* is even more precise than the English, *my body*, or the German, *mein Leib*, as the article, *to*, makes it all the more distinct that the one, well known, particular body, which was then and there visibly and palpably before the disciples, was what the words denoted. That the statement was not figurative speech, was likewise plain. For where should the figure be? It could not be in the subject *touto;* for no pronoun as such was ever or could ever be used tropically; it always really points to or represents that for which it stands, or it is not a trope, but an untruth. Nor is there any tropical concept in the preceding context for which *touto* might stand. The bread mentioned before was real bread. Jesus did not figuratively break and give, but He really broke and gave, when He distributed what was in His hand and which He would have His disciples really take and eat. There is nowhere a trope to be associated with *touto*. Nor could the trope be in the copula, *estin;* for the copula simply and solely indicates that the subject and the predicate are connected as subject and predicate. Hence, where this relation is clearly intended, the copula may be, and often is, entirely omitted. as in *megale he Artemis* (Acts 19, 28. 34. Cf. Mark 14, 36. Rom. 11, 16; 14, 21. 2 Cor, 1, 21. Phil. 4, 3, and many other places), or, where that relation does not really obtain, the copula, too, is not a trope, but an untruth, connecting what should not be connected as subject and predicate. When Christ says, *This is My body*, He really and truly and actually places the subject, *this*, and the predicate, *my body*, in the real and actual relation of subject and predicate, and this, and this only, is indicated by the copula, *is*. Since, then, neither the subject, *touto*, nor the copula, *estin*, admits of a tropical sense, the predicate only remains to be looked into, and this predicate, *to soma mou, my body*, is so far from containing a trope, that it is not even possible to smuggle a trope into this part of the proposition and keep it there with any show of right or reason. Jesus certainly had a real body, over which He was certainly free to dispose. That real body was present, in full view of the disciples to whom Jesus was speaking. The disciples might disbelieve, but they could not misunderstand, what Jesus said when He said, *my body*. The words could not be taken, either by the speaker or by the hearers, in a tropical sense. Or what might the words say figuratively? When Jesus said, *I am the vine, ye are the branches* (John 15, 5), this was tropical speech, and the context clearly shows the meaning of the words. There was a *tertium comparationis* underlying the trope. It was apparent from the preceding words, *As the branch cannot bear fruit of itself, except it abide in the vine, no more can ye, except ye abide in me* (John 15, 4), and from the subsequent words, *He that abideth in Me, and I in him, the same bringeth forth much fruit, etc.*, (John 15, 5), and here the rule, *ne tropus ultra tertium*, holds good. The *tertium* was not that the vine is one and the branches are many, or that the vine is stronger and the branches are weaker, but that the branches bear fruit only while they are in the vine. Again, when He says, *I am the door*, the meaning of the trope is plain, and the *tertium* appears from the subsequent context, *by Me if any man enter in, he shall be saved.* (John 10, 9). The tertium is this, that the door is the proper inlet and outlet of the sheepfold. When He says, *I am the good Shepherd* (John 10, 11, 14), the meaning, again, is plain, and the *tertium* is at once pointed out in each case. It is the faithfulness of the good shepherd as distinguished from the hireling (John 10, 11 ff.), and the familiarity of the good shepherd with all his sheep. (John 10, 14 f.). To extend the trope to the shepherd's crook and dog, or to the difference between the shepherd and the sheep, he being a man, and they being brutes, would do violence to the words and their meaning. When Jesus said, *I am the living Bread* (John 6, 51), the *tertium* is the nourishing, life-sustaining virtue of bread, and what Jesus would say is, that as bread sustains the physical life of the eater, so He sustains the higher life of those who partake of Him by faith that they live for ever. John 6, 50. 51; coll. v. 47). In all these instances, the trope lies in the predicate, and the point of comparison is plain from the words preceding or following the figure of speech. It was necessary to grasp the *tertium*, in order to understand the tropical speech. Hence, the Jews who failed to comprehend the point of comparison were at a loss what to make of the figurative words, and strove *among themselves, saying, "How can this man give us His flesh to eat?"* (John 6, 52). If they had understood that Jesus had stated the theme of His speech in v. 47, *Verily,*

verily, I say unto you, He that believeth in Me hath eternal life, and that all that followed was an enlargement on this theme in tropical speech, in which the life-sustaining power of meat and drink was the *tertium comparationis,* all would have been plain to them.

But it is remarkable that, while even His disciples, when they had heard this tropical exposition of the truth that faith in Christ gives everlasting life, had murmured and said, *This is a hard saying; who can hear it?* (John 6, 60), they too having failed to grasp the point of comparison, we do not hear of any slowness on their part to comprehend the meaning of the words, *This is My body.* Not that the disciples were particularly bright in that gloomy night. When Jesus had spoken of His going to the Father, and that a little while they should not see Him, they had said among themselves, *What is this He saith unto us?........We cannot tell what He saith* (John 16, 17 f.). And Jesus, knowing *that they were desirous to ask Him,* explained the meaning of His words. But here, when He said, *Take, eat, this is My body,* there is no such questioning. The words are plain as words can be. There is no trope to be interpreted or misinterpreted, no point of comparison which they might grasp or fail to grasp, no symbolism with a hidden meaning. If He had said, 'Take, eat, this bread is the staff of life,' there would have been a trope, and the meaning might have been, 'As a staff supports a pilgrim, so shall this bread support your life and give you strength on the way you are about to go.' But what trope could there have been in the words, *'my body'?* The *tertium compara-. tionis* in a trope must be some characteristic, some quality, state, or relation, inherent in or connected with the person or thing denoted by the word in its real signification. Thus when Jesus calls Herod a *fox* (Luke 12, 32), the *tertium* was the dangerous slyness of the real fox. When Jesus says, *I am the bread of life* (Vide supra), the *tertium* is the nourishing virtue of real bread. And if there be a trope in the predicate, *my body,* there must be some quality or relation of Christ's real body in view of which that body might serve as a symbol of what, in a tropical way, it should signify. Thus Christ's real body was the habitation of His soul, it was an organism, it had all the qualities of a human body. Should, then, the disciples understand Jesus to say, 'Take, eat, this is the habitation of a soul, this is an organism'? Should they look for some symbolism based upon some one of the many qualities of a human body in order to understand the hidden meaning of the Master's words? No, the assumption of a tropical sense in the words, *Take, eat, this is my body,* is simply nonsensical. If these words do not mean what they say in their real, proper significance, nobody in the world can say what they do mean, or even what they *might* mean. They simply cannot mean anything but what they properly say, *This, which I give you and bid you take and eat, is my body, my real body, the body which you see here before you, and which is about to be offered up for the sins of the world.*

And now, to make assurance doubly sure, we learn from St. Paul that Jesus added the words *to huper humon, which is for you,* (1 Cor. 11, 24), or, according to the still more complete record of St. Luke, *to huper human didomenon, which is being given for you.* (Luke 22, 19). These words are descriptive of the *real* body of Jesus, the body which was bound, and buffeted, and spit upon, and scourged, and crowned with thorns, and crucified, and laid in Joseph's tomb. All this was real. Jesus was not tropically or figuratively given for us; or we would still be unredeemed. If it was Christ's particular purpose to shut out every possibility of misinterpreting His words by forcing upon them a figurative sense, He most effectively achieved His purpose by adding the descriptive clause, *which is being given for you. No symbol of His body was symbolically given for us, but His real body was really given for us.* And this real body given *for* us in His suffering and death is, according to His plain words, really given *to* us in His sacrament. The words are so plain, and the meaning is so real that it is, in fact, hard to understand how anybody could deem it reasonable to depart from what the words say and still profess to believe that Jesus is the Truth as He is the Way and the Life. While they were eating, really eating, Jesus took, really took, bread, real bread, and gave, really gave, to His disciples, His real disciples, and said, really said, *Take, eat, this is my body.* When a man gives, and says, take, what can He mean but that they to whom he actually and really gives should actually and really *take?* When, at a supper, while He and His guests are eating, He gives an article of food and says, take, *eat,* what can He mean but that they should really *eat?* When, by the demonstrative pronoun, *this,* He points to what He really gives to be really taken and eaten, what can He mean but really *this* which he really gives? When he uses the copula, *is,* to connect the real subject and the real predicate of a sentence which He really speaks, what can he mean but that such subject and predicate should be really connected? And when He whose real body was about to be given, really given, for His real disciples and other real sinners, says, *my body which is being given for you,* what in the world can He mean but that real body? No manner or amount of ingenuity can really find in such words spoken under such circumstances even a semblance of a symbolism. Even an inversion of the terms of the proposition, while it would be a violent perversion of the statement, would not open a way to symbolism. For if the Savior were made to say, *My body which is being given for you,* is this, the subject, my body, would again stand for Christ's real body, the copula would again really connect the subject and the predicate, and *this* would again point to what was really given to be really taken; and even if *this* could point to *bread,* this bread was real bread really taken from the real table. In short, whatever the impugners of the Lutheran doctrine of the Lord's Supper may do, the words of Jesus stand as an adamantine wall and persistently refuse to admit of any interpretation which, with a view of satisfying reason and common sense, is nonsensical, defying the laws of interpretation, of language and of logic, of philosophy and theology alike. The words are fully as plain as the first words in Genesis, *In the beginning God created the heaven and the earth*, or as the last words in Revelation, *The grace of our Lord Jesus. Christ be with you all*, or any other words of Scripture between the two. That they have occasioned much controversy and a great variety of interpretation is no argument against, but in favor of, taking them, in their proper sense. The most general rule of interpretation, not only in theology, but everywhere, is, *The true meaning of words can be but one.* (Lieber, Legal and Political Hermeneutics, p. 158.) But the various endeavors to force upon these words a tropical sense have led to a multitude of contortions probably without a parallel in all history, Carlstadt, and Schwenkfeld, and Zwingli, and Oecolampad, and Calvin, and Beza, all disagreeing as to the meaning of the words, and only agreeing in the assumption that "This is my body" really meant "This is *not* my body." The multifarious attempts to pervert the true sense of the words are but so many evidences of the persistent refusal of the words to yield any other than the proper sense of the terms. The real difficulty lies not in the words, but in the substance of the statement, *This is my body.* The real cause of the refusal to accept what the words say is not in the words but in the readers and hearers of the words who, instead of saying with Queen Elizabeth, "And what the Word doth made it, that I believe and take it," persist in saying with the Jews of old, "How can this man give us His flesh to eat?"

How it was possible that Jesus, in the night in which He was betrayed, should give His body to His disciples, and His disciples should take and eat what He gave them, bread and His body, does not concern us here, our present object being to learn what, according to the Scriptures, took place when Christ instituted this sacrament. And that this was really what Jesus was about, the institution of an ordinance, also appears from the narratives. Having taken bread, blessed and given thanks, and distributed the bread, saying, *Take, eat, this is my body,* he continued, *Touto poieite eis ten emen anamnesin, This do in remembrance of Me.* (Luke 22. 19. 1 Cor. 11, 24). The pronoun *touto*, as the object of *poieite, do,* refers to the *action* which was then and there going on. And of this action, Jesus says, *do it in remembrance of Me.* To remember is to recall to the mind what is no longer present to the senses. Remembrance of things present belongs to the future. A departing friend asking to be remembered thinks of the future, of a time when he will be no longer where they could see and hear him. So Jesus, while yet present where they could see and hear him, looked forward to the time when he would have departed, (John 16, 5. 7. 28), and they should not see him. (John 16, 16-19). And then they were to remember him, and in remembrance of him they were to do what was now going on in his visible presence, enacted by him and them. According to this charge, *This do in remembrance of Me,* it was the will of the Master that His disciples should, after his departure, perform the act which was then being enacted at the paschal board. It was His will and covenant that in future assemblies of His disciples, He being invisibly in the midst of them, bread should be blessed and distributed, His words should be repeated, *Take, eat, this is My body which is given for you*, and by virtue of these words, His own words, he would give His body with the bread distributed to the guests at His supper, and they should eat the bread and what he would give them with the bread, His body given for them. And doing this, they should remember Him, as He was before them in the night in which he was betrayed, the Savior who was about to offer himself as the paschal lamb of the new covenant, of which the Jewish passover was a type and shadow. Thus should this sacred act be to them an ordinance whereby they were to be in a peculiar way reminded and assured of the atoning sacrifice once offered up for the sins of the world, as they should partake of the very body of the Lamb of God slain for an expiation of their sin and guilt. All this is implied in the words, *This do in remembrance of Me.*

But as the first Testament was not dedicated without blood (Heb. 9, 18), so also the new covenant must be sealed with blood. And the Lord Jesus, after He had done and said what has been considered, *after the same manner also took the cup.* Matt 26. 29, Mark 14, 25, and Luke 22, 18, we learn that the cup contained *to genema tes ampelou, the fruit of the vine.* This was not must, the unfermented juice of the grape. For it was in the days of Jesus, and is to this day, a matter of course in Palestine, as in other Oriental countries, to use *wine*, not must, as a beverage on festive occasions, and at no time was must used by the Jews at the Passover. Thus, also, we learn from 1 Cor. 11, that the wine used in the apostolic church was fermented wine, which, if taken to excess, would intoxicate. 1 Cor. 11, 21. Again Jesus *gave thanks*, and as he had given the bread, so he now gave the cup *edoken autois* (Matt. 26, 27. Mark 14, 23. Luke 22, 20), and said, Drink ye all of it. And of what he gave, and of what he bade them drink, he said, *This is My blood, the (blood) of the New Testament, shed for you, for many, for remission of sins.* (Luke 22, 20; Matt. 26, 27; Mark 14, 23), Jesus himself here tells His disciples what, as he gave them the cup and the wine therein contained, He gave them to drink. It was *His blood*, not the blood of a brute sacrifice, as the blood of the Old Testament had been, but the blood prefigured by the typical blood of the Levitical cult, the blood of the Lamb of which Isaiah had prophesied (Is. 53, 7), the blood of the New Covenant, shed for many, also for those especially who were to partake of it in the sacrament. Thus was this sacrament a seal of the *new covenant*, a covenant *in his blood* (Luke 22, 20. 1 Cor. 11, 25), not the old covenant in the blood of brutes, pointing forward to the coming Savior, but a covenant in the blood of the Savior who was now come to shed His own blood for the remission of the sins of the world. The words, *touto esti to aima mou* correspond to the words, *toutoesti to soma mou*, and must, of course, be taken in the same proper sense. The words, also aside from this parallelism, admit of no tropical signification. The blood of Jesus was real human blood. The blood which was shed for many as blood of the new covenant was not figurative, but real blood, really shed, not for a figurative, typical atonement, as in the Jewish ritual, but for the real atonement whereby the world should be reconciled with God. If what Jesus gave in the sacrament was the blood of the new covenant, it could not be a symbol of that blood. As it is in the nature of the type to be symbolic, it is equally in the nature of the antitype to be real, not again a symbol, but the thing itself. And this is precisely what the words say. Jesus not only plainly says, *this is My blood*, but by adding, *to tes kaines diathekes, that of the new covenant*, he expressly distinguishes His blood from the blood of the old covenant, which was indeed symbolic. And by adding the words, *to huper huemon, peri pollon, ekchunomenon, which is being shed for you, for many*, He describes what he gives as His real blood, the blood which flowed in His veins which were about to be opened by the scourge and the thorns and the nails and the spear. The blood of Jesus is nothing to us and for us, unless it is the real, true blood which was shed for us and for many for the remission of sins, our real sins.

But the words, *of the new covenant*, were significant in still another way. The new covenant established by the blood of Jesus was not intended for the twelve apostles only, but for all men, and not for that passover night only, but for all times. What Jesus enacted in that upper room was not a sacrifice, but a sacrament, whereby those who ate and drank were to be made partakers of the sacrifice about to be enacted in Gethsemane and on Golgotha. And as these benefits were to endure long after the night in which Jesus was betrayed, and to be enjoyed by many besides the twelve disciples, so also the means whereby such benefits were to be dispensed and appropriated should be of permanent endurance. Hence, as the Lord had said of the first part of the sacramental act, *This do in remembrance of Me*, so He also adds the words recorded by St. Paul, *This do, as oft as ye drink it, in remembrance of Me*, (1 Cor. 11, 25). When He should be no longer with them in visible presence, His disciples should, in remembrance of Him as their Savior, and of His obedience unto death, of His atoning sacrifice, celebrate this supper, wherein they should not only eat His body in with, and under the sacramental bread, but also drink His blood in with, and under the sacramental wine, and by virtue of the sacramental word, again and again drink His blood once shed for them for the remission of sins.

Thus did the Lord Jesus, in the night in which he was betrayed, institute the ordinance of the Lord's Supper. Of this ordinance, the Apostle says, *As often as ye eat this bread, and drink this cup, ye do show the Lord's death till he come,* (1 Cor. 11, 26). To the end of time, till the Son of man shall come to judge the quick and the dead, this sacramental bread shall be eaten, and men shall drink this sacramental cup, and in so doing shall voice forth the Lord's death. This sacrament shall be for all times a form of preaching Christ crucified, of setting forth the cardinal truth of the Gospel that in Christ Jesus we have forgiveness of sins, an efficacious means of grace. And wherever this sacrament shall be celebrated, it shall be what it was in the upper room at Jerusalem, not mere bread and wine; *but the cup of blessing which we bless is the communion of the blood of Christ, and the bread which we break is the communion of the body of Christ.* (1 Cor. 10, 16). *And whosoever shall eat of this bread, and drink of this cup of the Lord, unworthily, shall be guilty,* not of mere bread and wine, but *of the body and blood of the Lord* (1 Cor. 11, 27), *eating and drinking damnation to himself, not discerning the Lord's body.* (1 Cor. 11, 29). Wherever this sacrament is celebrated, it is what the Lord himself has once made it in the act of institution. Though men break the bread and bless the cup (1 Cor. 10, 16), speaking the words that Jesus spoke, they do not make the sacrament, they are not performing a work of their own, but are only repeating what Jesus did and whereof he said, *"this do";* i. e., repeat my acts and repeat my words, and also do as My disciples did at My bidding when I said, *take, eat, and drink ye all of it.* Nor is it the faith or unbelief of the communicants which makes or unmakes the sacrament; for the unworthy communicant also is guilty of the body and blood of Christ. When and where that is done whereof Christ says, *this do,* there is the sacrament with all the sacramental grace and efficacy, and no Judas among the communicants can undo it by his unbelief. And where that whereof Christ says, *this do,* is not done, there is no sacrament, and no amount of faith in the communicants can make it such. Where cider or water is used instead of wine, or where only a semblance of the words of institution is pronounced, while the meaning is professedly changed into "This signifies My body," there is no sacrament, though the celebrant and the communicants be believers in Christ and children of God by faith, every one of them. On the other hand, where the elements and words and acts essential to the sacrament are observed according to Christ's commandment, *this do,* a valid and efficacious sacrament is celebrated, though the communicants, on a given occasion, were hypocrites and rejected the grace offered by this means of grace, every one of them.

The Lord's Supper, then, is a means of grace, of reminding us of Christ, the Redeemer of the world, of assuring us that the sacrifice for the expiation of our sins was really and truly offered up by Him who was both the High Priest and the sacrifice. As in Baptism a visible element, water, is bound up with the word in the sacramental act, so in the Lord's Supper visible elements, bread and wine, are, by divine institution, bound up with the sacramental word.

And thus this sacrament too is of the nature of a seal. A memorial supper instituted by the primitive church, the apostles and other disciples of Jesus, would and could not have constituted a seal of divine grace, an assurance of the forgiveness of sins. But when Jesus, in His own words, solemnly assures us that His body is given for us, and His blood is shed for us, for the remission of sins, and in the same solemn act adds to His words the visible elements of bread and wine, again assuring us that with them he gives His body and blood to all those who eat and drink the elements thus given under His ordinance, this is to each recipient a solemn token and testimony of God's gracious will that He, the individual sinner, shall enjoy the benefits of Christ's redemption. As Baptism is the application of water bound up with words of divine promise, applying and securing that promise to the particular person to whom this sacrament is administered for establishing and confirming a personal relation, a covenant of grace, between that person and God, so in the Lord's Supper Christ would assure the individual sinner with whom He deals in this sacrament that He who hears the words and eats and drinks shall, by faith in these words and the visible tokens of his redemption attached thereto, have, hold, and enjoy what the words say and the tokens confirm. Thus, while this sacrament, too, is essentially Gospel, a means whereby the benefits of Christ's meritorious sacrifice are applied and appropriated to the individual sinner, this form of applying and appropriating what God's grace has provided and Christ has procured for all mankind is intended to emphasize this act of appropriation as a solemn transaction between God and the *individual* sinner.

Being essentially Gospel, a means of grace, the Lord's Supper does not confer grace *ex opere operato*. It is *organon dotikon*, the giving hand of God, which extends itself to an *organon leptikon*, a taking hand, which is faith. The efficacy of the sacrament is inherent in the sacrament. Here as everywhere the Gospel is *the power of God unto salvation* (Rom. 1, 16), but *unto every one that believeth*. The power exerted in and through the sacrament is God's, not man's, nor God's and man's working together, but God's alone. And here as everywhere the power of the Gospel is active as *vis collativa* and *vis effectiva*, giving and conferring what is offered and working or promoting the acceptance of such gift. The assurance of divine grace in Christ the Redeemer, which is so directly and impressively set forth to the communicant in the Eucharist celebrated *in remembrance* of Him who lived and died for the sinner who partakes of this memorial feast, is not only incidentally, but by divine intention, a means whereby the faith of the communicant shall be nourished and preserved. (1 Cor. 11, 25. 26. Luke 22, 20). But here again the sacrament works as a means of grace. While its power is everywhere and at all times efficacious, its efficacy is that of divine power exerted not by immediate but by mediate action. It operates in such a way that its effect can be, as it often is, frustrated by man's obstinate resistance. There are those who *eat this bread, and drink this cup of the Lord, unworthily* (1 Cor. 11, 27), who eat and drink, not life and salvation, but *damnation,* to themselves. (1 Cor. 11, 29. Luke 22, 21). And such should be warned not to partake of the sacrament, which was instituted as an assurance of divine grace in Christ for disciples of Christ (Matt. 26, 18. 26. Mark 14, 14. Luke 22, 11), and for them only. St Paul says: *Let a man examine himself, and so let him eat of that bread, and drink of that cup.* (1 Cor. 11, 28). And the apostle also states the reason for this injunction, as he continues: *For he that eateth and drinketh unworthily, eateth and drinketh damnation to himself.* (1 Cor. 11, 29) Since, then, the Lord's Supper was instituted and intended for Christ's disciples only, and those who examining themselves find, or should find, that they cannot worthily partake of this sacrament, are solemnly warned lest they eat and drink damnation to themselves, it is clearly incumbent on those who administer the sacrament to guard against its abuse by manifestly unworthy communicants, and to refuse access to the Lord's table to those who cannot or will not examine themselves, who do *not discern the Lord's body,* (1 Cor. 11, 29), or who by word or deed show that they are not disciples of Christ.

But there is still another aspect under which unity of faith must be considered a condition of admission to the same altar in the celebration of the Eucharist. While the Lord's Supper is in itself a sacrament, a means of divine grace, the celebration or use of this sacrament is in a certain sense a sacrificial act, not a propitiatory sacrifice as offering up the body and blood of Christ, but a sacrifice of praise and thanksgiving and a profession of faith. This was one of the purposes for which 'the Lord's Supper was instituted that........we might publicly confess our faith, and proclaim the benefits of Christ, as Paul says (1 Cor. 11, 26): *As often as ye eat this bread, and drink this cup, ye do show the Lord's death.'* (Apol. Aug. Conf. III, 6, 89). 'For', says the same Apology, 'just as among the sacrifices of praise, i e. among the praises of God, we include the preaching of the Word, so the reception itself of the Lord's Supper can be praise or thanksgiving.' (Ibid XII, 24, 33). Now, common confession of faith, as communion of worship generally, demands communion and unity of faith. Of the primeval church at Jerusalem it is said that *they continued steadfastly in the apostles' doctrine and fellowship, and in breaking of bread, and in prayers.* (Acts 2, 42). Especially does altar fellowship presuppose and demand unity of faith and doctrine concerning the Lord's Supper itself. By being *all partakers of that one bread* the communicants exhibit themselves as *one body* (1 Cor. 10, 17), and it is certainly improper that those who dissent and are divided on the very nature and sacramental character of *that one bread* should fellowship and exhibit unity by communing together where there is actually dissent and division concerning the very act in which they unite and which is to constitute a bond of unity. When Christ instituted and administered the sacrament, saying, *Take, eat, this IS My body*, he certainly did not want those to take and eat who hold and say that what they take and eat *is NOT His body*. Nor would He have His true disciples, who continue in His word, partake of a purported sacrament where the truth of His sacramental word is questioned or denied.'

That the Lord's Supper should not, as the sacrament of Baptism, be administered but once to any one person, but should be partaken of repeatedly by the worthy communicant, is apparent from the words of institution, *This do as oft as ye drink it*, (1 Cor. 11, 25), and by the words of St. Paul, *For as often as ye eat this bread, and drink this cup, ye do show the Lord's death till He come.* (1 Cor. 11, 26). Here the words, *hosakis esthiete kai pinete*, are addressed to the same persons, and we know that the church of the apostolic age, and in the days of Trajan (Plini epp. X, 97) and Marcus Aurelius (Justin, Apol. I, c. 65-67) so understood the words of Christ and of St. Paul.

'From the same words it also appears that the cup must not be withheld from any communicant in the sacrament. Jesus expressly said of the cup, *Drink ye ALL of it*, (Matt. 26, 27), and St. Mark expressly states that *they ALL drank of it.* (Mark 14, 23). And if it be said that there were no laymen among the first communicants, the argument, proving too much, proves nothing; for on the strength of it the bread also might or must be denied to the lay members of the church. Besides, the words of St. Paul, *As often as ye eat this bread and drink this cup*, (1 Cor. 11, 26), and the subsequent words (1 Cor. 11, 27-29), are addressed to the local congregation at large. (1 Cor. 1, 2). To the members of the congregation, as many as are able to examine themselves in their relations to God and their neighbor, and are known to be one with the congregation in the profession of true discipleship (John 8, 31) and in godliness of life, the sacrament, whole and entire, may and should be administered. And as this sacrament and all the means of grace are entrusted to the church as constituted in local congregations, it is proper and in accordance with the will of the Master that the Lord's Supper should be administered by the ministers of the church as the organs of the congregations. In this as in every other official function the minister is responsible to the congregation. But the church is not the mistress of the sacrament. It is the Lord's table, and must be administered according to the Lord's will and instruction as above set forth. And the pastor is also a minister of Christ and, therefore, responsible to the Lord over all as truly as he is to the church, his Master's bride, in the administration of the Lord's sacrament.

Such is the scriptural doctrine of the Lord's Supper. While this doctrine is plainly taught in its *sedes doctrinae*, the sacrament itself is a mysterious thing which no man's mind can fathom, and the doctrine

of the Lord's Supper is an article of faith. The doctrine of the person
of Christ is also clearly set forth in the Scriptures, and that doctrine
too, is an article of faith, the theanthropic person of the Redeemer being an inscrutable mystery even to the angels and archangels. How it
is possible that in a human nature the fulness of the Godhead should
dwell bodily in a perosnal union and with a real communication of attributes is far above all human understanding, and no amount of speculation can carry us nearer to the mystery. On the contrary, to specu-
late where we should simply believe is culpable in itself. Thus, also,
we cannot comprehend how it is possible that the body and blood of
Christ should, in the sacramental act, enter into a sacramental union
with the visible elements, bread and wine, and no amount of speculation can bring us nearer to a solution of this mystery. But the Lord's
Supper is not to be made the subject of physical or metaphysical,
physiological or mathematical enquiry, but must be and remain for all
time an object of faith. We know *that* even in the days of his humiliation, the Son of man, who was discoursing heavenly things with Nicodemus on earth, was at the same time in heaven, according to his
word (Jchn 3, 13), though we cannot comprehend the *how*. Nor is it
our business to comprehend this mystery; we simply believe what his
plain words plainly say. And we know *that* the same Son of man,
while bodily sitting with His disciples at the passover board discoursing
heavenly things and instituting His sacrament, gave unto the same disciples that same body with the sacramental bread, and *that* the same
Lord Jesus, who was visibly *taken up into heaven* (Acts 1, 9. 11), gives
His body and blood to all who, *till He come* (1 Cor. 11, 26. Cf. Acts
1, 11), do and shall partake of His sacrament, eating and drinking
with this bread and this cup, the body and blood of the Lord, though
we do not comprehend the *how*. Nor is it our business to comprehend
this mystery; we simply believe what his plain words plainly say, *Take,
eat, this is My body; take, drink, this is My blood*. We know that this
union of Christ's body and blood with the eucharistic elements is not a
natural union in a local or circumscriptive presence, and that the eating and drinking of such body and blood in the sacrament is not a
physical, Capernaitic (John 6, 52) eating and drinking; but the peculiar
mode and manner of such union and presence and eating and drinking
we do not know. We term it *sacramental*, not to explain it, but to
describe it as being peculiar to this sacrament, in accordance with and
by virtue of the sacramental word, which we believe. We do not con-
strue this sacramental presence from the doctrine of the person of
Christ and of the communication of attributes, especially of divine
omnipresence, to the human nature of Christ. We learn that *where
two or three are gathered together in Christ's name, there is He in the
midst of them* (Matt. 18, 20), and that He *is with us alway, even unto
the end of the world* (Matt. 28, 20), also according to His human
nature, according to which *all power is GIVEN unto Him in heaven
and in earth* (Matt. 28, 18); and this, too, we believe because He has

said it. But if He had said only this, and not the sacramental words recorded by the evangelists and St. Paul, there would be no doctrine of the Lord's Supper in Lutheran theology. We reject Nestorianism and Eutychianism, because both heresies are at variance with what the Scriptures teach concerning the personal union, the one separating and the other confounding what the Scriptures exhibit as personally united. And, likewise, we repudiate Zwinglianism and Calvinism on the one hand and Transubstantiation and Consubstantiation on the other because all of them are at variance with what the Scriptures teach concerning the sacramental union. We will not permit the sacramental bread and the body of Christ to be separated as, to use Beza's words, *summum coelum ab infirma terra.* Nor will we permit the bread to be changed into the body of Christ by transubstantiation, or the bread and Christ's body confounded into a new substance by a sacramental Eutychianism, consubstantiation. We refuse to accept the alternative constantly forced upon us of being either Zwinglians or Papists. We hold, teach and confess that *the cup of blessing which we bless is the communion of the blood of Christ, and the bread which we break is the communion of the body of Christ,* (1 Cor. 10, 16) ; that in a peculiar, sacramental way known to Christ and brought about by His divine power and will, we eat and drink in His holy sacrament His true body sacramentally present and united with the consecrated bread and His true blood sacramentally present and united with the consecrated wine by virtue of Christ's sacramental word, *Take, eat, this is My body; drink ye all of it, this is My blood."*

Ps. 33, 4. *The word of the Lord is right; and all His works are done in truth.*

Compare the explanation of this passage on page 88, Vol. I. There this text was used to prove the truthfulness of God. God cannot deceive us. His words mean what they say. Christ is true God who says of Himself: "I am the Truth". The words of the institution of the Lord's Supper proceed from the mouth of Him who is the King of Truth. John 18, 37. That we cannot comprehend the doctrine does not argue against the truthfulness of the sublime statements therein made. "Continue *in My word*—and ye shall *know the truth."* John 8, 30.

Eph. 3, 20, 21. *Now unto Him that is able to do exceeding abundantly above all that we ask or think, according to the power that worketh in us, unto Him be glory in the church.*

This text was studied when treating of the introduction to the Lord's prayer. (Qu. 223) God's, Christ's wisdom and power are unlimited. Observe the accumulation of the words to impress us with this fact: "He is able to do *exceeding abundantly above all that we ask or think."* This power we Christians have experienced. Now this God of unlimited powers has instituted this mysterious love feast—His Holy Supper—how can we entertain doubts as to His ability to do what He promises! Rather—this is our duty—intone a hymn of praise as does the Apostle here, saying: *"Unto Him be glory in the Church."*

1 Cor. 10, 16. *The cup of blessing which we bless, is it not the communion of the blood of Christ? The bread which we break, is it not the communion of the body of Christ?*

It would lead us too far afield to show why the Apostle speaks of the Lord's Supper in this environment. The words are plain in themselves as to the doctrine involved: "I speak as to wise men, judge ye what I say" v. 15. You are thoroughly competent to pass the proper verdict in the matter I am about to propose to you. It is a matter with which you are conversant. *"The cup of blessing which we bless, is it not the communion of the blood of Christ?"* Rhetorically Paul puts the question, knowing the answer to be: This is most certainly true.

"The entire passage breathes the consciousness, the certainty, of Christian fellowship, first in Christ in whom they participate through the wine and the bread, and secondly with the communicants, who partake of the same bread and of the same cup. We have here the essence of the Lord's Supper in one sentence: There are the earthly elements, bread and wine; there are the invisible blessings, the real presence of the body and blood of Christ; the heavenly gifts are present in, with, and under the earthly elements, for there is a communion of the two, in either case, and nothing is said of a change or a transubstantiation; the communion is with Christ, as the Author and Finisher of our salvation. There is no sacramental presence outside of the Sacrament; it is necessary that bread and wine be blessed and then partaken of in accordance with Christ's institution in order that the real presence be effective; he that partakes of the bread partakes of the body of Christ; and he that partakes of the cup partakes of the blood of Christ." Kretzmann Com. *in loco.*

Mark 14, 24. *This is My blood of the New Testament.*

For explanation see article: "The Four Records."

Gal. 3, 15. *Brethren, I speak after the manner of men. Though it be but a man's covenant, yet if it be confirmed, no man disannulleth, or addeth thereto.*

"The Apostle here offers the mystery of God in a human parable, incidentally addressing the Galatians in a kind and captivating tone: 'After the manner of man speak I.' In his endeavor to show that the promise alone brings salvation, he uses a comparison taken from the ordinary practise in regard to the last will or testament of a man, by which he disposes of his goods: Though it be but a man's, yet if it is ratified, no man sets aside a testament or adds thereto. If a man's last will and testament is duly witnessed and sealed, the disposal of his property is commonly regarded as being consummated; how much more then, ought this be true of the testament of God by which He made

Abraham and all his children heirs of the evangelical blessing!" *Fiat applicatio.* Kretzmann, Popular Com. *in loco.*

1 Cor. 11, 23-29. *For I have received of the Lord that which also I delivered unto you, that the Lord Jesus, the same night in which He was betrayed, took bread; and when He had given thanks, He brake it and said, Take, eat; this is My body, which is broken for you; this do in remembrance of Me. After the same manner also He took the cup when He had supped, saying, This cup is the New Testament in My blood; this do ye, as oft as ye drink it, in remembrance of Me. For as often as ye eat this bread and drink this cup, ye do show the Lord's death till He come. Wherefore, whosoever shall eat this bread, and drink this cup of the Lord unworthily, shall be guilty of the body and blood of the Lord. But let a man examine himself, and so let him eat of that bread and drink of that cup. For he that eateth and drinketh unworthily eateth and drinketh damnation to himself, not discerning the Lord's body.*

Various passages from this paragraph are cited in the following questions in the Catechism. We prefer to treat it in its entirety. The student may refer to this explanation as occasion demands.

Observe the solemn manner in which the Apostle introduces his instructions: *"I received of the Lord that which I also delivered unto you."* "Corinthian Christians", says the Apostle, "I delivered this doctrine unto you. I instructed you thoroughly in it. Hence you ought to know it. But your conduct just now shows that you have forgotten it, or else you are shamefully abusing it. Be it known to you, therefore, that the doctrine which I delivered unto you is not mine. I am an Apostle of Jesus Christ. Whatsoever I preach unto you I preach not in my own name, but in the name of the Lord. And especially of this doctrine—to show you its great importance—I solemnly affirm: I have received it of the Lord, that is to say, I have received a special revelation regarding it from the Lord Jesus Christ Himself, who instituted it. So you can rely upon my every word as coming from the Lord Jesus Christ Himself."

And who is this Lord Jesus? He is, as Paul writes to the Romans, "God over all." aye, as Isaiah says, "the Mighty God," who has ways and means to do that which He promises. He is the God-man, who has a body and blood that He can give. He is Truth itself, and therefore cannot lie. When He says, "This is My body", He speaks truly. He is the All-wise, who, looking down through the ages of time, knew that contentions would arise with respect to this ordinance, and therefore He used plain, unmistakable words, so that, whosoever is of the truth and will hearken to His words, can know the truth. He is, furthermore, the Almighty, who is able to do and give what He has promised.

*"The Lord Jesus, the same night in which He was betrayed, took
bread."* In that solemn night, a few hours before. He suffered and died
for the sins of the world, the Savior instituted this Sacrament as a rich
legacy to His disciples and all Christians. It was His last will. "This
is My body; this is My blood"—these words have the force and authority of such a document, of a last will or testament. In a matter of such
weighty importance, instituted at such a solemn time, our Lord would
use plain words. Figurative words, ambiguous words, have no place in
a testament. Paul says of a man's testament: "Brethren, I speak
after the manner of men. Though it be but a man's covenant, yet, if it
be confirmed, no man disannulleth or addeth thereto." Gal. 3, 15. So
sacred a man's testament is held to be; but, sad to say, when the Lord
of lords and King of kings makes a testament, there are sacrilegious
hands trying to destroy it.

*"The Lord Jesus, the same night in which He was betrayed, took
bread; and when He had given thanks, He brake it and said, Take, eat,
this is My body."* etc.

After the ordinary meal the Lord takes bread, gives thanks, thus
separating it from the ordinary use, and says: "Take, eat; this is My
body", indicating that something more exalted than ordinary bread was
given them, and likewise He did with the cup containing wine.

"It is plain that two objects are here spoken of as being present:
one is the body and blood of Christ, the other is bread and wine. The
body and blood are invisible, divine elements, while the bread and wine
are visible, earthly elements. The relation of the two elements is, that
the earthly is the means of the heavenly. That is, by using or appropriating this bread and this wine, the body and blood of Christ are
received and appropriated by the communicant."

Let us inspect the words: *"This is My body."* The word "is", according to the plain, natural understanding, does not mean "signifies"
or "represents" in any language of the civilized world, but "is" shows
that something really exists. "Body" means a true, essential body,
not an apparent body; and to remove all doubt, the Lord says: "My
body." That does away with all figurative language, and to cut off all
subterfuges, the Lord adds: "This is My body which is broken for
you." If any words in human speech are plain, these are.

The Lord does not say: "This is My *changed* body" so that the
bread were changed into the body of Christ, which is the Roman
Catholic error of Transubstantiation; and upon which they have built
that horrible doctrine of the so-called Mass, upon which again the whole
papal system rests. Further proof of the correctness of our version
we have in the text. Christ says: "For as aften as ye eat of *this
bread* and drink of *this cup*"; again: "Whosoever shall eat of this
bread and drink of *this cup*." He speaks of the elements *after* con-

secration, and still He says, "this bread" "this cup." Hence there is no change of the elements. The bread remains bread, and the wine remains wine.

Nor are the divine and the earthly elements separated, so that the body and blood are not received where the bread and wine are taken,— which is the error of other Protestant churches,—but the two are combined in an inseparable and yet unmixed union. Proof of this we find here also, v. 29: "For he that eateth and drinketh unworthily eateth and drinketh damnation to himself, not discerning the Lord's body." So the Lord's body is present, but not discerned by such as partake of the Sacrament unworthily. Again, v. 27: "Whosoever shall eat this bread, and drink this cup unworthily, shall be guilty of the body and blood of the Lord." Nothing can be plainer than that the body and blood of Christ are present, otherwise those partaking unworthily of the Supper could not be guilty thereof.

Based upon these plain Scriptures the Lutheran Church maintains the real presence of the body and blood of the Lord in the Holy Supper for the remission of sins. God says so: therefore it is true. How that is done we know not. It is sound theology to say: "We don't know"—when Scripture is silent. We know the fact; the manner is incomprehensible. The "how" we leave to God.

But does not Jesus say: *"This do in remembrance of Me?"* *"This do"* is a command. Do what? Consecrate bread and wine and under the consecrated bread and wine eat and drink My body and blood. "This do" and then remember at the same time that I gave My body and blood for the salvation of the world. Thus you do *"show forth the Lord's death."* In this visible way Christ crucified is preached, and in this visible way the cardinal truth of the Gospel is set forth, that by His death Jesus expiated the sin of the world, and by believing in Him we have forgiveness of sins. To assure us of this blessed fact again and again, He gives us that in the Holy Supper wherewith He redeemed the world—His body and blood.

We are told: If you accept the words in their literal sense you Lutherans are in the right. But *how* can this be? "That is the highest laudation one can give a Lutheran. For it remains true as Dr. Eck, a Catholic theologian at Luther's time, was told by one of his own faith. Dr. Eck was asked, "Can you refute the Lutherans?" Eck replied, "Whith the church-fathers—yes; with the Scriptures—no." He was told, "I see the Lutherans are entrenched within the Scriptures, and we are outside of them."

Do not let that "how" bother you. God speaks. Accept! You believe that God is one, yet three distinct persons. Can you explain the how? Why do you believe it? Because Scripture says so. Likewise do here.

We are surrounded by mysteries in daily life. We know the facts, not the manner. What is life? What is electricity? How is it possible to send your voice by means of the telephone in an instant from Springfield to Chicago? Edison does not know. How is blood produced in the body? The wisest doctor can not tell you.

Similar observations led Luther to remark: "They, (the opponents) want to know how Christ's body is in the bread, and if it can't be explained, they deny its presence, and yet the same men do not know how they open their mouths, move their tongues, or grasp their pens. I will say nothing about their not knowing how they see, hear or speak or live. All of these things we constantly observe, and yet we do not know *how* they are brought about,—yet they want to know *how* Christ's body is in the bread, and will not let Christ be the Master!"—We let Christ be the Master. He said: "This is My body; this is My blood." This we believe.

Matt. 26, 27. *Drink ye all of it.*

Mark 14, 23. *And they all drank of it.*

Transubstantiation, mentioned several times in preceding texts, is an erroneous doctrine of the Roman Catholic Church, devised several centuries after the birth of Christ, and confirmed at the fourth Lateran Synod by Pope Innocent III, A. D., 1215. This figment says that the bread and the wine, through the consecration of the priest becomes *changed, transformed, transubstantiated,* into the body and the blood of Christ, so that after the consecration there is no more bread and wine really present in the sacrament, but only the body and the blood of Christ; of the bread and the wine, nothing remains but the outward form, color, and taste. Cf. Conc. Trid. Sess. 13, ch. 1, and Canon 2, 4, 7.

A logical deduction from this doctrine and just as anti-scriptural, is their doctrine of *Concomitance.* "Concomitance" is derived from the Latin "concomitari", meaning *to accompany.* The Roman Catholic Church teaches that since the bread is transformed into the very body of Christ, and since Christ's body has blood, the communicant who receives the consecrated wafer, receives not only the body of Christ, but, by concomitance, also the blood of Christ. This rationalistic teaching has led to the taking away of the cup from the laity. Arbitrarily this church instituted two communions: the one for the laity—*communio sub una specie;* the other for the priests—*communio sub utraque specie.* The laity receives the consecrated wafer only; the priest both the consecrated wafer and wine. As an excuse for this procedure, which is contrary to the institution of Christ, the fear was expressed that in administering the cup to the communicants some of the consecrated wine, i. e., of the changed wine into the blood of Christ, might be spilt. Queries: May not the priest accidentally spill some of the consecrated wine? May not parts of the consecrated wafer be wasted accidentally? But it is not our purpose to enlarge upon this sacrilegious teaching. The Lutheran Christian knows that the sacramental union takes place during the eating and drinking by the communicants and affects only what he actually receives. Christ said to His disciples: *"Drink ye all of it"*, and we read: *"They all drank of it."* Christ instituted the sacrament. As Christ, the All-wise, has instituted it, so it should be administered.

Heb. 10, 14. 18. *For by one offering He hath perfected for ever them that are sanctified. Now where remission of sin is, there is no more offering for sin.*

The Catholic doctrine of Transubstantiation has bred another horrible doctrine of the same church—that of the Mass. In the Mass the officiating priest repeats in an unbloody manner that sacrifice that Christ offered in a bloody manner on the Cross. He takes the changed, transubstantiated wafer, i. e., the body of the Lord, and makes an offering of it in behalf of the living and the dead for the forgiveness of sins committed after baptism; while the sacrificial death of Christ on Calvary makes satisfaction for original sin only.—How blasphemous! How contradictory to the words of our dying Savior: "It is finished!"

Our text says: *"One* single offering Christ made, *one* single sacrifice He brought: but so great, so perfect was the value of this *one* offering that its perfection is indicated by the fact of Christ's sitting at the right hand of God (v. 12) as one who has quite finished His work and knows that its power and worth will last throughout eternity. —There is, then, no need of any further sacrifice: for by one offering He has perfected *for all times* them that are sanctified. The fact that He gave Himself into death as the Substitute of mankind *once,* the fact that He paid the price of all men's ransom with the price of His holy blood *once,* that is sufficient. No more need to be done, no more can be done. Salvation, the reconciliation of man with God, is secured forever. In the *one* sacrifice of Christ there is a cleansing sufficient for all men, both to bring them into fellowship with God by imputing to them the perfect righteousness and holiness of God through faith, and to keep them in this fellowship by renewing their hearts by daily contrition and repentance and causing them to dedicate themselves, their lives, to God anew with every further day of their lives." Kretzmann, Com. in loco.

1 Cor. 11, 26. *As often as ye eat this bread and drink this cup, ye do show the Lord's death till He come.*

The Lord's Supper should be received frequently. See previous explanation of 1 Cor. 11, 23-29; likewise the paragraph bearing on this topic in "The Four Records."

The student will do well to reread Luther's "Preface" to the Small Catechism, and to ponder especially the paragraph beginning: "Lastly, since the people are freed from the tyranny of the pope, they no longer desire to go to the Sacrament, but despise it," etc. Luther says the pastors are so to preach concerning this sacrament that the people will, as it were, "compel us pastors to administer the Sacrament. This is done", he proceeds, "by telling them that if a person does not seek nor desire the Lord's Supper at least some four times a year" (German: "zum wenigsten ein maler viere des Jahres") it is to be feared that he despises the Sacrament and is not a Christian, just as he is not a Christian who refuses to believe or to hear the Gospel. For Christ did not say, Omit this, or, Despise this; but, This do ye, as oft as ye drink it, etc. Truly, He wants it done, and by no means neglected or despised: "This do ye", is His command.

Matt. 11, 28. *Come unto Me all ye that labor and are heavy laden, and I will give you rest.*

All things pertaining to the Kingdom of God, to salvation, are delivered unto the Son by the Father. The Son stands in so intimate a connection with the Father that "no man knoweth the Son, but the Father; neither knoweth any man the Father, save the Son, and he, whomsoever the Son will reveal Him." v. 27. Thus the Son is the only Savior of mankind. To save man is His earnest will. Hence His gracious invitation: *"Come unto Me;"* Deute pros me=Hither to Me. This expression shows animation on the part of the speaker and a lively interest in the welfare of the people addressed: *"Hither to Me,"* at once, come immediately. Whom does He invite? *"Ye that labor and are heavy laden."* They that *labor, toil, kopiontes,* are they that labored hard at their task, that have become weary and discouraged, seeing that the task was too much for them. The *heavy laden, pefortismenoi,* are they upon whom a heavy burden has been imposed, who feel this burden, and know that they will break down under it.

Wherein does this *labor* and this *burden* consist? The Lord speaks of people with an alarmed conscience. By the Law they have come to a knowledge of sin; they have learned that they are violators of God's holy commandments, and now seek to appease the wrath of God by their so-called good works, by striving to live right and to do right and thus make themselves acceptable in His sight. And the more they try to fulfill the Law of God of their own power, the more they perceive their utter inability to do so, the more also they perceive how sinful they are. Such are they *"that labor and are heavy laden."* So to find rest for their souls these poor people had been taught by their teachers, the self-righteous Pharisees and Scribes. Of them Jesus said: "They bind heavy burdens, and grievous to be borne, and lay them on men's shoulders; but they themselves will not move them with their finger." Matt. 23. 4.

These poor sinners, who have labored very hard to obtain salvation through the deeds of the Law, and now sink weary and discouraged under their heavy burden, Jesus invites: "Hither to Me." And He wants *all* to come, all without exception. By inviting "all that labor and are heavy laden" to come to Him, Jesus does not mean to exclude any one from this privilege. "He would have all men to be saved." But before men will listen to and accept His gracious invitation they must "labor" and become "heavy laden", in other words they must come to a knowledge of their sinfulness and damnableness through the Law. They that are whole, need not a physician. Christ has not come to call the righteous but the sinners to repentance. But whosoever belongs to the class of those that labor and are heavy laden shall come to Jesus. And they shall come just as they are, with all their sins, with all their burdened consciences. Jesus' call is a gracious call. When He invites: "Come unto Me", at once, immediately, the sinner should make answer:

"Just as I am, and waiting not
To rid my soul of one dark blot
To thee, whose blood can cleanse each spot,
O Lamb of God, I come, I come."

And now observe the precious promise: "I will give you rest." *Come unto Me,* believe in Me as your Savior, as the One who has fulfilled the Law for you, who has borne the curse of the Law for you, *"I"*—said with emphasis—*"I will give you rest."* I will rid you of your burden, of your vain labor, I am your *Jesus*, your Savior, I have fulfilled the Law for you, "I am the end of the Law for righteousness to everyone that believeth", i. e., that comes to Me. Thus in Jesus, "in whom we have redemption through His blood," the poor sinner finds rest for his soul. He becomes a happy child of God, who now no longer "labors and is heavy laden," but who out of gratitude towards God cheerfully runs the way of His commandments. But such troubled consciences need consolation; their faith needs strengthening. One means to this end is the Lord's Supper.

How about those who are weak of faith? Should they approach the Lord's table?—Consider the following passages in the light of this question? See Qu. 349.

Mark 9, 24. *Lord, I believe, help thou mine unbelief.*

A father brought his lunatic child to Jesus to be healed. The poor child was terribly afflicted. He was not only *lunatic*, that is, epileptic, but he was also possessed with a devil. His obsession manifested itself especially in epileptic fits, which some attributed to the influence of the moon. The father appeals to Jesus for help. Thus he manifested his faith—he came to Jesus. His faith, however, was weak. In approaching Jesus, he prayed: *"If Thou canst do anything, have compassion*

on us and help us." This "if Thou canst" showed that he entertained
doubts in his heart. His spiritual condition was such as is described
by the hymn-writer:

> "Just as I am, though tossed about
> With many a conflict, many a doubt,
> Fightings and fears within, without,
> O Lamb of God, I come, I come."

Jesus answered: *"If Thou canst believe*—all things are possible
to him that believeth." The words fanned the embers of faith in the
father's heart. With tears in his eyes he immediately exclaimed:
"Lord, I believe; help Thou mine unbelief." The father received according to his faith. "He that believes with all his heart feels and
realizes how weak his faith still is, how the natural unbelief opposes
true faith, and therefore beseeches God to strengthen his faith."
(Stoeckhardt.) This father's faith was strengthened by Jesus' Word.
God strengthens our faith by His Word and sacrament. Far from de-
terring us from the use of the Lord's Supper, our recognized weakness
of faith should urge us to seek strengthening therein.

Ps. 22, 25. 26. *My praise shall be of Thee in the great congregation: I will pay my vows before them that fear Him. The meek shall
eat and be satisfied: they shall praise the Lord that seek Him: your
heart shall live forever.*

This text is taken from the greatest of Messianic psalms. The
Savior is the speaker. When His work of redemption shall have been
completed, He will "declare God's name unto His brethren; in the
midst of the congregation will He praise Him." The Savior shall see
of the travail of His soul. A large congregation will have been
gathered, a congregation of believers in the Messiah. In our text "New
Testament thoughts are dressed in an Old Testament garb. The suffering of the Messiah is viewed in the light of an offering. Christ has
offered Himself for us. Salvation, which He has merited by His sufferings and death, is the New Testament sacrificial feast. By the preaching of His Word the exalted Christ distributes the fruit of His passion,
distributes the gifts of salvation. To the Old Testament sacrificial
feasts widows, orphans and the poor in general were invited. Deut. 12,
18; 16, 11. They that participate in the New Testament feast are *"the
meek"*, i. e., the spiritually poor, who find no satisfaction in the things
of this world, who know their own unworthiness and hence ask and long
for the Lord and His grace. These sorrowing, grace-hungry souls eat
and drink with avidity what Christ, their Savior has merited and
offers to them in the Word and Sacrament—forgiveness of sin, life and
salvation. This salvation is prepared and ready for all. But only the
penitent, believing sinners actually accept this salvation in Christ and
become partakers thereof." Stoeckhardt, *Psalmen.*

Is. 42, 3. *A bruised reed shall He not break, and the smoking flax shall He not quench.*

This text, too, is from a Messianic prophecy. The person spoken of is Christ, "my Servant, whom I—Jehovah—uphold; my Elect, in whom my soul delighteth." This "Servant of the Lord" will work out the redemption of mankind. "He shall bring forth judgment"—justice —the righteousness that availeth before God—"to the Gentiles." How will He deal with the weak members that He has gathered about Himself? With the utmost compassion flowing from a merciful Savior's heart. Some—many—of the members of His flock are like "*a bruised reed*" and a "*smoking* flax." The considerate gardener does not break a "bruised", cracked, reed to pieces, but ties it up in order to save its life. So Christ deals with the bruised reeds in His garden—with the weak and depressed members of His flock. These He strengthens through His Word and grace. "The smoking flax", with its dying flame, with its dimly burning wick, the housewife trims, she replenishes it with a new supply of oil, and the once almost extinguished flax again burns briskly. So Christ by His Word and Sacrament fans the spark of faith into a flame of devotion by His tender ministration through the Gospel of His grace.

John 6, 37. *Him that cometh to Me I will in no wise cast out.*

Christ had miraculously fed the 5,000 on the eastern shore of the Sea of Galilee. Later in the synagogue at Capernaum, He discoursed on the Bread of Life. Here He met with opposition and unbelief on the part of the hostile Jews. His enemies. In the course of His sermon He informed them that He received His adherents as a gift from His Father who by His Holy Spirit operated through the Word upon the hearts of the hearers, and caused them to come to Him, i. e., to believe on Him. "All that the Father giveth Me, shall come unto Me." So His work of redemption will not fail. Next Christ utters the words of our text, which has brought sweet comfort, hope, and assurance to so many: "*Him that cometh to Me,*" ton erchomenon, everyone, none excepted, "coming to Me", in faith, "*I will in no wise cast out*", but receive him graciously, lovingly. *Fiat applicatio.*

To Whom Must the Lord's Supper Be Denied?

Matt. 7, 6. *Give not that which is holy unto the dogs, neither cast ye your pearls before swine.*

This text is taken from the Sermon on the Mount. The people addressed well knew the meaning of the expressions "the holy thing" and the "pearls". They knew that the Lord spoke of the sacred rites, ordinances, privileges, and blessings of God's house. In New Testament parlance "the holy thing" and "the pearls" are the precious Gospel and the Sacraments. St. Paul at Antioch in Pisidia acted in conformity with this command of our Savior, when he said to the hostile Jews, who contradicted the word of God and blasphemed: "It was necessary that the word of God should first have been spoken to you: but seeing you put it from you, and judge yourselves unworthy of everlasting life, lo, we turn to the Gentiles." Acts, 13. 46.

But now as to the bearing the text has in our Catechism we quote Zorn, Crumbs, p. 366.

"These are words of our blessed Lord. By 'that which is holy'. He also means the Lord's Supper, which is one of our 'pearls'. By 'dogs' and 'swine' He means' such as are known to be ungodly and impenitent; for after the manner of dogs and swine they abuse this most holy thing which the mercy of God has devised for us poor sinners. Is it not so? The Lord's Supper should be denied to such persons. They are unworthy of the Lord's Supper. And 'he that eateth and drinketh unworthily eateth and drinketh damnation to himself, not discerning the Lord's body', says the Holy Spirit. (1 Cor. 11, 29.) And when a pastor knowingly and intentionally out of indifference, from fear of men, or for the love of gain, admits such ungodly and impenitent persons to the Lord's Supper, he flatly disobeys the injunction of the Lord, and brings down upon himself the curse of God. And when church-members, for any reason whatsoever, demand that such persons be admitted to the Lord's Supper, they are of the same position. The Lord's Supper is instituted for Christians, for God's children, who repent of their sins, believe in Christ, and are earnestly resolved with the aid of God, the Holy Ghost, henceforth to amend their sinful lives. It is good and profitable for every one to take this to heart."

Acts 2, 42. *They continued steadfastly in the apostles' doctrine and fellowship, and in breaking of bread, and in prayers.*

We had occasion to comment on this passage previously. In this connection we call attention to the fact that it furnishes strong proof for close communion as practised in our Lutheran Church.—This truth the previous article "The Four Records" has duly stressed.—We rejoice over the fact that even among the heterodox dear children of God are to be found, but because they hold to false doctrine—though not aware of the fact—, and because altar-fellowship is a visible manifestation of unity of the faith and church-fellowship, we cannot commune at the same altar with them.—Restudy Rom. 16, 17; 2 Cor. 6, 14-16, et al., sub loco: The Proper Use of the Doctrine of the Church. See Vol. I, 257-260.

Matt. 5, 23, 24. *Therefore, if thou bring thy gift to the altar, and there rememberest that thy brother hath aught against thee; leave there thy gift before the altar, and go thy way; first be reconciled to thy brother, and then come and offer thy gift.*

The purpose of this text is to show that the Lord's Supper must not be given to people living at enmity with each other.—The passage has been studied previously under another *locus*—The Fifth Petition, Qu. 252. See the explanation and its application there.

1 Cor. 11, 28. *Let a man examine himself, and so let him eat of that bread and drink of that cup.*

The words under consideration here are: *"Let a man examine himself."* How this is to be done the answer to Qu. 348 shows.— Luther's "Christian Questions" furnish a valuable aid in this self-examination.—This Sacrament is to be denied, 1, to the ungodly and impenitent, Matt. 7, 6; 2, to the heterodox, i. e., to all holding to false teachings, Acts 2, 42; 3, to such as have given offense and have not made amends, Matt. 5, 23. 24; 4, to all unable to examine themselves— children, insane, and unconscious persons.

Soli Deo Gloria.

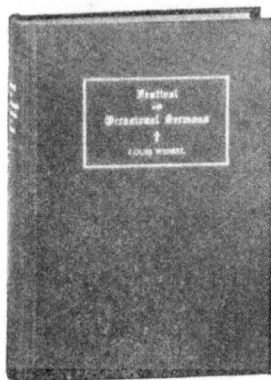

www.ingramcontent.com/pod-product-compliance
Lightning Source LLC
Chambersburg PA
CBHW030917150426
42812CB00045B/234